SPORTS IN SOCIETY

Issues and Controversies

Jay Coakley, PhD
University of Colorado, Colorado Springs

Elizabeth Pike, PhD
University of Chichester

The **McGraw·Hill** Companies

London Boston Burr Ridge, IL Dubuque, IA Madison, WI New York San Francisco
St. Louis Bangkok Bogotá Caracas Kuala Lumpur Lisbon Madrid Mexico City
Milan Montreal New Delhi Santiago Seoul Singapore Sydney Taipei Toronto

Sports in Society: Issues and Controversies
Jay Coakley & Elizabeth Pike
ISBN-13 9780077117443
ISBN-10 0077117441

Education

Published by McGraw-Hill Education
Shoppenhangers Road
Maidenhead
Berkshire
SL6 2QL
Telephone: 44 (0) 1628 502 500
Fax: 44 (0) 1628 770 224
Website: www.mcgraw-hill.co.uk

British Library Cataloguing in Publication Data
A catalogue record for this book is available from the British Library

Library of Congress Cataloguing in Publication Data
The Library of Congress data for this book has been applied for from the Library of Congress

Acquisitions Editor: Melanie Havelock
Senior Development Editor: Jack Fray
Marketing Manager: Vanessa Boddington
Senior Production Editor: James Bishop

Text Design by Hard Lines
Cover design by Jan Marshall
Printed and bound in Italy by Rotolito Lombarda

ISBN-13 9780077117443
ISBN-10 0077117441

Dedication

To Maddie, Ally, Cassidy, Alice and Charlie – each with their own way of doing sports

Brief Table of Contents

Preface ix

Acknowledgements xiv

About the authors xv

1 The sociology of sport: what is it and why study it? 1

2 Using social theories: how can they help us study sports in society? 32

3 Studying the past: does it help us understand sports today? 62

4 Sports and socialization: who plays and what happens to them? 98

5 Sports and young people: are organized schemes worth the effort? 136

6 Deviance in sports: is it out of control? 172

7 Violence in sports: how does it affect our lives? 224

8 Gender and sports: does equity require ideological changes? 265

9 Race, ethnicity and national identity: are they important in sports? 310

10 Social class: do money and power matter in sports? 348

11 Sports and the economy: what are the characteristics of commercial sports? 384

12 Sports and the media: could they survive without each other? 426

13 Sports, politics and globalization: how do governments and global processes influence sports? 469

14 Sports in the future: what can we create? 512

References 539

Index 583

Detailed Table of Contents

Preface   ix
Acknowledgements   xiv
About the authors   xv

1 The sociology of sport: what is it and
  why study it?   1
  About this book   2
  About this chapter   3
  Defining culture and society   4
  Defining sports   4
  What is the sociology of sport?   11
  Why study sports in society?   18
  What is the current status of the
  sociology of sport?   27
  Summary: why study the sociology of
  sport?   30

2 Using social theories: how can they
  help us study sports in society?   32
  What are theories and why do we need
  them?   34
  Functionalist theory: sports preserve
  the status quo   35
  Conflict theory: sports are tools of the
  wealthy   41
  Critical theory: sports are sites where
  culture and social relations are
  produced and changed   44
  Feminist theory: sports are gendered
  activities   49
  Interactionist theory: sports are given
  meaning as people interact with one
  another   51
  Figurational theory: sports are
  collective inventions   53
  Is there a best theoretical approach to
  use when studying sports?   57
  Summary: how can social theories help
  us study sports in society?   60

3 Studying the past: does it help us
  understand sports today?   62
  Understanding history while studying
  sports in society   64
  Sports vary by time and place   65

Contests and games in Ancient Greece:
beyond the myths (1000 BC to 100 BC)   66
Roman contests and games: spectacles
and gladiators (100 BC to AD 500)   68
Tournaments and games in medieval
Europe: separation of the masters and
the masses (500 to 1300)   70
The Renaissance, the Reformation and
the Enlightenment: games as diversions
(1300 to 1800)   73
The Industrial Revolution: the
emergence of organized competitive
sports (1780 to 1920)   77
Since 1920: struggles continue   87
Using history to think about the future   91
Summary: can we use history to
understand sports today?   94

4 Sports and socialization: who plays
  and what happens to them?   98
  What is socialization?   100
  Becoming and staying involved in
  sports   103
  Changing or ending sports
  participation   108
  Being involved in sports: what
  happens?   111
  What socialization research does not
  tell us   129
  Summary: who plays and what
  happens?   133

5 Sports and young people: are
  organized schemes worth the effort?   136
  Origin and development of organized
  youth sports   138
  Major trends in youth sports today   140
  Different experiences: informal, player-
  controlled sports versus organized,
  adult-controlled sports   148
  Sociological questions about youth
  sports   153
  Sports and education   159
  Recommendations for improving youth
  sports   163

Prospects for improving youth sports   *167*
Summary: are organized youth sports
schemes worth the effort?   *168*

6 Deviance in sports: is it out of
   control?   *172*
Problems faced when studying
deviance in sports   *174*
Defining and studying deviance in
sports: three approaches   *176*
A constructionist approach to deviance
in sports   *181*
Research on deviance among athletes   *197*
Performance-enhancing substances:
deviant overconformity in sports   *205*
Summary: is deviance in sports out of
control?   *220*

7 Violence in sports: how does it affect
   our lives?   *224*
What is violence?   *226*
Violence in sports through history   *227*
Violence on the field   *228*
Violence off the field   *243*
Violence among spectators   *250*
Summary: does violence in sports
affect our lives?   *262*

8 Gender and sports: does equity
   require ideological changes?   *265*
Participation and equity issues   *267*
Ideology and power issues   *291*
Summary: does equity require
ideological changes?   *308*

9 Race, ethnicity and national identity:
   are they important in sports?   *310*
Defining *race, ethnicity* and *national
identity*   *312*
Creating race and racial ideologies   *314*
Sports participation among minority
ethnic groups in the UK   *330*
The dynamics of racial and ethnic
relations in sports   *337*
Summary: are race, ethnicity and
national identity important in sports?   *344*

10 Social class: do money and power
    matter in sports?   *348*
Social class and class relations   *350*
Sports and economic inequality   *351*
Social class and sports participation
patterns   *358*

Global inequalities and sports   *371*
Economic and career opportunities in
sports   *373*
Sports participation and occupational
careers among former athletes   *378*
Summary: do money and power matter
in sports?   *380*

11 Sports and the economy: what are the
    characteristics of commercial sports?   *384*
Emergence and growth of commercial
sports   *386*
Commercialization and changes in
sports   *402*
Owners, sponsors and promoters in
commercial sports   *409*
Legal status and incomes of athletes in
commercial sports   *416*
Summary: what are the characteristics
of commercial sports?   *423*

12 Sports and the media: could they
    survive without each other?   *426*
Characteristics of the media   *428*
Sports and the media: a two-way
relationship   *438*
Images and narratives in media sports   *449*
Audience experiences with media
sports   *463*
The profession of sports journalism   *463*
Summary: could sports and the media
survive without each other?   *466*

13 Sports, politics and globalization: how
    do governments and global processes
    influence sports?   *469*
The sports–government connection   *472*
Sports and global political processes   *483*
Politics in sports   *501*
Summary: how do governments and
global processes influence sports?   *507*

14 Sports in the future: what can we
    create?   *512*
Envisioning possibilities for the future   *514*
Current trends related to sports in
society   *516*
Factors influencing trends today   *525*
Envisioning possibilities and creating
futures   *529*
Summary: what can we create?   *536*
References   *539*
Index   *583*

The United Kingdom (UK) is a complex country, constituted of the three home countries which make up Great Britain – England, Scotland and Wales – together with Northern Ireland, the Isle of Man and several small islands. The history of the British Empire has left a legacy of former colonial and Commonwealth links with nations including Australia, Canada and New Zealand, together with islands in the Caribbean and elsewhere, and the British monarch remains the head of state of the Commonwealth realms (although this is not always an easy or uncontroversial relationship). The UK is also a member state of the European Union, although it has not adopted the common currency of the euro; it has a permanent seat in the United Nations and is a member of the G8 and NATO. The UK was the first industrialized nation and has one of the largest economies in the world.

Sports in the UK reflect this complex history in several ways. For example, the history of many modern global sports can be traced back to the UK; the spread of sports such as cricket largely reflects colonization patterns from the British Empire; and the relationship with the European Union means the free movement of athletes between member states, resulting in diversity of members in club teams.

This textbook is an adaptation of Jay Coakley's book *Sports in Society: Issues and Controversies* – which largely takes as its focus sports in the United States of America (USA) – with revisions to the content of the original text in order to be more relevant to the UK context. In many ways, sports in the UK are very different from sports in the USA. For example:

- the history of sports in the two countries is very different
- the ways that sports are organized in schools and universities are very different
- the history of 'race' relations, the ethnic structure of the two countries and the ways in which this is manifested in the sports arena are quite different
- the economy and media are distinctly different in the two countries
- the political systems are very different, and legal issues, for example those related to children in sports, gender relations and drug abuse, are quite different.

There are also many similarities between the USA and the UK, so many lecturers and students have been able to use US-based sociology of sports textbooks when there were no appropriate British alternatives. The most popular of these has been Jay Coakley's *Sports in Society: Issues and Controversies*, which lecturers have often supplemented with British readings and materials.

Purpose of the text

Sports in Society: Issues and Controversies developed from discussions between the authors and other British colleagues, who agreed that while the US text was very useful to many British students, the differences in sports and society between the two countries meant there was a market for a UK-orientated edition of the text. This book has been written to meet this need, and the examples, images and some of the issues contained in this text are explicitly UK in focus.

There are three main aims of this first United Kingdom edition. First, it is designed to show British students the ways that sociology can be used to study sports in society. Second, it is written to evoke critical questions from students as they think about sports in their lives and the world around them. Third, it is organized to facilitate the use of research, theory and everyday experiences to learn about sports in society.

The chapters, organized around controversial and curiosity-arousing issues, present current research and theory in the sociology of sport so that readers may discuss and analyse those issues. Although popular sources are used in addition to sociological materials, the content of the book is grounded in sociological research and theoretical approaches. Therefore, the emphasis is clearly on sports and sports-related actions as they influence and are influenced by the social and cultural contexts in which they are created and played. Current issues and controversies are highlighted in 'Reflect on sports' boxes in each chapter, and these are designed to provoke student interest and stimulate critical thinking.

Throughout the book, we tend to use the term sports rather than sport. We do this to emphasize that the forms and meanings of sports vary from place to place and time to time. We want to avoid the inference that sport has an essential and timeless quality apart from the contexts in which people invent, develop, define, plan, package, promote and play sports.

For whom is it written?

Sports in Society is written for those taking their first look at the relationships between sports, culture and society. Each chapter is written to be accessible to college and university students who have not taken courses in sociology or sports science. Discussions of issues do not presume in-depth experiences in sports or a detailed knowledge of sports jargon and statistics. The primary goal is to assist students to identify and explore critical issues related to sports in their lives, families, schools, communities, societies and the world as a whole. To achieve this goal, we use concepts, theories and research as tools that enable us to visualize sports as activities that are inseparable from everyday life at the same time as they are more than mere reflections of the world in which we live.

The emphasis on issues and controversies makes the content of all chapters useful for people who are concerned with sports-related policies and administration of sports schemes. Our purpose is to assist those who wish to make sports more democratic and sports participation more accessible, especially to those who continue to be excluded or marginalized.

Given that there are limited books which focus explicitly on sports in the UK, we also believe that this United Kingdom edition will be useful for those from outside the UK who are interested in sports in British society, and for students and scholars who may be interested in taking a comparative approach to studying issues and controversies in sports in the UK and other societies.

What is new

This edition is a total adaptation of the tenth US edition; each chapter has been revised from start to finish so that it is easier for British readers to relate to and understand. We have preserved the most significant and relevant features of the tenth US edition, while including British research and examples, and drawing international comparisons where appropriate.

For the most part, the essential organization of the text has been preserved. However, there are two significant changes from the US edition. First, we have excluded religion from the United Kingdom edition and, second, we have combined the chapters on 'Sports and children' and 'Sports in high school and colleges' into one chapter on 'Sports and young people'. The reason for omitting the chapter on religion is because the relationship between sports and religion in the UK is very different to that in the USA, and we felt the issues could be more meaningfully explored within the discussions of ethnicity and national identity, and so they are incorporated throughout the book but, in particular, in Chapter 9. The decision to amalgamate the chapters on children and schools into one chapter on young people is because the inter-scholastic and inter-collegiate sports systems are less well developed in the UK, and we felt the discussion of young people's experiences of sports could not be meaningfully separated from discussions of the education system in the British context and so these are discussed within the same chapter. The overall organization of the book remains the same as the US edition, as follows.

- Chapters 1–3 deal with introductory materials: definitions, theories (with an extended discussion of figurational sociology) and the historical development of sports (with a more explicit focus on UK history).

- Chapters 4–7 deal with socialization and the character of sports, focusing on the involvement and experiences of young people in sports, and issues of 'deviancy' and violence.

- Chapters 8–10 deal with issues of equity and diversity; gender, 'race'/ethnicity and national identity, and social class, and how these affect participation in sports.

- Chapters 11–13 deal with social institutions and their relationships with sports: the economy, media and politics.

- Chapter 14 provides some concluding materials and proposals about how sports might look, and how we might make them look, in the future.

Online Learning Centre

Visit www.mcgraw-hill.co.uk/textbooks/coakley today!

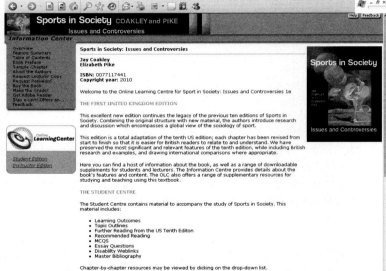

Website resources and the Online Learning Centre

Each chapter is followed by updated references to websites that are useful sources of information about the topics raised in the chapters.

The Online Learning Centre (OLC) contains supplementary materials associated with each chapter, as well as materials from previous editions of the US text and resources from the Canadian and Australia/New Zealand editions of this book. The website for the OLC may be found at www.mcgraw-hill.co.uk/textbooks/coakley.

Materials contained in the OLC include:

- annotated suggested readings
- updated URLs for website resources
- materials from past editions that add depth and background to current chapter topics
- learning objectives for each chapter
- a cumulative 2260-item bibliography from this and the last four editions of *Sports in Society*
- additional readings and current news articles
- a link to PageOut to help you create your own website.

Sports in Society blog

Read new articles, timely essays, and other relevant posts written by the authors and other subject matter experts at http://sportsinsociety.blogspot.com. You are encouraged to contribute comments of your own about the book or any aspect of sports in society.

Instructor's manual and test bank

An instructor's manual and test bank is available to assist those using *Sports in Society* in college courses. It includes the following.

- *Chapter outlines.* These are full outlines that provide a section-by-section overview of each chapter. They are useful for test reviews and organizing lectures, and they may be reproduced and given to students as study guides.
- *Test questions (multiple-choice).* These questions are designed to test students' awareness of the central concepts and ideas in each chapter. For the instructor with large classes, these questions are useful for creating formative assessments as well as final examinations.
- *Discussion/essay questions.* These questions can be used for tests or to generate classroom discussions. They are designed to encourage students to synthesize and apply materials in one or more of the sections in each chapter. None of the questions asks the students to simply list points or give definitions.

Computerized test bank

A computerized version of the test bank for the instructor's manual is available in both IBM and Macintosh formats to qualified adopters. This software provides a unique combination of user-friendly aids, and enables the instructor to select, edit, delete or add questions, and to construct and print tests and answer keys.

Acknowledgements

This book draws on ideas from many sources. Thanks go to students in our sociology of sport courses and others who have provided constructive criticisms. Students regularly open our eyes to new ways of viewing and analysing sports as social phenomena. Special thanks go to our families, friends and colleagues who influence our thinking, provide valuable source materials, and willingly discuss ideas and information. Peter Donnelly, Chris Hallinan and Steve Jackson deserve special thanks for exchanging ideas from the Canadian, Australian and New Zealand editions of this book.

Our appreciation goes to friends and colleagues in the sociology of sport community in the UK who reviewed individual chapters and whose suggestions were crucial in the planning and writing of this adaptation. They include:

Professor Dick Fisher, St Mary's University College
Professor Scott Fleming, University of Wales Institute Cardiff
Professor Ken Green, Chester University
Dr Udo Merkel, University of Brighton
Dr Alex Twitchen, University of Chichester
Dr Anita White

Thanks also to the staff at McGraw-Hill/Open University Press UK – in particular to Jack Fray and Melanie Havelock.

Finally, my personal thanks go to Jay Coakley for his selfless generosity, support and encouragement. Jay's textbooks have inspired and informed scholars in the sociology of sport throughout the world for more than three decades, and it has been a privilege to work with him on a United Kingdom edition of his work.

Elizabeth Pike
Chichester, UK

Jay Coakley

Jay Coakley is Professor Emeritus of Sociology at the University of Colorado in Colorado Springs. He received a PhD in sociology at the University of Notre Dame, and has since taught and done research on play, games and sports, among other topics in sociology. Dr Coakley has received many teaching, service and professional awards, and is an internationally respected scholar, author and journal editor. In 2004 the Citizenship Through Sport Alliance presented him with a national Citizenship Through Sport Award for his work to make sports and physical activities more inclusive. In 2007 the Institute for International Sport selected him as one of the 100 Most Influential Sports Educators, and the University of Chichester in West Sussex, England, awarded him an Honorary Fellowship in recognition of his outstanding leadership in the sociology of sport. A former inter-collegiate athlete, Coakley continues to use concepts, research and theories in sociology to critically examine social phenomena and promote changes that will make social worlds more democratic and humane. He currently lives in Fort Collins, Colorado.

Elizabeth Pike

Elizabeth Pike is a senior lecturer at the University of Chichester where she leads the sociology of sport field. She was awarded a PhD in the sociology of sport by Loughborough University, and has since researched and published on risk, injury, ageing and corporeality in sports. She has delivered presentations critically evaluating these phenomena in universities and conferences throughout Africa, the Americas, Asia, Australasia and Europe. Dr Pike is currently a member of the Executive Board of the International Sociology of Sport Association, and serves as the General Secretary of the association. She works as a reviewer for several journals and publishers, and is on the Editorial Board of the *International Review for the Sociology of Sport*. She lives in the City of Brighton and Hove, East Sussex.

Chapter 1

The sociology of sport: what is it and why study it?

Online *Learning* Centre Resources

Visit *Sports in Society*'s Online Learning Centre (OLC) at **www.mcgraw-hill.co.uk/textbooks/coakley** for additional information and study material for this chapter, including:

- Self-grading quizzes and essay questions
- Learning outcomes
- Related websites
- Additional readings

> Sport defines us as a nation. It teaches us about life. We learn self discipline and team-work from it. We learn how to win with grace and lose with dignity. It gets us fit. It keeps us healthy. It forms a central part of the cultural and recreational parts of our lives.
> *(Tessa Jowell, Secretary of State for Culture, Media and Sport, Game Plan, DCMS/Strategy Unit, 2002)*

1

Chapter contents

About this book
About this chapter
Defining culture and society
Defining sports
What is the sociology of sport?
Why study sports in society?
What is the current status of the sociology of sport?
Summary: why study the sociology of sport?

> *Now that the sports business is a massive arm of the international entertainment industry ... there's no way we can escape its economic, social and environmental footprints. ... [T]he growing involvement of big business, of the media and of advertisers has helped reshape the rules of many games – and, in the process, fuelled new forms of exclusion.*
>
> *(John Elkington, environmentalist, president of SustainAbility, 2004)*

About this Book

Most of you reading this book have experienced sports personally, as athletes or spectators or both. You are probably familiar with the physical and emotional experiences of playing sports, and you may know the rules and strategies of certain sports. You may even follow the lives of high-profile athletes in your city or on the national sports scene. Most of you have watched and read about sports, and discussed them with friends and family.

This book assumes that you are interested in some facet of sports, but it is written to take you beyond the scores, statistics and sports personalities. The goal is to focus on the 'deeper game' associated with sports, the game through which sports become part of the social and cultural worlds in which we live.

Fortunately, we can draw on our emotions and experiences as we consider this deeper game. Let us use our experiences with university sports in the UK as an example. When students play on a successful university team, we know that it may affect their status on campus and the treatment they receive from lecturers and fellow students. We know it may have implications for their prestige in the community, their self-images and self-esteem. We know it may affect their future relationships, opportunities in education and the workforce, and overall enjoyment of life.

Building on this knowledge enables us to move further into the deeper game associated with sports. For example, we might ask why people in the UK place such importance on sports and top athletes, including those representing universities such as Oxford and Cambridge whose annual rugby and boat race competitions are televised and watched by millions of viewers. We might question what this says about British values. We might study how varsity sports are organized and connected with ideas and beliefs about masculinity and femininity, achievement and competition, pleasure and pain, winning and fair play, and other important aspects of our culture. We might ask how sports influence the status structure that exists among university students and how athletes fit into that structure. We also might ask if the organization of varsity sports is influenced by corporate sponsorships, and examine student ideas about the corporations whose names and logos are on their tracksuits and sports hall walls.

The assumption underlying these questions is that sports are more than just games, meets and matches. They are important parts of social life and they have meanings and influence that go beyond scores and performance statistics. Sports are integral parts of the social and cultural contexts in which we live. They provide the stories and images that many of us use to explain and evaluate these contexts, our experiences, and our connections to the world around us.

People who study sports in society are concerned with the deeper meanings and stories associated with sports. They do research to understand (1) the cultures and societies in which sports exist, (2) the social worlds created around sports, and (3) the experiences of individuals and groups associated with sports.

Sociology is helpful when studying sports as social phenomena. This is because **sociology**[1] *is the study of social life, including all forms of social interaction and relationships.* The concepts, theories and research methods that have been developed by sociologists enable us to study and understand sports as they exist in our lives and as they are connected with history, culture and society. Sociology helps us examine social life *in context* and see connections between our lives and the larger social world. In this book, we use sociology to see sports as part of social and cultural life and understand social issues as we study sports.

The material in this book differs from material in blogs, talk radio, television news shows, match commentaries and everyday conversations about sports. It is organized to help you critically examine sports as they exist in people's lives and the social contexts where people live, play and work. We use research findings to describe and explain as accurately as possible the important connections between sports, society and culture. We try to be fair when using research to make sense of the social aspects of sports and sports experiences. This is why there is an extensive reference list of books and articles at the end of this book. Of course, we want to hold your attention as you read, but we do not exaggerate, distort, purposely withhold or present information out of context to impress you. In the process, we hope that you will develop or extend your critical thinking abilities so that you can assess the merits of what people say about sports in society.

About this Chapter

This chapter focuses on five questions:

1 What are culture and society?

2 What are sports and how might we distinguish them from other activities?

---

[1] Important concepts used in each chapter are identified in **boldface**. Unless they are accompanied by a footnote that contains a definition, the definition will be given in the text itself. This puts the definition in context rather than separating it in a glossary. Definitions are also provided in the index.

3 What is the sociology of sport?

4 Why study sports in society?

5 Who studies sports in society, and what are their goals?

The answers to these questions will be our guides for understanding the material in the rest of the book.

Defining Culture and Society

As we use sociology to study sports, it is important to define *culture* and *society*. **Culture** *consists of the ways of life that people create as they participate in a group or society*. These ways of life are complex. They are created and changed as people struggle over what is important in their lives, how to survive and accomplish everyday tasks, and how to make sense of their collective experiences. Culture encompasses all the socially invented ways of thinking, feeling and acting that emerge as people try to survive, meet their needs, and achieve a sense of meaning and significance in the process. Of course, some people have more power and resources than others in the culture-creation process, and sociologists study how people use power and resources in the social world.

Sports are elements of culture, and they have forms and meanings, which vary over time and from one group and society to the next. For example, traditional martial arts and sumo wrestling in Asia are organized differently and have different meanings and purposes than combat sports such as boxing and rugby in the UK. The meaning, organization and purpose of rugby have also changed considerably since the institution of the first written rules at Rugby School in 1845. These new rules restricted the physical violence which had been characteristic of the folk games from which rugby evolved. They also institutionalized the role of a referee, a defined boundary and a rule-enforcing body in the Rugby Football Union, which was formed in 1871. However, the game remained amateur for more than a century, finally becoming professionalized in 1995. William Webb Ellis, the Rugby School student who is often credited as the founder of rugby union (albeit incorrectly – as we will explain in Chapter 3), would not recognize the game if he were to see Ronan O'Gara kicking a penalty during the Six Nations tournament while millions of people watch on television and thousands of others pay up to hundreds of pounds per ticket to see the game in person. It is important to know about these cultural and historical differences when we study sports as parts of society.

The term **society** refers to *a collection of people living in a defined geographic territory and united by a political system and a shared sense of self-identification that distinguishes them from other people*. The UK, the USA, China, Australia and South Africa are societies. Each has a different culture and different forms of social, political and economic organization. It is important to know about these characteristics of society as we study the meaning and social significance of sports from one social context to another.

Defining Sports

Most of us have a good enough grasp of the meaning of sports to talk about them with others. However, when we study sports, it helps to define what we are talking about. For example, can we say that two groups of children playing beach cricket in Cornwall or tag rugby in a park in Cardiff are engaged in sports? Their activities are quite different from what occurs in connection with the International Cricket Conference (ICC) Cricket World Cup and International Rugby Board (IRB) Rugby World Cup matches. These differences become significant when parents ask if playing sports is good for their children, when community leaders ask if they should use tax money to pay for sports, or when school officials ask if sports contribute to the educational missions of their schools.

Students ask us if jogging and synchronized swimming are sports. How about weight-lifting? Hunting? Scuba-diving? Darts? Motor racing? Ballroom dancing? Chess? Professional wrestling? Skateboarding? The X Games? Paintball? A piano competition? Should any or all of these activities be called sports? In the face of such a question, some scholars use a precise definition of sports so that they can distinguish them from other types of social activities.

A traditional definition of *sports*

Although definitions of *sports* vary, many scholars agree that **sports** *are institutionalized competitive activities that involve rigorous physical exertion or the use of relatively complex physical skills by participants motivated by internal and external rewards*. Parts of this definition are clear, but other parts need explanation.

First, sports are *physical activities*. Therefore, according to the definition, chess probably is not a sport because playing chess is more cognitive than physical. Are snooker and pool physical enough to qualify as sports under this definition? Making this determination is arbitrary because there are no objective rules for how physical an activity must be to qualify as a sport. Pairs ice dancing is considered a sport in the Winter Olympics, so why not add ballroom dancing to the Summer Games? Members of the International Olympic Committee (IOC) asked this question, and ballroom dancing was included in the 2000 Sydney Olympic Games as a demonstration sport.

Second, sports are *competitive activities*, according to this definition. Sociologists realize that competitive activities have different social dynamics from co-operative or individualistic activities. They know that, when two boys compete in a game of 'keepy-uppy' on the grass outside their home, it is sociologically different from what happens when the England men's team plays Germany's national team in the FIFA World Cup™, so it makes sense to separate them for research purposes.

Third, sports are institutionalized activities. **Institutionalization** is a sociological term referring to *the process through which actions, relationships and social arrangements become patterned or standardized over time and from one situation to another*. Institutionalized activities have formal rules and organizational structures that guide people's actions from one situation to another. When we say that sports are institutionalized activities, we distinguish what happens when children dare each other to 'tombstone', which involves diving off cliffs, sea walls and piers, from what happens when a different child, Tom Daley, competed in the 2008 Olympic Games where his dives were evaluated and scored by officials and observed by the global television audience. In specific terms, institutionalization involves the following aspects.

- *The rules of the activity become standardized.* Sports have official rules applied whenever and wherever they are played.

- *Official regulatory agencies take over rule enforcement.* Representatives of recognized 'governing bodies' – such as the National Council for School Sport, British Universities and Colleges Sport (BUCS), the national governing bodies (NGBs) of individual sports and the International Olympic Committee – enforce the rules.

- *The organizational and technical aspects of the activity become important.* Sports occur under controlled conditions in which there are specific expectations for athletes, coaches and officials so that results can be documented, certified and recorded. Furthermore, equipment, technologies and training methods are developed to improve performance.

- *The learning of game skills becomes formalized.* Participants must know the rules of the game, and coaches become important as teachers; participants may also consult others – such as therapists, dieticians, sports scientists, managers and team doctors – as they learn skills.

The fourth point in the definition of *sports* is that sports are *activities played by people for internal and external rewards.* This means that participation in sports involves a combination of two sets of motivations. One is based in the internal satisfactions associated with expression, spontaneity and the pure joy of participation. The other motivation is based in external satisfactions associated with displaying physical skills in public and receiving approval, status or material rewards in the process.

When we use a precise definition, we can distinguish sports from both *play* and *dramatic spectacle*. **Play** is *an expressive activity done for its own sake.* It may be spontaneous or guided by informal norms. An example of play is three 5-year-olds who, during a break-time at primary school, spontaneously run around a playground, yelling joyfully while throwing playground balls in whatever directions they feel like throwing them. Of course, it makes sociological sense to distinguish this physical activity, motivated almost exclusively by personal enjoyment and expression, from what happens in sports.

Dramatic spectacle, on the other hand, is *a performance that is intended to entertain an audience.* An example of dramatic spectacle is a circus act where professional performers are paid to entertain spectators by staging skilled and cleverly choreographed gymnastic moves. It also makes sociological sense to distinguish this physical activity, motivated almost exclusively by a desire to perform for the entertainment of others, from what happens in sports. Sports are distinguished from play and spectacle in that they involve combinations of *both* intrinsic enjoyment and extrinsic rewards for performance. This means that all sports contain elements of play and spectacle. The challenge faced in some sports is to preserve a relatively even balance between these two elements.

Using a precise definition of sport has important advantages, but it also has potentially serious problems. For example, when we focus our attention only on institutionalized competitive activities, we may overlook physical activities in the lives of many people who have neither the resources to formally organize those activities nor the desire to make their activities competitive. In other words, we may spend all our time considering the physical activities of relatively select groups in society because those groups have the power to formally organize physical activities and the desire to make them competitive. If this happens, we privilege the activities of these select groups and treat them as more important parts of culture than the activities of other groups. This in turn can marginalize people who have neither the resources nor the time to play organized sports or who are not attracted to competitive activities.

Most people in the sociology of sport are aware of this possibility, so they use this precise definition of sports cautiously. However, some scholars reject the idea that sports can be defined once and for all time, and use an alternative approach to identifying and studying sports in society.

An alternative approach to defining *sports*

Instead of using a single definition of *sports*, some scholars study sports in connection with answers to the following two questions:

1 What activities do people in a particular group or society identify as sports?

2 Whose sports count the most in the ways they are funded and supported in a group or society?

Asking these questions opens the sociology of sport to a greater range of analysis than is possible when using a static, precise definition. These questions force researchers to dig into the social and cultural contexts in which people form ideas and beliefs about physical activities. The researchers must explain how and why some physical activities more than others are defined as sports and become important in the social and cultural life of a particular society.

Those who use this alternative approach do not describe sports with a single definition. When they are asked, 'What is sport?' they say, 'It depends on who we ask, when we ask, and where we ask research questions about sports.' They explain that not everyone has the same way of looking at and defining *sports*, and that ideas about sports vary over time and from one place to another. For example, they would note that people in Britain who raced horses and went fox-hunting during the 1870s would be horrified, confused or astonished by what Americans today consider to be sports. Similarly, the people who watch National Football League (NFL) football games today would look at many activities that were considered sports in nineteenth-century Britain and say they were not 'real' sports because participants did not train, compete according to schedules, play in leagues, or strive to set records and win championships. Maybe 90 years from now people will play virtual sports in virtual environments and see our sports today as backward, over-organized and funless activities that do not allow participants to combine movement with fantasies in ever changing environments.

Those who use this alternative approach to defining *sports* understand that there are cultural differences in how people identify sports and include them in their lives. For instance, in cultures that emphasize co-operative relationships, the idea that people should compete with one another for rewards is defined as disruptive, if not immoral (Kohn, 1986). At the same time, people in cultures that emphasize competition may see physical activities and games that have no winners as pointless. These cultural differences suggest that we should not let a definition of *sports* shape what is studied. Those who use this alternative approach do research based on what the people in particular cultural settings think is important in their own lives (see Bale and Christensen, 2004; Newbery, 2004; Rail, 1998; Rinehart and Syndor, 2003; Thornton, 2004; Wheaton, 2004a).

The assumption underlying this approach is that sports are **contested activities**, that is, *activities for which there are no timeless and universal agreements about meaning, purpose and organization.* This means that in the case of sports there are varying ideas about who will

What is a sport? This question cannot be answered without considering cultural values and power in a society. In the Olympics, rhythmic gymnastics is a sport although people in some societies believe that 'real' sports must reflect 'manly' attributes (Source: Colorado Springs Gazette)

participate, the circumstances under which participation will occur and who will sponsor sports for what reasons. The most important sociological issue to recognize when we use this approach is that people in particular places at particular times struggle over *whose* ideas about sports will count as *the* ideas in a group or society. A guide for thinking about these issues is in the box titled 'Sports as contested activities.'

Struggles over whose ideas count when it comes to the meaning, organization and purpose of sports are much more common than you might think. To illustrate this, consider the different ways that *sports* might be defined as people make decisions related to the following questions:

reflect on SPORTS — *Sports as contested activities*

When sociologists say that sports are contested activities, they mean that, through history, people have regularly disagreed about what sports could and should be. These disagreements have led to struggles over three major questions about sports and a number of related questions.

As you read the following questions, remember that there are many possible answers to each. Sociologists study how and why people in different places and times answer these questions in particular ways.

1 What are the meaning, purpose and organization of sports?

The struggles related to this question have raised other questions such as the following:

- What activities are defined as 'official' sports?
- How are sports connected with social values and people's ideas about one another, social relationships and the social worlds in which they live?
- What physical skills are valued in sports – are strength, size and speed, for example, more important than flexibility, balance and endurance?
- How are sports experiences evaluated – is emotional enjoyment more important than competitive success?
- What types of performance outcomes are important, and how is success defined, measured and rewarded?
- How is *excellence* defined – in terms of one's abilities to dominate others, all-round athletic abilities or one's abilities to maximize everyone's enjoyment in sports?

2 Who will participate in sports, and under what conditions will this participation occur?

The struggles related to this question have raised other questions such as the following:

- Will females and males play the same sports, at the same time, on the same teams, and should rewards for achievement be the same for females and males?
- Will sports be open to people regardless of social class and wealth? Will wealthy and poor play and watch sports together or separately?
- Will people from different racial and ethnic backgrounds play together or in segregated settings? Will the meanings given to skin colour or ethnicity influence participation patterns or access to participation?
- Will age influence eligibility to play sports, and should sports be age integrated or segregated? Will people of different ages have the same access to participation opportunities?
- Will able-bodied people and people with disabilities have the same opportunities to play sports, and will they play together or separately? What meanings will be given to the accomplishments of disabled athletes compared with the accomplishments of able-bodied athletes?
- Will gay men and lesbians play alongside heterosexuals?
- Will athletes control the conditions under which they play sports, and have the power to change those conditions to meet their own needs and interests? Will athletes be rewarded for playing, and how will rewards be determined?

3 How will sports be sponsored, and what will be the reasons for sponsorship?

The struggles related to this question have raised other questions such as the following:

- Will sports be sponsored by public agencies for the sake of the 'public good'? If so, who will determine what the public good is?
- Will sports be sponsored by not-for-profit organizations? If so, how will organizational philosophies influence the types of sports that are sponsored?
- Will sports be sponsored by commercial organizations? If so, how will the need for profits influence the types of sports that are sponsored?
- To what extent will sponsors control sports and athletes? What are the legal rights of the sponsors relative to those of the athletes and others involved in sports?

As you can see, many aspects of sports can be contested! Sports change depending on how people answer these questions. Furthermore, the answers are not permanent. New answers replace old ones as interests change, as power shifts, as the meanings associated with age, skin colour, ethnicity, gender and disability change, and as economic, political and legal forces take new and different forms.

This means that the definition of *sports* always reflects the organization of a society at a particular time. A precise definition of sports is helpful, but it should always be used with caution because truths about sports rest in people's lives, not sociological definitions. *What do you think?*

- Should children younger than 6 years old be allowed to play sports? If so, how should those sports be organized, and what will be their meaning and purpose?
- Should money from a local youth sports budget be given to a programme in which young girls are taught skipping or to a programme in which boys and a few girls compete in a football league?
- Should skateboarding be funded by a university student union?
- Should tenpin bowling and men's synchronized swimming be recognized as Olympic sports in London 2012?
- Should a permit to use a sports field in a public park be given to an informal group of frisbee players or to an organized hockey team that plays in an official local league?
- Should angling competitions be covered in the sports section of a local newspaper or in the lifestyle section?
- Should darts player Phil Taylor have been shortlisted for the 2006 BBC 'Sports' Personality of the Year award?

How these questions are answered depends on what activities are counted as sports in a society at a given time. These questions also remind us to be cautious in how we use a single definition of *sports*. For example, if sports are institutionalized competitive physical activities played to achieve internal and external rewards, then why are competitive dancing, aerobics and skipping not counted as sports? They fit the definition. The fact that they are not considered sports when it comes to important issues such as sponsorships, funding and formal recognition raises two questions: (1) what activities are defined as sports in a society, and (2) whose ideas and interests are represented most in those definitions?

Answering these questions requires a careful analysis of the social and cultural context in which decisions are made in everyday life. Asking what activities are identified as sports raises critical issues. These issues force us to look at the cultures in which people live, work and play together, and struggle over what is important and how they will live together.

What is the Sociology of Sport?

This question is best answered at the end of the book instead of the beginning. However, you should have a clear preview of what you will be reading in the following 13 chapters.

Most people who do the sociology of sport agree that the field is a sub-discipline of sociology that studies sports as parts of social and cultural life. Much research and writing in this field focuses on 'organized, competitive sports' although scholars also study other physical activities

Definitions of sports can be contested. The angling that this man is doing could be defined as a sport, a hobby or a job (*Source*: iStock)

that involve goals and challenges (Lewis, 2004; Palmer, 2004; Rinehart, 2000; Rinehart and Sydnor, 2003).

The people who do this work use sociological concepts, theories and research to answer questions such as:

1 Why have some activities rather than others been selected and designated as sports in particular societies?

2 Why have sports in particular societies been created and organized in certain ways?

3 How do people include sports and sports participation in their lives, and does participation affect who we are and our relationships with others?

4 How do sports and sport participation affect our ideas about bodies, masculinity and femininity, social class, race and ethnicity, work, fun, ability and disability, achievement and competition, pleasure and pain, deviance and conformity, and aggression and violence?

5 How are the meaning, purpose and organization of sports connected with culture, organization and resources in societies?

6 How are sports related to important spheres of social life such as family, education, politics, the economy, the media and religion?

7 How do people use knowledge about sports as they live their everyday lives?

8 How can people use sociological knowledge about sports to understand and participate in society as agents of progressive change?

Understanding the sociology of sport is easier if you learn to think of sports as **social constructions**, that is, *aspects of the social world that are created by people as they interact with one another under the social, political and economic conditions that exist in their society*. To stress this point, we generally use the term *sports* rather than *sport*. We do this to emphasize that the forms and meanings of sports vary from place to place and time to time. We want to avoid the inference that 'sport' has an essential and timeless quality apart from the contexts in which people create, play and change sports in society. Cartoon 1.1 illustrates that this approach may make some people uncomfortable because they have vested interests in sports as they are currently organized and played. They are not anxious for people to see sports as social constructions that are subject to change if people wish to organize and play them differently.

Differences between sociology and psychology of sport

An additional way to understand the sociology of sport is to contrast it with the psychology of sport. Psychologists study behaviour in terms of attributes and processes that exist *inside* individuals. They focus on motivation, perception, cognition, self-esteem, self-confidence, attitudes and personality. They also deal with interpersonal dynamics, including communication, leadership and social influence, but they usually discuss these things in terms of how they affect attributes and processes that exist inside individuals. Therefore, they would ask a research question such as, 'How is the motivation of athletes related to personality and self-perception of physical abilities?'

Sociologists study actions and relationships in terms of the social conditions and cultural contexts in which people live their lives. They focus on the reality *outside* and *around* individuals,

Cartoon 1.1 **If sports are social constructions, it means that we create them and that we can change them. The sociology of sport helps people identify things about sports that could or should be changed; other people, including those associated with sports, may resist this notion because they benefit from sports as they are currently organized**

and deal with how people form relationships with one another and create social arrangements that enable them to control and give meaning to their lives. Sociologists ask questions about the ways that actions, relationships and social life are related to characteristics defined as socially relevant by people in particular groups. This is why they often deal with the social meanings and dynamics associated with age, social class, gender, race, ethnicity, (dis)ability, sexuality and nationality. A sociologist would ask a question such as, 'How do prevailing ideas about masculinity and femininity affect the organization of sports programmes and the experiences of those who participate in sports?'

When psychologists apply their knowledge, they focus on the experiences and problems of particular individuals, whereas sociologists use their knowledge to focus on group experiences and the social issues that have an impact on entire categories of people. For example, when studying athletes' experiences of injury, psychologists look at factors that exist *inside* the athletes themselves. They may believe that athletes with particular personality types are more likely to seek thrills or to take risks (see Donnelly, 2004). When an athlete becomes injured, psychologists may assume that the damaged body is attached to the individual psychology and may lead to a damaged psyche. Psychologists focus on the emotional responses to injury, such as anxiety, fear, anger and depression. When applying this knowledge, they help athletes manage their injury and rehabilitation by developing coping skills, goal setting and personal approaches to pain management (see Sabo, 2004).

Sociologists, on the other hand, study injury in connection with the social reality that surrounds athletes. They focus on the organization of sports programmes and the relationships between athletes and other people, including family members, peers and coaches, who may pressure athletes to take risks and play while hurt. They may examine whether social characteristics, such as age, gender or social class, contribute to injury risk. Because athletes are influenced by the social context in which they play sports, the application of sociological knowledge emphasizes that to prevent athletes from being exploited and damaged by their sport, it is necessary to change the organization and culture of sports programmes and the dynamics of athletes' relationships so that athletes have more control over their lives and more experiences and relationships outside sports (see Roderick, 2006a, 2006b; Young, 2004a, 2004b).

Both approaches have value, but some people may see a sociological approach as too complex and disruptive. They feel that it is easier to change individual athletes and how they deal with pressure than it is to change the social conditions in which athletes live their lives. This is why many people who control sports programmes prefer psychological over sociological approaches. They do not want to change patterns of organization and control in their programmes. Similarly, many parents and coaches also prefer a psychological approach that focuses on controlling fear and managing pain rather than a sociological approach that focuses on changing their relationships with athletes and the organization of sports programmes.

Using the sociology of sport

The insights developed through sociological research are not always used to make changes in favour of the people who lack power in society. Like any science, sociology can be used in various ways. For example, research findings can be used to assist powerful people as they try to control and enhance the efficiency of particular social arrangements and organizational structures. Or they can be used to assist people who lack power as they attempt to change social conditions and achieve greater opportunities to make choices about how they live their lives.

Science is not a pure and objective enterprise. Therefore, sociologists, like others who produce and distribute knowledge, must consider why they ask certain research questions and how their research findings may affect people's lives. Sociologists cannot escape the fact that social life is complex and characterized by conflicts of interests between different groups of people. Like the rest of us, sociologists must deal with the fact that some people have more power and resources than others. Therefore, using sociology is not a simple process that always leads to good and wonderful conclusions for all humankind. This is why we must think critically about the potential consequences of sociological knowledge when we study sports.

As a result of our own thinking about sports in society, we have written this book to help you use sociology to do the following:

- think critically about sports so that you can identify and understand social problems and social issues associated with sports in society
- look beyond issues of physical performance and records to see sports as social constructions that influence how people feel, think and live their lives

- learn things about sports that you can use to make informed choices about your own sports participation and the place of sports in the communities and societies in which you live.

- think about the ways that sports in your editorial establishments and communities might be transformed so they do not systematically disadvantage some categories of people while privileging others.

 The rituals of sport engage more people in a shared experience than any other institution or cultural activity today

(Varda Burstyn, author, The Rites of Men, *1999)*

Controversies created by the sociology of sport

Research in the sociology of sport sometimes creates controversy. This occurs when research findings suggest that there should be changes in the organization of sports and the structure of social relations in society as a whole. These recommendations may threaten some people, especially those who control sports organizations, benefit from the current organization of sports or think the current organization of sports is 'right and natural'. These people have the most to lose if there are changes in the organization of sports and social life. People in positions of power and control know that changes in society could jeopardize their positions and the privilege that comes with them. Therefore, they prefer approaches to sports that blame problems on the weaknesses and failures of individuals. When theories put the blame for problems on individuals, solutions generally call for better ways to control people and teach them how to adjust to society as it is, rather than calling for changes in how society is organized (Donnelly, 1999; Scraton, 1999).

The potential for controversy that results from a sociological analysis of sports can be illustrated by reviewing research findings on sports participation among women around the world. Research shows that women, especially women in poor and working-class households, have lower rates of sports participation than do other categories of people. Research also shows that there are many reasons for this, including the following.

- Women are less likely than men to have the time, freedom and money needed to play sports regularly.

- Women have little or no control of the facilities where sports are played or the schemes in those facilities.

- Women have less access to transportation and less overall freedom to move around at will and without fear.

- Women often are expected to take full-time responsibility for the social and emotional needs of family members – a job that is never completed or done perfectly.

- Many sports programmes around the world are organized around the values, interests and experiences of men.

As a result of these reasons, many women do not see sports as appropriate activities for them to take seriously.

It is easy to see the potential for controversy associated with such research findings. For example, sociologists might use them to suggest that opportunities and resources to play sports should be increased for women, that women and men should share control over sports, and that new sports organized around the values, interests and experiences of women should be developed. Other suggestions would call for changes in ideas about femininity and masculinity, gender relations, family structures, the allocation of childcare responsibilities, the organization of work and the distribution of resources in society.

When sociologists say that increasing sports participation among women or achieving gender equity in sports programmes requires such changes, they threaten those who benefit from sports and social life as they are currently organized. In response, these people see the sociology of sport as too critical and idealistic, and often claim that these changes would upset the 'natural' order of things. However, good research always helps people think critically about the social conditions that affect our lives. Studying sports with a critical eye is easier if we have informed visions of what sports and society could and should be in the future. Without such visions, often born of idealism, what would motivate and guide us as we participate in our communities, societies and world? People who make a difference and change the world for the better have always been idealistic. This is illustrated in 'Breaking barriers'.

breaking BARRIERS

Cultural barriers – aren't we athletes?

Dame Tanni Grey-Thompson is Britain's most successful Paralympic athlete, having won 15 Paralympic medals. However, in 2003 she missed out on a World Athletics Championship race because she says she was not informed about the trial for the event by UK Athletics, which she believed was symptomatic of the treatment of disabled athletes. In a statement, she suggested that 'if this had happened to Paula Radcliffe [an Olympic athlete], there would have been an uproar'. She had previously had problems in acquiring kit, been excluded from team photographs, and booked into hotels and aboard flights that did not provide the wheelchair access that she requires:

> There is insufficient recognition or awareness of disabled athletes in the culture of our sporting organisations ... We need to have a wider discussion in British sport on what we are doing with the Paralympics and how we are treating disabled athletes.
>
> *(Dame Tanni Grey-Thompson, cited in Baker, 2003)*

Grey-Thompson's comments, combined with the relative invisibility of sports for athletes with a disability, raise a sociological question: whose sports count in society? The answer is that ideas and decisions about sports are based on multiple interactions that occur under particular cultural, political and economic conditions. For sociologists, this raises three additional questions: who is involved in and excluded from these interactions? Whose interests are represented or disadvantaged by the decisions made? How can cultural, political and economic conditions be changed so that decisions are more representative of all people in a social world?

Most readers of this book have never had friends whose physical or intellectual impairments made them 'disabled' and never met an athlete from the Paralympic Games or the Special Olympics. This means that if we asked you to close your eyes and imagine five different sport scenes, few of you would picture a scene involving athletes who have had a limb amputated, are in wheelchairs, blind, with cerebral palsy, or with intellectual or developmental disabilities.

This imagination exercise is *not* meant to evoke guilt. People's views of the world, including our own, are based on personal experiences, and our experiences are influenced by the meanings that are given to age, gender, race, ethnicity, social class, sexuality, (dis)ability and other characteristics that are defined as socially significant in our culture. Neither culture nor society forces us to think or do certain things, but the only way to mute their influence is to critically examine social worlds and understand the ways that cultural meanings and social organization create constraints and opportunities in people's lives, including people with disabilities.

In each of the following chapters, a 'Breaking barriers' box presents the voices and experiences of people with disabilities. If you are *currently* able-bodied, each box alerts you to social and cultural

Are these athletes? Their times in the 100- and 200-metre sprints are better than all but a handful of sprinters worldwide. Why are some sports defined as more real or more important than others? Who determines the standards? These three sprinters run on Ossur's Cheetah Flex-Foot. Does this matter in terms of a definition of sport? (Source: David Biene; photograph courtesy of Ossur)

barriers that constrain the lives of people with disabilities. If you have a disability, each box acknowledges the barriers that you, Tanni Grey-Thompson and millions of others face in the pursuit of sports participation.

These barriers, according to many people, are 'just the way things are'. Eliminating them is impossible or unrealistic because they require changes in the organization of relationships, schools, communities and societies. However, we are not victims of culture and society. If we have informed and idealistic visions of what sports could and should be, it is possible to identify and eliminate barriers. Fung Ying Ki, a triple gold medal winner in the 2000 Sydney Paralympics, knew that it was possible to break barriers when she said, 'I hope that, in the future, there will no longer be "disabled athletes" in this world, only "athletes"' (in Joukowsky and Rothstein, 2002b, p. 115).

Different approaches in the sociology of sport

Some scholars who study sports in society are more interested in learning about sports than society. They focus on understanding the organization of sports and the experiences of athletes and spectators. Their goal, in most cases, is to improve sports experiences for current participants, and make sports participation more attractive and accessible. They also may do research to improve athletic performance, coaching effectiveness, and the efficiency and profitability of sports organizations. These scholars often refer to themselves as **sports sociologists**, and see themselves as part of the larger field of **sports sciences**.

Scholars concerned primarily with social and cultural issues usually refer to themselves as sociologists who study sports or as cultural studies scholars. Their research on sports in society is often connected with more general interests in leisure, popular culture, social relations and social life as a whole. They use sports as windows into culture, society and social relationships, and they study sports as metaphorical stories that people tell themselves about themselves, thereby revealing their values, ideas and beliefs.

Differences between scholars are not unique to the sociology of sport. They occur in every discipline as researchers make decisions about the questions they will ask and the knowledge they seek to produce. Knowledge is a source of power, so our knowledge in the sociology of sport has practical and political implications. It influences the ways that people view sports, integrate them into their lives, and make decisions about the organization and place of sports in society.

Why Study Sports in Society?

This is a serious question for people in the sociology of sport. The answer that most of us give is that we study sports because they are given special meaning by particular people in societies, they are tied to important ideas and beliefs in many cultures, and they are connected with major spheres of social life such as the family, religion, education, the economy, politics and the media.

Sports are given special meaning in people's lives

We study sports in society because they are important parts of everyday social life around the world. As we look around us, we see that the Olympic Games, football's World Cup, the Tour de France, the tennis championships at Wimbledon and American football's Super Bowl are now worldwide events capturing the interest of billions of people. As these and other sports events are viewed in person or through the electronic media by people in over 200 countries, they produce vivid images and lively stories that entertain and inspire people, and provide them with the words and ideas that they use to make sense of their experiences and the world around them. Even when people do not have an interest in sports, their family and friends may insist on taking them to games and talking with them about sports to the point that they are forced to make sports a part of their lives. Sports images are so pervasive today that many young people are more familiar with the tattoos and body piercings of their favourite sports celebrities than they are with political leaders who make policies that have a significant impact on their lives.

People worldwide increasingly talk about sports – at work, at home, in pubs, on dates, at dinner tables, in school, with friends, and even with strangers at bus stops, in airports and on the street. Sports provide non-threatening conversation topics with strangers. Relationships often revolve around sports, especially among men, and increasingly among women. People identify with teams and athletes so closely that what happens in sports influences their moods, identities and sense of well-being. People's identities as athletes and fans may be more important to them than their identities related to education, career, religion or family.

Overall, sports and sports images and stories have become a pervasive part of our everyday lives, especially for those of us living in countries where resources are relatively plentiful and access to the media is widespread. For this reason, sports are logical topics for the attention of sociologists and anyone else concerned with social life today.

Sports are tied to important ideas and beliefs in many cultures

We also study sports in society because they are closely linked with how people think about and see the world. Sociologists try to understand these links by studying connections between sports and cultural ideologies.

Ideologies *are webs of ideas and beliefs that people use to give meaning to the world and make sense of their experiences.* Ideologies are important aspects of culture because they embody the principles, perspectives and viewpoints that underlie our feelings, thoughts and actions. However, ideologies seldom come in neat packages, especially in highly diverse and rapidly changing societies. Different groups of people in society often develop their own ideas and beliefs for giving meaning to the world and making sense of their experiences, and they do not always agree. These groups may struggle over whose ideologies provide the most accurate, useful or moral ways of giving meaning to and explaining the world and their experiences in it.

As various groups use and promote their ideologies in society, sports become socially relevant. As social constructions, sports can be organized to reinforce or challenge important ideas and beliefs. People create and organize sports around their ideas and beliefs about bodies, relationships, abilities, character, gender, race, social class, and other attributes and characteristics that they define as important in their lives. Usually, the most popular forms of sport in a society reinforce and reproduce the ideologies favoured and promoted by people with the most power and influence in that society. In the process, those ideologies often become dominant in that most people learn to use them as they make sense of the world and their experiences in it.

When this occurs, sports serve as cultural practices that support and solidify particular forms of social organization and power relations.

Gender ideology

We can use gender ideology to illustrate these points. **Gender ideology** consists of *a web of ideas and beliefs about masculinity, femininity and male–female relationships.* People use gender ideology to define what it means to be a man or a woman, evaluate and judge people and relationships, and determine what they consider to be natural and moral when it comes to gender. It also is used as people create, play and give meaning to sports.

Dominant gender ideology in most societies has traditionally emphasized that men are naturally superior to women in activities that involve strength, physical skills and emotional control. Through most of the twentieth century, this idea was used to establish a form of 'common sense' and a vocabulary that defined female inferiority in sports as 'natural'. Therefore, when a person threw a ball correctly, people learned to say that he or she 'threw like a boy' or 'like a man'. When a person threw a ball incorrectly, they learned to say that he or she 'threw like a girl'. The same was true when people were evaluated in terms of their abilities to run or do sports in general. If sports were done right, they were done the way a boy or man would do them. If they were done wrong, they were done the way a girl or woman would do them.

The belief that doing sports, especially sports that are physically demanding, would make boys into men has long been consistent with dominant gender ideology in many cultures, and especially in British culture. Consequently, when women excelled at these sports, many people claimed that they were 'unnatural'. Dominant gender ideology led them to assume that femininity and athletic excellence, especially in physically demanding or heavy contact sports, should not go together. As they tried to make sense of strong, competent women athletes, they concluded that such women must be male-like or lesbians. When this conclusion was combined with related ideas and beliefs about nature, morality and gender, many people restricted opportunities for girls and women to play sports.

This gender ideology was so widely accepted by people in sports that coaches of men's teams even used it to motivate players. They criticized men who made mistakes or did not play aggressively enough by 'accusing' them of 'playing like a bunch of girls'. As they made sense of sports and gender, these coaches inferred that being female meant being a failure. This ideology clearly served to privilege males and disadvantage females in the provision of opportunities and the allocation of resources to play sports. Although it has been challenged and discredited in recent years, the legacy of this gender ideology continues in many social worlds to privilege boys and men, and disadvantage girls and women.

Fortunately, ideology can be and sometimes is changed. People may question and struggle over it, and some people organize challenges that produce changes in deeply felt and widely accepted ideas and beliefs. In the case of gender ideology, sports have occasionally been *sites* or 'social places' for challenging dominant ideas about what is natural and feminine. The history of struggles over the meaning and implications of gender in sports is complex, but recent challenges by both women and men who do not accept traditional ideas and beliefs have led to important changes in gender ideology.

Women athletes have illustrated clearly that females can be physically powerful and capable of noteworthy physical achievements surpassing those of the vast majority of men in the world.

Furthermore, the accomplishments of women athletes have raised serious questions about what is 'natural' when it comes to gender. We will discuss issues related to gender ideology in sports in nearly every chapter, but especially Chapter 8. The box 'The body is more than physical: sports influence meanings given to the body,' presents issues related to another ideological issue in our lives: what do we consider to be natural when it comes to the body?

reflect on Sports   *The body is more than physical: sports influence meanings given to the body*

Until recently, most people viewed the body as a fixed fact of nature; it was biological only. But many scholars and scientists now recognize that a full understanding of the body requires that we view it in social and cultural terms (Blake, 1996; Brownell, 1995; Butler, 2004; Cole, 2000a; Evans et al., 2004; Hargreaves and Vertinsky, 2006; Petersen, 2007; Shilling, 1993, 2005a, 2005b; Turner, 1997). For example, medical historians explain that the body and body parts have been identified and defined differently through history and from one culture to another. This is important because it affects medical practice, government policies, social theories, sports participation and our everyday experiences (Fausto-Sterling, 2000; Laqueur, 1990; Lupton, 2000; Preves, 2005; Wahidin and Powell, 2003).

The meanings given to the body in any culture are the foundation for people's ideas and beliefs about sex, sex differences, sexuality, ideals of beauty, self-image, body image, fashion, hygiene, health, nutrition, eating, fitness, age and ageing, racial classification systems, disease, drugs and drug testing, violence and power, and other factors that affect our lives. Cultural definitions of the body influence deep personal feelings such as desire, pleasure, pain and other sensations that we use to assess personal well-being, relationships and quality of life. For example, people in Europe and North America during the nineteenth century identified insensitivity to physical pain as a sign that a person had serious character defects, and they saw a muscular body as an indicator of a person's criminal tendencies, immorality and lower-class status (Hoberman, 1992).

Cultural definitions of the body have changed so that today we see a person's ability to ignore pain, especially in the context of sports, as an indicator of strong moral character, and we see a muscular body as an indicator of self-control and discipline, not criminal tendencies, immorality and lower-class status. However, despite changes in the meanings given to the body, our identities and experiences are inherently embodied, and our bodies are identified in connection with social and cultural definitions of age, sex, sexuality, race, ethnicity and disability, among other factors.

Definitions of the body are strongly related to sports in many societies. For example, our conception of the 'ideal body', especially the ideal male body, is strongly influenced by the athletic body. Athletic bodies are used and displayed widely as models of health and fitness, strength and power, control and discipline, and overall ability. In today's competitive sports the body is measured, classified, typed, labelled, conditioned, trained, regulated and assessed in terms of its performance under various conditions. Instead of being conceived as a source of pleasure and joy, the body is more often viewed as a machine that is used to achieve instrumental rather than emotional goals. As a machine, its parts must be developed, co-ordinated, maintained, and fixed when they break down. Additionally, when the athletic body fails due to injuries, impairments and age, it is reclassified in ways that alter identity, relationships and status.

This way of defining, or *socially constructing,* the body emphasizes control and rationality. It leads people to accept and even seek forms of body assessment and regulation such as weigh-ins, the measurement of body-fat percentage, body and muscle size, tests for aerobic and anaerobic capacity,

The steroid-enhanced body of Arnold Schwarzenegger made bodybuilding popular worldwide. A cut-out of his pose as Mr Olympia is used to inspire the bodybuilding workouts of men who come to this gym in Ghazni, Afghanistan (in 2007). The man in this photograph may be comparing his own body image with that of Schwarzenegger and attempting to mirror the excessive muscularity which is highly valued in the social world of male bodybuilders. Although public displays of bodies are traditionally discouraged in Afghan culture, the notion that bodies can be sculpted in ways that change men's lives is increasingly accepted (Source: Musadeq Sadeq, AP Worldwide Photos)

physiological responses to various stressors, hormone testing, the ingestion of drugs and other chemical substances, drug testing, blood analysis and testing, diet restrictions, and on and on.

The cultural conceptions of *body as machine* and *sport as performance* make it likely that athletes will use brain manipulations, hormonal regulation, body-part replacements and genetic engineering as methods of disciplining and controlling their bodies. Measurable performance outcomes will be given priority over subjective experiences of bodily pleasure and joy (Pronger, 2002). As a result, the ability to endure pain and stay in the game will be used as an indicator of the 'disciplined body', and a body that is starved to reduce 'percentage of body fat' to unhealthy levels will be described as 'fit' and 'in shape'.

Once we realize that human life is embodied and that the body is socially constructed in all cultures, there are critical questions to be asked. These include the following:

- What are the origins of prevailing ideas about natural, ideal, and deviant bodies in sports and in culture generally?
- What are the moral and social implications of the ways that the body is protected, probed, monitored, tested, trained, disciplined, evaluated, manipulated and rehabilitated in sports?
- How are bodies in sports marked and categorized by gender, skin colour, ethnicity, (dis)ability and age, and what are the social implications of such body marking and categorization?
- How are athletic bodies represented in the media and popular culture, and how do those representations influence identities, relationships and forms of social organization?
- Who owns the body of an athlete, and what happens when it is used or sold as a billboard for advertising products and services?

These questions are seldom asked by people associated with sports because they challenge their taken-for-granted ideas about nature, beauty, health and competitive sports. But learning about sports in society requires that they be asked and investigated. *What do you think?*

Racial ideology

Sports are sites for important ideological struggles. For example, in the UK, they have been sites for either reproducing or challenging dominant ideas about race and the connections between skin colour and abilities, both physical and intellectual. **Racial ideology** consists of *a web of ideas and beliefs that people use to give meaning to skin colour and evaluate people in terms of racial classifications*. Racial ideologies vary around the world, but they are powerful forces in the social lives of many people. They are used to place people into racial categories, and they influence important social practices and policies that affect people's lives.

The connections between sports and racial ideologies are complex. Racial ideology is often used as a basis for evaluating athletic potential or explaining athletic success. The notion that light-skinned people cannot jump and that dark-skinned people are natural athletes are expressions of dominant racial ideology in certain cultures – an issue discussed in Chapter 9.

Class ideology, amateurism and professionalism

Class ideology consists of *a web of ideas and beliefs that people use to understand economic inequalities and make sense of their own position in an economic hierarchy in society*. British society has a long tradition of a social class hierarchy, and differential status and privileges available to its citizens. However, in recent years, sports in the UK have reflected broader social changes, which include the expansion of opportunities, the development of professionalism and increased media coverage, and this has created a sense of British society as a **meritocracy** *where deserving people become successful and success is achieved by those who deserve it*. As a result, sports are increasingly viewed as a legitimate career path. Sports provide many stories and slogans emphasizing that people can achieve anything through discipline and hard work, and that failure awaits those who are lazy and undisciplined. By extension, this ideology leads people to make positive conclusions about the character and qualifications of wealthy and powerful people, and negative conclusions about the character and qualifications of those who are poor and powerless. Winners are assumed to have strong character, whereas losers are assumed to have weak character. This way of thinking is used to explain and legitimize class inequality, and it connects sports positively with capitalism and its competitive system of economic rewards. This is discussed in Chapters 10 and 11.

Sports and ideologies: complex connections

As we think about sports and ideologies, it is important to know that ideology is complex and sometimes inconsistent, and that sports come in many forms and have many meanings associated with them. Therefore, sports are connected with ideologies in various and sometimes contradictory ways. We saw this in the example showing that sports are sites for simultaneously reproducing *and* challenging dominant gender ideology in society. Furthermore, sports can have many social meanings associated with them. For example, football is played by similar rules in South Africa and the UK, but the meanings associated with football and with athletes' performances are different in the two cultures because of ideological differences. In South Africa, the development of football has been a symbol of emancipation, and an inherent part of building a new national and non-racial identity in the post-apartheid era. In the UK, there has been resistance to the development of one national team for international competition, and football sometimes symbolizes a divided nation in an era of political devolution, with each home country having its own national team. The complex connections between sports and ideologies make it difficult to generalize about the role and consequences of sports in society. Sports have the social potential to do many things. This is another reason for studying them as social constructions.

> Using the undeniably strong forces of the Olympic movement in combination with other international and national bodies and organisations, I want to build a much stronger global alliance, using government and sports organisations, and businesses – to inspire youth to get into sport, to get into recreation – to make sure they enjoy it enough to stay in it; to strive to make clear the benefits of such involvement for them and their communities.
>
> *(Lord Sebastian Coe, Chair of London Olympic Games Organizing Committee, 2006)*

Sports are connected to major spheres of social life

Another reason to study sports in society is that they are clearly connected to major spheres of social life, including the family, the economy, the media, politics, education and religion. We discuss these connections in various chapters in this book, but it is useful to highlight them at this point.

Sports and the family

Sports are closely related to the family. In the UK, talented young people are being encouraged to become involved in a variety of organized sports activities in the build-up to the London 2012 Olympic Games. It is primarily their parents who organize their schedule, often coach or referee training, attend games and serve as 'taxi drivers' for child athletes. Family schedules are altered to accommodate training and games. These schedules also may be affected by sports participation among adult family members. The viewing of televised sports events sometimes disrupts family life and at other times provides a collective focus for family attention. In some cases, relationships between family members are nurtured and played out during sports activities or in conversations about them. Two of these situations are represented in Cartoon 1.2. Family issues are discussed in Chapters 4 and 5.

Sports, education and health

Sports are integral parts of school life in many countries. They are taught and played in physical education classes, and schools in a few countries have inter-scholastic sports teams that attract widespread attention among students and community residents. Physical education in the UK has its historical roots in the public health movement, and recent policies for physical education are grounded in a perceived need to challenge chronic diseases such as cardio-vascular problems, diabetes and obesity, through increasing children's physical activity levels.

Cartoon 1.2 **Families and family schedules often are influenced by sports involvement. Sometimes this involvement disrupts family life and interferes with family relationships (top); sometimes it brings family members together in enjoyable ways (bottom)**

In addition, specialist sports colleges and school sports partnerships aim to increase sports standards, improve competitions and develop links with sports clubs. These issues are discussed in Chapter 5.

Sports and the economy

The economies of most countries, especially wealthy post-industrial countries, are affected by the billions of pounds spent every year for match tickets, sports equipment, participation fees, club membership dues, and bets placed on favourite teams and athletes. Sports teams affect the economies of many communities. Most countries use public monies (taxes) to subsidize teams and events. In fact, sports and commerce have fused together so that corporate logos are linked with sports teams and athletes, and are displayed prominently in arenas, stadiums and other places where sports are played and watched. Sports stadiums, arenas and teams are now named after corporations: for example, the Leicester City football ground is named the Walkers Stadium after its sponsors, Walkers Crisps; and Bolton Wanderers' ground is the Reebok Stadium.

Some athletes make impressive sums of money from combinations of salaries, appearance fees and endorsements. When the former England football captain, David Beckham, transferred from Manchester United to Real Madrid in 2003, his transfer fee was £25 million. It is estimated that this was recouped by the club within a year from the sale of his Number 23 shirt, and that 'Brand Beckham' was responsible for half of Real Madrid's merchandise income in 2003–04 (*The Economist*, 2004). Beckham himself earned approximately £6 million per year in his salary from Real Madrid, but is also estimated to have paid himself around £19 million for the 2005–06 year from his own company, Footwork Productions Ltd, for his endorsements, which include Adidas, Gillette, Pepsi and Police sunglasses. Sponsorships and commercial associations with sports are so common that people now believe that, without Coca-Cola, McDonald's, Nike and other transnational corporations, sports could not exist. This indicates that sports are cultural practices deeply connected with the material and economic conditions in society. These issues are discussed in Chapters 10, 11 and 12.

Sports and the media

Television networks pay millions of pounds for the rights to televise major games and events. The BBC and ITV paid £160 million for the rights to the 2002 and 2006 FIFA World Cups[TM]. In the USA, NBC, owned by General Electric, paid the International Olympic Committee US$1.181 billion for the rights to the London Olympic Games of 2012. People in sports organizations that depend on spectators are keenly aware that without the media their lives would be different.

The images and stories presented in media coverage of sports also emphasize particular ideological themes, and they influence how people see and think about sports and social life. The media have converted sports into a major form of entertainment witnessed by billions of people. Athletes are global celebrities, and the corporations that sponsor sports inscribe their logos in people's minds as they promote lifestyles based on consumption. These issues are discussed in Chapter 12.

Sports and politics

People in many societies link sports to feelings of national pride and a sense of national identity. The complexity of this link in the UK is illustrated in the Olympic Games and other sports events for which athletes form a combined team of Great Britain and Northern Ireland, whereas in other events, such as the Commonwealth Games, each home country has its own national team, and in international rugby tournaments players from Northern Ireland and the Republic of Ireland combine for one team representing Ireland.

Most people around the globe have no second thoughts about displaying national flags and playing national anthems at sporting events, and some may quickly reject athletes and other spectators who do not think as they do about the flag and the anthem.

Political leaders at various levels of government promote themselves by associating with sports as participants and spectators. Former athletes, such as Sebastian Coe and Menzies Campbell, have been elected to powerful political positions in the UK by using their name recognition and reputations from sports to attract votes.

International sports have become hotbeds of political controversy in recent years, and most countries around the world have used sports actively to enhance their reputations in global political relationships. Furthermore, sports involve political processes associated with issues such as who controls sports and sports events, the terms of eligibility and team selection, rules and rule changes, rule enforcement and the allocation of rewards and punishments. Sports and sports organizations are political because they involve the exercise of power over people's lives. These issues are discussed in Chapter 13.

Sports and religion

There is an emerging relationship between sports and religion in certain cultures. Some sports clubs have a specific religious affiliation even in increasingly secular societies, for example the traditional conflict between the Scottish football teams, Celtic (Catholic) and Rangers (Protestant). Many athletes in the UK express religious beliefs and define their sports participation in religious terms. There are specific faith-based organizations for such sportspeople, such as Christians in Sport, whose mission includes playing sport in a way that honours God. These issues are discussed in Chapters 9 and 13.

What is the Current Status of the Sociology of Sport?

Prior to 1980, very few people studied sports in society. Scholars were not concerned with physical activities and thought that sports were unrelated to important issues in society. However, a few sociologists and physical educators in Europe and North America began to 'think outside the box' of their disciplines. They decided that sports should be studied because they were becoming increasingly important activities in many societies. During the last two decades of the twentieth century, the sociology of sport gradually came to be recognized as a legitimate sub-field in sociology and physical education/kinesiology/sports science.

Research and interest in the sociology of sport has increased dramatically over the past few decades. This is reflected in the rapid expansion of research and scholarly discussions of sports in society. For example, in 2000, when we searched for 'sports in society' books on Amazon.com, we received a list of fewer than 300 titles. The same search in mid-2007 turned up a list of over 5600 books! Similarly, the number of scholarly journals that publish articles in or related to the sociology of sport has increased, and these are listed in Table 1.1.

Table 1.1 **Publication sources for sociology of sport research**

Journals devoted primarily to sociology of sport articles
European Journal for Sport and Society (biannual)
International Review for the Sociology of Sport (quarterly)
Journal of Sport and Social Issues (quarterly)
Sociology of Sport Journal (quarterly)
Sport in Society (six times per year)
Sociology journals that sometimes include articles on or related to sports
American Journal of Sociology
American Sociological Review
British Journal of Sociology
International Sociology
Sociology
Sociology of Education
Theory, Culture, and Society
Interdisciplinary, sport science and physical education journals that sometimes include articles on or related to sociology of sport topics
Avante
Canadian Journal of Applied Sport Sciences
Sport in Society (formerly *Culture, Sport, Society*)
European Physical Education Review
Exercise and Sport Sciences Review
Journal of Physical Education, Recreation, and Dance
Journal of Sport Behavior
Journal of Sport Management
Journal of Sport Sciences
Physical Education and Sport Pedagogy
Quest
Research Quarterly for Exercise and Sport
Sport, Education, and Society
Sport Science Review
Women in Sport & Physical Activity Journal
Journals in related fields that sometimes include articles on or related to sociology of sport topics
Adolescence
Aethlon: The Journal of Sport Literature
The British Journal of Sport History
Canadian Journal of the History of Sport

European Sport Management Quarterly

The European Sports History Review

International Journal of the History of Sport

International Journal of Sport Psychology

Journal of Human Movement Studies

Journal of Leisure Research

Journal of the Philosophy of Sport

Journal of Popular Culture

Journal of Sport and Exercise Psychology

Journal of Sport History

Journal of Sport Media

Journal of Sports and Economics

Leisure Sciences

Leisure Studies

Managing Leisure

Olympika: The International Journal of Olympic Studies

Soccer and Society

Society and Leisure

Sport History Review

Sport Management Review

The Sport Psychologist

Sporting Traditions

Sport in History (formerly *The Sports Historian*)

Youth & Society

Sociology of sport organizations include the following.

- *The International Sociology of Sport Association (ISSA).* This organization, formed in 1965, meets annually and attracts international scholars. Since 1965 it has sponsored publication of the *International Review for the Sociology of Sport.*

- *European Association for the Sociology of Sport (eass).* This organization was formed in 2001, and has held regular conferences since then. It has sponsored the publication of the *European Journal for Sport and Society* since 2004.

- *Association for the Study of Sport and the European Union.* This organization was formed in 2005 to promote an inter-disciplinary understanding of the implications of the European Union for sport, and consequences for policies, law and society.

- *The British Sociological Association (BSA).* This association established a Sociology of Sport Study Group in 1995. The association has sponsored the journal *Sociology* since 1967.

- *The North American Society for the Sociology of Sport (NASSS).* This organization, formed in 1978, has held annual conferences every year since 1980 which attract many delegates from the UK, and it has sponsored publication of the *Sociology of Sport Journal* since 1984. Various other countries and regions also have their own associations for the study of the sociology of sport.

Growth in the sociology of sport will continue to occur if scholars in the field conduct and publish research that people find useful as they seek to understand social life and participate effectively as citizens in their communities and societies.

Summary: Why Study the Sociology of Sport?

Sociology is the study of social life, including all forms of social interaction and relationships. Sociologists are concerned with social issues, social organization and social change. Their goal is to enable people to understand, control and change their lives so that human needs are met at both individual and group levels.

Sociologists study sports as parts of culture and society. They look at sports in terms of their importance in people's lives and their connections to ideology and major spheres of social life. Research in the sociology of sport helps us understand sports as social constructions created by people for particular purposes. As social constructions, sports are related to historical, political and economic factors.

Some scholars in the field define *sports* as activities involving (1) the use of physical skill, prowess or exertion, (2) institutionalized competition, and (3) the combination of intrinsic and extrinsic reasons for participation. Using a single definition of sports is problematic if it leads us to ignore or devalue the lives of people who do not have the resources and the desire to develop formally organized and competitive physical activities. For this reason, many scholars now recommend that, instead of using such a definition, we should ask what activities are identified as sports in different groups and societies at different points in time. This approach forces us to recognize that sports are contested activities. Further, it focuses our attention on the relationship between sports and power and privilege in society, and leads more directly to concerns for transforming social life so that more people have resources to control their lives and make them meaningful.

When sociologists study sports in society, they often discover problems based in the structure and organization of either sports or society. When this happens, the recommendations that sociologists make may threaten those who want sports and sports programmes to remain as they are now. Therefore, sociology sometimes creates controversies. Continued growth of the sociology of sport depends primarily on whether scholars in the field do research and produce knowledge that makes meaningful contributions to people's lives.

Website resources

Note: Websites often change. The following URLs were current when this book was printed. Please check our website (***www.mcgraw-hill.co.uk/textbooks/coakley***) for updates and additions.

www.britsoc.co.uk/specialisms/123.htm This is the link to the Sociology of Sport Study Group of the British Sociological Association, and provides information on the activities of members of this group.

www.hlst.heacademy.ac.uk/Resources/resource_guides.html#sport This is the link to the Higher Education Academy's site for hospitality, leisure, sport and tourism programmes, providing a guide to texts, journals, websites and other resources. It is particularly useful for resources for sport development, sport history, the Olympic Games and comparative sport studies.

www.intute.ac.uk/socialsciences/sport/ This is a free online service providing links to websites and resources for a variety of subject areas related to the sociology of sport.

www.issa.otago.ac.nz The official site of ISSA, the International Sociology of Sport Association; this organization is a subcommittee of ICSSPE, the International Council of Sport Science and Physical Education, and is affiliated with UNESCO, the United Nations Educational, Scientific and Cultural Organization.

www.le.ac.uk/so/css Follow links to 'RESOURCES AND PUBLICATIONS' for a range of factsheets and publications that may be ordered online.

www.nasss.org The official site for the North American Society for the Sociology of Sport; the Resource Centre contains a list of experts in the field, along with graduate programmes specializing in the sociology of sport.

http://people.pwf.cam.ac.uk/dojr2/sportseu/accueil.html This is the site for the Association for the Study of Sport and the European Union, containing details of members, activities and a downloadable newsletter.

http://physed.otago.ac.nz/sosol The site for the Sociology of Sport Online: sosol is an international electronic forum with an archive of articles and book reviews published from 1998 to 2004 related to the sociological examination of sport, physical education and coaching; it is hosted by the School of Physical Education at the University of Otago in New Zealand.

www.pscw.uva.nl/sociosite/TOPICS/Leisure.html Click on 'SPORT'; this site, located in the Netherlands, provides excellent links to sites related to the sociology of sport, especially to international sites related to women in sports and to the Olympics.

www.studentzone.org.uk/sport/sportorgs.html This site provides links to a variety of sports organizations, including those providing downloadable materials on government policies, Olympic sport, women's sport and a range of governing bodies.

Chapter 2

Using social theories: how can they help us study sports in society?

Sport as an institution is just too economically big, too politically important, too influential in shaping people's lives not to be taken seriously as a subject for academic inquiry.

(Ellis Cashmore, Professor of Culture, Media and Sport, 2005, p. 2)

Online *Learning* Centre Resources

Visit *Sports in Society*'s Online Learning Centre (OLC) at **www.mcgraw-hill.co.uk/ textbooks/coakley** for additional information and study material for this chapter, including:

- Self-grading quizzes and essay questions
- Learning outcomes
- Related websites
- Additional readings

Chapter contents

What are theories and why do we need them?

Functionalist theory: sports preserve the status quo

Conflict theory: sports are tools of the wealthy

Critical theory: sports are sites where culture and social relations are produced and changed

Feminist theory: sports are gendered activities

Interactionist theory: sports are given meaning as people interact with one another

Figurational theory: sports are collective inventions

Is there a best theoretical approach to use when studying sports?

Summary: how can social theories help us study sports in society?

> The critical sociology of sport can therefore be conceptualized as theoretically eclectic, multidisciplinary, and dynamic; it draws on contributions from disciplines ranging from history to psychoanalysis; and it is consistently developing in responses to theoretical, political and social changes.
>
> *(Ian McDonald, sociologist of sport, 2002, p. 102)*

Those of us who study sports in society want to understand four things: (1) the social and cultural contexts in which sports exist, (2) the connections between those contexts and sports, (3) the social worlds that people create as they participate in sports, and (4) the experiences of individuals and groups associated with those social worlds. We are motivated by combinations of curiosity, interests in sports, and concerns about social life and social issues. Most of us also want to use what we know about sports in society to promote social justice, expose and challenge the exploitive use of power, and empower people so that they might resist and transform oppressive social conditions.

As we study and apply knowledge about sports, we use social and cultural theories. Theories provide frameworks for asking research questions, interpreting information, and uncovering the deeper meanings and stories associated with sports. They also enable us to be more informed citizens as we apply what we learn in our research to the world in which we live. Because those of us who study sports in society come from diverse academic backgrounds and because social life is complex, we use multiple theories to guide our work. The three goals of this chapter are to:

1   identify and describe the theories used most widely to study sports in society

2   explain the ways that theories help us understand sports and the society in which we live

3   demonstrate how theories influence our view of sports and the practical actions we take in connection with sports.

What are Theories and Why Do We Need Them?

Whenever we ask why our social world is the way it is and then imagine how it might be changed, we are 'theorizing' (hooks, 1992). **Theorizing** involves *a combination of description, analysis, reflection and application.* When we theorize, we are not required to use big words and complex sentences. In fact, the best theories are those we understand so clearly that they help us make sense of our experiences and the social world.

When we study sports in society, the best theories are those that describe and explain aspects of social life in logical terms that are consistent with systematic observations of the social world. Theories enable us to see things from new angles and perspectives, understand more fully the relationship between sports and social life, and make informed decisions about sports and sports participation in our lives, families, communities and societies.

Many people think that theories do not have practical applications, but this is not true. Most of our decisions and actions are based on our predictions of their possible consequences, and those predictions are based on our 'personal theories' about social life. Our theories may be incomplete, poorly developed, based on limited information and biased to fit our needs, but we still use them to guide our decisions and actions. When our theories are accurate, our predictions help us relate more effectively with others and control more effectively what happens in our lives. When people make decisions about sports, formulate policies or decide whether to fund or cut money from sport programmes, they base decisions on their personal theories about sports and society.

The theories discussed in this chapter are different from our personal theories about social life. This is because they are based on a combination of systematic research and deductive logic. They have been presented in books and articles so that others may evaluate, test, use and revise them. When logic or evidence contradicts them, theories are revised or abandoned.

People who study sports in society have used many theories to guide them as they ask research questions and interpret research findings. However, most scholarly work over the past half century has been based on one or a combination of six major theories:

1   functionalist theory

2   conflict theory

3 critical theory

4 feminist theory

5 interactionist theory

6 figurational theory.

Although there are important differences between these six theories, there are many points at which two or more of them converge and overlap. This is because people read and respond to the ideas of others as they do research and develop new explanations of society and social life. Therefore, theories are *emerging* explanations of what we know about social worlds at this time.

Several British sociologists have been at the forefront of the development of social theory to increase our understanding of sports in society. Eric Dunning led a tradition of figurational sociology from the University of Leicester, and this tradition is well represented in the UK by, among others, Joseph Maguire, Patrick Murphy and Ivan Waddington. John Sugden and Alan Tomlinson at the University of Brighton have argued convincingly for a more critical sociology of sport, and much of their work sits at the intersection of sociology and investigative journalism. British feminists have also contributed to the sociology of sport, perhaps most notably in the works of Ann Flintoff, Jennifer Hargreaves and Sheila Scraton. Advocates of conflict theory include John Hargreaves, while Alan Bairner at Loughborough University and Ian McDonald at the University of Brighton are founder members of the International Network for the Marxist Study of Sport.

Each of the six theories discussed in this chapter provides a different perspective for understanding the relationship between sports and society. This will be highlighted through the following: (1) a brief overview of each theory, (2) examples of the ideas and research that have been inspired by the theory, (3) explanations of how the theory can be used as we take actions and make policies about sports in our everyday lives, and (4) an overview of the major weaknesses of the theory.

Table 2.1 provides a summary of each theory and how it helps us understand sports in society. The table contains a large amount of material. It may look confusing at first, but, as you read through the chapter, you will find it to be a useful reference guide to each theory. Most important, it will help you identify and understand similarities and differences between the theories.

Functionalist Theory: Sports Preserve the Status Quo

Functionalist theory is based on the assumption that society is an organized system of interrelated parts held together by shared values and established social arrangements that maintain the system in a state of balance or equilibrium. The most important social arrangements are social institutions such as the family, education, the economy, the media, politics, religion, leisure and sport. If these social institutions are organized around a core set of values, functionalists assume that a society will operate smoothly and efficiently. When sociologists use functionalist theory to explain how a society, community, school, family, sports team or other social system works, they study the ways that each part in the system contributes to the system's overall operation.

Table 2.1 **Using social theories to study sports in society: a summary and comparison**

	Functionalist theory	Conflict theory	Critical theory	Feminist theory	Interactionist theory	Figurational theory
I. Assumptions about the basis for social order in society	Social order is based on consensus and shared values, which hold the interrelated parts of society together. All social systems operate efficiently when each part of the system stays in synchronization with other parts	Social order is based on economic interests and the use of economic power to exploit labour. Social class shapes social structures and relationships	Social order is negotiated through struggles over ideology, representation and power. Social life is full of diversity, complexities and contradictions	Social order is based primarily on the values, experiences and interests of men with power. Social life and social order is gendered and based on patriarchal ideas	Social order is created by people as they interact with each other. Social life is grounded in social relationships and the meanings given to social reality	Social order is based on interdependencies among individuals and groups. Connections between people take the form of social figurations
II. Major concerns in the study of society	How do the parts of social systems contribute to the satisfaction of 'system needs' and the efficient operation of the system?	How is economic power distributed and used in society? What are the dynamics of social class relations? Who is privileged and exploited in class relations?	How is cultural ideology produced, reproduced and transformed? What are the conflicts and problems that affect the lives of those who lack power in society?	How is gender ideology produced, reproduced and transformed? How do dominant forms of gender relations privilege men over women and some men over others?	How are meanings, identities and culture created through social interaction? How do people define the reality of their own lives and the world around them?	How do social figurations emerge and change? How do power balances within figurations influence relationships between individuals and groups?
III. Major concerns in the study of sport	How does sport fit into social life and contribute to social stability and efficiency? How does sport participation teach people important norms in society?	How does sport reflect class relations? How is sport used to maintain the interests of those with power and wealth in society? How does the profit motive distort sport and sport experiences?	How are power relations reproduced and/or resisted in and through sports? Whose voices are/are not represented in the narratives and images that constitute sports?	How are sports gendered activities, and how do they reproduce dominant ideas about gender in society? What are the strategies for resisting and transforming sport forms that privilege men?	How do people become involved in sports, become defined as athletes, derive meaning from participation, and make transitions out of sports into the rest of their lives?	How did modern sports emerge and become important in society? What social processes are associated with the commercialization of sports, expressions of violence in sports and forms of global sports?

Table 2.1 **Continued**

Functionalist theory	Conflict theory	Critical theory	Feminist theory	Interactionist theory	Figurational theory
IV. Major conclusions about the sport–society relationship					
Sport is a valuable social institution that benefits society as well as individuals in society. Sport is a source of inspiration on both personal and social levels	Sport is a form of physical activity that is distorted by the needs of capital. Sport is an opiate that distracts attention away from the problems that affect those without economic power	Sports are social constructions. Sports are sites at which culture is produced, reproduced and transformed. Sports are cultural practices that repress and/or empower people	Sports are grounded in the values and experiences of powerful men in society. Sports reproduce male power and distorted ideas about masculinity. Sports produce gendered ideas about physicality, sexuality and the body	Sports are forms of culture created through social interaction. Sports participation is grounded in the decisions made by people in connection with their identities and relationships	Sports are exciting activities that relieve boredom and control violence and uncivilized behaviour. Sports celebrate masculinity and male power. Global sports are complex activities with local and national significance
V. Social action and policy implications					
Develop and expand sport programmes that promote traditional values, build the type of character valued in society, and contribute to social order and stability	Raise class-consciousness and make people aware of their own alienation and powerlessness. Eliminate the profit motive in sports thereby allowing them to foster expression, creativity and physical well-being	Use sports as sites for challenging and transforming exploitative and oppressive forms of social relations. Increase the range and diversity of sport participation opportunities. Challenge the voices and perspectives of those with power	Use sports as sites for challenging and transforming oppressive forms of gender relations. Expose and resist homophobia and misogyny in sports. Transform sports to emphasize partnership over competition and domination	Allow individuals to shape sports to fit their definitions or reality. Make sports organizations more open and democratic. Focus on the culture and organization of sports when controlling deviance in sports	Develop a fund of valid knowledge, which can be used to enable people to control expressions of violence, exploitation and the abuse of power. Increase access to sport participation among those who have lacked power through history

Table 2.1 **Continued**

Functionalist theory	Conflict theory	Critical theory	Feminist theory	Interactionist theory	Figurational theory
		VI. Major weaknesses			
It does not acknowledge that sports are social constructions. It overstates the positive consequences of sport. It ignores that sport serves the needs of some people more than others	It ignores that sports can be a site for creative and liberating experiences. It overstates the influence of economic forces in society. It assumes that people who have economic power always shape sports to meet their interests	It does not provide guidelines to assess the effectiveness of particular forms of resistance as strategies for making progressive changes in social worlds. It often uses confusing vocabularies, making it difficult to merge critical ideas and theories	It does not provide guidelines to assess the effectiveness of particular forms of resistance as strategies for making progressive changes in social worlds. It sometimes uses confusing vocabularies making it difficult to merge critical ideas and theories	It does not clearly explain how meaning, identity and interaction are related to social structures and material conditions in society. It generally ignores issues of power and power relations in society	It gives too little attention to problems and struggles that affect day-to-day lives. It understates the immediate personal consequences of oppressive power relations. It gives little attention to the experiences of women and to gender inequities

For example, if Irish society is the system being studied, a person using functionalist theory wants to know how the Irish family, economy, government, educational system, media, religion and sport are related to one another and how they work together in contributing to the smooth operation of the society as a whole. An analysis based on functionalism focuses on the ways that each of these social institutions helps the larger social system to operate efficiently.

According to functionalist theory, social systems operate efficiently when they are organized to do four things: (1) socialize people so that they learn and accept important cultural values, (2) promote social connections between people so that they can co-operate with one another, (3) motivate people to achieve socially approved goals through socially accepted means, and (4) protect the overall system from disruptive outside influences. Functionalists assume that, if these four 'system needs' are satisfied, social order will be maintained and everyone will benefit. The first column in Table 2.1 summarizes functionalist theory.

Functionalist theory and research on sport

Functionalist theory leads people to ask research questions about the ways that sport contributes to the organization and stability of organizations, communities, societies and other social systems. Using functionalist theory, researchers have studied some of the questions and issues that are discussed in the following chapters. Examples include the following.

- Do sports and sports participation influence social and personal development? This issue is discussed in Chapters 4 and 5.
- Do sports and sports participation foster the development of social bonds and relationships in groups, communities and societies? This issue is discussed in Chapters 9, 13 and 14.
- Does playing sports have a positive impact on academic and occupational success, and does it teach people to follow societal rules as they strive for success? These issues are discussed in Chapters 4, 5, 10 and 11.
- Do sports contribute to personal health and wellness, and the overall strength and well-being of society? These issues are discussed in Chapters 4, 5, 13 and 14.

Functionalist theory focuses on the ways that sports contribute to the smooth operation of societies, communities, organizations and groups. This is why a functionalist approach is popular among people interested in preserving the status quo in society. They want sociologists to tell them how sports contribute to the smooth operation of the social systems in which they have been successful. Many people connected with organized competitive sports also prefer functionalist theory because it emphasizes the 'functions' of sports, and supports the conclusion that sports are a source of inspiration for individuals and societies.

Using functionalist theory in everyday life

Popularized forms of functionalist theory often are used when people in positions of power make decisions about sports and sports programmes at national and local levels. For example, a functionalist analysis of sports in society would support the following actions: promoting the development and growth of organized youth sports (to build values), funding inter-scholastic

Functionalist theory assumes that social order depends on maintaining social solidarity through established social institutions, including the institution of sport (Source: **USA Volleyball**)

sports programmes in schools and colleges (to promote organizational loyalty and attachments to schools), developing sports opportunities for girls and women (to increase achievement motivation among girls and women), including sports in military training (to increase military preparedness and the fitness of soldiers) and staging the Olympic Games (to build international goodwill and unity).

Functionalist theory generally leads to the conclusion that sports are popular in society because they maintain the values that preserve stability and order in social life. For example, in the UK it is assumed that sports are popular because they teach people to feel comfortable in tasks that involve competition, goal achievement and teamwork under the supervision of an authority figure. Furthermore, because functionalist theory leads to the conclusion that sports build the kind of character valued in society, it supports policies that recommend the growth of competitive sports programmes, the development of coaching education programmes, the establishment of training centres for top-level athletes, and increased surveillance and drug testing to supervise and control the actions of athletes. In the case of youth sports, functionalist theory supports actions to expand developmental sport schemes for children, establish criminal background checks and certification requirements for coaches, and build a sport system that trains young people to become elite athletes. Overall, functionalist theory inspires research questions about the ways in which sports contribute to the development of individuals and society as a whole.

Many people reading this book are attracted to functionalist theory because they like its emphasis on the positive aspects of sports in society. People in positions of power in society also favour functionalist theory because it is based on the assumption that society is organized for the equal benefit of all people and therefore should not be changed in any dramatic ways. The notion that the system operates effectively in its present form is comforting to people with power because it discourages changes that might jeopardize their privilege and influence. Because the functionalist approach is popular, it is important to know its weaknesses.

Weaknesses of functionalist theory

Functionalist theory has three major weaknesses. First, it does not acknowledge that sports are social constructions that take diverse forms because they are created and defined by people as they interact with one another. Functionalists see sport as a relatively stable social institution that always serves specific functions in societies. Such an approach overlooks the diversity of sports, the extent to which sports promote the interests of powerful and wealthy people more than others, and the possibility that sports may reproduce social outcomes that actually disrupt the smooth functioning of society.

Second, functionalist theory leads to overstatements about the positive effects of sports in society and understatements about their negative effects. For example, it does not help us understand that women in society are disadvantaged when sports are organized in ways that legitimize the use of physical power to dominate others.

Third, functionalist theory is based on the assumption that the needs of all groups within a society are the same. This overlooks the existence of real differences and conflicts of interest in society and cases when sports benefit some groups more than others. This limits our understanding of difference, conflict and the dynamics of change in societies.

Conflict Theory: Sports are Tools of the Wealthy

Conflict theory focuses on the ways that sports are shaped by economic forces and used by economically powerful people to increase their wealth and influence. It is based on the ideas of Karl Marx and his assumption that every society is organized around relationships and social arrangements that are shaped by economic factors. In the case of capitalist societies, relationships and social arrangements are organized around money, wealth and economic power.

Conflict theorists assume that all aspects of social life revolve around economic interests, and that people who control the economy use their power to coerce and manipulate workers and their families to accept the existence of economic inequality as a natural feature of social life. Conflict theorists often focus their research on **class relations**, that is, *social processes that revolve around who has economic power, how that power is used and who is advantaged or disadvantaged by the economic organization of society*. Studies of class relations focus on the consequences of social inequality in all spheres of social life.

The primary goal of conflict theory is similar to the goal of functionalist theory: to develop a general theory that explains the organization and operation of all societies. Conflict theory emphasizes that economic power in capitalist societies is entrenched so deeply that progressive changes are possible only if workers become aware of the need for change and take action to gain control over the organization of the economy. Sports, they argue, focus the attention and the emotions of the workers and have-nots in society on escapist spectator events that distract them from the economic issues and policies that reproduce their own powerlessness in society. Therefore, sports, especially mass spectator sports, are organized and sponsored by wealthy people and large corporations because they perpetuate capitalist values and a lifestyle based on competition, production and consumption. When people passively accept capitalist values, sport becomes an opiate in society – an element of culture that deadens their awareness of economic exploitation, and perpetuates the privilege and positions of people who control wealth and the economy.

Conflict theory and research on sport

Conflict theory is often used by people who study the connection between sports and the dynamics of power and privilege in society. Their research will be used in subsequent chapters as we discuss the following issues.

- Why do athletes become so alienated from their bodies that they will risk injury and physical well-being to play sports? This issue is discussed in Chapters 6 and 7.
- How are sports related to socio-economic inequality in society? This issue is discussed in many chapters – especially Chapters 10 and 11.
- What happens to sports when they become commercialized? This issue is discussed in Chapters 11 and 12.
- How do wealthy and economically powerful people use sports to further their interests? This issue is discussed in Chapters 11, 12 and 13.

Like functionalist theory, conflict theory is based on the assumption that society is a system of interrelated parts. However, those who use conflict theory focus on 'needs of capital' rather than 'general system needs'. Therefore, conflict theorists explain that a capitalist society cannot survive and grow without exploiting workers for the sake of boosting financial profits. Conflict theorists also focus on the ways that sports perpetuate the unequal distribution of power and economic resources in societies. Therefore, they often identify the negative consequences of sports and conclude that radical changes are needed in sports and society if fairness and justice are to prevail. Only when those changes are made will sports become sources of expression, creative energy and physical well-being.

Many people in countries with capitalist economies are not comfortable with the assumptions and conclusions of conflict theory. They say that the negative tone of conflict theory does not fit with their ideas about sports or society, and they are uneasy with conclusions that call for radical changes in the current structure and economic organization of sports and society. However, conflict theory calls attention to important economic issues in sports and forms of inequality that create conflict and tensions in society as a whole.

Using conflict theory in everyday life

Conflict theory focuses on the need to change the economic organization of sports and society. The goal of these changes is to give workers, including athletes, control over the conditions

Conflict theory calls attention to the possibility that sports can be sites for transforming social life. This 'pledge' for a martial arts group is designed to challenge the dominant values of power and performance sports (Source: Elizabeth Pike)

of their work. Problems in society and sports are attributed to the lack of power possessed by workers. Therefore, conflict theorists support policies and programmes that regulate or eliminate profit motives in sports and increase the control that athletes have over the conditions of their own sports participation. They also support policies that increase the element of *play* in sports and decrease the element of *spectacle* because it is designed to generate commercial profits. More play and less spectacle, they argue, would turn sport participation into a liberating and empowering experience for the masses of people in society.

In terms of specific issues, conflict theorists favour players' unions and radical changes in the control and economic organization of sports. Ideally, public resources would be used to sponsor sports designed to promote fun, fitness and political awareness; spectator sports would exist for enjoyment in local communities rather than as tools for creating celebrity athletes and financial profits for a few wealthy people.

Weaknesses of conflict theory

Conflict theory has three major weaknesses. First, it ignores the possibility that sports in capitalist societies may involve experiences that empower individuals and groups. Conflict theorists talk about sports being organized to maximize the control that wealthy people have over everyone else in capitalist societies. They see sports as activities through which athletes learn to define their bodies as tools of production, becoming alienated from their bodies in the process. This approach does not acknowledge that sports can take forms that could serve the interests of workers and have-nots in society, and it denies that sports participation can be a personally creative and liberating experience that inspires people to promote economic equality and eliminate the vast income and power gaps that exist in capitalist societies.

Second, conflict theory assumes that all aspects of social life are economically determined, that is, shaped by the profit motive and the needs of capital in society. It focuses on the inherent conflict between the economic haves and have-nots, and assumes that the haves always use their power to control and exploit the have-nots, who live in a state of powerlessness and alienation. These assumptions lead conflict theorists to focus exclusively on economic factors when they study sports. However, many sports, especially those emphasizing recreation and mass participation, are not completely shaped by economic factors or the interests of wealthy people in society.

Third, conflict theory underestimates the importance of gender, race, ethnicity, age, sexuality, disability and other factors when it comes to explaining how people identify themselves, relate to others and organize the social worlds in which they live. Therefore, it often leads people to overlook the possibility that power and inequalities in society are based on factors other than social class and economic differences.

Beyond the needs of society

Functionalist theory and conflict theory both focus on the structural foundation of society and how sports support that foundation. They give us a top-down view of society and the ways that sports fit into and perpetuate an integrated social system, but they do not help us explain or understand the ways that people integrate sports into their lives and actively participate in the processes through which sports and society are organized and changed. They ignore a bottom-up view of society, that is, from the perspectives of people who 'do' sports and give meaning to them in their everyday lives. They also ignore the complexities of everyday social life and the fact that sports and society are social constructions created by people as they interact and often struggle over what is important in their lives and how their collective lives should be organized. The theories that focus attention on these issues are critical, feminist and interactionist theories.

Critical Theory: Sports are Sites Where Culture and Social Relations are Produced and Changed

Critical theory comes in many forms, and it offers a useful alternative to the systems-based focus of functionalist and conflict theories.[1] It is based on the following three assumptions.

---

[1] This chapter is a basic introduction to using theories, and the goal is to provide a general explanation and overview of the valuable work done by scholars using multiple forms of critical theory to study sports in society. We attempt to pull together major ideas from the following critical theories and theoretical frameworks: *neo-Marxist theories*, *traditional critical theory* (combining ideas of Marx and Freud), *hegemony theory* (based on the ideas of Antonio Gramsci), *cultural studies* (as it focuses on cultural production, power relations, ideology and identity), *post-structuralism* (based on cultural studies, semiotics and forms of literary analysis dealing with language and the construction of power, meaning, representation and consciousness under the unstable, fluid, fragmented and often contradictory conditions of postmodern life), and *queer theory* (combining feminist cultural studies and post-structuralism). None of these theories or frameworks is specifically identified, but we cover issues raised by them.

1   Groups and societies are characterized by shared values *and* conflicts of interest.

2   Social life involves continuous processes of negotiation, compromise and coercion because agreements about values and social organization are never permanent.

3   Values and social organization change over time and from one situation to another as there are shifts in the power balance between groups of people in society.

Forms of critical theory were developed as people realized that societies are too messy, complex and fluid to be described as 'systems' and that it is unrealistic to focus scientific attention on developing one general explanation of social life that is applicable to all societies at all times in history.

Instead of focusing on society as a whole, critical theory focuses on the diversity, complexity, contradictions and changes that characterize social life as it is lived and experienced by people who interact with one another and struggle over how to organize their lives together. Although critical theory comes in many forms, it focuses primarily on the following three topics: (1) the processes through which culture is produced, reproduced and changed, (2) the dynamics of power and social inequalities in cultural processes, and (3) the ideologies that people use as they make sense of the world, form identities, interact with others and transform the conditions of their lives.

People using functionalist and conflict theories often say that 'sport is a reflection of society', but critical theorists explain that in addition to reflecting society, sports are sites where culture and social organization are produced, reproduced and changed. This makes sports much more than mere reflections of society. This issue is discussed in the box 'Sports are more than reflections of society' (p. 47).

Unlike functionalists or conflict theorists, critical theorists realize that there are many vantage points from which to study and understand social life, and that the relationship between sports and society is always subject to change. Therefore, they study sports in connection with changes in (1) the organization of government, education, the media, religion, the family and other spheres of social life, (2) cultural definitions of masculinity and femininity, race, ethnicity, age, sexuality and physical (dis)ability, and (3) the visions that people have about what sports could and should be in society.

Critical theory also encourages action and political involvement. It has been developed by scholars dedicated to identifying issues and problems for the sake of eliminating oppression and seeking justice and equity in social life. Critical theory is a valuable tool when identifying and studying specific social problems. People who use it assume that social relationships are grounded in political struggles over how social life should be defined and organized. They study sports to see if they are organized to systematically privilege some people over others. Their goal is to explain how sports have come to be what they are, and to inspire new ways to discuss, define, organize and play sports.

> Today, sports has come to pit race against race, men against women, city against city, class against class, and coach against player.
>
> *(Frank Deford, sports writer, 1998)*

Critical theories and research on sports

Those who use critical theory to study sports generally focus on one or more of the following research questions.

- Whose ideas about the meaning and organization of sports are used to determine funding priorities for sports, who will participate in them, how will they be covered in the media, and how will they be used for social, political and economic purposes?

- How are sports and sport experiences influenced by the dynamics of power in social life and how do sports reproduce or oppose patterns of privilege in society?

- How are sports related to people's ideas about economic success and failure, work and fun, physical health and well-being, gender and sexuality, race and ethnicity, and physical ability and disability, and what is 'natural' or 'deviant' in society?

- What are the ways that people struggle over the meaning, purpose and organization of sports in their lives?

- When do sports become sites where people challenge, resist and change prevailing ideas and the organization of social life?

- What are the narratives and images that people use to give meaning to sports and their sports experiences?

- Whose voices and perspectives are represented in the media coverage of sports?

- What strategies can be used to empower people who are regularly excluded from the processes through which sports are organized and played?

One or more of these issues are discussed in each of the following chapters. Critical theories inspire interesting and provocative research on sports in society. This research is based on the assumptions that sports are complex and sometimes internally contradictory activities, and that there are no simple or general rules for explaining them as social phenomena. The intent of research based on critical theories is to understand the structure, organization and meaning of particular sports in connection with changing relationships in and between groups that possess different amounts of power and resources over time and from one place to another.

Critical theorists also study how sports affect the processes through which people develop and maintain **cultural ideologies**, that is, *the webs of ideas and beliefs that they use to explain and give meaning to the social world and their experiences in it*. They want to know how and when sports become sites for questioning and changing dominant ideologies related to social class, gender, sexuality, race and ethnicity, age and (dis)ability. One of the mottos of critical theorists is a statement made by C.L.R. James, a native of Trinidad in the West Indies, who learned to play cricket after the British colonized his homeland. James said, 'What do they know of cricket who only cricket know?' (James, 1984, preface). Critical theorists would answer this question by saying, 'We know nothing about sports if sports is all we know.' This means that if we want to know about and understand sports, we must also know about the social and cultural contexts in which sports are created, maintained and changed.

'Sports are reflections of society.' This statement is true in that widely held ideas and values are usually represented in the sports of particular societies. However, sports also are social constructions that influence relationships and social organization in society as a whole. For example, sports in the UK are organized to represent traditional ideas and beliefs about masculinity and gender relations. But at the same time, sports are a social arena in which women athletes display physical strength and skills that contradict traditional ideas about gender and give rise to new ideas about femininity and body image in British society.

To understand that sports are *more* than a reflection of society let us shift our attention to families. Like sports, families are reflections of society, but our personal experience tells us that family life is more than that. Families are created by particular groups of people as they interact with one another in ways that are influenced by their abilities, resources and definitions of family life. Of course, the opportunities and choices available to the members of any particular family are influenced by factors in the larger society, including laws, economic conditions, government policies, and cultural beliefs about the appropriate roles of husbands, wives, parents and children.

This means that similarities exist between families in a society, but it does not mean that all families are destined to be the same or to simply reflect society. Real families are organized around relationships and practices that people create as they determine how they want to live with one another. This is why your family is different from many other families in British society. In addition, families may be sites (social locations) where people raise questions about widely accepted social arrangements and the meaning and organization of social life generally.

This means that what we do in each of our families becomes part of a general process of cultural production, the impact of which goes far beyond particular family households. For example, in the late twentieth and early twenty-first centuries, some people in the UK questioned the taken-for-granted legal structures of marriage and family. These questions and discussions ultimately led to reviews of marriage laws, including the status of 'common law marriages', and the introduction of legally recognized civil partnerships between same-sex couples. These changes encouraged people to rethink other ideas about intimate relationships, gender, gender equity, parent–child relationships, children's rights, and even the organization and delivery of community social services. In other words, families are more than mere reflections of society. They are the creations of human beings and sites for producing and changing social worlds and the ways of life that constitute culture.

This shows that human beings are active agents in the construction of social worlds – not just in their immediate family lives but also in the larger social settings in which they live. So it is with sports. People construct sports as they interact with each other. Social conditions influence the structure and dynamics of sports, but within the parameters set by those conditions, people can change sports or accept them as they are. People may even create and define sports in ways that oppose dominant ideas and norms and, in the process, turn sports into activities that introduce and promote changes in the culture and society of which they are a part.

This approach recognizes that people can create diverse forms of sports and give them many different meanings, that sports can have both positive and negative effects on participants, and that sports can serve to reproduce and change culture and society. This makes sports sociologically important. Instead of being mirrors that simply reflect society, they are the actual 'social stuff' out of which society and culture come to be what they are. When we understand this, we become aware of our potential to be agents of cultural production and/or social change. This helps us realize that we are neither victims of society, nor pawns destined to do sports as they are portrayed in the images promoted by adidas,

Gillette or Pepsi. We can create new, different and alternative forms of sports, if we think critically about the contexts in which we live and work with others to gain power in our social worlds. *What do you think?*

Using critical theory in everyday life

Critical theory is based on a desire to understand, confront and transform aspects of social life that involve exploitation and oppression. Critical theorists emphasize that changes in sports depend on more than simply shifting the control of sports to the participants themselves, because many of those participants accept sports as they are and know little about sports forms that have different meanings, purposes and organizational structures. Therefore, critical theorists emphasize the need for multiple and diverse forms of sport participation in society. This, they theorize, would increase participation, diversify images of sports and the stories told about them, and add to the voices represented in those images and stories. As a result, sports would become more humane and democratic, and less subject to the exclusive control of any particular category of people. This is exciting or threatening, depending on one's willingness to view and experience sports in new and different ways.

Weaknesses of critical theory

There are three general weaknesses associated with most forms of critical theory. First, most critical theory does not provide clear guidelines for determining when sports reproduce culture and social organization and when they become sites for resisting and transforming them. Although research describes cases when sports were believed to be sites for resistance, critical theorists do not outline the criteria they use to determine when resistance occurs and the conditions under which it is most likely to create enduring changes in sports and the organization of social life. This is partly because most critical theorists focus on specific problems and creating processes through which previously under-represented people can participate in social life. They assume that all knowledge is situation specific and that there is no single way to explain all societies or solve all social problems. This is a useful approach when dealing with a particular problem, but it does not provide guidelines for determining the effectiveness of oppositional actions or identifying the conditions under which opposition is most likely to produce changes that go beyond particular situations and problems.

Second, because critical theory emphasizes the need for actions that disrupt current forms of social organization, there is a tendency among those who use it to see value in all actions that violate prevailing norms or oppose prevailing ideas; this is especially true when critical theorists study the actions of marginalized or powerless people in society. However, prevailing norms are not always unfair or oppressive, and it is unrealistic to assume that the disruptive actions of all marginalized or oppressed people and groups have equal value when it comes to instigating progressive changes in social life. Critical theorists do not provide the criteria needed to identify the characteristics of effective forms of opposition and resistance. Therefore, they cannot assess the value of change-producing strategies from one situation to the next.

Third, some critical theories use confusing vocabularies that make it difficult to merge different critical ideas into theoretical frameworks that expand our knowledge of the strategies that, under certain conditions, are most likely to produce progressive change and transform sports and society.

Feminist Theory: Sports are Gendered Activities

Feminist theory is based on the assumption that knowledge about social life requires an understanding of gender and gender relations. It has grown out of a general dissatisfaction with intellectual traditions that base knowledge on the values, experiences and insights of men and do not take seriously the values, experiences and insights of women. Feminist theory explains the ways that women have been systematically devalued and oppressed in many societies, and they emphasize that women's rights and movement towards gender equity is a prerequisite for social development and progress.

There are many forms of feminist theory, but scholars in the sociology of sport tend to use *critical* feminist theory because it is well suited to asking questions about issues of power and the dynamics of gender relations in sports and social life in general.[2] Critical feminists focus on issues of power and seek to explain the origin and consequences of gender relations, especially those that privilege men over women and some men over other men (see Cartoon 2.1). They study the ways that gender ideology (that is, ideas and beliefs about masculinity and femininity) is produced, reproduced, resisted and changed in and through the everyday experiences of men and women.

Critical feminist research has shown that sports are *gendered activities*, in that their meaning, purpose and organization are grounded in the values and experiences of men and celebrate attributes associated with dominant forms of masculinity in society (Birrell, 2000; Burstyn, 1999). Therefore, in the world of sports, people are defined as 'qualified' as an athlete, a coach or an administrator if they are tough, aggressive and emotionally focused on competitive success. If people are kind, caring, supportive and emotionally responsive to others, they are likely to be seen as qualified only to be a team 'mum', a volunteer worker for the youth club or an assistant in marketing and public relations. Overall, qualities associated with femininity are equated with weakness and devalued in most sport organizations.

Critical feminist theory and research on sports

Critical feminist theory emphasizes the need to critique and transform sports, so that the structure and culture of sports and sports organizations at least partially represent the perspectives and experiences of women as well as men in society. Critical feminists argue that both structural and cultural changes are needed before there can be true gender equity in sports or society as a whole.

Studies based on critical feminist theory generally focus on one or more of the following research questions (see Birrell, 2000).

---

[2] There are many forms of feminist theory, including liberal, radical, gynocentric, socialist, Marxist, black and postmodern, among others. Critical feminist theory focuses on issues of ideology, power and change, and is most commonly used in the sociology of sport today.

'Feminists say that sports are organized around an ideology that emphasizes domination, conquest and male superiority. Isn't that ridiculous?!'

Cartoon 2.1 **Refusing to acknowledge the contributions of feminist theories leads people to overlook important and sometimes obvious aspects of sports**

- In what ways have girls and women been excluded from or discouraged from participating in sports, and how can gender equity be achieved without promoting sports that jeopardize the health and physical well-being of girls and women who play sports?

- How are sports involved in producing and maintaining ideas about what it means to be a man in society, and forms of gender relations that privilege tough and aggressive men over everyone else?

- How are women and men, gay and straight, represented in media coverage of sports, and how do those representations reproduce or resist dominant gender ideology?

- What strategies effectively resist or challenge the heterosexual, male-centred gender ideology that is promoted and reproduced through most competitive sports?

- How are sports and sport participation involved in the production of gendered ideas about physicality, sexuality and the body?

When critical feminists do research, they often focus on whether sports are sites for challenging and transforming oppressive forms of gender relations, including expressions of sexism and homophobia. For many critical feminists, the goal is to change the meaning, purpose and organization of sports so that caring for and competing *with* others is more important than dominating and competing *against* others (Duquin, 2000).

Using critical feminist theory in everyday life

Critical feminist theory has had a major impact on the sociology of sport. It has increased our understanding of sports as an element of culture and made us aware of gender-related issues in sports. For example, we know that gender equity is very difficult to achieve because it often requires that men share the resources that they have assumed are exclusively theirs. We know that homophobia influences the sports participation choices and training patterns of heterosexual women as much or more than it does lesbians. The fear of being called a lesbian is often greater among heterosexual women than among lesbians. Men's changing rooms in certain sports are sites for the expression of homophobia, gay-bashing jokes and comments that demean women (for research exploring each of these issues, see Caudwell, 2006). People are less concerned about the fact that nearly a quarter of male English professional rugby union players are injured at any time and players will spend, on average, a fifth of the year injured (Brooks et al., 2005) than they are about a single girl injured on a football pitch. People who consider themselves to be upstanding, moral, church-going mothers and fathers take their children to football games and cheer for young men charged and sometimes convicted of physical and sexual assault without thinking about the impact of their actions on their children. Finally, most people assume that men who play sports must be heterosexual and that it is respectful to refer to women's school and college teams as The Ladies team. Our awareness of and knowledge about these facets of our everyday lives has been inspired primarily by critical feminist theory and research in the sociology of sport. In fact, if we are not aware of these facets of everyday life and the reasons they exist, we cannot say that we know much about sports in society. Each of these issues is discussed in more detail in Chapter 8.

Weaknesses of critical feminist theory

Critical feminist theory has weaknesses similar to those of critical theory (see p. 48). Although critical feminists have become increasingly aware of the connections between gender and other categories of experience related to age, race and ethnicity, social class, disability, religion and nationality, they were slow to theorize these connections. Therefore, there remains a need for more research on the sports-related experiences of women of different ages, abilities, religions (for example, Muslim women) and nationalities (Hargreaves, 2000; Walseth and Fasting, 2003).

Interactionist Theory: Sports are Given Meaning as People Interact With One Another

Interactionist theory focuses on issues related to meaning, identity, social relationships and subcultures in sports. It is based on the idea that human beings, as they interact with one another, give meanings to themselves, others and the world around them, and use those meanings as a basis for making decisions and taking action in their everyday lives.

According to interactionist theory, we humans do not passively respond to the world around us. Instead, we actively give meaning to objects and events in our lives, and make decisions about our actions as we consider their potential consequences for us, the people around us and the social world in which we live. Culture and society, according to interactionists, are produced as our actions and relationships begin to form patterns that can be observed, studied and used as a basis for developing theories to explain the social organization and dynamics in particular situations.

According to interactionist theory, the ability that we humans have to define our actions and relationships as objects that we can think about and analyse enables us to develop **identity**, that is, *a sense of who we are and how we are connected to a social world*. Identities influence choices, actions, relationships and the processes through which people construct and change social worlds. They also are the foundation for self-direction and self-control. Identities are never formed once and for all time; they change as relationships change, and as we meet new people and face new situations.

Research based on interactionist theory helps us understand how people define and give meaning to themselves, their actions, other people and the world around them. It also helps us understand human beings as choice makers and as potential agents of change. The research carried out by interactionists involves observations of and interviews with people who are members of particular groups or identifiable cultures. The goal of this research is to develop an in-depth understanding of social worlds from the inside out – through the perspectives of the people who create, maintain and change them. Unlike functionalists and conflict theorists, interactionists view culture and society from the bottom up rather than from the top down.

Interactionist theory and research on sports

Interactionist theory is often used when people study the experiences of athletes, relationships between athletes and others, and the ways that athletes define and make sense of their sport participation. A relatively common goal of interactionist research is to reconstruct and describe the realities that exist in the minds of athletes, coaches, spectators and others involved in sports.

The data collection methods used in this research are designed to gather information about the ways that people define and give meaning to their experiences as they form identities and interact with others. Those who use interactionist theory to study sports focus on the following issues.

- What are the social processes through which people become involved in sports?
- How do people come to define themselves and be identified by others as athletes?
- How do people give meaning to and derive meaning from their sport experience?
- What happens when athletes retire and make the transition into the rest of their lives?
- What are the characteristics of sport cultures, how are they created, and how do they influence people's lives on and off the field?

One or more of these issues are discussed in all chapters. This is because interactionist research provides vivid, in-depth descriptions of sports experiences and the social worlds in which they occur.

Using interactionist theory in everyday life

Interactionist theory focuses on the meanings and interaction associated with sports and sports participation. It emphasizes the complexity of human action and the need to understand action in terms of how people define situations and give meaning to their experiences. Interactionists generally recommend changes that are based on the perspectives and identities of those who participate in sports. In many cases, recommended changes call for restructuring sports organizations so that participants are given opportunities to discuss issues related to the meaning, purpose and organization of the sports they play and to control the conditions of their sports participation. Therefore, interactionists support changes that make athletes more responsible for organizing and controlling their sports.

In the case of youth sports, for example, interactionists support organizational changes giving young people opportunities to create games and physical challenges that reflect their needs and interests, rather than the needs and interests of adults. Interactionists are likely to caution parents and coaches about burnout and other problems that occur when young people develop sports-related identities and relationships to the exclusion of other identities and relationships.

In the case of elite sports, interactionists support changes that discourage athletes from defining pain and injury as normal parts of the sport experience. Because the use of performance-enhancing substances is connected with issues of identity and the norms that exist in sport cultures, interactionists often argue that the use of these substances can be controlled only if there are changes in the norms and culture of sports; identifying substance users as 'bad apples' and punishing them as individuals will not change the culture in which athletes learn norms that encourage them to sacrifice their bodies for the sake of their team and their sport.

Weaknesses of interactionist theory

Interactionist theory has inspired many informative studies of meaning, identity, interaction and subcultures in sports. However, it has two primary weaknesses. First, it focuses our attention almost exclusively on relationships and definitions of reality without explaining the ways that interaction and the construction of meaning in sports are influenced by social organization, power and material conditions in society. Therefore, interactionist research often ignores power dynamics and inequality in connection with sports and sport experiences.

Second, interactionist theory has not been developed around a critical approach to social worlds. Only when it is combined with a form of critical theory do researchers have a basis for developing visions of the ways that sports and society could and should be organized. For this reason, many scholars who use interactionist theory now combine it with critical and critical feminist theory to take their analyses beyond mere descriptions of social worlds (Coakley and Donnelly, 1999).

Figurational Theory: Sports are Collective Inventions

The roots of figurational theory are based in European intellectual traditions, especially those grounded in the work of German sociologist, Norbert Elias. It is a comprehensive theory that has been used for over three decades by English-speaking scholars, primarily from the UK, as

Social life is complex and is best understood when viewed from multiple perspectives. Each theory in this chapter can be used to ask sociological questions about this scene. Afghan boys (no girls) are playing baseball organized by US ground troops after the US military had heavily bombed Afghanistan as it sought out terrorists. Adult male refugees watch as the soldiers teach the rules and the skills involved in the game (Source: Wally Santana, AP/Wide World Photo)

they form hypotheses, do research and synthesize research findings about social life and sports in society (Dunning, 1999).

Figurational theory, also known as process sociology, is based on the notion that social life consists of networks of interdependent people. Those who use this theory focus on the historical processes through which these networks or sets of interconnections, between individuals and collections of people emerge and change over time. These sets of interconnections are called 'figurations'.

Figurational theory assumes that human beings are 'more or less dependent on each other first by nature and then through social learning, education, socialisation, and socially generated reciprocal needs' (Elias, 1978, p. 261). In other words, human life continues to exist only because of and through sets of interconnections, and, if we wish to understand social life, we must study the ever-changing social figurations that emerge as social connections between people shift and change. According to figurational theory, human beings 'can be understood only in terms of the various figurations to which they have belonged in the past and which they continue to form in the present' (Goudsblom, 1977, p. 7).

Those who use figurational theory study the long-term processes through which the relatively autonomous actions of many individuals and collections of people influence and constrain each other. These processes are complex and dynamic, and they involve a wide range of outcomes, which no single individual or group has chosen, designed, planned or intended. These outcomes may be enabling or constraining for different individuals and collectivities, but they are never permanent. They shift and change as power and relationships within figurations shift and change over time. Power relationships tend to shift and change in connection with constantly emerging economic, political and emotional dimensions of social life (Murphy et al., 2000).[3]

Figurational theory and research on sports

Figurational theory has inspired much research and discussion about sports in society, predominantly in the UK and parts of northern and western continental Europe. In particular, figurational accounts of sports focus on links between sociology and history, and offer useful analyses of the following topics.

- What are the historical, economic, political and emotional factors that explain why modern sports emerged in much of Europe during the eighteenth and nineteenth centuries?
- What are the historical and social processes through which sports participation became increasingly serious in people's lives, and through which sports have come to be professionalized and commercialized in various societies during the twentieth and early twenty-first centuries?
- What are the historical and social dynamics underlying violence and efforts to control violence in sports, especially in connection with football in the UK and worldwide?
- How are relationships among sports, national identity and the dynamics of globalization processes involved in the media, economic expansion and consumerism that have become so socially important today?

Unlike many other social theorists, figurational theorists have long acknowledged the importance of sports in society. Sports, explain the figurationalists, are important because they are 'collective inventions' that provide people, especially men, in highly regulated, modern societies with forms of enjoyable excitement. This, in turn, reduces boredom at the same time as it also limits the excessive and destructive violence that characterized many folk games in pre-modern Europe (Dunning, 1999). Figurational research in the UK includes studies of the development of rugby, fox-hunting, boxing and the Highland Games (Jarvie, 2006).

Furthermore, the concept of figurations has been especially useful in studies of the complex economic, political and social processes associated with global sports. Figurational research on the global migration of elite athletes, the global sports industry, global media–sports relationships, the impact of global sports on national and local identities, and the manner by which sports are incorporated simultaneously into local cultures and global processes have helped us understand sports in a global perspective (Maguire, 1999, 2005).

---

[3] Figurational theory grew out of the work of Norbert Elias, a German Jew who fled Nazi Germany in 1933 and continued his sociological research in England until he died in 1990. Elias's theory of civilizing processes in Western Europe is based on extensive historical research (see Elias, 1978, 1982). When Elias turned his attention to sports and leisure, much of his work was done with Eric Dunning (Elias and Dunning, 1986). Dunning has influenced students around the world through his writing and his lectures at Leicester University in England and many other universities.

Figurational sociology focuses on the historical development of sports forms, including traditional cultural activities such as the Highland Games

Using figurational theory in everyday life

Figurational theory is based on the combined ideas that knowledge about social life is cumulative and that the goal of knowledge is to enable people to control expressions of violence, exploitation and power-driven relationships in their lives. Figurational theorists also emphasize that the application of knowledge in everyday social life is tricky, because applications are bound to produce unintended consequences, which may subvert intended positive and progressive outcomes. This, along with their desire to avoid the influence of ideology in their research, has led them to be cautious when it comes to social action and political intervention. Part of this caution is tied to their awareness of how science was appropriated and used during the Nazi era in Germany (1933–45).

Most figurational theorists say that their role in social action is to generate valid forms of knowledge and pass these to others in a critical framework so that people can use it to be meaningfully informed as they participate in society. When it comes to problem solving, the recommendations of figurationalists usually call for policies that increase meaningful participation among those who have historically lacked access to power in society. In the case of sports, their recommendations have traditionally supported the interests and participation of working-class men. In recent years they have increasingly supported participation opportunities for women and ethnic minorities, but rarely has this support been stated in explicit or assertive terms.

Weaknesses of figurational theory

The primary weakness of figurational theory is that its focus on long-term, historical interconnections between people minimizes attention to the immediate issues, current problems and day-to-day struggles that are the 'social stuff' of people's everyday lives. The historical framework that is the backbone of figurational theory tends to diffuse the urgency and painfulness of everyday issues and problems, because it frames and explains them in terms of complex, long-term processes. This is frustrating to those who wish to actively deal with the here-and-now problems and issues that affect people's lives.

Another weakness of figurational theory is that it focuses so much on the emerging dynamics of social interdependence between people that it understates the immediate personal consequences of oppressive power relationships and the need for concerted political actions to change the balance of power in particular relationships and spheres of social life. For example, figurational research offers powerful explanations for why modern sports serve as a 'male preserve' and how they reproduce a web of ideas and beliefs that privilege men in society, but it has paid little attention to the experiences of women in sports and the need for changes in the inequitable gender relations that characterize British society and sports organizations. This has prevented figurational theory from being readily combined with critical feminist theory, and it has discouraged many action-orientated theorists from working with colleagues who use figurational theory.

Is There a Best Theoretical Approach to Use When Studying Sports?

Each theory discussed in this chapter makes us aware of questions and issues that are important to us, the people with whom we work and play, and in the social worlds in which we live. In most of our research, we have used combinations of *interactionist*, *critical* and *feminist theories* because we have wanted to view sports from the inside, from the perspectives of those who decide to play or not to play and who integrate sports into their lives in various ways. As we view sports from the inside, we also want to be aware of the social, economic, political and historical factors that influence access to sports participation and the decisions that people make about sports in their lives.

Critical theories and critical feminist theories also help us think about very practical issues, such as whether to support or reject proposals for funding new sports facilities or a new stadium for a professional football team. They help us assess policies related to sport programmes for at-risk youth and to evaluate candidates for jobs at our universities which involve the delivery and management of student sport. More recently this combination of theories has guided much of our thinking about sports for people with disabilities, as is shown in the box 'Breaking barriers' (opposite).

Although neither of us has used *functionalist theory* and *conflict theory* in our research, we do use them to inform our general understanding of sports in society. For example, functionalist theory helps us understand the ways that many people currently think about sports in society. Even though functionalist theory does not help us identify social issues and controversies connected with sports in our communities and the sports organizations in which we work with coaches and administrators, we use it to understand the importance that many people attach to sports in their lives. Conflict theory alerts us to issues related to social class and economic exploitation as we use *critical theories* to help us understand (1) the dynamics of power in sports and society, (2) the ways that power is related to gender, race, ethnicity, disability and sexuality, and (3) the ways that people use ideologies as they explain and give meaning to the world and their experiences. Figurational theory helps us to understand historical and global issues more clearly, and the dynamics of power and politics in a global perspective.

Overall, our preference for a combination of interactionist, critical and critical feminist theories is based on our interest in making many forms of sports participation more accessible to a wider range of people in society. We are much more interested in increasing choices and alternatives for people in sports than we are in making sports a more efficient means of maintaining the status quo in society (a goal of functionalist theory) or in dismantling sports altogether (a goal of conflict theory). We think that many aspects of the status quo in the UK, the USA and other societies are in need of change, and that sports are sites at which we can learn strategies for effectively making creative and progressive changes. Creating alternative ways of doing sports requires an awareness of contemporary sports culture as well as a vocabulary for thinking critically about the future. A combination of interactionist, critical and critical feminist theories provides a guide for developing that awareness and vocabulary and creating new sports forms that offer human beings additional possibilities for physical and social experiences.

Our theoretical preferences often conflict with the preferences expressed by some students and people who work for sports organizations. Students who seek jobs in sports organizations know that most decision makers in those organizations see sports in functionalist terms, so they sometimes favour functionalist theory. However, we remind them that when they are employed in sports organizations it is important to understand issues related to power and culture. This enables them to critically assess organizational policies in terms of their impact on people in the organization and the general community and society. When we work with coaches and sports administrators, they often tell us that the critical approach that we use has helped them see sports and their involvement in them from a more fully informed perspective; this, they say, makes them more responsive and accountable decision makers.

Finally, theories continue to help us see that true empowerment in any social world involves enabling people to be critically informed actors so that they can effectively 'challenge and change unequal power relationships' (Mahiri, 1998). As we participate in social worlds, we find that combinations of critical, feminist and interactionist theories are especially helpful in making this happen.

breaking BARRIERS
Language barriers: don't call me handicapped!

Damon Rose is the editor of the BBC disability website, 'Ouch!', and is himself registered blind. In a discussion of the terminology often used to describe disabled people, including athletes, Rose has this to say: '"Handicapped" is a word which many disabled people consider to be the equivalent of nigger. It evokes thoughts of being held back, not in the race, not as good, weighed down by something so awful we ought not to speak of it' (Rose, 2004).

Rose is sensitive to the barriers created when people use the word *handicapped* to refer to physical and mental impairments and disabilities. Clear definitions of these words are necessary to understand and evaluate theories of disability.

An **impairment** *exists when a person has a physical, sensory or intellectual condition that potentially limits full participation in social and/or physical environments*. Many people have impairments and, as we get older, impairments generally increase in number and severity. This is part of normal, everyday life. None of us is physically or mentally perfect, and we regularly make personal adjustments to limit the impact of impairments on our lives. If we are lucky, we have access to technologies that make adjustments more effective. For example, we both wear eyeglasses that 'correct' our impaired vision. If we were world-class archers we could be a member of our national archery teams, despite our impairment. We would face no barriers as long as we were allowed to wear eyeglasses; therefore, we would not have a disability.

An impairment becomes a **disability** only *when accommodations in social or physical contexts are not or cannot be made to allow the full participation of people with functional limitations*. This means that disabilities are created when relationships, spaces and activities present barriers that limit opportunities and experiences for people with particular impairments. For example, prior to the late 1990s, if one of us had had our leg amputated below the knee and wore a prosthetic leg and foot, we could not have been a member of our national powerlifting team because the International Powerlifting Federation rules stated that 'Lifters without two real feet cannot compete in regular contests.' This rule created a barrier, making us disabled. However, after the rule was changed, the barrier was eliminated and our prosthetic leg and foot no longer made us disabled as a powerlifter. This shows that disability often has less to do with impairment and ability than with social, environmental, attitudinal and legal factors (Brittain, 2004; Hargreaves, 2000; Higgins, 1992; Morris, 1996; Oliver, 1996). Therefore, a person may be (dis)abled in one context but not in another (Friedman et al., 2004). Only when there are barriers that exclude or limit people with impairments do disabilities exist.

People become **handicapped** *when others define them as inferior and 'unable' due to perceived impairments* or, as Damon Rose suggests, not even able to be 'in the race'.

These three definitions are based on critical and interactionist theories. They locate handicaps and disabilities in the social processes through which (a) environments are organized to meet the needs of temporarily able-bodied people, (b) norms (rules) are created that disadvantage people with impairments, and (c) people learn to equate particular impairments with inferiority and inability.

Other definitions, based on medical and psychological theory, explain disability as a characteristic of individuals. Medical–psychological theories locate disability in the physical and cognitive 'abnormalities' of individuals and they lead to interventions emphasizing personal coping strategies and assistive technologies. Critical interactionist theories, on the other hand, locate disability in social and cultural barriers that limit participation; they lead to interventions emphasizing the elimination of cultural, organizational, legal and environmental barriers.

Both approaches are needed, but people too often overlook the need to eliminate external barriers. Personal coping strategies and assistive technologies are crucial for individuals, but eliminating external barriers reduces disability for entire categories of people (DePauw, 1997). Hilary Lister is a quadriplegic, paralysed from the neck down by reflex sympathetic dystrophy, a degenerative condition of the nervous system. She was the first quadriplegic to sail across the English Channel, gaining the world record for the longest solo voyage by a quadriplegic, which she was able to do by sucking and blowing into plastic straws to steer and control the sails. Lister says that sailing has 'given me my life again ... You have a freedom on water you don't have anywhere, well I don't. It's hard to explain what it's like being stuck in a wheelchair. Here I'm the boss. As well as steering, I can choose to sail flat, or go faster. It's wonderful to have choice again' (in Wollaston, 2005). The goal therefore is to create social and physical worlds that are like being on the water for Hilary Lister.

Summary: How Can Social Theories Help Us Study Sports in Society?

Theories are tools that enable us to ask questions, identify problems, gather information, explain social life, prioritize strategies to deal with problems, and anticipate the consequences of our actions and interventions. Different theories help us understand sports from multiple angles and perspectives. In this chapter, we discussed functionalist, conflict, critical, feminist, interactionist and figurational theories.

The purpose of the chapter is to show that each theory provides a framework that we can use as we think about sports in society and make decisions related to sports in our own lives. For example, functionalist theory alerts us to the connections between sports and other spheres of social life, and offers an explanation for positive consequences associated with sports and sport involvement. Conflict theory identifies problems as they are related to class relations and economic exploitation in sports. Critical theory shows that sports are cultural practices that are connected with social worlds in complex ways and that sports change as power and resources shift in the prevailing forms of social, political and economic relations in society. Critical feminist theory emphasizes that gender is a primary category of experience and that sports are sites for producing, reproducing and transforming gender ideology and power relations in society. Interactionist theory helps us understand the meanings, identities and social relationships associated with sport involvement. Figurational theory examines the complex and long-term social processes through which modern sports have emerged and changed in societies.

As we use these theories it is important to know their weaknesses. Functionalist theory exaggerates the positive consequences of sports and sports participation because it is based on the assumption that there are no conflicts of interest between groups within society. Conflict theory overstates the importance of social class and economic factors in society, and it focuses most of its attention on top-level spectator sports, which make up only a part of sports in any society. Critical theory provides no explicit guidelines for determining when sports are sites at which resistance leads to progressive transformations in society. Critical feminist theory has inspired little research on the connections between sports, gender and other categories of experience, including age, race, religion, nationality and disability. Interactionist theory does a poor job of relating issues of meaning, identity and experience in sports to general social conditions and patterns of social inequality in society as a whole. Figurational theory unintentionally diffuses the urgency of social problems by framing them in terms of complex, long-term processes and historical accounts of the changing balance of power in social relations.

Despite their weaknesses, social theories are helpful as we explore issues and controversies in sports and assess research and ideas about sports in society. We do not have to be theorists to use theory as we organize our thoughts and become more informed citizens in our social worlds. Nor do we have to identify ourselves with a particular theory in order to use it as a guide as we take a closer look at sports in society.

Website resources

Note: Websites often change. The following URLs were current when this book was printed. Please check our website (***www.mcgraw-hill.co.uk/textbooks/coakley***) for updates and additions.

www.mcgraw-hill.co.uk/textbooks/coakley Click on Chapter 2 for summaries of studies based on some of the theories discussed in this chapter.

www.feminist.org/sports/ This site has special coverage of 'Empowering women in sports'; this site not only is a good example of applied feminist theories but also highlights the issues that are most important in a feminist analysis of sports.

www.socqrl.niu.edu/FYI/theory.htm This site has valuable links to helpful sites on social theory.

http://socserv.mcmaster.ca/w3virtsoclib/theories.htm This site is a research source for information on sociological theory and theorists; it is not sports related, but it provides numerous links to sites around the world.

http://sportpolitics.blogspot.com/ This is the site for the Sport and Politics Specialist Group of the Political Studies Association, and contains information for the International Network for the Marxist Study of Sport.

www.sussex.ac.uk/spt/cst This is an advanced critical theory site.

www.usyd.edu.au/su/social/elias.html Site devoted to Norbert Elias and figurational theory; provides links to many European sources.

See the OLC, ***www.mcgraw-hill.co.uk/textbooks/coakley***, for an annotated list of readings related to this chapter. The OLC also contains a key concepts list, a review test and other helpful features.

Chapter 3

Studying the past: does it help us understand sports today?

Learning Centre Resources

Visit *Sports in Society*'s Online Learning Centre (OLC) at **www.mcgraw-hill.co.uk/textbooks/coakley** for additional information and study material for this chapter, including:

- Self-grading quizzes and essay questions
- Learning outcomes
- Related websites
- Additional readings

Of the thousands of evils ... in Greece there is no greater evil than the race of athletes. ...

Since they have not formed good habits, they face problems with difficulty.

(Euripides, Greek dramatist, fifth century BC)

Chapter contents

Understanding history while studying sports in society

Sports vary by time and place

Contests and games in Ancient Greece: beyond the myths (1000 BC to 100 BC)

Roman contests and games: spectacles and gladiators (100 BC to AD 500)

Tournaments and games in medieval Europe: separation of the masters and the masses (500 to 1300)

The Renaissance, the Reformation and the Enlightenment: games as diversions (1300 to 1800)

The Industrial Revolution: the emergence of organized competitive sports (1780 to 1920)

Since 1920: struggles continue

Using history to think about the future

Summary: can we use history to understand sports today?

They who laid the intellectual foundations of the Western world were the most fanatical players and organisers of games that the world has ever known.

(C.L.R. James, sociologist and West Indian cricket player, 1984)

To understand sports today, we need a sense of what physical games and sports activities were like in past times. This chapter presents brief overviews of sport activities in different cultural and historical settings. Our intent is *not* to provide an integrated overall history of sports. Such a history would look at the development and organization of physical games and sports across all continents from one cultural group to another over time. This is an ambitious and worthy project, but it is far beyond the scope of this chapter.

This chapter focuses on (1) the Ancient Greeks, (2) the Roman Empire, (3) the Middle Ages in parts of Europe, (4) the Renaissance through to the Enlightenment in parts of Europe, and (5) the Industrial Revolution through to recent times, with special emphasis on the UK. These times and places, often covered in history courses, are familiar to many of us, and they illustrate the ways that sports are connected with the social and cultural contexts in which they exist.

The goal of this chapter is to show that our understanding of sports depends on what we know about the social lives of the people who created, defined, played and integrated them into their everyday experiences. As critical theory suggests, it is important to study the ways that people use their power and resources as they create and participate in physical activities.

When we view sports history in this way, dates and names are less important than what we can learn about social life by studying sports and physical activities at particular times and places.

Understanding History While Studying Sports in Society

Many people think about history as a chronological sequence of events that gradually leads to a better and more 'modern' society. Many historical accounts are full of references to societies that are traditional or modern, primitive or civilized, underdeveloped or developed, pre-industrial or industrial. This terminology implies that history is always moving forward so that societies are improving and becoming more developed.

This approach to history enables some people to feel superior as they assume that they are the most modern, civilized and developed people in the world. However, this conclusion is not historically accurate. In the case of sports, there are literally thousands of 'histories' of physical activities among thousands of human populations in different places around the world. These histories sometimes involve patterns of changes that do not provide evidence of becoming more civilized or highly developed.

Research shows that physical activities and games have existed in all cultures. The specific forms of these activities and games, along with the meanings that people gave to them, were shaped through struggles over the meaning, purpose and organization of the activities, over who should play them and over the ways that they were to be integrated into people's lives. To say that physical activities and games over the years have evolved to fit a pattern of progress, or modernization, is to distort the life experiences of people all over the world (Gruneau, 1988).

There may be fewer contrasts among the sports and games that people play today, but this does not mean that sports are evolving to fit a grand scheme for how physical activities *should* be organized or what they *should* mean in people's lives (Maguire, 1999). Instead, it means that certain nations and corporations now have the power to define, organize and present through the media particular sport forms for the entire world to see. Therefore, when BMX (bicycle motocross) was approved as a new sport for the 2008 Summer Olympics in Beijing it was an example of wealthy countries and corporations using their power to promote a sport through international travel, social connections and access to resources. When BMX became commercially attractive to the International Olympic Committee, it was not part of a general pattern of progress in the history of sports.

Therefore, this chapter is not a story of progress. Instead, it is a sample of stories about people at different times and places struggling over and coming to terms with what they want their physical activities to be and how they wish to include them in their lives. There is historical continuity in these processes and struggles, but continuity does not mean that history follows a grand plan of progress. Progressive changes do occur, but they are the result of actions taken by collections of people with the power to make them happen and maintain them over time.

Sports Vary by Time and Place

People in all cultures, past and present, have used human movement in their ritual life. As we study history, we see that few cultures have had physical games that resemble the highly organized, rule-governed competitive games that we describe as sports today.

In prehistoric times, for example, there were no sports as we know them today. Physical activities were tied to the challenge of survival and religious beliefs (see Cartoon 3.1). People hunted for food, and sometimes used their physical abilities to defend themselves, establish social control and power over others, and appease their gods. The latter activities involved acting out events that had important meaning in their lives and, even though they may have taken the form of organized games, they were inseparable from sacred rituals and ceremonies. They often were performed as religious worship, and their outcomes were determined by religious necessity as much as the physical abilities of the people involved (Guttmann, 1978).

The first forms of organized games among humans probably emerged from this combination of physical challenges and religious rituals. From what we can tell, these games were connected closely with the power structures and belief systems of the societies in which they existed, and they usually re-created and reaffirmed dominant cultural practices in those societies. On rare occasions, they served as sources of protest or opposition to the status quo in particular groups or societies.

Historical and cultural variations in physical activities remind us that all cultural practices, even sports, serve a variety of social purposes. This raises the question of how the definition and organization of sports in any society promote the interests of various groups within that society. People create sports activities within the constraints of the social worlds in which they live. Therefore, everyone does not have an equal say in how those activities are defined and organized. People with the most power generally have the greatest impact on how sports are defined, organized and played in a group or society. Sports activities do not totally reflect their desires, but sports represent the interests of the powerful more than they represent the interests of others.

This approach to studying sports in history is based on critical theory. It calls attention to the existence and consequences of social inequality in societies. Inequalities related to wealth, political power, social status, gender, age, (dis)ability, and race and ethnicity have always had a

'You weren't playing football last night – it won't be invented for another million years!'
Cartoon 3.1 **In early human history, there were no sports as we define them. Physical activities occasionally were included in community and religious rituals, but their purpose probably was to appease the gods, rather than to entertain or build character**

significant impact on how sports activities are organized and played in any situation. We will pay special attention to these in the following discussions of times and places.

Contests and Games in Ancient Greece: Beyond the Myths (1000 BC to 100 BC)

The games played by early Greeks (*circa* 900 BC) were grounded in mythology and religious beliefs. They were usually held in conjunction with festivals that combined prayer, sacrifices and religious services with music, dancing and ritual feasts. Competitors in these games were from wealthy and respected Greek families. They were the only people who had the money to hire trainers and coaches, and the time and resources to travel. Sports events were based on the interests of able-bodied young males. They usually consisted of warrior sports such as chariot racing, wrestling and boxing, javelin and discus throwing, foot racing, archery and long jumping. Violence, serious injuries and even death were commonplace in comparison with today's sports (Elias, 1986; Kidd, 1984, 1996b; Mendelsohn, 2004). Greek women, children and older people occasionally played sports in these festivals, but they never played in the games held at Olympia.

The locations and dates of the Greek festivals also were linked to religious beliefs. For example, Olympia was chosen as one of the festival sites because it was associated with the achievements and activities of celebrated Greek gods and mythological characters. In fact, Olympia was dedicated as a shrine to the god Zeus about 1000 BC. Although permanent buildings and playing fields were not constructed until 550 BC, the games at Olympia were held every four years. Additional festivals involving athletic contests were also held at other locations throughout Greece, but the Olympic Games became the most prestigious of all athletic events.

Women were prohibited from participating as athletes or spectators at the Olympic Games. However, they held their own games at Olympia. These games, dedicated to the goddess Hera, the sister-wife of Zeus, grew out of Greek fertility rites. When women participated in sports, it was often to demonstrate their strength, sexually attract men and eventually bear strong warrior children (Perrottet, 2004). In general, physical prowess was inconsistent with dominant definitions of femininity among the Greeks. Women were seen as inferior to men. They could neither vote nor be Greek citizens. Wives were the property of their husbands and lived most of their lives in the confines of the home. Furthermore, women in Greece did not participate in political or economic affairs.

The men's games at Olympia took on political significance as they grew in visibility and popularity. Winning became connected with the glory of city-states. Physically skilled slaves and young men from lower-status backgrounds were forced to become athletes, or wealthy patrons and government officials hired them to train for the Olympics and other games. Victories brought cash prizes and living expenses for many of these slaves and hired athletes. Contrary to popular myths about the amateur ideals held by the Greeks, many male athletes saw themselves as professionals. During the second century BC, they even organized athletic guilds enabling them to bargain for rights, gain control over the conditions of their sports participation and enjoy material security when they retired from competition (Baker, 1988). Greek athletes were so specialized in their physical skills that they made poor soldiers. They engaged in warrior sports, but they lacked the generalized skills of warriors. Furthermore, they concentrated so much on athletic training that they ignored intellectual development. This evoked widespread criticism from Greek philosophers, who saw the games as brutal and dehumanizing, and the athletes as useless and ignorant beings.

Representatives of the modern Olympics have romanticized and perpetuated myths about Greek games to connect the modern games to a positive legacy. However, the ancient games were not tributes to mind–body harmony. Athletes were maimed and killed in the pursuit of victories and the rewards that came with them (Mendelsohn, 2004; Perrottet, 2004), fairness was not as important as honour, and athletic contests were connected with a cultural emphasis on warfare.

Physical contests and games in Greek culture influenced art, philosophy and the everyday lives of people wealthy enough to train, hire professionals and travel to events. However, Greek contests and games were different from organized competitive sports of today (see the box 'Dominant sport forms today', p. 69). First, they were grounded in religion; second, they lacked complex administrative structures; third, they did not involve measurements and record keeping from event to event. However, there is one major similarity: they often reproduced dominant patterns of social relations in society as a whole. The power and advantages that went with being wealthy, male, young and able bodied in Greek society shaped the games and contests in ways that limited the participation of most people. Even the definitions of excellence used to evaluate performance reflected the abilities of young males. This meant that the abilities of others were substandard by definition – if you could not do it as a young, able-bodied Greek man did it, you were doing it the wrong way. This legitimized and preserved the privilege enjoyed by a select group of men in Greek society.

Roman Contests and Games: Spectacles and Gladiators (100 BC to AD 500)

Roman leaders used physical contests and games to train soldiers and provide mass entertainment spectacles. They borrowed events from Greek contests and games, but they focused athletic training on preparing obedient soldiers. They were critical of the Greek emphasis on individualism and specialized physical skills that were useless in battle. Because Roman leaders emphasized military training and entertainment, the contests and games during the first century AD increasingly took the form of circuses and gladiatorial combat.

Chariot races were the most popular events during Roman spectacles. Wealthy Romans recruited slaves as charioteers. Spectators bet heavily on the races, and when they became bored or unruly, the emperors passed around free food and tickets for prizes to prevent outbreaks of violence. This strategy pacified the crowds and allowed the emperors to use events to celebrate themselves and their power. Government officials throughout the Roman Empire used similar events and strategies to control people in their regions.

As the power and influence of the Roman Empire grew, spectacles consisting of contests and games became increasingly important as diversions for the masses. By AD 300, half the days on the Roman calendar were public holidays because slaves did most of the work. Many Romans held only part-time jobs, if they worked at all. Activities other than chariot races and boxing matches were needed to attract and distract people.

Bear-baiting, bull-baiting and animal fights were added to capture spectator interest. Men and women were forced into the arena to engage in mortal combat with lions, tigers and panthers. Condemned criminals were dressed in sheepskins to battle partially starved wild animals. Gladiators, armed with various weapons, were pitted against each other in gory fights to the death. These spectacles achieved two purposes for Roman rulers: they entertained an idle populace and disposed of socially 'undesirable' people such as thieves, murderers, unruly slaves and outspoken Christians (Baker, 1988).

Some Romans criticized these spectacles as tasteless activities, devoid of value. However, their criticisms were based not on concerns for human rights as much as their objections to events in which wealthy people and peasants mingled together. Other than some activist Christians, few people criticized spectacles on moral or humanitarian grounds. The spectacles continued until the Roman economy went into a depression and wealthy people moved from the cities, taking their resources with them. As the Roman Empire deteriorated, there were not enough resources to support spectacles (Baker, 1988).

Women were seldom involved in Roman contests and games. They were allowed in the arenas to watch and cheer male athletes, but few had opportunities to develop athletic skills.

Within Roman families, women were legally subservient to and rigidly controlled by men. As in Ancient Greece, few women pursued interests outside the household.

Although local folk games and other physical activities existed in the Roman Empire, we know little about how they were organized and played and what they meant in people's lives. The gladiatorial spectacles did not capture everyone's interest, but they attracted considerable attention in major cities.

Roman contests and games differed from organized sports today because they sometimes were connected with religious rituals, and they seldom involved quantifying athletic achievements or recording outstanding accomplishments (review the box 'Dominant sport forms today').

 Just as the dominant class writes history, so that same class writes the story of sport.

(James Riordan, social historian and former football player, 1996)

reflect on SPORTS — *Dominant sport forms today: what makes them unique?*

The organized competitive sports so popular today are very different from the physical activities and games played in the past. Allen Guttmann's study of sports activities through history shows that today's *dominant sport forms* (DSFs) have seven interrelated characteristics, which have never before appeared together in physical activities and games. These characteristics are as follows.

1 *Secularism.* Today's DSFs are not directly linked to religious beliefs or rituals. They are sources of diversion and entertainment, not worship; they are played for personal gains, not the appeasement of gods; and they embody the immediacy of the material world, not the mysticism of the supernatural.

2 *Equality.* Today's DSFs are based on the ideas that participation should be open to everyone regardless of family or social background and that all contestants in a sport event should face the same competitive conditions.

3 *Specialization.* Today's DSFs involve athletes dedicated exclusively to participation in a single event or position within an event; excellence is defined in terms of specialized skills, rather than all-round physical abilities.

4 *Rationalization.* Today's DSFs involve formalized rules that regulate the conditions of participation and they are organized around rationally controlled strategies and training methods guided by 'sport sciences'.

5 *Bureaucratization.* Today's DSFs are governed by complex organizations and officials that control athletes, teams and events, enforce rules, organize events and certify records.

6 *Quantification.* Today's DSFs involve precise timing and measurements; scores and performance statistics are recorded and used as proof of achievements.

7 *Records.* Today's DSFs emphasize setting and breaking records; performances are compared over time to determine personal, national and world records.

One or some of these characteristics were present in the physical activities and games of previous historical periods, but not until the nineteenth century did all seven appear together in *modern* sports

Dominant sport forms today emphasize quantification. Performances are timed, measured and recorded. The clock is crucial, and digital scoreboards now show times in hundredths of seconds (Source: David Biene; photograph courtesy of Ossur)

(Dunning, 1999; Dunning and Sheard, 1979; Guttmann, 1978). This does not mean that today's organized competitive sports are superior to the games and activities of past times and other places. It means only that they are different in terms of how they are organized and integrated into people's lives. Sociologists study these differences in connection with the social and cultural contexts in which physical activities and sports are played. Table 3.1 summarizes Guttmann's comparison of games, contests and sport activities in each of the places and time periods discussed in this chapter. The table shows that the dominant sport forms that exist in many post-industrial societies today are different from the 'sports' played by people in times past. However, it does not explain why the differences exist or their social implications.

The seven characteristics identified by Guttmann are not found in all sports today. Sports are social constructions. They change as social, economic and political forces change, and as people seek and develop alternatives to dominant sport forms. The DSFs played 50 years from now are likely to have characteristics that are different from these seven characteristics. *What do you think?*

Tournaments and Games in Medieval Europe: Separation of the Masters and the Masses (500 to 1300)

Sport activities in medieval Europe consisted of folk games played by local peasants, tournaments staged for knights and nobles, archery contests and activities in which animals were brutalized (Dunning, 1999). The folk games, often violent and dangerous and sometimes organized to maim or kill animals, emerged in connection with local peasant customs. The

Table 3.1 **Historical comparison of organized games, contests and sport activities**

Characteristic	Greek contests and games (1000 BC to 100 BC)	Roman contests and games (100 BC to AD 500)	Medieval tournaments and games (500 to 1300)	Renaissance, Reformation and Enlightenment games (1300 to 1800)	'Modern' sports
Secularism	Yes and no*	Yes and no	Yes and no	Yes and no	Yes
Equality	Yes and no	Yes and no	No	Yes and no	Yes
Specialization	Yes	Yes	No	Yes and no	Yes
Rationalization	Yes	Yes	No	No	Yes
Bureaucratization	Yes and no	Yes	No	No	Yes
Quantification	No	Yes	No	Yes and no	Yes
Records	No	No	No	Yes and no	Yes

*This characteristic existed in some sports during this time, but not in others.

Source: Modified version of table 2 in Guttmann (1978)

tournaments and archery contests were linked with military training and the desire for entertainment among the feudal aristocracy and those who served them.

Some of the local games of this period have interesting histories. As Roman soldiers and government officials travelled around Europe during the fourth and fifth centuries, they built bathing facilities to use during their leisure time. To loosen up before their baths, they engaged in various forms of ball play. Local peasants during the early medieval period used the Roman activities as models and developed their own forms of ball games. They often integrated these games into local religious ceremonies and cultural events. For example, tossing a ball back and forth sometimes represented the conflict between good and evil, light and darkness or life and death. As the influence of the Roman Catholic Church spread through Europe during the early years of the medieval period, these symbolic rituals were redefined in terms of Catholic beliefs. In these cases, sports and religion were closely connected with each other.

During most of the medieval period, the Roman Catholic Church accepted peasant ball games, even though they occasionally involved violence. Local priests encouraged games by opening church grounds on holidays and Sunday afternoons. As games became a regular feature of village life, people played them during festive community gatherings that also involved music and dancing. The local ball games played on these occasions contained the roots for many contemporary games such as football, hockey, rugby, bowling, curling and cricket. However, the games in peasant villages had little structure and few rules. Local traditions guided play, and traditions varied widely from one community to the next.

The upper classes in medieval Europe paid little attention to, and seldom interfered in, the leisure of peasants. They saw peasant games and festivities as safety valves defusing mass social discontent. The sports activities of the upper classes were distinctively different from those of the peasants. Access to specialized equipment and facilities allowed them to develop early versions of billiards, tennis, handball and pelota. Ownership of horses allowed them to develop forms of horse racing, while their stable hands developed a version of horseshoes. On horseback, they also participated in hunting and hawking. Owning property and possessing money and servants clearly influenced their sports.

Throughout the medieval period, the most popular sporting events among upper-class males were tournaments consisting of war games to keep knights and nobles ready for battle. Some tournaments resembled actual battlefield confrontations. Deaths and serious injuries occurred, victors carried off opponents' possessions, and losers often were taken as prisoners and used as hostages to demand ransoms from opposing camps. Later versions of tournaments had lower stakes, but they also involved injuries and occasional deaths. Towards the end of the medieval period, colourful ceremonies and pageantry softened the warlike tournaments, and entertainment and chivalry took priority over military preparation and the use of deadly violence.

Women during this time seldom participated in physical games and sport activities. Gender restrictions were grounded in a male-centred family structure and Catholic teachings that women were inferior to men. A woman's duty was to be obedient and submissive; however, peasant women were involved in some of the games and physical activities that occurred during village festivals.

Among the aristocracy, gender relations were patterned so that men's and women's activities were clearly differentiated. Aristocratic women did little outside the walls of their dwellings, and their activities seldom involved rigorous physical exertion for fun. They sometimes engaged in 'ladylike' games but, because women were subject to men's control and often viewed as sex objects and models of beauty, their involvement in active pursuits was limited. Feminine beauty during this time was defined in passive terms: the less active a woman, the more likely she was perceived as beautiful.

Even though some sports in Europe and North America today can trace their roots back to the medieval period, the contests and games of that time were not much like today's organized sports. They lacked specialization and organization, they never involved the measurement or recording of athletic achievements, and they were not based on a commitment to equal and open competition among athletes from diverse backgrounds (review the box 'Dominant sport forms today,' p. 69). Historian Allen Guttmann has vividly described this last point:

> In medieval times, jousts and tournaments were limited to the nobility. Knights who sullied their honour by inferior marriages – to peasant girls, for instance – were disbarred. ... Peasants reckless enough to emulate the sport of their masters were punished by death. (1978, p. 30)

Although some characteristics of medieval sports activities can be seen in the games and contests of the Renaissance, the Reformation and the Enlightenment, these later periods involved important social transformations, which shaped the forms and meanings of physical activities and games.

'Why don't we settle this in a civilized way? We'll charge admission to watch!'

Cartoon 3.2 **Dominant sport forms in many societies have been organized to celebrate a particular form of masculinity, emphasizing aggression, conquest and dominance**

The Renaissance, the Reformation and the Enlightenment: Games as Diversions (1300 to 1800)

The Renaissance

Wars throughout Europe during the fourteenth and fifteenth centuries encouraged some monarchs, government officials and church authorities to increase their military strength and prohibit popular peasant pastimes. Those in authority felt that the peasants should spend less time playing games and more time learning to defend the lands and lives of their masters. But, despite the pronouncements of bishops and kings, the peasants did not readily give up their games. In fact, the games sometimes became rallying points for opposition to government and church authority.

At the time that peasants were subjected to increased control in many locations, the 'scholar-athlete' became the ideal man among the affluent. This 'Renaissance man' was 'socially adept, sensitive to aesthetic values, skilled in weaponry, strong of body, and learned in letters' (Baker, 1988, p. 59). Throughout the Renaissance period, women had relatively few opportunities to be involved in tournaments and sport activities. Although peasant women sometimes played physical games, their lives were restricted by the demands of work in and out of the home. They often did hard physical labour, but they were not encouraged to engage in public games and sports that called attention to their physical abilities.

Upper-class women sometimes participated in bowling, croquet, archery and tennis, but involvement was limited because women during this time were seen as 'naturally' weak and passive. Some of these 'Renaissance women' may have been pampered and put on figurative pedestals, but men maintained their power by tightly controlling the lives of women, partly by promoting the idea that women were too fragile to leave the home and do things on their own. The code of chivalry, popular during this time, had less to do with protecting women than with reproducing patriarchy and privileging men.

The Reformation

During the Protestant Reformation, growing negative attitudes about games and sport activities discouraged participation, especially where Calvinist or Puritan beliefs were popular. For example, between the early 1500s and the late 1600s, English Puritans tried to eliminate or control leisure activities, including physical contests and games. They were devoted to the work ethic and viewed sports in this way:

> [Sports] were thought to be profane and licentious – they were occasions of worldly indulgence that tempted men from a godly life; being rooted in pagan and popish practices, they were rich in the sort of ceremony and ritual that poorly suited the Protestant conscience; they frequently involved a desecration of the Sabbath and an interference with the worship of the true believers; they disrupted the peaceable order of society, distracting men from their basic social duties – hard work, thrift, personal restraint, devotion to family, [and] a sober carriage.
>
> *(Malcolmson, 1984, p. 67)*

The primary targets of the Puritans were the pastimes and games of the peasants. Peasants did not own property, so their festivities occurred in public settings and attracted large crowds. This made them easy for the Puritans to condemn and control. The Puritans did their best to eliminate festivities, especially those scheduled on Sunday afternoons. They objected to the drinking and partying that accompanied the games, and disapproved of physical pleasure on the Sabbath. The physical activities and games of the affluent were less subject to Puritan interference. Activities such as horse racing, hunting, tennis and bowling took place on the private property of the wealthy, making it difficult for the Puritans to enforce their prohibitions. As in other times and places, power relations had much to do with who played what activities under what conditions. Despite Puritan influence and social changes affecting the economic structure and stability of English village life, many peasants maintained participation in games and sports.

During the early 1600s, King James I formally challenged Puritan influence in England by issuing *The King's Book of Sports*. This book, reissued in 1633 by Charles I, emphasized that Puritan ministers and officials should not discourage lawful recreational pursuits among English citizens. Charles I and his successors ushered in a new day for English sporting life. They revived traditional festivals, and actively promoted and supported public games and sport activities. Consequently, cricket, horse racing, yachting, fencing, golf and boxing became highly organized during the late 1600s and the 1700s, although participation patterns reflected and reproduced social divisions in society.

During the Reformation period, England, as well as other European nations, attempted to secure colonies along the coast of America to increase their wealth. Many of the colonizers travelled to the 'New World' in order to escape religious persecution and, in colonial America, Puritan influence was strong. Many colonists were not playful people; hard work was necessary for survival. However, as colonists developed more routine lifestyles, more free time became available and Puritan beliefs became less important than the desire to include games from the their past into everyday life. Towns gradually abandoned the Puritan 'blue laws' that prohibited games and sports, and this made it possible for leisure activities, including sports, to grow in popularity.

During this time, the games of Native Peoples in the Americas were not directly affected by Puritan beliefs and cultural practices. Native Peoples in areas that now constitute eastern and north-eastern states in the USA continued to play the games that had been part of their cultures for centuries. In fact, sports and sports participation have many histories across North America. This alerts us to the issue of whose voices and perspectives are represented in historical accounts of games, contests and sports. The box 'Lessons from history' emphasizes that most historical accounts do not represent the experiences and perspectives of those who lack the power to tell their own stories and make them a part of dominant culture.

 Each sport's distinctive past matters to the people who play and follow it in the present.

(Martin Polley, historian, 2002, p. 49)

reflect on SPORTS   *Lessons from history: who tells us about the past?*

History is much more than a chronological series of events that revolve around the lives of male leaders. Historical research, when done thoroughly, should take us inside the lives of people who have lived before us. It should give us a sense of how people lived and gave meaning to their experiences and the events of their times. Therefore, when we study sports, it is important to be aware of whose voices and perspectives are used to construct historical accounts, as well as whose voices and perspectives are missing. This awareness is important when studying the physical activities, games and sports of Native Peoples in North America.

Prior to the arrival of Columbus and other Europeans, the histories of Native Peoples were often kept in oral rather than written forms; they were local and personal histories. It was not until the late eighteenth century that accounts of the lives and cultures of Native Peoples were recorded in English. However, those accounts were written by Europeans with limited knowledge of the diverse languages, cultures and complex social arrangements that made up the lives of at least 500 unique cultural groups of Native Peoples in North America. This social and cultural diversity was obscured by general accounts describing the lives and customs of 'Indians', as if all native cultures were the same. These accounts provide limited information about the diverse games and sports played by Native Peoples. In many cases, accounts were written after the lives and communities of Native Peoples had been disrupted and influenced by European explorers and settlers. This history provides little information about the ways that traditional games and sports were played and integrated into the diverse cultures that existed in North America.

Europeans were seldom able to observe authentic expressions of traditional native cultures. When they did make observations, it was often under strained circumstances, and Native Peoples were unwilling to reveal their customs while being watched by outsiders who often viewed them as 'oddities'. The fact that the most important games in native cultures were connected with religious rites made it even less likely that Europeans would be allowed to observe them in authentic, traditional forms or understand the meanings associated with them. By the time Native Peoples provided their own historical accounts in English, their cultures had changed in appreciable ways, and few people were willing to listen to their stories and publish them in forms that were considered 'real history'. In the meantime, experiences and meanings were lost for ever.

That we know so little about the many histories of games and sports among Native Peoples demonstrates that social, political and economic forces influence our knowledge of sport history and, even, our definitions of what constitutes 'real' knowledge. For example, if we wish to understand the importance of an event, such as the establishment of the Iroquois National Lacrosse Team in 1983, we must know the following:

- the histories and cultures of specific native societies and the six nations of the Iroquois Confederation
- the formal and informal political relationships between native societies and the US government
- the experiences of Native Peoples in North America as they struggled to maintain their cultures while others tried to strip them of their dignity, language, religion and customs.

Knowing these things enables us to initiate research on the significance of the Iroquois National Lacrosse Team in terms of those who formed it, participated on it and followed its matches.

The scarcity of information based on the perspectives of those who lack power diminishes our knowledge of sports history around the world. As British social historian James Riordan (1996, p. vii) has said, 'Just as the dominant class writes history, so that same class writes the story of sport.' Therefore, when our knowledge of the past does not go beyond the experiences and perspectives of those with the power to tell their own stories, it is always incomplete. In the worst case such stories reproduce stereotypes and justify discrimination against those with little power. This is why some people call for more cultural diversity in educational curricula and more materials representing the voices of those who previously were excluded from the knowledge production process. *What do you think?*

The Enlightenment

During the Enlightenment period (1700 to 1800), the games and sport activities in parts of Europe and North America began to resemble sport forms that are popular today. With some exceptions, physical games and sports during the Enlightenment were no longer grounded in religious ritual and ceremony. They involved a degree of specialization and organization, achievements sometimes were measured, and records occasionally were kept. Furthermore, the idea that events should be open to all competitors, regardless of background, became increasingly popular.

However, sport activities during the Enlightenment period were different from the dominant sport forms of today in at least one important respect: they were defined strictly as diversions – as interesting and often challenging ways to pass free time enjoyably. People did not see them as having a purpose beyond the immediate experiences of participants and the occasion on which they were played. No one thought that sports and sport participation were related to health, character development and the organization of social life. Therefore, people had no reason to organize sport activities for others or to create organizations to sponsor or govern sports. A few people formed clubs, and they occasionally scheduled contests with other groups, but they did not form leagues or national and international associations. But this approach to sports changed dramatically during the Industrial Revolution.

The Industrial Revolution: the Emergence of Organized Competitive Sports (1780 to 1920)

It is an oversimplification to say that the organized competitive sports of today are simply a product of the Industrial Revolution. They clearly emerged during the process of industrialization, but they were actually social constructions of people themselves – people who played their games and sport activities while they coped with the realities of everyday life in rapidly changing families, communities and societies. Of course, the realities of everyday life included economic, political and social forces, which either enabled or constrained people, depending on their position in society.

The development of factories, the mass production of consumer goods, the growth of cities and increased dependence on technology marked the Industrial Revolution. It involved changes in the organization and control of work and community life, and was generally accompanied by an increase in the number of middle-class people in the societies where it occurred. The Industrial Revolution first began in England around 1780, spreading quickly to urban areas of Scotland and the mining regions of Wales, and became a part of life after 1800 in other European countries and North America. Notably, Ireland did not experience a comparable Industrial Revolution, and this led to problems of unemployment and famine.

The early years: limited time and space for sports

During the early years of the Industrial Revolution, few people had regular opportunities to play games and sport activities. Farm and factory workers had little free time. The workdays, even for many child workers, were long and tiring. People in cities had few open spaces where they could play sports. Production took priority over play. Industrialists and politicians were not concerned with providing parks and public play spaces. Working people were discouraged from gathering in large groups outside the workplace. The authorities perceived such gatherings as dangerous because they wasted time that could be used for work. Additionally, they provided opportunities for workers to organize themselves and challenge the power of factory owners (Brailsford, 1991; Holt, 1989; Tranter, 1998).

In most industrializing countries, the clergy endorsed restrictions on popular games and gatherings. Ministers preached about the moral value of work and the immorality of play and idleness. Many even banned sports on Sundays and accused anyone who was not totally committed to work of being lazy. Work, they preached, was a sign of goodness. Not everyone agreed, but working people had few choices. For them, survival depended on working long hours, regardless of what they thought about work, and they had little power to change the conditions of their lives. The structure of working life was also changed to reduce the number of bank holidays per year from 17 to just four by 1834.

In most countries, games and sport activities during this period existed *despite* the Industrial Revolution, *not* because of it. People in small towns and farm communities still had opportunities to play games and sport activities during their seasonal festivities, holidays and public ceremonies. Local neighbourhood events that attracted crowds were often defined as illegal. For example, in Derby attempts were made to abolish the highly popular street football which was characteristic of many working-class pastimes: regulated by simple oral rules and played over several hours by hundred of participants who often used violent means to reach one of the goals situated at opposite ends of the town. It appears that resistance to this came from the middle classes, concerned about the working days lost for the event (see Delves, 1981; Guttman, 1978).

However, some communities have maintained their sporting rituals from this era. For example, in Leicestershire, bottle kicking (a form of football with beer kegs instead of a ball) is still played on Easter Monday. It has even been suggested that 'these archaic sports continue, perhaps because they appeal to other English virtues – of being drunk, of being violent and of beating the opposition' (Bull, 2007, p. 50)!

Most city people had few opportunities to organize their own games and sports, although the super wealthy lived highly publicized 'lives of leisure' (Veblen, 1899) including fox-hunting, cricket, horse racing and golf. Among the working classes, sport involvement seldom went beyond being spectators at new forms of commercialized sport events. These events varied by nation, but urban workers in most European and North American cities watched activities such as prizefighting in the form of boxing and wrestling, foot races, rowing and yachting races, circus acts, and various forms of animal contests including cockfighting, bull- or badger-baiting, among other things.

Some sports participation still occurred among urban workers, but it was relatively rare during the early days of the Industrial Revolution. However, between 1800 and 1850, some people in Europe and North America became concerned about the physical health of workers. This concern was partly based on the awareness that workers were being exploited and partly on the recognition that weak and sickly workers could not be productive. Consequently, there were growing calls for new open spaces and funding of 'healthy' leisure pursuits. Personal fitness was highly publicized, and there was an emphasis on callisthenics, gymnastics and outdoor exercises. Conflict theorists have suggested that such developments were a form of social control: to tame the workforce and ensure industrial progress (see Clarke and Critcher, 1985).

The sporting events which thrived tended to be organized commercial events which were approved in most industrial societies, even when they attracted large crowds. In fact, rules prohibiting crowds were suspended when people participated in controlled commercialized spectator events. These events were organized by and for the ultimate benefit of powerful and wealthy people, notably members of the aristocracy whose interests would be served by working-class involvement in these forms of sport. For example, prizefighters came from lower-class families, but the sport was patronized by people from the upper class who could profit by gambling on the outcome. Similarly, aristocratic gamblers were known to employ men from the lower social classes, ostensibly to work on their estate, but principally for their cricketing prowess to compete against other estates in matches which were watched by thousands. It was often the case that the aristocracy would socialize with the lower classes during such events, indicating a sense that they felt secure enough in their social power to socialize with the lower orders. This is in marked contrast to the nineteenth-century trend of social class distinction perpetuated through amateur statutes, which leave their legacy today.

The emergence of formally organized competitive sports and the maintenance of records of achievement would require more than increased freedom and limited support for healthy leisure activities, but this was the time during which the foundations for organized sports were established. Golby and Purdue (1984) suggest that the transformation of British sports were influenced by four main factors, particularly from the 1840s onwards: a reduced working week, with a half-day Saturday; increased real earnings providing unprecedented levels of disposable income; improved public transport, particularly in the form of the railway network; and the expansion of commercial provision in leisure. In discussing these, and other more recent issues related to sports in society, we focus on events throughout the UK.

Prizefighting was popular among urban workers during the early years of industrialism. The majority of participants were lower class, but the upper classes were keen spectators and frequently gambled on the outcomes of contests (*Source*: Bob Thomas/Popperfoto/Getty Images)

The later years: changing interests, values and opportunities

Over the past 150 years of UK history, there has been a growing emphasis on organizing all spheres of social life in a rational and systematic manner. For example, during the mid-1800s, newly formed clubs sponsored and controlled sports participation. Club membership usually was limited to wealthy people in urban areas and students at exclusive schools. However, the competitions attracted spectators from all social classes. The Young Men's Christian Association (YMCA), founded in England in 1844, was a clublike organization that had a less exclusive membership policy. During the late 1800s it began to change the popular notion that physical conditioning through exercise and sports was anti-Christian.

Central to the development of sporting forms at this time was the public school system. The sports culture of these institutions, epitomized by Thomas Arnold, the Headmaster of Rugby School from 1828 to 1842, was to turn out Christian gentlemen who could both govern themselves and the lower orders. Traditional games were transformed from popular folk games, such as football, into rationalized and 'gentlemanly' sports with codified rules. This process was largely responsible for the bifurcation of football into the two versions of soccer and rugby by the mid-1840s. The cult of athleticism was seen to underpin a healthy workforce, develop fit men for national defence and socialize male youth into the modern social order. By the 1860s, games were central to the school curriculum, and it was generally believed that boys who were active in strenuous sports would have 'a healthy mind in a healthy body': *mens sana in corpore sano* (Hargreaves, 1986).

As sports activities became more organized, they generally reinforced existing class distinctions in society. Upper-class clubs emphasized achievement and 'gentlemanly' involvement – an orientation that ultimately led to definitions of amateurism. The definition of *amateur*, which first appeared in England, became a tool for excluding working-class people from sports that were organized around the interests of upper-class people (Eitzen, 2003; Polley, 1998; Scambler, 2005). The activities of the working classes, by contrast, did not usually occur under the sponsorship of clubs or organizations, and they seldom received publicity. Instead, they generally involved local games and commercialized sports – a combination that ultimately led to professionalization. This dual development of amateurism and professionalization occurred in different ways in Europe and North America (Dunning, 1999).

the influence which bodily exercise, such as manly games and sports, has upon the character; these often develop a character as much as books, and when the young are engaged in them they are preserved from idleness, which is the root of much evil. England perhaps owes more than any country to its noble games.
(Reverend Maurice Ponsonby, 1879, cited in Collins, 1996a, p. 2)

The seeds of new meanings

Underlying the growing organization of sports activities in the decades after 1850 was a new emphasis on the seriousness of sports. Instead of defining sports simply as enjoyable diversions, people gradually came to see them as tools for achieving important goals such as economic productivity, national loyalty, and the development of admirable character traits, especially among males. This new way of viewing sports was fuelled by changes in every segment of industrial society: the economy, politics, family life, religion, education, science, philosophy and technology.

The growth of organized sports in the UK: 1880 to 1920

The years between 1880 and 1920 were crucial for the development of organized sports in the UK (Birley, 1995; Tranter, 1998). Wealthy people developed lives of leisure that often included sports, and they used participation in certain sports to prove that they were so successful that they could 'waste' time by playing non-productive games (Veblen, 1899). The wealthy often used sports to reinforce status distinctions between themselves and other social classes. For example, the well-documented division of rugby union from rugby league was largely a response of the upper classes to the numbers of working-class men who were taking up rugby during the 1870s and 1880s. The rugby hierarchy would not facilitate these men playing on an equal footing with wealthy gentlemen, and so forced a split of the two codes (Collins, 1996b). The wealthy also influenced how sports were played and organized by others, especially middle-class people whose status aspirations led them to emulate the rich and powerful.

In this way, the upper class influenced the norms for many players and spectators, the standards for facilities and equipment, and the way in which people throughout society defined and integrated sports into their lives. Specifically, wealthy people used their economic resources to encourage others to define sports as *consumer activities* to be played in *proper* attire, using the *proper* equipment in a *proper* facility and preceded or followed by *proper* social occasions separated from employment and the workplace. Because many people followed these norms, sports became connected with and supportive of the economy. This connection was subtle because sports involved both consumption *and* work-like orientations while being popularly defined as 'non-work' activities, separate from the economy.

The emergence of these ideas about the ways that sports 'should be' played was important. It enabled people with power to reproduce their privilege in society without overtly coercing workers to think and do certain things. Instead of maintaining their privilege by being nasty, people with economic power promoted forms of sports that were entertaining and supportive of the values and orientations that promoted capitalist business expansion. Critical theorists have noted that this is an example of how sports can be political and economic activities, even though most people see them as sources of excitement and enjoyment (Gramsci, 1971, 1988; Rigauer, 2000; Sage, 2000).

During the period of 1880 to 1920, middle- and working-class people, especially white males, had new opportunities to play sports. Trades unions, progressive government legislation and economic expansion combined to improve working and living conditions.

As the middle class expanded, more people had resources for leisure and sport participation. The spirit of reform at the turn of the twentieth century also led to the development of sports facilities, parks and open spaces in which games could be played by urban residents, especially boys and young men.

Ideas about sports participation and 'character development'

During the early 1900s, opportunities for sports involvement increased, but those opportunities were shaped by factors beyond the interests of the participants themselves. Important new ideas about human behaviour, individual development and social life led to an emphasis on organized competitive sports as 'character-building' activities.

Through the 1880s most people believed that the actions and development of human beings were unrelated to social factors. They assumed that fate or supernatural forces dictated individual development and that social life was established by a combination of God's will, necessity and coincidence. However, these ideas changed as people discovered that the social environment influenced people's actions and that it was possible to change patterns of individual growth and development by altering the organization of society.

This new way of thinking was a crucial catalyst for the growth of modern sports. It made sports into something more than enjoyable pastimes. Gradually, sports were defined as potential educational experiences – experiences with important consequences for individuals, communities and society. This change, based on behaviourist and evolutionary theories, which were popular at the time, provided a new reason for organizing and promoting sport participation. For the first time in history, people saw sports as tools for changing behaviour, shaping character, creating national loyalty and building unity.

People began to think about the meaning and purpose of sports in new and serious terms. For example, some religious groups, later referred to as 'muscular Christians', suggested a link between physical strength and the ability to do good works; therefore, they promoted sports involvement as an avenue for spiritual growth. The increased spending power which resulted from the rise in real wages around the turn of the century meant that the working classes saw increased affluence, and the muscular Christians attempted to persuade the workers and their children to invest their economic good fortune in active sports participation. Sport was seen as a means of character formation, teaching self-discipline and team spirit. In addition, this 'rational recreation' was offered as a counteraction to crime, gambling and alcohol (Vamplew, 1988). Many current football and cricket teams have their origins in religious affiliations.

In addition to the religious groups, people interested in economic expansion saw organized sports as tools for generating profits by introducing untrained workers to tasks emphasizing teamwork, obedience to rules, planning, organization and production. Sports, they thought, could create good workers who would tolerate stressful working conditions, maintain fitness, obey supervisors and meet production goals through teamwork on factory assembly lines. Despite this, participation in sports was not as popular among the working classes as the muscular Christians and employers might have anticipated. However, entrepreneurs were quick to realize that many workers were keen to watch others play, and to pay for the privilege, and the commercialization of spectator sport is one of the success stories of Victorian Britain, as we shall discuss later.

Organized sports and ideas about masculinity and femininity

The new belief that sports built character was applied primarily to males. The public schools routinely segregated boys from the influence of their family and from females, so ensuring the development of a chauvinistic masculine identity. Games were a medium for learning what it was to be 'gentlemanly'. Sports were used to counteract the negative influence of female-dominated home lives on the development of young males from middle- and upper-class backgrounds. The goal was to turn 'over-feminized' boys from affluent families into assertive, competitive, achievement-orientated young men who would become effective leaders in business, politics and the military. In these ways, contemporary sports were heavily grounded in the desire of people with power and wealth to control the working classes, while preparing their own sons to inherit their positions of power and influence (Burstyn, 1999; Kidd, 1996b).

Although women's sport participation increased between 1880 and 1920, many sports programmes ignored females. Organizers and sponsors did not see sports participation as important in the character development of girls and women. They sometimes included girls with boys in organized games at playgrounds, but they discouraged sex-integrated sports among children nearing the age of puberty. It was widely believed that if boys and girls played sports with one another, they would become good friends and lose their interest in being married, having children, and maintaining beliefs in male superiority and female inferiority.

When boys were taught to play sports on playgrounds in the early 1900s, girls were told to sit in the shade and preserve their energy. Medical doctors during this time warned that playing sports would sap the energy that young women needed to conceive and bear healthy children. In 1887, the chair of the British Medical Association proposed that women should be denied education and other activities which might cause constitutional overstrain, and that this was in the interests of the 'progressive improvement of the human race' (cited in Hargreaves, 1994, p. 45). Many middle-class women were keen to follow the dictates of fashion and so wore restricting clothes, ate very little and did not take any exercise. It is no surprise that many became ill, fainted frequently and behaved submissively, so reinforcing the stereotype of the delicate female. Luther Gulick, who shaped the recreational philosophy of the YMCA at that time, wrote, 'It is clear that athletics have never been either a test or a large factor in the survival of women; athletics do not test womanliness as they test manliness' (1906, p. 158). Gulick also felt that strenuous activities were harmful to the minds and bodies of females. This was the gender ideology of the time.

Organized activities for girls often consisted of domestic science classes to make them good wives, homemakers and mothers. In many ways, the development of 'rational recreation' for males was paralleled by the development of 'rational domesticity' for females (Clarke and Critcher, 1985). When playground organizers provided opportunities for girls to play games and sports, they designed activities that would cultivate 'ladylike' traits, such as poise and body control. This is why so many girls participated in gymnastics and other 'grace and beauty' sports (Burstyn, 1999; Hart, 1981). Another goal of the activities was to make young women healthy for bearing children. Competition was eliminated or controlled so that physical activities emphasized personal health, the dignity of beauty and good form. In some cases, the only reason games and sports were included in girls' lives was to give them the knowledge they would need to introduce sports to their future sons.

Limited opportunities and a lack of encouragement did not prevent women from partici-pating in sports, but they certainly restricted their involvement (Vertinsky, 1994). Some middle- and upper-class women engaged in popular physical exercises and recreational sport activities, such as quoits, skittles and gentle forms of tennis and badminton. However, they had few opportunities to engage in formal competitive events. Instead, they reinforced male sporting superiority by watching men participate in regattas and cricket matches. The sporting oppor-tunities for working-class girls were largely limited to the introduction of Swedish gymnastics in state schools, which involved drill-like activity to teach discipline and obedience, thus consolidating social class divisions. Ideas about femininity changed between 1880 and 1920, but traditional gender ideology and many misconceptions about the physical and mental effects of strenuous activities on females prevented the 'new woman' of the early twentieth century from enjoying the same participation opportunities and encouragement received by males (Lenskyj, 1986). Medical beliefs supported this ideology by providing 'scientific evidence' showing that women's bodies could not tolerate vigorous activities. These faulty beliefs and studies damaged the health of women during these years (Vertinsky, 1987).

Organized sports and ideas about national identity

The latter part of the nineteenth century was a crucial time in Anglo-Irish relations, much of which was played out in sports. Ireland and Britain were formally linked under the Act of Union from 1800 although, in reality, the Irish had been under British control for much longer. Throughout the nineteenth century, Irish nationalism was underpinned by a desire

Leisure activities among wealthy people in the early twentieth century included sports. However, physical activities and sports for girls and women often stressed balance and co-ordination, which were defined as 'ladylike' qualities. Girls and women were often trained to be graceful and co-ordinated so that they might become 'ladies' (Source: McGraw-Hill)

for independence and freedom from Britain. This was particularly the case following the Irish famine of the 1840s (for which the British were largely blamed) through to the problematic division of Ireland under the Anglo-Irish Treaty of 1921. Nationalists were keen to compare the history of prosperity under an Irish Ireland, to the poverty and problems of the British colonial era. They formed cultural organizations which celebrated Irishness and resisted the customs of the colonizer. Such groups included the Gaelic League and the Gaelic Athletic Association, formed in 1884, which promoted and supported traditional Irish sports. In particular, there was a desire to revive the fortunes of traditional rural pastimes, such as Gaelic football and hurling, which had declined during the years of famine.

In 1906 a ban was brought on playing 'imported' sports and, while this did not last long, it was indicative of nationalistic fervour. The authorities were particularly concerned by the success of the Gaelic Athletic Association which was seen as a front for insurrectionist activities. In 1912, the All-Ireland Gaelic Football Final was watched by 18 000 people, and the hurling final by 20 000 (Cronin, 1999). By 1913 there were several rule changes, consistent with the codification of sports taking place in Britain, which increased attendance at games and helped those with a commercial interest in sports. However, many teams lost players who were more interested in military than sporting pursuits, and who subsequently joined the Irish Volunteers.

Gaelic sports were also the focus of one of the most famous tragedies of the Anglo-Irish conflict, when British troops killed 13 people (including one player) at Croke Park, the venue for a Gaelic football match between Dublin and Tipperary in 1920. While the Gaelic Athletic Association was not involved in the events surrounding the 'Bloody Sunday' atrocity, it gained legendary status as being central to the connection between national violence and national sport. Croke Park remained closed as a venue for 'British' sports until a vote at the Gaelic Athletic Association conference in 2005 revoked the rule.

Gaelic sport did not completely usurp British sports and, in fact, the modernization of the games took place largely along lines influenced by developments in British society. Notably, while the Gaelic Athletic Association was still in formative stages, the English football code was established among Irish Catholic working classes, as well as its more traditional supporters in the north and Protestant areas. Football became a central focus for working-class sectarian conflict, with tense and sometimes violent rivalry between the nationalist Catholics and loyalist Protestant supporters, and this tension continues today. (For a more detailed discussion of the relationship between sport and Irish identity, see Bairner, 2005; Hassan, 2003; Tuck, 2003a.)

Organized sports and ideas about age and disability

Ageing involves biological changes, but the connection between ageing and sports participation depends largely on the social meanings given to those changes. Developmental theory in the early 1900s emphasized that all growth and character formation occurred during childhood and adolescence. Therefore, it was important for young people to play sports, but older people were already 'grown ups' and no longer needed the character-building experiences provided by sports.

Medical knowledge at the time also discouraged older people from engaging in sports. Strenuous activities were thought to put excessive demands on the heart and organs in ageing bodies. This did not prevent some older people from playing certain sports, but it did prevent the establishment and funding of organized sports programmes for older people. Furthermore, when older people were physically active, they participated by themselves or in age-segregated settings.

People with observable physical or mental impairments were denied opportunities to play sports and were often told that strenuous physical activities would upset their well-being. During this time, widely accepted definitions of mental and physical disability gave rise to fears and prejudices that led many people to think it was dangerous to allow people with disabilities to become physically active or excited. Therefore, programmes to build their bodies were discouraged. This meant that people born with certain disabilities were isolated and destined to be physically inactive; obesity and problems caused by a lack of physical activity shortened their life expectancy. People with 'acquired disabilities', usually those injured in war or accidents, were treated with physical therapy in the hope of some degree of rehabilitation. As explained in the 'Breaking barriers' box overleaf, sports for most people with disabilities did not exist until after the Second World War.

breaking BARRIERS

'Other' barriers: *they found it hard to be around me*

Danny was 21 years old, a popular and able-bodied rugby player. Then came the accident, the amputation of his right arm just below the shoulder, the therapy and, eventually, getting back with friends. But reconnecting with friends after suddenly acquiring a disability is not easy. Danny describes his experience with these words: 'A lot of them found it very difficult ... to come to terms with it ... And they found it hard to be around me, friends that I'd had for years' (in Brittain, 2004, p. 437).

Chris, an athlete with cerebral palsy and one of Danny's teammates on the British Paralympic Team, explains why his friends felt uncomfortable: 'They have very little knowledge of people with a disability and [they think that] if I leave it alone and don't touch them and don't get involved, then it's not my problem' (in Brittain, 2004, p. 437). Chris raises a recurring issue in the history of disability: what happens when people define physical or intellectual impairments as 'differences' and use them to create 'others' who are distinguished from 'us normals' in social worlds?

Throughout history, people with disabilities have been described by words inferring revulsion, resentment, dread, shame and a world of limitations. In Europe and North America, it took the Second World War and thousands of returning soldiers impaired by injuries before there were widespread concerns about the words used to describe people with disabilities. Language has changed so that people with intellectual disabilities now have opportunities to participate in the Special Olympics, and elite athletes with physical disabilities may qualify for the Paralympics ('para' meaning *parallel with*, not *paraplegic*). Words like *retard*, *spaz* (spastic), *cripple*, *freak*, *deaf and dumb*, *handicapped*, *gimp* and *deformed* have largely been abandoned. However, they are not gone, and people with disabilities are still described as 'others' – such as 'she's a quad', 'he's a CPer', 'they're amputees' and 'what a retard!'

Improvements have occurred, but when people with disabilities are defined as 'others', encountering disability raises questions about personal vulnerability, ageing and mortality. It also highlights the faulty assumptions of normalcy around which we construct social worlds. Therefore, those identified as 'normal' often ignore, avoid or patronize people with disabilities, and this subverts the possibility of ever seeing the world through their eyes.

The fear of 'otherness' is powerful, and people in many cultures traditionally restrict and manage their contact with 'others' by enlisting the services of experts. These include doctors, mental health workers, psychiatrists, healers, shamans, witchdoctors, priests, exorcists and all professionals whose assumed competence gives them the right to examine, test, classify and prescribe 'normalizing treatments' for 'others'. Therefore, the history of disability is also the history of giving meaning to difference, creating 'others', and using current knowledge to treat 'otherness' (Foucault, 1961/1967; Goffman, 1963).

As noted in 'Breaking barriers' in Chapter 2, cultural traditions in the UK have long emphasized treatment-orientated approaches to fix impairments or help people adjust to living with disabilities. Only recently have these approaches been complemented by transformational approaches focused on creating barrier-free social spaces in which disabilities become irrelevant and 'others' are no longer created. This is an idealistic project, and it requires actions that disrupt the 'normal' order of social worlds. But Jean Driscoll, eight-time winner of the Women's Wheelchair Boston Marathon, has experienced such worlds, and she says that 'when sports are integrated, the focus turns from the person with a disability to the guy with a great shot or the gal with a fast 800-metre time. Integration provides the perfect venue where "actions speak louder than words"' (in Joukowsky and Rothstein, 2002b, p. 28). And we would add that interactionist theory helps us understand that words are the foundation for action.

Since 1920: Struggles Continue

By 1920 major connections between sports and British society had been firmly established. Sports were a growing part of people's everyday lives, and they were linked to major social institutions such as the family, religion, education, the economy, the government and the media. Since 1920 the rate of change and the expansion of the visibility and importance of sports in people's lives have intensified. The past nine decades have been a time of many 'firsts' in UK sports. They have also been a time for continuing struggles over the following:

- the meaning, purpose and organization of sports
- who plays sports under what conditions
- how and why sports are funded.

As explained in Chapter 1, sports are social constructions *and* contested activities. Therefore, we can outline social trends and patterns in recent history by focusing on issues and events related to these three realms of struggle. They serve as useful reference points for discussing social history, and we use them to guide our choice of materials in the following chapters. They also provide a useful framework for understanding patterns and trends during the twentieth century.

Table 3.2 highlights events related to major struggles and changes in sports, providing a feel for the social side of what has happened in recent sports history. Of course, the timing, dynamics and outcomes of these struggles and changes were related to larger historical events and trends, such as wars, economic recessions, the growth of universities, the women's movements, the development and expansion of the electronic media and other technologies, globalization, and the growing concentration of corporate power and influence around the world. (For a list of specific events and trends, see the OLC at www.mcgraw-hill.co.uk/textbooks/coakley).

Connections between the recent history of sports and these trends and events are too complex to discuss in this chapter. But it is possible to outline some of the major struggles that have occurred since 1920.

AT YOUR *fingertips*

For more information on sports as contested activities and social constructions, see pages 7–11.

Struggles over meaning: do sports encourage or challenge social divisions?

Sports have always had multiple meanings, and these meanings change over time. Sports in the UK have a long history of amateurism which, in turn, ensured a social class distinction between those who needed to be paid and those whose social position enabled them to play without financial reward. Amateurs controlled sport throughout the nineteenth century but the words 'amateur' and 'professional' had become largely meaningless by the end of the twentieth century. However, the changes were treated differently within different sports. While sports such as football chose to accept professionalism within its organization in order to control it, sports such as rugby union rejected professionalism and so lost control of that part of the game when it separated from the amateur body.

The meanings given to sports often vary from one region of a country to another. Professional sports took hold in many northern areas faster than in the south, largely due to economic differences. While rugby has been associated with public schools and the upper classes in England and Scotland, Welsh rugby has been a unifying force played by all social classes and immigrant groups, enabling a sense of nationhood. Gaelic sports have been popular in areas of Ireland keen to resist British culture. Similarly, in Scotland, it is argued that the revival of the Highland Games was to raise national consciousness against the cultural invasiveness of the English (Jarvie, 1991).

The meanings given to sports generally reaffirm the values and lifestyles of those who play and watch them, and this has certainly been true since 1920. Boxing is an example of a sport which reflects the social conditions in which it flourishes. Boxing has been particularly popular in inner-city areas where working-class boys, and specifically those from ethnic minorities, have had to fight for financial necessity because of social and racial oppression.

Struggles over purpose: is winning the only thing?

Meaning and purpose are closely aligned. On a general level, the central purpose of most sports between the 1920s and 1960s was to foster fitness and fair play. However, as occupational success and social mobility became increasingly important in a growing capitalist economy during the 1950s, there was a gradual turn towards an emphasis on competitive success and winning in sports. There was particular concern that Britain's international sporting performance appeared to be declining, not least because of the successes from the 1950s to 1980s of the Communist nations of the former Soviet Union and the German Democratic Republic.

As sports teams and sports events were linked to communities and the nation, the primary purpose of sports continued to shift from participation and fair play to wins that brought prestige to sponsors. By the 1960s, many people felt that 'winning is not the most important thing – it is the *only* thing'. This was particularly significant in competitions between the home countries, which offered the opportunity for Scotland to beat England in the rugby Calcutta Cup, and Northern Ireland to play against the Republic of Ireland in football. With the 1970s and the dramatic growth of media coverage, entertainment became an increasingly important purpose of sports. Entertainment and winning were closely linked because winners filled stadiums and generated revenues for sponsors and owners.

There is never complete agreement on the purpose of sports. For example, physical educators emphasize fitness and health, whereas people associated with the commercial media emphasize entertainment. This and other disagreements occur today as people struggle to define the purpose of sports in their schools and community-based youth programmes.

Struggles over organization: who is in control?

Since 1920 there has been a clear trend towards organizing sports in formal and 'official' ways. Mainstream sports are increasingly organized around standardized rules enforced by official governing bodies. Some people have resisted increased organization and rationalization, but resistance has not slowed or reversed this trend. Even many alternative and recreational sports have become increasingly organized as people try to make them safer, more accessible or more commercially profitable. Hundreds of sports organizations have come and gone over recent years, but the emphasis on organization has become more prevalent.

Sports have also been taken increasingly seriously by governments, particularly as the period since the 1920s saw relative parliamentary stability which enabled the government to turn its attention to wider aspects of social life. Sports were encouraged partly for capitalist interests and partly as an integral aspect of welfare reform. In particular, there was an increasing concern that the activities of young people needed to be curtailed, especially the privileged young men in the south who were visible in urban disorder such as the clashes in Brighton and Margate between 'mods' and 'rockers'. The Wolfendon Report of 1960 was seen to reflect a 'moral panic' regarding such behaviour (see Cohen, 1972), and it promoted sport as a means of controlling youth activities. This will be discussed further in Chapters 5 and 13.

The Wolfendon Committee recommended the establishment of an Advisory Sports Council, which was set up in 1965 to co-ordinate policy development and sports provision. This has remained a quasi-governmental organization, and classic and sometimes bitter struggles have taken place over who controls sports so that they will be organized consistently over time. In the process, governing bodies, coaches and other officials have become key 'players' in sports at all levels. In fact, many children today grow up thinking that sports cannot exist without coaches and referees.

Struggles over sports participation: can everyone play?

Some of the most contentious struggles in sports since the 1920s have revolved around who participates in formally organized, mainstream sports programmes. Most sports were initially organized around various forms of exclusion and segregation based on social class, race, ethnicity, gender, age and (dis)ability. In particular, the period immediately following the mid-1920s saw persistent social inequalities in British society which were mirrored in divided leisure experiences. The decline in heavy industry and increased investment in light engineering, chemical and electrical industries meant that there became a north–south divide, with many in the south experiencing relative affluence and those in northern areas experiencing hardship. Men from relatively well-to-do white families have consistently had the greatest access to sport participation opportunities throughout their lives.

There were other changes in the make-up of society which impacted on sports. The relationship of Britain with its former colonies influenced sport in two main ways. First, there was the 'exportation' of sports which were spread through imperial conquest, most notably cricket in countries such as India and the Caribbean. And, second, the 'importation' of persons from the British colonies had a significant impact on the cultural make-up of British society. The key time for these changes took place from the mid-1950s when inducements were offered by employers to immigrants from the West Indies and the Asian subcontinent. The backlash against this by many white British people included ethnic segregation to exclude 'the coloureds', including from sporting contexts. However, by the 1970s, there were some visible black British sports heroes and there was gradual diffusion of immigrant cultures into British society. These processes will be discussed in more detail in Chapter 9.

There have been constant struggles to expand participation opportunities for ethnic minorities, women, people from low-income families and neighbourhoods, people with physical and intellectual disabilities, and people labelled as gay or lesbian. Complex histories are associated with each of these struggles, but the general trend between 1920 and the early 1980s was to open sport participation to more people, especially through sports funded by public money and played in public facilities. The formation of the Sports Council in 1965 was largely in response to pressure on the state to address social deprivation and exclusion. However, private clubs and organizations have maintained exclusionary membership criteria over the years, and most continue to do so today. Increased privatization since the 1980s has made it more financially difficult for many people to initiate or maintain regular sport participation, and this trend suggests that sports will be characterized by increased socio-economic segregation in the future.

Struggles over who participates under what conditions have been further complicated by the diversity of goals among the people involved, illustrated in the various feminist sociologies of sport. Feminist theorists have long argued that involvement in sport can enable substantial benefits for women, including a sense of exercising self-control over their own lives independent of male influences (Deem, 1986; Kay, 2003; Talbot, 1986). Scraton and Flintoff (2002) identify the different goals of liberal feminists, who seek equality of access and opportunity, in contrast to radical feminists whose concerns are with structural power relations in sport. This is considered further in Chapter 8. These differences illustrate how some groups of people have fought to be integrated fully into organized, mainstream sports, whereas others have fought to have separate opportunities that meet their specific needs and interests. For instance, not everyone wishes to play sports developed and organized around the interests and experiences of young, able-bodied, white, heterosexual males. Many struggles have occurred around the funding of new or alternative sport participation opportunities.

Struggles over funding: who pays, who gains?

In the period following the First World War, the UK, along with many other European nations, was influenced by the approach to sport and physical education used in the USA. Sports festivals were developed, and sport spectatorship steadily increased, largely due to increased radio coverage of sports fixtures. Football was particularly popular, especially with working-class men, and the introduction of two additional divisions in 1922 extended the appeal beyond the northern and Midlands regions. It was in the shift to the south, and particularly with the rise of Arsenal, that the economic base of the contemporary game was established. A more organized management structure appeared, investment in grounds followed and transfer fees rose rapidly, all to the benefit of those who owned the clubs (Clarke and Critcher, 1985). In the 1960s, the Professional Footballers' Association threatened strike action in order to remove the maximum wage restriction for players and enable them to gain from the increased revenue provided by television coverage.

One particular feature of sport at this time was the expansion of the gambling culture. The football pools became a business in their own right. Also, animal sports such as horse racing and greyhound racing were able to develop a place in the betting world as a combined result of increased disposable income among some classes and improved circulation of the popular press which contained fixtures and results. In today's society, it is possible to gamble on almost any sports event, providing a lucrative business for bookmakers.

The move towards a more competitive and professional era was global as well as local. Relations with the USA and the former colonies increased international competitions, and in 1948 London hosted the Olympic Games. The development of sports on a global scale has meant that sports needed to find sources of funding beyond government support. The fact that these large-scale competitions were of interest to television companies, means that corporate sponsors have been only too happy to provide large sums of money in return for media coverage and the association of their product with an appealing sporting image. Corporate sponsorship of sports, teams, events and individuals is now an integral part of the sporting scene, as we will discuss in Chapters 11 and 12.

This new form of sponsorship has had a major impact on the types of sports that have become popular and who has had opportunities to participate in them. Instead of being based on ideas about 'the common good' – such as the reduction of obesity, for example – sports today often are sponsored in connection with the commercial interests of corporations. Struggles over sports sponsorships have recently involved corporations that sell tobacco, alcohol, fast foods, products made in sweatshops and services defined by some people as immoral (related to gambling, strip clubs and escort services). These struggles will continue as long as the sports that people want to play and watch require large amounts of capital and as long as people do not approve of their tax money being used to sponsor public sports and sport facilities. Eventually, this could raise the question of whether people want to play and watch sports that require external sponsors. If this happens, people may decide that it is possible to have fun playing and watching sports that they can organize and maintain by themselves, if there are accessible public spaces in which sports can be played.

Using History to Think about the Future

As we study the past, we learn that struggles over the meaning, purpose and organization of sports always occur in particular social, political and economic contexts. Sports history does not just happen; it always depends on the actions of people working with one another to construct sports to match their visions of what sports could and should be in their lives. Many people in recent history have ignored what others say is practical or realistic and pursued choices based on idealistic notions of what sports could be. These are the people who have inspired new opportunities for girls and women, new programmes for people with disabilities, the recognition and acceptance of gay and lesbian athletes, and new sport forms that are playful and accessible to nearly everyone. Table 3.2 does not do justice to those people and the struggles they have waged to turn their idealistic visions into realities. Each of those struggles has its own history, and those of us who choose to be actively involved in creating future histories will shape them.

Table 3.2 **UK social history time line**

Since 1920 thousands of sports organizations have come and gone, hundreds of legal decisions have regulated and deregulated sports, and thousands of important struggles have occurred over (1) the meaning, purpose and organization of sports, (2) who plays sports under what conditions, and (3) how and why sports are funded. This selective time line highlights events related to these struggles and the issues and controversies discussed in this book.

1922	Formation of the Women's Amateur Athletics Association
1924	The first live radio coverage of the Olympic Games was broadcast (from Chamonix, France); the first Deaflympics (called the Silent Games) were held in Paris; the Federation Sportive Feminine Internationale organized the first Women's Olympic Games in Paris; Suzanne Lenglen set new trends at Wimbledon, wearing short, light skirts which scandalized society
1925	Foundation of the National Playing Fields Association, to improve sports facilities
1926	Gertrude Ederle swam the Channel two hours faster than the best male swimmer
1927	First BBC live coverage of sports events on the radio
1928	Women entered the Olympics in Amsterdam, although were not permitted to run races longer than 800 metres as these were thought too strenuous for them – when some competitors appeared physically distressed at the end of the 800-metre race, this confirmed male opinion of them; British women stayed away from the Olympic Games to protest the lack of women's Olympic events, forming the only feminist boycott in Olympic history
1930	The British Deaf Sports Council was formed
1933	Carnegie Physical Training College was established, the first college to train male physical education specialists
1935	The Central Council of Recreative Physical Training was established, to act as an umbrella organization for all agencies concerned with sport; the fourth and last Women's Games were held in London
1936	The Olympics were held in Berlin; Jesse Owens (an African-American) won four gold medals and challenged Hitler's ideas about race and white supremacy
1937	The first screening of sport on British television occurred with the BBC coverage of Wimbledon in June
1948	London hosted the first summer Olympic Games after the Second World War; Fanny Blankers-Koen of the Netherlands was the first mother to be an Olympic gold medallist; the British Wheelchair Sports Association was founded
1954	Roger Bannister was the first person to run a sub-four-minute mile, in Oxford
1957	Althea Gibson was the first black player to win a title at Wimbledon
1960	The Wolfendon Committee report *Sport and the Community* led to the development of a National Sports Development Council, government involvement in the financing of sport and a programme for increased facilities
1961	The International Olympic Committee established a Medical Commission, in part to regulate drug taking
1963	County cricket abandoned the distinction between amateur and professional players; the first annual National Multi-Disability Games were held
1964	The Olympic Games in Tokyo were the first to be televised

1965	Formation of a Sports Council to act on behalf of the government in providing sporting opportunities
1966	FIFA conducted drug testing at the World Cup; England won the final, beating West Germany, with Geoff Hurst scoring a hat-trick although one of the goals remains famously contested
1968	Many black athletes boycotted the Olympic Games in Mexico City in protest at racial discrimination; Tommy Smith and John Carlos (both African-Americans) supported the boycott by raising gloved fists and standing barefoot on the victory podium at the Olympics; Mexican students protested against using public money for the Olympic Games, and police killed over 30 protesters; Enrigueta Basilio was the first woman to light the Olympic flame; Olympic drug testing began; the first Special Olympics was held, for athletes with intellectual disabilities; women athletes in the Olympics were forced to 'prove' that they were females by 'passing' a chromosome-based sex test; Wimbledon was opened to professionals
1970	Drug testing was introduced in the Commonwealth Games
1971	The International Olympic Committee produced the first list of banned substances and practices; Evonne Cawley (Goolagong) was the first aboriginal Australian to play in the Wimbledon tennis final
1976	The Sports Aid Foundation was established to provide financial support for elite athletes preparing for international competition; 29 nations, mostly from Africa and Asia, boycotted the Olympic Games in Montreal to protest New Zealand's sporting ties with white supremacist South Africa
1977	The all-male IOC prohibited women from running the 3000-metre race to protect women from physical damage
1978	Three sociology of sport textbooks were published, including the first edition of *Sport in Society: Issues and Controversies.*
1980	More than 50 nations boycotted the Olympic Games in Moscow because the Soviet Union unilaterally (and without United Nations approval) invaded Afghanistan in 1979. Athletes from Great Britain and Northern Ireland attended, but without government support
1981	Two new national disability sports associations were founded and recognized by the Sports Council: Cerebral Palsy Sport and the United Kingdom Sports Association for the People with Mental Handicap (which in 1995 became the English Sports Association for People with Learning Disabilities)
1984	The Soviet Union and 13 other nations said they did not trust US security and boycotted the Olympic Games in Los Angeles; the Los Angeles Games were the first to create a profit for the host city, and this intensified competition among cities bidding to host future Games; the women's marathon was introduced into the Olympics
1985	In the European Football Cup Final between Liverpool and Juventus, 39 fans were killed in Heysel Stadium when a wall collapsed during riots
1989	At the FA Cup semi-final between Liverpool and Nottingham Forest, 96 football supporters were killed in Hillsborough Stadium prior to the start of the game, mostly crushed to death by the fencing when supporters surged into a small area of the ground; the Council of Europe published the Anti-Doping Convention

1990	The Taylor Report was published, providing safety recommendations for football following the tragedies at Heysel and Hillsborough; British Les Autres and Amputee Sports Association founded
1991	The World Student Games were held in Sheffield
1992	The National Lottery Bill was established, which determined that the allocation of funding to sport was to be distributed between home country Sports Councils; the FA Premiership was formed
1993	'Let's kick racism out of football' was launched by the Commission for Racial Equality and the Professional Footballers' Association; an obsessive fan of Steffi Graf jumped from the stands during a tennis tournament in Germany and stabbed Monica Seles, ranked number one in the world at the time
1994	The Sports Council policy document 'Black and ethnic minorities and sport' recognized disadvantage and discrimination as the basis of racial inequality and a need for positive action; the Brighton Declaration of Women and Sport made a range of recommendations for equality of opportunities, and this was adopted by the International Olympic Committee in 1995
1995	The Bosman Ruling invalidated the restrictions of the number of players from the European Union in a European sports club/team, in line with European legislation offering freedom of workers to travel within the EU; rugby union was professionalized
1996	The European Football Championships were hosted in the UK, attracting 280 000 spectators and media, who spent £120 million; 'Tackle racism in rugby league' was set up by the Commission for Racial Equality and Rugby Football League; 'Hit racism for six' was established by the England and Wales Cricket Board
1998	The English Federation of Disability Sport was formed; Sporting Equals was created by the Commission for Racial Equality and Sport England to work with governing bodies to understand, and develop policies to address, racism in sport; Manchester United was the first British sports club to have its own television channel (MUTV)
1999	World Anti-Doping Agency (WADA) formed
2000	The Racial Equality Charter for Sport was signed by the Chief Executives of the Rugby Football League, Rugby Football Union, UK Athletics, England and Wales Cricket Board, English Basketball, the Amateur Swimming Association and the National Coaching Foundation; Steven Redgrave's gold medal in rowing at the Sydney Olympics was his fifth in five successive Games
2001	The government's Plan for Sport was produced, with the aim of tackling social exclusion
2003	A Russian billionaire, Roman Abramovich, invested $140 million in Chelsea Football Club to secure a majority stake, and making Chelsea the wealthiest club in the world
2005	London was awarded the right to host the 2012 Summer Olympic Games

Summary: Can We Use History to Understand Sports Today?

Our selective look at different times and places shows us that physical games and sports are integrally related to social contexts in which they exist. As social life changes and power shifts in any society, the meaning, purpose and organization of games and sport activities also change.

Two significant events in recent British history were the first sub-four-minute mile, achieved by Roger Bannister in 1954, and England hosting and winning the men's football World Cup, beating the former West Germany 4–2 in 1966

In Ancient Greece, games and contests were grounded in mythology and religious beliefs. They focused on the interests of able-bodied young men from wealthy segments of society. As the outcomes of organized games took on political and social implications beyond the events, athletes were recruited from the lower classes and paid to participate. The existence of professional athletes, violence and an emphasis on victory show us a side of sports in Ancient Greece that contradicts many popular beliefs. It also demonstrates that sports may not represent the interests of everyone in a society.

Roman contests and games emphasized mass entertainment. They were designed to celebrate and preserve the power of political leaders and pacify masses of unemployed and underemployed workers in Roman cities and towns. Many athletes in Roman events were slaves or 'troublemakers' coerced into jeopardizing their lives in battle with one another or wild animals. These spectacles faded with the demise of the Roman Empire. Critically assessing the contests and games of this period makes us more aware of the interests that powerful people may have in promoting large sport events.

Folk games and tournaments in medieval times clearly reflected and reproduced gender and social-class differences in European cultures. The peasants played local versions of folk games in connection with seasonal events in village life. Knights and nobles engaged in tournaments and jousts. Other members of the upper classes often used their resources to develop games and sports activities to occupy their leisure time. Studying the history of sports during this time period shows that gender and class issues should not be ignored as we analyse sports and sports experiences today.

Patterns from the medieval period continued through the Renaissance in parts of Europe, although the Protestant Reformation generated negative attitudes about activities that interfered with work and religious worship. Peasants were affected most by these attitudes because they did not have the resources to resist the restrictive controls imposed by government officials inspired by Calvinist or Puritan orientations. The games and sports of the wealthy generally occurred in the safe confines of their private grounds, so they could avoid outside control. The Enlightenment was associated with increased political rights and freedom to engage in diversionary games and physical activities. Studying these historical periods shows us the importance of cultural ideology and government policies when it comes to who plays sports under what conditions.

During the early days of the Industrial Revolution, the influence of the Puritans faded in Europe and North America, but the demands of work and the absence of spaces for play generally limited sport involvement to the wealthy and rural residents. This pattern began to change in the UK from the late 1800s through the early 1900s when the combined influence of progressive legislation and economic expansion led to the creation of new ideas about the consequences of sport participation and new opportunities for involvement. However, opportunities for involvement were shaped primarily by gender ideology and the needs of an economy emphasizing mass production and consumption. It was in this context that people developed organized competitive sports. Studying this period shows us that the origins of today's sports are tied closely to complex social, political and economic factors.

Sports history since 1920 has revolved around continuing struggles over (1) the meaning, purpose and organization of sports, (2) who participates in sports under what conditions, and (3) who funds sports and why. These struggles have occurred in connection with major historical events, trends and patterns. In most cases, powerful economic and political interests have prevailed in these struggles, but in a few cases, people motivated by idealistic visions of what sports could and should be like have prevailed. Every now and then, the visions of idealists have become reality, but struggles never end. As we study current issues and controversies in sports, our awareness of past struggles is useful.

Website resources

Note: Websites often change. The following URLs were current when this book was printed. Please check our website (***www.mcgraw-hill.co.uk/textbooks/coakley***) for updates and additions.

See the OLC, ***www.mcgraw-hill.co.uk/textbooks/coakley***, for an annotated list of readings related to this chapter.

http://cain.ulst.ac.uk/issues/sport/source.htm The official site of Conflict Archive on the Internet, providing a list of resources for information on politics in Northern Ireland, and the relationship of sport with 'The Troubles'.

www.cureourchildren.org/sports.htm A helpful site for anyone looking for information and creative ideas about sports and recreation for people with disabilities; links to dozens of related sites.

www.deaflympics.com Official site of the Deaflympics, established in 1924 as the Silent Games; this was the first international competition for athletes with disabilities.

http://depthome.brooklyn.cuny.edu/classics/gladiatr/index.htm This site was developed by Roger Dunkle, an expert on Roman sports; excellent information and visuals related to the spectacles in which gladiators participated.

www.hickoksports.com/index.shtml An easy-to-use site with many search options covering a wide range of history topics, events, athletes and other sport personalities; tends towards the popular rather than academic, although there is an excellent bibliography of sports history books.

www.nassh.org North American Society for Sport History.

www.studies.org The Institute for Mediterranean Studies; site summarizes and sells audiotapes on the Olympic Games in Ancient Greece and on sports in the Roman world.

www.umist.ac.uk/sport/ishpes.html International Society for the History of Physical Education and Sport and the British Society of Sports History, provides links to many other sites for sports history.

www.wsf.org.uk A good site for obtaining information on the history of women in sports in the UK.

Chapter 4

Sports and socialization: who plays and what happens to them?

(*Source*: Elizabeth Pike)

" Without sport I would not be the person I am today. It isn't the level at which I race that is important because at any level sport teaches us. Athletics has taught me about myself, both my strengths and weaknesses ... What I have learned in sport is applicable to everyday life and it has helped me to make more of my life. "

(Paula Radcliffe, 2005, pp. 1–2, world record holder, women's marathon)

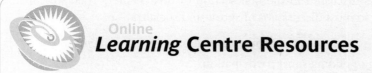

Learning Centre Resources

Visit *Sports in Society*'s Online Learning Centre (OLC) at **www.mcgraw-hill.co.uk/ textbooks/coakley** for additional information and study material for this chapter, including:

- Self-grading quizzes and essay questions
- Learning outcomes
- Related websites
- Additional readings

Chapter contents

What is socialization?
Becoming and staying involved in sports
Changing or ending sports participation
Being involved in sports: what happens?
What socialization research does not tell us
Summary: who plays and what happens?

> Competitive school sport matters to learning and health. Importantly, it also builds character and teamwork. Lessons should be fun and inspire every child to take an interest, not only in their fitness, but in sport outside school.
>
> *(Ruth Kelly, Education Secretary, DCMS, 2005)*

Socialization is a popular topic in discussions about sports. We deal with socialization issues whenever we discuss the following questions:

- Why are some people fanatically interested in playing and watching sports, whereas others do not seem to care about sports?
- How and why do some people see themselves as athletes and dedicate themselves to playing sports?
- When and why do people stop playing competitive sports, and what happens to them when they do?
- What impact do sports and sports participation have on people's lives?

Many of us in the sociology of sport have done research to find answers to one or more of these questions. The search for answers has taken us in different directions, depending on the theories that we use to guide our thinking about sports and sports participation. The influence of theoretical perspectives is discussed in the first section of this chapter. Then we consider three topics that are central to most discussions of sports and socialization:

1   the process of becoming involved and staying involved in sports
2   the process of changing or ending sport participation
3   the impact of being involved in sports.

As these topics are discussed, we provide tentative answers to the socialization questions that have been asked by researchers in the sociology of sport. As you read the chapter, you will see that most of the answers are incomplete and many others are so complex that discussions about them will carry over into other chapters.

The chapter closes with information about new approaches to socialization. These approaches are based on critical, feminist and interactionist theories that emphasize socialization as a community and cultural process as well as an individual and personal process.

What is Socialization?

Socialization *is a process of learning and social development, which occurs as we interact with one another and become acquainted with the social world in which we live.* It involves the formation of ideas about who we are and what is important in our lives. We are *not* simply passive learners in the socialization process. We actively participate in our own socialization as we form relationships and influence those who influence us. We actively interpret what we see and hear, and we accept, resist and revise the messages that we receive about who we are, about the world and about our connection with the world. Therefore, socialization is *not* a one-way process of social influence through which we are moulded and shaped. Instead, it is an interactive process through which we actively connect with others, synthesize information and *make decisions* that shape our own lives and the social world around us.

This definition of *socialization*, which we use to guide our research, is based on a combination of *critical* and *interactionist theories*. Therefore, not all sociologists would agree with it. Those using functionalist or conflict theory approaches, for example, would define *socialization* in slightly different terms. Like the definition we use, their definitions have an impact on the questions that they ask about sports and socialization, the research methods that they use to gather data and the way that they make sense of their research data.

A functionalist approach to socialization

Scholars using *functionalist theory* view socialization as a process through which we learn what we must know to fit into society and contribute to its operation. This approach to socialization is based on an *internalization model* (see Coakley, 1993, 2007a). In other words, as we grow up in our families, attend school, interact with peers, and receive images and messages from the media, we learn the rules we should follow and the roles we should play in society.

When researchers use an internalization model to guide their studies, they focus on four things: (1) the characteristics of the people who are *being* socialized, (2) the people who *do* the socializing, (3) the *contexts* in which socialization occurs, and (4) the specific *outcomes,* or results, of socialization. In studies of sports and socialization, researchers focus on athletes as the people being socialized and on the **agents of socialization** *who exert influence on athletes.* Agents, or 'social-izers', generally include fathers, mothers, brothers, sisters, teachers, coaches, peers and people used as role models. The most central and influential socializers are described as *significant others.* In some cases, contexts in which socialization occurs, such as the family, education, peer groups and the media, are also studied in connection with sports participation. The socialization outcomes, or results, that are studied include personal attitudes, values, skills and behaviour patterns, especially those that are seen as contributing to the operation of society as a social system.

Those who use a functionalist approach also study what causes people to participate in sports and how participation influences them and the patterns of their lives. This research generally uses surveys to collect data. Researchers have done literally hundreds of studies by sending questionnaires to people. Their analyses compare those who do and do not play organized sports, and their goal is to discover the socialization experiences that lead to and result from sport participation (see Cartoon 4.1).

Until recently, this research has provided us with inconsistent and contradictory findings about why people play sports and what happens to them when they do. However, more recent research, using large data-sets collected through well-funded regional and national studies, has begun to provide more consistent and detailed analyses of the complex connections between sport participation and processes of socialization (Office for National Statistics, 2004a; Sport England, 2001b, 2003a, 2006; Vine and Aust, 2006). These studies provide us with many snapshots rather than videos of socialization as it occurs over the course of people's lives. But multiple snapshots can be used to identify general patterns and guide further research that is designed to study the specific details of socialization processes. The rest of this chapter uses both past and current research findings – the snapshots and the videos – to explain what we know about sports and socialization today.

A conflict theory approach to socialization

Scholars using conflict theory also view socialization in terms of an internalization model. However, they focus on the ways that economic factors influence sports participation and the consequences of sports participation for the economic organization of society. For example, studies based on conflict theory investigate questions such as these:

- Does participation in organized competitive sports reproduce capitalist economies by creating conservative, militaristic, sexist and racist orientations among players and spectators?
- Are people from low-income and working-class backgrounds systematically denied oppor-tunities to play sports on their own terms and in their own ways?
- Are athletes, especially those from poor, minority backgrounds, victims of a profit-driven, win-at-all-cost sports system in which they have no rights?
- Do people with money and power control the conditions of sport participation and exploit others to make money and maintain their own interests?

There are fewer studies based on conflict theory than functionalist theory. Where such studies have been conducted, the samples have been so small that research findings provide only fuzzy

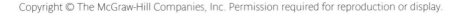

'I know this is starting early, bit I can't let him get too far behind the other kids if he's ever going to make a school team'

Cartoon 4.1 **Research guided by functionalist theory has focused on who influences the sport participation patterns of children. Fathers and other family members have usually been identified as *significant others* who influence when, how and where children play sports**

snapshots telling us little about the details of sports-related socialization. In general terms, these fuzzy snapshots do show us that economic resources are related to the organization of sports and the dynamics of sports participation, and that the people who control economic resources often use them to promote their own interests.

Unfortunately, the large data-sets that enable scholars to examine questions based on functionalist approaches seldom include information about the ways that economic resources and power influence who does and does not play sports and what happens to them when they do play. Fortunately, new approaches to socialization help us understand some of these issues.

New approaches to socialization

Sociologists today are unlikely to view socialization as a process through which culture is passively internalized as it is transmitted from one generation to the next. Instead of using an internalization model of socialization they prefer an **interactionist model** *based on the idea that socialization involves participatory learning through which people are involved in larger processes of cultural production, reproduction and change.* Researchers who use an interactionist model generally use qualitative rather than quantitative research methods. Instead of using questionnaires to obtain statistical data from large numbers of people, they use in-depth interviews and field observations. Their goal is to obtain detailed descriptions of sports experiences as they occur in people's lives. They seek information on the processes through which people make decisions about their sports participation and give meanings to their sports experiences. Finally, they seek to connect those decisions and meanings with the larger cultural context in which sports and sports participation exist. This approach, they argue, captures the complexity of processes related to becoming and staying involved in sports, changing or ending sports participation and incorporating sports into people's lives. The rest of this chapter draws on old and new approaches to outline what we know about sports and socialization today.

Becoming and Staying Involved in Sports

Research based on functionalist and conflict theories indicates that sports participation is related to three factors: (1) a person's abilities, characteristics and resources, (2) the influence of significant others, including parents, siblings, teachers, peers, and role models, and (3) the availability of opportunities to play sports in ways that are personally satisfying. These are the snapshots that we have of *socialization into sports.* However, a fuller description of the ongoing process of becoming and staying involved in sports emerges when we obtain detailed stories from people about their sport participation. These stories are more like videos than snapshots.

Studies using in-depth interviews, fieldwork, participant observations and strategic conversations indicate that sports participation is connected with multiple and diverse processes that make up people's lives, and it occurs as people make decisions about and give meaning to sports. Therefore, decisions and meanings associated with sports are not permanent. As social conditions change, so do sports-related decisions and meanings. Furthermore, as people stay involved in sports, their reasons for participating on one day may be different from reasons for participating on the next day. When there is no reason, they may discontinue or change their sports participation.

To understand how and why people become and stay involved in sports, it is helpful to review research on these issues. The following studies give us three sociological videos of the decision-making processes related to playing sports.

Example 1: the process of becoming an elite athlete

Chris Stevenson is a sociologist of sport interested in how people become elite athletes. Using interactionist theory to guide his research, he interviewed and collected stories from elite athletes about how they were introduced to their sports and became committed to sports participation. As he analysed the stories, he noticed that they sounded much like descriptions of careers. In other words, they had identifiable beginnings, followed by a process of development and, ultimately, an end. Stevenson felt that he could understand these careers in terms of the decisions that people made about sports participation and how those decisions were related to important issues and relationships in their lives over time.

In one of his studies, Stevenson (1999) interviewed 29 international athletes from England and Canada. At first, he was struck by the diversity of the stories the athletes told him. But as he analysed the data, he identified two processes that were common to nearly all the stories. First, there was a process of *introduction and involvement,* during which young people received

Participation in sports is usually sponsored through important social relationships. This boy's participation in golf is likely to be influenced by his grandfather, an agent of socialization and a significant other in his life. However, continued participation also requires a combination of developing a commitment to the sport, receiving material and emotional support, and establishing social relationships and an identity related to the sport (Source: Elizabeth Pike)

support as they tried certain sports. His interviewees talked about being introduced to sports bit by bit over time through important relationships in their lives. MacPhail et al. (2003) identified similar processes through their ethnographic study of the junior section of an English athletics club. They found that the children began their socialization into sports through a process of testing out a variety of sports, which they refer to as the process of 'sampling'.

Second is a process of *developing a commitment* to sport participation, which may involve choosing to focus on one particular sport. MacPhail et al. (2003) describe this as a shift from sampling to 'specializing'. This process occurs as the athletes developed a sense of being personally connected with the people associated with the sport, and gradually establishing personal reputations and identities as athletes with the potential for success in their sports. Their relationships and identities figured prominently in how they set priorities and made decisions about sports participation. Staying involved in their sports depended on active and thoughtful efforts to develop identities as athletes. This occurred as people who were important in their lives recognized and defined them as athletes. Over time, this social recognition led them to become more deeply committed to their sports and their lives as athletes.

These studies found that these processes did *not* occur automatically. The young people themselves helped them happen. Becoming and staying involved in sports was a complex process. The young people realized that they could not take for granted the social support that they received for playing sports or continued reaffirmation of their identities as athletes. They knew that the resources needed for participation could disappear and that changes in other parts of their lives could force them to alter the importance of sports participation. Therefore, they made decisions to stay involved in sports day after day, and as they stayed involved, they impressed and influenced those who supported and influenced them.

MacPhail et al.'s and Stevenson's research shows that the socialization process is *interactive* and that each of us participates in our own socialization as we make decisions and become committed to particular identities. Furthermore, these findings demonstrate that, for those who stay involved in sport, this is also conducive to the success of public health and elite sport development goals, even if this happens unintentionally.

Example 2: the process of being accepted as an athlete

Peter Donnelly and Kevin Young are sociologists who have studied sports as social worlds, or subcultures in which people develop ways of doing things and relating to each other. In their research, they have paid special attention to how people become accepted members of those subcultures. Consequently, they have taken a closer look at some of the processes studied by MacPhail et al. and Stevenson (Donnelly and Young, 1999).

On the basis of data that Donnelly collected from rock climbers and Young from rugby players, they concluded that playing sports occurs in connection with complex processes of identity formation. They explain that entering and becoming an athlete in a particular sport subculture occurs through a four-phase process:

1 acquiring knowledge about the sport
2 associating with people involved in the sport
3 learning how those people think about their sport, and what they do and expect from each other
4 becoming recognized and fully accepted into the sports group as a fellow athlete.

These details of sports socialization indicate that becoming involved in a sport depends on learning to 'talk the talk and walk the walk' so that one is identified and accepted as an athlete by others who are athletes. This process of identification and acceptance does not happen once and for all time; it is continuous. When we lose touch and are no longer able to talk the talk and walk the walk, acceptance wanes, our identities become difficult to maintain, and overall support for our participation becomes weak. We are not athletes for ever.

To illustrate the findings of Donnelly and Young's studies, take the example of windsurfers provided by Wheaton's (2004b) ethnographic study of a community on Silver Sands, a coastal location in the south of England. Wheaton found that acceptance into the windsurfing culture involved displays of sporting prowess, through a stylistic performance of difficult moves. One particularly valued skill was 'looping' (involving a 360-degree aerial jump). Participants who could do such moves would often choose to surf in an area of the beach where they would have the largest audience, in order to ensure their 'beach cred'. However, subcultural status involved more than sporting skill. The windsurfers were mostly white males, and displayed a particular attitude towards female participants, which became part of their subcultural identity. For example, the majority of males at Silver Sands were middle class and aged between 30 and 40, and they were keen to embrace females as participants in their sport, not least by way of demonstrating that this differentiated them from participants in other, more sexist, sports such as rugby and football. However, Wheaton explains that there were also other windsurfers, particularly younger elite males, who gained subcultural acceptance partly through a display of heterosexual prowess through the conquest, and occasional denigration, of women.

The studies of Donnelly, Young and Wheaton demonstrate that different sporting groups have their own vocabulary and ways of referring to their members and what they do. The terms they use are not found in dictionaries. They also have unique ways of thinking about and doing their sports, and they have special understandings of what they can expect from others in their groups. New participants in these sports may be tested and 'pushed' by the 'veterans' before being accepted and defined as true players, climbers or surfers. Vocabularies may change over time, but this process of becoming accepted and gaining support for participation exists in all sports. Many people have discovered that, if they do not establish social connections and acceptance in a sport, their participation may be difficult to maintain over time. Becoming involved in sports clearly is part of a complex, *interactive* socialization and identity-formation process.

Example 3: to participate or not to participate?

Anita White is a sociologist of sport and former director of sports development at Sport England. Before she began working at Sport England, Anita and Jay did a study of sport participation among British adolescents in a working-class area east of London (Coakley and White, 1999). Their goal was to provide coaches and programme organizers with information on why some young people participated in government-sponsored sports programmes, whereas most did not.

The in-depth interviews indicated that sports participation was the result of decisions based on a combination of factors, including the following:

- their ideas about the ways that sport participation was related to other interests and goals in their lives
- their desires to develop and display competence so they could gain recognition and respect from others
- social support for participation and access to the resources needed for participation (time, transportation, equipment and money)
- memories of past experiences with physical activities and sports
- sports-related cultural images and messages that they had in their minds.

Coakley and White (1999) found that young people decided to play sports when it helped them extend control over their lives, achieve development and career goals, and present themselves to others as competent. They also found that young women were less likely than the young men to imagine that sport participation could do these things for them. Therefore, the young women participated in organized sports less often and less seriously.

The young people in the study did not simply respond to the world around them. Instead, they actively thought about how sports might be positively incorporated into their lives and then made decisions based on their conclusions. Their sports participation patterns shifted over time, depending on their access to opportunities, changes in their lives and changes in their identities. Therefore, socialization into sports was a *continuous, interactive process* grounded in the social and cultural contexts in which the young people lived.

The interviews also indicated that people make decisions to participate in sports for different reasons at different points in their lives. This fits with theories telling us that developmental tasks and challenges change as we move through childhood, adolescence, young adulthood and adulthood. Therefore, the issues considered by 7-year-olds who make decisions about sports participation are different from the issues considered by 14-year-olds, 40-year-olds or 60-year-olds (Porterfield, 1999; Stevenson, 2002). Furthermore, when 7-year-olds make decisions about sports participation today, they do so in a different cultural context than the context in which 7-year-olds lived in 1970 or will live in 2020.

Sports participation decisions at all points during the life course and through history also are tied to the perceived cultural importance of sports and the links between playing sports, gaining social acceptance and achieving personal goals. Therefore, studies of socialization into sports must take into account the ways in which sports participation is related to individual development, the organization of social life, and the ideologies that are prevalent in a culture (Ingham et al., 1999; Jarvie, 2006; Kirk, 2003).

In summary, this study and the two previously discussed provide three videos about becoming and staying involved in sports. They show that sports participation is grounded in decision-making processes involving self-reflection, social support, social acceptance and cultural factors. People do not make decisions about sports participation once and for all time. They make them day after day as they consider how sports are related to their lives. In fact, they sometimes make them moment by moment when coaches are making them do hypoxic training and they are gasping for air at the end of the session! These decisions are mediated by the social and cultural contexts in which the people live. Therefore, social meanings attached to gender, class, skin colour, ethnicity, age and physical (dis)abilities influence sports participation decisions, and these meanings are influenced by political, economic, social and cultural forces.

Changing or Ending Sports Participation

Questions about becoming and staying involved in sports often are followed by questions about changing or ending involvement. Much of the research on this latter issue has been guided by 'role theories' inspired by functionalist theory or 'alienation theories' inspired by conflict theory (see Coakley, 1993).

Researchers using *functionalist theory* have been concerned with identifying who drops out of sports and what can be done to keep them in sports so that they can learn the positive lessons taught through participation. This was a popular research topic when millions of baby boomers (born between 1946 and 1964) were flooding playgrounds and primary schools, and parents wanted to know how to control and build character in their children. Research based on functionalist approaches also focuses on how to make sports programmes more efficient in developing skills and preparing young people to move to higher levels of competition. This is currently a popular topic among people who have an interest in creating successful athletes and sports teams.

Researchers using *conflict theory* generally focus on the ways that rigidly organized, win-orientated programmes turn children off participation. They have hypothesized that these programmes, along with autocratic, command-style coaches, alienate young athletes and cause them to drop out. Similarly, adolescent and adult athletes drop out because of injuries or alienation caused by years of being exploited. Their studies explore the ways that elite athletes are victims of exploitation and alienating experiences that damage their bodies and leave them unprepared for life after sport.

Studies grounded in functionalist and conflict theories tell us the following important things.

- When people drop out of particular sports, they do not drop out of all sports for ever, nor do they cut all ties with sports; many people play different and less competitive sports as they become older, or they move into other sport roles such as coach, administrator or sports businessperson.

- Dropping out of sports is usually connected with developmental changes and transitions in the rest of a person's life (changing schools, graduating, getting a job, getting married, having children, and so on).

■ Dropping out of sports is not always the result of victimization or exploitation, although injuries and negative experiences can and do influence decisions to change or end participation.

■ Problems may occur for those who end long careers in sports, especially those who have no identities apart from sports, and lack social and material resources for making transitions into other careers and relationships.

Recent studies, especially those using qualitative research methods and based on critical theory and interactionist models of socialisation, have built on these findings and extended our understanding. The following are three examples of these studies.

Example 1: burnout among young athletes

Jay's work with coaches and interest in identity issues led him to do a study of young people who, after being age-group champions in their sports, had decided to stop playing (Coakley, 1992). People described these young people as 'burned out', so Jay decided to interview former elite athletes identified by themselves or others as cases of burnout; all were adolescents.

Data collected through in-depth interviews indicated that burnout during adolescence was grounded in the organization of high-performance sports. It occurred when young athletes felt they no longer had control over their lives and could not explore, develop and nurture identities apart from sports. This led to increased stress and decreased fun when doing sports. Burnout occurred when stress became so high and fun declined so much that athletes no longer felt that playing their sport was worth their effort.

The data also indicated that stress increased and fun decreased when sports programmes were organized so that successful young athletes felt that they could not accomplish important developmental tasks during adolescence. Jay's conclusion was that burnout could be prevented only if sports programmes were reorganized so that athletes had more control over their lives. Stress management strategies could be used to delay burnout, but they would not change the underlying organizational and development causes of burnout. Overall, the study indicated that ending sports participation during late adolescence sometimes occurs when young people feel that staying in sports prevents them from developing the autonomy and multiple identities that mark people as adults.

Jay's study is significant in a time when the UK is targeting young athletes who may be potential Olympic medal winners, as part of the vision to at least maintain the third place achieved in the medal table in the 2008 Beijing Olympics at the 2012 Summer Olympic Games, and the second place achieved in the 2008 Paralympic Games, and sustain team and individual world rankings in the top five of a range of identified 'popular' sports (DCMS/Strategy Unit, 2002; Sport England, 2004; UK Sport, 2007). This strategy involves identifying potential world-class talent up to eight years before they would compete in an Olympics, and structuring their training, coaching, competition and scientific support to maximize their chances of success, in what has been termed a 'No Compromise' approach (UK Sport, 2007). This, according to Jay's research, is precisely the kind of programme that would produce high rates of burnout!

> The Framework for Sport in England provides the strategic direction and policy priorities that unite sport in its commitment to make England the most active and successful sporting nation in the world by 2020.

(Sport England, 2004, p. 2)

Example 2: getting out of sports and getting on with life

Konstantinos Koukouris (1994) is a physical educator from Greece who wanted to know why people who had been seriously committed to sports decided to end or reduce their sports participation. After analysing questionnaire data from 157 former national athletes, Koukouris identified 34 who had ceased or reduced sport participation between the ages of 18 and 24. In-depth interviews with these people enabled him to construct case studies illustrating the process of disengaging from sports.

The data indicated that athletes voluntarily decided to end or change their participation. But this decision was part of a long-term process during which they stopped playing and then started again more than once. In other words, they had not gone 'cold turkey' as they withdrew from sport. The decision to end or change their sport participation was usually associated with two practical factors: (1) the need to obtain a job and support themselves and (2) realistic judgements about their sports skills and the chances of moving to higher levels of competition. As they graduated from school or college, the athletes faced the expectation that they should work and be responsible for their own lives. But jobs interfered with the time they needed to train and play sports at a serious level. Furthermore, as they spent money to establish adult lifestyles, they did not have enough left to pay for serious training. At the same time, their sports-training programmes were organized so rigidly that sports participation was difficult to fit into their new adult lives.

As serious training ended, many of these young adults sought other ways to be physically active or connected with sports. They sometimes experienced problems but, as they faced new challenges, most of them grew and developed in positive ways, much like people who had never been serious athletes. Disengaging from serious sports training was perceived as part of inevitable, necessary and usually beneficial developments in the lives of these young adults.

Example 3: changing personal investments in sports careers

Garry Wheeler from the University of Alberta is concerned with the careers of athletes with disabilities and what happens when their playing careers end. Building on a previous study (Wheeler, 1996) of Paralympic athletes, Wheeler and his fellow researchers gathered data through interviews with 40 athletes from the UK, Canada, Israel and the USA (Wheeler, 1999). Data indicated that athletes in each of the countries became deeply involved in playing sports and often achieved a high level of success in a relatively short time. Through sports they developed a sense of personal competence and established identities as elite athletes.

Withdrawing from active sports participation and making the transition into the rest of life often presented challenges for these athletes. Retirement often came suddenly and forced them to reinvest time and energy into other spheres of their lives. As they reconnected with family members and friends, returned to school and resumed occupational careers, some individuals experienced emotional problems. However, most stayed connected with sports and sports organizations as coaches, administrators or recreational athletes. Those few who hoped they might compete again often experienced serious difficulties during the retirement transition, whereas those who accepted the end of their competitive careers had fewer adjustment problems.

In summary, research shows that ending or changing sports participation often involves the same interactive and decision-making processes that occur during the process of becoming and staying involved in sports. Just as people are not simply socialized into sports, neither are they simply socialized out of sports. Changes in participation are grounded in decisions associated with other life events, social relationships and cultural expectations related to development. This means that theories explaining why people play sports and change their participation over time must take into account identity issues and developmental processes that are part of the social and cultural contexts in which people make decisions about sports in their lives (Dacyshyn, 1999; Drahota and Eitzen, 1998; Jarvie, 2006; Maguire et al., 2002; Swain, 1999; Wheaton, 2004a). Furthermore, the theories must consider the personal, social and material resources that athletes have as they make transitions to other relationships, activities and careers. Some people have problems when they retire from sports, but to understand those problems, we need information about the ways that sports participation has been incorporated into their lives and the resources that can be used as changes occur and challenges are faced. Research suggests

Many factors influence the decisions to drop out of sports or shift participation from one sport to another. Identity changes, access to resources and life-course issues are involved. As our circumstances change, so do our ideas about ourselves and about sports and sport participation (*Source*: Elizabeth Pike)

that, if sports participation expands a person's identity, experiences, relationships and resources, changes and retirement transitions will be smooth. Difficulties are most likely to occur when a person has never had the desire or the chance to live outside the culture of elite sports (Murphy et al., 1996; Spitzer, 2006).

Being Involved in Sports: What Happens?

Beliefs about the consequences of sports participation vary from culture to culture, but the beliefs that playing sports builds character and improves health and well-being are widely accepted in many cultures. These beliefs are used as a basis for encouraging children to play sports, funding sports programmes in school, building stadiums, promoting teams and leagues, and sponsoring a wide range of community, regional, national and international sport events.

Do sports build character?

For over half a century, researchers have examined the validity of the belief that 'sport builds character'. Many of the studies have involved comparisons of the traits, attitudes and behaviours of people who play organized sports and people who do not play them. To a large extent, these comparisons are grounded in the legacy of 'muscular Christianity' and a belief that a strong, healthy body provides the vessel for mental and spiritual growth and the ability to do good works. These snapshot comparisons have produced inconsistent and confusing findings. This is because there are many different definitions of 'character', and researchers have used inconsistent measures of *character* in their studies (Stoll and Beller, 1998). Furthermore, many researchers base their studies on two faulty assumptions (McCormack and Chalip, 1988). First, they mistakenly assume that *all* athletes have the same or similar experiences in *all* organized competitive sports. Second, they mistakenly assume that organized sports provide learning experiences that are not available to people in any other activities.

These faulty assumptions cause researchers to overlook the following important things when they study sports and socialization.

- Sports offer many *different experiences*, both positive and negative, to participants because sports programmes and teams are organized in vastly different ways. Therefore, we cannot make general statements about the consequences of sport participation. This point is explained in 'Reflect on sports', pages 114–116.
- People who choose or are selected to participate in sports may have different traits than those who do not choose or are not selected to participate. Therefore, sports may not *build* character as much as they are organized to *select* people who already have certain character traits that are valued by coaches and compatible with highly organized, competitive activities.
- The meanings given to sports experiences vary from one athlete to the next, even when they play in the same programmes and on the same teams. Therefore, the lessons that athletes learn and the ways they apply those lessons to their lives vary greatly.
- The meanings that people give to their sports experiences change over time as they grow older and view themselves and the world in new ways. Therefore, people revise their evaluation of past sports experiences as they develop new ideas and values.

- Socialization occurs through the social interaction that accompanies sport participation. Therefore, the meaning and importance of playing sports depend on a person's social relationships and the social and cultural contexts in which participation occurs.
- The socialization that occurs in sports may also occur in other activities. Therefore, people who do not play sports can have the same developmental experiences that athletes have.

Owing to these oversights, studies that compare 'athletes' with 'non-athletes' produce inconsistent and sometimes misleading evidence about sports and socialization. Our review of these studies leads us to conclude that sports participation is most likely to have positive socialization consequences for people when it provides the following:

- opportunities for exploring and developing identities apart from playing sports
- knowledge-building experiences that go beyond the changing room and the playing field
- new relationships, especially with people who are not connected with sports and do not base their interaction on a person's status or identity as an athlete
- explicit examples of how lessons learned in sports may be applied to specific situations apart from sports
- opportunities to develop and display competence in non-sport activities that are observed by other people who can serve as mentors and advocates outside of sports.

Hilary Rose, a former England and Great Britain hockey international, expressed some of these points when she said,

> Sport doesn't last forever and athletes must consider what they want when their sporting career has ended ... It is also useful to have a support network outside of sport, such as friends from university; otherwise athletes can become isolated by sport.
>
> *(English Institute of Sport, 2006).*

Research also suggests that when playing sports *constricts* a person's opportunities, experiences, relationships and general competence apart from sports, it is likely to have limited, or even negative, consequences for overall development. For example, Pike and Beames (2007) undertook a study of young people from the UK who travelled to Africa on an organized expedition which involved a combination of adventure sports and community work. While the participants believed that the expedition would enable them to develop character, Pike and Beames (2007, p. 156) concluded that in reality the activities were so restricted and involved such a high degree of forced conformity that participants were unlikely to experience forms of identity development that would have long-term implications for their lives.

Therefore, we cannot make a general statement that sports build *or* undermine character development. Neither positive nor negative character is automatically developed in sports. This is because sport experiences are defined and incorporated into people's lives in various ways depending on the social and cultural contexts in which they live.

This conclusion does *not* mean that sports and sports participation are irrelevant in people's lives. We know that discourses, images and experiences related to sports are vivid and powerful in many cultures today. Sports do impact our lives and the world around us. However, we cannot separate that impact from the meanings that we give to sports and the ways that we integrate them into our lives. Therefore, if we want to know what happens in sports, we must study sports experiences in the social and cultural contexts in which they occur. This type of research is exciting and provides insights into the complex connections between sports and socialization. Unfortunately, the uncritically accepted belief that 'sports build character' has prevented this research from being taken seriously. Additionally, this belief has prevented people from recognizing that if we want sports to build character we must critically examine sports and determine the types of sports experiences that are sites where positive socialization outcomes are most likely to occur.

reflect on Sports   *Power and performance versus pleasure and participation: different sports, different experiences, different consequences* • • • • • • • •

Sports experiences are diverse. It is a mistake to assume that all sports are defined in the same way, organized around the same goals and orientations, and played in the same spirit. In the UK, for example, there are highly organized competitive sports, informal sports, adventure sports, recreational sports, extreme sports, alternative sports, co-operative sports, folk sports, contact sports, artistic sports, team sports, individual sports, and so on. The *Framework for Sport in England* identifies 'Priority Sports' and 'Development Sports' as the basis of a co-ordinated approach to national planning for sport. The Priority Sports include athletics, cycling, football, gymnastics, rowing, rugby and swimming (see Sport England, 2004). It is clear from the model presented that, at this point in history, the dominant sport form in the UK is organized around a *power and performance model*.

Power and performance sports are highly organized and competitive. Generally, they emphasize the following:

- the use of strength, speed and power to push human limits and dominate opponents in the quest for victories
- the idea that excellence is proved through competitive success and achieved through dedication, hard work, sacrifices, risking personal well-being and playing in pain
- the importance of setting records, and using technology to control and monitor the body
- trials and selection systems based on physical skills and competitive success
- hierarchical authority structures in which athletes are subordinate to coaches and coaches are subordinate to owners and administrators
- defining opponents as enemies to be conquered, especially when they are confronted on 'home turf'.

These points exaggerate the characteristics of power and performance sports, but our purpose is to show that experiences in such sports are very different from experiences in sports with other characteristics. Although the power and performance model has become the standard for defining 'real' sports in global achievement sport culture, some people have maintained or developed other forms of sport. Some of these are revisions of dominant forms, whereas others represent alternative or even oppositional sport forms. The sports that are the most oppositional are organized around a *pleasure and participation model*. Pleasure and participation sports generally emphasize the following:

- active participation revolving around connections between people, mind and body, and physical activity and the environment
- a spirit of personal expression, enjoyment, growth, good health and mutual concern among teammates and opponents
- personal empowerment created by experiencing the body in pleasurable ways
- inclusive participation based on accommodating differences in physical skills among players
- democratic decision-making structures characterized by co-operation and sharing power, even in coach – athlete relationships
- an emphasis on competing *with* others and defining opponents as partners who test skills.

Again, these points exaggerate the characteristics of pleasure and participation sports, but they show that experiences in these sports would be very different from experiences in power and participation sports.

These two sport forms do *not* encompass all the ways that sports might be defined, organized and played. Many people play sports that contain elements of both forms and reflect diverse ideas about what is important in physical activities. However, power and performance sports remain dominant today in the sense that they receive the most attention and support. When people play or watch these sports, their socialization experiences are likely to be different from their experiences when playing or watching pleasure and participation sports.

Why are power and performance sports dominant today? Critical theory tells us that sports are parts of culture and that people with the needed resources to sponsor sports usually want them to be organized and played in ways that promote their interests. They want sports to fit their view of the world, and celebrate the relationships, orientations and values that reproduce their privileged positions in society. Today, power and performance sports fit the interests of people with wealth and influence.

Wealthy and influential people in societies around the world use different strategies to maintain their privileged positions. Some use coercive strategies such as police or military force, but most use cultural strategies designed to create the belief that wealth and power are distributed in legitimate and acceptable ways in society. For example, in the UK, the privileged position of the royal family usually is explained in terms of its birthright. Kings and queens maintain their privileged positions as long as people in society believe that birthrights represent legitimate claims to wealth and power. This is why the Church and State are closely aligned in societies with monarchies and why – since the Parliamentary Acts of the 1530s which marked the English Reformation – Henry VIII and all subsequent kings and queens have also held the title 'Defender of the Faith and Supreme Governor of the Church of England'. In this way, British sovereigns are able to use their association with divine external forces to legitimize their wealth and power.

In societies organized around democracy rather than monarchy, most people use *merit* as a standard when judging whether wealth and power are legitimate. Therefore, status and privilege in democracies are maintained only when most people believe that rewards go to those who have earned them. When there is widespread inequality in a democratic society, people with wealth and power must promote the idea that they have earned their privileged positions through hard work and intelligence, and that poverty and powerlessness are the result of laziness and a lack of intelligence. An effective strategy to promote this idea is to emphasize that *competition* is a natural part of social life and a fair means of determining who gets what in the society. If people accept this idea, they will also believe that those with wealth and power deserve what they have.

This connection between wealth, power and an emphasis on competition helps us understand why power and performance sports are so widely promoted and supported in many countries today. These sports are based on a class ideology that celebrates winners and idealizes the domination of some people over others. These sports also promote the idea that competition is the only fair and natural way to distribute rewards and that people with wealth and power deserve status and privilege because they have competed successfully – they are the winners.

Power and performance sports often are popular in democratic societies where there are widespread and highly visible economic inequalities between classes of people. These sports have also expanded globally as wealthy and powerful transnational corporations seek strategies to promote the idea that global economic competition is a good thing. Corporate executives collectively allocate billions of pounds annually to sponsor power and performance sports. They want people to agree that rewards should go to winners, that the winners deserve wealth and power, and that the ranking of people on the basis of wealth and power is not only fair but also natural. In other words, their sponsorships are based on concerns about ideology as well as financial profits that might be generated by sports.

Pleasure and participation sports and other sport forms that challenge this way of thinking may be popular among some people, but they generally do not receive sponsorships and support from people with money and power. For example, sponsorships and support are not given to alternative sports unless they are reorganized around the power and performance model. This is illustrated by the conversion of free-flowing, expressive alternative sports into the X Games or Olympic snowboarding and BMX events, organized around a power and performance model that fits the interests of wealthy corporate sponsors, *not* the interests of participants and spectators. *What do you think?*

Pleasure and participation sports may involve competition, but the primary emphasis is on connections between people and on personal expression through participation (Source: Jay Coakley)

Do sports improve health and physical well-being?

If something is said often enough, many people accept it as true. This has certainly been the case with the statement, 'sports are healthy activities'. However, what constitutes a healthy level of activity varies depending on which documents you read. For example, the government's target for sports is based on people participating in sporting activities for 30 minutes of moderate intensity at least five times a week (DCMS/Strategy Unit, 2002). However, when Sport England (2006) subsequently conducted a survey of participation rates, they concluded that people were active if they had engaged in 30 minutes of moderate intensity sport or active recreation on at least one in the previous 28 days, and were considered 'regular' participants if this reached three days a week: rather a different definition! Others have questioned the health value of sports altogether, given that the injury risks associated with nearly all competitive sports are so high that participation often creates more health costs than benefits (Waddington, 2007; White, 2004; Young, 2004a).

The sport–health connection

The relationship between sports, exercise and health is complex. However, many people who describe the health benefits of sports often ignore this complexity when they assume that sports are the same as all forms of regular physical exercise in people's lives. After reviewing dozens of studies on this topic, sociologist Ivan Waddington (2000a, 2000b, 2007) explains that the healthiest of all physical activities are rhythmic, non-competitive exercises in which individuals control and regulate their own body movements. Health benefits decline when there is a shift from self-controlled exercise to competitive sports; in fact, the health costs of competitive sports are relatively high, due primarily to injuries. This benefit–cost ratio becomes even less favourable when there is a shift from non-contact to contact sports and from mass sports to elite sports in which players train intensely, put their bodies at risk and play while injured. Overall, Waddington concludes the following:

> The health-related arguments in favour of regular and moderate physical activity are clear, but they are considerably less persuasive in relation to competitive, and especially contact, sport and very much less persuasive in relation to elite, or professional sport.
>
> *(Waddington, 2007, p. 2095)*

Other scholars in the sociology of sport have made similar points. For example, Eric Dunning (1986) notes that many sports are mock battles during which aggressive and violent acts are common (see Chapter 7, for a discussion of violence in sports). Following the work of North American researchers (e.g. Messner, 1992; Nixon, 1993a; Young, 1993) several British sociologists of sport have examined the implications of this for athletes in the UK. For example, in heavy-contact sports, male athletes are seen to routinely turn their bodies into weapons and use them in ways that injure themselves and opponents (Howe, 2004a, 2004b; Malcolm, 2006). According to research by Sheard (2006a, 2006b), debates over the health implications of some sports have been extended into discussions within Parliament and the medical profession with, for example, some practitioners calling for a ban on combat sports such as boxing. There is also a growing body of research which explains that female athletes often participate in contexts where there are group pressures to engage in risky and unhealthy actions as they seek success and live up to the expectations of coaches and teammates (see Charlesworth and Young, 2004, 2006; Pike, 2004, 2005a, 2005b; Pike and Maguire, 2003). Howe (2006) has also investigated how injury takes on particular connotations when the athletes are Paralympians.

Although risks are highest in elite sports, they also exist in mass sports where injury rates are regularly higher than in other everyday activities. In fact, researchers in England found that when they compared the health benefits and costs of exercise and sports, the health benefits outweighed costs for people 45 years old and over. However, the costs outweighed benefits for people 15 to 45 years old. In financial terms, this meant that every young adult who regularly participated in exercise and sports 'created' £25 per year of costs more than if they had not participated regularly (Nichol et al., 1993). In other words, the 'disease prevention benefits' were lower than the medical fees for treating exercise and sports-related injuries in younger adults.

These findings about benefits and costs do not consider difficult-to-measure social and psychological benefits that result from being active and having 'good workouts' in competitive sports. But they clearly indicate that we cannot say that 'sports improve health and physical well-being' without qualifying what we mean.

    Neglecting ... rules of health, [athletes] spend their lives like pigs – over-exercising, over-eating and over-sleeping ... Athletes rarely live to old age, and if they do, they are crippled by disease

(Galen, Greek physician, AD 180)

The sport – obesity connection

Like the connection between sports and health, the connection between sports and weight is complex. Some sports emphasize extreme forms of weight control; gymnastics and rowing are prime examples of this. Other sports emphasize weight gain for some or all of the athletes involved. For example, players in certain rugby positions, bodybuilders and heavyweight boxers may be encouraged to 'bulk up'. Sport in its most generic form is, however, often promoted as the solution to one of the most widely publicized health issues of contemporary developed societies: obesity. Nearly every discussion of this issue ends with the conclusion that eating right and exercising is the best way to avoid unhealthy weight gains. This is of course true, and research consistently supports the value of exercise in controlling body weight.

It would be nice if we could say that as sports become increasingly popular in society, obesity rates go down. But data suggest otherwise: obesity rates have increased at the same time and in the same cultures that competitive sports, especially those organized around the power and performance model, have become increasingly popular. This does not mean that playing sports causes obesity, but it does mean that the popularity of sports in a society does not inspire more than a few people to embrace forms of exercise that enable them to avoid gaining weight. However, we continue to see suggestions that public bodies should promote sporting activities to address the so-called 'obesity epidemic', without considering this apparently contradictory evidence or, indeed, individual's rights to make their own lifestyle choices. For example, the Women's Sport and Fitness Foundation UK has recommended that the government needs to commit proactively to increasing the participation of women in sport as a 'legitimate health intervention' in tackling obesity (Donohoe, 2003), but it did not specify the forms of sports participation that might be most effective in accomplishing this goal.

In Western countries, the age of 24-hour entertainment and instant fame presents young people with a host of obstacles standing in the way of the inspiration and role models which sport offers. Today's children live in a world of conflicting messages and competing distractions. Their landscape is cluttered. Their path to sport is often obscured.

[That t]he modern lifestyle of millions of children from the developed world is … coming at a cost … of poor public health and physical inactivity, leading to rapidly increasing obesity levels is now beyond dispute.

(Lord Sebastian Coe, Chair of London Olympic Games Organizing Committee, 2006)

How do sports affect our lives?

Sports and sport participation impact the lives of many people around the world. We are learning more about this impact through three types of studies based on a combination of critical, critical feminist and interactionist theories:

1. studies of sports experiences as explained through the voices of sport participants
2. studies of social worlds, or subcultures, that are created and maintained in connection with particular sports
3. studies of sports as sites, or 'social locations', where dominant ideas and ideologies are expressed and sometimes challenged and changed.

Taken together, these studies have helped many of us in the sociology of sport to rethink socialisation issues. Now we view sports as *sites for socialization experiences*, rather than as *causes of specific socialization outcomes*. This is an important distinction. It highlights two things. First, sports are social locations rich in their potential for providing memorable and meaningful personal, social and cultural experiences. Second, sports *by themselves* do not cause particular changes in the character traits, attitudes and actions of athletes or spectators. Therefore, when positive or negative socialization outcomes occur in connection with sports, we do not simply say that they were caused by sports; instead, we view sports as sites for influential experiences and then search for and explain the specific social processes through which particular socialization outcomes occur.

The following summaries of selected studies illustrate how this approach to socialization helps us understand what happens in sports and how sports are connected with social issues and forces in society.

Real-life experiences: sports stories from athletes

The following examples provide three socialization videos. They illustrate what happens in sports from the perspectives of the participants themselves, and they show us how people give meaning to sports experiences and integrate them into their lives on their own terms.

Example 1: stories of disordered eating

Sociologists Emma Rich, Rachel Holroyd and John Evans (2004) studied several young women who were receiving treatment for anorexia nervosa. Their research focuses on the ways in which schooling, including messages from physical education classes, may undermine girls' sense of competence and control in such a way that they may develop disordered eating behaviours.

They found that the messages that teachers presented to students were grounded in health discourses of being active and achieving the right size, often related to the perceptions of the so-called 'obesity epidemic' in developed societies. The central point was a moral responsibility to exercise regularly and have the correct diet. The participants in this study heard and interpreted these messages in terms of their views as young women concerned with being valued by peers and learning what it means to be accepted in British school culture. They learned that there was a hierarchy of bodies according to size, shape and weight, with a higher value on slenderness, which they then reproduced in their own behaviour. Thus, socialization was an interactive process in which the young women played key roles in what and how they learned. What happened to them as they progressed through the education system resulted from a combination of adult influence, the developmental issues associated with adolescence, and the social reality of being teenagers in the UK at the beginning of the twenty-first century.

The schooling the young women received did not *cause* their anorexia, but it was one of the sites where they considered various ideas about what it meant to have a desirable body. Exercise and diet were resources to cope with the cultural demands placed on them by teachers and peers. The impact of the messages received from within the school network was accentuated because they reinforced other cultural messages that the women received in their relationships and through the media.

We know that these young women's stories are mirrored by athletes, most commonly female rather than male participants in a range of sports, who also receive messages regarding what constitutes a desirable athletic body. The relationship between sports and disordered eating therefore may be twofold: first, as we have seen in the stories told by the young women in Rich et al.'s study, sports may be used as a means of achieving an ideal weight; and, second, the loss of weight may, in turn, be desirable if it is related to improved athletic performance. For example, this is often seen in sports with weight categories (such as lightweight rowing), those in which performers are advantaged by low body weight (such as long-distance running), and sports where performers are judged on aesthetic considerations, which usually require slenderness (such as gymnastics). These messages are reinforced when participants are surrounded by a peer group of athletes who are very slim. The high incidence of disordered eating among young athletes has caused such concern that UK Sport has produced guidelines on eating disorders and sports for practitioners working with high-performance athletes. This is the *socialized lived body* in an extreme form.

Example 2: stories from the changing room

Anthropologist P. David Howe (2004a, 2004b) spent two and a half years studying an elite men's rugby union team in Wales. As he observed and interviewed team members, he noticed the ways in which the sporting community dealt with the ambiguous nature of pain and injury. Their experiences and attitudes to injury were related to the fact that, in South Wales, rugby union maintains strong support from the local community, such that an injury to a key player is felt by the wider community as well as within the club itself. In addition, Howe (2004a, 2004b) suggested that the professionalism of the game had transformed players into commodities. Within this overall sports structure, the men developed particular strategies for revealing and discussing pain and injuries.

Howe found that the changing room was a key place for these discussions, where teammates would bond with each other and talk openly about pain and the time that may be required to return to training after an acute injury. However, such injuries were rarely discussed outside the changing room, since the idea of injury suggests an imperfect body, and may provide the basis for a player losing his place on the team, and therefore his match fee, if it was known by club officials. In contrast to this, players would more openly discuss playing with pain, since this demonstrated commitment to the sport and provided an excuse if the player's performance in a match was less than might be expected of them.

Such trends were sometimes reinforced by the medical team and club officials, with some players being declared 'match fit' before full recovery. In this way, the team became a community with its own dynamics and internal organization. Within this constructed community, the athletes learned things about the expectations of professional rugby, and influenced the meanings that the players gave to their pain and injury experiences.

Howe's study shows us that playing sports is a social as well as a physical experience. Rugby was a site for experiences, but it was *through social relationships* that those experiences were given meaning and incorporated into the men's lives. Howe focused on relationships between the athletes and the medical professionals, but also important were relationships with coaches, managers and even members of the local community. If we want to know what happens in sports, we must understand what happens in those relationships. It is through them that athletes are socialized.

Example 3: stories of gay male athletes

The meanings given to sport experiences emerge in connection with social relationships. But those meanings vary from one person to another because social relationships are influenced by social definitions given to age, gender, socio-economic status, ethnicity, skin colour, (dis)abilities and sexuality. This point is highlighted in Price and Parker's (2003) study of gay and bisexual male rugby players in the UK. Price and Parker felt it was important to give voice to gay men in sports, and hear what they had to say about themselves and their sports experiences. Using data collected from an ethnographic study, Price and Parker tell the stories of members of one amateur rugby club whose membership comprised primarily gay and bisexual men, in keeping with its status as the world's first gay rugby team.

The stories indicate that gay men are especially cautious about coming out in sports. Many of the players had experienced homophobia prior to joining the gay-friendly club, and perceived mainstream rugby to be hostile to gay men. Successfully combining a gay identity with an athletic identity had been a challenging process for nearly all the interviewees. Most of the men joined the new club because it provided a sense of community which contrasted with the feeling of estrangement they had experienced on mainstream teams. Some had also joined for sexual motives and the opportunity to meet other gay men. Being out was liberating for most of the men because this was an organization which supported them on and off the field. However, it was also the case that they were not treated seriously by other rugby teams. As a result, during the course of Price and Parker's research, the club had started to recruit heterosexual players as part of an attempt to secure more league victories and to be accepted as a serious club. For some of the players, this devalued the ideological importance of the club's existence, and reinforced heterosexist stereotypes that gay men cannot play 'masculine' sports and needed heterosexual men to help them win games.

Despite similarities between the experiences of gay and straight men in sports, the meanings given to those experiences and how they are integrated into people's lives differ because of how *heterosexuality* and *homosexuality* are defined by many people. Those definitions influence the meaning and impact of sport experiences; as those definitions change, so will the meanings given to the experiences that people have in sports (see also Anderson, 2000, 2002, 2004; Jarvis, 2006).

Social worlds: living in sports

Although sociologists study sports mostly as parts of the societies and cultures in which they are played and watched, some studies focus on sports as **social worlds**, a term used in interactionist theory to refer to *a way of life and an associated mindset that revolve around a particular set of activities and encompass all the people and relationships connected with the activities*. These studies are based on the assumption that we cannot understand who athletes are, what they do and how sports influence their lives unless we view them in the context of the social world in which they give meaning to sport experiences. Unless we know about these contexts, we have difficulty making sense of sport experiences and their impact on socialization. This is especially true when we study people whose lives revolve completely around a particular sport – that is, when the social world of their sport is their entire world.

Studies of social worlds created in connection with specific sports provide useful information about socialization processes and experiences. Following are five examples.

Example 1: learning to be a hero

Christopher Cushion and Robyn Jones undertook a sociological analysis of English male youth football by spending a season with the coaches and players of the youth sections of a Premiership club. Cushion and Jones (2006) focused on the interactions between the coaches and the athletes. The players were part of an academy of talented young athletes, who had the potential to be offered a professional contract if they performed well during their time in the academy. As a result, both the youth players and coaches were constantly scrutinized by the club management. In turn, the young men became increasingly engulfed in their athletic roles as they committed to identities based on playing football, and their football identities became the context for how they viewed appropriate behaviour patterns.

Cushion and Jones (2006) found that coaching practices were authoritarian, frequently to the point of being aggressive, which was viewed as necessary for preparing the young players for the demands of the adult professional game. The players were denied autonomy or individuality, with all aspects of their occupational lives, as well as their academy-based social lives, being directed by coaches. Players who conformed experienced favouritism, including a greater chance of being offered a professional contract, than those who were not viewed by coaches to have a good attitude. These young men developed unquestioning acceptance of the practices within the academy, as it served as their gatekeeper to success in the professional game.

Among other things, the players learned to define *being a professional athlete* in terms of toughness and dominance, and this was also gendered as it incorporated an expression of disdain for feminine characteristics. What made football significant was that these emerging ideas about being tough and aggressive were clearly endorsed by coaches and peers. Toughness and aggression were promoted in connection with team strategies, player evaluations and peer acceptance. There is no immediate evidence to suggest whether athletes apply these lessons to other aspects of their lives, or whether the social world of the football academy separates these players from the rest of life so much that the lessons learned in that social world stayed there. There remains a need for further studies on how such role engulfment influences the socialization experiences of athletes from different backgrounds and in different sports (Miller and Kerr, 2003).

Example 2: realizing image is not everything

Social scientists Andrew Sparkes, Joanne Batey and David Brown (2005) studied the social world of competitive bodybuilding through the experiences of one elite black male bodybuilder. They found that Jessenka (a pseudonym) learned to project a public image of power and strength as a sign of respected masculinity. This masked serious personal doubts about his identity and self-worth, related to his small stature and being black in a community where racial tensions ran high.

The social world of bodybuilding supported Jessenka's need for attention and approval from others which originated from the insecurities about his size and skin colour that he experienced in his youth. Winning the British Championship confirmed Jessenka's athletic identity within a framework of ideas about masculinity approved by the social world of bodybuilding, and he proudly referred to himself as a 'short monster'. While his body size and hard muscles may, from the outside, appear to be an exaggerated caricature or comic-book depiction of masculinity, for Jessenka this was a positive self-image which contrasted with the fragile sense of self he had in his youth. His identification with bodybuilding was so strong that he stated: 'Life *was* bodybuilding. Jessenka *was* bodybuilding' (Sparkes et al., 2005, p. 145).

Jessenka's bodybuilding career was cut prematurely short after an injury from a car accident meant he could no longer compete. As his body shrank in size, so his sense of masculinity diminished. Additionally, the respect that he received as a British Champion had enabled him to feel accepted as a black person in a racist society. When he lost his champion status and hyper-muscular body, he not only lost his athletic identity but his racial identity was also brought into sharp relief, making him realize that having the image of a bodybuilder did not increase racial tolerance or acceptance in society in any sustained or meaningful way.

Example 3: living in the shadow of a man's world

Sociologist Katie Liston (2006a) spent 10 years studying the social world of women's football as both a player and an ethnographer. Her research has focused on females playing in the Republic of Ireland. She found that the profile of women's football in Ireland is lower than other women's sports, and sports more generally; specifically men's football. As one of her interviewees explained, it has 'been the poor relation of men's football for years. I mean in terms of the financial and social investment in the game' (Liston, 2006a, p. 371). While there have been attempts to incorporate women's football within male structures to enable female players to have access to better facilities, organization, support staff and spectators, it remains the case that the women's game continues to be largely dependent on voluntary networks of people to organize matches and undertake the administration of coaching and development.

The differential experiences of the men's and women's games are reflected in the way that players express their identities as football players. Many talked of having to negotiate their contradictory identities as footballer and female, particularly as they made the transition from 'teenage tomboy' to adulthood. Their stories indicated their awareness of the male dominance of football, but simultaneously the importance of sport in their individual biographies.

The women in Liston's study reflect a broader 'feminization' of many sports, whereby female athletes have become increasingly visible and accepted in many societies. However, issues of sexuality continue to be discussed quietly, if they are discussed at all, and even highly successful female footballers such as those representing their country receive much less media attention than most of their male (and often less successful) counterparts.

Example 4: surviving in a ghetto

Sociologist John Sugden (1996) spent more than a decade studying the social world of boxers in a variety of gyms around the world. One of his case studies involved spending a year in a boxing club in Belfast, Northern Ireland. His ethnographic work helped him to uncover the ideas and meanings that constitute the life and craft of boxing in a divided and troubled society. He explains that the social world of the boxing gym is very complex: it is created in connection with the social forces in a sectarian society and its violent street culture, but it also operates as a sanctuary, avoiding allegiance to either side of the conflict and sheltering young pugilists from the full destructive impact of those forces. As a result, Catholics and Protestants were able to mix in this sport without fear of sectarian repercussions.

The experience of living in the social world of the boxing gym enabled some men to experience life, and socialize with people, outside the sectarian conflict intrinsic to life in Belfast at this time. Most of the boys in the club saw boxing as fun rather than having a desire to become professional competitors, but their involvement with the club kept them away from the dangers of their violent neighbourhoods. Within the clubs, the boys and men learned to respect disciplined toughness but not gratuitous violence, in no small part in order to ensure that the wildness of street culture did not contaminate the sport. For those who did become serious boxers, this was viewed as an opportunity to leave their social roots and violent society behind. While individual athletes were able to reject the sectarianism and political violence, there is no sense that boxing provides any challenge to the community conflict. For these boys and men, boxing was a powerful socialization experience, but it cannot be understood apart from the context of their everyday lives.

Example 5: sport worlds portrayed in the media

Ian Brittain (2004) is a sociologist who has studied the experiences of British Paralympic athletes. His research helps us to understand how the media reinforces many of the perceptions of disability and disabled athletes. The athletes in his study comment on the relative lack of media coverage of the Paralympic Games compared with the Olympic Games, which indicates the limited value placed on sports for disabled athletes and is in itself a form of discrimination. Some of the athletes told stories of how the language used to describe disabled athletes has often been patronizing and has bordered on the offensive (see Chapter 12).

The lack of exposure of disability sport within the UK limits the visibility of such events and so reduces available role models for young disabled persons who may be interested in sport. If such young people then turn to able-bodied sportspeople for role models, they end up comparing themselves to a conception of sports based on able-bodied and predominantly male norms, and so may perceive their own performances to be less worthy and internalize stereotypes that disability sport is inferior. Brittain (2004) suggests that the amount and content of media coverage needs to be addressed, in order to challenge the underlying perceptions of athletes with disabilities.

Like the social worlds described in the previous four examples, Paralympic sports are sites where influential socialization processes occur. Understanding those processes and the experiences involved in them requires knowledge of the particular social worlds in which they occur. Once we have a deep understanding of a social world associated with a sport, once we delve into it through good research, the things that athletes think and do become meaningful and understandable to us, regardless of how they appear to people who are not part of those worlds. This does not mean that we approve of everything that occurs in those worlds, but it enables us to understand why things occur, and what might be done to make sports safer and more humane places for athletes to be.

Ideology: sports as sites for struggling over how we think and what we do

Socialization research has focused mostly on what occurs in the lives of individuals and small groups. However, as researchers have combined critical theories with cultural studies and post-structuralism,[1] they have done creative studies of *socialization as a community and cultural process*. Their research goes beyond looking at the experiences and characteristics of athletes. Instead, it focuses on sports as sites where people in society collectively create and learn 'stories', which they use to give meaning to and make sense of the world and their lives. The stories that revolve around sports and athletes have their own vocabularies and images. The meanings in these stories shift, depending on who tells and hears them, and they often identify important cultural issues in everyday life. Researchers identify these stories and study how they fit into the culture and how people use them in connection with what they think and do.

Researchers also are concerned with whose stories about sports become dominant in the culture because so many stories *could* be told about sports. These stories are culturally important because they identify what is natural, normal and legitimate, and therefore give priority to ideas and orientations that privilege some people more than others. For example, the vocabulary and stories that frequently are associated with sports revolve around heroic figures who are big, strong, aggressive, record-setting champions. Political scientist Varda Burstyn (1999, p. 23) says that these stories celebrate the notion of 'higher, faster, stronger' that today serves the interests of capitalist expansion and traditional manly values associated with conquest. This is an important way in which comprehensive forms of socialization occur in connection with sports.

---

[1] Post-structuralism is a theoretical and methodological perspective based on the assumption that culture today revolves around language and rapidly changing media representations. Functionalists and conflict theorists consider material production and empirical reality to be the foundation of culture and society; post-structuralists focus on language and media representations because they assume that social life in today's postmodern culture is constantly negotiated, constructed, challenged and changed through language and images that represent people, ideas and things. Research done by post-structuralists often deals with the media and focuses on how images, identities, symbols and meanings are fabricated through media representations that constitute the contexts of our lives. Post-structuralists often do scholarly work that is intended to disrupt meanings and representations that oppress some people and privilege others.

Researchers are also concerned with whose stories are not told and whose voices are silenced or 'erased' from the stories that are told in the dominant culture. For example, the media coverage of sports might be studied to learn what is *not* contained in narratives and images as much as what is contained in them. This is because we can learn about culture by seeing what is *not* represented in narratives and images as well as seeing what is represented.

This type of research is difficult to do because it requires a knowledge of history and a deep understanding of the settings in which sports and sport stories come to be a part of people's lives. But it is important to do this research because it deals with the influence of sports in the culture as a whole, rather than in the lives of individuals and small groups.

The politics of socialization as a community and cultural process

Research on socialization as a community and cultural process is partly inspired by the ideas of Italian political theorist, Antonio Gramsci. When fascists in Italy imprisoned Gramsci for speaking out against their oppressive policies, he used his time in prison (1928–35) to think about why people had not revolted against exploitive forms of capitalism in Western societies. Gramsci concluded that it was important to understand how people in society form their notions of common sense and ideas about how society ought to be organized socially, politically and economically. He explained that powerful people could influence and win the support of the people over whom they exercised power by providing them exciting and pleasurable experiences.

Gramsci suspected that most people use the cultural messages associated with the sources of excitement and pleasure in their lives to inform their notions of common sense and their ideas about the organization and operation of society as a whole. Therefore, existing forms of power relations in society could be maintained if people with power organized and sponsored exciting and pleasurable activities that promoted their perspectives and interests.

Gramsci's analysis helps us understand why large corporations spend billions of pounds every year to sponsor sports and present advertisements in connection with sports. For example, Coca-Cola and McDonald's have each spent hundreds of millions of pounds sponsoring and presenting advertising messages during the 1996, 2000, 2004 and 2008 Olympic Games. Similarly, Famous Grouse and Brains have sponsored, respectively, the Scottish and Welsh men's rugby union teams. These expenditures were made to promote sales but, more important, they were made to use sports as vehicles for delivering cultural messages that corporate executives wanted people in the world to hear. They wanted people watching the Olympics or Rugby Union World Cup to agree that competition is the best way to allocate rewards, and that wealthy and powerful people (and corporations) deserve what they have because they are the best at what they do.

The people who run Coca-Cola and Famous Grouse and Brains want people to drink their products, but they also want people to develop lifestyles in which excitement and pleasure are associated with consumption and in which social status is associated with corporate brands and logos. They want people to say, 'These large companies are important to us because without them we would not have the sports we love so dearly.' They want people to believe that their excitement and pleasure depends on large corporations and their products. They want to establish consumption as the foundation for measuring progress and defining prosperity. Their profits and power depend on it, and their marketing people use sports to promote an ideology of competition and consumption. To the extent that people in society accept this ideology, the power of corporations increases in society.

Many sociologists refer to this process of forming consent around a particular ideology as the process of establishing hegemony. In political science and sociology, **hegemony** is a *process of maintaining leadership and control by gaining the consent of other groups, including those who are being led or controlled.* For example, British hegemony in the world existed when people in the former British Empire and its colonies worldwide accepted British control as legitimate. Hegemony is never permanent, as illustrated in the fall of the British Empire, but it can be maintained in a society as long as most people feel that their lives are as good as can be expected and that there is no strong reason to change the way social worlds are currently organized. Similarly, corporate hegemony is maintained as long as most people accept a view of the world that is consistent with corporate interests. People in corporations know that their interests depend on establishing 'ideological outposts' in people's heads. Sports, because they are exciting and pleasurable activities for so many people, are important tools for building such outposts. Once established, these outposts are useful to corporations because they serve as terminals through which many corporate messages can be delivered into people's minds. To paraphrase Gramsci's conclusion about hegemony, it is difficult to fight an enemy that has outposts in your head.

Research on socialization as a community and cultural process

It is difficult to understand socialization as a community and cultural process unless we see it in action. The following examples of research highlight this informative approach to sports and socialization.

Sociologist Alan Bairner (2003) studied the connection between sports and community socialization processes in an area of Belfast which reflects the broader sectarian conflict. His study focused on a planned junior football match between Donegal Celts, a team based in nationalist West Belfast, and the Royal Ulster Constabulary, who represented the British military presence in Ireland. People in the local community were divided, with some feeling the game should be allowed to proceed in order to represent the interests of nationalist football fans in the area, and others arguing that it would offend the community if the club had dealings with those representing an unacceptable police force. Those involved in the debate, which culminated in the game being cancelled, included members of the club, political groups and the media. Bairner's findings indicate that football was personally important and a source of national identity for many individuals in the area. As a 'foreign' sport, many purists reject football as indicative of the culture of the colonizer, instead supporting Gaelic sports as integral to their sense of Irishness. However, for others, it is possible to embrace football without experiencing a sense of compromise to their Irish identity. This one game reaffirmed the ongoing broader political agenda and divisions between different social groups, while affecting individual lives in the process. As Bairner (2003, p. 167) argues, 'Soccer has long been used by Irish nationalists in Belfast as a vehicle for promoting communal identity and engaging in cultural resistance. It has seldom been solely a medium for assimilation or accommodation.'

Gill Clarke's (2004) biographical research with lesbian physical education teachers in England demonstrates how schools may be sites of compulsory heterosexuality within which physical educators create identities that influence how they present themselves in public, relate to others and evaluate themselves. The subject matter of physical education, which focuses on the performance of students' bodies, creates particular anxieties for teachers of physical education which is not experienced by teachers of other subjects. As a result, many were careful to conceal their true sexual identity from their colleagues, often adopting vocabularies and behaviour which supported homophobic inequalities and perpetuated heterosexual privilege. Clarke concludes that physical education in schools may serve as a space within which people's identities are limited and policed by the heterosexual borders of the school environment.

Scott Fleming (1995) undertook an in-depth case study of South Asian males in a school in London in order to analyse the sports–ethnicity dynamic. He identified that there were several different lifestyle groups, largely related to the interplay of ethnicity and social class. These groupings influenced the young men's experiences of racism and their participation in sport. While recognizing these differences, Fleming identified a general trend of religious and cultural identity influencing leisure choices, which led to a degree of continuity within and between generations. This sense of ethno-cultural identity provided the basis for significant socialization processes in two main ways. First, racism and discrimination denied real equality of opportunity for South Asians to engage in sport. A few of the young men made the choice to engage in sports as a direct strategy for dealing with this racism. However, the second factor was that many of the South Asians studied did not wish to emulate white middle-class sports participation patterns. Their refusal to conform to the dominant pattern of formalized sport, but instead to participate in culturally relevant activities, enabled a challenge to the dominant (racist) culture in a way that was personally empowering. This made their sports experiences very different from the experiences of others who play power and performance sports. Additionally, it demonstrated that sports can be played in ways that challenge dominant ideas. When this happens, socialization in sports may involve changes in how entire groups of people think about what is important in life and how social relationships can and should be organized.

Other studies also have focused on the ways that popular images connected with sports become influential cultural symbols as they are represented in the media and everyday conversations. For example, Ben Carrington (2001) used critical and post-structuralist theories to study the connection between racial ideology in the UK and the cultural stories created around the former England footballer, Ian Wright. Carrington's analysis of the development of Wright's media and commercial image show how the 'genealogy of Wright' included a commodification of blackness. Wright's celebrity career has incorporated an appearance of political resistance to racism, but manufactured in such a way that white British society can comfortably identify with him. Carrington uses historical information about race and the development of Wright's media career, which has included public declarations of black politics, to argue that we cannot understand Wright's status and impact as a cultural icon without knowing how racism operates in the UK.

Carrington's research and similar studies done by others emphasize that *none of us lives outside the influence of ideology* (Andrews, 1996a, 1996b; Smart, 2005). This research is based on the premise that sports, because they are popular sources of excitement and pleasure in people's lives, are significant sites at which people learn and sometimes raise questions about ideology. This research holds the promise of showing us how sports influence widely held ideas in a culture and how people can disrupt that influence when it promotes stereotypes and exploitation (see Andrews and Jackson, 2001).

When corporations spend money to have their names, logos and products associated with sports, they are looking for more than sales. In the long run, their executives hope that people will believe their enjoyment of sports depends on the corporations. If this happens, people are more likely to support, and less likely to interfere with, corporate interests (*Source*: Elizabeth Pike)

What Socialization Research Does Not Tell Us

Existing research does not tell us all we want to know about sports and socialization. We have many research snapshots and a few videos to help us understand parts of socialization processes related to sports, but we lack information about the ways that these processes operate in the lives of people from various ethnic groups and social classes. In the UK, research on Asian Britons, continental European migrants and travelling communities in sports is especially needed. We also need studies of sports participation in high-income and low-income communities, as well as among wealthy and poor individuals and families.

We know that an 11-year-old white girl from a wealthy English family playing tennis in an exclusive suburban club has different sports experiences than an Asian boy playing in a street cricket game in a Welsh former mining town where his parents are minimum-wage factory workers. Clearly, we need to know more about variations in sport experiences and how people from different social and cultural backgrounds give those experiences meaning and integrate them into their lives at various points in their life course. We cannot talk about the socialization consequences of sports without putting sports experiences into real-life contexts (see Cartoon 4.2). That is why your sports participation has had a different impact on you than ours has had on us, and that is why it is senseless to argue about whether all sports build character or whether all athletes are role models. Neither socialization nor sports are that simple, and research cannot give us unconditional yes or no answers about what sports do to us or to our communities and societies.

We also need research on sports participation careers among children and on how those careers are linked to overall social development, especially among girls, children with disabilities and children from ethnic minority backgrounds. Similarly, we need research on older people, especially those considering or trying sports for the first time or resuming participation after decades of not playing. We need research on how people make participation decisions about different types of sports. Sports come in many forms, and the socialization processes related to power and performance sports are different from experiences related to pleasure and participation sports.

If we knew more about each of these topics, we could provide sports participation opportunities that fit into the lives of a greater number of people. This would help us make sports more democratic and less subject to the commercial forces that make them exclusive and elitist (Donnelly, 1993, 1996b). This is the focus of the 'Breaking barriers' box on pages 131–132.

We also need research on the emotional dimensions of socialization processes. Few sociologists have considered emotions in their research, but most of us know that decisions about sports participation are clearly connected with our feelings, fears and anxieties. For example, some decisions may be linked with 'psyching up', the emotional experience of forming expectations about what a person will encounter in sports. These expectations are based on memories and the stories about sports that exist in the culture as a whole. Stories about the emotional side of sports have been collected by social psychologists who have studied 'flow experiences' among athletes (Jackson and Csikszentmihalyi, 1999). Flow occurs when we face a challenge that requires us to use all of our skills and, in the process, lose track of time and get carried along by the activity itself. The 'runner's high', 'peak experiences' and 'that game when everything just seems to click' are examples of flow in action. Even though flow is a personal experience, it is tied to sociological issues such as how activities are organized and the amount of control that participants have over their involvement in those activities.

Finally, we need more research on the ways that the vocabulary used in certain sports influences sports participation decisions and the meanings given to sports experiences. When words constantly refer to opposition, hostility, rivalries, confrontations, warriors, domination and mastery over others, they set the stage for memories, fantasies and identifications that serve as powerful sources of personal identity and social dynamics. This vocabulary tells us much about the organization and spirit of sports. For example, given the words that many people use when they talk about sports, it is not surprising that young women in UK colleges and universities are less likely than their male counterparts to be interested in or try out for and stay on varsity teams. If the language of sports is based on traditionally masculine images and orientations, many girls and women may not find certain sports very appealing. Furthermore, what types of boys and men are likely to be attracted to sports described as forms of 'warfare', requiring aggression, toughness and the desire to dominate others? Sociologists, especially those interested in gender equity and gender relations, would like to know answers to these questions.

'I don't think these guys agree about the meaning of boxing'

Cartoon 4.2 **Meanings given to sports vary from one person to another. However, many power and performance sports are organized to encourage orientations that emphasize domination over others. Those who do not hold this orientation may not fit very well in these sports**

In practical terms, when we learn more things about sports and socialization, we can become wiser parents, coaches, teachers, managers and sports administrators. Then we can create sports that offer a wider array of challenging and satisfying experiences.

Breaking barriers

Socialization barriers: *living in the empire of the normal*

Popular images of bodies embedded in our culture, the media and our minds are images of able bodies. Seldom do we see images of impaired bodies, except in notices for fund-raising events to 'help the disabled'. Images that represent disability as an embodied form that is valuable, beautiful, healthy, fit or athletic are practically non-existent (Seeley and Rail, 2004). This is because we live in an 'Empire of the Normal' where productive, healthy, fit, beautiful and ideal bodies are *able bodies* (Couser, 2000).

In the Empire of the Normal, the existence of a disabled body causes people to ask, *'What happened to you?'* People in the empire demand an explanation for a disabled body – a story that accounts for its difference from normal bodies. As people with disabilities are asked incessantly to tell their stories, their identities come to be organized around their accounts of 'why my body is different from your body' (Thomson, 2000, p. 334).

This information helps us understand socialization and sports in more detail. For example, when people with disabilities make decisions to play sports, the *significant others* in their lives include physical therapists, physical educators, athletes with disabilities, sport scientists and doctors as well as family members and peers (Schilling, 1997). In fact, the origin of today's Paralympics was in Stoke Mandeville, a British medical centre for war veterans with spinal cord injuries. Ludwig Guttmann, the neurosurgeon in charge of the centre, was convinced that sports could be used as therapy for patients. His idea to schedule public games for people with disabilities at the same time as the 1948 Olympics in London was radical. People in the Empire of the Normal became uncomfortable when they were confronted with disabled bodies. 'Out of sight, out of mind' has always been a norm in the empire.

After a person with a disability becomes involved in sports, decisions to stay involved are related to how other people define their bodies and treat them as athletes. Also important are participation opportunities, resources for transportation and adapted equipment, knowledgeable coaches, and programmes that inspire achievement and success.

Changing or ending sports participation occurs in connection with many of the same factors that lead able-bodied athletes to disengage from sports. Injuries, a sense of reaching one's goals or hitting one's limits, responsibilities related to work and family, a lack of resources, and new opportunities to coach or work in sports influence decisions to alter or end sport participation.

The issue of what happens to people with disabilities when they play sports has seldom been studied. As with able-bodied athletes, socialization experiences among athletes with disabilities depend on their relationships, the general social and cultural context in which participation occurs, and the meanings given to participation.

In societies where power and performance sports predominate, people with disabilities seldom play with or alongside able-bodied athletes. Power and performance sports are exclusive: only able bodies are defined as 'fit' for participation. This forces athletes with disabilities to play in segregated or 'special' programmes or leads them to prefer those programmes. This influences the meanings given to their sport participation.

Among many athletes with disabilities, sports are perceived as sites for challenging body images in the Empire of the Normal. Among a few, sports are sites for planning how to break through the empire's walls, open gates for others, and rebuild its foundation so that people no longer see disabled bodies as needing to be cured, fixed, regulated or separated from other bodies (Thomson, 2002, p. 8).

Tricia, a British powerlifter, questions the notion of normality when she says:

> Normality is what I am. I can barely remember what life was like when I wasn't disabled, so disability is normal to me and all I have known … Who is normal? Everyone is different, but to them that difference is normal. Society puts normal labels on people. I am a different individual, yes, but who isn't?
>
> *(in Huang and Brittain, 2006, p. 362)*

Considering Tricia's questions just might hasten the fall of the Empire of the Normal.

When people see a body with a disability, they often want to hear the story that accounts for its difference from 'normal' bodies. Over time this may lead to the development of an identity organized around a person's account of 'why my body is different from your body' (*Source:* David Biene; photograph courtesy of Ossur)

Summary: Who Plays and What Happens?

Socialization is a complex, interactive process through which people learn about themselves and the social worlds in which they participate. This process occurs in connection with sports and other activities and experiences in people's lives. Research indicates that playing sports is a social experience as well as a physical one.

Becoming involved and staying involved in sports occur in connection with general socialization processes in people's lives. Decisions to play sports are influenced by the availability of opportunities, the existence of social support, processes of identity formation and the cultural context in which decisions are made.

Studies of socialization into sports show that sports participation decisions are related to processes of individual development, the organization of social life and cultural ideology. People do not make decisions about sports participation once and for all time. They make them day after day, as they set and revise priorities in their lives. Research on sports-related decisions helps us understand the social dynamics of early experiences in sports and who influences those experiences. The reasons for staying in sports change over time as people's lives change, and it is important to study the complexities of these processes.

Changing or ending active sport participation also occurs in connection with general socialization processes. These processes are interactive and influenced by personal, social and cultural factors. Changes in sport participation are usually tied to a combination of identity, developmental and life-course issues. Ending sports participation often involves a transition process, during which athletes disengage from sports, redefine their identities, reconnect with friends and family members, and use available resources to become involved in other activities and careers. Just as people are not socialized into sports, they are not simply socialized out of sports. Research shows that changing or ending a career as a competitive athlete occurs over time and is often tied to events and life-course issues apart from sports. These connections are best studied by using research methods that enable us to identify and analyse long-term transition processes.

Socialization that occurs as people participate in sports has been widely studied, especially by people wanting to know if and how sports build character. Much of this research has produced inconsistent findings because it has been based on oversimplified ideas about sports, sport experiences and socialization. Reviews of this research indicate that studies of sports and socialization must take into account variations in the ways that sports are organized, played and integrated into people's lives. This is important because different sports involve different experiences and produce different socialization patterns. For example, the experience and meaning of playing power and performance sports is different from the experience and meaning of playing pleasure and participation sports. The visibility and popularity of power and performance sports are related to issues of status and ideology: these sports fit the interests of people who have the wealth and power to sponsor and promote sports.

We know that sports have an impact on people's lives. The most informative research on what happens in sports deals with (1) the everyday experiences of people who play sports, (2) the social worlds created around sports, and (3) community and cultural processes through which ideologies are created, reproduced and changed. As we listen to the voices of those who participate in sports, study how they live their lives in connection with sports and pay special attention to the ideological messages associated with sports, we learn more about sports and socialization.

Most scholars who study sports in society now see sports as sites for socialization experiences, rather than causes of specific socialization outcomes. This distinction recognizes that powerful and memorable experiences may occur in connection with sports, but it emphasizes that these experiences are given meaning through social relationships, and these meanings are influenced by the social and cultural contexts in which sports are played. Therefore, the most useful research in the sociology of sport focuses on the importance of social relationships and the contexts in which sport experiences are given meaning by a wide and diverse range of people who play or watch sports in some form or another.

Website resources

Note: Websites often change. The following URLs were current when this book was printed. Please check our website (*www.mcgraw-hill.co.uk/textbooks/coakley*) for updates and additions.

www.mcgraw-hill.co.uk/textbooks/coakley Click on Chapter 4; see information on the concept of competition, the relationship between competition and culture, and the persistent belief that sports build character.

www.activepeoplesurvey.co.uk The results of the largest survey in Europe of physical activity participation rates in England.

www.disabilitysportwales.org The website of the Federation of Disability Sport Wales, with links to national and sport-specific disability sport groups.

www.dsni.co.uk This site has advice and information for disability sport in Northern Ireland.

www.efds.net The official website of the English Federation of Disability Sport, with downloadable research materials and links to other sites.

www.excite.co.uk/directory/Society/Gay,_Lesbian,_and_Bisexual/Sports A directory of gay, lesbian and bisexual sports groups in the UK.

www.scottishdisabilitysport.com A website covering issues affecting disability sport in Scotland.

www.sogb.org.uk/index.asp The website of Special Olympics Great Britain, which provides sports opportunities for people with learning disabilities. Provides links to organizations that support specific learning disabilities.

www.sportdevelopment.org.uk/dupearly.pdf This is a paper which reviews the importance of early learning experiences for continuing in sport, and suggests ways of improving opportunities for children in marginalized groups.

www.sportengland.org/national-framework-for-sport.pdf This is the link to the Framework for Sport in England, explaining the aims and partnerships involved in the vision for sport for 2020.

Sports and young people: are organized schemes worth the effort?

(*Source*: **Elizabeth Pike**)

> In recent years, it has been very noticeable that, while the children turn up in much more expensive kit than ever before, they can hardly kick a ball ... these kids have nobody to teach them.
>
> *(Trevor Brooking, former Chief Executive of Sport England, 1999)*

> Unlike many jobs, the road to become a professional starts from an early age, sometimes as young as nine, through involvement with a club ... It has become unusual for players above school age to be signed as professional footballers.
>
> *(The Football Association, 2001)*

Learning Centre Resources

Visit *Sports in Society*'s Online Learning Centre (OLC) at **www.mcgraw-hill.co.uk/ textbooks/coakley** for additional information and study material for this chapter, including:

- Self-grading quizzes and essay questions
- Learning outcomes
- Related websites
- Additional readings

Chapter contents

Origin and development of organized youth sports

Major trends in youth sports today

Different experiences: informal, player-controlled sports versus organized, adult-controlled sports

Sociological questions about youth sports

Sports and education

Recommendations for improving youth sports

Prospects for improving youth sports

Summary: are organized youth sport schemes worth the effort?

 Kids don't go to the playground anymore. When they practice there's a coach telling them what to do and how to do it. What happens to the kids' passion and heart in all this?

(Ken Ravizza, sport psychologist, 2002)

When, how and to what end children play sports are issues that concern parents, community leaders and child advocates in national and international organizations. When sociologists study youth sports, they focus on the experiences of participants and how those experiences vary depending on the organization of schemes and the social and cultural contexts in which they exist. Research done by sociologists and others has influenced how people think about and organize youth sports, and it continues to provide valuable information that parents, coaches and sports development officers can use when organizing and evaluating youth schemes.

This chapter summarizes part of that research as we discuss six topics that are central to understanding youth sports today. These are:

1   the origin and development of organized youth sports

2   major trends in youth sports

3   differences between informal, player-controlled sports and formally organized, adult-controlled sports

4   commonly asked sociological questions about youth sports, including

   (a) When are children ready to play organized competitive sports?

   (b) What are the dynamics of family relationships in connection with organized youth sports?

   (c) How do social factors influence youth sport experiences?

5   the relationship between youth sports and education

6   recommendations for changing children's sports.

An underlying question that guides our discussions of these topics is this: are organized youth sports worth the massive amount of time, money and effort that people put into them? We first asked this question when the children in our families played sports during childhood, and we continue to ask it as we talk with parents and work with coaches and policy makers who make extensive commitments to organizing sports for young people.

Origin and Development of Organized Youth Sports

During the latter half of the nineteenth century, people in Europe and other developed nations began to realize that the social environment influenced child development. This created a movement to organize children's social worlds. The goal was to build character and virtue among children and socialize them to be hard-working, productive adults in rapidly expanding capitalist economies (Chudacoff, 2007). It was not long before sports for young boys were organized and sponsored by schools, communities and church groups. The organizers hoped that sports, especially team sports, would teach boys from working-class families to obey rules and work together productively. They also hoped that sports would toughen middle- and upper-class boys and socialize them to be competitive men despite the 'feminized' values they learned from stay-at-home mothers. At the same time, girls were provided with activities that taught them to be good wives, mothers and homemakers. The prevailing belief was that girls should learn domestic skills rather than sports skills when they went to schools and playgrounds. There were exceptions to these patterns but, after the Second World War, youth sports schemes were organized this way in Western Europe and North America.

The post-war baby boom and the growth of youth sports

The baby-boom generation was born between 1946 and 1964. Young married couples during these years were optimistic about the future and eager to become parents. As the first wave of baby boomers moved through childhood during the 1950s and 1960s, there was a growth in organized youth sports. Parents also entered the scene, eager to have their sons' characters built through organized competitive sports. Fathers became coaches and club committee members. Mothers washed the kit, prepared meals and became chauffeurs so that their sons were on time for training and games.

Most schemes were for boys aged 8 to 14 years old, and they were organized in the belief that playing sports would prepare them to participate productively in a competitive economy. Until the 1970s, girls were largely ignored by these organizers. Girls were relegated to being spectators during their brothers' games. Then came the women's movement, the fitness movement and government legislation prohibiting sex discrimination. These changes stimulated and mandated new sport schemes for girls. During the 1970s and early 1980s, these schemes grew rapidly, to the point that girls had nearly as many opportunities as boys. However, their participation rates have remained lower than rates for boys – for reasons we discuss in the section, 'How do social factors influence youth sport experiences?' (p. 156), and in Chapter 8. Participation in organized youth sports is now a valued part of growing up in most wealthy nations. Parents and communities with resources to sponsor, organize and administer schemes have created a variety of youth sports. Some parents question the benefits of schemes in which winning seems to be more important than overall child development, whereas other parents seek out the win-orientated schemes, hoping their children will become the winners. A few parents also encourage their children to engage in unstructured, non-competitive physical activities, an alternative that many children prefer over organized schemes that are controlled by adults. Research shows that these 'alternative sports' have become increasingly popular among children in many countries (Midol and Broyer, 1995; Rinehart, 2000; Rinehart and Grenfell, 2002; Rinehart and Syndor, 2003).

Social changes have influenced the growth of organized youth sports

Since the 1950s, an increasing amount of children's after-school time and physical activity has occurred in adult-controlled organized schemes. This growth is partly related to changing ideas about family life and childhood in neo-liberal societies, that is, societies in which individualism and material success are highly valued. The following five changes are especially relevant to the growth of organized schemes.

First, the number of families with both parents working outside the home has increased dramatically. This has created a demand for organized and adult-supervised schemes after school and during school holidays. Organized sports have grown because many parents believe they offer their children opportunities to have fun, learn adult values, become physically fit and acquire positive status among their peers.

Second, since the early 1980s, there has been a major cultural shift in what it means to be a 'good parent'. Good parents today are those who can account for the whereabouts and actions of their children 24 hours a day, every day. This expectation is a new component of parenting ideology, and in recent years it has led many parents to seek organized, adult-supervised schemes for their children. Organized sports are favoured by parents because they provide adult leadership for children, predictable schedules and measurable indicators of a child's accomplishments. When their children succeed, parents can claim that they are meeting cultural expectations. In fact, many mothers and fathers feel that their moral worth as parents is associated with the visible achievements of their children in sports – a factor that further intensifies parental commitment to youth sports (Coakley, 2006; Dukes and Coakley, 2002).

Third, there has been a growing belief that informal, child-controlled activities inevitably lead to trouble – much like what occurs in the novel, *Lord of the Flies*. In its extreme form, this belief leads adults to view children as threats to social order (Sternheimer, 2006). Therefore, organized sports are seen as ideal activities because they keep children occupied, out of trouble and under the control of adults.

Fourth, many parents, responding to the fear-producing stories highlighted in media news, now see the world outside the home as dangerous for their children. They regard organized sports as safe alternatives to informal activities that occur outside the home's locked doors and fenced gardens. Even when sports have high injury rates and coaches use methods that border on abuse, parents still feel that organized schemes are needed to protect their children (Gorman, 2005; Nack and Munson, 2000; Nack and Yaeger, 1999; Pennington, 2005).

Fifth, the visibility of high-performance and professional sports has increased people's awareness of organized competitive sports as a valued part of culture. As children watch sports on television, listen to parents and friends talk about sports, and hear about the wealth and fame of popular athletes, they often see organized youth sports, especially those modelled after professional sports, as attractive activities. This also means that children expect high standards of their sporting activities, to match what they see on television, and may drop out if they are not satisfied. As a result, when children say they want to be gymnasts or tennis players, parents often look for the best organized schemes in those sports (see Cartoon 5.1; Opdyke, 2007). Therefore, organized youth sports have become popular because children see them as enjoyable and culturally valued activities that will gain them acceptance from peers and parents alike.

Together, these five social changes have boosted the popularity of organized youth sports in recent decades. Knowing about them helps to explain why parents invest so many family resources into the organized sports participation of their children. The amount of money that some parents spend on club membership, participation fees, equipment, travel, coaching and other things defined as necessary in many schemes has gone through the roof in recent years (Bick, 2007; Giordana and Graham, 2004; King, 2002; MacArthur, 2008; Moore, 2002; Poppen, 2004; Sokolove, 2004a; Wolff, 2003). The father of Greg Rusedski, the British-Canadian tennis player, mortgaged his house to support Rusedski's playing career and estimated that it cost approximately £200 000 to maintain him for four years. Rusedski did, of course, eventually earn money from his tennis career, but most are not so fortunate.

One of the troubling issues raised by these changes is that mothers and fathers in working-class and lower-income households are increasingly defined as irresponsible or 'bad' parents because they lack the resources to put their children in adult-supervised after-school sport schemes, as wealthier parents do. When these parents lack the time and other resources needed to volunteer and coach in youth sport schemes, they are seen as uninterested in nurturing the dreams of their children. In this way, organized sports for children become linked to political issues and debates about family values and the moral worth of parents in lower-income households.

Major Trends in Youth Sports Today

In addition to their growing popularity, youth sports are changing in five socially significant ways. *First*, organized schemes have become increasingly privatized. This means that more youth sports today are sponsored by private and commercial organizations, and users have

Cartoon 5.1 **When children have schedules that are full of organized youth sports, they have little time to be with their parents. The irony is that many parents spend more time making it possible for their children to play sports than they spend with their children.**

to pay to participate in these schemes. *Second*, organized schemes increasingly emphasize the 'performance ethic'. This means that participants in youth sports, even in recreational schemes, are encouraged to evaluate their experiences in terms of the progress they make in developing technical skills and progressing to higher personal levels of competition. *Third*, there has been an increase in private, elite sports-training facilities, which are dedicated to producing highly skilled and specialized athletes who can compete at the highest levels of youth sports. *Fourth*, parents have become more involved in and concerned about the participation and success of their children in organized youth sports. This has turned youth sports into serious activities for adults and children, and adults are more likely to act in extreme ways as they advocate the interests of their children. *Fifth*, participation in alternative and action sports has increased. This means that many young people prefer unstructured, participant-controlled sports such as skateboarding, rollerblading, snowboarding, BMX biking, surfing, playing frisbee and other physical activities that have local or regional relevance in their lives.

These five trends have an impact on who plays and what happens in organized youth sports. This is discussed in the following sections and in the box 'Sponsorship matters' (p. 144).

The privatization of organized schemes

Privatization is a prevalent and sometimes alarming trend in youth sports today. Although organized sports have become more popular in recent years, there are few publicly funded schemes with free and open participation policies. Most sports in the UK come under the jurisdiction of sports authorities which are private entities given state subsidies. However, when local governments face budget cuts, various social services, including youth sports, are often downsized or eliminated. Some publicly funded schemes have tried to survive by imposing participation fees, but many have been forced to drop schemes altogether. In connection with these changes, private-profit sport schemes have become major providers of youth sports. These organizations depend on membership fees, corporate sponsorships and fund-raising. The instruction and experience offered by these schemes is usually good.

However, there is a negative consequence associated with this trend towards privatizing youth sports. These privatized schemes often reproduce the socio-economic inequalities that exist in the larger society. Unlike public schemes, they depend on the resources of participants rather than entire communities. Low-income and single-parent families often lack money to pay for dues, travel, equipment and other fees. These schemes therefore offer sport opportunities for children in well-to-do families and neighbourhoods, but they are too expensive and inconveniently located for children in low-income families and neighbourhoods. This, in turn, creates or accentuates social-class divisions in communities.

An additional dimension of youth sports being 'sold out' to private companies for economic interests has been the selling of school playing fields – mostly to businesses that subsequently build and sell private housing on the site. This process started under the Conservative government in the 1980s but continued under the subsequent New Labour government. It is estimated that in the two decades since such sales were encouraged more than 6000 playing fields have been sold, and there are some regions of the country where there is not a single school with green playing areas. Many argue that these sales have exacerbated the decline of sports in schools, and that this impacts most on those in state schools in lower-income areas, rather than private schools with extensive sports facilities. Surveys suggest that approximately one-third of primary school children do not reach minimum levels of physical activity, and two-thirds of children will drop out of sports altogether when leaving school (see Wigglesworth, 2007).

These trends demonstrate that, when privatization occurs, market forces become primary factors shaping who plays youth sports under what conditions. Wealthy people do not see this as a problem because they can pay for their children to play under the conditions that they choose. But people with few economic resources find themselves in a double bind: they cannot pay to support their children's activities, and they are often defined as negligent parents because their children do not experience the same successes as their wealthier peers. There are obvious problems associated with privatization, and they disproportionately affect poor people with little political power; therefore, they receive little attention.

Emphasis on the performance ethic

The performance ethic is an orientation based on the idea that the quality of the sport experience can be measured in terms of improved skills, especially in relation to the skills of others. It has become increasingly important in youth sports schemes where fun is now defined in terms of becoming a better athlete, becoming more competitive and being promoted into more highly skilled training and competition categories. Often, the categories have names that identify skill levels, so there may be gold, silver and bronze groups to indicate a child's status in schemes.

Many large corporations sponsor youth sports so that young people and their families will link the name of the company with a healthy, wholesome activity and want to buy their products. These children are playing an adapted game of football, where the equipment has been provided by the fast-food chain McDonald's (*Source: Elizabeth Pike*)

Many parents like this because it enables them to judge their child's progress and prove to themselves and others that they are 'good parents'. (Review the box 'Sponsorship matters: variations in the purpose of organized youth sports', p. 144.)

Private and commercial schemes emphasize the performance ethic to a greater degree than do public schemes, and many market themselves as 'centres of athletic excellence'. This approach attracts parents willing and able to pay high fees for membership, participation and instruction. Another way to sell private schemes to parents who can afford the cost is to highlight the profiles and achievements of successful athletes and coaches who have trained or worked in the scheme.

Parents of physically skilled children sometimes define fees, equipment, travel and training expenses, which can be shockingly high, as *investments* in their children's future. They are concerned with skill development, and as their children get older, they use performance-orientated schemes as sources of information about adult sports and networks for contacting coaches and sport organizations. They approach their children's sport participation rationally, and see clear connections between participation and their children's future development and success in adult life.

Of course, the application of the performance ethic is not limited to organized sports; it influences a range of organized children's activities (Chudacoff, 2007; Elkind, 2007; MacArthur,

reflect on SPORTS *Sponsorship matters: variations in the purpose of organized youth sports* • • • • • • • • • • • • • •

The purpose of organized youth sports often varies with the goals of those who pay for them. Forms of sponsorship differ from one scheme to another, but they generally fall into one of the following four categories.

1 *Public, government-supported community recreation organizations.* This includes local parks and recreation departments and community centres, which traditionally have offered a range of free or low-cost organized sports schemes for children. These schemes are usually inclusive and emphasize overall participation and general physical skill development as it relates to health and enjoyment.

2 *Public, non-profit community organizations.* These include the Guide and Scout movements, activities related to Duke of Edinburgh Awards and other community-based clubs, which traditionally have provided a limited range of free or low-fee organized sport schemes for children. The goals of these schemes are diverse, including everything from providing children from particular neighbourhoods with a 'wholesome, Christian atmosphere' for playing sports to providing 'at-risk children' with activities to keep them off the streets.

3 *Private, non-profit sport organizations.* These include local sports clubs which operate either independently or through connections with larger sport organizations, such as national sports federations. These might include swimming, gymnastics or athletics clubs who train at local authority venues. These organizations usually offer more exclusive opportunities to groups of children who usually come from families who can afford relatively costly participation fees.

4 *Private commercial clubs.* These include tennis, squash, golf and many other sports clubs and training schemes. Many of these organizations have costly membership and participation fees, and some emphasize intense training, progressive and specialized skill development, and elite competition.

Because these sponsors have different missions, the youth sports that they provide are likely to appeal to different people and offer different types of experiences. Therefore, their impact on children and families is also likely to vary (King, 2002). This makes it difficult to generalize about what happens in organized youth sports and how participation affects child development and family dynamics.

When there are cuts in government spending, this limits the amount that local authorities can invest in youth sport schemes – the type in category 1. Wealthy people seldom object to this because they have the money to fund private schemes and pay membership fees in commercial schemes. However, reducing public schemes has a range of effects. It limits opportunities available to children from low-income families, and funnels those with strong interests and top skills into one or two sports for which public schemes remain. Additionally, it creates a market for private, commercial schemes that cater to those with the money to pay for their services.

Overall, this means that the opportunities and experiences available to young people are influenced by local and national politics, especially those related to taxation and public spending. At present, opportunities and experiences are strongly influenced by voters and political representatives who say that local government budgets and council tax money should not be used to fund sports for children. *What do you think?*

2008; Rosenfeld and Wise, 2001). Childhood in some segments of wealthy nations has been changed from an age of exploration and freedom to an age of preparation and controlled learning. Children's sports reflect this larger trend (Sokolove, 2004a; Wolff, 2003).

New, elite, specialized sports training schemes

The emphasis on performance is also tied to a third trend in youth sports – the development of elite, specialized training schemes (Bick, 2007; King, 2002; Sokolove, 2004a; St Louis, 2007; Wolff, 2003). Many private and commercial schemes encourage early specialization in a single sport because these schemes have year-round operating expenses that are paid from membership fees through the year.

Therefore, they develop rationales to convince parents and athletes that they must make year-round commitments to participation. As more parents accept these rationales, 'high-performance' clubs and schemes continue to grow. Commercial schemes in football, tennis, swimming, golf and other sports now boast an explicit emphasis on making children into headline-grabbing, revenue-producing sports machines. Children in these schemes even become marketing tools for scheme managers and symbols of the moral worth of parents, who pay the bills and brag to friends about their children's accomplishments and how much they have done to make their children successful (Dukes and Coakley, 2002; Mahany, 1999; Rinehart and Grenfell, 1999).

Children in high-performance training schemes work at their sports for long hours week after week and year after year (King, 2002; Wolff, 2003). They compete regularly and often generate revenues (directly and indirectly) for their coaches and families. In a sense, they become child labourers because the livelihoods of coaches and other adults often depend on their performances (Donnelly, 1997, 2000). When Formula One motor racing team McLaren signed Lewis Hamilton in 1998, he was only 15 years of age and did not have a driving licence. McLaren paid US$2 million for Hamilton, a small sum in the world of motor racing, and secured themselves a future profit-making celebrity. Jackie Stewart, a member of Jaguar's racing team, responded that: 'It's a very good idea and we could do it too … It is a small investment that can become very profitable' (in David, 2005, p. 136).

While football is the most popular and wealthiest of sports in the UK, even Premier League clubs need to produce enough professional players to trade to other clubs and use the money raised to reinvest in the system. For example, Liverpool Football Club invested more than £10 million in its academy which opened in 1999. They accept children from the age of 7 in order to train them from a very young age to reach a high standard of play, so that they are a useful commodity to be traded for commercial gain, and the club can reap the benefits of its investment. Of course, the reality is that very few players will make it into the professional game and, if they have sacrificed their education, they have limited alternative career options when the club decides that they are no longer useful to them. While this is recognized by the Football Association, the practice still continues:

> Not all players who are successful in gaining entry to Football Academies and Centres of Excellence, will make it as established professionals. Some will be 'released' by their clubs. Boys and parents/guardians need to be realistic and appreciate the extremely small chance of successfully overcoming all the obstacles to become an established professional.
>
> *(The Football Association, 2004)*

Existing child labour laws in many post-industrial societies prevent adults from using children as sources of financial gain in other occupations, but these laws have not always been applied to sport. In many nations, there remain limited government regulations to protect the child athletes' interests, bodies, health and overall psychosocial development.

In the UK, the Children (Performances) Regulations Act 1968 stated that children under 16 must be licensed if they require absence from school or receive payment for performing in their sport. Once licensed, any income received from the child's performances can only be spent by their parents for maintenance, protection and education, the rest is put into a trust for when the child becomes an adult. This legislation is designed to protect the child athlete from financial exploitation. In 2001, the Child Protection in Sport Unit was established in partnership with the National Society for the Prevention of Cruelty to Children (NSPCC). This was the first of its kind in the world, and focuses on providing education, training and advice for protecting child athletes, as well as dealing with any allegations of abuse. Any sports association which applies for public funding must have a child protection policy in place to be eligible. And some individual sports have extended this: for example, if a club or scheme wishes to become a Football Association (FA) Academy or Centre of Excellence, it must comply with a charter for quality which includes staff screening, a child protection policy and periodic inspections. The Code of Conduct of such schemes is designed to ensure that the activities offered are appropriate to the age, maturity and experience of the child (see David, 2005).

Despite these advances, it remains difficult to enforce standards regulating what child athletes do or what happens to them in these elite specialized schemes. For example, coaches often need no credentials. This is particularly the case in sports which depend on volunteer coaches. They can use fear, intimidation and coercion to turn a few children into medal-winning athletes and damage other, 'less talented' children in the process. The results of this situation are sometimes frightening, resulting in illness, injury and, in some cases, sports have been used by people who want to gain easy access to children for illegal sexual activities (see Chapter 6; Coakley, 1994; Coakley and Donnelly, 2004; David, 2005; Ryan, 1995). The emphasis on elite specialized training even takes place within some schools. Specialist Sports Colleges have been established during the twenty-first century, with a stated aim 'to give pupils the opportunity to achieve their potential in sport' (DCMS, 1999). These, along with fee-paying public schools, routinely recruit accomplished sports performers, and many have large budgets for school sports, including paying for full-time coaches and high-standard facilities. Sociologists, some parents and others now are asking serious questions about how this new emphasis on elite training affects the health and development of children (Brackenridge, 2001; Brackenridge et al. 2007a; David, 2005; Gorman, 2005; Pennington, 2005; Sokolove, 2004a).

 To deliver a successful Olympic Games and Paralympic Games with a sustainable legacy and get more children and young people taking part in high quality PE and sport.

(PE and Sport Strategy for Young People, 2008)

Increased involvement and concerns among parents

Youth sports have become serious business in many families. The expectation that good parents control the actions and nurture the dreams of their children 24 hours a day has made parenthood today more demanding than ever before. Many parents now feel compelled to find the best organized youth sports schemes for their children and ensure that their children's interests are being met in those schemes.

Even though many factors influence child development today, many people attribute the success or failure of children entirely to their parents. When children are successful in sports, their parents are perceived to be parenting the correct way. For example, when Lewis Hamilton began winning races, everyone labelled Anthony Hamilton, his father, as a good and wise parent. The same thing is happening with Judy Murray, the mother of tennis players Andy and Jamie Murray, and Rob Daley, the father of diver Tom Daley, who was the youngest member of the Great Britain Olympic team in Beijing 2008 at age 14. When children succeed, parents are labelled 'good parents' and are even asked by other parents how they did it. When a child fails, people question the moral worth of the parents.

Under these conditions, a child's success in sports is especially important for many parents. Youth sports are highly visible activities and become sites where mums and dads can establish and prove their moral worth as parents. This greatly increases the stakes associated with youth sports. When parental moral worth is linked with a child's achievements in sports, parents take youth sports very seriously.

The stakes associated with youth sports are increased even further when parents expect their children to benefit financially, earn professional contracts as athletes, or gain social acceptance and popularity in school and among peers. When parents think in these terms, the success of their children in youth sports is linked to anticipated social and financial pay-offs.

As the moral, financial and social stakes associated with youth sports participation have increased, youth sports have become sites for extreme actions among some adults (Engh, 1999; Farrey, 2008; Nack and Munson, 2000). Parents may be assertive and disruptive as they advocate the interests of their children with coaches and organizers of youth sport schemes. Some parents are belligerent and disruptive as they scream criticisms of coaches, referees, players and their own children. A few have even attacked other people over sports-related disagreements (see Chapter 6). The child athlete may then also be affected by this, as illustrated in the words of one British gymnast who explained how she did not feel able to give up the sport: 'It would break my dad's heart if I gave up. It means everything to him' (cited in David, 2005, p. 218).

These cases have led to calls for parent education combined with new rules and enforcement procedures to control adults associated with youth sports. These are appropriate strategies, but to be successful they must be administered with an understanding of the context in which parenting occurs today. As long as parental moral worth is linked to the achievements of their children, and parents feel morally obliged to nurture the sports dreams of their children, mothers and fathers will be deeply involved in and concerned about their children's youth sports participation. Furthermore, when parents make major financial sacrifices and invest vast amounts of time in their children's sports without receiving from local authorities the support that families through history have always needed to thrive, their actions will be difficult to control. When cultural ideology emphasizes that parents are solely responsible for their children, mothers and fathers will assertively advocate the interests of their children. If they do not, who will? Under these cultural circumstances, many parents conclude that it is their moral obligation to put pressure on anyone standing in the way of their child's success in sports.

Increased interest in alternative and action sports

As organized schemes have become increasingly exclusive, structured and performance orientated, some young people have sought alternatives allowing them to engage more freely in physical activities on their own terms. Because organized youth sports are the most visible and widely accepted settings for children's sport participation, these unstructured and participant-controlled activities are referred to as alternative sports – alternatives, that is, to organized sports.

Alternative sports, or 'lifestyle' or 'action' sports as they are also known, encompass a wide array of physical activities. Their popularity is based in part on children's reactions against the highly structured character of adult-controlled, organized sports. For example, when legendary skateboarder Tony Hawk was asked why he chose to skateboard rather than do other sports, he said, 'I liked having my own pace and my own rules … and making up my own challenges' (in Finger, 2004, p. 84). When we observe children in action sports, we are regularly amazed by the physical skills that they develop without adult coaches and scheduled practices and contests. Although we are concerned about injury rates and the sexism that often is a part of these activities, we are impressed by the discipline and dedication of children who seek challenges away from adult-controlled sports settings. The norms in these participant-controlled activities vary from one location to another, but most young people use them as guides as they share the spaces used in their sports (Rinehart and Grenfell, 2002).

Mark Shaw, winner of the first International Mountain Board Championships in 2000, explained that action sports often are attractive to young people because the older and more skilled participants teach tricks and give helpful advice to those with less experience. He explained, 'I look forward to helping young skaters … at the park each weekend almost as much as I look forward to skating and my own progression on the board' (2002, p. 3). Many young people find this orientation and the sense of community it creates to be more welcoming than what occurs in organized youth sport schemes.

Participation in alternative and action sports has become so widespread that media companies and corporations wishing to turn young people into consumers have sponsored competitive forms of these sports and now hype them as 'extreme' and high-risk activities. These sponsored events, such as the X Games, provide exposure and material support for athletes, but they alter the activities by making them more structured and controlled. At this point, we need research on the ways that this occurs and its implications for the participation experiences of young people. Adult intervention in these activities remains relatively limited, but in the future we will see skateboard and BMX coaches and organized schemes. If this occurs, some children will seek other opportunities to play sports on their own terms.

Different Experiences: Informal, Player-Controlled Sports Versus Organized, Adult-Controlled Sports

We have interviewed many children about their sports experiences and watched children play sports in different settings. We have learned that individual children define and interpret personal experiences in many ways. But we have also discovered that experiences among children differ, depending on whether sports are informally organized and controlled by the players themselves or are formally organized and controlled by adults.

Many children seek alternatives to adult-controlled youth sports. Some of these are related to the 'extreme' sports seen in televised events and the videotapes that are made, duplicated and circulated by the participants themselves. When you create your own sports, you have experiences very different from that of organised youth sports (*Source: Rocky Mountain News*)

Our findings indicate that informal, player-controlled sports are primarily action centred, whereas formal, adult-controlled sports are primarily rule centred. This means that, when children create their own activities and games, they emphasize movement and excitement. But when they play sports that are organized and controlled by adults, the adults emphasize learning and following rules.

The different experiences in these two versions of youth sports have important implications for what children learn, the meanings they give to their experiences and the ways they integrate sports into their lives (Baker and Coté, 2006). Despite this, research on this issue has been scarce after the 1980s. This is due to three factors. First, there has been a rapid and continuous decline in the informal games played by children. Second, parents have increasingly objected to anyone studying their children's lives. Third, the 'human subjects' and Research Ethics Review Committees at most universities have regularly demanded that researchers obtain written approval from all parents whose children might be interviewed or observed in a study – even when the study involves hundreds of children on dozens of teams, or children who spontaneously create games played in parks, school grounds, streets, car parks, driveways and gardens.

AT YOUR *fingertips*:
See the OLC – Additional Readings for Chapter 5 – for a summary of Coakley's research on informal games and organized sports.

For these reasons, most recent studies focus on organized youth sports but seldom involve in-depth or spontaneous conversations with children playing informal games. There is no recent research that compares the experiences of young people in organized, adult-controlled sports with their experiences in other types of sports and physical activities. However, we can use research from a variety of disciplines to identify the full range of experiences available to young people and to think critically about the merits of organized schemes. This will help us determine whether the organized sports that exist today are worth all the time, money and effort that adults put into them. The following sections provide more complete descriptions of these two types of participation setting.

Informal, player-controlled sports

We have observed informally organized, player-controlled sports in gardens, parks, car parks and school playgrounds, and we have interviewed hundreds of children. The data indicate that when children create games and play on their own, they are interested in four things:

1 action, especially action leading to scoring
2 personal involvement in the action
3 a challenging or exciting experience (for example, a close score in a competitive contest)
4 opportunities to reaffirm friendships during games.

Informal games usually had 2 to 12 players, all or mostly boys. The players often knew each other from games played previously. In most cases, they formed teams quickly, using skill differences and friendship patterns as criteria for choosing teams. Initiating and maintaining games usually involved complex dynamics; success depended on the players' abilities to manage interpersonal relationships and make decisions accepted as fair by their peers.

Games and game rules often resembled those used in organized schemes, but they contained modifications to maximize action, scoring and personal involvement, while keeping the scores close. Action-producing strategies involved eliminating free throws in basketball, reducing the distance between stumps in cricket, and adapting the size of the goal in football. Similar action-producing rules existed in other informal games, and they generally resulted in extremely high scores.

Personal involvement was maximized through rule qualifications and handicap systems. Restrictive handicaps were sometimes used to keep highly skilled players from dominating games, for example, a player in cricket would be removed after they had scored a certain number of runs or bowled out a player. Other handicaps advantaged less skilled players, by, for example, giving them second chances to serve in tennis or volleyball or compensate for the effects of their mistakes on the outcomes of games. This saved them personal embarrassment and preserved their integrity as contributing members of their teams. It also kept game scores close. The overuse of these special rules was usually discouraged through jests and teasing. When children were asked to name the biggest source of fun in their games, they almost always referred to hitting, catching, kicking, scoring or another form of action in which they were personally involved.

Maintaining order in informal games depended on the extent to which players were committed to maintaining action. Usually, when children were personally involved in the game, they were more committed to maintaining action. Social control strategies were used most often to keep players from disrupting action in the games. Players joked around and even ignored rules, but norm violations were allowed unless they interfered with the flow of action.

Our observations of these games uncovered many performance styles and 'moves', and these were accepted as normal if they did not disrupt action in the games. The players with the greatest skill also had the most freedom to be creative because they usually could do so without upsetting game action or interfering with the personal involvement of other players.

Social status among players was important because it determined which individuals became involved in decision-making processes during the games. The older or more skilled players usually had the highest status. Disagreements were usually resolved in creative ways and seldom destroyed the games. When children played together often, they became more skilled at solving conflicts.

A word of caution: these summary descriptions of informal sports do not apply to all occasions when children create their own games. Problems in informal games do occur. Bigger and stronger children occasionally exploit smaller and weaker ones. Girls sometimes are patronized or dismissed when they try to play with groups of boys, and children excluded from games often feel rejected by their peers.

Additionally, the dynamics of games usually vary with the availability of play spaces and equipment. For example, when a large group uses the only basketball court in a neighbourhood, the games exclude many children who want to play. The team that wins takes on challengers, rather than giving up the court to others, and those with less developed skills are not given concessions when it comes to participation. Taking turns is rare when there are more players than spaces to play. However, when there are many courts and only a few players, the goal is often to accommodate everyone's interests so that nobody leaves and forces the game to end. This is a major reason that the informal games of children in low-income areas with few facilities and resources are often different from the games played by children in higher-income areas where facilities are more plentiful and there is little or no competition for space (Carlston, 1986). Clearly, then, external conditions in the society as a whole have important effects on the way children play informal games. Most of the children who we observed and interviewed were from neighbourhoods where competition for space was not a major issue.

Formal, adult-controlled sports

Our observations and interviews done in connection with formally organized, adult-controlled sports focused on children between 8 and 12 years old. The data indicated that, even though the children valued action and personal involvement, they were concerned about playing well and winning games. Most apparent in these games was that they were strictly regulated by formal rules. Adults, including coaches, umpires, referees and other game officials, enforced these rules.

Children in these sports often were concerned with the positions they played on their teams. They even referred to themselves as 'goalkeepers' or 'strikers', as 'forwards' or 'backs', as 'bowlers' or 'wicketkeepers'. The importance of positions was also emphasized by the coaches and spectators, who encouraged players to 'stay in position' during games. This happened regularly in all sports in which the players were constantly on the move, such as football and rugby.

Adult-controlled schedules governed organized sports. Individual playing time varied by skill levels, and less skilled children played least often. Every player was in the game for at least

Organized youth sports are a luxury item in most of the world. The parents of this 10-year-old Kenyan boy do not have the resources to nurture his sports dreams. But using his bare feet and a ball of rags bound with twine, he has managed to develop impressive football skills. The meaning he gives to kicking this ball likely differs from the meanings that privileged 10-year-old British boys give to kicking dozens of 'official footballs' provided by parents (*Source*: Kevin Young)

a short time, but the children whose playing time was low often seemed uninterested in what occurred on the pitch. The highly skilled players showed strong interest in games and expressed disappointment when they were taken out of the line-up.

A consequence of adult control and organization was the visible absence of arguments and overt displays of hostility between players from opposing teams. There were occasional arguments between officials and coaches or spectators, and between teammates. Arguments between teammates usually were caused by a player's inability to remember game rules, stay in position or carry out the strategies developed by the adults.

Adult control and **formal structure** (that is, *established rules plus roles or positions*) kept children organized, but they also seemed to limit visible displays of affection and friendship during the games. This made it difficult to determine which children were friends. However, interpersonal relationships among the players had little to do with how the games were played because players made so few decisions.

The major purpose of game rules was to standardize the competition and control the players. Rules and rule enforcement regularly caused breaks in the action, but the players did not seem to resent this. The only signs of displeasure came when delays were caused by penalties called against a player's team. Rule enforcement (social control) in these games was based on players' self-control and obedience, but it ultimately rested in the hands of adults: coaches, referees and game officials. Adults usually applied the rules universally and seldom made exceptions, even when there were differences in players' abilities and characteristics. The coaches' strict application of rules restricted players' freedom, but players seldom violated rules.

When deviance occurred, it was more often caused by players forgetting or not knowing what to do than by blatantly ignoring the rules. On the playing field, rule infractions usually were accompanied by formal sanctions, even if they did not affect game action or outcomes. Off the field, rules varied from one team to another, and violations usually involved 'joking around' or exhibiting a lack of interest in the game or the team. Responses to these actions also varied. Coaches and parents used verbal and non-verbal sanctions to control players, preserve the organization of the game and maintain the authority of referees and coaches.

The children in organized sports were serious about their games, and they wanted to win although they were seldom obsessed with winning. Those most concerned with winning were the highly skilled players and members of the most successful teams. Although they had other goals, the principal goal of most players was to have fun. However, they usually knew their win–loss record and the place of their team in league standings. The players were disappointed if they did not get to play as much as they thought they deserved. Playing time was very important because it was related to the children's reputations among peers. Status on the teams, however, usually depended on relationships with coaches or parents who were active in organizing the clubs or teams.

Finally, the games in organized sports were extremely stable. Games did not end until the rules said they were over, regardless of the quality of play or enjoyment among the players. Adults' whistles, along with verbal encouragement, commands and advice, were ever present in these games.

Analysis of differences

The personal experiences of children in these two sports forms are very different. Informal sports are action centred, whereas organized sports are rule centred. Which of these experiences is more valuable in the development of children? The answer to this question is important to children and the adults who invest so much time, money and energy in organized schemes.

Research on this issue indicates that each experience makes different positive contributions to the lives of children, and neither experience is without problems. However, people traditionally overrate the contributions of participation in organized sports and underrate the contributions of participation in informal sports (Schultz, 1999).

Playing informal sports clearly involves the use of interpersonal and decision-making skills. Children must be creative to organize games and keep them going. They encounter dozens of unanticipated challenges requiring on-the-spot decisions and interpersonal abilities. They learn how to organize games, form teams, co-operate with peers, develop rules, and take responsibility for following and enforcing rules. These are important lessons, many of which are not learned in adult-controlled organized sports. Although we do not know how or to what extent the learning that occurs in these informal sports carries over to other settings, we can assume that children are influenced by their experiences.

Playing organized sports, on the other hand, involves different experiences. Organized sports help children learn to manage relationships with adult authority figures. Children also learn the rules and strategies used in activities that are defined as important in the culture and, through their participation, they often gain status that carries over to other parts of their lives. When they play organized sports, they learn about formal structures, rule-governed teamwork and adult models of work and achievement (Adler and Adler, 1998). A possible problem in organized sports is that children may learn to view the world in passive terms, as something that is given rather than created. If this occurs, children grow up thinking they are powerless to change the world in which they live.

It is important to recognize that some games fall between the two types described in this section. For example, there are informal games in which an adult provides subtle guidance to children, who control most of what occurs. There are also organized games in which adults let children handle many things on their own. These 'hybrids' are valuable contexts for learning. The adults in such games often say that it takes tact and patience to put up with children's mistakes and oversights. They also say that it is a joy to see the creativity and compassion shown by many children, who respond to adult suggestions and subtle encouragement.

Sociological Questions about Youth Sports

Dozens of questions could be raised in this section, and we have chosen three that people who work with children ought to be able to answer as they plan schemes and make policies related to youth sports.

When are children ready to play organized competitive sports?

Development issues are a concern for many parents who want to know when their child should begin playing sports. In general, it is *never* too early for a child to engage in expressive physical activities. In fact, the more activity, the better; and the more socially and physically diverse the activities, the better (American Academy of Pediatrics, 2000). But to put 4- and 5-year-olds in organized competitive sports is much like creating a system of arranged marriages for 12-year-olds – children at this age have not learned what they love, nor are they ready to make commitments based on their choices. Additionally, when children begin playing organized sports early and specialize in one or two sports year round they are more likely than other children to suffer overuse injuries and burnout (Coakley, 2008; Côté and Fraser-Thomas, 2007).

Contributing to burnout and dropout is the fact that most children under 8 years old do not yet have the cognitive and social abilities they need to fully or meaningfully comprehend competitive relationships (Côté and Fraser-Thomas, 2007; Selman, 1971). A prerequisite for understanding competition is being able to form and nurture co-operative relationships, which are the foundation of orderly competitive sports. When children are signed up for competitive schemes before they have had the chance to play informal games, they often lack the experience they need to understand their role in creating fair and ethical competition in organized games. This can make them difficult to coach and lead to frustrations, causing them to drop out (Coakley, 2008).

Coaches unwittingly contribute to burnout and dropout when they try to teach complex team strategies to children under 12 years old (Côté and Fraser-Thomas, 2007). For example, to understand one's position in any team sport a player must do three things simultaneously: (1) mentally visualize the ever-changing locations of all teammates and opponents over the entire field, (2) assess the spatial relationships between all players relative to the ball, and (3) synthesize this information to determine where one's position should be. Because most children younger than 12 do not have the cognitive ability and social experience to think in these terms, coaches must condition them to stay 'in position'. But doing the repetitive drills and plays over and over again to condition the players makes training so boring that children often lose interest; at their age they cannot appreciate the need for such an approach. To make things worse, when they play games, the coaches and their parents are constantly yelling at them to 'spread out' and 'get in position'. This is so distracting that many children do not fully enjoy the experience of participation.

Research shows that informal games help children learn to co-operate and express themselves through a wider range of movements than they would try if coaches were evaluating them (Ginsburg, 2007; Henricks, 2006). For example, André Mérelle, the director of youth football development in France, explains why they emphasize the importance of unstructured play and informal games for French children:

> Everyone wants to win games. That's good. But *how* do you win? If you're too focused on winning games, you don't learn to play well. You get too nervous, because you're always afraid to make errors.
>
> *(In Farrey, 2008, p. 75)*

The French developmental approach emphasizes informal play – no uniforms, positions, lined fields, game clocks, league standings or adults yelling instructions from the sidelines, and the success of the national team and players like Thierry Henry and Zinadine Zidane would suggest it works. Without the constraining structures and adult expectations that characterize organized youth sports, young people learn to improvise, feel the joy of intrinsic satisfaction and develop a playing style and personality that makes them unique. This allows them to claim ownership of football rather than feeling that football owns them. Further, as French coaches explain, informal games are the places where children develop a personal 'feel' for the game and a vision for what occurs and is possible on the field of play – things that are not learned as readily in organized, adult-controlled games in which the structure and rhythm of play are dictated by rules, coaches and referees. This was the basis of the 'teaching games for under-standing' model, developed by British physical education lecturers David Bunker and Rod Thorpe in the 1980s, which stresses that young people need to learn to play through modified games which they develop themselves as they see the outcome of actions and behaviours, rather than more traditional and directive styles of play.

Consensus among sport development experts worldwide is that children under 8 years old should not play highly organized sports or on (football) teams with more than five players (Farrey, 2008). From 8 to 14 years old, games can be increasingly organized, but positional play should not be emphasized, there should be no more than one game per week or 30–35 games per year. Most important, say the experts, is that all coaches must complete a coaching education course and be regularly re-certified through continuing coach education. When coaches learn about child development they can facilitate participation opportunities through which young people are likely to develop a passion for the sport and the awareness that the sport enables them to be creative and expressive.

Developmental research supports the approach used in French football (Bloom, 1985; Côté and Fraser-Thomas, 2007). When Benjamin Bloom, a noted educational psychologist, studied 120 individuals who were recognized world-class talents in classical piano, sculpting, mathematics, Olympic swimming, professional tennis and neurological research, he concluded that talent development occurred over a long period of time under special conditions. In all cases, the talent development process began with exploration, play and expressive fun. It did not begin with structured activities organized by other people, early specialization or childhood commitments to long-term goals. Nor did it begin with pep talks about hard work, sacrifice, dedication and the need to practise constantly. It began with opportunities to freely and playfully explore an activity and discover that it permitted them to be creative and expressive. Talent development ultimately depended on whether the young people emotionally bonded with the activity, claimed it as their own and identified what they wanted to learn so they could master a set of skills. When this occurred, the young people came to be driven by the feelings of exhilaration that occurred as they met and mastered new challenges. Bloom found that this process took at least 10 years to occur but, when it did, the young people, usually in their mid-teens, were ready to specialize and make the commitments required to excel. At this point, fun merged with the hard work of mastering skills, and this merger fuelled the passion and drive that enabled them to achieve excellence.

Bloom's findings have been widely supported by other scholars who study the development of excellence in sports (Côté and Fraser-Thomas, 2007). For example, we know that the existence of informal games and sports requires and fosters creativity, interpersonal skills and problem-solving abilities among the players (Côté and Fraser-Thomas, 2007; Elkind, 2007, 2008). Creating games requires knowledge of game models, but maintaining them in the face of multiple unanticipated challenges requires keen conflict resolution skills and an ability to develop on-the-spot solutions to problems. Players must understand the basic requirements of an organized activity so they can create games to fit here-and-now circumstances; additionally, they must form teams, co-operate with peers, develop rules and take responsibility for following and enforcing rules (Adler and Adler, 1998). These are important lessons, and we need research to explain when and how children learn them in different types of sports experiences, and whether the learning that occurs in sports is used by children in their relationships and activities apart from sports.

What are the dynamics of family relationships in connection with organized youth sports?

Organized youth sports require time, money and organizational skills, and these usually come from parents. Therefore, playing organized sports is often a family affair. However, few sociologists have done research on how youth sports participation affects family relationships.

Anecdotal information and a few studies indicate that youth sports can bring family members together in supportive ways or create problems in family relationships. Parents may become so emotionally involved with sports that they put pressure on their children or fail to see that their children perceive their encouragement as pressure to play well and stay involved in sports. When children feel such pressure, they face a triple dilemma: (1) if they quit sports, they fear that their parents may withdraw support and attention; (2) if they play sports but do not perform well, they fear their parents will criticize them; (3) if they perform well, they fear that their parents will treat them like 'mini professionals' and never let them do other things.

Organized youth sports have an impact on families and family relationships in other ways as well. Research shows that organized sport schemes for children could not exist without the volunteer labour of parents, especially mothers (Chafetz and Kotarba, 1999; Thompson, 1999a, 1999b). Mothers drive children to training and games, prepare meals at convenient times, wash dirty training clothes and uniforms, and make sure that equipment is ready. They undertake fund-raising activities for clubs, and purchase, prepare and serve food at social events. Mothers also manage the activities of brothers and sisters who are not playing games, and they provide emotional support for their child-athletes when they play poorly or when coaches or fathers criticize them. Fathers also provide labour, but it is devoted primarily to on-the-field and administrative matters such as coaching, and serving on committees.

When parental labour occurs in this pattern, youth sports reproduce a gendered division of labour in families, clubs and the minds of children, especially the boys who are treated as 'son-gods' as they play organized sports. More research is needed on this and other aspects of family dynamics that exist in connection with youth sports. For example, we know little about fatherhood and sports, a topic that is important to consider as expectations for parents become more demanding and wives demand more assistance from their husbands (Coakley, 2006).

How do social factors influence youth sport experiences?

Children make choices about playing sports, but they have little control over the context in which they make their choices. Many factors, including parents, peers and the general social and cultural contexts in which they live, influence the alternatives from which they choose, and how they define and give meaning to their choices. For example, children from low-income backgrounds generally have many fewer sports participation opportunities than other children. Children who live in rural areas may have greater freedom than those living in inner-city areas, but they often suffer from poor transport and long distances to get to facilities, and less variety in what is available in their area. Children with able bodies have more opportunities and receive more encouragement to play sports than do children with disabilities. Choosing to play a contact sport, such as rugby or boxing, is seen by most people around the world to be more appropriate for boys than for girls. Boys who want to do gymnastics or dance do not receive the same encouragement from peers as girls receive. Racial and ethnic stereotypes often influence the sports participation choices made by people who learn to associate certain sports and physical skills with various skin colours and cultural backgrounds (for a comprehensive review of each of these social factors, see Hayes and Stidder, 2003).

None of these statements is earth-shaking. People know these things. They know that, as children make sport choices and give meaning to their experiences, they and the people around them are influenced by prevailing cultural beliefs about age, gender, sexuality, race and ethnicity, ability and disability, and social class. This is how social forces influence youth sports experiences. This is highlighted in the 'Breaking barriers' box on pages 158–159.

Research shows that sports choices and experiences are influenced by dominant definitions of gender in society. These definitions influence early childhood experiences when it comes to physical activities (see Wellard, 2007). For example, in the UK, fathers play with their sons more often and in more physically active ways than they play with their daughters. Furthermore, the physical activity messages that most young boys receive differ from the messages many young girls receive, both inside and outside family settings (Beal, 1994; Hargreaves, 1994; Hasbrook, 1999; Kay, 2000; Kirk, 2004). Because of these messages, most children have definite ideas about their physical skills and potential before they even think about playing sports. For example, boys are more likely than girls to *think* they are better than they actually are as athletes. This affects their self-confidence and willingness to be physically active and express an interest in playing youth sports. Overall, girls learn to minimize the physical space that they occupy, sexualize their bodies through modifying appearance and movement, and accept the notion that boys are physically superior to them. And boys learn to present themselves as physically big and strong, act in ways that claim physical space around them, and assume power and control over girls in sports (Hasbrook, 1999; Hasbrook and Harris, 1999).

Gender-related expectations may be one of the reasons why boys' ball games often dominate the space on school playgrounds and in other public places. This pattern extends through the life course. For instance, observe the playing fields and gyms on a university campus and measure the amount of time that young men or young women appropriate those spaces for themselves. It is often difficult to change these male-dominant patterns because they are deeply rooted in the culture as a whole. In the case of children, it is important to focus on variations in their experiences rather than simply looking for differences related to gender, ethnicity, ability and social class. As we see how experiences vary, we learn how social forces interact with each other and influence children's lives on and off the playing field.

breaking BARRIERS

Mainstreaming barriers: *will they let me play with my brace?*

Ally was born with physical impairments – no fine motor movement in her left hand, a left leg that had to be stabilized by a brace, and a loss of 40 per cent of her left-side peripheral vision. She did not see her impairments as disabilities because she learned that every person's body was unique and capable of many things. Like other children, she developed physical skills and learned about her strengths and weaknesses. After playing football informally with her parents and sisters, and watching her older sister play on a local team, she said she wanted to play on an organized team; then she asked, 'Will they let me play with my brace?'

Ally's brace had never been an issue in her family. But as she watched sports on television, and watched her mum and sister play in local events, she had never seen athletes with leg braces. As a 6-year-old she had seen enough to wonder if there was space for her in sports.

The youth football scheme where Ally lived was covered by disability legislation which states that sports schemes cannot exclude children with disabilities unless there are direct threats to the health and safety of able-bodied participants. These threats must be real, based on objective information, and unavoidable, even *after* reasonable efforts have been made to eliminate them. In Ally's case, it was initially easy to follow the law: she wore one shin pad on the front of her leg and another on the back, and her participation did not require the league to make accommodations causing 'undue burden' or 'fundamental alteration' of the scheme (Block, 1995).

According to the law, if a team was being selected for competition, the coach could not exclude Ally because she had a disability, but Ally *could* be left out of the team for skills-related reasons. For example, her coaches could not say that all players must be able to run without a limp to make the team, but they could say that running was a prerequisite for team eligibility.

Ally had a great time playing her first year, despite surgery to lengthen her Achilles tendon and playing part of the season wearing a walking boot over her cast. But during her season as a 7-year-old, the coaches and parents put more emphasis on the performance ethic. When Ally's lack of peripheral vision caused her to collide with others and sustain a few minor injuries, she became discouraged. Her coach helped everyone on the team understand the implications of Ally's vision impairment, but it was difficult to do this with members of opposing teams. As the season progressed, some parents of Ally's teammates expressed concern that accommodating Ally was jeopardizing the team's success.

When it came time to sign up for the next season, Ally said she did not want to play. Her main complaint was not that she felt inferior in terms of skills or that she had frequent collisions, but that opposing players never asked her if she was OK after collisions left her lying on the field. Her parents explained that children playing football were not expected to say they were sorry when they knock opponents down, but Ally was not willing to accept this, especially after she had been taught to always say she was sorry if she knocked someone down. Two years later, when she began to understand this qualification, she resisted playing because she felt her skills were not as good as those of her peers. Additionally, she had seen her sister's team play and knew that 'the performance ethic' pervaded the culture of youth football. Her parents knew that even the 'recreational' teams in town emphasized the performance ethic to a degree that would make it difficult to accommodate a player with special needs and skills that would not help win games.

Ally's story is not unique: children with disabilities generally have only two options if they wish to play sports: find an organized adapted scheme, or play informal games in which peers are willing and able to develop adaptations. Unfortunately, very few communities have adapted youth sport schemes, and informal games are scarce and seldom involve children who know how to quickly or easily include a child with disabilities. As a result most children with disabilities are excluded from youth sports. Without advocates they remain on the sidelines.

This outcome was noted by a 10-year-old boy with cerebral palsy when he said that other kids 'like me but ... if I'm trying to get in a game without a friend, it's kind of hard' (in Taub and Greer, 2000, p. 406). In other words, without a friend who has enough power with peers and enough experience with disabilities to facilitate a process of adaptation and inclusion, this 10-year-old does not play sports.

Other children with disabilities describe their experiences with these statements: (a) '[Kids] try and shove me off the court, [and] tell me not to play', (b) 'they just don't want me on their team', and (c) 'there's a couple of people that won't let me play' (in Taub and Greer, 2000, p. 406). When these things occur, children with disabilities miss opportunities to make friends and participate in activities that have 'normalizing' effects in a culture where sports often are contexts for gaining social acceptance and self-validation.

Although the achievement of inclusion requires sensitivity, experience and effort, it is worth it when children – in this case, children with cerebral palsy – say things like this:

> [Playing games] makes me feel good 'cause I get to be with everybody … and talk about how our day was in school while we play.

> Playing basketball is something that I can do with my friends that I never thought I could do [with them], but I can, I can!
>
> *(In Taub and Greer, 2000, pp. 406, 408)*

Eliminating barriers to mainstreaming is a challenge, but when we are creative and open to expanding our experiences, it is not impossible.

Sports and Education

Physical education and school sports

Physical education in schools in the UK has come a long way since the early days of the military-style 'drill' activities of the nineteenth century, and the free-standing Ling gymnastics of the early twentieth century. These activities were largely grounded in a belief that young children, particularly those from the working classes, needed to be disciplined and controlled. Meanwhile, physical education in public schools enabled upper-class children to develop character and leadership skills through team games.

By 1933, a new physical education (PE) syllabus identified a relationship between exercise and health, encouraging physical activity for all school-aged children. During the 1950s, PE became increasingly gendered and was segregated on the grounds of sex, with boys playing football and cricket, and girls being offered hockey and netball.

The British education system changed dramatically during the 1990s, largely as a result of the new National Curriculum and Education Reform Act. The current National Curriculum for Physical Education (NCPE) requires schools to deliver six categories of activities: athletics, dance, games, gymnastics, outdoor and adventurous activities, and swimming and water safety. The curriculum area has also been 're-branded' as physical education and school sports (PESS) to move away from traditional and confusing attempts to distinguish between 'PE' and 'sport'. Schools have been required to deliver a minimum of two hours of physical education and school sports per week to pupils within and beyond the curriculum. Physical education and sports studies are now examinable subjects, with GCSE and A level qualifications available in schools. (For an overview of the development of physical education and school sports, see Armour and Kirk, 2008; Craig and Beedie, 2008.)

Many secondary schools have successfully applied for 'specialist' status, becoming Specialist Sports Colleges, and these now constitute approximately 10 per cent of all secondary schools in the UK. Since 2000, these have been connected to other secondary schools and their primary feeder schools through the school sport co-ordinator (SSCo) programme. The SSCo's role is to work with a 'family' of schools to plan and deliver sport and physical education programmes, and to develop links with clubs and the wider community.

There are now four key elements within physical education and school sport: lifelong activity, lifelong participation, sports development and talent development. These are to be delivered within the curriculum, in school but outside the formal curriculum, in competitive school sports, and through links with local clubs (see Figure 5.1).

In 2002, the government launched a national strategy for Physical Education, School Sport and Club Links (PESSCL), and in 2008 this strategy was extended to increase opportunities for children to take part in more sports. The new PE and Sport Strategy for Young People (PESSYP) makes a 'Five Hour Offer'. This aims to provide children with a minimum of two hours of physical education and sport at school, and a further three hours of sporting activity through school or community providers, each week. The government claims to be investing more than £2 billion in this strategy.

A particular trend in the UK has been the increasing prominence of competitive elite-level sport for young people since 2005 when London was awarded the rights to host the 2012 Summer Olympic Games. The government has a stated ambition to implement a high-quality school sport national competition framework by 2010. This includes a National School Sport Week, the UK School Games (a multi-sports event for the most talented school-age athletes), a National Talent Orientation Camp and a network of Young Ambassadors to promote Olympic and Paralympic values. Various funding opportunities have been made available to enable school and college students to combine study with elite performance. These include the Talented Athlete Scholarship Scheme (TASS), Sports Aid, Gifted and Talented Programme, World Class Pathway Programme (WCPP) and Girls4Gold, aimed at talent identification and development for females aged between 17 and 25.

Underpinning these developments and policies appears to be an assumption that increasing the amount of sport that children do in schools will be inherently 'good for them', physically,

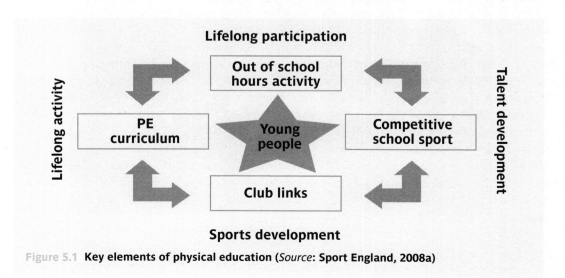

Figure 5.1 **Key elements of physical education (*Source*: Sport England, 2008a)**

psychologically, socially, educationally and morally. This is epitomized in the words of the Prime Minister as he launched National School Sport Week:

> We need to put school sport back where it belongs – playing a central role in the school day. National School Sport Week is a great opportunity to do just that and I'm confident that it will help get young people fit and physically healthy. Whatever their natural ability and whatever their age, sport and activity can make our children healthier, raise self-confidence and self-esteem. It develops teamwork, discipline and a sense of fair play. Values that will stand young people and the country in good stead in the years to come.
>
> *(Gordon Brown, British Prime Minister, 2008)*

We have questioned these assumptions earlier in this chapter, and in the next section we consider ways to improve youth sports.

Student athletes in further and higher education

The new PE and sport strategy extends to young people aged 16–19, to help them to participate in three hours each week of sporting activities through colleges or local clubs. In addition, the government has invested £16 million into extending School Sports Partnerships so that they include sport co-ordinators for further education to try to encourage higher levels of sporting

In 2008, the first National School Sport Week was held to engage young people in physical education and sport. Various competitions and festivals were held, including this one in the City of Brighton and Hove (*Source*: Elizabeth Pike)

physical activity among teenagers, who have traditionally had high 'dropout' rates from sport once it ceases to be compulsory at school. Recreational sports at universities are largely organized by the Students' Union through student-run clubs.

At the competitive level, sports are organized by British Universities and Colleges Sport (BUCS). The number of funded student-athletes has increased in recent years. There is currently limited research into the experiences of these young people in the UK, but some preliminary studies indicate that students struggle to balance the demands of academic and sporting commitments with competing pressures from their lecturers and coaches (Wightwick, 2008). This is consistent with findings from the USA where scholarship programmes for student-athletes are more extensive and established (see Coakley, 2007b). Whether at school, college or university level, it is clear that the organization and delivery of sports still could be improved to better meet the needs and requirements of young people.

Recommendations for Improving Youth Sports

Improving informal, alternative and action sports

Informal, alternative and action sports are unique because they are not controlled directly by adults. Many children opt for these sports because they seek activities without organized structures and adult control. Further, there are ways that adults can foster safety and partici- pation opportunities for children interested in action sports. For example, instead of passing laws to prohibit skateboarding or rollerblading, adults can work with young people to design and provide safe settings for them to create their own activities. If adults are not supportive of alternative sport forms, their children will use the extreme models of the X Games and other made-for-television spectacles as sole sources of inspiration.

The challenge for adults is to be supportive and provide guidance without controlling alter- native sports. Children need their own spaces in which they can be creative and expressive while they engage in physical activities. Adult guidance is crucial in making those spaces safe and open for as many children as possible – for boys and girls as well as children with disabil- ities and from various ethnic and social class backgrounds.

As the tradition of informal games has nearly disappeared among young people today, there is a need to consider ways to revive it and also to develop what might be called **hybrid sports** that *combine features of player-controlled informal games and adult-controlled organized sports*. Hybrid games have not been studied, but they come in at least two forms. *First*, there are informal games in which adults provide subtle guidance to children, who create and control most of what occurs as they play games in safe settings that are familiar and accessible to young people. *Second*, there are organized sports teams on which parents and coaches encourage unstructured or semi-structured play and games, and include children in processes of making decisions, establishing team rules, resolving conflicts and organizing relationships with teammates. As more adults learn that child development depends, in part, on engaging in play and informal games, there will be attempts to facilitate them.

Improving organized sports

When considering improvements for organized youth sports, most people agree that schemes should meet the needs of the children who participate in them. This means that children are valuable sources of information about possible changes. If children seek fun emphasizing action, involvement, close scores and friendships in their informal games, it makes sense that organized schemes also should emphasize these things. The following recommendations are based on this assumption.

Increasing action

Children emphasize *action* in their games. Much activity occurs around the scoring area, and scoring is usually so frequent that it is difficult to keep personal performance statistics. Organized sports, although they contain action, strongly emphasize rules, order, standardized conditions and predictability. The strategy of many organized teams is to prevent action, rather than stimulate it. Parents and coaches often describe high-scoring games as undisciplined free-for-alls caused by poor defensive play. The desired strategy in the minds of many adults is to stop action: bowl or catch out every batter (cricket and rounders), stall the game when you are in the lead (football and hockey), and use a safe running play to gain territory and maintain possession (rugby union and rugby league). These tactics may win games, but they limit action and scoring – the things that children define as the most exciting aspects of playing sports.

It is easy to increase action and scoring in most sports, as long as adults do not view game models as sacred and unchangeable. Bigger or more goals, smaller playing areas and fewer

Many sport schemes for younger children have decreased the size of playing fields and teams. This football scheme has three-on-three teams, there are no goalies and no scores are recorded, although some parents keep track of scores and team records. The 4- and 5-year-olds in the league are most interested in running around and kicking the ball somewhere, even if it is in the wrong direction (*Source*: Jay Coakley)

rules are the best means to increase action. Why not have two goals at each end in football and hockey, make all players eligible to receive passes and shoot in netball, and use a 6-foot basket in a half-court basketball game?

Many adults resist such changes that they think will alter game models – that is, the models used in elite, adult sports. They want children to play 'the real thing' and they forget that children are more interested in having fun than mimicking adults following institutionalized rules.

Increasing personal involvement

Children do not sit on the bench in informal games. They use rule qualifications and handicap systems to maximize personal involvement and promote action. Less skilled players may not contribute to the action as much as their more skilled peers, but they play the whole game. If they are treated badly or excluded, they leave without being branded as quitters or given lectures on commitment by their parents.

In organized games, playing time is often limited for all but the most skilled players, and the substitution process creates problems for coaches and pressure on players. Specialization by position further restricts involvement by limiting the range of experiences for players. Improvements would involve rotating players to different positions and co-ordinating group substitutions with opposing teams. Team size could be reduced (as is already done in many sports for very young children) to create more opportunities for players to be involved in the action. In football, hockey and rugby, games could be played across the width of the pitch, thereby allowing three times as many teams to compete at the same time. In basketball, the first teams could play a half-court game at one basket, while the second teams played at the other basket, and a combined score would determine the winner. These and many other revisions of games would increase personal involvement.

Creating close scores

'Good games' are those for which the outcomes are in doubt until the last play; games that go into extra time are often the best. Lopsided scores destroy the excitement of competition. Children realize this, so they usually keep their informal games close. Because motivation depends on perceived chances for success, a close game usually keeps children motivated and satisfied. Just like adults who use handicaps to keep competition interesting in golf and other sports, children adjust their games to keep them close.

In organized games, lopsided scores are common, and team records are often uneven. Keeping players motivated under these circumstances is difficult. Coaches are forced to appeal to pride and respect to motivate players in the face of lopsided scores and long, losing seasons. Ironically, when coaches urge players to develop a 'killer instinct' by taking big leads during games, it often undermines motivation among all players in the long run.

Many adults hesitate to make changes that affect the outcomes of games, but some possibilities are worth consideration. For example, they could encourage close scores by altering team rosters, using handicap systems during games or by giving the underdog an advantage such as having extra players. Many changes could keep games close; however, when game models are viewed as unchangeable, possibilities are not discussed, even though children make such changes when they play informal games.

Maintaining friendships

When children play informal and alternative sports, the reaffirmation of friendships is important. Friendships influence processes of selecting teams and the dynamics of problem-solving processes during games and activities. Organized sports provide contexts for making friends, but players need more than adult-controlled practices and games to nurture relationships with teammates and peers on other teams.

To foster friendships, coaches could help groups of players plan game tactics or coach training sessions. They could enable players to talk and interact with opponents in supportive ways during games. Too often, relationships between opponents are impersonal or hostile, and players do not learn that games have a human component that is central to having fun in competitive relationships. Most important, players should be expected to enforce game rules so that they understand why rules are necessary and how collective action depends on co-operation related to following rules. Many people claim that self-enforcement would never work (although it does in tennis). However, if organized schemes do not teach young people how to co-operate to the extent needed to play games on their own, then those schemes are *not* worth our time and effort. If young people do not learn how to play games without coaches and referees, how can adults claim that sports teach young people leadership, discipline, decision-making skills or character?

Improving high-performance sport schemes

Many of the worst problems in youth sports occur in high-performance schemes. To deal with these problems, sociologist Peter Donnelly (1993) has called on the governing bodies of all sports to do two things:

1 change their policies, procedures and rules to account for the rights and interests of children

2 create less controlling sport environments designed to promote children's growth, development and empowerment

Because people in sports organizations often have vested interests in maintaining the status quo, Donnelly advocates that some form of child labour laws be developed and enforced so that children might be protected from overzealous parents and coaches (see Cartoon 5.2). This is a suggestion that deserves serious consideration as overuse and other injury rates increase among children in elite sports schemes. Past experience in the UK and many other nations indicates that, when the status and incomes of adults depend on the work or performance of children, children need formal protection from an agency that is concerned with their well-being more than the medals and championships they win.

In football, the 'Give Us Back Our Game!' campaign has been designed by people who are concerned with these very issues. The aim of this campaign is to provide a safe environment for children to play football and experiment with playing styles as free as possible from adult intervention. It summarizes its concerns as follows:

> Football for children is now very different from earlier generations when the only adult involvement was a call from your mum that your tea was ready. Football is no longer beautiful for our kids: it's ugly.

> ('Give Us Back Our Game!', 2008)

In addition to the national Child Protection in Sport Unit, many governing bodies of sport have also developed their own child protection accreditation programmes. For example, in football there is the FA Charter mark and in gymnastics the Gym mark. The Swim 21 and Aquamark schemes in swimming were developed by the Amateur Swimming Association after a coach, Paul Hickson, was found guilty of abusing swimmers in his charge (see Chapter 6). In Ireland, the Irish Sports Council and the Sports Council for Northern Ireland opted to adopt a Code of Ethics and Good Practice for Children's Sport in Ireland. This promotes a child-centred approach to sport, taking into account the United Nations Convention on the Rights of the Child, stating: 'As citizens, adults have a responsibility to protect children from harm and to abide by government guidelines in responding to and reporting child protection concerns' (in David, 2005, p. 243). Each of these schemes is designed to improve high-performance sports while protecting the well-being of the young people involved in these schemes.

Prospects for Improving Youth Sports

Many youth sport schemes have made changes that reflect a concern for the needs and well-being of children. Research identifies excellent models for making creative and progressive changes in youth sports (Chalip and Green, 1998; Morris and Stiehl, 1989; Murphy, 1999; Torbert, 2004, 2005). However, the approach most often used to guide changes in youth sports

'How many times have I told you to practise your basketball before you even think of homework?'

Cartoon 5.2 **The fame and fortune of some professional athletes may encourage some parents to overemphasize youth sports in the lives of their children. Might this turn young athletes into 'child workers'?**

is grounded in functionalist theory (see Chapter 2), and focuses primarily on increasing the efficiency and organization of existing schemes and maximizing the physical skills of athletes.

A functionalist orientation often leads to an emphasis on coaching education schemes and tough rules regulating the actions of parents, spectators, players and coaches. But, at the same time, it also leads to increased emphasis on the performance ethic and more tournaments and championships, which has been especially the case in the UK since the award of the 2012 Olympic Games to London. Furthermore, as local schemes align with national organizations, the people who run those organizations decide how to define 'improvements' and what should be changed in youth sports. Most of these organizations run schemes that are commercial and 'excellence orientated', and they appeal to parents who mistakenly equate excellence in sports with overall child development.

Coaching education schemes could be a tool for changing this trend in youth sports. Most coaching education emphasizes putting athletes' needs ahead of winning, but it never teaches coaches how to critically assess the sports schemes or general organizational contexts in which they work with young people. It does not teach coaches how to make structural changes in schemes or create alternatives to existing schemes. Instead, coaching education generally assumes that existing youth sports schemes are pretty good, but they could be better if coaches were more organized and used more applied sports science as they work with child athletes. The dependence on win–loss records to measure coaching effectiveness intensifies this approach.

One thing to be avoided in coaching education is a 'techno science approach' emphasizing control and skill development rather than human development. If this happens, coaches become 'sports efficiency experts' rather than teachers who help young people become responsible and informed decision makers about physical activity and sports in their lives. Unfortunately, we do not yet know of any organized youth sports scheme or coaching education scheme with a mission statement declaring that the goal is to help child athletes become decision makers who control their sport lives and the contexts in which they play sports. Such a mission statement would be based on critical rather than functionalist theory.

Summary: Are Organized Youth Sports Schemes Worth the Effort?

Although physical activities exist in all cultures, organized youth sports are a luxury. They require resources and discretionary time among children and adults. They exist only when children are not required to work and only when adults believe that experiences during childhood influence overall growth and development. Youth sports have a unique history in every society in which they exist. However, they characteristically emphasize experiences and values that are central to the dominant culture of the society in which they exist.

The growth of organized sports in the UK and much of the rest of Europe, as well as elsewhere in the developed world, is associated with changes in the family that occurred during the latter half of the twentieth century. Many parents now see organized sports as vehicles to control children and ensure that boys and girls have access to important developmental experiences.

Major trends in youth sports today include the privatization of organized schemes, an emphasis on the performance ethic, the development of high-performance training schemes

'I'll say this only once, Dad. You turn on the camera, I walk off the court.'

Cartoon 5.3 Many children who play sports do not enjoy videotapes of their games, meets and matches. They would rather remember their experiences in their own terms. Too often, the tapes are used to identify mistakes and make youth sports more important than children want them to be

and increased involvement among parents. In response to these trends, some young people have turned to informal, alternative and action sports that they can control on their terms.

Children's sport experiences vary with levels of formal organization and the extent to which they are participant controlled or adult controlled. The dynamics of sports participation and the lessons learned during participation are different in informal games than in organized youth sports. Involvement across a range of participation settings is best for the overall development of children. Interactionist research in the sociology of sport helps us understand that, prior to 8 years old, children do not have the developmental abilities to fully participate in organized competitive sports, especially team sports in which complex strategies are used. Such abilities are not fully developed until 12 years of age in most children. Research also describes and helps us understand some of the family dynamics associated with organized youth sports, especially in terms of how they affect family relationships, family schedules and the lives of mothers and fathers. Studies guided by critical theories illustrate how social factors influence youth sport experiences, including the participation choices available to children and the meanings given to various sport experiences.

Recommendations for improving organized youth sports emphasize that there should be action, involvement among all participants, exciting competition, and opportunities for children to form and nurture friendships with peers – just as there are in many informal games.

When coaches and parents constantly shout directions to children during games, it is unlikely that they will feel comfortable engaging in personally expressive actions. This makes it nearly impossible for them to emotionally bond with and begin claiming ownership of a sport. Instead, many of them view organized sports as an adult thing that they will eventually outgrow – much like braces on their teeth (Farrey, 2008) (*Source*: Jay Coakley)

Adults inhibit the prospects for change because they often have vested interests in maintaining schemes as they are currently organized. This is especially true in high-performance sport schemes, even though these are the ones in which improvements are most needed. Coaching education schemes could facilitate critical thinking among those who work most directly with children in these schemes, but coaching education is based on functionalist rather than critical approaches to sports.

No sports scheme can guarantee that it will make children into models of virtue, but the adults who organize and control youth sports can make improvements to existing schemes. This means that organized sports for children *are* worth the effort – when the adults put the children's interests ahead of the scheme's organizational needs and their own needs to gain status through their association with successful and highly skilled child athletes.

Website resources

Note: Websites often change. The following URLs were current when this book was printed. Please check our website (***www.mcgraw-hill.co.uk/textbooks/coakley***) for updates and additions.

www.mcgraw-hill.co.uk/textbooks/coakley Click on Chapter 5 to find information on studying gender in children's sports, observation guide for studying a youth sports event, comparison of informal games and organized sports, in-depth discussion of when children are ready to play sports; materials on parent–child relationships and youth sports, discussion of social factors influencing youth sports.

www.afpe.org.uk/ The website of the Association for Physical Education, which provides links and resources for those providing physical education within schools or the wider community.

www.thecpsu.org.uk/Scripts/content/Default.asp This is the site of the Child Protection in Sport Unit, with resources for parents, children and professionals.

www.culture.gov.uk/3096.aspx This website promotes the work of the Department for Culture, Media and Sport for schools and sport for young people.

http://deepfun.com/junkyard-sports.html This site, maintained by Bernie De Koven, contains practical descriptions of how play and games can be done in any environment by using creativity rather than special equipment.

www.righttoplay.com Right To Play, headquartered in Toronto, Canada, is an international humanitarian organization that uses sport and play to encourage the overall health and development of children in high-poverty regions of the world; the focus is on community development in connection with sport schemes, and it provides a practical evaluation system that youth sports administrators can use to assess schemes and teams, identify and anticipate problems among spectators and with coaches and players, and provide corrective action when there are problems.

www.sportdevelopment.org.uk/html/rg_education.html The site promotes sports development and contains several sports and education resources, including information about school sports funding, the school sports partnership impact and the government's specialist schools programme.

www.sportengland.org/index/get_resources/school_sport.htm The Sport England website contains information for all areas of sport but the above link gives directions to information about competitions within schools, how to get funding and the future of sport within schools.

www.sportsthinktank.com/youth%20sport%20report_sportsthinktank.pdf A document providing information on the structure, organization, priorities and issues facing youth sports in the UK.

www.standards.dfes.gov.uk/specialistschools/what_are/sports/ A site of the government Department for Children, Schools and Families which explains specialist schools status and provides a comprehensive list of all Specialist Sports Colleges within the UK.

www.teachernet.gov.uk/teachingandlearning/subjects/pe/ A website for teachers; includes school sports surveys and information on the new National Curriculum for Physical Education, which started in September 2008.

www.youthsporttrust.org/ A website dedicated to promoting a brighter future for young people through sport.

Chapter 6

Deviance in sports: is it out of control?

Learning Centre Resources

Visit *Sports in Society*'s Online Learning Centre (OLC) at **www.mcgraw-hill.co.uk/ textbooks/coakley** for additional information and study material for this chapter, including:

- Self-grading quizzes and essay questions
- Learning outcomes
- Related websites
- Additional readings

Chapter contents

Problems faced when studying deviance in sports
Defining and studying deviance in sports: three approaches
A constructionist approach to deviance in sports
Research on deviance among athletes
Performance-enhancing substances: deviant overconformity in sports
Summary: is deviance in sports out of control?

There is a murky quality to sport at the moment. We are in a time of flux. The rules are ambiguous. Everything is a little suspect … A very narrow tunnel leads to success at the very top levels of sport … The temptation to cheat is human. In the realm of elite international sport, it can be irresistible.

(Michael Sokolove, journalist, 2004a, p. 28)

The old adage that sport builds character is a fallacy actually. What sport does is it exposes character. You have an opportunity in your career as a sports person to choose various routes and that's the test of sport.

(Damon Hill, British and World Champion Formula One racing driver, 2007, in Sport's, Dirty Secrets, *video)*

Today, there is scarcely a major sport that is not tainted by drugs scandals … Can the drugs cheats be stopped? Perhaps not. But we must try to stop them, all the same. If we don't, we are condemning so many children to certain abuse at the hands of malevolent coaches.

(Jason Cowley, journalist, 2004, p. 1)

Deviance among athletes, coaches, agents and others connected with sports attract widespread attention. Media stories about on-the-field rule violations and off-the-field criminal actions have become so common that many people think that deviance in sports is out of control. News about drug and substance use among athletes promotes this perception. For those who cling to the myth that sports build character, these stories lead them to conclude that the moral fabric of society itself is eroding. They say that money, greed and undisciplined athletes have destroyed the 'natural' purity of sport and the existence of ethics and fair play.

Because many people think this way, the purpose of this chapter is to examine deviance in sports. We focus on four questions as we deal with this issue:

1 What problems do we face when studying deviance in sports?
2 What is deviance and how does sociological knowledge about it help us understand sports as social phenomena?
3 Are rates of deviance among athletes (on and off the field), coaches and others connected with sports out of control?
4 Can sociology help us explain the use of performance-enhancing substances in sports and develop strategies to control it?

These questions direct our attention to important issues in the study of sports in society.

Problems Faced When Studying Deviance in Sports

Studying deviance in sports presents problems for four reasons. First, *the types and causes of deviance in sports are so diverse that no single theory can explain all of them.* For example, think of the types of deviance that occur just among male university athletes: talking back to a coach during training, running wind sprints to the point of vomiting, violating rules or committing fouls on the playing field during a match or game, taking performance-enhancing substances, initiation ceremonies with fresher team members – demeaning them and forcing them to do illegal things, binge drinking and fighting in pubs, harassing women, engaging in group sex, sexual assault, turning in coursework prepared by others, betting on sports, playing with painful injuries and using painkillers to stay on the field. This diverse list would be greatly expanded if we also included all athletes as well as coaches, administrators, team owners and spectators. Therefore, it is important to study deviance in the contexts in which it occurs and not expect that a single theory will explain all or even a significant part of it.

Second, *actions accepted in sports may be deviant in other spheres of society, and actions accepted in society may be deviant in sports.* Athletes are allowed and even encouraged to do things that are outlawed or defined as criminal in other settings. For example, some of the things that athletes do in contact sports would be classified as criminal assault if they occurred on the streets. Boxers would be criminals outside the ring. Rugby players would be arrested for actions they define as normal during their games. Racing drivers would get points on their licence for speeding and careless driving. Speed skiers and motocross racers would be defined as criminally negligent outside their sports. Consider the 'TT' (Tourist Trophy) event on the Isle of Man: this series of motorbike races consists of mostly amateur participants racing at otherwise illegally high speeds on roads across the island, and is regarded as the most dangerous motorbike race in the world with more than 200 deaths of participants and spectators in its history. However, even when serious injuries or deaths occur in sports such as the TT, criminal charges are seldom filed, and civil lawsuits asking for financial compensation are rare and generally unsuccessful if they ever reach a courtroom.

Coaches treat players in ways that most of us would define as deviant if teachers treated students or employers treated employees similarly. Fans act in ways that would quickly alienate friends and family members in other settings or lead people to define them as mentally deranged.

On the other hand, if athletes take the same drugs or nutritional supplements used by millions of normal citizens, they may be banned from their sports and defined as deviant, even by the people using those drugs and supplements to maintain their performance in their jobs. Athletes who miss training or games due to sickness or injury often are defined as deviant by coaches and teammates, even though taking 'sick days' is accepted as normal outside sport. Young athletes may be substituted if they miss training to attend a family picnic despite the value given to family outside sports. The fact that norms seem to be applied and enforced differently in sports makes it difficult to use studies of deviance in other contexts to understand what occurs in sports.

Norms in sports often are different from norms in other social worlds, and responses to deviance by athletes may be different from responses to others who engage in deviance. For example, athletes often are praised for their extreme actions that risk health and well-being, and inflict pain and injury on others, whereas non-athletes would be defined as deviant for doing the same things. We tend to view the motives of people in sports, especially athletes, as positive because their actions are directed towards the achievement of success for their team, school, community, country or corporate sponsor. Therefore, those actions, even when they clearly overstep generally accepted limits in society as a whole, may be tolerated or even praised rather than condemned. Athletes often are seen as different and deviant in ways that evoke fascination and awe rather than repulsion and condemnation. Most sociological theories about deviance do not adequately explain many actions that occur in sports and the meanings given to them.

Third, *deviance in sports often involves an unquestioned acceptance of norms, rather than a rejection of norms.* Athletes often go overboard in their dedication to sport and their willingness to pay the price, play with pain and live their dreams. Their attitudes and actions are *supranormal* in the sense that they over-conform to norms widely accepted in society as a whole. Instead of setting limits on what they are willing to do as athletes, they evaluate themselves and their peers in terms of their dedication to the game and their unqualified willingness to put health and well-being on the line as they play it.

This 'over the top deviance' is often dangerous, but athletes learn to accept it as part of the game they love to play and as the basis for being accepted into the culture of high-performance sports. When normative overconformity takes the form of extreme dedication, commitment and self-sacrifice, it brings praise rather than punishment from coaches and fans. It is even used to reaffirm cultural values related to hard work, competition, achievement and manliness. In the process, people overlook its negative consequences for health, relationships with family and friends, and overall well-being.

This concept of overconformity to norms makes much of the deviance in sports difficult to understand because it does not fit the belief that deviance always involves *subnormal* or underconforming attitudes and actions based on a rejection of norms. However, both *supranormal* and *subnormal* attitudes and actions are *abnormal*, that is, deviant. When people do not distinguish between these different forms of deviance they often define athletes as role models, even though much of what athletes do is dangerous to health and well-being, and beyond the limits of acceptance in other spheres of life.

Fourth, *training and performance in sports are now based on such new forms of science and technology that people have not yet developed norms to guide and evaluate the actions of athletes and others in sports.* Science and medicine once used only to treat people who were ill are now used regularly in sports. The everyday challenge of training and competition in sports often pushes bodies to such extremes that continued participation requires the use of new medical treatments and technologies just to stay on the field. The use of nutritional supplements is now standard practice in nearly all sports. As one journalist explains:

> Most top sportsmen and women are fanatics; they push themselves beyond toler-
> able limits and then push themselves some more. Most of them already take more
> vitamins, dietary supplements and pills than the average Aids patient. They take
> almost anything, if it is legal, to secure competitive advantage. And many will risk
> taking illegal substances too. The truth is, the drugs do work.
>
> *(Cowley, 2004, p. 3)*

A survey of the ads for performance-enhancing substances in any *Flex, Men's Fitness* or *Muscle and Fitness* magazine leads to the conclusion that 'Strength and high performance (and an attractive body) are just a swallow away'! Online promotions push protein drinks, amino acids, testosterone boosters, human growth hormone boosters, insulin growth factor, vitamins and hundreds of other supplements that will help athletes get the most from their workouts, recover more quickly from injuries and build a body that can adjust to overtraining and become stronger in the process. If you do not like to swallow, there are rub-on creams and patches that do the job. Using the Internet to obtain various substances has occurred since the early 1990s (even though this was not discovered by government officials until much later – see Denham, 2007a). In the meantime, it has become much more difficult to determine just what actions are deviant and what actions are accepted parts of athletic training; in fact, 'normal training' is now an oxymoron, because all training involves excess, and ignoring limits and boundaries is accepted as normal in society as a whole.

Defining and Studying Deviance in Sports: Three Approaches

Approaches to identifying, defining and controlling deviance in sports vary depending on the theoretical framework used. We focus on approaches based on functionalist theory, conflict theory, and a combination of interactionist and critical theories.

Using functionalist theory: deviance disrupts shared values

According to functionalist theory, social order is based on shared values. Shared values give rise to shared cultural goals and shared ideas about how to achieve those goals. Deviance occurs when actions demonstrate a rejection of cultural goals and/or the accepted means of achieving

It is difficult to study deviance in sports because athletes often engage in actions that would not be accepted in other settings. For example, actions that are acceptable in boxing, rugby, football and other sports would get you arrested or sued if you were to engage in them off the field

them. In other words, deviance involves a departure from cultural ideals: the greater the departure, the more disruptive the action, the greater the deviance. Conversely, conformity to cultural ideals reaffirms the social order and is seen as the foundation of ethics and morality.

Most functionalists see deviance as a result of faulty socialization or inconsistencies in the organization of society. Deviance occurs because people have not learned and internalized cultural values and norms, or because there are conflicts and strains built into the structure of society. Therefore, reforming socialization processes, and eliminating structural conflicts, strains and inconsistencies in social systems is the best control for deviance.

Deviance in sports, according to a functionalist approach, occurs when an athlete rejects the goal of improving skills or the expectation that the means to achieve goals is to work harder than others. A problem with this approach is that it becomes difficult to identify deviance when there is a lack of agreement about the importance of various goals. For example, if we think that the goal in sports is to play fair but you think that it is to win, then we will see any violation of the rules as deviant, whereas you will see some violations as 'good fouls' if they contribute to winning. If we regard sports as a form of play in which intrinsic satisfaction is the reason for participation but you regard sports as 'war without weapons' fought for external rewards such as trophies and cash prizes, then we will see violent actions as deviant, whereas you will see them as signs of courage and commitment. Because we do not share beliefs about the ideals of sports, we do not define *deviance* in the same way.

Another problem with a functionalist approach is that it leads many people to think that controlling deviance always calls for policies and programmes that increase conformity among individuals. This usually involves establishing more rules, making rules more strict and consistent, developing a more comprehensive system of detecting and punishing rule violators, and making everyone more aware of the rules and what happens to those who do not follow them. For example, Graeme Obree, commonly known as 'The Flying Scotsman', was a cyclist who built his own bike and developed new streamlined cycling positions (the 'tuck' and the 'superman' styles). However, because these were different he was banned from competing by the Union Cycliste International, cycling's governing body (of course, these styles were later copied by other riders). As Obree's experience demonstrates, this approach to controlling behaviour often subverts creativity and change, and it assumes that all conformity, especially extreme conformity, is a cultural ideal. This assumption is questionable because obsessive and excessive conformity can be dangerous, a possibility discussed in the section on interactionist and critical theories (p. 180).

Despite these problems, many people use a functionalist approach when they discuss deviance in sports. When actions do not match their ideals they define them and their perpetrators as deviant. The solution, they say, is to 'get tough', make punishments more severe and throw out the 'bad apples'. This solution is based on the idea that people violate rules because they lack moral character and that 'normal' people in normal situations are not deviant. This approach may be useful when people are unaware of norms, but it ignores the influence of powerful social processes in sports and leads people to label athletes unjustly as moral failures when, in fact, most athletes are 'hyperconformers' whose main fault is that they have not learned to critically assess norms or set limits on what they will do to conform to norms in sport. We will say more about this throughout the chapter.

Using conflict theory: deviance interferes with the interests of wealthy people

According to conflict theory, social order is based on economic interests and the use of economic power by those who own the means of production in society. Therefore, social norms reflect the interests of those people, and any actions, ideas or people violating those norms are defined as deviant.

Those who use this approach assume that all people act in their own interests and that people in power use their position to turn their ideas of right and wrong into the official definitions of conformity and deviance in a society. Those who lack economic power in society have nothing to say about the content or enforcement of rules and they are more likely to be identified as deviant than people with wealth and power. Furthermore, legal processes are organized so that people who lack power do not have the resources to resist being labelled as deviant when their actions do not conform to the standards of the rule makers.

Conflict theorists assume that rules in sports reflect the interests of owners and sponsors and ignore the interests of athletes and most fans. Therefore, they see deviance among athletes as a result of rules that discriminate against them and force them to follow the expectations of those

'If they had more rules and better enforcement, all this deviance would stop.'

Cartoon 6.1 **Many people use a functionalist approach when they think about deviance in sports. They call for more rules and better enforcement. This approach has only limited usefulness in sports today**

in power, even though their health and well-being may be harmed in the process. Athletes are viewed as victims of a profit-driven system, in which progressive change requires rejecting and remaking the rules.

A problem with conflict theory is that deviance in sports is always assumed to be the result of biased norms and law enforcement processes controlled by wealthy owners and sponsors who convince everyone that their rules are the only rules. For instance, conflict theorists cannot explain why deviance exists in non-revenue-producing sports in which the athletes themselves may be in positions of power and control. Furthermore, many athletes voluntarily use dangerous growth hormones and other substances because they seek acceptance from teammates, not sponsors and team owners. Therefore, it is unlikely that all deviance in sports would disappear if athletes were in charge. Athletes should have more control over their sports participation, but without the critical consciousness needed to eliminate the profit motive and transform sports, it is unlikely that shifting more power to athletes would eliminate deviance in sports. Explaining all forms of deviance in economic terms is difficult. Although the commercialization of sports and financial motives may account for certain forms of deviance, other factors and dynamics must be considered to understand why deviance occurs in sports that are neither commercialized nor driven by profit motives.

Using interactionist and critical theories: deviance as a social construction

Although functionalist and conflict theories call attention to socialization and economic factors, they overlook the possibility that much of the deviance in sports involves overconformity to the norms that athletes use to evaluate themselves and others.

Most people who violate rules in sports cannot be classified as morally bankrupt, as functionalists often conclude, or as exploited victims, as conflict theorists often conclude. For example, it is not accurate to say that young people lack moral character when they accept without qualification the notion that athletes are dedicated to the game and willing to do what it takes to become and remain an accepted participant of a sports culture, even if it means going beyond normal limits as they train. Nor is it accurate to define all athletes who engage in deviance as passive victims of an exploitive, profit-driven sports system; after all, athletes participate in the creation and maintenance of the norms that guide their decisions and actions in sports. This means that we need an alternative explanation of deviance in sports, an explanation that takes into account the experiences of athletes within the actual contexts in which they play sports.

In searching for such an explanation, most sociologists now use a constructionist approach based on interactionist and critical theories. This approach focuses on two issues: (1) the meanings that people give to actions, traits and ideas, and (2) the ways that people use those meanings to 'construct' their definitions of what and who is deviant. It acknowledges that norms change over time and from situation to situation so that it is possible for something or someone to be considered deviant at one time or place and not at other times and places. For example, Linford Christie tested positive for the stimulant ephedrine after the 1988 Olympics men's 100m final. This is the race made famous by the Canadian athlete, Ben Johnson, winning the gold medal and then subsequently being stripped of his title when he was found to have used anabolic steroids. However, although Christie also tested positive for a banned substance in the same race, he was cleared of wrongdoing when he convinced a panel that the stimulant was present in the ginseng tea he had been drinking and that he had not deliberately cheated. In 1999, Christie was suspended from competition for two years by the International Association of Athletics Federations (IAAF) when he tested positive for high levels of the steroid nandrolone, even though the British Federation cleared him on the basis that they could not prove his guilt 'beyond reasonable doubt'. Christie has used his reputation as an athlete to develop a successful career as a television presenter, and in 2006 he was appointed by UK Athletics to coach medal hopefuls for the London 2012 Olympics. Those who employ him use a constructionist approach to deviance as they have decided to judge him by the belief in his potential innocence by the British board, rather than the construction of his wrongdoing by the International Federation.

People who assume that social reality contains absolute truths about right and wrong and good and evil reject a constructionist approach to deviance. They believe that unchanging moral truths are the foundation for all norms. Therefore, every norm represents an ideal, and every action, trait or idea that departs from that ideal is deviant, immoral or evil. When this 'absolutist' approach is used, deviance becomes increasingly serious as the departure from the ideal increases. For example, if using drugs violates an absolute principle of fairness in sports, any use of drugs at any time or place would be deviant, and if the drug use continued, use over time would be defined as immoral or evil. People using an absolutist approach do not accept that norms and deviance are social constructions. They cling to the notion of absolute moral truths and use it to divide the world into good and evil, and to make decisions about deviance and social control in everyday life. For example, media commentators who discuss criminal cases or drug use in sports often use an absolutist approach when they say without qualification that athletes today lack moral character to the point that they cannot distinguish right from wrong.

breaking BARRIERS

Acceptance barriers: *what is deviance and who defines it?*

Oscar Pistorius is a record-setting sprinter from South Africa. Sometimes identified as 'Blade Runner' and 'the fastest man on no legs', he was born without a fibula bone in both legs. The fibula is the long, slender bone that goes from the knee to the ankle alongside the tibia, or shin bone. Oscar's parents determined that a below-the-knee prosthetic leg and foot would enable him to live more normally. So, in late 1987 they arranged surgery in which doctors amputated the legs of their 11-month-old son below the knee.

As an active, athletic boy, Oscar dreamed of playing elite rugby. Never experiencing a body without prosthetic legs, he did everything his friends did. Through middle and high school he wrestled, and played cricket, rugby, water polo and tennis. But after he shattered his knee playing rugby in late 2003 his doctor told him to use running as physical therapy. In January 2004 at the age of 17 he began to train as a sprinter. Two months later he competed in his first 100-metre race, winning a gold medal and setting a world record time of 11.51 seconds!

Through the summer he continued to compete and set records. In September he competed in the 2004 Paralympic Games in Athens, Greece, where he won a silver medal in the 100 metres and a gold medal in the 200 metres. Overall, he set four world records at those games.

Between 2005 and early 2008 (as we write this), Pistorius has competed in many open/able-bodied meets as well as T43 and T44 races – the categories used for runners with both legs amputated below the knee and with one leg amputated below the knee, respectively. Breaking his own records over 25 times, he holds all world records in the T43 and T44 100-, 200- and 400-metre sprints, and he has steadily improved his placement against elite international able-bodied sprinters in the 200- and 400-metre races. As of early 2008 his best time in the 100 metres was 10.91 seconds, and his best time in the 400 metres was 46.34 seconds, just 2.34 seconds slower than the 2004 Olympic men's gold medal time of 44.00 seconds.

Team Ossur, the company that makes the carbon-fibre Flex-Foot® Cheetah prosthesis (see photograph), sponsors Pistorius and other record-setting Paralympic sprinters. The Flex-Foot replicates the hind leg of a cat with a small-profile foot that extends and reaches out to contact the ground while the large thigh muscles pull the body forward. These prosthetic legs return about 95 per cent of the energy put into them by the runners' upper legs, whereas a human lower leg returns about 200 per cent of the energy put into them. Ossur researchers hope to eventually duplicate the running power of a human leg, but they say that reaching their goal will take some time.

In 2007 Pistorius adopted a new training regime similar to the one that elite, able-bodied sprinters use. He feels that his hard work will improve his performance, especially in the 400-metre sprint. However, his hopes of qualifying for and competing in the 2008 Olympics in Beijing were dashed when the International Association of Athletics Federations (IAAF), the global governing body for track and field, banned him. Research commissioned by the IAAF concluded that his prosthetic legs give him an advantage over able-bodied runners (IPC, 2008; Tucker and Dugus, 2007a, 2007b, 2007c, 2007d, 2008) and the members of the IAAF board defined Pistorius as deviant – his body, they said, was abnormal.

Pistorius appealed the IAAF decision and asked the International Court of Arbitration for Sport to consider research that went beyond laboratory tests which had focused only on the carbon-fibre leg apart from the human leg. He felt there should be field tests on a track and tests on the leg in use and on Pistorius himself as he ran under race conditions. He knew from experience that the blade-like legs slow him at the start of a race, provide poor traction on a wet track, produce rotational forces that are difficult to control, and they supply none of the manoeuvrability and control that is supplied by the human lower leg, ankle and foot (Longman, 2007; McHugh, 2007; Ossur, 2008).

Independent researchers conducted further studies, and after the international court reviewed all the data, they overturned the IAAF ban in May 2008 and ruled that Pistorius was eligible to qualify for the Olympics and to participate in other international events (Director, 2008). In response, Pistorius said, 'It's not just about me, it's about the extra opportunity for amputee athletes.'

This case raises provocative issues about what counts as deviance in sports. The merger of sports and technology has led to heated debates over where to draw the line between what is acceptable and unacceptable in sports. Pistorius knew that it was risky to challenge the 'Empire of the Normal' as it existed in the IAAF. But he also knew that definitions of deviant and normal are social constructions, and that baseball players have 'assistive' laser eye surgery to improve their vision; that football and tennis players have 'assistive' elbow and knee reconstructions using stronger ligaments taken from other parts of their bodies; that endurance athletes sleep in 'assistive' hyperbaric chambers to enhance the oxygen-carrying capacity of their red blood cells (to increase their endurance); and that swimmers wear NASA-designed, ultra-light, seamless, water-resistant, full-body 'assistive' swimsuits

In 2008 Oscar Pistorius (No. 1853) was banned from racing in the Olympics. International track and field officials concluded that his carbon-fibre legs gave him an unfair advantage over able-bodied runners. While his ban was overturned on appeal, he did not qualify for the 2008 Olympic Games (*Source*: David Biene; photograph courtesy of Ossur, www.ossur.com)

that improve their times and enable competitors like Michael Phelps to break multiple world records in the Beijing Olympics.

Pistorius did not qualify for the 2008 Olympics in Beijing – missing by seven tenths of a second in the 400 metres (46.25 vs 45.55), but he will train to run in the 2012 Games in London. Even if he does not qualify in 2012, his case has shown us that the line between normal and deviant shifts and changes depending on who draws it and what criteria they use. It also forces us to reconsider the meaning of 'assistive', our notion of what athletes look like, and why we separate people into able-bodied and disabled categories when real bodies are so much more complicated than that.

As technologies enable people with various impairments to compete more frequently at elite levels, officials who determine eligibility must think more clearly and critically about their definitions of normal and deviant and their conception of human perfection. But can this occur if none of the decision makers has had experiences like those of Oscar Pistorius? *What do you think?*

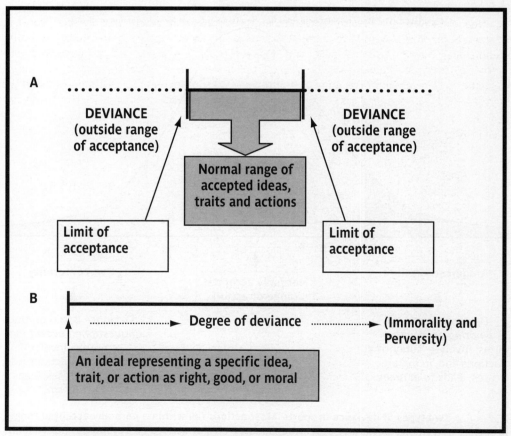

Figure 6.1 **A constructionist (A) versus an absolutist (B) approach to deviance in sports**

A Constructionist Approach to Deviance in Sports

Deviance always involves violating a norm. But sociologists using a constructionist approach say that a definition of deviance must take into account the process of *identifying* and *responding to* actions, traits and ideas. Therefore, they define **deviance** as *an action, trait or idea that falls outside a range of acceptance as determined by people with the power to enforce norms in a social world.* This definition emphasizes the following points about deviance.

■ Norms are socially constructed as people interact with each other and determine a range of accepted actions, traits or ideas that are consistent with their values; norms *do not* represent absolute ideals against which all actions are evaluated. This point is illustrated in Figure 6.1 where line A shows that norms are constructed in ways that permit variations within accepted limits so that everyone is not required to act, look and think exactly alike to conform to values and avoid being labelled as deviant. Line B, on the other hand, illustrates an absolutist approach in which every norm is based on an ideal that identifies a specific action, trait or idea as right, good and moral; and any departure from the ideal represents a degree of deviance, immorality or perversity.

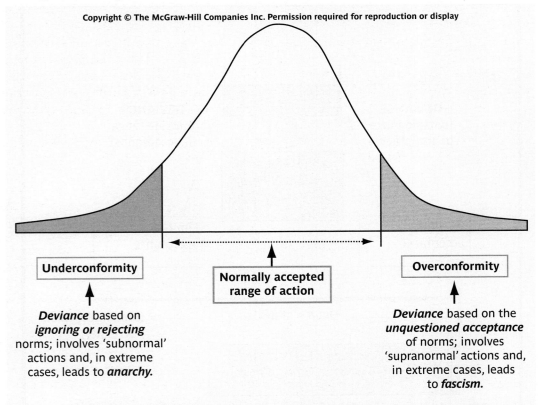

Underconformity

Deviance based on *ignoring or rejecting* norms; involves 'subnormal' actions and, in extreme cases, leads to *anarchy.*

Normally accepted range of action

Overconformity

Deviance based on the *unquestioned acceptance* of norms; involves 'supranormal' actions and, in extreme cases, leads to *fascism.*

Figure 6.2 **Two types of deviance in sports. Most actions fall within a normally accepted range in society as a whole. Deviance occurs when ideas, traits, or actions go beyond normative limits on either side of this range**

■ Deviance is socially constructed as people negotiate the boundaries of their acceptance. The ideas, traits and actions that fall outside those limits are unacceptable, or deviant. However, boundary negotiation occurs continuously, and the vertical hash lines move one way or the other over time as norms change. An example of this negotiation process is highlighted in 'Breaking barriers' (pp. 183–185).

■ Power relations influence the process of negotiating normative limits because limits are seldom meaningful unless they can be enforced. Therefore, people who possess the power to administer sanctions (that is, punishments or rewards) generally have the most influence in determining normative limits.

■ Most actions, traits and ideas in a social world fall into a normally accepted range, and those that fall outside this range involve deviant underconformity *or* deviant overconformity, as illustrated in Figure 6.2.

As represented in Figure 6.2, a constructionist approach is useful when studying deviance in sports, especially when it involves the use of performance-enhancing substances and other extreme actions that most people in society define as outside the normal range of acceptance. **Deviant underconformity** *consists of subnormal ideas, traits and actions that occur when people ignore or reject norms*, such as fighting in a pub or sexual assault. **Anarchy** is *the social condition that exists when widespread underconformity creates general lawlessness*. **Deviant overconformity** *consists of supranormal ideas, traits and actions that occur when people uncritically accept norms and conform to them without recognizing boundaries*, such as playing with broken bones and torn ligaments, or using painkilling drugs to stay in the game. **Fascism** *is the social condition that exists when widespread overconformity creates unlimited obedience to norms or the commands of leaders*.

Both types of deviance involve abnormal ideas, traits or actions, and both can be dangerous, just as both anarchy and fascism are dangerous.

Deviant over conformity in sports

Research shows that deviant over conformity is a significant problem in sports. When American sociologists Keith Ewald and Robert Jiobu (1985) studied men seriously involved in bodybuilding or competitive distance running, they found that some of the men engaged in unquestioned over conformity to norms related to training and competition in their sport. They trained so intensely and so often that their family relationships, job performance and/ or physical health deteriorated, yet they never questioned what they were doing or why they were doing it.

Ewald and Jiobu's study was published over 20 years ago in the USA, but athletes today are just as likely, if not more likely, to ignore normative limits and do anything it takes to train and participate in sports. For example, many elite athletes in the UK now prepare so intensely for their sports that they ignore aspects of their own health as well as the needs of family members. As a Welsh elite distance runner explained to David Howe, 'When I was wrapped up in my world of training and racing I didn't care about anything other than getting the miles in. It was about getting ready for the next race. I could not have cared less about anything other than running' (cited in Howe, 2004a, p. 150). This also appears to be true of amateur athletes, whose lives may also be dominated by their sport. In a study of female rowers, a lightweight sculler explained how non-rowing friendships become problematic and are often sacrificed for the sport: 'the ones that don't row, it is difficult to fit in with them' (Clare, cited in Pike, 2004, p. 158). One of the coaches in this same study agreed, suggesting that 'rowers marry rowers because there's no time for anything else' (Max, cited in Pike, 2004, p. 158).

Research has identified other forms of deviant overconformity, such as self-injurious overtraining, unhealthy eating behaviours and weight control strategies among female athletes in university and other elite amateur sports (Brackenridge, 2001; Charlesworth and Young, 2006; Fasting et al., 2000; Yorganci, 1993), extreme dedication to training among runners (Howe, 2004a), and uncritical commitments to playing sports with pain and injury.

When we use a critical, constructionist approach to study deviance in sports, we see that it is important to distinguish between actions based on indifference or a rejection of norms and actions based on a blind acceptance of norms and a willingness to follow them without question or limits. This is done by closely examining the organization and dynamics of sports cultures and the meanings that athletes give to their sport participation. For example, within the culture of high-performance sports, athletes are expected to live by a code that stresses dedication, sacrifice and a willingness to put one's body on the line for the sake of their sport and their teammates. Following this code to an extreme degree is seen as a mark of a true athlete, one who is respected by peers (Howe, 2004a; Malcolm and Sheard, 2002; Murphy and Waddington, 2007; Roderick, 2004; Waddington, 2006). Because of this, much of the deviance among athletes (and coaches) involves *unquestioned acceptance of* and *overconformity to* norms embodied in the ethos of contemporary power and performance sports.

The sports ethic and deviance in sports

An **ethic** is *an interrelated set of norms or standards that are used to guide and evaluate ideas, traits and actions in a social world*. Research suggests that elite athletes and coaches use a **sports ethic** to guide and evaluate attitudes and actions in the social world of power and performance sports (Hughes and Coakley, 1991). This ethic is formed around four general norms (see Figure 6.3).

1 *Athletes are dedicated to 'the game' above all other things.* This norm stresses that athletes must love 'the game' and prove it by giving it top priority in their lives. They must have the proper attitude and demonstrate their unwavering commitment to the game by meeting the expectations of fellow athletes, making sacrifices to stay in sport, and facing the demands of competition without backing down. Coaches' pep talks proclaim the importance of this norm. For example, the coach of English rugby league team Wigan, told the team in a pre-match talk: 'It doesn't matter what's wrong with you when you're injured … I don't care if the [physiotherapist is] out there and he wants to examine you and all that stuff. That's not important. What's important is … you've got twelve team-mates tackling their guts out, defending … I don't care what's wrong with you … if the opposition's got the ball, I want you on your feet and in the defensive line … There are no exceptions to that rule' (John Monie, cited in Murphy and Waddington, 2007, p. 241). Tony McCoy, a Northern Irish jump jockey explained this norm with these words: 'I've broken pretty much everything there is to break and I'm still here. I have no feeling down the left side of my face … I am well aware that I'm not going to be in great shape when I'm older.

Maybe I'll feel differently when I'm older but at the moment the pain is worth it … If you worry about that sort of thing you shouldn't be riding a horse' (in Honeyball, 2006, p. 58). Athletes often make statements like these, and retired athletes talk about missing the game and wanting to give back to it, even when playing it left them with disabilities.

2 *Athletes strive for distinction.* The Olympic motto *Citius, Altius, Fortius* (swifter, higher, stronger) captures the meaning of this norm. Athletes are expected to relentlessly seek to improve and achieve perfection. Winning symbolizes improvement and establishes distinction; losing is tolerated only because it increases the desire to win and magnifies winning as a sign of distinction in the culture of high-performance sports. Breaking records is the ultimate mark of distinction because it reaffirms that athletes are a special group dedicated to climbing the pyramid, reaching for the top, pushing limits, excelling, exceeding others and being the best they can be no matter what it takes. This norm is highlighted by Rebecca Seal, a British former gymnast who explained that 'Being a gymnast is about conquering fear and embracing danger. It is about pushing your body to the edge of the possible. Gymnastics is scary, fast and completely addictive' (Seal, 2005, p. 63). Similarly, during the 2006 Football World Cup, David Beckham vomited midway through a game between England and Ecuador, but continued to play and scored the only goal of the game. His commitment to success regardless of his own well-being was positively reinforced by the media, with headlines in the tabloid papers including: 'The Spewtiful Game', 'Here We Throw' and 'A Game of Two Barfs' (*Daily Mirror*, 26 June 2006).

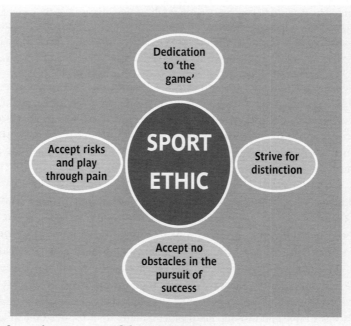

Figure 6.3 **The four primary norms of the sports ethic**

3   *Athletes accept risks and play through pain.* According to this norm, athletes are expected to endure pressure, pain and fear without backing down from competitive challenges. When athletes talk about this, they simply say that 'this is part of the game'. But in sociological terms, it shows that athletes are participants – along with coaches, trainers, owners and others – in a **culture of risk** *where a player's willingness to compete in pain while subjecting one's body to danger on the field is the mark of a true athlete* (Liston et al., 2006; Murphy and Waddington, 2007). The language used in sports emphasizes the importance of this norm. Furthermore, coaches look for players willing to take risks and play through pain; they like injured players in the line-up because it shows teammates that overconformity to the norms of the sport ethic is valued on their teams. When asked about playing with serious injuries and pain, a professional football player explained that 'They think it's fantastic. Brilliant. He's out there dying for the club. Dying for the club … if you go out with an injury and you play for ninety minutes and it's doing you more harm than good, you know, you're Braveheart, you're brilliant' (in Roderick et al., 2000, p. 169). Bradley Wiggins (2004), a British world champion cyclist reaffirmed this norm when he said of the Giro d'Italia (Tour of Italy) that it 'takes your pain tolerance to a different level … I've learnt how to suffer much more'. Athletes like Wiggins are encouraged to increase their power and endurance in order to improve their chances of winning and, in some events, contribute to the success of their teams. Therefore, it has become common for cyclists to go too far in conforming to expectations that are a key part of sport culture (see Waddington, 2000b).

> It's very easy to do it. It's very very very hard to not do it. Especially when you're surrounded by it. You do just get to a point where you give up fighting, you give up hope that it's going to change.
> *(David Millar, British cyclist banned for two years for testing positive for the performance-enhancing substance EPO, 2007, in* Sport's Dirty Secrets, *video)*

4   *Athletes accept no obstacles in the pursuit of possibilities.* This norm stresses 'the dream' and the obligation to pursue it without question. Athletes do not accept obstacles without trying to overcome them and beat the odds; dreams, they say, are achievable unless one quits. Overconformity to this norm was clearly illustrated by Jason Leonard, an English rugby union player, who described how he played on despite serious, and potentially disabling, nerve and spinal damage in his neck:

> I should have stopped playing as soon as I felt the tingles down my arm but of course I left it until I was practically crippled before I did anything about it … I battled through the Wales match with pain and numbness in my right arm that was so severe that I could not lift my arm above my waist. Whenever I scrum-maged, Jeff Probyn would have to pull my arm around Brian Moore and lock it in because I couldn't hold my arm up myself. 'Bind me in,' I said to Jeff. 'My arm's buggered, I can't hold it up'. Such was the attitude of players at the time, that Jeff's reaction was simple and instant. 'No problem, mate,' and he pulled me in with all his might, holding the scrum straight single-handedly.
> *(Leonard, 2004).*

Similarly, Jonny Wilkinson, the England rugby union player who scored a record number of points in the 2003 World Cup which was won by England, barely played rugby for the following two years and did not represent England again until 2007 due to a series of injuries and surgery. His repeated attempts to overcome his injuries and play for both his club and national team were explained by Jonathan Davies, a Welsh national: 'Every No. 10 is brave. You have to be. Brave and intelligent' (in the *Observer*, 16 January 2005, p. 9).

To understand the connection between the sports ethic and deviance in sports, three points must be kept in mind. *First*, the norms of the sports ethic are widely accepted in cultures in which people believe that it is important to be dedicated to what you do, strive for improvement, make sacrifices to achieve goals, push yourself even when things are difficult or painful, and pursue dreams despite obstacles. For example, in the UK these norms are taught to children by parents, incorporated into academic curricula, emphasized in motivational speeches and self-help books, and portrayed on posters hung on office walls. *Second*, it is expected that those who wish to be accepted as athletes in sports cultures will conform to these norms. *Third*, people with power in sports take great care to control deviant underconformity, but they often ignore or encourage overconformity, even though it may lead to injuries and have long-term negative implications for the health and well-being of athletes. Therefore, in the culture of high-performance sports, these norms are accepted uncritically, without question or qualification, and often followed without recognizing limits or thinking about the boundaries that separate normal from deviant.

This is illustrated in the words of a climber who had never been able to climb for more than nine months in a year due to a series of injuries which stopped him climbing for up to eight weeks at a time. He explained: 'I probably take risks with what I do … I don't give up. So I keep trying something, trying something, keep trying something until I either do it or my body's falling apart … till your fingers are bleeding whatever. I just keep going … I like being obsessive' (35-year-old climber cited in Robinson, 2004, p. 120). Even though climbing is an individualistic and primarily non-competitive sport, this climber's story illustrates how the sports ethic translates into a range of different sports forms. His attitude also demonstrates how dangerous forms of deviance can occur when athletes do not critically assess the sports ethic and the context in which deviant overconformity becomes commonplace. This lack of critical assessment allows this type of deviance to exist even though it is one of the biggest problems in sports today. Deviant underconformity is also a problem, but when athletes reject norms or refuse to take them seriously, they are immediately reprimanded or dropped from teams. Players who underconform to the norms of the sports ethic are not accepted as athletes by others associated with high-performance sports. For example, an English Premiership football player described how:

> we have another player here who's from (another country) and his attitude is any little niggle, 'That's it, I'm not playing'. Even in warm-ups before playing he walks off. Everyone's attitude towards him is 'He's a poofter, he doesn't want to play, no heart'. You know, the manager says in front of the players, 'Look at him over there, he's pulled out of the game again. There is a big game coming up … so he's pulled out'. It might be because he has genuinely got an injury. Only the player knows. But his title is that he's a f****** wuss, you know, he hasn't got the right attitude.
>
> *(Cited in Roderick et al., 2000, p. 169)*

But reactions to deviant overconformity are different. When players overconform to the norms of the sports ethic, they are praised and hailed as models, even if they risk their safety and well-being in the process. Media commentators glorify these athletes, praising those who play with broken bones and torn ligaments, endure surgery after surgery to play the game and willingly submit to injections of painkilling drugs to stay in the game. Spectators often express awe when they hear these stories, even though they realize that athletes have surpassed normative boundaries as defined in the society as a whole. Fans like to see deviance as long as it reaffirms an acceptance of values; they condemn deviance when it is based on a rejection of values. In light of the way that many people respond to the actions and traits of athletes, it is not surprising that many of them uncritically overconform to the norms of the sports ethic without question or qualification, even when it creates problems, causes pain, disrupts family life, jeopardizes health and safety or shortens their life expectancy (Murphy and Waddington, 2007; Roderick, 2006b). This type of deviance raises interesting and important sociological questions.

This type of 'overdoing-it deviance' is dangerous, but it is based on a desire to fit in and maintain an athletic identity through excessive dedication and commitment. This is sociologically different from *antisocial deviance* grounded primarily in alienation and a rejection of norms. Athletes accept without question the norms that define what it means to be an athlete, and their deviance often involves overconformity to those norms, not a rejection of them. Therefore, taking a drug to meet expectations in sports is very different from taking a drug to escape reality and expectations. The athlete overconforms when taking drugs to improve performance and gain acceptance from teammates; the alienated youth underconforms when mainlining heroin. This difference is important when we study and try to explain the origins of deviance in sports.

The greatest athletes want it so much, they run themselves to death. You've got to have an obsession, but if unchecked, it's destructive. That's what it is with [US athlete, Mary Decker Slaney]. She'll kill herself unless you pull the reins back.

(Longman, 1996, p. B11)

Why do athletes engage in deviant overconformity?

Many athletes overconform to the norms of the sport ethic, but some do not. The main reasons for overconformity are as follows.

- Playing sports is so exciting and exhilarating that athletes will do almost anything to stay involved.

- Being selected to play high-performance sports often depends on a perceived willingness to overconform to the norms of the sports ethic; coaches praise overconformers and use them as models on their teams.

- Exceeding normative boundaries infuses drama and excitement into people's lives because it increases the stakes associated with participation and bonds athletes together through a 'bunker mentality' in which putting one's body on the line is mutually expected.

reflect on SPORTS   *'Crock watch': the sport ethic in the mass media*

The media often use journalistic strategies in which they depict and glorify deviant overconformity to the norms of the sport ethic, especially when it takes the form of pain and injury (Nixon, 1993b). They assume that this attracts attention and sells their products. Trujillo (1995) suggests that this is particularly the case with male athletes, whose bodies are reproduced in the media as weapons, tools or an object of gaze. A study of the coverage of the men's football World Cup in 2002 indicates that the journalists and commentators appeared to celebrate the behaviour of athletes who took risks and played hurt during the tournament (Munday, 2003). For example, when Wilmots, a Belgian player, received a facial injury, the commentator stated that 'it adds to your bravery barometer having a blood-stained shirt'.

British sociologist Gill Lines (2001) suggests that the media constructs sporting heroes, villains and fools. Heroes are those who demonstrate strength, bravery and competitiveness. This is illustrated by the commentary during the 2002 World Cup. For example, Jeremies, a German player, was described as: 'a hard man and it must be a serious injury to keep a hard man down, he is a man of steel'. Sporting heroes are also equated with war heroes, risking their bodies for their country. Several commentators used 'warrior' analogies, such as when Alexandersson, a Swedish player, returned to the game with stitches in a head injury: 'here comes the injured warrior'; and similarly the commentary regarding a Costa Rican player: 'Martinez has picked up a facial wound ... he is really patched up just like a warrior in the name of his country'. Such commentary is in contrast to those depicted as 'fools', such as Silva of Uruguay, who was described as 'becoming an embarrassment. "Cry baby" comes to mind. The French are suggesting he is a wimp.' During the same tournament, several of the tabloid newspapers (notably, the *Daily Mirror*, the *Sunday Mirror* and the *Sun*) also carried an ongoing 'Crock watch' section in the paper to follow the injury careers of athletes throughout the competition.

Recent advertisements for everything from cars to soft drinks show young people, usually young men, in extreme sports engaging in actions that clearly fall outside the range of normal acceptance. The media coverage of sports events, combined with the images and narratives in many advertisements, show that people in the media and corporate advertising understand the sports ethic and the tendency among athletes to overconform to its norms. This coverage and these advertisements are problematic because they glorify and encourage dangerous forms of deviance. *What do you think?*

For these reasons, athletes often use cases of deviant overconformity as standards to define and evaluate their sports experiences. 'Just do it', the tag line of Nike advertisements, is fine, even commendable, but 'just overdo it' until you vomit, bleed, lose consciousness, need surgery or die is generally defined as deviant. However, most athletes do not see overconformity to the sports ethic as deviance because it is required to reaffirm their identities as athletes and retain membership in a special group, separated from normal everyday people who live boring lives and never test their limits. When writer Tom Wolfe (1979) studied astronauts and fighter pilots, he found that pilots who overconformed to norms similar to those constituting the sports ethic, were defined as having 'the right stuff' to move up the pyramid and become one of a special few in the world. Dangerous overconformity, said Wolfe, was a small price to pay to live such an exciting life.

Of course, all athletes are not equally likely to overconform to the sports ethic. Those most likely to do so are the following:

- players with low self-esteem and a deep need to be accepted as athletes by their peers in sport

- players who see achievement in sports as their only way to get ahead and be treated with respect in the world at large

- male players who link together their identities as athletes and as men so that being an athlete and being a man become one and the same in their minds.

Therefore, athletes whose identities or future chances for recognition and success depend exclusively on sports participation are most likely to engage in deviant overconformity. An athlete's vulnerability to group demands, combined with the desire to gain or reaffirm group membership, is a critical factor underlying this form of deviance. Many coaches realize this and create team environments that keep athletes in a perpetual state of adolescence – a developmental stage characterized by identity insecurities and a strong dependence on peer acceptance. This encourages a never-ending quest to confirm identity and eliminate self-doubt by going overboard to make the coach happy and earn respect in the changing room. This dependency-based overconformity to the sports ethic increases the likelihood of dangerous forms of deviance. If coaches wanted to control all forms of deviance on their teams, they would help athletes set limits on their conformity to the norms of the sport ethic. This is done by encouraging athletes to ask themselves why they do what they do in sports, and how they want their sports participation to be integrated with the rest of their lives.

It would hurt me so much to run across the floor and do a round-off into back-flip, but it hurts me so much more that I cannot.

(Rebecca Seal, British former gymnast, forced to retire aged 14 due to recurrent injuries, 2005, p. 60)

Deviant overconformity and group dynamics

Being an athlete is a social experience as well as a physical one. At elite levels of competition, players develop special bonds with each other, in part due to their collective overconformity to the norms of the sport ethic. When team members join together and collectively dedicate themselves to a goal, and willingly make sacrifices and endure pain in the face of significant challenges, they often create a social world in which overconformity to their norms and ideas becomes 'normalized', even as it remains deviant in society as a whole (Curry, 1993; Howe, 2004a; Liston et al., 2006; Malcolm and Sheard, 2002; Pike, 2004; Waddington, 2006). As they test their limits together, the bonds between players become extraordinarily powerful. This is because their overconformity sets them apart and separates them from the rest of the community, and it leads them to assume that 'outsiders' cannot understand them and their lives. Athletes may appreciate fan approval, but they do not look to fans for reaffirmation of their identity as athletes because fans are ignorant of what it takes to pay the price day after day, face risk and pain, subordinate one's body and total being to the needs of the team, and do anything required to be among a select few who can perform as no others in the world can perform. Only other athletes understand this, and this makes everyone else peripheral to an athlete's life in sports.

The separation between athletes and the rest of the community makes the group dynamics associated with participation in high-performance sports very powerful. However, they are not unique. Other selective and exclusive groups, usually groups of men, experience similar dynamics. Examples are found in the military, especially among Special Forces units. Former soldiers sometimes talk about these dynamics and the powerful social bonds formed while they faced danger and death with their 'teams'. Tom Wolfe (1979) explains that trusting your life to fellow pilots when a small mistake or misjudgement means death creates special bonds, along with feelings that you and your peers are special. These bonds may exist in university sports teams where 'freshers' voluntarily submit to systematic initiation ceremonies designed to emphasize that membership in this special group must be earned by paying the price. In fact, rituals have long been part of the initiation into groups that see themselves as special and separate from the rest of the community. Sports teams often have pre-season initiation (known in North America as 'hazing') rituals, during which freshers must obey the commands of team veterans, no matter how demeaning, sickening, painful or illegal the 'mandated' actions are (Bryshun and Young, 2007; Dunning and Waddington, 2003; King, 2000; Tinmouth, 2004). The bonds in these groups and the need for group acceptance and approval can be so strong that they prevent group members from reporting deviant and criminal activities to people outside the group.

As high-performance athletes endure the challenges of maintaining their membership in select groups and teams at the highest level of accomplishment in their sports, they develop not only extremely strong feelings of unity with other athletes but also the sense that they are unique and extraordinary people. After all, they are told this day after day by everyone from coaches to autograph seekers. They read it in newspapers and magazines, and they see it on television and the Internet.

When the sense of being unique and extraordinary becomes extreme, as it does among many high-profile athletes in certain settings, it can take the form of pride-driven arrogance, an inflated sense of righteousness and power, and a public persona that communicates superiority and even insolence. The Greeks used the word **hubris** to describe this *expression of self-importance and the accompanying sense of being separate from and above the rest of the community.* Hubris is so common in some sports that it has become a key dimension of the public personas of many athletes. A few athletes even market it and use it to attract attention and make people remember them, whereas others may be very selective in choosing when to express it.

The dynamic leading to hubris among athletes is clear. First, athletes bond together in ways that encourage and normalize deviant overconformity. Second, collective overconformity creates a sense of specialness and separates athletes from the rest of the community at the same time that it inspires awe and admiration from fans. Third, the unique experiences associated with team membership lead athletes to feel a sense of entitlement. Fourth, athletes see people outside their sports culture as incapable of understanding them and their lives, and therefore undeserving of their concern or, in some cases, their respect.

This process is not driven by the desire to win or make money; instead, it is driven by a powerful desire to play the game, gain the respect of peers in the changing room, maintain an identity as an athlete and remain an accepted member in an elite athletic group. This is not to say that winning and money are irrelevant to elite athletes; they are important, but they do not explain deviant overconformity. Therefore, this overconformity also occurs on teams and among athletes who will never win championships, achieve public fame or receive professional contracts (Liston, 2007). The roots of deviant overconformity are not grounded in exploitation of athletes' desires to win or make money. Instead, they are grounded in the culture and social organization of sports – tied to processes of identity development and group dynamics, and nurtured by the failure of coaches and administrators to effectively control deviant overconformity. Fines and jail sentences seldom control this form of deviance. Throwing out the so-called bad apples may help in the short run, but the social processes that operate in the social world of many sports guarantee that the apples in the orchard will look the same next season. It is the soil and trees that are the source of the problem, not the apples.

Deviant overconformity and deviant underconformity: is there a connection?

An important topic that has not been studied in the sociology of sport is the possible connection between deviant overconformity and rates of deviant underconformity. This connection is illustrated in Figure 6.4. Questions related to this topic are these:

- If the social bonds created in sports are powerful enough to normalize deviant overconformity that jeopardizes health and well-being among athletes, are they powerful enough to foster other forms of deviance in and by groups of athletes?

- If the actions of athletes separate them from the rest of the community, do athletes come to disdain or disrespect non-athletes to the point that they might be likely to harass or assault them?

Cartoon 6.2 **Winning is important to athletes. But winning and standing on the victory podium are usually secondary to the goal of being defined and accepted as true athletes by their peers in sports**

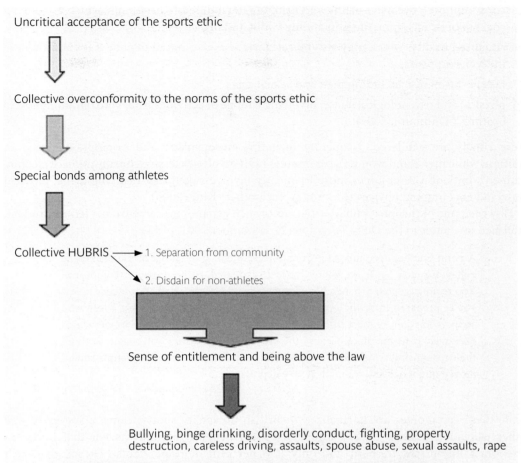

Uncritical acceptance of the sports ethic

Collective overconformity to the norms of the sports ethic

Special bonds among athletes

Collective HUBRIS ⟶ 1. Separation from community

2. Disdain for non-athletes

Sense of entitlement and being above the law

Bullying, binge drinking, disorderly conduct, fighting, property destruction, careless driving, assaults, spouse abuse, sexual assaults, rape

Figure 6.4 **Hypothesized relationship between deviant overconformity and deviant underconformity**

- If athletes develop hubris, might they feel entitled to the point of concluding that community standards and rules do not apply to them?
- If fans and others in the general community view athletes with awe and fascination because of their displays of deviant overconformity, are those people less likely to enforce laws and other community standards when athletes, especially high-profile athletes, violate them?

Research is needed on these questions. Our sense is that long-term overconformity to the sports ethic creates social conditions and group dynamics in sports that encourage notable forms of deviant underconformity such as binge drinking, academic cheating, group theft and property destruction, drunken and careless driving, sexual harassment, physical assault, spousal abuse and sexual assault.

For example, initiation ceremonies in sports teams have subjected prospective teammates to demeaning and even criminal treatment. There seem to be four broad categories of such rituals:

1 consumption – excessive eating and drinking, including of 'dirty pints' which are often a cocktail of drinks, sometimes including vomit and urine

2 ritualized nudity, which may also be categorized as a criminal offence if it entails public indecent exposure

3 task performance, including theft and sexual acts

4 physical and psychological abuse, involving a range of activities from verbal humiliation to beatings (Tinmouth, 2004).

These rituals are gendered, frequently including misogynistic and homophobic acts. In addition, while men's and women's ceremonies both involve excessive consumption of alcohol, the men's initiation ceremonies more frequently involve nakedness, drinking urine, physical abuse and encouraging novices to vomit on each other (King, 2000).

However, one of the most public criticisms of such ceremonies came from a female student, published in a letter to the *Daily Telegraph* (21 November 2001, p. 23):

> A point that has been missed in your correspondence about the drinking and vile behaviour at L＿＿, from where I've just graduated, is the pressure to conform. You're not accepted as a member of a sports team or even a hall of residence unless you're prepared to drink to excess and, preferably, until you vomit. Those who support this culture most enthusiastically get elected to the students' union, which effectively runs the place because the university authorities don't seem to think their responsibility extends beyond teaching. I dropped out of the tennis squad, moved out of hall and found it all very depressing.
>
> *(Cited in Bryshun and Young, 2007, p. 309)*

While these ceremonies are normalized in British university sports teams, a survey of one higher education establishment found that 89 per cent of respondents felt that initiation ceremonies humiliated freshers, and only 17.6 per cent of respondents believed that such rituals promoted team-building. This university banned all initiation ceremonies in 2001 and, in the following two years, there was a 27 per cent increase in students' participation in sport, and the university achieved an all-time highest ranking in the British University Sports Association list (Tinmouth, 2004).

Controlling deviant overconformity in sports

Deviant overconformity presents special social control problems in sports. Coaches, managers, owners and sponsors – people who exercise control and enforce norms – often benefit when athletes overconform to the norms of the sports ethic. In their eyes, athletes who willingly put their bodies on the line for the team are a blessing, not a curse. In the eyes of the athletes their overconformity is proof of their dedication and commitment; and in the eyes of fans and media people it is seen as exciting, a way to win games and a wonderful boost to media ratings. Therefore, deviant overconformity goes unpunished, even though it often consists of dangerous actions that everyone sees as falling outside normative boundaries.

The issue of social control is further complicated by the tendency to promote overconformers into positions of power and influence in sports. Because they have proved willing to do anything it takes to win as players, they are seen as ideal candidates for certain jobs in sports, especially coaching jobs. This creates a situation in which deviance and related ethical infractions among athletes are rooted in the organization of sports and in athletes' relationships with each other, and the wilful neglect of coaches and managers.

Controlling deviant overconformity requires that athletes be taught how and when to set limits as they play sports. This is difficult to do because it conflicts with an ethos of overconformity that is common in sports. Controlling deviant underconformity is less difficult because it is quickly identified by authority figures, and everyone understands that it will be punished. Deviant overconformity, however, is more subversive because it is widely ignored. For example, when a 14-year-old gymnast is late for practice, her coach immediately sanctions her for being deviant. However, when the same gymnast loses weight and becomes dangerously thin as she strives for distinction and pursues her sports dream, many coaches, parents and judges do not see possible deviance as much as they see the mindset of a champion and the culture of excellence in the gym – that is, until stress fractures or anorexia interfere with competition and put their athlete daughter in hospital.

Another barrier to controlling deviant overconformity is that people associated with sports resist asking critical questions about the goals, purpose and organization of sports. Without asking critical questions, dangerous forms of deviance will persist, including the use of performance-enhancing substances. But many coaches encourage deviant overconformity by telling athletes that the team is their family and that family members put their bodies on the line for each other when they go to battle. Similarly, they may claim that 'outsiders are out to get us'. This, in turn, promotes hubris and further separates athletes from the surrounding community and its laws.

Fans also want athletes to exceed normative limits and put their bodies on the line. They see this as exciting and entertaining because it heightens the stakes associated with competition. But fans also want athletes to reaffirm the myth that sports build character. But they cannot have it both ways: accept deviant overconformity and you are likely to get deviant underconformity along with it.

The most effective strategy for controlling deviant overconformity is to directly assist athletes in setting limits that foster their long-term health and in meaningful connections with the rest of the community. This also is an important step in controlling deviant underconformity because it makes athletes feel less like outsiders and identify with the community and its norms.

Research on Deviance among Athletes

Media stories about deviance among athletes have become an everyday thing. But do athletes have higher rates of deviance than other people? Few studies have tried to answer this question, and no studies make distinctions between deviant overconformity and underconformity, because the former is rarely identified and counted as deviance.

At present, we would argue that deviant overconformity is out of control, especially if the use of performance-enhancing substances is considered to be this form of deviance – an issue discussed later in the chapter. Most people focus attention on deviant underconformity, and highlight lists of arrest records and criminal charges filed against athletes. They claim that this form of deviance is out of control in sports, but they cannot say if rates are higher today than in the past, or if rates of deviance in sports are higher than rates among comparable people outside of sports.

Most media reports focus on the deviance of athletes rather than coaches, administrators, team owners and other off-field personnel. They use reports of deviance to attract attention, and without doing any analysis, blame deviance on the character weaknesses of athletes and the greed of everyone associated with sports. Ignored is the possibility that deviance is grounded in the culture and organization of sports and the social dynamics that exist in the social worlds that are created around sports. If these latter factors were acknowledged, the reports would identify a need to make deep structural and cultural changes in sports. Such changes would serve the health and well-being of sports participants, but they would jeopardize the viability of spectator sports – something that media people do not want to do.

When we discuss deviance among athletes, it is important to distinguish the actions that occur on the field and in the immediate realm of sports from the actions that occur off the field and away from sports. They are related to different types of norms and rules, and they have different causes and consequences.

 When you grow up being competitive and trying to win, not just for yourself but for your team as well, I guess that after a while that pressure to succeed, not the money but just the pressure to be a winning athlete, maybe blurs the lines between what you should do and what you shouldn't do.

(James Richardson, sports broadcaster, 2007, in Sport's Dirty Secrets, *video)*

Deviance on the field and in the realm of sports

This type of deviance includes cheating (such as ball tampering in cricket, or Maradona's famous 'hand of God'), gambling, throwing games or matches, engaging in unfair conduct, fighting, taking illegal performance-enhancing drugs, and generally finding ways to avoid rules of the game. Some people claim that these types of deviance have become serious today because the personal and financial stakes have become so great in sports. But historical research indicates that cheating, dirty play, fighting and the use of violence are less common today than in the days before television coverage and high-stakes commercialization (Dunning, 1999; Guttmann, 2004; Maguire, 1988; Scheinin, 1994). This research also shows that sports today are more rules governed than in the past and that on-the-field deviance today is more likely to be punished and publicly criticized. Therefore, saying that these particular forms of deviance are out of control and blaming television and money for the problems is not justified.

Not even the photographers managed to capture what really happened. And Shilton, jumping with his eyes shut, was outraged! I like this goal. I felt I was pick-pocketing the English.

(Maradona, 2006, p. 24, on 'handballing' a goal for Argentina against England in the quarter finals of the 1986 men's football World Cup)

Comparing rates of on-the-field deviance among athletes from one time period to another is difficult because rules and enforcement standards change over time. Research shows that

There is no evidence that rates of deviance on the field are higher today than in the past. What is different today is the media coverage and video technology, which enable us to see rule violations in slow motion, stop action, and replay after replay after replay. Actually, many forms of deviance were more prevalent and blatant 80 years ago when the technology of enforcement was limited

athletes in most sports interpret rules very loosely during games and they create informal norms, which stretch or bend official rules (Shields and Bredemeier, 1995). But this is not new. Athletes in organized sports have traditionally 'played to the level' permitted by umpires and referees – that is, they adjust their actions according to the ways that referees enforce rules during a match. However, this does not mean that players ignore rules or that deviance is out of hand. Nor does it mean that we ought to ignore this form of deviance when it occurs.

The perception that deviance has increased on and around the field is partly due to the constant addition of new rules in sports. Rule books in sports organizations today have hundreds of rules that did not exist a generation ago. International sports organizations now provide catalogues of banned substances. Today, there are more ways to be deviant in sports than at any time in history! Furthermore, the forms of surveillance used today and the increased emphasis on rule enforcement means that more rule violators are caught today than ever before. For example, consider the complex regulations classifying Paralympic athletes according to functional ability in their sport. This is designed to ensure fair competition, but in the 2000 Sydney Paralympic Games the rules were breached when it was discovered that the Spanish basketball team included 10 out of the 12 players who had no disability.

Finally, evidence shows that athletes in power and performance sports expect and engage in certain forms of on-the-field deviance, such as 'professional fouls' and 'cheating when you can get away with it' (Anonymous, 1999; Pilz, 1996; Shields et al., 1995). This is most prevalent at higher levels of competition, it increases with the number of years that people play sports, and it is more common among men than women. These patterns are consistent with other research suggesting that participation in power and performance sports does not generally promote moral development or moral decision making (Stoll and Beller, 1998, 2000). However, there are no historical studies showing that deviant underconformity on and around the field is more common now than in the past and this form of deviance does not seem to be out of control. However, deviant underconformity does exist in sports and efforts should be made to control it without violating individual rights and principles of due process. The form of sports-related deviance that is more prevalent today than in the past is deviant overconformity in the form of using banned and illegal performance-enhancing substances. This is clearly a serious problem that has been out of control for some time, and is discussed later in the chapter (pp. 205–220).

Deviance off the field and away from sports

Off-the-field deviance among athletes attracts widespread media attention (Blackshaw and Crabbe, 2004). When athletes are arrested or linked to criminal activity, they make headlines and become lead stories on the evening news. Media reports of athletes driving under the influence, fights and assault charges appear regularly (Starr and Samuels, 2000). The incidence of sexual assault (including stories of 'roasting', 'dogging' and rape) among male athletes is an especially important topic, and is discussed in Chapter 7. There are limited systematic studies of these forms of deviance, and research does not tell us if rates of off-the-field deviance have gone up or down or if general crime rates are higher among athletes than among comparable people in the general population. However, there have been studies which focus on excessive alcohol use among athletes, as a form of deviancy in its own right, and as a potential cause of other forms of violent and deviant behaviour.

Underage and excessive alcohol consumption is not limited to athletes. However, research suggests that sport and alcohol have a long-standing mutually supportive relationship. In a cultural history of this trend, Collins and Vamplew (2002) indicate that British ale houses in the sixteenth century were well established as arenas for sporting events from cricket and tennis, and bowls and quoits, to cockfighting. The boom in football at the end of the nineteenth century was largely enabled by breweries supporting clubs such as Manchester United and Liverpool. Many teams and tournaments continue to be sponsored by alcohol companies; for example, Carling, Tennants and Bass-Worthington have sponsored football, and Courage and Heineken have sponsored rugby. Indeed, sports trophies themselves are cups, designed to facilitate the alcoholic celebrations of the victor. Dunning and Waddington suggest that this relationship extends beyond mere practicalities, arguing that young men, particularly in the post-war years,

> were socialized into an acceptance of the idea that it is 'manly', not only to play physical contact sports such as football and painful, physically dangerous sports such as cricket, but also to drink beer and to be able to 'hold your ale', that is to drink copious quantities of alcoholic beverages without becoming visibly drunk and losing control.
>
> *(2003, p. 356)*

It should not, therefore, be surprising that a study of university students in the UK found that 61 per cent of males and 48 per cent of females exceeded the recommended limits for alcohol consumption (Webb et al., 1996). As we have already identified, this is often associated with sports events, including initiation ceremonies, as epitomized in the case of a member of an English university ski club who died in 2001 after what was described as a 'monstrous drinks binge'. The response to this of the university's student union was that the 'drinking culture is exactly the same as twenty five years ago', and that they would be 'highly sceptical about any draconian attempt' to restrict the alcohol consumption of students (cited in Tinmouth, 2004). In other words, the university accepted that excessive drinking was part of the culture of student sporting life. Further studies of university male sports teams confirm that alcohol consumption and misogynist attitudes to women are expected behaviour in such subcultures (see Clayton and Humberstone, 2006).

Research on this topic is important because alcohol use and abuse is related to other forms of deviance. Studies are needed to see if the group dynamics of alcohol use and binge drinking at the college level are related to the dynamics underlying overconformity to other group norms among athletes. Slamming drinks and getting drunk with fellow athletes may not be very different, sociologically speaking, from playing with pain to meet the expectations of teammates: 'Have another shot of tequila – it's what we teammates who take risks together are doing tonight. Are you a part of this special group or not?' Again, research is needed to see if, why, when and how often this occurs.

> I get drunk every night. Depends what you call drunk, really. I never fall over. Darts is a drinking man's game ... All darts players drink. They can hold it, you see. The more you drink, the more you can take it. Just because modern players don't drink on the telly, doesn't mean they don't have a few pints two or three hours before their match.
>
> *(Eric Bristow, five-times World Darts Champion, 2004, p. 51)*

Off-the-field deviance: a final comment

The point of this section is that there is limited research evidence to support the attention-grabbing headlines which suggest that off-the-field deviance and crime rates among British athletes are out of control and in excess of comparable peers. At the same time, rates for alcohol abuse, binge drinking and certain forms of assault may be higher among athletes.

But until we have good theories to explain these data, we can only speculate on why these patterns exist.

Interestingly, despite the perception that sports may be sites for deviant behaviour, sports schemes have also been designed as 'interventions' for 'at-risk youth'. In a review of this issue, Geoff Nichols (2003) notes that we lack a clear theory to explain how and why we might expect sports-based intervention schemes to be effective in reducing delinquency or producing other positive effects. Most of these schemes have little effect because they do nothing to change the unemployment, poverty, racism, poor schools and other delinquency-related factors that exist in most neighbourhoods where sports for at-risk youth are offered (Coakley, 2002).

We know from Chapter 4 that we cannot make generalizations about athletes because sports experiences vary from scheme, to scheme, and sport participation constitutes only a part of a person's experiences. Therefore, when someone says that 'playing sports kept me out of trouble', we need to investigate what that means and if there are ways to organize sports and sports experiences that provide young people with opportunities to identify positive alternatives for their lives. Until more of this research is done, we must say that sports participation creates neither 'saints nor sinners', although both may play sports. This issue is discussed further in the section 'Is sports participation a cure for deviant behaviour?'

Why focus on deviance only among athletes?

This chapter focuses almost exclusively on deviance among athletes. This is an important issue. However, athletes are not the only people in sports who violate norms. The following list identifies other examples of sports-related deviance:

- coaches who hit players, treat them inhumanely, use male players' insecurities about masculinity to motivate them, sexually harass women in and out of sports, subvert efforts to follow sex discrimination legislation that mandates equal participation opportunities for girls and women in sports, and violate other organizational rules

- sport administrators (including those on the International Olympic Committee and related organizations) who take bribes and gifts in return for favours, and who violate public trust and organizational principles by making decisions clearly based on their personal interests (see Jennings, 1996a, 1996b; Jennings and Sambrook, 2000)

- judges and other officials in events such as figure skating, gymnastics and boxing who take bribes or make agreements with others to alter the outcomes of events

- managers, such as Luciano Moggi of Juventus football club, who have been found guilty of influencing the selection of opposing teams, referees, timing of matches and media coverage in order to ensure success; notably, Juventus, along with three other Italian teams, was deducted points and relegated from Serie A in 2006 when its match-fixing was exposed

- media promoters and commentators who deliberately distort and misrepresent sports events so that they can generate high television ratings or newspaper/magazine sales

- agents who mislead athletes, misrepresent themselves or violate rules as they represent professional athletes

- managers and agents colluding in making irregular payments for the transfer of players, accusations of which led to the controversial and expensive Stevens Inquiry into British football transfers between 2004 and 2006

- parents/spectators who berate, taunt and fight with each other, referees and players as they watch their children in youth sports

- spectators who attack or throw objects at athletes, fight with each other, destroy property as they mourn a loss or celebrate a win, place illegal bets on sports and sell forged autographs of athletes.

Some of these and other examples of deviance are discussed in Chapters 5, 7, 11 and 12.

> The tempting and very profitable prospect for a corrupt sportsman is that working alone or with others he can fix the outcome of a sporting event or indeed part of it and achieve a very significant healthy coup.
> *(Lord Condon, Chair of the International Cricket Council's Anti-Corruption Unit, 2007 in* Sport's Dirty Secrets, *video)*

When a football player loses his temper, throws a ball in anger and appears ready to fight, many people 'see' deviance and worry about it. When a coach does similar things – shouts at the referee, throws rolled-up programmes and appears ready to fight – many people 'see' him (Sir Alex Ferguson, for example) as a legend, as an authority figure who controls subordinate players with tactics that might be defined as criminal if a teacher used them in the classroom. How do people define deviance in sports? Are roles (authority) related to these definitions? These questions must be answered for a full understanding of deviance in sports

Is sports participation a cure for deviant behaviour?

We often hear that sports keep young people off the streets and out of trouble, and build character in the process. Such ideals are promoted in policy documents, which make claims that sports will be used, for example, 'to reduce anti-social behaviour, crime and drug use among 10–16 year olds within local neighbourhoods' (Sport England, 2000, p. 1). Then we hear about athletes who get into trouble and prove that years of playing sports have not turned them into models of character. How do we make sense out of this conflicting information?

Geoff Nichols (2003) suggests that the success of sports programmes in reducing crime may depend upon the type of programme and the mechanisms that are used. He identifies three categories of programme: primary – where there is an attempt to modify criminal conditions, for example, by providing sporting opportunities in areas of deprivation; secondary – these are programmes which intervene in the lives of those who live in circumstances likely to lead to crime (for example, youth offenders before they engage in serious crime); tertiary – where the programme is aimed at the prevention of recidivism for those who have already offended. With respect to the mechanisms used for reducing crime, Nichols also suggests three styles: diversion – programmes such as the 'Splash' schemes, which aimed to reduce street crime and robbery by providing diversionary activities for 9–17-year-olds during the summer holidays (DCMS/Strategy Unit, 2002); deterrence – opening sporting facilities and leisure centres for longer hours on the premise that if they are being used for sport, they will not be vandalized; positive development of individuals – using sport to teach pro-social values and offer social support.

Unfortunately, there is very little evidence for the success of any of these schemes (Collins and Kay, 2003; Dunning and Waddington, 2003; Nichols, 2007). For example, while it is possible that sporting activities do provide excitement and so limit the boredom which may lead to criminal behaviour, it is also possible that sports may be morally neutral or even provide a context for deviant behaviour and promote negative social values (Nichols, 2003; Pike, 2007; Ramella, 2004; Smith and Waddington, 2004).

This was explored in a study by American sociologist Michael Trulson (1986) who suggested that *only certain types of sports and sport participation* can lower delinquency rates among young people. Trulson worked with 34 young men, aged 13 to 17, who had been classified as delinquents. He tested them for aggression and personality adjustment, and divided them into three groups matched on important background characteristics. For six months, each group met three times a week for training sessions with the same instructor. Group 1 received traditional tae kwon do training, taught with a philosophy emphasizing respect for self and others, the importance of physical fitness, self-control, patience, perseverance, responsibility and honour. Group 2 received 'modern' martial arts training, emphasizing free-sparring and self-defence techniques, and the coach provided no philosophy in connection with the physical training. Group 3 received no martial arts training but jogged and played basketball and football under the instructor's coaching and supervision.

Trulson's findings indicated clear changes in group 1. After six months, the young men in this group had fewer delinquent tendencies, less anxiety and aggression, improved self-esteem and social skills, and more awareness of commonly held values. Those in group 2 had increased delinquent tendencies and were more aggressive and less adjusted than when the study began. Those in group 3 showed no change in delinquent tendencies or on most personality measures, but their scores on self-esteem and social skills improved over the six months.

On the basis of these findings, it seems that sport participation might keep young people out of trouble when it emphasizes (1) a philosophy of non-violence, (2) respect for self and others, (3) the importance of fitness and control over self, (4) confidence in physical skills, and (5) a sense of responsibility. When these five things are absent, sport participation will seldom keep young people out of trouble. Simply taking them off the streets is just the beginning. If they play sports that emphasize confrontation, dominating others, using their bodies as weapons and defining masculinity or success in terms of conquest, we *cannot* expect rates of deviance to decrease. Changing behaviour is a complex process, and to do it in connection with sports participation requires a clear programme of intervention in the lives of young people. Certainly it seems likely that short-term 'diversionary' schemes may not impact beyond the event, and that higher-risk clients need longer-term goals than are provided in some of these schemes. This does not mean that all sports must be turned into treatment programmes, but it does mean that playing sports cannot be expected to keep young people out of trouble unless participation connects them with people who can support them and advocate their interests, and provides them with opportunities to make choices that do not involve deviance (see Nichols, 2007).

These studies show that neither virtue nor deviance is *caused* by sports and sports participation. Sports are sites where young people often have powerful and exciting physical and social experiences. When experiences are organized so that young people receive thoughtful guidance from adults who can help them develop self-respect and become connected to the rest of the community, good outcomes are likely. However, when playing sports separates athletes from the rest of the community and fosters overconformity to the norms of the sports ethic, good outcomes are unlikely. Bonds formed among athletes can take them in many directions, including deviant ones. Sport programmes are effective only when they enable people to live satisfying lives in the world beyond sports; simply taking people off the streets for a few hours a week so that they can bounce basketballs does little more than provide temporary shelter. Further research is clearly needed in order to learn whether such projects have any enduring impact.

    How different is steroid use from cosmetic surgery for the male TV newsies reporting these stories, from Botox for actresses, beta blockers for public speakers[?]

(Robert Lipsyte, journalist, 2005)

Performance-Enhancing Substances: Deviant OverConformity in Sports

Stories about athletes using performance-enhancing substances are no longer shocking; they appear regularly in the media. However, many people do not know that drug and substance use in sports has a long history (Dimeo, 2007). For centuries athletes have taken a wide variety of everyday and exotic substances to aid their performances, and this has occurred at many levels of competition. In fact, research suggests that athletes in past centuries would have taken the same substances that athletes take today if the substances had been available (Hoberman, 1992, 2004; Todd, 1987). This makes it difficult to say that money, television and the erosion of traditional values are the causes of this form of deviance. The use of performance-enhancing substances *pre-dates* commercial sports and television, and it occurred regularly when

Off-the-field deviance among athletes may decrease if they are taught a philosophy of non-violence, respect for self and opponents, self-control, confidence in their abilities, and responsibility. This can happen in a variety of sports, even those involving heavy physical contact (*Source*: McGraw-Hill)

reflect on SPORTS   *Are some sports forms deviant? Field 'sports'* • • •

Many modern sports forms have their roots in hunting activities. Indeed, in the 1900 Paris Olympic Games, the live pigeon-shooting event was won by a Belgian athlete, Leon de Lunden, who killed 21 birds. Similarly, fox-hunting was one of the first activities to which the term 'sport' was attached, and the pleasure in the hunt was enhanced by the utilitarian pleasure of killing and eating the prey (Elias and Dunning, 1986). During the eighteenth century, animal racing in the form of fox-hunting, or dogs that would chase and kill a hare, remained popular, but adopted what figurational sociologists would call a more 'civilized' form. The difference at this time was that the foxes were killed for 'sport', rather than any utilitarian purpose, and the kill was made by the dogs rather than the gentleman hunter (Dunning, 1993). Increasingly, people have come to view violent activities and killing as uncivilized, and athletes today engage in actions of chasing, catching, shooting or throwing a weapon in ways which are more symbolic than 'real'.

For example, hunting with dogs was banned by the Scottish Parliament in 2001, and in England and Wales in 2005. However, this legislation has met with resistance, and certain hunting activities have been controversially maintained in some areas of the UK. On the first day of hunting after the ban in England and Wales, 91 foxes were 'legally' killed (shot or killed underground by terriers ostensibly to protect game birds). The pro-hunting lobby argues that such activities serve a utilitarian purpose of controlling the animal population and contributing to the rural economy and, perhaps more controversially, many argue that hunting is a legitimate form of 'sport'. The philosopher Roger Scruton offers this opinion:

> By describing hunting and fishing as sports, our ancestors intended to distinguish them from the mere games we play with each other. Football, cricket and tennis were pastimes; the contest with the quarry was a way of life … It is difficult for many people today to understand how you can be bound by a code of honour and sympathy to an animal that you are intending to kill; but this is exactly what was once understood by chivalry and it is perhaps the function of sport to cultivate the spirit of chivalry in those who engage in it. For chivalry limits wars, gives quarter to enemies, controls aggression and brokers peace … chivalry is not only a necessary virtue but one that is best acquired through sport … Through country sports we are reunited to our hunter-gatherer past. We are granted a glimpse of another world, a world that we share with the animals, who are dignified as antagonists, worshipped as totems and pursued as quarry. You may welcome this or you may deplore it; but it is what sport really means.
>
> *(2004, pp. 62–7)*

The debate over whether the pursuit and killing of an animal is morally acceptable as a sporting practice is illustrated in the case of 'sporting estates', which are private hunting reserves maintained in Scotland. These estates are governed under land laws which have been implemented to protect game but also

Hunting is a controversial sport which is supported by many, but described by others as cruel and 'deviant' (*Source*: Elizabeth Pike)

ensure that these are elitist areas which exclude much of the local indigenous population from hunting for food. The most widespread are maintained for deerstalking, and they cover more than a third of all privately owned land in Scotland. While Scottish National Heritage recognizes hunting as a form of country or field 'sport', sportscotland refuses to recognize any field sports on ethical and moral grounds (Wightman et al., 2002). The contradiction in the views of these two bodies provides a good example of the controversy in associating hunting activities with sporting recreation. As Wightman et al. (2002, p. 60) explain: 'Hunting is no straightforward form of outdoor recreation. It is associated (at least in the public mind) with elite endeavour, class delineation and morally questionable practices'. *What do you think?*

traditional values were widely accepted. Therefore, we must look beyond these factors to explain why athletes use performance-enhancing substances.

Research also suggests that drug and substance use is not caused by defective socialization or lack of moral character among athletes. In fact, substance use often occurs among the most dedicated, committed and hard-working athletes in sports. Nor are all substance users helpless victims of exploitive coaches and trainers, although coaches and trainers who push the sports ethic without question may indirectly encourage the use of performance-enhancing substances. At this point, it appears that most substance use and abuse is tied to an athlete's uncritical acceptance of the norms of the sports ethic. Therefore, it is grounded in overconformity – the same type of overconformity that occurs when injured distance runners continue training, even when training may cause serious injuries; when young female gymnasts control weight by cutting their food intake to dangerous levels; and when rugby players use painkilling drugs and risk their already injured and surgically repaired bodies week after painful week (Roderick, 2006a).

Sports provide powerful and memorable experiences and many athletes are willing to 'set no limits' in their quest to maintain participation and their identities as members of a select group sharing lives characterized by intensity and challenge. Athletes seek victories because winning enables them to stay involved, but their desire to win is secondary to their desire to play and keep the respect of other athletes. These dynamics encourage overconformity to the norms of the sports ethic, and they affect athletes at various levels of sports – from local gyms to the changing rooms of professional sports teams; they affect both women and men across many sports, from the 100-metre sprint to the marathon and from tennis to football.

The point here is that athletes use substances, legal and possibly illegal, for reasons that are different than the reasons that an alienated 25-year-old shoots methanphetamines to get high and 'zone out' as he rejects society's norms. Athletes use drugs because they accept norms blindly and overconform to them. Therefore, we need different explanations to understand the athletes and control their actions. The explanations and methods of control used to deal with people who reject norms and use heroin, cocaine and methanphetamines are not relevant when trying to limit the use and abuse of performance-enhancing substances in sports.

Defining and banning performance-enhancing substances

Defining *performance-enhancing substances* is difficult. They can include anything from aspirin to heroin; they may be legal or illegal, harmless or dangerous, natural or synthetic, socially acceptable or unacceptable, commonly used or exotic. Furthermore, they may produce real physical changes, psychological changes, or both (see Cartoon 6.3). Problems with definitions are faced whenever a sports organization develops an anti-drug or no-doping programme. For example, until 1999, the International Olympic Committee (IOC) defined doping in this way:

> [Doping is] the administration of or use by a competing athlete of any substance *foreign* to the body or any *physiological substance* taken in *abnormal quantity* or taken by an *abnormal route of entry* into the body with the *sole intention* of increasing in an *artificial* and *unfair* manner his/her performance in competition. When necessity demands *medical treatment* with any substance that, because of its nature, dosage, or application, is able to boost the athlete's performance in competition in an artificial and unfair manner, this too is regarded by the IOC as doping.
>
> *(USOC, 1992, p. 1, emphasis added)*

'Hey smart guy, did you mix the growth hormones with the "miracle seaweed extract" I bought online?'

Cartoon 6.3 **The negative side effects of various combinations of substances are difficult to identify. Controlled studies of banned substances are difficult to do because it may not be ethical to experiment with the same dosages that athletes use. This means that the side effects of many substances are unknown**

This definition may sound good, but the IOC had difficulty defining all the terms in italics. For example, what is a substance 'foreign' to the body, and why are the 'foreign' substances of aspirin and ibuprofen not banned, whereas the 'natural' hormone testosterone and naturally grown marijuana are banned? What is an 'abnormal' quantity or an 'abnormal' route of entry? Why are megadoses of vitamins not banned, whereas small amounts of decongestants are banned? Why can athletes be stripped of medals when they swallow medications without intending to enhance performance, whereas other athletes keep their medals after having intravenous needles inserted into their veins to be rehydrated during competitions?

With scientific discoveries being made every day and applied to sports, what is artificial and what is unfair? Why are needles permitted to drain fluid from the knees of weightlifters and inject their bodies with painkillers, whereas the same needles are considered dangerous and artificial when used to inject a cyclist's or distance runner's own 'natural' red blood cells into a vein (blood doping)? Why is the electronic stimulation of muscles not banned? Is it not artificial? Is it fair to compete with knees strengthened with surgically inserted synthetic ligaments after natural ligaments were torn beyond repair? Why are biofeedback and other psychological technologies defined as 'natural' and 'fair', whereas certain naturally grown herbal teas are defined as 'unnatural' and 'unfair'? Are vitamins natural? Amino acids? Caffeine? Human growth hormone? Gatorade? Protein drinks? Creatine? Eyeglasses? What if an athlete could wear contacts that would boost vision acuity from 20-20 to 20-5?

How about so-called natural herbs, chemicals and compounds now stacked floor to ceiling in stores that sell nutritional supplements with the promise of performance enhancement? Is it natural to deprive yourself of food to make weight or meet the demands of a coach who measures body fat every week and punishes athletes who eat 'normal' diets? Should athletes who binge and purge, become anorexic or exercise in saunas wearing rubber suits to lose weight be considered normal? In fact, what is normal about any of the social, psychological, biomechanical, environmental and technological methods of manipulating and changing athletes' bodies and minds in today's high-performance sports? Are marathon runners deviant if they wear high-tech 'ice suits' before a race in hot weather to drop their core body temperature? Is this not performance-enhancing? Is it normal, safe? How about 12-year-old gymnasts who pop a dozen anti-inflammatory pills every day so that they can train through pain? Are they deviant? Are they different from endurance cyclists who take caffeine pills to get extra energy during an event?

How about footballers who became addicted to painkillers after being regularly prescribed them by team doctors? Why do we call athletes heroes when they use an intravenous procedure to play in ungodly heat, or take large injections of painkilling drugs to keep them training and playing, and then condemn the same athletes when they take drugs to help them build muscles damaged by overtraining or take other drugs to help them relax and recover after their bodies and minds have been pushed beyond limits in the pursuit of dreams?

Why do many athletes see the use of drugs as a noble act of commitment and dedication, whereas many spectators see it as a reprehensible act of deviance yet pay big money to watch athletes do superhuman things requiring extreme training regimes and strategies made possible only by drugs or random genetic mutations? These and hundreds of other questions about what is artificial, natural, foreign, fair and abnormal show that any definition of *doping* will lead to endless debates about the technical and legal meaning of terms (Shapin, 2005). For this reason, the IOC changed its definition of doping in 1999. Now the Olympic Movement Anti-Doping Code defines doping in accordance with World Anti-Doping Agency (WADA) policy as: the presence of a prohibited substance in an athlete's bodily specimen; use, or attempted use, of a prohibited substance or prohibited method; failing to produce a sample; missing a test; tampering with doping control; possessing, trafficking or administering prohibited substances or methods (World Anti-Doping Agency, 2003). However, even this simplified definition, along with the 30 pages in which prohibited substances and prohibited methods are described, raises many questions. A new body, the International Intergovernmental Consultative Group on Anti-Doping in Sport (IICGADS), has, therefore, been formed to help generate a common international response to issues of doping and the funding of the WADA (see Houlihan, 2004).

Meanwhile, physicians, pharmacists, chemists, inventors and athletes continue to develop new and different aids to performance – chemical, 'natural' and otherwise. For example, Anthony Almada and former partner Bill Phillips, founders of EAS (Experimental and Applied Sciences), a major supplement producer and distributor, made many millions of pounds by knowing all the loopholes in every sport's drug policy and creating substances that fit through the holes. Now we have a seemingly endless game of scientific hide-and-seek, which persists despite new definitions and drug policies. This game will become even more heated and controversial as scientists manipulate the brain and nervous system, and use genetic manipulation and engineering to improve athletic performance. With new performance-enhancing technologies, we are approaching a time when defining, identifying and dealing with doping and drugs will be only one of many strategies for manipulating athletes' bodies and improving performance (Bjerklie and Park, 2004).

Further complicating decisions about which substances to ban is confusion about their effects on athletic performance. Ethical and legal considerations have constrained researchers who study the impact of megadoses and multiple combinations of substances that are 'stacked and cycled' by athletes. Athletes learn things in changing rooms faster than scientists learn them in the laboratory, although the validity of changing-room knowledge is questionable at best. Furthermore, by the time researchers have valid information about a substance, athletes have moved on to others, which are unknown to researchers. This is why most athletes ignore 'official statements' about the consequences and dangers of doping – the statements are about two to five years behind the 'inventors' who supply new substances.

As the market for substances and the wealth of athletes have grown, so have the laboratories that are dedicated to 'beating the system' with 'designer drugs', undetectable substances, and masking agents that hide certain molecules in the testing process. Perhaps most famous is Balco, the San Francisco-based Bay Area Laboratory Co-Operative, which has provided support for many British athletes, including the sprinter Dwain Chambers who received a two-year ban and lifetime Olympic ban in 2003 for use of the designer steroid tetrahydrogestrinone (THG) provided by this laboratory. There are dozens of other 'designer substances' rumoured to be available for the right price (Assael, 2003, 2005; Sokolove, 2004b).

The Internet has made information about and access to substances immediately available to athletes worldwide (see website resources at the end of this chapter). Muscle, fitness and bodybuilding magazines provide dozens of references to these sites. Despite anti-doping policies in sports, most athletes know that those who control sports organizations are not eager to report positive tests because it jeopardizes the billions of dollars that corporate sponsors and television networks pay for events that are promoted as 'clean and wholesome' (*ESPN The Magazine*, 2005; Jennings and Sambrook, 2000). Testing, therefore, remains a challenge in most sports organizations (Keating, 2005). In fact, if there were a law that mandated random testing of all professional athletes across all major sports by an independent enforcement agency, it would cost billions of pounds to test all international, Olympic-level, national and elite club-level athletes over the next decade.

Finally, some people ask why drugs should be banned in sports when they are widely accepted in society, and used to improve performance or treat conditions that interfere with performance at home, work or play. The majority of adults in most wealthy, high-tech societies use tranquillizers, pain controllers, mood controllers, antidepressants, decongestants, diet pills, birth control pills, insulin, caffeine, nicotine, sleep aids and/or alcohol. Doctors readily prescribe prohormone and hormone therapies to improve strength and counteract the negative effects of ageing; these include thyroid hormone, testosterone, anabolic steroids, human growth hormone (HGH), HGH stimulants, and rostenedione, DHEA and creatine. Every six months, the list changes and grows longer as new discoveries are made and new supplements are manufactured. In fact, if people really did say no to drugs, life in most Western societies would change dramatically. When a 55-year-old man takes HGH to maintain strength so that he can outperform others in his highly paid job, why should his 25-year-old son not take HGH to perform in the Commonwealth Games swimming championships (Weise, 2003)?

These issues lead to an important question: why control athletes in ways that other people are not controlled? After all, do colleges have rules banning caffeine and other drugs that students use so that they can study all night and be mentally primed to take a biology test? Do teachers make students sign an oath to avoid drugs that might enable them to perform better in a course? Do employers tell executives not to use hormone therapies that will keep them fit for work? Are men told by their partners not to take Viagra or other substances that elevate sexual performance? Why should athletes be tested and denied access to substances, when others competing or working for valued rewards are often encouraged to take similar substances? As these questions are asked, it remains difficult to define drugs, doping and substance abuse in sports.

Why is the challenge of substance control so great in sports today?

Many factors contribute to the tendency among today's athletes to seek substances for the edge that they need to pursue their dreams and stay involved in the sports they love and the jobs for which they are paid. These factors include the following.

- *The visibility and resources associated with sports today have fuelled massive research and development efforts and increased the number and availability of performance-enhancing substances.* Entrepreneurs and corporations have developed performance-enhancing substances as forms of 'alternative medicine' that make them substantial profits. Ageing baby boomers (the massive population cohorts born between 1946 and 1964) see these substances as health aids and tools for preserving youth. This creates a market consisting of 20 million Britons that pushes the supplement industry to make available an ever-expanding array of substances.

■ *People in post-industrial societies are deeply fascinated with technology and want to use it to extend human limits.* Advertising messages that promote hyper-consumption as a lifestyle encourage this fascination. Athletes, because they live in these societies and seek to excel in their sports, hear those messages loud and clear. Like many of us, they use consumption as a tool to pursue their dreams. Consuming substances is simply another manifestation of their overconformity to the norms of the sport ethic, and they see it as part of their dedication and willingness to pay the price to stay in the game.

■ *The rationalization of the body has influenced how people conceptualize the relationship between the body and mind.* People in post-industrial societies see the body as a malleable tool serving the interests of the mind. Separating the body from the mind is common in cultures with Judeo-Christian religious beliefs, and it leads people to objectify their own bodies, view them as machines and use them as tools for doing what the mind commands. Using substances to improve the body and what it can do fits with this orientation and is consistent with the way that athletes use their minds to ignore or redefine physical pain and injury (Grant, 2002a, 2002b).

■ *There is a growing emphasis on self-medication.* People in wealthy post-industrial societies increasingly seek alternatives to mainstream medicine. They use friends, advertisements and the Internet for medical information, and they are open to experimenting with substances that can be purchased online and over the counter without licensed medical advice or approval. A study of injured athletes found that many turned to complementary and alternative medicines (CAMs) as a result of their dissatisfaction with traditional forms of medicine in treating sports-related injuries. In particular these athletes enjoyed being actively involved in their own treatment, which contrasted with the passivity of traditional allopathic healthcare and was more consistent with their identity as an active athlete. Furthermore, the study found that women particularly enjoyed the holistic nature of alternative medical treatments, which were experienced as more 'feminine' than orthodox medicine (Pike, 2005a).

■ *Gender relations are changing in contemporary society.* As traditional ideas about masculinity and femininity have been challenged, the threat of change has fuelled a desire among some men to do whatever it takes to develop a physique that reaffirms an ideology of male strength and power. At the same time, the promise of change has fuelled a desire among many women to revise their notions of femininity and do whatever it takes to achieve strength, power and physical ability, and to lose weight at the same time. Therefore, men and women define performance-enhancing substances as valuable in their quests to preserve or challenge prevailing gender ideology.

■ *The organization of power and performance sports encourages overconformity to the norms of the sports ethic.* Many sports are organized so that continued participation at the level needed to sustain an 'athlete identity' requires competitive success – *making the cut*, so to speak. The desire to maintain participation makes winning personally important to athletes and fuels their search for performance-enhancing substances. There was also the famous case in France in 2003 of Christophe Faviau, a father of two tennis players, who spiked the drinks of his children's opponents without their knowledge, because he was so determined to maintain his children's athletic successes. One of the players he drugged with a tranquillizer fell asleep while driving home from a game, and was killed in the ensuing road traffic accident.

■ *Coaches, sponsors, administrators and fans clearly encourage deviant overconformity.* Athletes who make sacrifices and put their bodies on the line for the sake of the team, the community or the nation are defined as heroes. Athletes realize this and many willingly take substances as they 'do their duty'. For example, Sandra, a track and field athlete, talked of how she had weekly cortisone injections to reduce the inflammation caused by a back injury, on the advice of her impatient coach: 'I think I knew that it wasn't really doing me any good, but I also knew that if I wanted to compete then I had to somehow numb the pain. My coach said that the best way for me to do that was to have cortisone injections' (cited in Charlesworth and Young, 2006, p. 94). When Rio Ferdinand, an English Premiership footballer, was banned from a lucrative European championship tournament, his sponsors ensured that he was able to compensate for his financial loss by giving him the opportunity to appear in television commercials which parodied his drugs ban, and simultaneously undermined any message that drug taking is 'wrong' (see Cashmore, 2005).

■ *The performance of athletes is closely monitored within the social structure of elite sports.* Elite sports are organized to emphasize (a) control, especially control over the body, (b) conformity, especially to the demands of a coach, and (c) shame, especially when an athlete lets down teammates, parents, schools, communities, clubs and corporate sponsors. This creates a powerful incentive to do whatever it takes to succeed on the field.

When the above factors are combined, access to substances and the willingness to use them are high. Such conditions exist today, and this makes it more difficult than ever to control substance use.

Drug testing as a deterrent

Drug testing is controversial. There are powerful arguments for and against it. The arguments in favour of testing are as follows.

■ Drug testing is needed to protect athletes' health and reduce the pressures that they feel to take substances to keep up with competitors. In elite cycling, the blood-boosting drug erythropoietin (EPO) was implicated in the deaths of about 20 riders from Europe between 1988 and 2000 (Zorpette, 2000), and seven of the eight elite cyclists who died over a 13-month period in 2003 and early 2004 were victims of heart attacks, often caused by circulatory problems (Henderson, 2004). Erythropoietin causes a person's blood to thicken and clot, and it can be fatal when taken in high doses. Furthermore, the use of steroids and other substances may partially account for the rising injury toll in certain sports in which severe muscle and tendon tears and bone fractures are common (Keating, 2004; Verducci, 2002). Other serious health risks are associated with various substances, including ephedrine; steroid precursors, such as androstenedione; diuretics; epogen; and beta-blockers (Meyer, 2002).

■ Drug testing is needed to achieve a level playing field where competitive outcomes reflect skills and training rather than access to substances. Many athletes and spectators believe that some of the most visible and talented athletes today owe part of their success to drugs.

This damages the integrity of sports and jeopardizes sponsorships, television rights fees, and the willingness of spectators to buy tickets and pay cable and satellite fees so that they can see games.

■ Requiring people to submit to drug tests is legally justified because the actions of those who take substances affect the lives of other people. If drug users are not caught, they influence the chances of success for athletes who are not taking drugs. For example, in the year after Dwain Chambers was banned for use of the drug THG, several US athletes were missing from the Olympic team in Athens. There was speculation that some of these athletes were also using banned substances provided by Balco, the same company used by Chambers. If this were the case, banning Chambers and forcing the withdrawal of any other drug users enabled a greater chance of success for their non-drug-using competitors.

■ Drug testing is part of normal law enforcement because drug use is illegal and must be controlled, as other criminal acts are controlled. This means that punishments must be clearly explained, fairly administered and severe enough to deter future substance use.

■ Drug tests must be expanded to preserve the current meaning of sports and athletic achievements. According to a member of the World Anti-Doping Agency (WADA), if doping and other technologies cannot be controlled it will mark 'the end of sport as we know it' (Swift and Yaeger, 2001, p. 91). Unless drug testing succeeds, there will be no precedent for controlling future technologies, such as genetic manipulation, that will turn sports into circus-like spectacles in which genetic engineers compete against each other to produce the most superhuman bodies. These technologies already exist, and many athletes are eager to try them (Reynolds, 2007; Wilson, 2008). For example, there are reports of top professional soccer players storing stem cells from the umbilical cords of their newborn children so the cells can be used in future treatments to restore the players' bodies after serious injuries (Cannella, 2006). Testing is the only hope of preventing such things.

The arguments against testing are equally powerful. They emphasize the following points.

■ Testing is ineffective because athletes are one step ahead of rule makers and testers (see Cartoon 6.4). By the time certain substances are banned and tests are developed to detect them, athletes are taking new substances that tests cannot detect or are not calibrated to detect (Assael, 2005, 2007a, 2007b, 2007c; Sokolove, 2004b; Zorpette, 2000). Don Catlin, head of the University of California at Los Angeles (UCLA) laboratory that does all the tests for the WADA, says, 'You may think testing is wonderful and great, but ... [athletes] have little trouble beating the test and there are many doctors telling them how to do it' (in Patrick, 2005, p. 7c). An additional concern is that the test results may not always be correct. For example, the British runner Diane Modahl was banned from competition in 1994 for four years after failing a drug test, but following an appeal and subsequent investigation, reasonable doubt was cast on the testing procedures and her ban was lifted. Modahl sought up to £305 000 in damages from the British Athletics Federation, which became bankrupt in 1997 (Cashmore, 2005). Similarly, the British tennis player Greg Rusedski tested positive in 2004 for nandrolene, but was also subsequently cleared when it was found that trainers in the Association of Tennis Professionals may have inadvertently given him, and several other players, contaminated supplements.

'Don't worry, most of these are legal and the others won't show up on the drug tests!'

Cartoon 6.4 Some athletes take vast amounts of various substances in many combinations. The industries that produce performance-enhancing substances are now located worldwide. They have stayed ahead of the testers in sports, and probably will continue to do so

- Requiring people to submit to drug tests without cause violates rights to privacy and sets precedents for invasive testing programmes that produce medical and biological information that could be used against a person's interest apart from sports (Malloy and Zakus, 2002). If protocols for future tests require blood samples, muscle biopsies, genetic testing and DNA analysis, test results could lead some people to be stigmatized as 'impure', 'contaminated' or abnormal for medical or biological reasons. There are also particular issues related to child athletes, given that there are increasing examples of young athletes taking drugs and yet few explicit references in the World Anti-Doping Code to how the Code should be applied to a minor. For example, should children bear the same responsibility for understanding doping rules as an adult athlete, should their names be publicly disclosed if they are found to have violated these regulations (even if it is possible that they did not knowingly take a banned substance), and should there be an organization acting as an advocate and taking responsibility for protecting the interests of child athletes in such cases (see Houlihan, 2004)?

- Drug tests are expensive and drain resources that could be used to fund health education programmes for athletes. The test administered to athletes in Olympic sports by the

WADA costs well over £150 per athlete every time it is administered. Testing 100 000 potential Olympic athletes around the world once a year would cost about £15 million. Furthermore, athletes taking substances are unlikely to be deterred by a test administered only once a year, especially if it is set up to detect only a limited number of substances. Furthermore, athletes could still take the substances during the off-season while they train and then stop prior to the season when they would be tested. This would teach athletes nothing about health and how to set health priorities in sports.

- Drug tests often cannot detect substances that are designed to match substances naturally produced by the body. Erythropoietin, HGH, IGF-1 (insulin-like growth factor-1) and testosterone are powerful performance enhancers produced by the body, and normal levels of these substances vary from person to person. This makes it difficult to determine an amount of each substance that would be considered illegal for all bodies. And, once legal levels are determined, athletes who test positive frequently use lawsuits to challenge the limits in individual cases (Zorpette, 2000).

- Drug tests provide an incentive for developing forms of genetic engineering that alter physical characteristics related to performance (Assael, 2005; Longman, 2001; Parrish, 2002; Sokolove, 2004b; Sweeney, 2004; Swift and Yaeger, 2001; Zorpette, 2000). When genetic engineering occurs, it will make steroids and other drugs obsolete. Gene therapies are seen as crucial treatments to deal with the negative effects of ageing and to cure or reduce the symptoms of certain diseases. These therapies will make 'gene doping' possible for athletes – therapies to enhance muscle size, strength and resiliency. Gene doping and other forms of genetic manipulation will be difficult if not impossible to detect, and tests will cost at least £500 per athlete (Sweeney, 2004). Chuck Yesalis, an American professor who has studied drugs in sports for many years, argues that drug testing will be made irrelevant by 'genetic engineering' (in Patrick, 2002, p. 6C).

In the face of arguments for and against drug testing, many athletes have mixed feelings about testing policies and programmes. They realize that political and economic interests can cloud the validity and reliability of testing programmes. They also know that drug testing is an enormously complicated bureaucratic process and that mistakes can occur at many points. This has already provoked legal challenges to test results. These challenges are complicated because they often cross national borders where judicial processes and definitions of individual rights and due process are inconsistent. In the meantime, athletes know that fellow athletes continue to overconform to the sports ethic and seek creative ways to push their bodies to new limits in the pursuit of dreams.

When drug testing is done by the same organizations that promote and profit from sports, athletes have good reason to have mixed feelings. Promoting, profiting and policing just do not go together. To avoid conflicts of interest, international athletes in Olympic sports are tested by 'independent' agencies formed in 1999. The World Anti-Doping Agency conducts random, unannounced tests around the world. UK Sport (2005) developed the *UK National Anti-Doping Policy* with a stated aim to 'protect an athlete's fundamental right to participate in doping-free sport and thus promote health, fairness and equality for athletes in the UK' (UK Sport, 2005, p. 4). Within this policy framework, UK Sport is responsible for overseeing tests similar to the WADA procedures on British athletes wherever they are training around the world. These two agencies work together. However, the testing of samples collected by the UK Sport programme takes place in WADA-accredited laboratories and so is also partly funded by WADA. This causes some people to wonder about how independent the body is. Both agencies have an educational emphasis, which may be more important than the tests they conduct, if educational programmes are expanded to emphasize the control of all forms of deviant overconformity in elite sports. But this is unlikely.

Controlling substance use in sports: where to start

Today's athletes, like their counterparts in the past, seek continued participation and excellence in sports. When they overconform to norms promoting sacrifice and risk in the pursuit of distinction and dreams, they are not likely to define the use of performance-enhancing substances as deviant. Even Ben Johnson, the Canadian sprinter who lost his gold medal for the 100-metre sprint in the 1988 Seoul Olympics, said this in 1993: 'You can never clean it up. People are always gonna be doing something. They feel good about themselves, and they feel it's right to do it' (in Fish, 1993, p. A12). A physician who works with athletes makes Johnson's point in another way; he observes that 'athletes don't use drugs to escape reality – they use them to enforce the reality that surrounds them' (DiPasquale, 1992, p. 2).

This forces everyone who uses sports for entertainment to ask if they are being reasonable when they praise athletes as warrior-heroes when they take injections of cortisone (a type of steroid) and other painkilling drugs to stay on the field, and then condemn them as cheaters for taking steroids, HGH and other substances to heal injuries more quickly, rebuild muscles damaged by overtraining, or relax and recover after exhausting and tightly scheduled competitions (Farrey, 2007; Olney, 2006). Similarly, is it reasonable to condemn athletes for failing to be positive role models for children, when we expect them to do anything to stay on the field and sacrifice their bodies in sports that involve brutal body contact and gruelling physical challenges?

A central point in this chapter is that athletes use performance-enhancing substances not because they lack character or are victims of evil coaches, but because they uncritically accept and overconform to the norms of the sports ethic in an effort to remain in sports and be accepted as athletes. This is why tougher rules and increased testing have not been effective. Moral panics over drug use and oversimplified solutions will not stop athletes from using substances that they see as essential to do what they must do to maintain their identities and continue experiencing the exhilaration of playing elite sports.

The use of performance-enhancing substances and future forms of genetic manipulation cannot be eliminated from elite sports cultures as they are organized today. Effective control requires both cultural and structural changes in sports so that athletes, coaches and others critically assess the sports ethic and control deviant overconformity, or redefine the sports ethic to include new norms (Shogan and Ford, 2000). Here are some suggestions on where to begin these processes.

■ *Critically examine the deep hypocrisy involved in elite power and performance sports.* It is not possible to effectively control the use of performance-enhancing substances when federations and teams encourage general overconformity to the norms of the sports ethic. Therefore, there is a need for critical discussions of limits on the use of currently accepted performance-enhancing strategies, such as injecting painkilling drugs, vitamin B-12, hydration therapies, playing with pins in broken bones and with high-tech 'casts' to hold broken bones in place during competition, and using special harnesses to restrict the movement of injured joints. These practices are common, and they foster a sport culture in which the use of performance-enhancing substances is defined as logical and courageous.

- *Establish rules indicating clearly that certain risks to health are undesirable and unnecessary in sports.* When teenagers who compete with training-induced stress fractures in professional football are turned into national heroes and poster children for corporate sponsors, we promote deviant overconformity in sports. This sets up athletes for permanent injuries and disabilities. This is clearly unnecessary, and sports organizations should not allow it to occur.

- *Establish a 'harm reduction' approach in which athletes are not allowed to play until certified as 'well' (not simply 'able to compete') by two independent physicians or medical personnel.* This approach differs from current practices in which therapists and medical personnel do what they can to get injured athletes on the field as quickly as possible (*ESPN The Magazine*, 2005; Safai, 2003; Waddington, 2000a, 2000b, 2006). Too many team doctors and physiotherapists have divided loyalties because they are paid by teams or by medical organizations that have contracted with teams or leagues (Howe, 2004a; Malcolm, 2006; Roderick et al., 2000). Therapists and doctors also must be able to identify the ways that athletes hide injuries and be prepared to negotiate strategies for healthy recoveries. They should be health advocates paid by someone other than team management. The focus of a player health advocate would be protecting the long-term well-being of athletes. Therefore, instead of testing for drugs, athletes should be tested to certify that they are healthy enough to participate. If drugs damage their health or make it dangerous for them to play, they would not be certified. Only when their health improves and meets established guidelines would they be allowed back on the field. This would be a major step in creating a new sports culture.

- *Establish health and injury education programmes for young athletes.* This is a first step in establishing a sport culture in which *courage* is defined in terms of recognizing limits and accepting the discipline necessary to accurately and responsibly acknowledge the consequences of deviant overconformity and sports injuries. Learning to be in tune with one's body rather than to deny pain and injury is important in controlling the use of potentially dangerous performance-enhancing substances.

- *Establish codes of ethics for sport scientists.* Too many sport scientists assist athletes as they overconform to the norms of the sports ethic, rather than helping them raise critical questions about how deviant overconformity is dangerous to their health and development. This makes scientists become part of the problem rather than part of the solution. For example, sports psychology should be used to help athletes understand the consequences of their choices to play sports, and reduce the extent to which guilt, shame and pathology influence participation and training decisions. This is the alternative to the technique of 'psycho-doping', which encourages deviant overconformity by making athletes more likely to give body and soul to their sports without carefully answering critical questions about *why* they are doing what they are doing and *what* it means in their lives.

- *Make drug and substance use education a key part of larger deviance and health education programmes.* Parents, coaches, managers, therapists and athletes should participate in formal educational programmes in which they consider and discuss the norms of the sport ethic and how to prevent deviant overconformity. Unless these people understand their roles in reproducing a culture supportive of substance use and abuse, the problems will continue. Such a programme would involve training to do the following:

- create norms regulating the use of new and powerful technology and medical knowledge that go beyond the use of drugs
- question and critically examine values and norms in sports, as well as set limits on conformity to those values and norms
- teach athletes to think critically about sports so that they understand that they can make choices and changes in sports
- provide parents, coaches and athletes with the best and most recent information available on performance-enhancing technologies so that they can make informed decisions about if and how they will be used.

We now face a future without clearly defined ideas about the meaning of achievement in sports. There are new financial incentives to succeed in sports, athlete identities have become central in the lives of many sports participants, and performance-enhancing technologies have become increasingly effective and available. Therefore, we need *new* approaches and guidelines. Old approaches and guidelines combined with coercive methods of control have not been effective. Trying to make sports into what we believe they were in the past is futile. We cannot go back to an imagined past. We face new issues and challenges, and it will take new approaches to deal with them effectively (Kix, 2007). As described in Breaking barriers (pp. 183–185), this is evident in the Paralympics, where new technologies have created a number of challenges related to fairness.

Widespread participation is needed if sports cultures are to be successfully transformed. At present, both nation states and corporate sponsors have appropriated the culture of power and performance sports and used it to deliver messages that foster forms of deviant overconformity that promote their interests. There is no conspiracy underlying this, but it creates a challenge that can be met only through collective awareness of what needs to be done and collective efforts to do it. Even then changes will be incremental rather than revolutionary, but changes are possible if we work to create them in our sports, schools and communities.

Summary: Is Deviance in Sports Out of Control?

The study of deviance in sports presents challenges due to four factors: (1) the forms and causes of deviance in sports are so diverse that no single theory can explain all of them; (2) actions, traits and ideas accepted in sports may be defined as deviant in the rest of society, and what is permitted in society may be defined as deviant in sports; (3) deviance in sports often involves uncritically accepting norms rather than rejecting them; (4) training in sports has incorporated such new forms of science and technology that people have not had the opportunity to develop norms to guide and evaluate the actions of athletes and others in sports.

Widely used conceptual frameworks in sociology do not offer useful explanations of the full range of deviance in sports, nor do they offer much help in devising ways to control it. Problems are encountered when functionalist theory is used. Functionalists define deviance as the failure to conform to ideals, and deviants are seen as lacking moral character. But ideals are difficult to identify, and athletes often violate norms as they go overboard in their acceptance of them, not because they lack character.

Similarly, problems occur when conflict theory is used. Conflict theorists define deviance as actions violating the interests of people with money and power, and deviants are seen as exploited victims of the quest for profits. But people with power and money do not control all sports, and it is not accurate to define all athletes as victims.

Sociologists today generally use a constructionist approach to study and explain deviance in sports. This approach, based on a combination of cultural, interactionist and structural theories, emphasizes that norms and deviance are socially constructed through social interaction as it occurs in a particular social and cultural context. This approach emphasizes that the dynamics of sports participation are grounded in the social worlds created around sports and that people in sports make choices and can act as agents of change in sports and the culture as a whole. The use of a constructionist approach in this chapter highlights the distinction between cases of deviant underconformity and overconformity. Such a distinction is important because the most serious forms of deviance in sports occur when athletes, coaches and others overconform to the norms of the sports ethic – a cluster of norms that emphasizes dedication to the game, making sacrifices, striving for distinction, taking risks, playing with pain and injury, and pursuing dreams. When little concern is given to setting limits in the process of conforming to these norms, deviant overconformity becomes a problem.

Research supports this explanation. Most on-the-field and sports-related actions fall within an accepted range; when they fall outside this range, they often involve overconformity to the norms of the sport ethic. Rates of off-the-field deviance among athletes are generally comparable with rates among peers in the general population; when rates are high, as they are with binge drinking and sexual assault, they often are connected with the dynamics and consequences of overconformity to the sports ethic.

The use and abuse of performance-enhancing substances is a form of deviance that is reportedly widespread among athletes, despite new rules, testing programmes, educational programmes and strong punishments for violators. Historical evidence suggests that recent increases in rates of use are due primarily to increases in the supply and range of available substances rather than changes in the values and moral characters of athletes or increased exploitation of athletes. Most athletes through history have sought ways to improve their skills, maintain their athlete identity and continue playing their sports, but today their search is more likely to involve the use of widely available performance-enhancing substances.

Despite new enforcement efforts by sports organizations, athletes using performance-enhancing substances have generally stayed one jump ahead of the rule makers and testers. When one drug is banned, athletes use another, even if it is more dangerous. If a new test is developed, athletes switch to an undetectable drug or use masking drugs to confuse testers. The use of HGH, blood doping, testosterone and many new substances still escapes detection, and testing programmes are often problematic because they are expensive and can violate privacy rights or cultural norms in many societies. However, many people are strongly committed to testing, and new testing procedures have been developed. The prospect of 'gene doping', or performance-enhancing genetic manipulation, will present significant challenges for testing in the future. In the meantime, testers are struggling to stay ahead of athletes who continue to overconform to the norms of the sports ethic.

Controlling deviant overconformity requires a critical assessment and transformation of the norms and social organization of sports. The goal is to strike a balance between accepting and questioning norms and setting limits on conformity so that athletes who engage in risky and self-destructive forms of deviant overconformity are not defined and presented as heroes. The existence of new forms of performance technologies can be controlled only through new strategies that recognize the existence and dynamics of deviant overconformity.

An effective transformation of sports also requires that all participants be involved in a continual process of critical reflection about the goals, purpose and organization of sports. Controlling deviance requires an assessment of the values and norms in sports, as well as restructuring the organizations that control and sponsor sports. Critical assessment should involve everyone, from athletes to fans. It is idealistic but it is worth trying.

Website resources

Note: Websites often change. The following URLs were current when this book was printed. Please check our website (***www.mcgraw-hill.co.uk/textbooks/coakley***) for updates and additions.

www.mcgraw-hill.co.uk/textbooks/coakley Click on Chapter 6 for information on the history of performance-enhancing drug use and drug testing in high-performance sports, and for information on recent cases of athletes testing positive for certain drugs.

http://bodybuilding.com/store/hardcore.htm The site lists more than 200 producers of 'nutritional supplements', chemical compounds and what many consider to be performance-enhancing drugs; this is where bodybuilders and athletes who cannot afford designer drugs choose among over 200 different substances to aid their training and stay ahead of drug testers.

http://bodybuilding.com/store/hgh.html The site provides information on HGH and other substances for which there are no tests being used in most sports.

www.countryside-alliance.org.uk/ This is the website of the major pro-hunting organization, providing details of hunting campaigns and events.

www.league.org.uk/ This is the website of the League Against Cruel Sports, with information on a range of activities including hunting and bullfighting, and containing educational resources.

www.SportsEthicsInstitute.org A non-profit corporation that fosters critical information and discussions about ethical issues in sports; site provides news, information and links to online resources.

www.sportslaw.org The Sports Lawyers Association often refers to deviance in sports in terms of the legal issues raised; this site lists articles and recent cases.

www.supportfoxhunting.co.uk/ This site provides reports, news and statistics supporting fox-hunting, and contains a section covering issues related to game shooting and angling.

www.t-nation.com/ The site of Testosterone Nation; widely used by people who take bodybuilding compounds and drugs, seek information on what drugs to use, how to obtain them, and what others say about them.

www.uksport.gov.uk/pages/testing_programme_design_operation/ Details of the UK Sport drug-testing programme.

www.uksport.gov.uk/pages/drug_test_results/ A database of the results of drug tests on athletes, providing information on the sport, individual, substance and action taken by the governing body.

www.wada-ama.org The site of the official worldwide drug- and substance-testing agency; online materials illustrate how the agency is presenting regulatory and educational materials.

www.wada-ama.org/web/standards_harmonization/code/list_standard_2004.pdf The World Anti-Doping Code: the 2004 Prohibited List, International Standard, updated 17 March 2004, 10 pages.

Chapter 7

Violence in sports: how does it affect our lives?

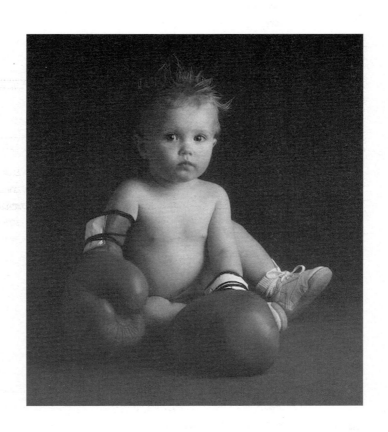

Learning Centre Resources

Visit *Sports in Society*'s Online Learning Centre (OLC) at **www.mcgraw-hill.co.uk/ textbooks/coakley** for additional information and study material for this chapter, including:

- Self-grading quizzes and essay questions
- Learning outcomes
- Related websites
- Additional readings

Chapter contents

What is violence?
Violence in sports through history
Violence on the field
Violence off the field
Violence among spectators
Summary: does violence in sports affect our lives?

> Rugby is a game of violence. It is supposed to be. Both codes. It is a game of brutal physical confrontations: individual against individual, group against group … Without violence, rugby is nothing … Violence is the setting, the context. Without violence there is no courage, without mayhem there is no grace, without pain there is no exalted relief in victory.
>
> *(Simon Barnes, journalist, 2005)*

> It's art. Brutal, but art. You can't headbutt, gouge out your opponent's eye or kick him in his private parts. It's perfectly safe.
>
> *(Sid Gore, President of World Cage-Fighting Championships, 2006, p. 22)*

> Anything that celebrates or trivialises hooliganism in any form is deplorable. The Premier League and our clubs have worked tirelessly to try and eradicate violence from the game.
>
> *(Premier League spokesman, 2006, commenting on the development of a new toy figurine of 'Little Hooliganz')*

Discussions of violence in sports, like discussions of deviance, are often connected with people's ideas about the moral condition of society as a whole. When violence occurs in sports, many people are quick to use it as an indicator that the moral foundation of society is eroding and that people, especially children, are learning a warped sense of morality as they watch athletes and use them as models for their own actions.

Statements about violence in sports are often confusing. Some people say that violence is an inherent part of many games, whereas others say that it destroys the dynamics of games. Some people say that violence in sports reflects natural tendencies among males in society, whereas others say that men use violence in sports to promote the idea that physical size and strength is a legitimate basis for maintaining power over others. Some say that violence in sports is worse today than ever before, whereas others say it is less common and less brutal than in the past.

Contradictory statements and conclusions about violence in sports occur for four reasons. *First*, many people fail to define important terms in their discussions. They use words such as *physical, assertive, tough, rough, competitive, intense, intimidating, risky, aggressive, destructive* and *violent* interchangeably. *Second*, they may not distinguish players from spectators, even though the dynamics of violence differ in these two groups. *Third*, they categorize all sports together, despite differences in meaning, purpose, organization and amount of physical contact involved. *Fourth*, they may not distinguish the immediate, short-term effects of experiencing or watching violence in sports from more permanent, long-term effects.

The goal of this chapter is to enable you to include information based on research and theories in your discussions of violence in sports. Chapter content focuses on five topics:

1 a practical definition of *violence* and related terms
2 a brief historical overview of violence in sports
3 on-the-field violence among players in various sports
4 off-the-field violence among players and the impact of sports violence on their lives apart from sports
5 violence among spectators who watch media coverage of sports and attend events in person.

In connection with the last three topics, we will make suggestions about how to control violence and limit its consequences on and off the field.

What is Violence?

Violence *is the use of excessive physical force, which causes or has the potential to cause harm or destruction.* We often think of violence as actions that are illegal or unsanctioned, but there are situations in which the use of violence is encouraged or approved in most groups or societies. For instance, when violence involves deviant underconformity based on a rejection of norms in society, it is often classified as illegal and sanctioned severely. However, when violence occurs in connection with enforcing norms, protecting people and property or overconforming to widely accepted norms, it may be approved and even lauded as necessary to preserve order, reaffirm important social values or entertain spectators. Therefore, violence is often, but not always, tolerated, or even glorified, when soldiers, police and athletes are perceived to be protecting people, reproducing accepted ideologies or pursuing victories in the name of others.

When violence occurs in connection with the widespread rejection of norms in a social world, it is often described as anarchy or lawless mayhem. When it occurs in connection with extreme methods of social control or extreme overconformity to norms, it often is associated with a sense of moral righteousness, even when it produces harmful or destructive consequences. Under certain political conditions, this latter expression of violence is tied to fascism and fascist leaders.

In the case of sports, pushing a referee who penalizes you or a coach who reprimands you is violence based on a rejection of norms. These actions are defined as illegal and punished severely by teams and sports organizations, even if the referee or coach was not seriously injured. However, it is different when a rugby player delivers a punishing tackle, breaking the ribs or blowing out the knee of an opposing winger after his coach told him to be aggressive and put his body on the line for the team. Such violence involves (over)conformity to norms and is seen as entertaining, highlighted on video replays, and used by teammates and other rugby players as a mark of one's status in rugby culture. The player might feel righteous in being violent, despite the harmful consequences, and would not hesitate to be violent again. His violence is not punished because it helps achieve a valued goal for the team and the people it represents. Furthermore, his ability to do violence and endure it when perpetrated by others is used to affirm his identity as a rugby player.

The term **aggression** is used in this chapter to refer to *verbal or physical actions grounded in an intent to dominate, control or do harm to another person.* Aggression is often involved in violence, but violence may occur inadvertently or carelessly without aggressive intent. This definition allows us to distinguish aggressive actions from other actions that we might describe as assertive, competitive or achievement orientated. For example, a very competitive person may use violence during a game without the intent to dominate, control or harm others. However, there is often a difference between being aggressive and simply being assertive or trying hard to win or achieve other goals. The term **intimidation** is used to refer to *words, gestures and actions that threaten violence or aggression.* Like aggression, intimidation is used to dominate or control another person. These definitions focus our discussion, but they will not eliminate all conceptual problems.

Violence in Sports through History

Violence is not new to physical activities and sports (Dunning, 1999; Guttmann, 1998, 2004). As noted in Chapter 3, so-called blood sports were popular among the Ancient Greeks and throughout the Roman Empire. Deaths occurred regularly in connection with ritual games among the Mayas and Aztecs. Tournaments in medieval and early modern Europe were designed as training for war and often had warlike consequences. Folk games were only loosely governed by rules, and they produced injuries and deaths at rates that would shock and disgust people today. Bear-baiting, cockfighting, dogfighting and other 'sporting' activities during those periods involved the treatment of animals in ways that most people today would define as brutal and violent.

Research indicates that, as part of an overall civilizing process in Europe and North America, modern sports were developed as more rule-governed activities than the physical games in previous eras (see Cartoon 7.1). As sports became formally organized, official rules prohibited certain forms of violence that had been common in many folk games. Bloodshed decreased, and there was a greater emphasis on self-control to restrict physical contact and the expression of aggressive impulses often created in the emotional heat of competition (Dunning, 1999).

Social historians, who study these changes, also explain that rates of sports violence do not automatically decrease over time. In fact, as actions and emotional expression have become more regulated and controlled in modern societies, players and spectators view the 'controlled' violence in sports as exciting. Furthermore, the processes of commercialization, professionalization and globalization have given rise to new forms of instrumental and 'dramatic' violence in many sports. This means that goal-orientated and entertainment-orientated violence have increased, at least temporarily, in many Western societies.

Sociologist Eric Dunning (1999) notes that violence remains a crucial social issue in modern sports because their goal is to create tension rather than relieve or discharge it. Additionally, violent and aggressive sports serve, in patriarchal societies, to reproduce an ideology that naturalizes the power of men over women. Overall, historical research shows that sports are given different meanings by time and place and that we can understand violence in sports only when we analyse it in relation to the historical, social and cultural context in which it occurs.

Violence on the Field

Violence in sports comes in many forms, and it is grounded in social and cultural factors related to the sports ethic, commercialization, gender ideology and ideas about masculinity, the

'Now that we've invented violence, we need a sport so we can use it without being labelled as uncivilized.'

Cartoon 7.1 **Violence in sports is not new. However, this does not mean that it is a natural or inevitable part of sports.**

dynamics of social class and race, and the strategies used in sports. Violence also has significant consequences for athletes and presents challenges for those who wish to control it. As we discuss these topics, it is useful to consider the different types of violence that occur in sports.

Types of violence

The most frequently used typology of on-the-field violence among players was developed by the late Mike Smith, a respected Canadian sociologist (1983; see Young, 2000, 2002, 2007a). Smith identified four categories of violence that occur in sports.

1 *Brutal body contact.* This includes physical practices common in certain sports and accepted by athletes as part of the action and risk in their sports participation. Examples are collisions, hits, tackles, blocks, body checks and other forms of forceful physical contact that can produce injuries. Most people in society define this forceful physical contact as extreme, although they do not classify it as illegal or criminal, nor do they see a need to punish it. Coaches often encourage this form of violence. For example, one coach was reported by an opposing football team for the tactics he was encouraging in his players: 'The girls had an issue at a match with another manager who was actually from a Charter Standard club who was telling his girls to use their elbows and kick' (in Brackenridge et al., 2007a, p. 131).

2 *Borderline violence.* This includes practices that violate the rules of the game but are accepted by most players and coaches as consistent with the norms of the sports ethic and as useful competitive strategies. Examples are the forcefully placed elbow or knee in football and basketball, the strategic bump used by distance runners to put another runner off stride, and the fist fight in rugby. Take, for example, the following comment on a British university's 'Sports and Soc' website encouraging members to join the men's basketball team by describing the reasons for the success of the team in the previous season: 'with a fight and a scuffle along the way, (I don't encourage violence but it was bloody funny)' (www.aston guild.org.uk, 2006). Although these actions are expected, they may provoke retaliation by other players. Official sanctions and fines are not usually severe for borderline violence. However, public pressure to increase the severity of sanctions has grown in recent years, and the severity of punishments has increased in some sports.

3 *Quasi-criminal violence.* This includes practices that violate the formal rules of the game, public laws and even informal norms among players. Examples are cheap shots, late hits and flagrant fouls that endanger players' bodies and reject the norm calling for dedication to the game above all else. Fines and suspensions are usually imposed on players who engage in such violence. For example, in 2006 Manchester City player, Ben Thatcher, elbowed an opposing Portsmouth player, Pedro Mendes, in the face, knocking him unconscious. At the time, Thatcher only received a yellow card, prompting then Portsmouth manager Harry Redknapp to ask whether a player had to kill someone to be sent off, not least because Thatcher has a history of similar incidences. Most athletes condemn quasi-criminal violence and see it as a rejection of the informal norms of the game and what it means to be an athlete. In the case of Thatcher, he was eventually suspended and fined by his club, but this was not treated as a criminal assault.

4 *Criminal violence.* This includes practices that are clearly outside the law to the point that athletes condemn them without question and law enforcement officials may prosecute them as crimes. Examples are assaults that occur after a game and assaults during a game that appear to be premeditated and severe enough to kill or seriously maim a player. Such violence is relatively rare, although there is growing support that criminal charges ought to be filed when it occurs. This support grew recently after Lee Bowyer attacked his Newcastle United teammate Kieron Dyer. He was banned and fined by his club but, controversially, the case was also dealt with by the Crown Prosecution Service as a public order offence. While Graham Taylor, the Chief Executive of the Professional Footballers' Association, argued that this event should have been 'dealt with within football', the chief Crown Prosecutor for the region stated that 'the criminal law doesn't cease to operate once you cross the touchline of a sports field' (Nicola Reasbeck, in *The Times*, 6 July 2006, p. 3). In 2006, James Cotterill of Barrow AFC became only the second player to be jailed for grievous bodily harm (GBH) caused during a football match when he punched an opposing player and shattered his jaw. Previously, Duncan Ferguson of Scotland and Rangers had been jailed for head-butting an opponent during a game in 1995.

Canadian sociologist Kevin Young (2002, 2004b, 2007a) has noted that this is a useful general typology but that the lines separating the four types of violence shift over time as norms change in sports and societies. Furthermore, the typology fails to address the origins of violence and how violent acts are related to the sports ethic, gender ideology and the commercialization of sports. Despite these weaknesses, this typology enables us to make distinctions between various types of violence discussed in this chapter.

Violence as deviant overconformity to the norms of the sports ethic

During the 1991 men's Rugby World Cup, the England team manager famously played the Harfleur speech from Shakespeare's *Henry V* to the players on the coach on their way to the game. The speech includes the following words, which include the kind of references to rage, bloodshed and warfare that many athletes in heavy-contact sports have heard during their careers:

Once more unto the breach, dear friends, once more;
Or close the wall up with our English dead.
… when the blast of war blows in our ears,
Then imitate the action of the tiger;
Stiffen the sinews, summon up the blood,
Disguise fair nature with hard-favour'd rage;
Then lend the eye a terrible aspect;
… Now set the teeth and stretch the nostril wide,
Hold hard the breath and bend up every spirit
To his full height. On, on, you noblest English.
Whose blood is fet from fathers of war-proof!
… Be copy now to men of grosser blood,
And teach them how to war. And you, good yeoman,

Whose limbs were made in England, show us here
The mettle of your pasture; let us swear
That you are worth your breeding; which I doubt not;
For there is none of you so mean and base,
That hath not noble lustre in your eyes.
I see you stand like greyhounds in the slips,
Straining upon the start. The game's afoot:
Follow your spirit, and upon this charge
Cry 'God for Harry, England, and Saint George!'

Many coaches do not use such vivid vocabulary because they know it can inspire dangerous forms of violence. However, there are coaches and team administrators who seek athletes who think this way. When athletes do think this way, violence occurs regularly enough to attract attention. Journalists describe it, sociologists and psychologists try to explain it and athletes brag or complain about it. When an athlete dies or is paralysed by on-the-field violence, the media present stories stating that violence is rampant in sports and in society, and then they run multiple replays or photographs of violent acts knowing that this will increase their ratings or sales.

Although players may be concerned about brutal body contact and borderline violence in their sports, they generally accept them. Even when players do not like them, they may use them to enhance their status on teams and popularity among spectators. Athletes whose violence involves overconformity to the sport ethic become legends on and off the field. Athletes who engage in quasi- and criminal violence often are marginalized in sports, and they may face criminal charges, although prosecuting such charges has been difficult and convictions are rare (Young, 2000, 2002, 2004b, 2007a).

Violence as deviant overconformity is also related to insecurities among athletes in high-performance sports. Athletes learn that 'you're only as good as your last game', and they know that their identities as athletes and status as team members are constantly tested. Therefore, they often take extreme measures to prove themselves, even if it involves violence. Violence becomes a marker of self-worth and leads other athletes to reaffirm your identity. This is why athletes who do not play in pain are defined as failures, whereas those who do are defined as courageous. Willingly facing violence and playing in pain honours the importance of the game and expresses dedication to teammates and the culture of high-performance sport.

It is important to understand that violent expressions of deviant overconformity are not limited to men, although they are more common among male athletes than female athletes. Women also overconform to the norms of the sports ethic, and when they play contact sports, they face the challenge of drawing the line between physicality and violence. For example, when sociologist Lone Friis Thing (2001) studied the sports experiences of female ball players in Denmark, she discovered that the women loved the physicality of their sports. As two ice hockey players explained:

I enjoy it, I enjoy it ... I can shoot hard, or I can give the other participants 'a shoul-der' ... without anybody feeing that it is strange.

When she tried to run towards the goal for the first time, the only way that I could stop her, was to run into her ... a head-on collision ... I was the one who fell down

onto the ice. But she didn't get around me and she didn't score. I bit myself in the
lip so it was bleeding. But it was good.

(In Thing, 2001, pp. 280–2)

The experience of dealing with the physicality of contact sports and facing its consequences creates drama, excitement, strong emotions and special interpersonal bonds among
female athletes just as it does among men. Despite the risk and reality of pain and injuries,
many women in contact sports feel that the physical intensity and body contact in their
sports make them feel alive and aware. Although many women are committed to controlling
brutal body contact and more severe forms of violence, the love of their sport and the
excitement of physicality can lead to violence grounded in overconformity to the norms of
the sports ethic.

Commercialization and violence in sports

Some athletes in power and performance sports are paid well because of their ability to do
violence on the field. However, it is difficult to argue that commercialization and money in
sports cause violence in sports. Violent athletes in the past were paid very little, and athletes in
schools, colleges and sports clubs today are paid nothing, yet many of them do violence, despite
the pain and injuries associated with it.

Commercialization and money have expanded opportunities to play certain contact sports
in some societies, and media coverage makes these sports and the violence they contain
more visible than ever before. Some sociologists note that the media sometimes make events
appear more violent than they actually are (see Poulton, 2005; Weed, 2001) – a point covered
in Chapter 12. Children watch this coverage and may imitate violent athletes when they play
informal games and organized youth sports, but this does not justify the conclusion that
commercialization is the cause of violence in sports.

Athletes in heavy contact sports engaged in violence on the field long before television
coverage and the promise of big salaries. Players at all levels of organized rugby maimed each
other at rates that were far higher than the death and injury rates in rugby today. There are more
injuries in rugby today because there are more people playing rugby. Violence in certain sports
is a serious problem that must be addressed, but to think that it is caused mainly by professionalization, commercialism and money is a mistake.

This is an important point because many people who criticize sports today blame violence
and other problems on money and greed. They claim that, if athletes were true amateurs and
played for love of the game instead of money, there would be less violence. However, this
conclusion contradicts research findings, and it distracts attention from the deep cultural and
ideological roots of violence in particular sports and societies. This means that we could take
money away from athletes tomorrow, but violence would be reduced only if there were changes
in the culture in which athletes, especially male athletes, learn to value and do violence in
sports.

Many people resist the notion that cultural changes are needed to control violence because
it places the responsibility for change on all of us. It is easy to say that wealthy and greedy team
owners, athletes without moral character and television executives seeking high viewer ratings

are to blame for violence in sports. But it is more difficult to critically examine our culture and the normative and social organization of the sports that many people watch and enjoy. Similarly, it is difficult for people to critically examine the definitions of *masculinity* and the structure of gender relations that they have long accepted as part of the 'natural' order of things. But these critiques are needed if we wish to understand and control violence in sports.

> I'm challenging Laila Ali ... Kicking [her] butt will be a walk in the park ... And if she wants a rematch, I'll dust her off again.
>
> *(Jacqui Frazier-Lyde in Farhood, 2000, online)*

> The FA have given me a pat on the back. I've taken violence off the terracing and onto the pitch.
>
> *(Vinnie Jones, 1992, www.saidwhat.co.uk, former professional football player, who held the record for the fastest receipt of a yellow card in a match, after only 5 seconds)*

The point in this section is that commercialization is not the *primary* cause of violence in sports. But money is not irrelevant. Consider the following statements made by a boxer and a football player:

These are two among dozens of similar statements from popular sports publications. They express the language and rhetoric that have come to be used in certain commercial sports. Therefore, when images of intimidation are used by Jacqui Frazier-Lyde (daughter of former heavyweight boxing champion Joe Frazier) as she challenges Laila Ali (daughter of Muhammad Ali) to a prize fight with a big pay-off, and when football players who have been involved in the production of a video offering footage and advice on violent play make statements of pride in their acts, their violent rhetoric tells us less about the way they *play sports* than it does about how they want us to *think* they play sports.

Professional athletes are entertainers, and they now use a promotional and heroic rhetoric that presents images of revenge, retaliation, hate, hostility, intimidation, aggression, violence, domination and destruction. These melodramatic images attract attention and serve commercial purposes. They sell videos, such as Vinnie Jones's *Soccer's Hard Men*, that present image after image of glorified violence in slow-motion close-ups accompanied by the actual sounds of bodies colliding, bones and tendons snapping on impact, and players gasping in agony and pain. In true promotional fashion, the same media companies that sell or promote these videos also publish articles that condemn violence and violent players. Vinnie Jones was fined £20 000 for his role in his video, further cementing his own celebrity status, which eventually developed into an acting career playing 'hard men'. The marketing people know that violence *and* moral outrage about violence attracts audiences and generates profits.

Does this commercially inspired rhetoric represent real on-the-field orientations among athletes, or is it part of a strategy to attract attention and create personas which have commercial value? Research is needed on this, but our sense is that most athletes do not relish hurting opponents and seeing them bleed. At the same time, some athletes have become experts at using violent rhetoric to enhance the entertainment value of what they do and the events in which they participate. When the American boxer Mike Tyson, who is renowned for his own violence in the ring, refereed the cage fighting world championships in Manchester in 2006, he is said to have stated that he would not stop a fight until there was an eyeball rolling across the canvas. According to Tyson, cage fighting (also known as mixed martial arts, ultimate fighting and no holds barred):

> Is basically bone against bone, so there's probably going to be some blood and broken bones. It's a bit gory, not for the weak to watch.
>
> *(In the* Observer, *19 March 2006, p. 22)*

Such rhetoric is part of the spectacle dimension of sports, similar to dramatic storylines delivered by paid announcers, sexy cheerleaders and Formula One 'grid girls', and toy axes for the symbolic 'chopping' of opponents. However, it raises this question: how far can the spectacle be emphasized before people conclude that a particular sport has lost its authenticity as a game and has become choreographic violence devoid of play? Professional wrestling (e.g. WWE) crossed this line long ago, and cage fighting seems to be crossing it now. Many people

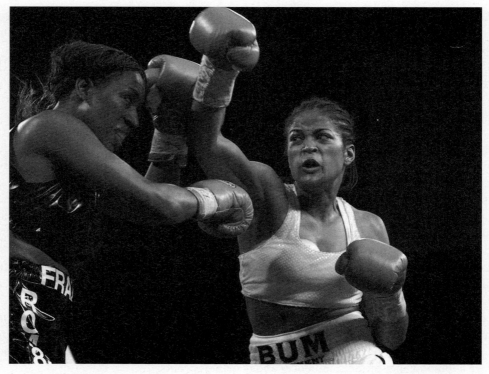

Both men and women are capable of violence on and off the playing field. However, women may not connect violent actions to their identities in the same way that some men do. Prevailing definitions of *masculinity* lead many people to feel that violence is more 'natural' for men than for women, and it may lead men to feel comfortable with violence in their sports

will watch violence in the context of an authentic game, but few will pay to watch violence week after week when it is not part of a goal-orientated structure that gives it meaning beyond the blood and gore.

Violence and masculinity

Violence in sports is not limited to men. However, research based on critical feminist theory indicates that, *if we want to understand violence in sports, we must understand gender ideology and issues of masculinity in culture.* American sociologist Mike Messner explains:

> Young males come to sport with identities that lead them to define their athletic experience differently than females do. Despite the fact that few males truly enjoy hitting and being hit, and that one has to be socialized into participating in much of the violence commonplace in sport, males often view aggression, within the rule-bound structure of sport, as legitimate and 'natural'.

(1992, p. 67)

Messner notes that many male athletes learn to define injurious acts as a necessary part of the game, rather than as violence, as long as they are within the rules of the game and within the informal norms the players use to judge and evaluate each other.

In many societies today, participation in power and performance sports has become an important way to prove masculinity. Boys discover that, if they play these sports and are seen as being able to do violence, they can avoid social labels such as *pussy, lady, fag, wimp* and *sissy* (Ingham and Dewar, 1999). Similarly, in a study of English Premiership footballers, Roderick (2006b) notes that, if players refuse to play through pain and injury, they are stigmatized as a 'wuss' and 'poofter'.

Boys and men who play power and performance sports learn quickly that they are evaluated in terms of their ability to do violence in combination with physical skills (Lance, 2005). This learning begins in youth sports, and by the time young men have become immersed in the social world of most power and performance sports, they accept brutal body contact and borderline violence as part of the game as it is played by 'real' men. Studies of coaching tactics used in professional football demonstrate that violence, intimidation and abuse are key aspects of the control of male players (see Cushion and Jones, 2006; Kelly and Waddington, 2006). For example, when a mistake by a goalkeeper led to a late equalizing goal, in the post-match talk the coaches told the players, 'You should have taken his fuckin' head off from that corner, just fuckin' knocked his head off' . . . 'Bunch of fuckin' tarts, that's what y'are, all of ya' (in Cushion and Jones, 2006, p. 149). When gender is viewed in these terms, the ability to do violence becomes 'one of the cornerstones of masculinity' (White and Young, 1997, p. 9).

When women do violence in sports, it may be seen as a sign of commitment or skill, but it is not seen as proof of femininity. Dominant gender ideology in many cultures links manhood with the ability to do violence, but there is no similar link between womanhood and violence. Therefore, female athletes who engage in violence do not receive the same support and rewards that men receive – unless they wrestle in the WWE or mixed martial arts where the sport personas of female athletes are constructed to shock or titillate spectators (Berra, 2005; Blumenthal, 2004). The emergence of women's boxing provides a context in which female athletes are rewarded for doing violence, but most female boxers do

breaking BARRIERS

Ideological barriers: *the hit isn't real unless it bends steel*

Wheelchair rugby is unique. It is four-on-four competition with players in wheelchairs customized to function like mini-chariots: angled wheels, bucket seats, safety harnesses, and protective metal bars that shield legs and feet during crashes. Using a volleyball on a basketball court, the teams engage one another in a contest that resembles a mix of rugby, team handball and American football that was organized by an X Games promoter.

While it is officially called wheelchair rugby, participants informally refer to the sport as 'murderball'. Many people also call it quad rugby because participants have quadriplegia or limited use of three or four limbs. Each of the 12 members of a team is rated in terms of upper-body muscle function, from 0.5 to 3.5 (least impaired). During games the four players on the court from each team may not exceed a cumulative rating of 8.0 points. Participation is open to men and women, but men only comprise most teams and Josie Pearson made history by becoming the first British woman to play in wheelchair rugby in the Paralympics in Beijing 2008. During the four 8-minute quarters, points are scored when a player possessing the ball crosses the opponents' end line.

Wheelchair rugby was invented in Canada (1981) and first played in the Paralympics in 1996. It immediately became popular among people with multiple limb impairments, especially those who favoured power and performance sports involving heavy physical contact. Paul Davies, a former player and now manager of the British national team, describes wheelchair rugby as 'a real in your face sport [resembling] chess with violence' (BBC Sport Academy, 2005).

Many wheelchair rugby players have impairments caused by accidents in risky activities, including high-risk sports. They like wheelchair rugby because it differs from other sports in the Paralympics. When players and other insiders refer to the sport as murderball, it implies a closer connection to able-bodied heavy-contact sports than there is for other Paralympic sports.

Some athletes say that murderball allows them to express their aggression and therefore gain a sense of control over their bodies. But as one member of the US team said, 'Of course, you're gonna have healthy aggression and unhealthy aggression.' And then one of his teammates added, 'But when you can use your body and your chair just to go knock the shit out of somebody, it helps' (in Anderson, J., 2005; from the documentary film, *Murderball*).

Although other Paralympic sports are organized so that violence is inconsistent with the strategy and rhythm of participation, some athletes with disabilities want to play a violent sport and reaffirm their identities as athletes and men by doing violence. For example, when the US team faced Canada in the gold medal game of the 2002 Wheelchair Rugby World Championships, the coach reminded the players that, 'It's not buddy-buddy time anymore, guys.' And when a member of the US team was asked about their goal for the 2004 Paralympics in Athens, he quickly replied, 'We're not going for a hug, we're going for a f___ing Gold Medal' (in *Murderball*, 2004).

'Hugs' are associated with the Special Olympics, which are organized to emphasize play and personal accomplishment among athletes with intellectual disabilities. There is little emphasis on competitive success in the Special Olympics and none on dominating opponents. Volunteer coaches frequently hug athletes who complete an event, regardless of the outcome.

Many Paralympians, influenced by the ideology of ableism, want to distance themselves from the Special Olympics because it does not match dominant sport forms in society and it perpetuates the idea that people with disabilities cannot play 'real' sports – that is, the sports played by able-bodied athletes. **Ableism** is a *web of ideas and beliefs that people use to classify bodies perceived as unimpaired as normal and superior and bodies perceived as (dis)abled as subnormal and inferior*. This ideology is

Wheelchair rugby (also known as quad rugby and murderball) is played in the Paralympics. Pictured are the Portland Pounders, one of the many teams in North America. Some wheelchair rugby players use a highly masculinized vocabulary to describe the intimidation and violence that occur in their games. Wheelchair rugby challenges stereotypes about people with a disability, but it also reaffirms a gender ideology in which manhood is defined in terms of the ability to do violence. When sports embody contradictory ideological themes, making clear sense of them is difficult (*Source*: Jason E. Kaplan Photography, Portland, Oregon)

widespread in society and many people, including some with disabilities, use it to evaluate themselves and others. Similarly, some murderball athletes use traditional gender ideology to connect power, status and male identity with the ability to do violence, as expressed through words on a player's T-shirt: 'The hit isn't real unless it bends steel' (Grossfeld, 2005, p. 1). This is not surprising because none of us lives outside the influence of ideology.

not feel that doing violence in the ring makes them more of a woman than the boxers they defeat. Overall, none of us lives outside the influence of ideology. This point is highlighted in connection with the rapidly growing sport of wheelchair rugby. Some participants call this sport 'murderball', and it is the focus of 'Breaking barriers' on pages 236–237.

AT YOUR *fingertips*:

See the OLC – Additional Readings for Chapter 7 – for the authors' review of the documentary film, *Murderball.*

The institutionalization of violence in sports

Certain forms of violence are built into the culture and structure of particular sports (Guilbert, 2004). Athletes in these sports learn to use violence as a strategy, even though it may cause them pain and injury. Controlling institutionalized violence is difficult because it requires changes in the culture and structure of particular sports – something that most people in governing bodies are hesitant to do. These are the topics discussed in the following sections.

Learning to use violence as a strategy: non-contact sports

In some non-contact sports, participants may try to intimidate opponents, but violence is rare. For example, tennis players have been fined for slamming a ball to the ground in protest or talking to an official or opponent in a menacing manner. A survey of British male athletes found that approximately one-third admitted to 'swimming pool rage', 'cricket rage' and 'golf rage', with one in 10 arguments leading to actual violence (BBC, 2001). However, players in non-contact sports are seldom, if ever, rewarded for violent actions. Therefore, it is doubtful that playing or watching these sports teaches people to use violence as a strategy on the field.

Some athletes may use violent images as they describe competition, for example of wanting to 'kill their opponent', but they do not have actual opportunities to convert their words into deeds. Men who play non-contact sports use violent images in their descriptions of competition much more often than women use them. The use of a 'language of violence' is clearly linked to masculinity in most cultures. Women may use it on occasion, but men use it more frequently. It may be that many women realize that a language of violence reaffirms a version of gender ideology that privileges men, works against their interests, and subverts the health and well-being of everyone in society.

Learning to use violence as a strategy: men's contact sports

Athletes in heavy-contact and collision sports learn to use intimidation, aggression and violence as strategies to achieve competitive success on the field. Success in these sports depends on the use of brutal body contact and borderline violence. Research shows that male athletes in these sports readily accept certain forms of violence, even when they involve rule violations, and this acceptance increases with the frequency and force of collisions in a sport (Pilz, 1996; Shields and Bredemeier, 1995; Weinstein et al., 1995; White and Young, 1997). These athletes routinely disapprove of quasi-criminal and criminal violence, but they accept brutal body contact and borderline violence as long as it occurs within the rules of the game. They may not intend to hurt, but this does not prevent them from doing things that put their bodies and the bodies of opponents in jeopardy.

In boxing, rugby and other heavy-contact and collision sports, athletes also use intimidation and violence to promote their careers, increase drama for spectators and enhance the publicity for their sports and sponsors (see Cartoon 7.2). These athletes realize that doing violence is expected, even if it causes harm to themselves and others. This is illustrated in the creation of the International Rules sporting hybrid of Australian Rules football and Gaelic football. During the 2006 tournament in Ireland, two players had to be 'sin binned' for fighting before the game even started. During play, one Australian player needed stitches to a headwound when he was kneed by Irish player Graham Geraghty. In the second leg of the match, Geraghty was knocked unconscious and stretchered off the field following a tackle described by the Australians as 'great'. Interestingly, the game had more than 82 000 spectators, the highest recorded figure of any international sports fixture on Irish soil.

Violence is also incorporated into game strategies when coaches use players as designated agents of intimidation and violence for their teams. These players are expected to protect teammates and strategically assist their teams by intimidating, provoking, fighting with or injuring opponents. Such tactics have become an accepted part of certain sports. For example, Peter Stead, a cultural historian and television presenter, suggested that Welsh rugby 'has become one of the most violent sports in the world with coaches more determined to have players smash into each other with great force rather than side-step and run for the line' (in Turner, 2006).

Some players continue to be paid primarily for their ability to do violence. However, every time they maim or come close to killing someone on the pitch, people raise questions about this form of institutionalized violence in sports. Football, rugby and boxing have taken actions to control certain forms of institutionalized violence. However, once violence is built into the culture, structures and strategies of a sport, controlling or eliminating it is difficult.

 Football is a game for gentlemen played by hooligans, while rugby is a game for hooligans played by gentlemen.

(Oxbridge college master, 1890s)

Learning to use violence as a strategy: women's contact sports

Information on violence among girls and women in contact sports remains scarce even though more women are participating in them (Lawler, 2002; Young, 2007a). This creates the possibility for cases of violence among female athletes, but there are few studies that tell us if and why this is true.

Women's programmes have undergone many changes over the past 30 years. They have become more competitive with a greater emphasis on power and performance and higher stakes associated with success. Today, as women become increasingly immersed in the social world of elite power and performance sports, they become more tolerant of rule violations and aggressive actions on the playing field, but this pattern is less clear among women than men (Nixon, 1996a, 1996b; Shields and Bredemeier, 1995; Shields et al., 1995; Tucker and Parks, 2001; Young, 2007a).

'We know of no biological reasons that would prevent women from using intimidation and violence or being as physically aggressive as men' (Dunn, 1994). However, most girls and women become involved in and learn to play sports in ways that differ from the experiences of most boys and men. As women compete at higher levels, they often become similar to men in the way they embrace the sports ethic and use it to frame their identities as athletes. Like men, they are willing to dedicate themselves to the game, take risks, make sacrifices, pay the price, play with pain and injury, and overcome barriers. However, it is rare for them to link toughness, physicality and aggression to their gender identities. In other words, women do not tie their ability to do violence to their definitions of what it means to be a woman in society. Similarly coaches do not try to motivate female athletes by urging them to 'go out and prove who the better woman is' on the field. Therefore, at this time, women's contact sports are less violent than men's contact sports.

With this said, there are many research questions that have not been answered: do elite female athletes develop the same form of hubris (pride-based arrogance) that many elite male athletes develop? If so, how is it linked to their identities, and how do they express it in sports? Do female athletes use a rhetoric of violence when they talk about sports? Some studies suggest that they do not (Nelson, 1994, 1998; Theberge, 1999; Young and White, 1995), but more information is needed. A good place to start might be with the women now playing heavy-contact sports such as football, rugby and boxing, or participating in dramatic spectacles such as cage fighting and professional wrestling.

Becky Zerlentes took a shot to the head above her left eye, then staggered forward and fell to the canvas ... [She] never regained consciousness and died, becoming the first female boxer to die in a sanctioned event.

(CBS News, 5 April 2005)

Learning to use violence as a strategy: animal sports

While most animal and blood sports have been outlawed in the UK, as in many other nations, greyhound racing remains a popular leisure pursuit. Greyhounds were used in the eighteenth century for slaughtering native populations in the British and French colonies. Their sporting prowess was subsequently employed in greyhound coursing, a popular English aristocratic pastime in the nineteenth century, where two dogs would compete to chase and kill a hare in open ground. Today, racing takes place at tracks with an electronic 'hare', and is primarily a social and gambling event. While this may appear to be a more 'civilized' version of the former activities of these dogs, Atkinson and Young (2005) have identified four major types of violence faced by many racing greyhounds in the interests of 'sporting' performance: during breeding, housing, training and disposal.

For example, there is evidence that dogs who are deemed unsuitable for racing are abandoned or culled at a very young age. Those who are more successful are often stored in cramped, inhumane conditions, isolated from human contact, where they may be exposed to contagious diseases. On the track, many successful dogs are raced beyond recommended levels,

'When are you gonna learn when it's necessary to use unnecessary roughness?'
Cartoon 7.2 **Physical intimidation and violence are used as strategies in men's contact sports. They have been effective in winning games and building the reputations of players and teams**

such that they experience pain and injury similar to overtrained human athletes. Some will also die during collisions with other dogs, generally smaller female dogs trampled by larger males. In many cases, dogs will not receive treatment, as it is economically more efficient for the owner to abandon the dog and buy a new one than offer treatment to an ill or injured animal. There is also evidence that some have been injected with performance-enhancing substances. Many dogs are not neutered in order to maintain high energy levels and breeding capacity, but will have metal devices inserted into their genitalia to prevent energy wastage through coitus. Once a dog has ended its racing career, they are often disposed of, sometimes through neglect leading to death, sometimes through inhumane euthanasia.

While this is not true of all racing dogs, Atkinson and Young (2005) argue that there is evidence that greyhounds, as with many human athletes, experience violent abuse and victimization such that their well-being is sacrificed in the interests of sporting performance. We should also be aware that this is not the only example of animal sports continuing in the UK: in 2004, a police operation broke up an apparent dogfighting ring, while pigeon-racing, polo and horse-racing (with many animal deaths each year) remain popular legal sports (see Cashmore, 2005).

Pain and injury as the price of violence

Many people think about sports in a paradoxical way: they accept violence in sports, but the injuries caused by that violence make them uneasy. They seem to want violence without consequences – like the fictionalized violence they see in the media and video games in which characters engage in brutality without being seriously or permanently injured. However, sports violence is real, and it causes real pain, injury, disability and even death (Dater, 2005; Farber, 2004; Leahy, 2008; Rice, 2005; Smith, 2005; Young, 2004a, 2004b).

Research on pain and injury among athletes helps us understand that violence in sports has real consequences. As noted in Chapter 6, studies indicate that professional sports involving brutal body contact and borderline violence are among the most dangerous workplaces in the occupational world (Leahy, 2008; Nixon, 2000; Waddington, 2000a, 2000b; White, 2004; White and Young, 1997; Young, 1993, 2000, 2004a). Rates of disabling injuries vary by sport, but they are high enough in many sports to constitute a serious health issue (see Chapter 4, p. 117). The 'normal' brutal body contact and borderline violence in contact sports regularly cause arthritis, concussions, bone fractures, torn ligaments and other injuries. In other words, the violence inherent in power and performance sports takes a definite toll on the health of athletes (Leahy, 2008; Young, 2004a).

The consequences of violence in sport are perhaps most clearly illustrated in boxing. In 2003, Michael Watson was awarded the Helen Rollason Award for courage and achievement in the face of adversity at the British Sports Personality ceremony. Watson was critically injured in 1991 in a super-middleweight fight against Chris Eubank, and remains partially paralysed and brain damaged. Nigel Benn, another British super-middleweight boxer and former world champion, was seriously injured in a fight in 1995 against the American Gerald McClellan. Benn recovered from his injuries, but McClellan was left permanently paralysed, blind and hearing impaired. Benn has since argued that 'There are much worse sports than boxing', and the British Boxing Board of Control also defended the outcome of the fight by claiming that boxing is no more dangerous than other risk sports. However, Benn's choice to be known by the name 'The Dark Destroyer', demonstrates an awareness that it is possible, and even desirable, to 'destroy' one's opponent (see Parry, 2006). Notably, in the same year as Benn's fight against McClellan, James Murray died after a British bantamweight title fight against Drew Docherty in Glasgow.

Research shows a close connection between dominant ideas about masculinity and the high rate of injuries in many sports. Ironically, some power and performance sports are organized so that players feel that their manhood is up for grabs. Men who define *masculinity* in terms of physically dominating others often use violence in sports as an expression of this code of manhood. Until they critically examine issues related to gender and the organization of their sports, they will mistakenly define *violence* as a source of rewards rather than a source of chronic pain and disabilities that constrain and threaten their lives.

Controlling on-the-field violence

The roots of violence on the playing field are deep. They are grounded in overconformity to the sports ethic, processes of commercialization and definitions of *masculinity*. Therefore, many of the men who control and play power and performance sports resist efforts to control violence. As sports are currently organized, they understand that their identities depend on approving of and doing violence, and that competitive success in sports depends on the use of strategic violence.

Brutal body contact is the most difficult type of violence to control. It is grounded in the culture of power and performance sports and dominant gender ideology. Unfortunately, about 90 per cent of the serious injuries in power and performance sports occur *within the rules* of those sports. This means that many men pay the price for their destructive definitions of *sports* and *masculinity*.

Efforts to control brutal body contact require changes in certain sports cultures and gender ideology. This requires relentless strategies that call attention to the dangers and absurdity of the actions and the language that men and women use to reproduce violent sport cultures and the gender ideology that supports them. People should demand and keep accurate records and publish information on injuries on a team-by-team, league-by-league and sport-by-sport basis.

Controlling brutal body contact and certain forms of borderline violence is challenging. In basketball, for example, there is a fine line between a 'hard foul', as encouraged by many coaches, and a flagrant or intentional foul, as defined by league rules. However, when enforced consistently, rules can limit some forms of violence

Parents should be informed of these rates before they enlist their children in the service of reproducing patriarchy and a gender ideology that jeopardizes health and development. People should also calculate the cost of injuries due to brutal body contact and other types of violence in terms of medical expenses, lost work time and wages, days missed in college classes, disability payments, family problems and even loss in life expectancy. This will help us understand better the connections between sports participation and health.

One example of a sport which has been investigated for permitting violence *within the rules* is boxing. The British Medical Association began to campaign for the abolition of boxing in 1984. By the mid-1990s this campaign was linked to broader social debates about violence in society, including discussions of fox-hunting (see Chapter 6, p. 206) and related to concerns with violent gun crimes such as the Dunblane massacre. The argument for banning boxing is grounded in a belief that, unlike many other sports, injuries are *intentionally* inflicted by violent acts, and that this is morally questionable (see Jones, 2001). This argument in itself is complex, since many other sports have higher injury rates than boxing, and sometimes these are caused intentionally, and yet there are no calls to ban, for example, rugby. In addition, the measures introduced to limit the violence in boxing may actually increase injury rates. For example, providing pugilists with padded gloves actually protects their hands and so enables a harder punch. Similarly, the use of head guards makes the head heavier which means that when the head is punched there is likely to be a greater swirling movement, which increases the risk of brain damage (see Sheard, 2006a, 2006b). The debate over boxing continues, and it illustrates the complexities of 'legal' violence within sports.

It is less difficult to control borderline, quasi-criminal and criminal violence in sports, although many people continue to resist taking necessary actions. Players who are hired explicitly for their ability to do violence on the field should be eliminated by suspending them without pay, prohibiting teams from replacing suspended players, and fining coaches and team owners for the violence of their players. Unless these or similar actions are taken, owners will simply replace one violent player with another. When team owners think that violence boosts their profits, they have little incentive to control it unless they lose money when their players cross the line. Suspensions prevent players from doing what they love to do, and, if they cannot be replaced on teams, the suspensions also hurt coaches and team owners, who have some of the power needed to discourage violence on the field.

Violence off the Field

When athletes in contact sports are arrested for violent crimes, many people assume that their violence off the field is related to the violent strategies they have learned to use on the field. For example, the American boxer and convicted rapist Mike Tyson compared hitting his ex-wife in the face with his sporting prowess, by describing it as 'one of the best punches I ever threw'. Similarly, when the English footballer Paul Gascoigne was found guilty of hitting his wife, he was supported by George Best, the former Northern Irish football player, who had also beaten his own wife. Best suggested that this might be common behaviour among football players stating: 'I think we all give the wife a smack once in a while' (in Viner, 2005).

These quotes, as well as statements in a study of professional ice hockey players (Pappas et al., 2004), suggest that the violence used strategically on the field carries over into athletes' lives off the field. However, research on the carry-over issue is difficult to do, and good studies are rare. When people refer to statistical correlations that show a relationship between playing certain sports and high rates of off-the-field violence, it does not prove that playing violent sports causes people to be violent outside sports. There are other issues that must be considered before causality can be established.

First, the people who play violent sports may have used violence to establish status or cope with problems prior to their sports participation. In other words, violent sports attract people who already feel comfortable about doing violence. *Second*, off-the-field violence among athletes may be due to unique situational factors encountered by athletes more than other people. For example, athletes known for their toughness on the field may be encouraged, dared or taunted by others to be tough on the streets. In some cases, they may be challenged to fight because of their reputations in sports. This is most likely to occur when athletes who grew up in high-crime neighbourhoods return home and are identified as 'marks' by locals who push drugs or run scams to make money. If athletes hang out in those neighbourhoods, they may also attract locals who define them as 'sell-outs' to big money and corporate sponsors. Some of these locals would like nothing better than to enhance their own credibility on the streets by successfully confronting an athlete known for his toughness. If trouble occurs and an athlete is arrested for fighting in these circumstances, it is misleading to say that their actions were caused by what they learned in sports.

Control versus carry-over

Does playing sports teach people to control violent responses in the face of adversity, stress, defeat, hardship and pain? Or does it create identities, personal orientations and social dynamics that make off-the-field violence more likely?

Trulson's research, which was summarized in Chapter 6 (p. 204) showed that aggressive tendencies among male juvenile delinquents decreased after they received training in the philosophy and techniques of tae kwon do. The philosophy emphasized respect for self and others, confidence, physical fitness, self-control, honour, patience and responsibility. Similar young men who received martial arts training *without* the philosophy actually measured higher on aggressive tendencies after a training period, and young men who participated in running, basketball and football with standard adult supervision did not change at all in terms of their aggressive tendencies.

Sociologist of Sport John Sugden studied these issues when he 'hung out' at a boxing club for a year in Belfast. During that time, he observed, interviewed and documented the experiences and lives of the boys and their trainers, becoming immersed in the social world in which the boxers lived and competed. He found that the social world formed around this gym was one in which the boxers learned to respect disciplined toughness but devalued any gratuitous violence such as that witnessed daily on the streets of their neighbourhoods. The club was based in an inner-city, low-income housing estate where familiar problems of violent crime, drug and sexual abuse, combined with sectarian conflict and political violence, gave the trainers a greater incentive to work with the young members.

When Sugden (1996) explored the connections between boxing and violence, the responses he heard included a desire to protect the boys from the violence of the society in which they lived, and to learn discipline and respect for others irrespective of the political and religious beliefs which fuelled the sectarian conflict. Two of these responses are as follows:

> There's a lot of bad things go on in Belfast, in all areas, Catholic and Protestant. If the kids stay at the club, come training here three or four times a week, they're not getting into trouble with the police, getting involved in mischief, or falling into the wrong hands (Morris, trainer, in Sugden, 1996, p. 101).

> We've got simple rules and basic discipline, the same as when the club was set up in 1948. No swearing and no political talk. You leave the political talk outside the door. When you come in here your business is boxing. We don't care what colour you are, what religion you are or anything like that so long as you come to train and box. Hopefully, when they grow up they remember those things (Storey, manager, in Sugden, 1996, p. 108).

These statements are not meant to support professional boxing. However, the statements, along with other findings in the studies by Trulson and Sugden, suggest that participation in sports, even martial arts and boxing, can teach people to control violence. Of course, this depends greatly on the conditions under which sport participation occurs. *If* the social world formed around a sport promotes a mindset and norms emphasizing non-violence, self-control, respect for self and others, physical fitness, patience, responsibility and humility (the opposite of hubris), then athletes *may* learn to control violent behaviour off the field. Those most likely to benefit seem to be young men who lack structured challenges and firm guidance as they navigate their way through lives where there are many incentives to engage in violence.

Unfortunately, many sports are not organized around these norms. Instead, most sports cultures emphasize hostility, physical domination and a willingness to use one's body as a weapon. They are also organized to produce hubris, separate athletes from the community and encourage athletes to think that others do not deserve their respect. For example, recent research on 13- to 17-year-olds in American schools shows that sports participation, especially for young men in contact sports, is associated with fighting and delinquency off the field (Kreager, 2007; Portes, 1998; Roche, 1999; Wright and Fitzpatrick, 2006). Sociologist Derek Kreager (2007) used data from 6397 young men in a nationwide study and sample, and found that high school gridiron football players and wrestlers were over 40 per cent more likely to be involved in fights than peers who did not play high school sports. Playing basketball and baseball were unrelated to fighting, and male tennis players had a 35 per cent *lower* risk of fighting than male peers who did not play sports. The likelihood of fighting increased with the proportion of football players in a young man's friendship network.

Another recent national study in the USA (Wright and Fitzpatrick, 2006) found that certain high school sports were associated with status dynamics that created or intensified in-group versus out-group differences among young people. Other research suggests that these status differences frequently take the form of a social hierarchy that is sustained, in part, through harassment, bullying and fighting; in many cases, athletes from certain sports were the perpetrators of these actions (ESPN, 1999).

More research is needed to understand the social worlds of athletes in particular sports, the meanings that athletes attach to their actions, and the place of violence in sport cultures.

Similarly, we need to know more about issues of identity, group dynamics among athletes, ideological issues and social factors associated with the incidence of violence. Sports participation does not automatically teach people to control violence, nor does the aggression and violence used in certain sports inevitably carry over to other relationships and settings. Instead of seeking examples of carry-over or control, perhaps we should look for cultural connections between sports and ideologies associated with high rates of violence. This is discussed in the box 'Violence on the field'.

reflect on SPORTS   *Violence on the field: does it distort our ideas about gender?*

'Men are naturally superior to women': this is a contentious statement today. However, many people still believe it, mostly because the hierarchical structure of gender relations depends on the extent to which people in a society accept it as true.

The ideology of male superiority is clearly reaffirmed through sports such as ultimate fighting, boxing, football, wrestling, ice hockey, rugby and other heavy-contact sports that are valued and viewed worldwide (Burstyn, 1999; Connell, 1995; Messner, 2007). The violence in those sports supports the belief that hierarchical distinctions between men and women are grounded in nature and have relevance for gender relations.

Power and performance sports emphasize sex *difference* in terms of physical strength, *control* through domination, and *status* as an outcome of victories over others. This serves to 'naturalize' hierarchical differences and reaffirm the belief that power differences are inevitable and that success depends on one's rank compared with others. These ideas and beliefs are perpetuated through the stories that people tell about power and performance sports, and the way that victories and championships have been won by using strength and strategy to overcome or dominate others, often using violence in the process (Burstyn, 1999).

The gender ideology formed around these ideas and beliefs has had a strong influence in UK culture. The stakes associated with preserving this ideology are so high that male boxers are paid millions of pounds for 3 to 36 minutes of brutalizing one another in the ring. Heavyweight boxers are among the highest-paid athletes in the world because they promote the idea that one-on-one violent confrontations are 'nature in action', even though the combatants often lose millions of brain cells in the service of 'proving' male superiority.

The irony in this approach is that, if gender were truly fixed in nature, there would be no need for sports to reaffirm 'natural' differences between men and women. Gender would simply exist without painting our children's bedrooms different colours and spending so much time and effort to teach them how to be girls or boys. Power and performance sports serve as valuable aids in this teaching and learning process, and the men who play them sometimes serve as the teachers. For example, when it was believed that Joe Calzaghe, the British super-middleweight champion boxer, had broken his hand during a fight in 2007, a comment on the Boxing Daily website suggested that: 'ya boy is a bitch who hits like a girl and then breaks a hand with those bitch slaps ... breaks his little fairy hand' (Wes, www.boxingdaily.co.uk, 6 June 2007). In his comment, Wes is suggesting that a boxer who breaks a bone during a fight is weak, and associates weakness with femininity. Wes is assuming that men are superior to women because they have 'superior' ability to do violence, and failure to do violence 'well' should bring into question their masculinity.

Some men celebrate sports in which violence and aggression are common because these sports reaffirm a gender order in which men are privileged over women. These often are the same people who reject rules against fighting. For example, when rules were passed to partially limit fighting in ice hockey, Tie Domi, an American player with a reputation for being violent, complained: 'If you take out fighting, what comes next? Do we eliminate checking? Pretty soon, we will all be out there in dresses and skirts' (Domi, 1992, p. C3). Domi's point was that, unless men can do violence in ice hockey, there will be nothing that makes them different from women, and the perception is that nothing is worse for a man than being like women – except, perhaps, being gay.

When women participate in violent sports they potentially disrupt the 'logic' that many people use to reaffirm traditional gender ideology. This causes some people to argue that women should not participate in these sports – that there should be rules to prevent their participation. Others simply treat women athletes in these sports as jokes, oddities, or freaks of nature; they may watch as women box, cage fight or wrestle, but they do not take them seriously. Still others may accept women in these sports but only if they present themselves in sexualized terms that reaffirm the 'logic of sex differences' on which traditional gender ideology is based (see www.fatalfemmesfighting.com/).

The participation of women in violent sports often creates a dilemma for people who wish to change traditional gender ideology. Participation can contradict the ideological belief that women are frail and vulnerable, but when participation is sexualized, it reaffirms the beliefs that have traditionally disadvantaged women through history. For this reason, some women advocate equal opportunities in sports at the same time that they seek alternatives to violent sports. Their goal is to promote sports in which women can be strong and assertive without being violent.

These issues and controversies illustrate that sports have an impact on our lives regardless of our own involvement in them as athletes or spectators. *What do you think?*

Assaults and sexual assaults by athletes

Highly publicized cases in which athletes are accused or guilty of assault, sexual assault, rape, gang rape and, even, murder have led many people to think that the violence in certain sports influences off-the-field actions and relationships, especially relationships with women. Athletes are public figures and celebrities, so when they are accused, charged, arrested, tried and found guilty or innocent, we hear and read about it time and time again. This repetition also contributes to the belief that many athletes are violent and misogynist.

Violent crimes by athletes are a serious problem. On this, there is no question (Armstrong and Perry, 2008a, 2008b, 2008c; Benedict, 1997, 1998, 2004; Lefkowitz, 1997; Robinson, 1998). Furthermore, the victims of these crimes are often subject to various forms of character assassination and harassment to a degree that may exceed victims of similar crimes by men who are not celebrity athletes (Hnida, 2006). Therefore, there is a clear need for sport teams and organizations to directly and assertively address this issue. But there is also a need to understand the role of sport participation in connection with violent off-the-field actions and crimes. Without this understanding, the efforts of teams and organizations may be ineffective.

As noted above, some research indicates that high school athletes in certain sports are involved in fighting more frequently than their peers (see above, p. 246), but we lack studies that compare specific rates of off-the-field violence for athletes of different ages with rates for similar men or women who do not play elite sports. For example, people in the UK read time and time again about sexual assault accusations made against George Best and Paul Gascoigne, but these reports said nothing about a systematic connection between sports participation and involvement in assaultive actions.

Research on the conversations and biographies of athletes has presented important information suggesting that the social worlds created around men's power and performance sports subvert respect for women and promote the image of women as 'game' to be pursued and conquered (Clayton and Humberstone, 2006; Curry, 1991, 1996, 1998; Lefkowitz, 1997; Messner and Stevens, 2002; Nack and Munson, 1995; Reid, 1997).

How do we make sense of this? In a critical assessment of the debate about sexual exploitation in sport, sociologist Celia Brackenridge (2001) reviewed all the published research on the issue. Her review indicated that the majority of sexual assaults are by male athletes against women. The imperative for male athletes to demonstrate active heterosexuality, inflict and tolerate pain, and avoid any suggestion of inferiority or femininity goes some way to explaining sexual assault. When this is combined with excessive alcohol consumption and sexually explicit initiation rituals (see Chapter 6, p. 174), athletes may lose their inhibitions and sexual assault may become normalized as part of the sporting experience. Those who engage in such assault are then able to rationalize their behaviour through a variety of coping strategies, including denial that it happened (or that they cannot remember it), minimizing the seriousness of the assault, and blaming the victim as 'asking for it'.

Violence against women is a serious social problem, but it is important to recognize that most acts are perpetrated by men who are not currently playing competitive sports. We, therefore, need to understand this problem within the broader context of British culture and forms of gender relations that exist in sports and other spheres of society if we wish to significantly cut the rates of sexual assault and rape. Building on the framework developed by Brackenridge and combining it with other research on patterns of violence in all-male groups, it appears that violence against women by male athletes is associated with the extent to which the culture of men's sports:

- supports the belief that violence is an effective strategy for establishing one's manhood, achieving status as an athlete and controlling women
- fosters social bonds and a related sense of hubris that separates athletes from the rest of the community
- creates a sense of privilege based on the beliefs that people outside the fraternity of elite athletes do not deserve respect and that elite athletes live outside the norms of the general community
- supports the belief that women, apart from mothers and sisters, are celebrity-obsessed 'groupies' who can be exploited for sexual pleasure without consequences
- is viewed with such awe and idealism that people and institutions in the general community fail to hold elite athletes accountable for violations of community norms and rules.

Research on these factors will help us understand violence against women *in the full social and cultural contexts in which it occurs.*

As noted in Chapter 6, the social dynamics in certain all-male sports groups encourage athletes to demean and humiliate those who do not match their unique, elite status. This suggests that off-the-field violence is not simply the result of carry-over from on-the-field violence. Instead, it is action grounded in complex social processes related to the social worlds in which athletes live, define their identities and deal with their social relationships. As athletes are increasingly separated from the rest of the community, it becomes more important to understand these processes, if we wish to explain assault rates among athletes.

When discussing this issue, it is important to remember that even if studies indicated that male athletes had higher sexual assault rates than other categories of people, this would not change the fact that 'non-athletes' perpetrate nearly all violence, including violence against women. Jackson Katz, a violence prevention expert, explains that it would be useful to explain why some male athletes assault women, but this is only part of what we need to know when trying to answer the main question of why 'stockbrokers, teachers, priests, auto mechanics, and … students also commit rape' (Katz, 2003). Although people from all racial and ethnic groups, social classes and occupational categories perpetrate violence, it is clear that men commit nearly all rapes.

Finally, the focus on athletes should not distract attention away from other sports-related assault issues. For example, sexual assaults, including statutory rape, by coaches have a greater impact in sports and on people's lives than sexual assaults by athletes (Brackenridge, 2001; Brackenridge and Fasting, 2003; Fasting et al., 2004). The first significant case against a British coach was in 1995 when Paul Hickson, a former Olympic swimming coach, was convicted of 15 sexual offences, including two rapes, of teenage swimmers in his care. He was sentenced to 17 years in prison, the longest rape sentence imposed in an English court. The 'Hickson case' has been identified as a defining moment in the history of sexual exploitation in British sport (Brackenridge, 2001, 2004). While Hickson was found guilty of abusing female athletes, in 2001 another British swimming coach, Mike Drew, was jailed for eight years for sexually abusing five boys in his care, who were aged between 13 and 15 at the time of the abuse. The issues of assault and sexual assault are complex, and they also go far beyond the realm of sport. They are part of a larger issue in many societies, including in the UK.

Violence among Spectators

Do sports incite violence among spectators? This is an important question because sports capture widespread public attention around the world and spectators number in the billions. To answer this question, we must distinguish between watching sports on television and attending events in person. Further, we must study spectators in context if we wish to understand the emotional dynamics of identifying with teams and athletes and the meanings that spectators give to particular sports, events and the circumstances under which watching sports occurs.

Violence among television viewers

Most sports watching occurs in front of the television. Television viewers may be emotionally expressive during games and matches. They may even get angry, but we know little about whether their anger is expressed through violence directed at friends and family members at home.

We also know little about violence among those who watch televised sports in public settings such as bars, pubs and around large video screens in public areas. Most people who collectively watch media sports restrict emotional expressions to verbal comments. When they do express anger, they nearly always direct it at the players, coaches, referees or media commentators rather

'Hey, watch it, pal! You stepped on my foot'.
Cartoon 7.3 **The language used by some spectators often refers to violence, but it is not known if such language actually incites violent actions.**

than fellow viewers. Even when emotional outbursts are defined as too loud or inappropriate, fellow viewers usually try to control the offender informally and peacefully. When fans from opposing teams watch an event in a local place, there often are sources of mutual identification that defuse differences and discourage physical violence, although verbal comments may become heated.

Since the mid-1990s, there has been an increase in cases when people, usually men who have been watching sports in a bar or other public place, engage in celebratory violence after the favoured team wins a big game or championship. Predicting such violence is difficult, but a combination of heavy alcohol consumption and the presence of peers who encourage extreme actions increases its likelihood.

The belief that watching sports is associated with violence has led some people to wonder if watching sports is associated with temporary spikes in the rates of domestic violence in a community or the nation as a whole. During the 2006 men's football World Cup, a 'positive arrest' policy was adopted by British police forces, grounded in a belief that increased television viewing during major sports events leads to domestic tension and the related high levels of alcohol consumption increase the incidence of domestic violence. This led to raised visibility of support groups and a campaign under the slogan: 'Give domestic violence the red card'. While it is possible that high levels of alcohol consumption along with anger caused by something in a televised sports event *could* be factors in particular cases of domestic violence, we should also recognize that violence in the home is a complex phenomenon, and to blame it on watching sports overlooks more important factors. Furthermore, we do not know enough about the ways that spectators integrate televised sport content into their lives to say that watching sports does anything in particular (Coakley, 1988–89; Crawford, 2004).

Violence at sports events

Spectators attending non-contact sport events seldom engage in violence. They may be emotionally expressive, but violence directed at fellow fans, players, coaches, referees, stewards or police is rare. The attack and wounding of American tennis player Monica Seles during a tournament in Germany in 1993 stands out as one of the only violent incidents at a non-contact sports event, and that had more to do with celebrity stalking than with the dynamics of a sport event. Of course, there are occasions when fans use hostile words or engage in minor skirmishes when someone unintentionally drops a drink onto another person's head, but such cases of violence are usually controlled effectively by the fans themselves. The exception is when there are pre-existing hostilities between particular fans who are eager to confront each other.

Spectators attending contact sports tend to be vocal and emotional, but most of them have not been involved in violent actions. However, crowd violence occurs with enough regularity and seriousness in certain sports to be a problem for law enforcement and a social issue for

Diverse fans gathered around public video screens when the 2007 Rugby World Cup was hosted in Paris. These fans, mostly French, with groups from England, Ireland, Australia and New Zealand, were expressive but violence was not observed by the author who took this photograph (Source: Jay Coakley)

which it would be helpful to have an explanation (Lewis, 2007; O'Neill, 2004; Pearson, 2000; Perryman, 2001; Young, 2007b).

Historical background

Media reports of violent actions at sports events around the world, especially at football matches in Europe, have increased our awareness of crowd violence. However, crowd violence is not new. Data documenting the actions of sports spectators through the ages are scarce, but research suggests that spectator violence did occur in the past and much of it would make crowd violence today seem rare and tame by comparison (Dunning, 1999; Guttmann, 1986, 1998; Young, 2000).

Roman events during the first five centuries of the first Christian millennium contained especially brutal examples of crowd violence (Guttmann, 1986, 1998, 2004). Spectators during the medieval period were not much better, although levels of violence decreased in the late medieval period. With the emergence of modern sports, violence among sport spectators decreased further, but it remained common by today's standards. Malcolm (1999, 2002) outlines the frequency of spectator disorder at cricket matches during the eighteenth and nineteenth centuries in England, with some matches having to be abandoned due to pitch invasions. More recently, a football match in 1909 between Glasgow and Celtic ended in a riot when the officials declined the fans' demand to play extra time to settle a draw score. Fifty-four policemen were injured when 6000 spectators joined the riot, which also caused extensive damage within and outside the ground. Following a survey of reports of incidents in the pre-war years, Hutchinson (1975, p. 22) concluded that: 'Riots, unruly behaviour, violence, assault and vandalism, appear to have been a well-established, but not necessarily dominant pattern of crowd behaviour at football matches at least from the 1870s.'

During the inter-war years there was a relative decline in the intensity of violence on the football terraces. What did occur was largely precipitated by excessive violence by players, such that the Football Association issued a warning to the players in 1936 to stop any form of rough play. Other incidents were related to protests against administrative rulings such as the sale of the best players, and abuse of referees.

Prior to the Second World War, spectator behaviour continued to be fairly peaceful, possibly due to continued high levels of national solidarity. This is not to suggest that violence disappeared from the terraces altogether. For example, in 1924 in Brighton, the pitch was invaded, the referee chased by the crowd and a policeman knocked unconscious. In 1934, Leicester City fans vandalized a train returning from a match in Birmingham. And in 1935, the police had to lead a baton charge against stone-throwing fans during a match between Linfield and Belfast Celtic (see Frosdick and Marsh, 2005).

During the 1960s, an enquiry into the state of football in the UK was commissioned. The ensuing Chester Report of 1966 suggested that incidences of football violence had doubled in the first five years of the 1960s compared with the previous 25 years. This was followed by a succession of government enquiries into spectator violence at football matches, including the Harrington Report 1968, the Lang Report 1969, the McElhone Report on Scotland 1976 and the Popplewell Report 1985. The violent behaviour of British spectators had an international impact when 39 fans, mostly Italians, were killed in Heysel, Belgium, as they tried to escape rioting English supporters in the Champions' Cup Final between Juventus and Liverpool. In 1989 the

Taylor Report was commissioned following the tragedy at Hillsborough, Sheffield, which is regarded as Britain's worst sporting disaster, when 96 fans died during the FA Cup semi-final between Liverpool and Nottingham Forest.

By now, violence by football spectators had become known as 'The British Disease' even though similar behaviour has been common elsewhere in Europe and other parts of the world, and many cases have been far worse than incidents involving British fans (see Scambler, 2005). Various theories have been proposed in these reports and by academic scholars to explain contemporary spectator violence. These include racial tensions since immigrants who arrived during the 1950s were the target of much of the violence in this era, the increased availability of televisions which provided publicity for hooligan behaviour and so encouraged others to become involved, and the general rise of counterculture youth movements. These are examined below.

These examples are not meant to minimize the existence or seriousness of crowd violence today. They are mentioned here to counter the argument that violence is a bigger problem today than in the past, that coercive tactics should be used to control unruly fans and that there is a general decline of civility among fans and in society as a whole (Saporito, 2004). Some spectators do act in obnoxious and violent ways today. They present law enforcement challenges and interfere with the enjoyment of other fans, but there is no systematic evidence that they are unprecedented threats to the social order or signs of the decline of civilization as we know it.

Celebratory violence

Oddly enough, some of the most serious and destructive crowd violence occurs during the celebrations that follow victories in important games (Lewis, 2007). Such displays have included

Cartoon 7.4 **We need research on so-called celebratory riots. Research on other forms of collective action suggests that celebratory riots may not be as spontaneous and unplanned as many people think**

ransacking seats and throwing objects onto the field. In the wake of injuries and mounting property damage associated with these displays, authorities have banned or limited alcohol sales in stadiums and arenas, and they now use police and security officials to prevent fans from rushing onto the playing field when games end. Cases of celebratory violence still occur, but new social control methods have been reasonably successful in stopping them from happening *inside* the stadium.

Celebratory violence is not exclusive to elite professional sport. For instance, a parent supporting his child at a youth football game explained:

> Last season I was actually put out of work for five weeks when I was attacked. I was attacked at a football game, and it's been dealt with by the police. I was kicked to the ground from behind, simply for celebrating, clapping my son scoring at the end of the game. I was proud … next thing I know I've just hit the floor … I was put out of work through damaged shoulder and ribs.
>
> *(In Brackenridge et al., 2007a, p. 93)*

Sociologists have studied crowds and crowd dynamics, but scholars in the sociology of sport usually do not have the resources to study sport-related celebratory violence. However, if celebratory violence continues to occur, there will be resources for law enforcement research. Furthermore, professional sports teams will develop strategies to defuse violence through announcements by highly visible players and respected coaches, bar owners will be asked to control drinking and contain the movement of their customers, and universities will attempt to control the binge drinking that accompanies most celebratory violence. Fans will be encouraged to BIRG, that is, 'bask in the reflected glory' of the moment, but the goal is to facilitate the formation of norms that discourage violence in connection with BIRGing.

Research and theories about crowd violence

Most of the available research on sports crowd violence has been carried out by British scholars, and their studies have focused almost exclusively on football and 'football hooliganism'. One of the difficulties in identifying a cause of such behaviour is that 'hooliganism' itself has no clear definition. The term is commonly believed to originate from an Irish family of the same name who wreaked havoc in their local community. Football hooliganism is now an umbrella term used to define any violent or criminal behaviour which takes place in connection with a football event. There have been several theories proposed to explain this behaviour.

Studies grounded in social psychological theories largely emerged from the 'Oxford School'. This stance emphasizes that displays of intimidation and aggression at football matches have involved ritual violence, consisting of fantasy-driven status posturing by young males who want to be defined as tough and manly (Marsh, 1982; Marsh and Campbell, 1982). These studies are interesting, and they describe classic examples of ritualistic aggression, or what they refer to as 'aggro', but they have understated the serious and occasionally deadly violence perpetrated by football fans, especially during pre- and post-game activities.

Research inspired by various forms of conflict theory has emphasized that violence at football matches is an expression of the alienation of disenfranchised working-class men (Taylor, 1982a, 1982b, 1987). In addition to losing control over the conditions of their work lives, these men also feel that they have lost control of the recently commercialized clubs that sponsor elite football, particularly in England. Taylor modified his theories during the 1980s to suggest that the working class itself was being dislocated as a result of Thatcherite policies, and that this exacerbated the hooligan problem. This research helps us understand that certain forms of violence may be associated with class conflict in society, but it does not explain why violence at football matches has not increased proportionately in connection with the declining power of the working class in England.

Research inspired by interactionist and critical theories has emphasized a variety of factors, including the importance of understanding the history and dynamics of the working-class and youth subcultures in British society and how those subcultures have been influenced by the professionalization and commercialization of society as a whole and football in particular (Critcher, 1979). However, the data presented in this research from the 'Birmingham School' (the Centre for Contemporary Studies at Birmingham) are not very strong, and more work is needed to develop critical analyses of crowd violence across various situations. Much of the recent research on football violence has been based on figurational theory, from scholars at the 'Leicester School'. This is an explanatory framework that is grounded in a synthesis of approaches based on biology, psychology, sociology and history.

Much of this work, summarized by Dunning (1999), Dunning et al. (1988, 2002) and Young (2000), emphasizes that football hooliganism is grounded in long-term historical changes, which have affected working-class men. In contrast to the work of Taylor, which suggests that hooligan groups are largely from the 'upper' sector of the working classes, the thesis of Dunning and his colleagues is that hooligan groups largely comprise those who experience the greatest deprivation, or what they call the 'rough' working classes. This deprived social condition impacts on their relationships with each other and their families, and their definitions of community, violence and masculinity. Taken together, these changes have created a context, or social figuration or a set of historically concentrated social processes, in which football represents the collective turf and identity of people in local communities, especially young British men. Football then becomes a site for these men to defend and/or assert community and identity through violence directed at the new status quo. This research provides valuable historical data and thoughtful analyses of the complex social processes in which particular forms of sports violence are located. It has also been used as a guide by those who have formulated recent policies of social control related to football crowds in England and around Europe.

As the police have become more sophisticated in anticipating violence associated with football crowds, young men, some of whom may not be avid football fans, take it as a challenge to outsmart them and create discord and violent confrontations with rival groups. Research indicates that current forms of hooliganism involve semi-organized confrontations that are strategically staged to cause havoc and avoid arrest. The police in this situation play the role of umpire between groups, and attempt to confine confrontations to spaces where they are prepared to deal with them and make arrests before serious injuries and property damage occur (Armstrong, 2006; Brown, 1998; Dunning et al., 2002; Giulianotti and Armstrong, 2002). Mobile phones, handheld Global Positioning System (GPS) devices, and other communications technology used by the young men to formulate on-the-spot strategies and escape detection and arrest, fuel this cat-and-mouse scenario. The police use similar technologies and surveillance cameras to contain violence. The dynamics associated with this form of violence are not related to sports to the same degree that so-called hooliganism was in the past. Today, football matches and tournaments are not the primary focus of those involved in the violence; instead, the men simply use football matches as occasions for seeking excitement through violence.

General factors related to violence at sports events

Crowd violence at sport events is a complex social phenomenon. Research shows that it is related to three general factors:

1 the action in the sports event itself
2 the crowd dynamics and the situation in which the spectators watch the event
3 the historical, social, economic and political contexts in which the event is planned and played.

Violence and action in the event

If spectators perceive players' actions on the field as violent, they are more likely to engage in violent acts during and after games (Smith, 1983). This point is important because spectators' perceptions often are influenced by the way in which events are promoted. If an event is hyped in terms of violent images, spectators are more likely to perceive violence during the event itself, and then they are more likely to be violent themselves. This leads some people to argue that promoters and the media have a responsibility to advertise events in terms of the action and drama expected, not the blood and violence.

Research by Daniel Wann and his colleagues (1999, 2001a, 2001b, 2002, 2003, 2004) has shown that the perceptions and actions of spectators heavily depend on the extent to which they identify with teams and athletes. Highly identified fans are more likely than others to link their team's performance to their own emotions and identities. Although, by itself, this does not cause violence, it predisposes fans to take action if and when they have opportunities to do something that they think might help their team. This is important because teams and venues encourage fans to believe that they can motivate home team players and distract visiting team players. Although most fans restrict their 'participation' to cheering, stomping and waving objects, some fans and groups of fans systematically harass and taunt opposing players.

Taunts from fans are not new, but they have become increasingly obscene and personal in recent years. Players are expected to ignore taunts, but there are occasions when they have gone into the stands to attack an obnoxious fan. One of the most highly publicized cases took place in 1995 in a football match between Manchester United and Crystal Palace. Eric Cantona, a Manchester United player from France, jumped into the stands with both feet in what has become known as 'Cantona's Kung Fu Kick', kicking a spectator in the chest and then punching the fan before being removed by security personnel. Cantona alleged that his actions were a response to the spectator chanting racist abuse related to his French nationalism and spitting at him. He was fined £20 000, banned from football for nine months, stripped of the French national captaincy and served community service. More recently, Trevor Brennan, an Irish international rugby player, attacked a spectator when Toulouse, the French club that he plays for, had a match against the Irish club Ulster in 2007. Brennan entered the stands and repeatedly hit an Ulster supporter, who it is alleged was verbally abusing him. Brennan was suspended from playing rugby union for five years, fined 250 000 euros, and ordered to pay 5000 euros compensation to the spectator.

In sociological terms, these incidents highlight the need to manage player–fan relationships more carefully. This is a challenge under current circumstances. Fans pay high prices for tickets, expect players to give them their money's worth and often detest what they perceive as arrogance displayed by highly paid players; further, venue managers encourage them to be emotionally involved in the action. From the players' perspective, there is a strong sense of vulnerability when standing amid thousands of fans who could kill or main them in minutes if a mass brawl occurred.

Also important in the sports event are the calls made by officials. When fans believe that a crucial goal or a victory has been 'stolen' by an unfair or clearly incompetent decision made by a referee or an umpire, the likelihood of violence during and following the event increases (Murphy et al., 1990). This is why it is important to have competent officials at crucial games and matches, and why it is important for them to control game events so that actions perceived as violent are held to a minimum.

The knowledge that fan aggression may be precipitated by a crucial call in a close, important contest puts heavy responsibility on the officials' shoulders. Sometimes this aggression is directed at the official themselves. For example, in recent years two well-respected international football referees have retired citing threatening behaviour from supporters as the reason for the termination of their career. In 2004 Urs Meier, a Swiss referee, retired following a media-fuelled hate campaign against him, which included death threats, when he disallowed a goal for England in the European Championship semi-final against Portugal, which England subsequently lost. In 2005 Anders Frisk, a Swedish referee, also retired after receiving death threats from Chelsea supporters after he refereed their losing game against Barcelona in the Champions League. The Football Association introduced a ruling in 2005 that clubs could be fined up to £250 000 if their players abused referees, following a spate of incidents of referees being abused, threatened, physically assaulted and even confronted with guns, both on and off the pitch.

Evidence of officials having to deal with violence in sport is not only witnessed at the elite level. In 2005, a referee had to abandon a game between two Brighton-based teams of 15-year-old boys because of the abuse and threats from spectating parents, some of whom were encouraging the boys to kick the referee in the head and 'take him out'. The importance of good refereeing at the amateur level of play is supported by the parent of a youth footballer interviewed in a study by Brackenridge et al., who claimed:

> It is the poor standard of refereeing which leads to problems on the pitch ... In the last three matches this had led to violence on the pitch between players which has only been brought about because referees were either biased or weren't observant enough to see when fouls and things were happening off the ball.
>
> *(2007a, p. 101)*

These incidents emphasize that officials are important when it comes to controlling violence, but they sometimes do so at the risk of their own personal safety.

Violence, crowd dynamics and situational factors

The characteristics of a crowd and the immediate situation associated with a sports event also influence patterns of action among spectators. Spectator violence is likely to vary with one or more of the following factors:

- crowd size and the standing or seating patterns of spectators
- composition of the crowd in terms of age, sex, social class and racial/ethnic mix
- importance and meaning of the event for spectators
- history of the relationship between the teams and among spectators
- crowd-control strategies used at the event (police, police dogs, surveillance cameras or other security measures)
- alcohol consumption by the spectators
- location of the event (neutral site or home site of one of the opponents)
- spectators' reasons for attending the event and what they want to happen at the event
- importance of the team as a source of identity for spectators (class identity, ethnic or national identity, regional or local identity, club or gang identity).

Instead of discussing each factor in detail, the following comparison of two game situations is used to illustrate how they might influence spectator violence.

The *location of an event* is important because it influences who attends and how they travel. If the stadium is generally accessed by car, if spectators for the visiting team are limited due to travel distance and expense, and if tickets are costly, it is likely that the local people attending the game have a vested interest in maintaining order and avoiding violence. On the other hand, if large groups of people travel to the game in buses or trains and if tickets are relatively cheap and many of the spectators are young people more interested in creating a memorable experience than simply seeing a game, confrontations between people looking for exciting action increase, as does the possibility of violence. If groups of fans looking for excitement have consumed large amounts of alcohol, the possibility of violence increases greatly.

If spectators are respected and treated as valued guests rather than bodies to be controlled, and if stadium norms emphasize service as opposed to social control, people are less likely to engage in defensive and confrontational actions, which could lead to violence. If the stadium or arena is crowded and if the crowd itself is composed mostly of young men rather than men and women of all ages, there is a greater chance for confrontations and violence, especially if the event is seen as a special rivalry whose outcome has status implications for the communities or nations represented by the teams.

Spectator violence, when it does occur, takes many forms. There have been celebratory riots among the fans of the winning team, fights between fans of opposing teams, random property destruction carried out by fans of the losing team as they leave town, panics incited by a perceived threat unrelated to the contest itself, and planned confrontations between groups using the event as a convenient place to face off with each other as they seek to enhance their status and reputation or reaffirm their ethnic, political, class, national, local or gang identities. Each of these has different dynamics and requires specific methods of control.

Whenever thousands of people gather together for an occasion intended to generate collective emotions and excitement, it is not surprising that crowd dynamics and circumstances influence the actions of individuals and groups. This is especially true at sport events where collective action is easily fuelled by what social psychologists call *emotional contagion*. Under conditions of emotional contagion, norms are formed rapidly and may be followed in a nearly spontaneous manner by large numbers of people. Although this does not always lead to violence, it increases the possibility of potentially violent confrontations between groups of fans and between fans and agents of social control, such as the police.

Violence and the overall context in which events occur

Sports events do not occur in social vacuums. When spectators attend events, they take with them the histories, issues, controversies and ideologies of the communities and cultures in which they live. They may be racists who want to harass those they identify as targets for discrimination. They may come from ethnic neighbourhoods and want to express and reaffirm their ethnicity, or from particular nations and want to express their national identity. They may resent negative circumstances in their lives and want to express their bitterness. They may be members of groups or gangs in which status is gained partly through fighting. They may be powerless and alienated and looking for ways to be noticed and defined as socially important. They may be young men who believe that manhood is achieved through violence and domination over others. Or they may be living lives so devoid of significance and excitement that they want to create a memorable occasion they can discuss boastfully with friends for years to come. In other words, when thousands of spectators attend a sports event, their actions are grounded in factors far beyond the event and the stadium.

When tension and conflict are intense and widespread in a community or society, sports events may become sites for confrontations. For example, during the European men's football World Cup in 2006, there were several reports of England fans living in Scotland being physically assaulted and having their property damaged by Scotland fans if they were wearing the England shirt or displaying the St George's Cross in their cars or around their homes. Similarly, when the 'ultras', organized groups of fans prevalent in Italy during the 1990s, attended football games, they often used violence to express their loyalty to peers and the teams they followed (Roversi, 1994). The 'ultras' have developed in recent years into commercial enterprises run by businessmen. However, the violence continues and recent events for which they have been credited include hospitalizing four Leeds fans in a visit to Milan in 2000, and stabbing to death a policeman in 2007.

Finally, it must be noted that nearly all crowd violence involves men. This suggests that future research on this topic must consider the role of masculinity in crowd dynamics and the actions of particular segments of crowds (Hughson, 2000). Female fans generally do not tip and set cars on fire or throw chairs through windows when they celebrate a victory. They may become involved in fights, but this is relatively rare. Crowd violence may be as much a gender issue as it is a racial or social class issue, and controlling it may involve changing notions of masculinity as much as hiring additional police to patrol the sidelines at every event.

Controlling crowd violence

Effective efforts to control spectator violence are based on an awareness of each of the three factors previously discussed. *First*, the fact that perceived violence on the field is associated with crowd violence indicates a need to control violence among players during events. If fans do not define the actions of players as violent, the likelihood of crowd violence decreases. Furthermore, fans are less likely to perceive violence if events are not promoted as violent confrontations between hostile opponents.

Perceived hostility and violence can be defused if players and coaches make public announcements to emphasize the skills of the athletes involved in the event and their respect for opponents. High-profile fans for each team could make similar announcements.

The use of competent and professionally trained officials is also important. When officials maintain control of a game and make calls the spectators define as fair, they decrease the likelihood of spectator violence grounded in anger and perceived injustice. Referees also could meet with both teams before the event and explain the need to leave hostilities in the changing rooms. Team officials could organize pre-game unity rituals involving an exchange of team symbols and displays of respect between opponents. These rituals could be covered by the media so that fans could see that athletes do not view opponents as enemies. These strategies conflict with media interests in hyping games as wars without weapons, so we are faced with a choice: the safety of fans and players versus media profits and gate receipts for team owners. Until now, media profits and gate receipts have been given priority.

Second, an awareness of crowd dynamics and the conditions that precipitate violence is critical. Preventive measures are important. The needs and rights of spectators must be known and respected. Crowd-control officials must be well trained so that they know how to intervene in potentially disruptive situations without creating defensive reactions or escalating violence. Alcohol consumption should be regulated realistically, as has been done in many venues worldwide. Venues and the spaces around them should be safe and organized, to enable spectators to move around, while limiting contact between hostile fans of opposing teams. Exits should be accessible and clearly marked, and spectators should not be herded like animals before or after games. Encouraging attendance by families is important in lowering the incidence of violence.

Third, an awareness of the historical, social, economic and political issues that often underlie crowd violence is also important. Restrictive law-and-order responses to crowd violence may be temporarily effective, but they will not eliminate the underlying tensions and conflicts that often fuel violence. Policies dealing with oppressive forms of inequality, economic problems, unemployment, lack of political representation, racism, and distorted definitions of *masculinity* in the community and in society as a whole are needed. These factors often are the root of tensions, conflicts and violence. As noted in the box 'Terrorism' (p. 263), dealing with the threat of political terrorism at sports events also requires an awareness of these factors on a global level. For example, current and past wars often create the tensions that will precipitate sports-related violence under particular conditions.

In addition to strategies in each of these three categories, social control can be maintained by establishing visible and meaningful connections between teams and the communities in which they are located. These connections can defuse potentially dangerous feelings among groups of spectators or community residents. This does not mean that teams merely need better public relations. There must be *actual* connections between the teams (players) and the communities in which they exist. Effective forms of community service are helpful, and team owners must be visible supporters of community events and schemes. Teams must develop schemes to assist in the development of local neighbourhoods, especially those around their home stadium or arena. The goal of these strategies is to create anti-violence norms among spectators and community residents. This is difficult but it is more effective than using metal detectors, moving games to remote locations, hiring hundreds of security personnel, patrolling the stands, using surveillance cameras, scheduling games at times when crowds will be sparse, and recruiting armed police and soldiers. Of course, some of these tactics can be effective, but they destroy part of the enjoyment of spectator sports. Therefore, they are last resorts or temporary measures taken only to provide time to develop new spectator norms.

Summary: Does Violence in Sports Affect Our Lives?

Violence is not new to sports. Athletes through history have engaged in actions and used strategies that cause or have the potential to cause injuries to themselves and others. Furthermore, spectators through history have regularly engaged in violent actions before, during and after sport events. However, as people define violence in sports as controllable rather than as a fact of life, there is a tendency to view it as a problem in need of a solution.

Violence in sports ranges from brutal body contact and borderline violence to quasi-criminal and criminal acts. It is linked with overconformity to the sports ethic, commercialization and cultural definitions of *masculinity*. It has become institutionalized in most contact sports as a strategy for competitive success, even though it causes injuries and permanent physical impairments to athletes.

Controlling on-the-field violence is difficult, especially in men's contact sports, because it is often tied to players' identities as athletes and men. Male athletes in contact sports learn to use violence and intimidation as strategic tools, but it is not known if the strategies learned in sports influence the expression of violence in off-the-field relationships and situations.

Among males, learning to use violence as a tool within a sport is frequently tied to the reaffirmation of a form of masculinity that emphasizes a willingness to risk personal safety and a desire to intimidate others. If the boys and men who participate in certain sports learn to perceive this orientation as natural or appropriate, and receive support for this perception from sources inside sports and the general community, then their participation in sports may contribute to off-the-field violence, including assault, sexual assault and rape. However, such learning is not automatic, and men may, under certain circumstances, learn to control anger and their expressions of violence as they play sports.

The most important impact of violence in sports may be its reaffirmation of a gender ideology that assumes the 'natural superiority of men'. This ideology is based on the belief that an ability to do violence is an essential feature of manhood.

Female athletes in contact sports also engage in aggressive and violent acts, but little is known about the connections between these acts and the gender identities of girls and women at different levels of competition. Many women prefer an emphasis on supportive connections between teammates and opponents, and regulation of the power and performance aspects of sports. Therefore, aggression and violence do not occur in women's sports as often or through the same identity dynamics as they occur in men's sports.

Violence occurs among spectators consuming sports through the media as well as those attending live events. Research is needed to explain the conditions under which violence occurs in crowds watching or listening to media representations of events. Studies of on-site violence indicate that it is influenced by perceived violence on the field of play, crowd dynamics, the situation at the event itself, and the overall historical and cultural contexts in which spectators give meaning to the event and their relationships with others in attendance. Isolated cases of violence, including celebratory violence, are best controlled by improved crowd management, but chronic violence among spectators usually signals that changes are required in the culture and organization of sports and/or the social, economic and political structures of a community or society.

Terrorism in the form of planned, politically motivated violence at sport events is rare, but the threat of terrorism alters security policies and procedures at sports venues. The terrorist attack at the 1972 Olympic Games reminds us that global issues influence our lives, even when we attend our favourite sports events. Just as violence in sports affects our lives, the social conditions in the rest of our lives affect violence in sports.

reflect on SPORTS   *Terrorism: planned political violence at sports events*

The visibility of sport events and the concentration of many people in one place make sports venues a possible target of terrorist attacks. After deadly terrorist attacks in New York, Washington, DC, London, Madrid and other cities worldwide, most people today have a heightened awareness of terrorism and its possible impact on their lives.

An integral part of planning major sports events today is establishing effective security measures at arenas and stadiums. Spectators often are searched as they enter venues, and rules regulate what they may bring with them. However, most security measures are discretely enacted and take place behind the scenes in the form of bomb searches, electronic surveillance and undercover tactics.

As sports teams and venues deal with security issues, their costs increase. In fact, it is estimated that world organizers of sports events spend around US$2 billion per year on security. During the 2004 Summer Olympic Games in Athens, nearly US$1.5 billion was spent on security. The day after London was awarded the summer Olympic Games for 2012, London itself was the target of a terrorist attack. The cost of security for these Games rapidly rose and it is estimated that final costs for this event will be £900 million.

Although the threat of political terrorism may be new in the minds of people in the UK, others around the world have lived for many years with the threat and reality of terrorism. Furthermore, terrorism has occurred in connection with sports in the past. For instance, during the early morning hours of 5 September 1972, members of a Palestinian terrorist group called Black September entered the Olympic Village in Munich, Germany. Dressed in athletic warm-up suits and carrying sports bags containing grenades and automatic weapons, they entered a bedroom that housed Israeli athletes participating in the Summer Olympic Games. They shot and killed a wrestling coach and a weightlifter, and captured nine other Israeli athletes.

After a 21-hour stand-off and a poorly planned rescue attempt, 17 people were dead – 10 Israeli athletes and one coach, one West German police officer and five terrorists. The remaining terrorists were sought out and killed by Israeli commandos. The Olympics were suspended for a day, but events resumed and the closing ceremonies occurred as planned. About US$2 million had been spent on security during the Olympics in Munich; 32 years later Athens spent 750 times that amount.

Although the terrorism in Munich is remembered by those who plan the Olympic Games, it is seldom mentioned in the media coverage of the Olympics. The reasons for this are complex, but it is clear that many people do not want their favourite sports events disrupted or defined in connection with the nasty realities of everyday life, even though sports cannot be separated from the world in which they exist.

Because terrorism occurs regularly, it is useful to remember that sports cannot be separated from the policies, events and material conditions of life that create deeply felt resentment and hatred around the world. This means it is in everyone's interest to learn more about the world and how peace might be achieved. This takes time and commitment on our part, and it will not be easy to change the conditions that precipitate terrorism. In the meantime, none of us can escape the threat of terrorism, not even at the sports events that we attend. *What do you think?*

Website resources

Note: Websites often change. The following URLs were current when this book was printed. Please check our website (***www.mcgraw-hill.co.uk/textbooks/coakley***) for updates and additions.

www.mcgraw-hill.co.uk/textbooks/coakley Click on Chapter 7 for information and critique of instinct theory and frustration-aggression theory as applied to violence in sports; discussion of cultural patterning theory and violence associated with sports.

www.answers.com/topic/violence-in-sports Encyclopaedia-like information about violence in sports; good links to sites on specific topics.

www.coe.int/t/dg4/sport/violence/Default_en.asp Council of Europe site, presents documents stating the council's official position on spectator violence, mostly in connection with football matches.

www.thecpsu.org.uk/Scripts/content/Default.asp The Child Protection in Sport Unit, overviews the problem in the UK and elsewhere, and provides resources and links to other organizations.

www.un.org/Depts/dhl/resguide/r58.htm Links to two UN resolutions: 'Building a Peaceful and Better World Through Sport and the Olympic Ideal' (A/RES/58/6) and 'Sport as a Means to Promote Education, Health, Development and Peace' (A/RES/58/5).

www.un.org/sport2005/ The site for the UN International Year for Sport and Physical Education 2005; also a link to the Sport for Development and Peace report entitled, 'Sport as a Tool for Development and Peace: Towards Achieving the United Nations Millennium Development Goals' (33 pages).

Gender and sports: does equity require ideological changes?

(*Source*: McGraw-Hill)

Online Learning Centre Resources

Visit *Sports in Society*'s Online Learning Centre (OLC) at **www.mcgraw-hill.co.uk/ textbooks/coakley** for additional information and study material for this chapter, including:

- Self-grading quizzes and essay questions
- Learning outcomes
- Related websites
- Additional readings

Chapter contents

Participation and equity issues
Ideology and power issues
Summary: does equity require ideological changes?

> Football is a game of hard, physical contact, a form of combat. It is, and must remain, a man's game. Women have no place in it except to cheer on their men, wash and iron their kit, and prepare and serve refreshments.
>
> *(Ted Croker, former secretary of the FA, in Dunning, 2007, p. 325)*

> Girls are growing up believing it is more important to be attractive than active with many women inhibited from exercising because of low body confidence. Sport is still seen by some women as unfeminine, and girls' earliest experiences of sport are often off-putting.
>
> *(Sue Tibballs, Chief Executive, Women's Sport and Fitness Foundation, 2007)*

> Elite athletes are still nervous about negative exposure if they come out, and worried that they will lose sponsorship if they do ... One woman on the English discus team wanted to participate in the Gay Games, then pulled out at the last minute, scared to be recognized.
>
> *(Gay Games organizer, in Hargreaves, 2007, p. 362)*

Gender and gender relations are central topics in the sociology of sport. It is important to explain why most sports around the world have been defined as men's activities, why half the world's population generally was excluded or discouraged from participating in many sports through history, and why there have been dramatic increases in women's participation in recent years. To explain these things we must understand the relationship between sports and widespread beliefs about masculinity, femininity, homosexuality and heterosexuality.

Discussions and research on gender relations and sports usually focus on two interrelated issues. One is fairness and equity, and the other is ideology and power. *Fairness and equity issues* revolve around topics such as:

- sports participation patterns among girls and women
- gender inequities in participation opportunities, support for athletes, and jobs in coaching and administration
- strategies for achieving equal opportunities for girls and women.

Ideology and power issues revolve around topics such as:

- the production and reproduction of gender ideology in connection with sports
- the ways in which prevailing gender ideology constrains people's lives and subverts the achievement of gender equity
- the cultural and structural changes required to achieve gender equity and democratic access to participation in sports.

The goal of this chapter is to discuss these two sets of issues and show that, even though many people deal with them separately, they go hand in hand in our lives. We cannot ignore either one if we define sports as important in the lives of human beings.

Participation and Equity Issues

The single most dramatic change in sports over the past two generations is the increase in participation among girls and women. This has occurred mostly in wealthy post-industrial nations, but there have been increases in some developing nations as well. Despite resistance against change, more girls and women now participate in sports than ever before.

Reasons for increased participation

Since the mid-1960s, five interrelated factors account for the dramatic increases in sports participation among girls and women:

1. new opportunities
2. government legislation and policies mandating equal rights
3. the global women's rights movement
4. the health and fitness movement
5. increased media coverage of women in sports.

New opportunities

New participation opportunities account for most of the increases we have witnessed in sports participation among girls and women. Young women today may not realize it, but the opportunities they enjoy in their schools and communities were not available to many of their mothers or any of their grandmothers. Teams and schemes developed during and since the second half of the twentieth century have inspired and supported interests ignored in the past. Girls and women still do not receive an equal share of sports resources in most organizations and communities, but their increased participation clearly has been fuelled by the development of new opportunities. Many of these opportunities owe their existence to some form of political pressure or government legislation.

Government legislation and policies mandating equal rights

Although many people complain about government regulations, literally millions of girls and women would not be playing sports today if it were not for local and national policies mandating equal rights. Legislation and rules calling for gender equity exist today mostly because of persistent political action focused on raising legal issues and pressuring political representatives. Activist individuals and groups often have been feminists committed to achieving fairness in society.

In the UK, the Sex Discrimination Act was passed in 1975, making sex discrimination unlawful in employment and vocational training, education, the provision and sale of goods, facilities, services and premises, including those for sport. It also covers discrimination against someone on the grounds of being married and of gender reassignment. In 2007, the Gender Equality Duty came into force, requiring all public authorities, including those providing sporting opportunities, to demonstrate that they are promoting equality for women and men and that they are eliminating sexual discrimination and harassment. Additional public policies, legislation and financial issues affecting girls physical education in schools and sport in the broader community are discussed in Chapters 5 and 13.

Governments in many nations now have laws and policies that support equal rights for girls and women in sports. Women around the world have formed the International Working Group on Women and Sport (the IWG; see www.iwg-gti.org) to promote the enforcement of these laws and policies, and pressure resistant governments and international groups to pass equal rights legislation of their own. Political power in these nations and organizations rests in the hands of men, and they often think that if girls and women played sports it would disrupt their ways of life and violate important moral principles grounded in nature and/or their religious beliefs.

The women and men working to produce changes in these settings have had to be persistent and politically creative to achieve even minor improvements. Progress has been made in some nations, but at least half the women in the world today lack regular access to sport participation opportunities.

The global women and sports movement

The global women's movement over the past 40 years has emphasized that females are enhanced as human beings when they develop their intellectual *and* physical abilities. This idea has encouraged women of all ages to pursue their interests in sports, and it has inspired new interests among those who, in the past, never would have thought of playing sports (Fasting, 1996).

The women's movement also has initiated and supported changes in the occupational and family roles of women. These changes have in turn provided more women the time and resources they need to play sports. As the goals of the women's movement have become more widely accepted and as male control over the lives and bodies of women has weakened, more women choose to play sports. More changes are needed, however, especially in poor nations

reflect on SPORTS · *Women's football: possibilities of gender equity?*

Football remains the most popular sport in the UK and is considered to be the fastest-growing sport for female participants. In 2005, England hosted the Women's European Championships, and this event had television viewing figures of more than 8 million and 100 000 spectators attending games (see Brackenridge et al., 2007a). This apparent 'success story' should be understood in the context of more than a century of struggle, and ongoing marginalization and discrimination.

Football is not a 'new' sport for women, with the first recorded game in Britain taking place in 1888, and an association for female players founded in 1894. However, by 1921 the Football Association (FA) had banned women from playing on league grounds on the basis that 'the game of football is quite unsuitable for females and should not be encouraged' (cited in Williams, 2003, p. 33). This ban remained in place for 50 years, until action from the Union of European Football Associations (UEFA) caused the FA to rescind it in 1971. It took a further 20 years before Rule 37 was changed, finally allowing girls to play in mixed-sex teams up to the age of 11.

Psychologist Kate Russell has undertaken an extensive research project with players, parents, coaches and administrators in women's football. She found that most people agree that there is little immediate possibility of widespread professionalism in the women's game. As a result, there is limited financial and structural support for female players. In turn, this discouraged motivation for training and reaching the standards achieved by men in professional football. Additionally, despite the success of Hope Powell as the England women's football coach, there are relatively few female coaches, and those who qualified as coaches felt that they would always receive worse treatment than male coaches (in Brackenridge et al., 2007a).

Do gender inequities continue to exist only because the sports participation interests of girls and women do not match those of boys and men, or are inequities due primarily to differential patterns of socialization and encouragement, and a general cultural devaluation of women's sports relative to men's sports? It is likely that sports interests among girls and women would increase if they did not feel that they were perceived as second class and if sporting excellence was not equated with 'being like a man'. However, as long as sports are 'social places' organized exclusively around the values and experiences of men, struggles over gender equity in football and other sports will last long into the future. *What do you think?*

and among low-income women in wealthy nations, but the choices now available to women are less restricted than they were a generation ago.

The global women's movement has fuelled both national and international political action. Many politically influential women's sports organizations have emerged in connection with the women's movement. For example, the Women's Sport and Fitness Foundation in the UK and the USA, together with similar organizations in other nations, have become important lobbyists for change. The IWG emerged from a 1994 conference, which brought women delegates from 80 countries to Brighton to discuss 'women, sport, and the challenge of change'. After three days of discussion and debate, the delegates unanimously passed a set of global gender equity principles now known as the 'Brighton Declaration'. This document, updated and reaffirmed at world conferences on women in sport in Windhoek, Namibia (1998), Montreal, Canada (2002), and Kumamoto, Japan (2006), continues to be used by people as they pressure governments and sports organizations to create new opportunities for girls and women in sports.

Lobbying efforts by representatives from these and other organizations led to the inclusion of statements related to sports and physical education in the official Platform for Action of the United Nation's Fourth World Conference on Women, held in Beijing, China, in 1996. These statements called for new efforts to provide sport and physical education opportunities to promote the education, health and human rights of girls and women in countries around the world. This has developed into a widely accepted global effort to promote and guarantee sports participation opportunities for girls and women. For example, the IOC 'World Conference on Women and Sport' was held in the Middle East for the first time when Jordan hosted this event in March 2008. However, a fifth World Conference on Women has not yet been scheduled because the goals of the 1996 conference were far from being achieved in 2008.

The health and fitness movement

Since the mid-1970s, research has made people more aware of the health benefits of physical activities (Sabo et al., 2004). This awareness has encouraged women to seek opportunities to exercise and play sports. Although much of the publicity associated with this movement has been influenced by traditional ideas about femininity, and tied to the prevailing feminine ideal of being thin and sexually attractive to men, there also has been an emphasis on the *development of physical strength and competence*. Muscles have become increasingly accepted as desirable attributes for women of all ages. Traditional standards for body image remain, as illustrated by clothing fashions and marketing strategies associated with women's fitness, but many women have moved beyond those standards and focused on physical competence and the good feelings that go with it rather than trying to look like anorexic models in fashion magazines.

Many companies that produce sporting goods and apparel also have recognized that women can be serious athletes. They continue to sell apparel and equipment, but they now focus on function in their designs and marketing approaches. For example, they have produced advertisements that appeal to women who see sports participation and achievements as symbols of independence and power. In the process, they have encouraged and supported sports participation among girls and women at the same time that they do the opposite in other advertisements (Wearden and Creedon, 2002).

Increased media coverage of women in sports

Even though women's sports are not covered as often or in the same detail as men's sports, girls and women now can see and read about the achievements of female athletes in a wider range of sports than ever before (also see Chapter 12). This encourages girls and women by publicly legitimizing their participation (Heywood and Dworkin, 2003). For example, while research indicates that only approximately 5 per cent of newspaper articles are devoted to female sports, television coverage is improving, even if this is predominantly on cable and satellite channels. For example, in 2006, Sky Sports broadcast the Rugby Women's World Cup and secured a deal with England Netball to show weekly coverage of the Netball Superleague. The qualification of the England women's football team for the 2007 World Cup was also featured on several BBC channels. There are also increasing numbers of female sports reporters on the television, although only approximately 10 per cent of the members of the Sports Journalist Association of Great Britain are women (Women's Sports Foundation, 2007a).

As girls grow up, media images help them envision possibilities for developing athletic skills. This is important because the media present so many other images and messages that emphasize versions of femininity that are inconsistent with playing sports and being identified as a serious athlete. For example, studies of the media coverage of players in the Wimbledon tennis tournament confirm that female players are trivialized as athletes and sexualized to appeal to a predominantly male readership (Harris and Clayton, 2002; Vincent, 2004). Similarly, British Olympic gold medallist heptathlete Denise Lewis appeared on the cover of *Total Sport* magazine, topless apart from body paint of her Olympic kit, which she claimed was the result of pressure from her sponsors. But despite mixed messages, media coverage of everything from women's hockey to synchronized swimming helps girls and young women conclude that sports are human activities, not male-only activities.

Media companies, like their corporate counterparts that sell sporting goods, now realize that women make up half the world's population and therefore half the world's consumers. The American company that televised the 1996 Olympic Games in Atlanta, NBC, experienced high ratings when it targeted women during its 175 hours of coverage. Many men complained about this, but Olympic coverage since 1996 has continued this approach of covering female athletes and acknowledging female viewers.

Women's sports will continue to be covered in the media, and this will influence the images that all of us associate with women's sports and the achievements of female athletes. The most influential coverage occurs when female athletes demonstrate physical skills and present body images and forms of self-presentation that push traditional ideas and beliefs about the characteristics and potential of women on and off the field (Lafferty and McKay, 2004; Thomsen et al., 2004).

> The sponsors design the kit and they want you to look a certain way. It makes you feel awful … Why am I showing off my boobs? … I need a proper sports kit to perform, I have boobs that need support, not tiny thin straps like the anorexic Russian tennis players wear, I can't be holding my boobs every time I take a shot.
>
> *(Gail Emms, British badminton champion, 2006, p. 12)*

Reasons to be cautious when predicting future participation increases

Increases in the sports participation rates of girls and women have not come easily, and they will not be given up without a fight. They are the result of dedicated efforts by many individuals and groups. Progress has been remarkable, but gender equity does not exist yet in many sports programmes in most parts of the world. Furthermore, there are six reasons to be cautious about the pace and extent of future sport participation increases:

1 budget cuts
2 backlash among people who resent changes that threaten dominant gender ideology
3 under-representation of women in decision-making positions in sports
4 continued emphasis on 'cosmetic fitness'
5 trivialization of women's sports
6 homophobia and the threat of being labelled 'lesbian'.

Budget cuts

Gender equity is often subverted by budget cuts. Compared with sports for boys and men, schemes for girls and women often are vulnerable to cuts because they are less well established, they have less administrative support, a smaller fan base and they have less revenue-generating potential. Overall, they often are seen as less important by many sponsoring organizations. As one woman observed, 'It seems like the only time women's programmes are treated equally is when cuts must be made.'

Because sports schemes for girls and women often are relatively new, they have start-up costs that long-standing and well-established programmes for boys and men do not have. Therefore, 'equal' budget cuts cause women's sports to fail at a faster pace than men's because they have not developed institutional support or market presence. Many programmes for boys and men are less vulnerable because they have had more than 100 years to develop legitimacy, value, support and an audience. Today, many of them can raise funds to sustain themselves, whereas many girls' and women's sports cannot.

Setbacks have already occurred in women's football, even though this is the fastest-growing sport for females in the UK. When men's teams are relegated and the club has to make financial cuts, it is often the women's team that suffers. For example, in 2007 Charlton Athletic men's team was relegated from the Premier League, while its women's team had placed third in their Premier League and reached their FA Cup final. Despite the club being awarded several millions pounds in 'parachute' payments and making extra millions through the sale of some male players, the club withdrew its funding of the women's squad. This meant that in the 2007–08 season, the more successful women's team had to agree a special dispensation to make a late start to the season while it found a private sponsor, and now shares administrative resources with a variety of schemes as part of the club's 'community' initiative. In contrast, the less successful men's team did not experience any similar inconvenience or threat to its status. Other women's teams have had similar experiences, at Birmingham, Bristol City and Fulham.

Backlash among people who resent changes that threaten dominant gender ideology

When women play certain sports, they become strong. Strong women challenge the prevailing gender ideology that underlies the norms, legal definitions and opportunity structures that frame the conditions under which men and women form identities, live their lives and relate to each other. Those who are privileged by the prevailing gender ideology in society see strong women as a threat. They seek to discredit most women's sports and strong female athletes, and they call for a return to the 'good old days', when men played sports and women watched and cheered. Private sports clubs have the right to maintain policies of gender (or racial) exclusion, and many golf clubs exclude women from taking out membership, gaining access to some social areas or playing at peak times.

A variation of backlash occurred in 2006, when Luton Football Club manager, Mike Newell, criticized the presence of a female assistant referee in a professional men's football match. Newell was quoted as saying:

> She should not be here. I know that sounds sexist, but I am sexist, so I am not going to be anything other than that. We have a problem in this country with political

correctness, and bringing women into the game is not the way to improve refereeing and officialdom. It is absolutely beyond belief. When we reach a stage when all officials are women, then we are in trouble. It is bad enough with the incapable referees and linesmen we have, but if you start bringing in women, you have big problems. It is tokenism, for the politically correct idiots.

(Cited in Sharp, 2006, p. 2)

Newell's words demonstrated that he strongly objected to any changes threatening a dominant gender ideology that supports the power and privilege of men. The presence of a female referee was ideologically intolerable for him and his response was indicative of backlash by a powerful man against equity claims that challenged the male-dominated status quo (Nylund, 2003; Roberts, S., 2004). To the extent that other men in positions of power in sports organizations think this way, progress towards gender equity will be slowed.

Under-representation of women in decision-making positions in sports

Despite increased sports participation among girls and women, women are not achieving equity in leadership and coaching of sports programmes. For example, only approximately one-third of the board members of the UK Sports Councils are female, and some national governing bodies (such as British Cycling, and the England and Wales Cricket Board) have no women on their boards. Similarly, the numbers of elite female coaches are disproportionately low compared with the attendance of female athletes at international events. In Ireland, the affiliation of women's sports organizations, such as the Irish Women's Rugby Football Union and the Women's Football Association of Ireland, to the traditional male-governed organizations had the unintentional consequence of allowing more men to control women's sports as administrators and coaches (see Liston, 2006a). Women who are successful still often have lower status, power and salaries than their male counterparts (Women's Sport Foundation, 2007b, 2007c).

Many men do a good job of coaching and administering women's sports, but unless girls and young women see women in decision-making positions in their sports, they will be reluctant to define sports and sports participation as important in their futures. If women are not visible leaders in sports, some people conclude that women's abilities and contributions in sports are less valued than men's. This conclusion certainly limits progress towards gender equity (Ligutom-Kimura, 1995).

Continued emphasis on 'cosmetic fitness'

There are competing images of female bodies in many cultures today. Girls and women receive confusing cultural messages that they should be 'firm but shapely, fit but sexy, strong but thin' (Markula, 1995, p. 424). Although they see images of powerful female athletes, they cannot escape the images of fashion models whose bodies are shaped by food deprivation and multiple cosmetic surgeries. Girls and women also hear that physical power and competence are important, but they see disproportionate rewards going to women who look young, vulnerable and non-athletic. They are advised to 'get strong but lose weight'. They learn that muscles are good but too many muscles are unfeminine. They are told that athletic women are attractive, but they see men attracted to pop singers and celebrity models with breast implants and airbrushed publicity photos. They also see attractive athletes, such as Russian tennis player Maria Sharapova, 'packaged and sold as the … giggly gal who just wants to have fun: Hillary

Duff with a forehand' (Glock, 2005, p. 66). They might know that Sharapova earned more than US$20 million in endorsements in 2006, more than other players who had greater success in tennis. Therefore, they may conclude that even if you are a good athlete, it is hot looks that bring fame. And they know that Anna Kornikova turned her looks, not her success in tennis, into fame, and they see that her fame has lasted far longer than her tennis skills would have lasted.

Despite cultural messages that promote athletic performance, they are outnumbered and out-hyped by cultural messages promoting appearance and beauty (Hargreaves, 1994; Heywood and Dworkin, 2003). Effective commercial messages for everything from make-up to clothing are based on the well-established marketing assumption that insecurities about appearance promote consumption, whereas positive body image does not. Therefore, even many advertisements that show women doing sports are carefully staged to make women feel insecure rather than confident about their bodies.

A related cultural message is that having muscle tone is acceptable but only when it attracts men. For example, when the US women's football team was described as 'Babe City' by a popular US television talk-show host, it was clear that, underlying all the adulation of strong, physically competent women, there was the inference that men still retain the prerogative to judge women by their appearance and assess women's bodies as objects of men's pleasure (Solomon, 2000). Even when American player, Brandi Chastain, pulled off her football shirt in spontaneous jubilation after scoring a shootout goal to win the 1999 World Cup and revealed a sports bra, people sexualized Chastain and her action – even though women have worn such bras for years as they have worked out, and male football players for decades have pulled off their shirts when celebrating goals. It was as if many people in 1999 did not have a frame of reference to see Chastain's gesture as a joyous celebration of achievement rather than a titillating striptease to please or shock everyone (Caudwell, 2003; Chastain, 2004; Schultz, 2004; Solomon, 2000).

Messages about feminine and sexy bodies are so powerful that some women avoid sports until they are thin enough to look 'right' and wear the 'right' clothes; other girls and women combine participation with pathogenic weight-control strategies to become dangerously thin. Research shows that some female athletes use laxatives, diet pills, diuretics, self-induced vomiting, binges and starvation diets in conjunction with their training (Beals, 2000; Hawes, 2001; Johns, 1997; Madison and Ruma, 2003; Wilmore, 1996). This increases the probability of injuries, jeopardizes health and keeps alive the idea that women must conform to media-based beauty standards or be rejected by men and women who use those standards to evaluate females of all ages.

Although most female athletes do not develop eating disorders, they may choose sports and/or monitor their appearance and actions in light of the standards of cosmetic fitness. Participation statistics demonstrate that girls and women choose to participate in non-competitive physical activities rather than sports, as these forms of exercise prioritize appearance and fashion, so enabling the development of sexual attractiveness (Horne, 2006; Jarvie, 2006; Sport England, 2006; sportscotland, 2005). Overall, the tensions between cosmetic fitness and being strong and physically skilled create for many girls and women the challenge of negotiating the meanings they and others give to their bodies (Dworkin, 2001; Garrett, 2004; Heywood and Dworkin, 2003; Shakib, 2003; Wedgewood, 2004; Young, 1998). This challenge is especially daunting for female athletes with disabilities, as explained in 'Breaking barriers'.

When the goal of playing sports is cosmetic fitness, women may define their participation as a means of achieving an unrealistic body image, burning calories so that they can eat without guilt, or punishing themselves when they have eaten too much (Krane et al., 2001). Additionally, young women seeking cosmetic fitness sometimes drop out of sports if they gain weight while they train, and others drop out after they achieve weight-loss goals. Overall, it appears that cultural messages about cosmetic fitness will interfere with future increases in sports participation.

breaking BARRIERS

Narrative barriers: *I was too ashamed of my body*

Anna was born with underdeveloped arms and feet. Despite encouragement and support from a close friend, she resisted going to the gym and becoming involved in sports. She explained her resistance in the following way:

> I really wanted to go – inside, I was dying to be physical, to have a go at 'pumping iron' ... But at the time I just couldn't say yes ... I was too ashamed of my body ... It was the same thing with swimming. I just couldn't bear the thought of people looking at me. I felt *really* vulnerable.
>
> *(In Hargreaves, 2000, p. 187)*

Anna's fear of her body being seen and judged is not unique. Negotiating the meanings that we and others give to our bodies is a complex and challenging process. But in contemporary cultures it is more challenging for women than men and for people with disabilities than their able-bodied peers.

In cultures where femininity is tied to physical attractiveness and sexual desirability, the women who accept dominant gender ideology often make choices that interfere with sports participation. For example, a young woman who has had a leg amputated may choose a prosthesis that is more natural looking, rather than one that is more functional and better suited to sport participation. As one woman explained, 'It's one thing to see a man with a Terminator leg[1] ... It may inspire people to say, "Cool". But body image for women in this country is model thin and long sexy legs' (in Marriott, 2005, p. F1). In agreement, Nick, a 20-year-old American college student who lost his legs after contracting a rare bacterial disease at a summer camp when he was 14, says, 'I love my Terminator legs', and he does not think twice about plugging them in to the nearest electrical outlet when they run short on their charge.

Although Nick loves his 'Terminator legs', negotiating the meaning given to one's body is more challenging for men with disabilities than for most able-bodied men. This is especially true when they accept a gender ideology that ties masculinity to power and the ability to outperform or dominate others. For example, after filling his car with petrol and putting his wheelchair in the back, Mark had trouble starting his car. A man who had just driven up behind him pressed his horn and shouted obscenities. Mark said that before the accident that paralysed his legs 'I would have got out of the car and ... laid him out, but now I'm useless ... This is why I say my manhood has been shattered' (in Sparkes and Smith, 2002, p. 269).

[1] 'Terminator leg' is a term some people use to describe the cyborg-like appearance of high-tech prosthetic legs that have not been disguised to look like flesh and bone, so-called after the cybernetic character in the film of the same name.

Although Mark did not use the same words that Anna used, he also felt vulnerable. When men with disabilities feel vulnerable, some may do what Anna did and avoid sports participation, whereas others may view sports as a site for asserting or reaffirming masculinity.

Sociologists Brett Smith and Andrew Sparkes (2002) point out that people create identities, including feminine and masculine identities, through narratives – that is, the stories that they show and tell others about themselves. Their research indicates that playing power and performance sports is a masculinizing narrative – a story in which manhood is constructed through physical accomplishments and dominance over other men. Such narratives are the foundation of dominant gender ideology.

When alternative or oppositional narratives are not available to women with disabilities, they often avoid sports because sports do not contain femininity narratives. Similarly, some men like Mark may avoid sports for fear that they will not be able to overpower other men. Therefore, males and females with disabilities would benefit if they had access to new, counter-narratives that construct gender in less constraining terms (Thomas, 1999). When there are multiple ways to be a woman or a man, people with visible disabilities have more options for negotiating the meanings that they and others give to their bodies. Maybe this would enable Anna to become more physical and have a go at pumping iron. And maybe it would enable Mark to accept help and still feel like a man.

Trivialization of women's sports

'Okay. Women play sports, but they are not as good as men and people want to see the best.' Statements like this assume that 'real' sports involve 'manly' things, such as intimidation, violence and physical domination over others, and that women's sports are second rate. This orientation is widespread enough that it interferes with achieving gender equity in sports (Laurendeau, 2004; Vincent, 2004). For example, it was only in 2007 that Wimbledon agreed to equal prize money for male and female players. Previously, women earned approximately 15 per cent less than men based on the argument that men play the best of five sets, whereas women play the best of three. But, as Billie Jean King argued, other entertainers do not get paid by the hour: 'If Elton John does a concert, it could last one hour or four hours – it's a done deal' (in Aldred, 2006, p. 25).

Power and performance sports are historically grounded in the values and experiences of men, and they use evaluative standards that disadvantage women. Women play rugby, but they do not hit as hard as men do. They play basketball, but they do not dunk. They do sports, but they do not do them as men do them. Therefore, they do not do them well enough to receive equal support. An extension of this 'logic' was used in 2004 by the president of FIFA (Fédération Internationale de Football Association), the world-governing body for football, when he told international women players that more spectators would watch them if they would wear tighter shorts (Christenson and Kelso, 2004). He assumed that the women's game was trivial, compared with the men's game, and using sex appeal would make it more fan friendly.

When enough people trivialize women's sports by dismissing competent female athletes or defining them primarily as sex objects, it is difficult to generate gate receipts and commercial sponsorships to sustain elite and professional sports. This is why women's Premier League football and other professional women's sports have not been successful. Even though most people know they should not say that a person 'throws like a girl' when he or she does not throw well, many people continue to think that playing like women is by definition second rate. This form of trivializing women's sports and female athletes continues to interfere with achieving gender equity at all levels of sport.

> If I wanted to wear a bikini I would have chosen to play beach volleyball.

(Solveig Gulbrandsen, professional football player, Norway, in Christenson and Kelso, 2004)

Homophobia and the threat of being labelled 'lesbian'

Homophobia is *a generalized fear or intolerance of lesbians, gay men and bisexual people* (Griffin, 1998). It is based on the notion that homosexuality is deviant or immoral, and it supports prejudice, discrimination, harassment and violence directed towards those identified or believed to be homosexual or bisexual. Homophobia is a powerful cultural factor that has discouraged many girls and women from playing certain sports or making sports an important part of their lives.

Homophobia causes some parents to steer their daughters away from sports that they believe attract lesbians and away from teams or schemes in which lesbians are believed to play or coach. Homophobia and public expressions of homophobic discourse influence and often limit the sports participation choices available to women (Dworkin, 2003; Howe, 2003; Veri, 1999). When women fear the label of *lesbian* or fear being associated with lesbians, they sometimes avoid certain sports, limit their commitment to sports, de-emphasize their athletic identities or emphasize their heterosexuality. Closeted lesbians may fear the loss of secrecy so much that they limit their relationships with others and become lonely and isolated in the process (Bredemeier et al., 1999; Clarke, 2004; Griffin, 1998; Lenskyj, 2003; Swoopes, 2005).

Heterosexual men may use homophobic discourse to tease female athletes and control all women who are intimidated by it. This occurs in some schools and colleges, and it can cause women to become defensive and give sports participation a lower profile in their lives. Effectively challenging homophobic discourse and forcing others to confront their homophobia is a daunting task. Some people, gay and straight, are good at this, but most people lack the experience to do it effectively.

In the meantime, many female athletes go out of their way to emphasize traditional feminine attributes and even say in interviews that being an athlete is not nearly as important as eventually getting married, settling down, having children and becoming a nurturing homemaker. Like athletes, people who market women's sports often avoid acknowledging lesbians for fear that it will decrease attendance among potential spectators who are homophobic. Players know this and often say that if a woman wants to make a team, she had better grow her hair long and talk about wanting to be married and have children. As one international player said, it is well known that team officials 'don't want a bunch of dykes representing our country' (Hall, 2002, p. 200).

Homophobia affects all women, lesbian and straight alike; it creates fears, it pressures women to conform to traditional gender roles, and it silences and makes invisible the lesbians who manage, coach and play sports (Clarke, 2002; Griffin, 1998; Hall, 2002; Lenskyj, 1999; Nelson, 1998).

These Barbie dolls are a classic example of sport images mixed with the notion of cosmetic fitness. The beauty myth remains strong in popular ideas about femininity. Does Barbie reproduce those myths? (*Source*: Jay Coakley)

Gender and fairness issues in sports

Sports participation among girls and women will not continue to increase automatically. Without continued efforts to achieve gender equity, there is a tendency in most cultures to give priority to men's sports and male athletes. This is because sports worlds are usually organized to be:

- *male dominated* so that the characteristics of men are used as standards for judging qualifications
- *male identified* so that the orientations and actions of men are used as standards for defining what is right and normal
- *male centred* so that men and men's lives are the expected focus of attention in sports programmes, stories, legends and media coverage.

Therefore, female athletes, coaches, officials and administrators are considered qualified if they play or do their jobs 'like a man'. If a woman in sports does not think and act like a man, she is not likely to be defined as right or normal. And when people talk about athletes and sports in such a social world, it is assumed that they are talking about men and men's sports unless they specify otherwise – such as saying that they are talking about women's teams, women's records, the best female athletes, the Women's World Cup and so on.

The impact of social organization that is male dominated, male identified and male centred is illustrated through a review of information on sports participation, support for athletes and jobs for women in sports.

 It's unfortunate that [some golf clubs have policies that exclude women and minorities], but it's just the way it is.

(Tiger Woods, professional golfer, in Dodd, 2002, p. 1C)

Participation opportunities: organized and mainstream sports

It was not until the second half of the twentieth century that significant numbers of people began to question the male-dominated/identified/centred organization of sports. Many people believed that females were naturally frail and unsuited for most sports participation. When girls and women were encouraged to be physically active, they were steered into figure skating, gymnastics, swimming, tennis, netball and other sports that were assumed to not require strength, power and speed – the traits associated with masculinity. Some girls and women ignored these assumptions and played sports involving strength, power and speed – and they lived with the consequences, which often involved some form of social rejection. But overall, there were limited opportunities for girls and women to play sports.

Over the past 50 years, female athletes demonstrated clearly that notions of female frailty were grounded in ideology rather than nature. They expanded ideas about what girls and women could and should be encouraged to do in sports. Today, most people in the UK and many nations agree that women should have opportunities to play sports. But there continue to be disagreements about girls and women playing certain contact sports, playing certain sports with men and having access to the same resources that men have.

These disagreements have perpetuated inequities in participation opportunities in many international sports. For example, there are still fewer sports for women than for men in the Olympics and other international events. The only completely successfully integrated sport, where men and women compete together and on the same terms at all levels, is equestrianism.

Although important changes have occurred since the early 1980s, female athletes remain under-represented in international competitions. The data in Table 8.1 (p. 280) illustrate that women in the modern Summer Olympic Games have always had fewer events than men have had, and there have always been fewer women participants than men. The International Olympic Committee, which from 1894 to 1981 had no women members, did not approve a women's 1500-metre event until the 1972 Games in Munich. It was not until the 1984 Games in Los Angeles that women were allowed to run the marathon. Women waited until 1988 to run the Olympic 10 000-metre race and 1996 to run the 5000-metre race. But despite these changes, the French Minister of Sports observed at the start of this century that 'women's involvement in sports [around the world] is characterized by deep inequalities'. The Paralympic Games also have fewer events open to women than men, and in Athens 2004 only 31 per cent of the total number of competitors were women.

Equity sometimes is difficult to achieve because of fundamentalist religious beliefs in certain cultures. For example, strict Islamic beliefs in certain nations forbid women from publicly exposing any surface of their bodies to the sight of men (see Chapter 9). Women in traditionally Catholic nations have not faced moral restrictions, but they have often lacked the power and resources to play sports traditionally played only by men. Women in traditional and poor societies often face barriers that preclude or discourage sports participation as well as limit the extent to which any woman could take sports seriously enough to train at an elite level. These barriers are both ideological and structural. In other words, they are related to (1) *webs of ideas and beliefs* about what is and is not appropriate for girls and women to do (*gender ideology*), and (2) the organization of *opportunities* and the distribution of *resources* to take advantage of opportunities (*social structure*).

Opportunities to play professional sports always have been scarce for women. Until recently, many people did not believe that spectators would pay to watch women play anything but 'ladylike' sports in which they competed alone (figure skating, golf) or with nets separating the opponents and preventing physical contact (tennis, volleyball). Norms in some countries began to change in the 1980s, but many people still doubted that spectators would pay to watch women play sports that went beyond the limits of dominant definitions of *femininity*. Although these limits have been pushed and broken, there remains 'cultural encouragement' to highlight traditional notions of femininity. Therefore, many female athletes are still referred to as 'ladies', and any recognition of the participation of lesbians is carefully erased in the media profiles of teams and leagues. The media emphasis is on heterosexual habits, lifestyles and 'looks'; children and husbands are made visible and discussed often. Homophobia continues to shape the public image of women's sports, and lesbians have been made invisible despite their strong presence in many sports. Opportunities for women at the professional level will continue to be limited until ideas and beliefs about femininity expand to embrace multiple notions of womanhood.

Table 8.1 **Male and female athletes in the modern Summer Olympic Games, 1896–2008**

Year	Place	Countries represented	Male athletes	Female athletes	Percentage female
1896	Athens	14	241	0	0.0
1900	Paris	24	975	22	2.2
1904	St Louis	12	645	6	0.9
1908	London	22	1971	7	1.8
1912	Stockholm	28	2359	48	2.0
1916	Olympics scheduled for Berlin cancelled (First World War)				
1920	Antwerp	29	2561	65	2.5
1924	Paris	44	2954	135	4.4
1928	Amsterdam	46	2606	277	9.6

1932	Los Angeles	37	1206	126	9.5
1936	Berlin	49	3632	331	8.4
1940	Olympics scheduled for Tokyo cancelled (Second World War)				
1944	Olympics cancelled (Second World War)				
1948	London	59	3714	90	9.5
1952	Helsinki	69	4436	519	10.5
1956	Melbourne	72	2938	376	11.3
1960	Rome	83	4727	611	11.4
1964	Tokyo	93	4473	678	13.2
1968	Mexico City	112	4735	781	14.2
1972	Munich	122	6075	1059	14.8
1976	Montreal	92	4824	1260	20.7
1980	Moscow	81	4064	1115	21.5
1984	Los Angeles	140	5263	1566	22.9
1988	Seoul	159	6197	2194	26.1
1992	Barcelona	169	6652	2704	28.9
1996	Atlanta	197	6806	6806	34.0*
2000	Sydney	199	6582	4069	38.2
2004	Athens	201	6452	4412	40.6
2008	Beijing	204	6450	4746	42.3

Notes:

*26 countries sent only male athletes to the 1996 Summer Games.

These data show 108 years of gradual progress towards gender equity. At this rate, the 2016 or 2020 Summer Games may have equal numbers of men and women. The number of athletes participating in 1976, 1980 and 1984 was lower than expected, due to boycotts.

Source: www.olympic.org/uk/games/index_uk.asp

Participation opportunities: informal and alternative sports

Gender and fairness issues are not limited to formally organized, mainstream sports. Informal games often have gender dynamics that present girls and women with special challenges for gaining access to participation and claiming identities as athletes. Similar challenges exist in alternative sports, both informal and formal. This is because boys and men generally control who plays and who is defined as a 'fellow' athlete.

Regardless of where informal sports participation occurs – back gardens, driveways, local parks, school playgrounds, gyms and playing fields at schools and universities, or on the streets – the contexts are male dominated/identified/centred. This often discourages the participation of girls and women, and it creates a situation in which they must be exceptionally good athletes and have clever inclusion strategies to be given the chance to play and be accepted as an athlete by male peers. In many cases, the best inclusion strategy is to be 'sponsored' by an influential boy or man who vouches for a girl's or a woman's 'right' to demonstrate what she can do as an athlete. Gender equity laws do not apply to these settings. Therefore, changes come more slowly than they do in formal sport settings.

Forms of excluding or restricting the participation of girls and women in informal sports have received little attention in the sociology of sport. However, we do know that girls and women face unique participation and identity challenges in both informal and alternative sports, and that there are equity and fairness issues related to who plays under what conditions (Wheaton and Beal, 2003). The most important consequence of these issues is that many girls and women feel that they are not welcome to develop and display their skills. This leads many boys and men to say that they should receive priority when using sports facilities or resources because girls and women are not interested in sports. It's a 'Catch-22' situation for girls and women: they have fewer opportunities than men to develop interests and skills, and then they are denied opportunities to play because they have fewer interests and skills!

Research on alternative sports shows that they are clearly organized around the values and experiences of boys and young men (Anderson, 1999; Honea, 2007; Rinehart and Syndor, 2003). Observations at nearly any open, non-commercial skateboard park will reaffirm this point. Girls and young women are usually spectators, or 'skate groupies', or they are cautious participants earning the right to be taken seriously (Beal and Weidman, 2003) – and a disproportionate number of girls are in-line skaters, which puts them lower in the skateboard park status hierarchy. The few girls who do claim space for themselves in bowls or ramp areas have earned the 'right' to participate, but they have done so on terms set by the boys. As one hard-core mountain biker noted as he described expert women riders: 'Testosterone is contagious' (in Bridges, 2003, p. 181). In sociological terms, this means that to be accepted as an authentic athlete in alternative sports, a female must perform 'like a guy'.

Alternative sports have emerged in connection with the lifestyles of boys and young men who value, among other things, facing one's fears, taking risks and pushing normative limits. The boys and young men in these sports say that inclusion is based on skill, guts and aggressiveness, not gender (see, for example, Wheaton's 2004b study of English windsurfers). But when pressed on this point, one skater said with a swagger, 'It takes too much coordination for a girl, and it's too aggressive' (in Beal and Weidman, 2003, p. 345). Therefore, the girls who are identified as athletes in the 'extreme' versions of alternative sports are those who demonstrate 'Kodak Courage' – that is, enough skill and guts to attempt and occasionally accomplish creative and dangerous unique tricks that others want to see in person or on film (Kay and Laberge, 2003; Wheaton, 2004b).

The consequences of the male-dominated/identified/centred culture and organization of alternative sports are seen in media-created, corporate-sponsored versions such as the X Games

(Kilvert, 2002). For example, there were 56 female athletes in the 1995 X Games but only 26 in 2003; in 2005 only four of the 54 *invited* participants were females. Patterns vary from one alternative sport to another, but gender inclusion is relatively rare in the case of participation opportunities.

Support for athletes

Female athletes in most British sports seldom receive the same support enjoyed by the boys and men. This is also the case in sports-sponsoring organizations around the world. Historically, serious inequities have been in the following areas:

- access to facilities
- quality of facilities (playing surfaces, changing rooms, showers and so on)
- funding to operate schemes
- provision and maintenance of equipment and supplies

Girls and women are eager participants in alternative sports such as climbing. However, in many 'action sports', boys and men control who plays and who is defined as an athlete, and girls and women are seldom treated seriously in those sports unless they do things like the boys and men do them (*Source*: Jay Coakley)

- scheduling of events and training times
- travel, board and food expenses
- numbers of coaches assigned to teams
- salaries for administrators, coaches and other staff
- provision of medical and training services and facilities
- publicity for individuals, teams and events.

Inequities in some of these areas remain a problem in sports at all levels, and yet they often go undetected unless someone digs through data from a range of events. Access to facilities, the number of teams and events available, and the staff assigned to girls' and women's sports, are the most likely areas of inequity in sports in the UK and around the world.

Most people today realize that a lack of support for female athletes subverts sports participation among girls and women. For well over a century, men developed their sports, shaped them to fit their interests and values, generated interest in participation, sold them to sponsors and marketed them to potential spectators. Girls and women want only the same treatment. As American sociologist, Mary Jo Kane, says, 'Women are not asking for a handout, we're just asking for an investment. Just put the same investment in us that you put into men. Then we'll see what happens' (in Lamb, 2000, p. 57). For those who believe in fairness, it is difficult to argue with this point.

Jobs for women in coaching and administration

Most sport are controlled by men. Although women's sports have increased in number and importance around the globe, women often have lost power over them. For example, while the overall membership and staffing numbers in many key sports organizations suggest reasonable equity, this is largely because women appear in relatively large numbers in lower-level administrative and secretarial roles (see White and Kay, 2006). However, women do not appear to have equal opportunities when it comes to more senior jobs in coaching or administration, and women remain under-represented at the highest levels of power in sports. Surveys by the Women's Sports Foundation (2007b, 2007c) documented gender trends for UK sports coaching and administration between 2005 and 2007 as follows.

- In 2006, women accounted for 37 per cent of all qualified sports coaches.
- However, the higher the performance level of the athlete, the more likely they are to have a male coach (see also Fasting and Pfister, 2000). For example, at the 2004 Olympics, even though women constituted 30 per cent of the British athletes, only 10 per cent of the British coaches were female.
- The proportion of female coaches at the Commonwealth Games declined between 2002 and 2006.
- 35 per cent of board members of the UK Sports Councils between 2005 and 2007 were women.
- Of the national governing bodies of sport, 22 per cent of board members were women. Within this figure there is great variation, from the Welsh Hockey Union, which had a 60 per cent representation of women on its board, to tennis with only 7 per cent, and British

Cycling and the England and Wales Cricket Board, both of which had no female members on their boards.

- The boards of selected sports organizations, such as the Youth Sport Trust, the British Paralympic Association and Sportscoach UK had, on average, 27 per cent of key decision makers who were female.

While there have been improvements since the seminal study of White and Brackenridge in 1985 which concluded that British sport was 'firmly in the hands of men' (p. 105), these figures indicate that parity is still a long way off. It is also interesting to consider what men would say if three-quarters of the administrators and almost all the top-level coaches *in men's sports* were women. They would be outraged! They would claim a breach of the Gender Equality Duty and demand affirmative action to achieve fairness – and they would be justified in doing so.

The coaching and administration situation is much the same in other nations and on a global level. Systematic data on coaches are not easy to collect from nation to nation, but over 80 per cent of all national team coaches are men. In 2007, only a quarter of the members of the European and International Federations of Sport were female. The IOC, the most powerful administrative body in global sports, had had *no* women members from 1896 until 1981. In response to widespread charges of sexism, the IOC in 1997 announced that its goal was to have 10 per cent of all decision-making positions in the IOC, all national Olympic committees (NOCs) and all international federations (IFs) of sports held by women by the end of 2000; by 2005 women would hold 20 per cent of those positions. However, in 2006 the IOC membership was composed of 99 men and 14 women, and its executive committee had 14 men and one woman. Therefore, as of 2006 it had not reached its goal for 2000. The NOCs and IFs have worse records than the IOC, especially in their most powerful positions (White and Henry, 2004). The goal of having women in 20 per cent of the decision-making positions in sports organizations around the world by 2005 was not reached, and at the current rate of change it will not be reached for many years in many nations and many sports.

The reasons for the under-representation of women in coaching and administrative positions in women's sports have been widely debated and studied (Shaw, 2007; White, 2003; White and Brackenridge, 1985; White and Kay, 2006; Women's Sports Foundation, 2007b). The major reasons appear to include the following.

- Men use well-established connections with other men in sports organizations to help them during the job recruitment process.
- Compared with men, most female applicants for coaching and administrative jobs do not have the strategic professional connections and networks to compete with male candidates.
- Job search committees often use ideologically based evaluative criteria, making it likely that female applicants for coaching and administrative jobs will be seen as less qualified than men.
- Support systems and professional development opportunities are scarce for women who want to be coaches or administrators, and for women already in coaching and administrative jobs.

- Many women know that it is difficult to work in sports that have corporate cultures organized around the values and experiences of men (see Cartoon 8.1).
- Sports organizations are seldom organized in family-friendly ways.
- Sexual harassment is more often experienced by women than by men, and female coaches and administrators often feel that they are judged by more demanding standards than are men.

These factors affect aspirations and opportunities. They influence who applies for jobs, how applicants fare during the recruitment process, how coaches and administrators are evaluated, who enjoys their job, and who is promoted into higher-paying jobs with more responsibility and power.

People on job search committees seek, interview, evaluate and hire candidates who they think will be successful in sports programmes that are male dominated/identified/centred. After looking at objective qualifications, such as years of experience and win–loss records, search committee members subjectively assess such things as a candidate's abilities to recruit and motivate players, raise money, command respect in the community (among fans and sport reporters), build toughness and character among players, maintain team discipline and 'fit' in the athletic department or sport organization.

None of these assessments occurs in a vacuum, and some are influenced by gender ideology in addition to the facts. Although people on search committees do not agree on all things, many think in terms that favour men over women (Hovden, 2000). This is because coaching and other forms of leadership in sports often are seen to be consistent with traditional ideas about masculinity: if you 'coach like a girl', you are doing it wrong; if you 'coach like a man', you are doing it right. In a male-dominated and identified organizational culture, this is taken for granted.

Under these conditions, women are hired only when they present compelling evidence that they can do things as men have done them in the past. In sports organizations where men have routinely been hired and women have been ignored, there may be pressure to recruit and hire women so that charges of discrimination can be deflected. When a woman is hired in such circumstances, it is often said that, 'We had to hire a woman.' But the more accurate statement is this: 'We have favoured men for so long that people were going to rightfully accuse us of gender discrimination if we did not hire a woman or two.'

When women are hired, they are less likely than men to feel welcome and fully included in sports organizations. Therefore, they often have lower levels of job satisfaction and higher rates of job turnover (Pastore et al., 1996). When turnover occurs, some people accuse women of being secretive and defensive and not having what it takes to survive in the 'real' world of sports. But this ignores that expectations for coaches and administrators have been developed over the years by men who often had wives who raised their children, provided them and their teams with emotional support, hosted social events for teams, co-ordinated their social schedules, handled household finances and maintenance, made sure they were not distracted by family and household issues, and faithfully attended games season after season. If female coaches and administrators had the opportunity to develop schemes and coach teams under similar circumstances, job satisfaction would be high and turnover would be low, and there would certainly be childcare provided for the children of coaches and administrators (McKay, 1999).

Finally, some sports organizations have records of being negligent in controlling sexual harassment and responding to complaints from women who wish to be taken seriously in the structure and culture of sports organizations. This means that people working in sports must critically assess the impact of male-dominated/centred/identified forms of social organization on both males and females. Unless this is done and changes are made, gender equity will never exist in the ranks of coaching and administration.

Strategies to achieve equity

Most men support the idea of gender equity, but few of them are willing to give up anything to achieve it. This resistance has forced proponents of gender equity to ask governments for assistance. Governments have been helpful, but they often are slow to respond, and if legal action is required this involves costs and long-term commitments. Therefore, Donna Lopiano, former executive director of the US Women's Sport Foundation (WSF), has identified strategic political organization and pressure as the key for achieving gender equity. This involves the development of grass-roots organizations to systematically support and publicize sporting opportunities for girls and women. As these organizations publicly recognize the achievements of female athletes and their sponsors, more people will see the value of women's sports and join their efforts to achieve equity. The WSF and other organizations in the UK and elsewhere have

'Yes, I'll make your tea straight away, sir.'

Cartoon 8.1 **Women traditionally have been expected to play support roles for men in sports as well as in society at large. This is changing but these roles are still present in the gendered social structures of many societies**

facilitated this process with their resources, and they have been effective in fostering progressive changes.

Lopiano (1991) has urged people in sports organizations, including those in the UK, to use the following strategies to promote gender equity.

- Confront discriminatory practices in your organization and become an advocate for female athletes, coaches and administrators.
- Insist on fair and open employment practices in your organization.
- Keep track of equity data and have an independent group issue a public 'gender equity report card' every three to four years for your organization.
- Learn and educate others about the history of discrimination in sports and how to recognize the subtle forms of discrimination that operate in sport worlds that are male dominated, male identified and male centred.
- Object to practices and policies that decrease opportunities for women in sports and inform the media of them.
- When possible, package and promote women's sports as revenue producers, so there will be financial incentives to increase participation opportunities for women.
- Recruit female athletes into coaching by establishing internships and training programmes.
- Use women's networks when seeking coaches and sports administrators.
- Create a supportive work climate for women in your organization and establish policies to eliminate sexual harassment.

These are useful suggestions. They emphasize a combination of public relations, political lobbying, pressure, education and advocacy. They are based on the assumption that increased participation and opportunities for women will not come without struggle and that favourable outcomes depend on organization and persistence. More important, they have already produced varying degrees of change in many organizations.

Those who use critical and critical feminist theories to study sports in society have argued that gender equity cannot be achieved in contexts that are organized by men who are unwilling to critically assess dominant gender ideology. Therefore, real equity requires cultural and structural changes in existing sports combined with the development of new models of sport participation and sports organizations that acknowledge the values and experiences of women (Birrell, 2000; Nelson, 1998; Theberge, 2000). This is discussed below in the section 'Ideology and power issues' (pp. 291–308).

Girls and women as agents of change

Some people assume that women are empowered when they play sports and that empowered women become effective agents of gender equity in sports and in society as a whole. Research supports this claim, but only to a point (Eitle and Eitle, 2002; Stoelting, 2004).

Sports participation provides girls and women with opportunities to connect with the power of their bodies. This is important because social life sometimes is organized to encourage girls and women to see themselves as weak, dependent and powerless. Additionally, many images of women in society present the female body as an object to be viewed, evaluated and consumed, and girls and women learn to objectify their bodies as they view and assess themselves through the eyes of others (Fredrickson and Harrison, 2005; Young, 1990). Because identity and a personal sense of power are partly grounded in one's body and body image, sports participation can help women overcome the feeling that their bodies are objects. Furthermore, the physical skills and strength often gained through sports participation go beyond simply helping a woman feel fit. They also can make her feel less vulnerable, more competent and independent, and more in control of her physical safety and psychological well-being (see Chastain, 2004; Ference and Muth, 2004; Frederickson and Harrison, 2005; Pelak, 2002, 2005; Roth and Basow, 2004; Theberge, 2000; Wedgewood, 2004).

Empowerment does not occur automatically when a girl or woman plays sports, nor is a sense of empowerment always associated with a desire or an ability to actively promote fairness and equity issues in sports or other spheres of life. Feeling competence as an athlete does not guarantee that women will critically assess gender ideology and gender relations or work for fairness and equity in sports or society at large. For example, some female athletes express negative attitudes towards feminism and distance themselves from social activism related to women's issues. In other words, those who play elite-level sports are not likely to be 'boat rockers' critical of the gender order (McClung and Blinde, 1998; Young and White, 1995). There are four possible reasons for this.

1 Female athletes may feel that they have much to lose if they are associated with civil and human rights issues for women because others might identify them as ungrateful, or marginalize them by tagging them with labels such as *radical, feminist* or *lesbian*.

2 The corporation-driven 'celebrity feminism' promoted through media sports today focuses on individualism and consumption rather than everyday struggles faced by ordinary girls and women who want to play sports but also are concerned with obtaining childcare, healthcare and a decent job (Cole, 2000b).

3 The 'empowerment discourses' associated with fitness and sports often emphasize individual self-empowerment through physical changes that enhance feminine beauty (Eskes et al., 1998; MacNeill, 1999); they do not emphasize social or cultural changes.

4 Female athletes, even those with high media profiles and powerful bodies, have little control over their own sports participation and little political voice in sports or society as a whole (Lowe, 1998).

Similarly, women hired and promoted into leadership positions in major sports organizations are expected to promote power and performance sports in society. The men who control many sports organizations are not usually eager to hire women who put *women's issues* on the same level as *sports issues*. Of course, not all female leaders become uncritical cheerleaders for power and performance orientations in sports and society. However, it takes effort and courage to critically analyse sports and use one's power to change the culture and structure of sports. But without this effort and courage, gender inequities tend to persist.

Boys and men as agents of change

Gender equity is not just a woman's issue. Equity also involves creating options for boys and men to play sports that are not based exclusively on a power and performance model. Sports

Developing physical skills often improves health and provides girls and women with a sense of empowerment. This is true for Reshma, a 7-year-old in Dhaka, Bangladesh. But if the culture and social structure in Bangladesh do not provide Reshma with opportunities to express her sense of empowerment as a woman, beating all the boys in this race will not enable her to participate in society as they will when they become adults (Source: photograph courtesy of The Hunger Project, www.thp.org/)

that emphasize aggression and domination often encourage orientations and actions that lead to chronic injuries, an inability to relate to women, fears of intimacy with other men, homophobia and a compulsive concern with comparing oneself with other men in terms of what might be called 'life success scores' (Burstyn, 1999; White and Young, 1997).

Sports privilege men over women, but they also privilege some men over others. When men realize that some sports constitute cultural contexts that constrain and distort their relationships with one another and with women, they are more inclined to view sports critically. Bruce Kidd, a former Olympic runner and now a physical educator and social scientist, used his experiences to suggest the following:

> Through sports, men learn to cooperate with, care for, and love other men, in [many] ways, but they rarely learn to be intimate with each other or emotionally

honest. On the contrary, the only way many of us express fondness for other men
is by teasing or mock fighting.

(1987, p. 259)

Men who want to move beyond an expression of fondness based on teasing and mock
fighting have good reason to join with those women concerned with critically assessing
dominant sport forms in their society (Anderson, 2005; Pronger, 1999; Wheaton, 2004b).

Ideology and Power Issues

Ideology often is so deeply rooted in our social worlds that we seldom think about it and almost
never raise questions about it. We take it for granted and use it as a form of 'cultural logic' to
make sense of the world. This is especially the case with gender ideology.

Gender is a central organizing principle of social life, and gender ideology influences how
we think of ourselves and others, how we relate to others and how social life is organized at
all levels, from families to societies. It influences what we wear, how we walk, how we present
ourselves to others and how we think about and plan for our future. Most people take gender
ideology as a 'given' in their lives; they do not question it because it is so deeply rooted in their
psyches and the way they live their lives.

The tendency to ignore ideology is a serious problem when we deal with gender equity in
sports. The achievement of equity requires changes in the gender ideology that has been used to
organize, play and make sense of sports. The following sections critically examine the prevailing
gender ideology in society, its effects on our lives, its connection with sports and some strategies
for changing it as well as how power is distributed in sports.

Gender ideology in society

Gender ideology varies from culture to culture. In most societies in which men have been
privileged in terms of legal status, formal authority, political and economic power and access
to resources, gender ideology is based on a *simple binary classification model*. According to
this model, all people are classified into one of two **sex categories**: *male or female* (see Figure
8.1). These categories are defined in biological terms, and they are conceptualized to highlight
difference and opposition; they are commonly identified as 'opposite sexes'. All people in the
male category are believed to be naturally different from all people in the female category, and
they are held to have different normative expectations when it comes to feelings, thoughts and
actions. These expectations outline the basis for the ways that people define and identify **gender**,
that is, *what is considered masculine and what is considered feminine in a group or society*. This
classification and interpretation model is so central to the way that many people see the world
that they resist thinking about gender in new ways and they often feel uncomfortable when
people do not fit neatly into one sex category or the other.

It takes dedication and hard work to maintain a simple binary classification model because
it is inconsistent with biological evidence showing that anatomy, hormones, chromosomes and
secondary sex characteristics vary in complex ways and cannot be divided neatly into two sex
categories, one male and one female. As biologist Anne Fausto-Sterling explains, 'A body's sex is
simply too complex. There is no either/or. Rather, there are shades of difference' (2000, p. 3). Real

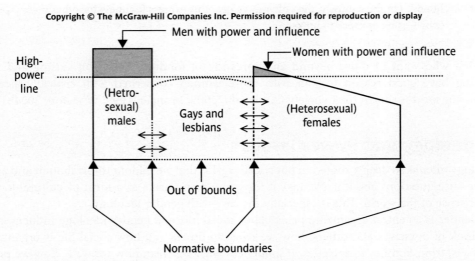

Figure 8.1 **The two-category gender classification model: a representation of gender construction in UK culture.**
Note: Heterosexual masculinity and heterosexual femininity are depicted as separate, non-overlapping categories. Each has clearly marked normative boundaries that limit what is defined as normal. The 'FEMININITY' category is wider than the 'MASCULINITY' category because girls and women have more latitude in what they can do without being out of bounds. Other forms of sexuality are in a grey area that many people define as being outside the normative boundaries of the two gender categories widely perceived as 'natural'. People in this grey area include lesbians, gay men, bisexuals, the intersexed and transsexuals.

The short double arrows indicate two processes: (1) movement into and out of the categories of heterosexual male and female, and (2) efforts to push normative boundaries to make space for different expressions of masculinity and femininity, create new sexual categories or to transcend sexual categories by making them socially irrelevant.

The 'high-power line' indicates that heterosexual men are more likely to occupy high-power and influential positions, such as heads of state, Members of Parliament, CEOs, and top-level leaders and decision makers in religious organizations, education, media and sports. The high-power line can also be viewed as a representation of the 'glass ceiling' for women, although a few women have cracked through it in certain spheres of social life.

bodies have physiological and biological traits, which are distributed along continua related to these dimensions of biochemistry and appearance.

This natural sexual variation does not fit with a binary classification model. Therefore, when people are born with physical traits that do not fit ideology-based definitions of *male* and *female*, genitals and reproductive organs usually are surgically 'fixed' to make them fit (Fausto-Sterling, 2000).

Hormones vary from one person to the next, and both men and women have testosterone and oestrogen in their bodies. However, testosterone is identified as a 'male hormone' and oestrogen as a 'female hormone'. This way of thinking about and referring to hormones is misleading, but it enables people to maintain their two-category gender classification model without asking critical questions about it. Even chromosomal patterns do not always fit neatly into two distinct categories. Nor do secondary sex characteristics, which vary greatly. But we do our best to cover variations with sex-appropriate clothes and forms of body management that highlight characteristics that identify us as male or female. Most people spend considerable time, energy and money to ensure that their physical characteristics and appearance fit general expectations based on the two-category gender classification model. Those who ignore these expectations risk being marginalized or treated as if they are 'out of gender bounds' (Fenstermaker and West, 2002). A woman who does not remove natural hair growth above her upper lip or on other parts of her body risks being ridiculed, and a slender man with 'fine' features who does not avoid wearing clothes defined as effeminate risks serious ridicule in many situations.

Physical variation is real, and to say that all variation can be reduced to two separate and 'opposite' categories forces biology to fit socially constructed definitions of what males and females are 'supposed to be' in physical terms (Butler, 2004; Caudwell, 2003).

Being 'out of bounds': a problem for gays and lesbians

Another problem created by a binary classification model is that the model comes with relatively fixed ideas and expectations about how men and women are supposed to think, feel and act. These ideas and expectations emphasize *difference*, and they are the foundation for gender. A binary gender classification model is based on the assumption that heterosexuality is natural and normal and that those who express feelings, thoughts and actions that do not fit neatly into the two socially constructed categories of masculine and feminine are 'out of bounds' when it comes to gender (review Figure 8.1).

When gender ideology is based on this classification model, many people, including gay men, lesbians, bisexuals and transsexuals do not fit into either of the two categories, so they usually are defined as deviant. A two-category model provides no legitimate social space or recognition for those who are neither heterosexual males nor heterosexual females. This, in turn, serves as a foundation for **homophobia**, *a general fear and/or intolerance felt for those who are 'out of bounds' in the classification model.*

Power in society: gender ideology in action

Another important aspect of a binary classification model is that the two categories are seldom equal. As represented in Figure 8.1, males have access to higher levels of privilege, power and influence than do females, and men occupy the highest levels of power and influence in greater numbers than do women. However, there is a social and personal cost that comes with access to and possession of power.

When a two-category gender classification model exists in cultures that emphasize equal rights and freedom of expression, the accepted range of feelings, thoughts and actions for men often is more restricted than it is for women. This means that the normative boundaries associated with masculinity are more restrictive and more closely regulated than the normative boundaries associated with femininity. Masculine characteristics are believed to be consistent with positions of power and influence; therefore, men have more to lose collectively if they do not conform to gender expectations. This is why men strictly police their gender boundaries and sanction those who push or move outside them. Women, on the other hand, have less to lose and more to gain if they push boundaries, although they must do so carefully.

What this means in everyday life is that men have less social permission to express the feelings, thoughts and actions associated with femininity than woman have to express the feelings, thoughts and actions associated with masculinity. This is why boys are teased for being 'sissies', whereas girls are praised for being 'tomboys'; it's also why male ballet dancers are less likely to be socially accepted in society than female athletes have been (Laberge and Albert, 1999).

To demonstrate this point, ask the women in a gender-mixed group how many of them have bought clothing for themselves in a men's store or the men's section of a department store; most will say they have done so. Then ask the men how many of them have bought clothing for themselves in a women's store or a women's section of a department store and listen to the laughter caused by the tension of thinking about the question. The responses illustrate that men face more restrictive normative boundaries related to gender than women face. However, the pay-off for men is that they have more access to power, although some men have more access than others.

Challenging gender ideology: blurring the old boundaries

A binary classification model has socially constructed normative boundaries. However, not everyone accepts or conforms to them. The double arrows in Figure 8.1 represent efforts by men and women to push, erase, pass through and revise normative boundaries. Of course, women do more pushing and passing through than men, although there are potential costs associated with challenging gender boundaries (that is, 'gender bending'). However, as boundary pushers and crossers raise issues that promote revised definitions of *masculinity* and *femininity*, the normative boundaries for women and men change. Change comes slowly, though, because most people have vested interests in the two-category gender classification model. After all, they have learned to use the model as a guide for perceiving and making sense of themselves, their relationships and the world around them.

For example, when Annika Sorenstam became the first woman to compete on the traditionally male only PGA Tour, a PGA golfer was threatened and declared, 'I'll do what men do, and she should do what women do' (*Newsweek*, 2004, p. 122). After Sorenstam beat him by three strokes, his assumptions about sex differences and male superiority were shown to be wrong but he could use football or rugby to maintain his ideas about gender and male superiority (Caudwell, 2003; Messner, 1992). Similarly, when golfer Michelle Wie played in her first men's tournament in 2005, an analyst for the Golf Channel wondered if her presence would turn the PGA into 'a freak show' (Kensler, 2005).

Gender ideology in sports

Ideas and beliefs about gender are a crucial part of the foundation on which sports are organized, promoted and played. Sports are sites for reaffirming beliefs about male–female *difference* and valorizing masculine characteristics. At the same time, women's sports often are marginalized because they are not seen as 'real' or as good as men's sports, and female athletes sometimes are marginalized or seen as deviant because they violate femininity norms. Sports also are sites for challenging and revising gender ideology, a fact that makes gender interesting to study when trying to understand sports in society.

Traditional gender ideology is reproduced in many men's sports. Some of those sports inspire fantasies and symbols of a heroic manhood in which playing the role of warrior is the substance of being a man. Do these fantasies and symbols influence how these men define *masculinity*? (*Source*: photograph courtesy of Peter Holton)

Celebrating masculinity

Gender is not fixed in nature. Therefore, gender ideology grounded in a binary classification model can be preserved only if people work hard to police gender boundaries and maintain them through myths, rituals and everyday cultural practices. People must 'do' gender to keep the model viable, and the model is most effectively maintained when gender categories become embodied dimensions of people's lives – that is, when they are built into the way people move and experience the world with and through their bodies (Fenstermaker and West, 2002). This is how and why sports become important in connection with gender (Messner, 2002).

Sports have been important sites and activities for preserving gender ideology in most cultures. The meaning of gender and its application in people's lives have been symbolized and powerfully presented in the bodily performances that occur in sports. Men's achievements in power and performance sports have been used as evidence of men's aggressive nature, their superiority over women, and their rights to claim social and physical space as their own. American sociologist Doug Hartmann explains this issue in this way:

> [Sport] makes male advantages and masculine values appear so normal and 'natural' that they can hardly be questioned. Therein may lie the key to the puzzle connecting men and the seemingly innocent world of sports: they fit together so tightly, so seamlessly that they achieve their effects – learning to be a man, male bonding, male authority, and the like – without seeming to be doing anything more than tossing a ball or watching a Sunday afternoon game.
>
> *(2003a, p. 20)*

Hartmann's words help us understand why Bruce Kidd (1987) describes sports stadiums and domed arenas as 'men's cultural centres'. These facilities, often built with public funds, host events that present a manhood based on aggression, physical power and the ability to intimidate and dominate others. In such spaces, sports are able to reproduce a gender ideology that privileges the interests of men and favours a particular form of manhood.

Political scientist Varda Burstyn (1999) explains that the major men's sports in most societies provide people with a vocabulary and a set of stories that erase diverse and contradictory masculinities and present a homogenized manhood in which the heroic warrior is the model of a real man. For example, when television sports announcers give special recognition to a male athlete, they often refer to him as 'a warrior' (see Chapter 6, p. 191). As sociologist Garry Whannel (2007, p. 11) suggests, sports are, therefore, practices which are able to unite men, but also divide men according to dominant and residual masculinities:

> Dominant masculinity is experienced by many men as a strait-jacket; a set of conventions of behaviour, style, ritual and practice … in which the men are competitive and acquisitive, the women are objectified, and the male bodies exploited and abused in the training and medication process.

Girls and women as invaders

When girls and women play certain sports, they are seen to be invaders of male turf. This is why they have been excluded from some sports while at the same time they have been encouraged to play sports that emphasize grace, beauty and co-ordination. Through most of the twentieth century, this exclusion was rationalized by experts and educators, who told women that if they played strenuous sports, they would damage their uteruses and breasts, and experience problems endangering their abilities to give birth and nurture their children (Coakley, 1990). Today's college students laugh at these myths from the past because they have information that refutes them. However, it has taken many years to refute the myths and challenge traditional gender ideology. Unfortunately, myths continue to be widely believed in cultures where literacy rates are low and men control the production and distribution of knowledge.

The legacy of traditional gender ideology has not disappeared, even in post-industrial societies (McGarry, 2005). American journalist Joan Ryan writes about this in the following description of women's gymnastics and figure skating:

> Talent counts, but so do beauty, class, weight, clothes and politics. The anachronistic lack of ambivalence about femininity in both sports is part of their attraction, harkening back to a simpler time when girls were girls, when women were girls for that matter: coquettish, malleable, eager to please. In figure skating especially, we want our athletes thin, graceful, deferential and cover-girl pretty. We want eyeliner, lipstick and hair ribbons.
>
> *(1995, p. 5)*

Women who do sports such as figure skating, gymnastics, tennis and some track and field events, are socially valued because they present athletes in ways that do not force viewers to deal with the ideologically threatening issues of sexuality, power and gender relations. When TAG Heuer campaigned to raise money for the Wheelchair Sports Worldwide Foundation in 2000, five years after Ryan's analysis, it brought together some of the world's most famous sports performers to be photographed in fashion clothing. While male athletes such as Colin Jackson appeared in warrior-like armour, gold shields and chain mail tunics, emphasizing strength and aggression, female athletes such as Marion Jones and Monica Seles were scantily clad and adopted sexually provocative poses which were more about eroticism than athleticism (see Maguire et al., 2002).

In a study of female football players, Caudwell (2003) identifies the challenge that many meet in trying to maintain the physical prowess of being an athlete while still looking feminine. For example, a media feature prior to an international match between England and Ukraine was entitled 'England's Angels' and included three England players in a photo shoot posing as *Charlie's Angels*. One of the players stated:

> It is very nice, I mean for people to see us like a lady as well ... I mean a lot of names are said about women that play football, but it's proven a point really that they can look like ladies and play football.
>
> *(Katie Chapman, cited in Caudwell, 2003, p. 380)*

When female athletes challenge traditional gender ideology, they have pushed gender boundaries to make more cultural space for girls and women in sports. Another player interviewed by Caudwell pushed boundaries when she was told she looked like a tomboy. Her response to this was positive and she said that her tomboyishness 'just encouraged me to do the activities I did, like kick the can and football and make go-carts' (2003, p. 382). This player's statement expands notions of femininity in society. However, some young women still hear messages indicating that being a tomboy violates expectations for heterosexual attractiveness, lifestyles and self-presentation. Playing most sports is widely accepted today, but the cuteness of being a tomboy still begins to fade during adolescence. If young female athletes do not conform to dominant definitions of *femininity*, they may experience certain forms of social rejection or less credit than they deserve.

Forever 'ladies'?

Female athletes deal with the consequences of traditional gender ideology in various ways (Cox and Thompson, 2000; Harris, 2005; Krane et al., 2004). For example, young women who play contact and power sports sometimes discover that, unless they are seen as 'ladylike', the *tomboy* label may change to *lesbian*. Therefore, they sometimes try to be more feminine by wearing hair ribbons, ponytails, makeup, dresses, high heels, or engagement or wedding rings; by saying how they like to party with heterosexuals in heterosexual clubs; and by making statements about boyfriends or husbands and their desire to eventually settle down and have children. In the absence of these heterosexualized 'femininity insignias', some people define women in contact and power sports as threats to their ideas about 'nature' and morality. This illustrates how the two-category gender classification model fuels homophobia in sports and the lives of female athletes (Griffin, 1998; Krane, 1996). The dynamics of this process are discussed in the box 'Female bodybuilders'.

The pressure to be 'forever ladies' was intensified in the mid-1960s through the late 1990s when many international sport events, including the Olympics, demanded that female competitors take 'gender tests' to prove that they were women (see www.pponline.co.uk/encyc/0082.htm). The assumption was that, if they were really good in sports, they might not be real women! At first, the female athletes were required to present themselves, naked, to a panel of doctors. But the all-male IOC decided that for the 1968 Olympics in Mexico City they would use a Barr body test to establish the gender of female athletes. Each competitor had cells scraped from inside her cheek so that a testing laboratory could determine if she had a female, or XX, chromosome profile. But chromosome profiles do not always match the socially constructed two-gender classification model used by IOC officials. For example, some people with only one X chromosome grow up as females, others have two X chromosomes and one Y and grow up as men, and there are 'XX males and XY females whose sex doesn't match their chromosomes' (Lehrman, 1997). This meant that some athletes who had lived their lives as women failed the Barr body test and were disqualified from the Olympics. This surprised the parents and friends of the athletes, who knew that they were women.

Most female athletes continued to object to gender testing, and the tests were eliminated by most international sports organizations in the 1990s. However, all 3500 female athletes at the 1996 Olympic Games in Atlanta were required to take the Barr body test or show their 'fem card' from a previous test certifying that they were 'real' women. The IOC continued testing through 1999 but dropped it before the 2000 Sydney Games in response to protests from female lobby groups and scientific research that challenged the test's validity.

reflect on SPORTS   *Female bodybuilders: expanding definitions of femininity?*

Female bodybuilders have been described as powerful women, unfeminine freaks, the ultimate hard bodies, new women, gender benders, entertainers and sideshows for real sports. Descriptions have varied over time and from one group to another as gender ideology has changed.

Until the late 1970s, there was no such thing as competitive women's bodybuilding. It did not exist because it so totally contradicted dominant definitions of femininity and what people saw as 'natural' muscular development for women. The first bodybuilders challenged those definitions of femininity, pushed boundaries of social acceptance and raised questions about what is natural and normal when it comes to the bodies of women (Lowe, 1998).

Many people continue to see female bodybuilders as rebels, deviants and freaks of nature. According to the gender ideology used by most people, females are the 'weaker sex' when it comes to muscles and strength. Leslie Heywood, a lifelong athlete and currently a professor of English and a bodybuilder, explains that female bodybuilders challenge this ideology and threaten dominant ideas about gender and nature. She describes women's bodybuilding as:

> an in-your-face confrontation with traditional roles, an unavoidable assertion of ... unequivocal self-expression, an indication of women's right to be, for themselves ...

not for anyone else. In a culture that still mostly defines women's purpose as service for others, no wonder female bodybuilding is so controversial.

(1998, p. 171)

Therefore, bodybuilders have been accused of being unfeminine because they are 'too muscular', too like men. Of course, not everyone accepts this gender ideology, and for those seeking new or expanded definitions of femininity, women's bodybuilding provides exciting and provocative new images. These images challenge notions of 'female frailty' and raise questions about the biology of gender difference.

Like others who challenge hegemonic ideologies, female bodybuilders have discovered that careful strategies are required to change widely accepted ideas. The first female bodybuilders were careful to be 'feminine' and not 'too muscular'. They emphasized a toned, symmetrical body displayed through carefully choreographed graceful moves. Their goal was to stay within the boundaries of femininity as determined by contest judges. However, even this approach presented problems because definitions of femininity have never been set permanently. Definitions changed and judges could not provide unchanging guidelines for what type of body symmetry was needed to look 'feminine' and what exactly was 'too muscular'.

Many female bodybuilders have been frustrated as they try to anticipate changing guidelines (Lowe, 1998). For example, one bodybuilder observed that:

When you compete, your muscularity is all, but the judges insist on [us] looking womanly. They try to fudge the issue with garbage about symmetry, proportion and definition. What they really want is tits and ass.

(In Bolin, 2003, p. 115)

Some bodybuilders try to live with the confusion caused by dominant ideas about gender by making clear distinctions between how they present themselves during competitive posing and what they do in their workouts (Bolin, 1998, 2003). In the gym, they focus on bodywork and muscle building. As Heywood notes, 'The gym remains a place where the female body, unlike other places, can, by getting strong, earn a little respect' (1998, p. 187). Serious training overrides concerns about how gender is defined outside the gym. Workouts are not 'gendered', and bodybuilders, both women and men, train in similar ways.

The public arena of competitive posing is different, and the women try to neutralize the socially imposed stigma of having too many muscles. They use 'femininity insignias' to carefully construct a presentation of self that highlights the 'look' of dominant femininity as it is defined today. They may dye their hair blonde, wear it in a long, fluffy style, and adorn it with a ribbon. They manicure fingernails and toenails and polish them or glue on false fingernails. They employ make-up artists, carefully choose posing bikinis for colour and material, wear earring studs and an engagement or wedding ring, shave all body hair, and perhaps use plastic surgery to soften the contours of their faces. When they pose, they may walk on their toes, use graceful dance moves and smile incessantly. They try to be seen with husbands or male friends, and they cautiously flirt with male judges. They do all this to appear 'natural' according to dominant definitions of femininity (Bolin, 2003).

Of course, none of this is natural in biological terms. When female bodybuilders walk on stage, the femininity insignias they inscribe on their bodies contrast with their muscularity to such an extent that it is difficult for anyone who sees them not to realize that femininity is a social construction rather than a biological fact. The contestants in women's events today are clearly more muscled than 99 per cent of the men in the world, and they challenge the notions that women are the 'weaker sex', and that femininity implies frailty and vulnerability.

Female bodybuilders provide living examples that nature is more variable than prevailing gender ideology would indicate. In the process, they make it possible for women to view muscles and strength as a source of personal empowerment. This empowerment focuses on personal change rather than the development of progressive and collective politics among women, but those personal changes serve to challenge dominant definitions of femininity. At the same time, women who are 'too muscular' repulse many people, and this creates challenges to personal identity for some participants, causing many to drop out of the sport altogether (Probert et al., 2007). *What do you think?*

In women's bodybuilding, there is clear tension between muscularity and femininity. It is created when a woman's muscles place her outside normative boundaries. This tension did not exist for Arnold Schwarzenegger when he was judged the most muscled man in the world. Muscles and masculinity go together in ideological terms, but women with muscles cause ideological confusion, even when they wear long hair and ponytails, polish their nails and accessorize with 'feminine' jewellery. Arnold Schwarzenegger was elected to be a State Governor in the USA. Could you imagine voting for this woman as your local Member of Parliament? (Source: **Steve Wennerstrom,** Women's Physique World Magazine)

Sports as sites for change

Although female athletes still live with the consequences of traditional gender ideology and homophobia, their achievements have challenged certain ideas and beliefs, and encouraged many people to think in new ways about masculinity, femininity and gender relations (Theberge, 2000). When this occurs, women's sports are important sites for pushing the normative boundaries of *femininity*. For example, author Leah Cohen points out that 'any girl who boxes challenges, unwittingly or not, the idea of what it means to be a girl in our culture' (2005, p. xiii). In some cases, female athletes even encourage people to question the validity of the two-category gender classification model and rethink the meaning of gender in society. For example, in 2004 IOC executive board members revised their thinking about gender when they approved a proposal to allow athletes who have undergone sex change operations to participate in the Olympics (Hui, 2004). The athletes must have had their new gender legally recognized and had post-operative hormone therapy for at least two years. Although this decision assumes a two-gender classification model, it recognizes that gender is changeable. This is a significant change that now applies worldwide in international sports.

 Gender is much more than a biochemical construct. It's bizarre to think you can determine whether someone is male or female based on [laboratory] tests.

(Andrew Pipe, former president of the Canadian Academy of Sports Medicine and chair of the Canadian Centre for Ethics in Sport, in Lehrman, 1997)

When a two-category classification model is used to define *gender*, the identities and actions of lesbians, gay men, bisexuals and transsexuals (LGBTs) are outside normative boundaries (refer to Figure 8.1). This ideology was legalized in the UK by a Conservative Local Government Act clause in 1988, known as 'Section 28', which was a right-wing attempt to regulate homosexual behaviour and caused many groups to limit or censor their activities. The clause was not completely revoked throughout the UK until 2003 under a New Labour government. As a result of such ideologies, LGBTs are sometimes marginalized, feared or seen as oddities or sinners. They may be harassed and, in extreme cases, physically attacked (Smith, 2005; Wertheim, 2005).

Discussions about the identities and lives of those who live outside normative boundaries established in connection with a two-gender classification model sometimes evoke strong emotions, defensive reactions and moral judgements. Exceptions to this exist when people do not accept such a model or define *gender* in normative terms that reflect the reality of people's lives (see Figure 8.2).

The same is true in sports. Lesbians, gay men, bisexuals and transsexuals play sports but they are seldom recognized. When discussions do occur, many people express ambivalence, mixed feelings and inconsistencies. There is also evidence of institutionalized homophobia in some sports. For example, a study of women's football in France found that some of the clubs' managers operated policies aiming to 'clean up' the sport by organizing 'girls days', where players had to wear skirts, and paying for boyfriends to attend matches with the players (Mennesson and Clement, 2003). Homophobia also operates less formally, although equally powerfully, in less structured sporting situations. A survey of bullying in schools in the UK indicated that half of homophobic bullying incidents occurred in the context of sport. This influences boys and

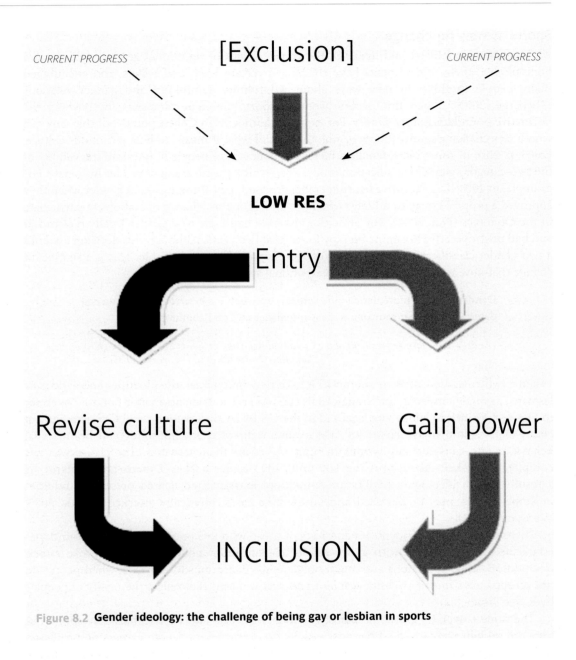

Figure 8.2 **Gender ideology: the challenge of being gay or lesbian in sports**

girls in different ways: for boys, they are encouraged to conform to hyper-masculine sporting ideals and denigrate those who deviate from this norm as 'poofs'; for girls homophobic bullying discourages participation in sport altogether (see Brackenridge et al., 2007b; Clarke, 2004; Rivers, 2004).

Despite this, acceptance of LGBTs has increased in society as a whole *and* in sports (Anderson, 2000, 2002, 2005). Today, there are teams and sport events in which LGBTs are accepted and supported by heterosexual athletes and coaches, and there are more teams and events exclusively for those with sexualities that are not heterosexual (Elling et al., 2003). But significant challenges remain for both lesbian and gay athletes, and even when acceptance occurs, it is defined on terms set by heterosexual athletes, not terms preferred by gay and lesbian athletes (Anderson, 2002; Brackenridge et al., 2007b). Therefore, many LGBT athletes remain closeted, pass as heterosexual, cover their identity, or selectively reveal identity to trusted others and in situations where their sexuality is accepted (Caudwell, 2003; Griffin, 1998). Because of different levels of acceptance, identity management strategies often differ between athletes in women's and men's sports.

Lesbians in sports

Acceptance of homosexual, bisexual and transsexual athletes is greater in women's than men's sports. When the first high-profile female athletes came out as lesbians in the 1980s, they were the focus of praise, hostility, and endless media discussions and debates. When tennis star Martina Navratilova came out, it is estimated that she lost over US$10 million in endorsement contracts – a major price to pay in the 1980s. Today, she receives endorsement offers *because* of her sexuality. As other top-level female athletes come out today, they face short-term media attention, some negative reactions from fans and other athletes, and the personal challenges that most women face when they come out with friends and family (Griffin, 1998). But they are also likely to find people who will support them, even if most corporations are hesitant to sign them to endorsements (Swoopes, 2005).

Pat Griffin's ground-breaking book *Strong Women, Deep Closets: Lesbians and Homophobia in Sports* (1998) provides clear evidence that 'sports and lesbians have always gone together' (p. ix). She notes that this evidence has been ignored in the popular consciousness, largely because of cultural myths about lesbians. Although most myths have been challenged and discredited, some remain. For example, some people think that lesbians are predatory and want to 'convert' others to their 'way of life', which is imagined to be strange, immoral or downright evil. To the extent that lesbian athletes fear such people, they may turn inward and experience isolation and loneliness. This has also been found to be the experience of physical education teachers, who fear being viewed as predators on the young girls in their charge, and so hide their sexual orientation, at least within the school setting (see Clarke, 2002, 2004). When heterosexual athletes believe these myths or even wonder about their veracity, they avoid lesbian athletes and coaches; when coaches and administrators believe them, they are less likely to hire and promote lesbians in coaching, teaching and sports management.

Some women's sports and teams are characterized by a 'don't ask, don't tell' atmosphere in which lesbians work to hide their identity so that they may play the sports they love without being marginalized or harassed. However, such a strategy has costs, and it does not encourage changes that might defuse and even eliminate homophobia in women's sports. Ethics educator Pat Griffin (1998) makes a good case for being open and truthful about sexual identity, but she also notes that open lesbians must be prepared to handle everything from hostility to cautious acceptance when they come out. She notes that handling challenges is easier when friends, teammates and coaches provide support; when there are local organizations that challenge homophobia and advocate tolerance; and when there is institutionalized legal protection for gays and lesbians in organizations, communities and society.

> (the man) threw punches at Ali ... he eventually backed off. 'Come on Mick it's only a bunch of women' 'It's not a woman it's a lesbian'. (He) backed off shouting abuse, threatened to come back and get us 'fucking bunch of lesbians'.
>
> *(Minutes from a women's football club meeting, in Caudwell, 2006a, p. 150)*

Gay men in sports

In men's sports, changes are not as visible as in women's sports. The culture of many men's sports continues to support a vocabulary of exclusion, marginalization and homophobia, but this vocabulary does not always predict the responses of heterosexual athletes when a teammate comes out (Anderson, 2005; Bull, 2004). Men's sports have always been key sites for celebrating and reproducing dominant ideas about masculinity. Playing sports has been a rite of passage for boys to become men, and many people define male athletes in contact and power sports as the epitome of what it means to be a heterosexual man in society. Therefore, there is much at stake in maintaining the silence about gay men in sports and in discouraging gay male athletes from revealing their identities. This is necessary to maintain the integrity of existing normative gender boundaries and the privilege that is available to some men as long as the two-gender classification model is widely accepted (Pronger, 1999, 2002). Therefore, men in changing rooms use a vocabulary that reaffirms the norms of heterosexual masculinity. Policing gender boundaries preserves the glorified status of male athletes and men's access to power and influence in society as a whole.

It is due to these issues that the message to boys and men in sports is loud and clear: 'do not be a poof' and 'do not play like a girl'. The message to gay males of all ages is also clear: 'Do not challenge the two-category gender classification model because it works for us men and has given some of us privilege and power in sports and in society.' These messages create a combination of commitment to the cult of masculinity and deep fears of homosexuality in men's sports (Anderson, 2005; Tuaolo, 2002).

These messages also create a context in which boys and men feel ashamed about feelings of affection towards other men and feel compelled to mimic violent caricatures of masculinity to avoid being labelled 'poofs' (Roderick, 2006b). This maintains the norm that 'real' men play with pain and injuries, never admit that they are afraid, and never, never confide affectionately in other men, even – or especially – when they care deeply for another man. Instead, connections between male athletes are expressed through punches, mock fights, fist touching and other ritualistic actions that disguise and belie intimacy. Of course, for gay male athletes, the sporting situation offers very real intimate and often homoerotic experiences (see Owen, 2006).

Increasingly, gay men are choosing to form separate 'gay' clubs and teams, where they can be open about their sexual orientation, enjoy their sport in a non-threatening environment and have the opportunity to meet potential sexual partners. For example, there are gay rowing clubs (see Owen, 2006), gay rugby clubs (see Price and Parker, 2003) and gay tennis clubs (see Wellard, 2006). However, the power of gender ideology among male athletes means that very few men have come out as gay in mainstream sports. In men's professional football, there are currently no 'out' gay players. This is not surprising when both players and male fans of clubs based in cities which have a large gay population, such as Brighton and Hove Albion, suffer homophobic abuse regardless of their actual sexual orientation.

However, reactions to other gay male celebrities in, for example, the music and television industries, suggest that were a player to come out in a major men's team sport, he will also be guaranteed celebrity status. He will be seen as a hero by closeted and openly gay men of all ages. He will be on every talk show on television and radio. His website will receive millions of hits. Corporations that market to the gay demographic will knock down his door with endorsement deals. He will eventually be defined as a hero who stood up for a principle that would later be taken for granted in the culture as a whole.

So why are dozens, even hundreds, of high-profile athletes taking a pass on this status and fame? Research by sociologist Eric Anderson (2005), who in 1993 was the first openly gay male high school coach in the USA, indicates that all male athletes, including gays, have learned to see themselves in strict ideological terms and they conform to the norms of hegemonic masculinity in cult-like ways, even when they would benefit by leaving the cult. This explanation makes sense, and it highlights the point that problems for gay athletes are ultimately grounded in a sports culture organized around a two-category gender classification model. Furthermore, when the only openly gay professional British football player, Justin Fashanu, received horrendous abuse throughout his footballing career in the 1990s and later committed suicide, players have good reason to believe that remaining closeted is the best form of action. Therefore, solutions rest in finding strategies to change gender ideology and the ways we do sports.

> Football is a male society and it actively defines itself by means of homophobia.
>
> *(Simon Barnes, journalist, 2006)*

Strategies for changing ideology and culture

Gender equity in sports ultimately depends on transforming gender ideology, including ideas and beliefs about *masculinity* and *femininity*, and changing the ways we do sports in society. These are complex and challenging tasks.

Alternative definitions of masculinity

Dominant gender ideology today normalizes and naturalizes the idea that masculinity involves aggressiveness and a desire to physically dominate others. Men with the power and willingness to do whatever it takes to dominate others are lionized and defined as heroes in sports, business and politics. Men seen as nurturing and supportive of others are defined as weak and emasculated.

As boys and men apply this ideology to their lives, they learn to view manhood in terms of things that jeopardize the safety and well-being of themselves and others. They may drive cars at breakneck speeds, play various forms of 'chicken', drink each other under the table, get into fights, use violence in sports as indicators of manhood, use dangerous substances to build muscles, avoid interacting with women as equals, keep sexual scores in heterosexual relationships, and physically control girlfriends and wives (see Chapters 6 and 7). Some men learn that size and toughness allow them to violate norms and control others through fear and physical coercion.

Despite the dangers and socio-emotional isolation caused by this ideology, male athletes are seldom criticized for using it to guide their words and actions in sports. Coaches do not make athletes run laps for hitting someone too hard or showing no feeling when they have blown out someone's knee, knocked someone unconscious, or paralysed – even killed – an opponent (as in boxing). Instead, coaches want athletes who can hurt others without hesitation or remorse and simply see it 'as part of the game'. But in the larger social and cultural context, does this ideology destroy men's ability to empathize with others and feel their pain, even the pain of opponents? Does it discourage the development of intimate and supportive relationships with other men or with women? Does it lead to high assault and sexual assault rates in society?

The frightening record of men's violence suggests that it would be useful to answer these questions and create new cultural space for alternative definitions of *masculinity*. The dual notion that hormones irrationally drive boys and that 'boys will be boys' continues to be closely associated with seriously dangerous actions in many societies around the world. If dominant forms of sport in today's society prevent people from questioning and transforming this gender ideology, it is important to critically examine sports in society. David Beckham is known to prefer to spend time with his family rather than drinking and clubbing with other players, and when he once missed an international training session to be with his sick child, he explained: 'I'm not scared of my feminine side and I think quite a lot of the things I do come from that side of my character' (in Lemos, 2002). This is an example of an alternative definition of *masculinity* on a football team, which includes a commitment to empathy and integrity.

 Being a gay icon is a great honour for me. I'm quite sure of my feminine side.

(David Beckham, in Wahl, 2003)

Alternative definitions of femininity

The experiences of many female athletes also suggest a need to develop additional definitions of *femininity*. This process has already begun but requires commitment to maintain. For example, how are girls socialized to avoid objectifying their bodies to the point that they refrain from becoming physically skilled in a wide range of sports? We know that parents and others monitor the bodies and actions of girls more closely than they do for boys, even during infancy. Does this pattern of protectiveness continue through the entire life course and, in the process, limit physical skill development and participation in sports? Research suggests that it does (Frederickson and Harrison, 2005; Young, 1990). Therefore, alternative definitions of femininity are needed. This does not mean that girls and women should become like men as much as they should explore and connect with the power of their bodies across many activities, including competitive sports. In the past, large and/or strong girls and women without traditionally feminine characteristics and mannerisms have challenged the two-gender classification model, and sport seems to be a context for extending this challenge to the point of transforming gender ideology. If this occurs, there will be new femininities that recognize and support more women than are now supported by traditional notions of femininity.

Changing the way we do sports

Gender equity involves more than socially constructing new ways to define and perform masculinity and femininity. It also depends on changes in how sports are defined, organized and played. New and creative sport events, new vocabularies to describe those sports, new images that people can associate with sports, and new ways to evaluate success and enjoyment in sports are the foundation of such changes (Burstyn, 1999; Hargreaves, 2000). When women and men who participate in sports as athletes, coaches and administrators can critically assess sports and sports organizations from the inside, changes are more likely to occur (see Chapter 14).

One strategy for achieving gender equity is to change the way that we do sports. Possibilities include organizing sports so that they:

- promote lifetime sports participation and emphasize combinations of competition and partnership, individual expression and teamwork, and health and skill development
- embody an ethic of care and connection between teammates and opponents (Duquin, 2000)
- provide coaching and administrative opportunities for lesbians, heterosexual women, and gay men, thereby adding new voices in decision-making processes, expanding ideas about the organization and purpose of sports, and opening sports to a wider range of participants
- bring boys and girls, men and women, and heterosexuals and LGBTs together in shared sport experiences that promote new ideas about gender and sports in society
- offer spaces in which females can express themselves free of male-dominated/identified/centred sports, such as single-sex physical education classes for girls in schools and women-only classes for Muslim females (see also Chapters 5 and 9).

In addition, strategies to effect change require that people realize that there may be political challenges associated with them. These include the following.

- When women's sports are structured differently than men's, it is difficult to determine if there are equal opportunities for girls and women.
- New sports schemes for girls and women run the risk of being perceived as 'second class', thereby perpetuating notions of female inferiority.
- New sports are difficult to promote, and it is easier to apply pressure for equal resources in schools and other organizations when asking for comparable activities rather than new ones.
- Sports that do not reproduce dominant gender ideology often are devalued and defined as 'not real' and are (under)funded accordingly.

In the long run, gender equity depends on maintaining both approaches simultaneously. This means that changes will occur if those who participate in existing sports can envision and work towards creating alternatives for the future. Likewise, those who envision and favour new sports forms will contribute to changes if they establish credibility and gain access to the power and resources needed to develop new possibilities.

All of us participate in ideological and cultural change when we critically assess how we talk about and do sports. This occurs when we:

- eliminate the language of difference and domination associated with sports and sport participation

- refrain from using labels such as *sissy*, *tomboy*, *poof* and *wimp* in conversations and relationships
- object to coaches who motivate young men by telling them to go out and prove their masculinity on the playing field
- speak out against language that bashes gays and demeans women
- discourage the use of military metaphors that masculinize descriptions of sports (for example, 'he/she is a warrior', 'bringing out the big guns' and 'punishing opponents').

Rule changes in sports are also useful strategies to achieve gender equity. For example, rules to restrict violence in football, rugby and boxing create contexts where female athletes are more likely to be taken seriously. Men will object to this by saying such rules make sports into 'girls' games', but such comments only reaffirm that the rules are necessary. Similarly, rules that support rituals that bring opponents together in ways that emphasize partnership rather than hostility and rivalry can provide images that change ideas about the goals and purposes of sports.

Gender equity depends on seeing and doing sports that reflect the values and experiences of everyone, including women and the men who do not identify themselves in terms of the dominant definition of *masculinity*. Therefore, gender equity does not automatically mean that the goal is to have girls and women play sports just as men have played them. Full equity means that people have a wide range of choices when it comes to organizing, playing and giving meaning to sports.

Summary: Does Equity Require Ideological Changes?

Sports participation among females has increased dramatically in the past half-century. This is the result of new opportunities, equal rights legislation, the women's movement, the health and fitness movement and increased publicity given to female athletes.

Despite this recent trend of increased participation, gender equity is far from being achieved, and future increases in sports participation among girls and women will not be automatic. In fact, there are reasons to be cautious when anticipating more changes in the future. These reasons include budget cuts, backlash in response to changes favouring strong women, a relative lack of female coaches and administrators, a cultural emphasis on cosmetic fitness among women, the trivialization of women's sports, and the existence of homophobia.

More women than ever are playing sports and working in sports organizations, but gender inequities continue to exist in participation opportunities, support for athletes, jobs for women in coaching and administration, and informal and alternative sports. This is because sports have traditionally been organized to be male dominated, male centred and male identified.

Even when sports participation creates feelings of personal empowerment among women, the achievement of full gender equity is impossible without a critical analysis of the gender ideology used in sports and society as a whole. Critical analysis is important because it gives direction to efforts to achieve equity and it shows that there are reasons for men to join women in trying to achieve equity.

The major point of this chapter is that gender equity in sports is integrally tied to ideology and power issues. Gender equity will never be complete or permanent without changes in how people think about masculinity and femininity, and in how sports are organized and played. The Gender Equality Duty which came into force in 2007 was the biggest change to legislation in the UK since the 1970s, and obliges public authorities and other bodies not only to prevent discrimination but also to actively monitor and promote equality. This should improve the provision of sports in communities, but may not impact on dominant gender ideologies.

Dominant sports forms in society are currently based on a two-category gender classification model, which leads to the conclusion that girls and women are by definition inferior to boys and men. The gender ideology based on this classification model includes beliefs about male–female differences that 'naturalize' the superiority of men over women, and erase the existence of gay men, lesbians, bisexuals and transsexuals from cultural images about sports and athletes. Therefore, sports celebrate a form of masculinity that marginalizes women and many men. As this form of masculinity is celebrated through sports, sexism and homophobia are built right into the structure of sports and sports organizations.

When gender ideology and sports are organized around the values and experiences of heterosexual men, real and lasting gender equity depends on changing dominant definitions of masculinity and femininity and the way we do sports. Useful strategies include developing new sports and sports organizations and changing existing sports from the inside and through outside actions and pressure.

Changes also depend on strategies such as these: using new ways to talk about sports, developing new rules to control violence and injuries and foster safety for all players, and creating new rituals and orientations based on the pleasure and participation approach to sports rather than the power and performance approach. Unless gender ideology and sports change, gender equity will never be completely and permanently achieved. This is why those interested in gender equity in sports should be interested also in gender and gender relation issues outside of sports.

Website resources

Note: Websites often change. The following URLs were current when this book was printed. Please check our website (***www.mcgraw-hill.co.uk/textbooks/coakley***) for updates and additions.

www.mcgraw-hill.co.uk/textbooks/coakley Click on Chapter 8 for a discussion of myths about the impact of strenuous exercise on women, and other gender issues.

www.feminist.org/sports/ Numerous links to sites dealing with girls and women in sports; links include many sites related to gender equity.

www.gssf.co.nr/ The site of the Gender Sport and Society Forum, a site maintained by Emma Rich, at Loughborough University; contains an excellent bibliography of recent published books and articles on gender and sports, among other helpful resources.

www.iwg-gti.org The site of the International Working Group on Women and Sport; contains information on programmes, policy issues and problems faced by girls and women in more than 100 nations.

www.wsf.org.uk/ The site of the most recognized sports organization for women in the UK; contains excellent links to many sites.

Chapter 9

Race, ethnicity and national identity: are they important in sports?

(*Source*: **AFP/Getty**)

> Football is the game of the masses, which is why it is increasingly a game of colour ... Football offers a level playing field for the poor ... and it is difficult to think of another walk of life where those not only of African descent but also largely from poor countries are so admired and acclaimed.

(*Martin Jacques, journalist, 2004, p. 55*)

Learning Centre Resources

Visit *Sports in Society*'s Online Learning Centre (OLC) at **www.mcgraw-hill.co.uk/
textbooks/coakley** for additional information and study material for this chapter, including:

- Self-grading quizzes and essay questions
- Learning outcomes
- Related websites
- Additional readings

Chapter contents

Defining *race, ethnicity* and *national identity*
Creating race and racial ideologies
Sports participation among minority ethnic groups in the UK
The dynamics of racial and ethnic relations in sports
Summary: are race, ethnicity and national identity important in sports?

> I speak for the majority of blues when I say Everton are white and should remain
> so. Quite simply we don't want any coons, pakis, wops, dagos or little yellow friends
> pulling on the royal blue shirt … Everton are a club of great tradition and we do
> not want to see any banana chewing wogs at Goodison. Quite simply the majority
> say keep Everton white.
> *(Letter to Everton football club fanzine, cited in Fleming and Tomlinson, 2007, p. 306)*

Sports involve complex issues related to race, ethnicity and national identity, and these terms are even problematic in themselves as we will discuss in this chapter. These issues are increasingly relevant as global migration and political changes bring together people from different racial and ethnic backgrounds, and create new challenges for living, working and playing together. These social developments also create challenges to traditional definitions of nationality and people's constructions and experiences of national identity (Carrington, 2004a). The challenges created by racial and ethnic diversity are among the most important that we face in the twenty-first century (Edwards, 2000).

Ideas and beliefs about race, ethnicity and nationality influence self-perceptions, social relationships and the organization of social life. Sports reflect this influence and are sites where people challenge or reproduce racial ideologies and existing patterns of racial and ethnic relations in society. As people make sense of sports and give meaning to their experiences, they often take into account their beliefs about skin colour and ethnicity. The once-popular statement, 'White men can't jump', is an example of this.

Not surprisingly, the social meanings and the experiences associated with skin colour and ethnic background influence access to sports participation, decisions about playing sports, the ways that people integrate sports into their lives, and the organization and sponsorship of sports. People in some racial and ethnic groups use sports participation to express their cultural or national identity and evaluate their potential as athletes. In some cases, people are identified and evaluated as athletes, coaches or media commentators because of the meanings given to their skin colour, ethnic background or nationality.

Sports also are cultural sites where people formulate or change ideas and beliefs about skin colour, ethnic heritage and national characteristics, and then use them as they think about and live other parts of their lives. This means that sports are more than mere reflections of racial and ethnic relations in society; they are also sites where racial and ethnic relations occur and change. Therefore, the depth of our understanding of sports in society depends on what we know about race, ethnicity and national identity, and the ways that they are intertwined in the UK (Gilroy, 2001).

This chapter focuses on the following topics:

- definitions of *race, ethnicity* and *national identity,* as well as the origins of ideas about race in contemporary cultures
- racial classification systems and the influence of racial ideology in sports
- sport participation patterns among racial and ethnic minorities in the UK
- the dynamics of the relationship between racial, ethnic and national identities in sports

Defining *Race, Ethnicity* and *National Identity*

Discussions about race, ethnicity and national identity are confusing when people fail to define their terms. In this chapter, **race** refers to *a population of people who are believed to be naturally or biologically distinct from other populations.* Race exists only when people use a classification system that divides all human beings into distinct categories, which are believed to share genetically based physical traits passed from one generation to the next. Racial categories are developed around the meanings that people give to real or assumed physical traits that they use to characterize a racial population.

Ethnicity is different from race in that it refers to *a particular cultural heritage that people use to identify a particular population.* Ethnicity is *not* based on biology or genetically determined traits; instead, it is based on cultural traditions and history. This means that an **ethnic group** is *a category of people regarded as socially distinct because they share (i) a way of life, and/or (ii) a collective history, and/or (iii) a sense of themselves as a people.* Of course, these terms are complicated by the fact that many people have more than one racial and/or ethnic heritage.

Confusion also sometimes occurs when people use the term *minority* as they talk about racial or ethnic populations. In sociological terms, a **minority** is *a socially identified population that suffers disadvantages due to systematic discrimination and has a strong sense of social togetherness based on shared experiences of past and current discrimination.* Therefore, *not* all minorities are racial or ethnic populations, and *not* all racial or ethnic populations are minorities. For example, whites in the UK often are identified as a race, but they would not be a minority unless another racial or ethnic population had the power to subject them to systematic discrimination that would collectively disadvantage whites as a population category in British society. Irish people in London are considered an ethnic population, but they are no longer considered a minority (although they have previously experienced discrimination, as we discussed in Chapter 3). British Asians, on the other hand, are an ethnic population that also is a minority due to historical *and current* discrimination experienced by many Asians and British Asians. In the UK, the term **visible minority** is often used to differentiate minority groups who are identifiably different (usually by skin colour and forms of dress) from other ethnic groups.

Black Britons often are referred to as a race because of the meanings that people have given to skin colour in the UK; additionally, they are referred to as an ethnic group because of their shared cultural heritage. This has led many people to use *race* and *ethnicity* interchangeably without acknowledging that one is based on a classification of physical traits and the other on the existence of a shared culture. Sociologists attempt to avoid this conceptual confusion by using the term 'race' only to refer to the social meanings that people have given to physical traits. These meanings, they say, have been so influential in society that shared ways of life have developed around them. Therefore, many sociologists today focus on ethnicity rather than race, except when they study the social consequences of widespread ideas and beliefs about race. This is also why 'race' appears in quotation marks in some literature, to identify that it is a social construction and not a biologically meaningful concept. We do not do this in this text in order to identify the very real social significance of the meanings people attach to physical characteristics such as skin colour.

One consequence of racial ideologies is related to definitions of British national identity. We use the term **national identity** in this chapter to refer to *feelings of attachment to a nation's history and traditions which create unity and a sense of 'we-ness' among citizens.* We discuss this further in Chapter 13 when we explain the ways that governments and other organizations use sports to create national unity. However, national identity has relevance here because many visible black and minority ethnic (BME) groups have been portrayed as being outside British national culture, even posing a threat to national identity. These views, and the resultant racist behaviour which is often played out in sporting contexts, need to be understood in the historical context of the British Empire, which practised racist traditions such as slavery (see Chapter 3, p. 67). As a result, being black and British has presented something of a paradox for many people (see Alexander, 1996; Jones, 2002).

This information about race confuses many people in the UK because they have been socialized to take for granted that race is a biological reality. To be told that race is based on social meanings rather than biological facts is difficult for them to accept until they learn about the origins of the concept of race and the development of racial ideologies.

> Science has a long and disreputable history of making false extrapolations from inconclusive hard data – extrapolations that merely parrot the prejudices of the age.
>
> *(Gary Kamiya, executive editor,* Solon, *2000)*

Creating Race and Racial Ideologies

Physical and cultural diversity is a fact of life, and people throughout history have categorized one another, often using physical appearance and cultural characteristics to do so. However, the idea that there are distinct, identifiable races is a relatively recent invention. Europeans developed it during the seventeenth century as they explored the world and encountered people who looked and lived unlike anything they had ever known. As they colonized regions on nearly every continent, Europeans developed classification systems to distinguish the populations that they encountered. They used the term *race* very loosely to refer to people with particular religious beliefs (Hindus), language or ethnic traditions (the Basque people in Spain), histories (indigenous peoples such as New World 'Indians' and 'Aborigines'), national origins (Chinese) and social status (chronically poor people, such as Gypsies in Europe or the Untouchables in India).

More specific ideas about race emerged in connection with religious beliefs, scientific theories, and a combination of political and economic goals (Fredrickson, 2003; Omi and Winant, 1994; Winant, 2001, 2004, 2006). And, over time, people in many societies have come to use the term *race* to identify populations that they believe are naturally or biologically distinct from other populations. This shift from a descriptive to a biology-based notion of race occurred as light-skinned people from northern Europe sought justification for colonizing and exercising power over non-white ethnic groups around the world. Intellectuals and scientists in the seventeenth century through to the twentieth century facilitated this shift by developing appearance-based racial classification frameworks that enabled them to 'discover' dozens of races, sub-races, collateral races and collateral sub-races – terms that many scientists used as they analysed the physical variations of people in colonized territories and other regions of the world.

Faulty 'scientific' analyses combined with the observations and anecdotal stories told by explorers led to the development of racial ideologies. As we noted in Chapter 1, **racial ideology** consists of *a web of ideas and beliefs that people use to give meaning to skin colour and evaluate people in terms of racial classifications*. The racial classification models developed in Europe were based on the assumption that the appearance and actions of white Europeans were normal and that all deviations from European standards were strange, exotic, primitive or immoral (Carrington, 2007a; Carrington and McDonald, 2001). In this way, the 'whiteness' of northern Europeans became a standard against which the appearance and actions of *others* ('those people') were measured and evaluated. In other words, the regions that were white dominated also became white identified and white centred in a social and cultural sense.

 It's very bad to hear when people boo players because of the colour of their skin.

(Sven Goran Eriksson, former manager of England men's football team, 2004)

Racial ideology in the UK

Racial ideology in the UK emerged during the sixteenth and seventeenth centuries when the first European overseas expeditions led to the conquering and exploitation of several countries.

In particular, the people of Britain felt that it was their biological and cultural destiny to colonize and rule other parts of the world, in particular in Africa, South and East Asia, and the Caribbean. They were driven to such a degree that they conquered over half of the globe as they formed the British Empire! These white colonizers used racial ideology to conclude that black and Asian people around the world were primitive beings driven by brawn rather than brains, instincts rather than moral codes and impulse rather than rationality. Through this way of thinking, whites gave themselves 'moral permission' to exploit, subjugate, enslave and even murder dark-skinned peoples without guilt or the sense that they had sinned (Carrington, 2007a; Carrington and McDonald, 2001; Fredrickson, 2003; Hoberman, 1992; Smedley, 1997, 1999; Winant, 2001, 2004, 2006).

By the early nineteenth century, this 'racial science' had developed into a set of ideas, and many whites believed that race was a mark of a person's humanity and moral worth. Africans and Asians, they concluded, were subhuman and incapable of being civilized. By nature, these 'collared peoples' were socially, intellectually and morally inferior to light-skinned Europeans – a fact that was unchangeable (Smedley, 1997). This ideology became popular for two reasons. *First*, it provided a justification for imperial expansion. *Second*, white Britons used the 'accepted fact' of black inferiority to justify the imposition of British customs and ways of life on these colonies in order to 'civilize' the 'native' peoples (see Carrington, 2007a). For example, some whites came to view black people as pagans in need of spiritual salvation. They worked to save souls, and in the process, dark-skinned people came to be known as the 'white man's burden'.

Patterns of immigration changed during the nineteenth century, with large numbers of Irish workers settling in Britain in the second half of the century, and substantial Jewish immigration to the East End of London at the end of the nineteenth century. Although these were not always visible minorities, both groups faced discrimination. This led to a certain amount of sectarianism, including the formation of separate sports and social clubs, many of which remain today (see Chapters 3 and 13).

The majority of immigration into the UK after the Second World War took place in the 1950s and 1960s from the West Indies and the Indian subcontinent. These were people supported by the British government to make up labour shortages, mostly in public services. They were, therefore, regionally concentrated, primarily in areas of London, the Midlands, West Yorkshire and South Lancashire. The main difference with these immigrants from the previous white-European settlers in the UK was that they were distinguishable by skin colour, and this provided the basis for considerable racial prejudice. This manifested itself in sports, with private clubs largely refusing membership to non-white members, and the black community forming their own teams and leagues, mostly in sports which were cheap and accessible such as athletics and football (Holt and Mason, 2000).

In the later twentieth century and early years of the twenty-first century, immigration into the UK has been dominated by refugees and asylum seekers from countries with unstable and often violent domestic situations, or experiencing natural disasters, and by people moving within the European Union, particularly from Eastern countries. This is discussed further in the section on 'Sport participation and national identity in the "United" Kingdom'. The dominant ethnic groups currently in the UK are illustrated in Table 9.1.

Although Britain has never had formal segregation, such as that enforced in the USA, South Africa and other nations, it has not achieved complete racial integration, largely because

British-born whites have carefully policed racial boundaries to maintain their privilege in UK culture and society. As a result, whiteness and national identity have gone hand in hand. Additionally, the traditional belief that whiteness is a pure and innately special racial category has, through the past century, created a deep cultural acceptance of inequality and strong political resistance to policies that are designed to deal with the existence and legacy of these facts of British life.

The problem with race and racial ideology

Research since the 1950s has produced overwhelming evidence that the concept of race is not biologically valid (Graves, 2002, 2004; Omi and Winant, 1994). This point has received powerful support from the Human Genome Project, which demonstrates that external traits such as skin colour, hair texture and eye shape are not genetically linked with patterns of internal differ-

Table 9.1 **Population of the UK by ethnic group, April 2001**

	Total population		Non-white population (percentages)
	(Numbers)	(Percentages)	
White	54 153 898	92.1	
Mixed	677 117	1.2	14.6
Indian	1 053 411	1.8	22.7
Pakistani	747 285	1.3	16.1
Bangladeshi	283 063	0.5	6.1
Other Asian	247 664	0.4	5.3
All Asian or Asian British	2 331 423	4.0	50.3
Black Caribbean	565 876	1.0	12.2
Black African	485 277	0.8	10.5
Black Other	97 585	0.2	2.1
All black or black British	1 148 738	2.0	24.8
Chinese	247 403	0.4	5.3
Other ethnic groups	230 615	0.4	5.0
All minority ethnic population	4 635 296	7.9	100.0
All population	58 789 194	100	

Source: National Statistics, 2001

ences among human beings. We now know that there is more biological diversity within any one so-called racial population than there is between any two racial populations, no matter how different they may seem to be on the surface (AAA, 1998; Williams, 2005).

Noted anthropologist Audrey Smedley (2003) explains that the idea of race has had a powerful impact on history and society, but it has little to do with real biological diversity among human beings. This is because the concept of race identifies categories and classifications that people use to explain the existence of social differences and inequalities in social worlds. In this sense, race is a biological myth based on socially created ideas about variations in human potential and abilities that are assumed to be biological.

This conclusion is surprising to most people in the UK because they have learned to 'see' race as a fact of life and use it to sort people into what they believe to be biology-based categories. They have also used ideas and beliefs about race to make sense of the world and the experiences of various people. Racial ideology is so deeply rooted in British culture that many people see race as an unchangeable fact of nature that cannot be ignored when it comes to understanding human beings, forming social relationships and organizing social worlds.

To put biological notions of race aside requires a major shift in thinking for many people. This is difficult to do because it complicates the world, and changes our sense of how it is organized and how it operates. But when we move beyond the lens of traditional racial ideology in the UK, we see that definitions of race and approaches to racial classification vary widely across cultures and over time. Thus, a person classified as black in the UK may not be identified as 'black' in Brazil, Haiti, Egypt or South Africa where approaches to racial classification have been created under different social, cultural and historical circumstances. For example, Yannick Noah, a pop singer and former professional tennis player, is classified as white in Cameroon because his mother is a light-skinned woman from France, but he is classified as black in his native France because his father is a dark-skinned man from Cameroon in Central West Africa. Brazilians use over 100 different terms when asked to identify their race. Less than 5 per cent of Brazilians classify themselves as black, even though people in the UK would say that half of all Brazilians are black according to the way they define race. These cultural and historical variations indicate that race is a social construction instead of an objective, unchanging biological fact.

Another problem with race is that racial classification models force people to make clear racial distinctions on the basis of *continuous traits* such as skin colour and other physical traits possessed to some degree by all human beings. Height is an example of a continuous physical trait: all humans have some height, although height measurements vary along a continuum from the shortest person in the world to the tallest. If we wanted to classify all human beings into particular height categories, we would have to decide where and how many lines we should draw along the height continuum. This could be done only if the people in charge of drawing the lines could develop shared agreements about the meanings associated with various heights. But the agreements made in one part of the world would likely vary from the agreements made in other parts of the world, depending on social and cultural factors that influenced the relevance of height. Therefore, in some societies a man who stood at 1.8 metres would be classified as tall, whereas 'tall' in other societies might mean being in excess of 2 metres. To make classification matters more complicated, people sometimes change their ideas about what they consider to be short or tall, as British people have done through the twentieth century. Additionally, evidence clearly shows that the average height of people in different societies changes over time as diets, lifestyles and height preferences change, even though height is a physical, genetically based trait for individuals (Bilger, 2004). This is why British people are now taller, on average, than Americans and people in many continental European countries.

Like height, skin colour also is a continuous physical trait. It varies from *snow white* at one end of the skin colour continuum to *midnight black* at the other, with an infinite array of colour shades in between. When skin colour is used to identify racial categories, the lines drawn to mark off and identify races are based on the meanings given to skin colour by the people who are doing the classifying. Therefore, the identification of races is based on social agreements about where and how many racial dividing lines to draw; it is not based on objectively identifiable biological division points.

An example of the trouble with trying to draw distinct racial lines is that 'mixed-race' people are erased in British history and in sports. This occurred in the UK census up until 2001 when it added the category of 'mixed race' for the first time. Clinging to traditional definitions of race also has created confusing social and identity issues. For example, when American golfer Tiger Woods was identified as 'black', he said he was 'Cablinasian' – a term he invented to explain that he is one-quarter Thai, one-quarter Chinese, one-quarter African-American, one-eighth Native American and one-eighth white European (Ca-bl-in-asian = *Ca*ucasian + *Bl*ack + *In*dian + *Asian*). Woods was not about to deny his diverse ancestry by accepting a classification system that traditionally identified people as black if they were not 'pure' white, with qualifications in the case of those who also have Asian ancestry. This is why mixed-race persons in sports are constantly described as black, even though a parent or multiple grandparents are white. This is illustrated by the 2006 England men's World Cup football squad on which six of the seven players defined as 'black' were actually mixed race. Similarly, Lewis Hamilton, who many describe as the 'Tiger Woods of Formula One', and Dame Kelly Holmes, the track and field

(*Source*: **Alamy**)

Dame Kelly Holmes and Lewis Hamilton have a white mother, yet they are often identified as black because of the way race has been defined by most people in the UK

double Olympic gold medallist, are also described as black even though they both have white British mothers. Perhaps worse still is the use of the term 'half-caste' which many mixed-race athletes say continues to be used to describe them; 'caste' is a derivative of the Latin word 'castus' which is used to indicate racial purity. (The British Sociological Association (www.britsoc. co.uk) provides useful guidelines on appropriate language when discussing issues of 'race' and ethnicity.)

To say that race is a social construction does not deny the existence of physical variations between human populations. These variations are real and some are meaningful, such as those having medical implications, but they do not correspond with the skin-colour-based racial classification models widely used in the UK and some other cultures. Additionally, scientists now know that physiological traits, including particular genetic patterns, are influenced by the experiences of particular individuals and the long-term experiences of particular populations. Therefore, a population that has lived for centuries in a relatively isolated mountainous region in Africa may have more or less of a specific trait than a population of people who have lived for centuries in Norway, but this does not justify classifying these populations as different races on the basis of skin colour.

Even though race is not a valid biological concept, its social significance has profoundly influenced the lives of millions of people for three centuries. As people have developed webs of ideas and beliefs around skin colour, the resulting racial ideologies have become deeply embedded in many cultures. These ideologies change over time, but they continue to exert a powerful influence on people's lives.

The primary problem with race and racial ideologies is that they have been used for three centuries to justify the oppression and exploitation of one population by another (Carrington, 2007a; Fredrickson, 2003; Klein, 2008; Smedley, 1997, 1999; Winant, 2001, 2006). Therefore, they have fuelled and supported **racism**, defined as *attitudes, actions and policies based on the belief that people in one racial category are inherently superior to people in one or more other categories*. In extreme cases, racial ideology has supported racist beliefs that people in certain populations are (1) childlike beings in need of external control, (2) subhuman beings that can be exploited without guilt, (3) forms of property that can be bought and sold, or (4) evil beings that should be exterminated through **genocide**, or *the systematic destruction of an identifiable population*.

Another problem with race and racial ideologies is that they foster the use of **racial stereotypes**, or *generalizations used to define and judge all individuals who are classified in a particular racial category*. Because stereotypes provide ready-made evaluative frameworks for making quick judgements and conclusions about others, they are widely used by people who do not have the opportunity or are not willing to learn about and interact with those who have experiences that are influenced by popular beliefs about skin colour. Knowledge, when used critically, undermines racial stereotypes, and gradually subverts the ideologies that support them and the racism that accompanies them.

> The challenge in sports in the 21st Century is going to be diversity.
>
> *(Harry Edwards, sociologist/activist, 2000, p. 29)*

Race, racial ideology and sports

None of us is born with a racial ideology. We acquire it over time as we interact with others and learn to give meanings to physical characteristics such as skin colour, eye shape, the colour and texture of hair, or even specific bodily movements. These meanings become the basis for classifying people into racial categories and associating categories with particular psychological and emotional characteristics, intellectual and physical abilities, and even patterns of action and lifestyles.

This process of creating and using racial meanings is built into the cultural fabric of many societies, including the UK. It occurs as we interact with family members, friends, neighbours, peers, teachers and people we meet in our everyday lives (see Chapter 4). And it is reproduced in connection with general cultural perspectives as well as images and stories in children's books, textbooks, popular films, television programmes, video games, song lyrics and other media content. We incorporate these perspectives, images and stories into our lives to the extent that we perceive them to be compatible with our experiences.

The influence of race and racial ideologies in sports has been and continues to be significant in the UK (Brown et al., 2005; Buffington, 2005; Carrington, 2004a, 2007a; Woodward, 2004). For example, through the nineteenth century and much of the twentieth century when black Britons engaged in clearly courageous acts, many whites used racial ideology to conclude that such acts among blacks were based on ignorance and desperation rather than *real* character. Some white people went so far as to say that blacks, including black athletes, did not feel pain in the same way that whites did and this permitted black people to engage in superhuman physical feats and endure physical beatings as in the case of boxers (Mead, 1985). Many whites concluded that the success of black athletes was meaningless because they were driven by simple animal instincts instead of the heroic and moral character that was used to account for the achievements of white athletes. For example, when legendary American boxer Joe Louis defeated a 'white' Italian for the heavyweight championship of the world in 1935, the wire service story that went around the world began with these words:

> Something sly and sinister and perhaps not quite human came out of the African
> jungle last night to strike down [its opponent] ...

(Cited in Mead, 1985, p. 91)

Few people today would use such blatantly racist language, but traditional ideas about race continue to exist. Therefore, when eight black athletes line up in the Olympic finals of the 100 metres or contest the world heavyweight boxing title, many people talk about 'natural speed and power'. Black football players have also described how white players and coaches assume that they will be 'naturally' fast, but that their performance will be likely to suffer in cold weather (Jones, 2002). As a result, some scientists want to study dark-skinned bodies to discover the internal physical traits that allow them to perform well – that is, *better than whites*. On the other hand, Asians are stereotyped as frail, lacking the physical robustness or strength of character required for vigorous contact sports (Fleming, 2001).

When white athletes do extraordinary physical things, dominant racial ideology leads people to conclude that it is either expected or a result of fortitude, intelligence, moral character, strategic preparation, coachability and good organization. Therefore, few people want to study white-skinned bodies. Rarely do we even hear white athletes referred to by their physical characteristics, unlike their black athletic counterparts; and so while Lewis Hamilton is referred to as the *black* Formula One driver, we did not read of the *white* David Beckham's transfer to LA Galaxy. When all the finalists in multiple Olympic Nordic (cross-country skiing) events are 'white', and white skiers from Austria and Switzerland win nearly all World Cup championships year after year, people do not say that they succeed because their white skin is a sign of genetic advantages. Everyone already knows why the Austrians and Swiss are such good skiers: they live in the Alps, they learn to ski before they go to school, they grow up in a culture in which skiing is highly valued, they have many opportunities to ski, all their friends ski and talk about skiing, they see fellow Austrian and Swiss skiers winning races and making money in highly publicized World Cup competitions, and their cultural heroes are skiers. But this is a cultural explanation, not a biological one.

When athletes are white, racial ideology focuses attention on *social* and *cultural* factors rather than biological and genetic factors. This is why scientists do not do studies to identify genes that give Scottish curlers instinctive hand–eye co-ordination and the ability to endure cold climates. Dominant racial ideology prevents people from seeing 'whiteness' as an issue in these cases because it is the taken-for-granted standard against which everything else is viewed.

When dominant racial ideology serves as the cultural foundation of a white-dominated, white-identified and white-centred society, the success of white athletes is seen as 'normal' – the way it always has been. At the same time, the success of black athletes is seen as an invasion or a takeover – a 'problem' in need of an explanation focused on dark-skinned bodies. This way of thinking about skin colour was clearly apparent in 1997 when the white editors of the American magazine *Sports Illustrated* decided that a feature-length cover story should be titled, 'What happened to the white athlete?' (Price, 1997). The story was based on their belief that blacks had taken over sports and that white athletes were fast disappearing. However, the story focused only on the most visible revenue-producing sports and ignored the fact that white athletes made up all or nearly all participants in dozens of other sports at all levels of competition. Similarly, in the UK since the 1980s, the success of black British athletes in football and track and field athletics has been linked with broader concerns about the threat posed to British national culture and identity by the black 'foreigner', and this has been fuelled by newspaper stories of these performers with headlines such as 'Black power' (see Cashmore, 2005; Jones 2002). This illustrates that when racial ideology influences how topics are chosen and stories are told in the media, race-related ideas and beliefs become self-perpetuating, even when they portray reality in distorted and inaccurate terms.

Like all of us, if scientists and editors do not ask critical questions about racial ideology, it will influence their explanations of human performance in sports. These explanations are based on three things: (1) the facts people choose to examine, (2) the ways that people classify and organize those facts, and (3) the theories people use to analyse and interpret the facts that have been classified and organized. Therefore, if people are not critically self-reflective as they observe, analyse and explain the actions of human beings, racial ideology will influence the process of producing knowledge (St Louis, 2003). This issue is discussed further in the box '"Jumping genes" in black bodies' (overleaf).

reflect on SPORTS *'Jumping genes' in black bodies: why do people look for them, and what will it mean if they find them?*

When people seek genetic explanations for the achievements of black athletes, sociologists raise questions about the validity and purpose of the research. Let us use the search for 'jumping genes' to explore whether these questions are justified. Our questions about research on this issue are based on two factors: (1) many current ideas about the operation and effects of genes are oversimplified and misleading, and (2) jumping is much more than a simple physical activity.

Oversimplified and misleading ideas about genes

Most people have great hopes for genetic research. They see genes as the building blocks of life that will enable us to explain and control everything from food supplies to human feelings, thoughts and actions. These hopes have inspired studies seeking genes for violence and intelligence as well as genes that enable people to sprint fast, run record-setting marathons and jump high.

According to Robert Sapolsky (2000), a professor of biology and neurology at Stanford University in the USA, this notion of the 'primacy of the gene' fosters deterministic and reductionist views of human action and social problems. The actions of human beings, he explains, cannot be reduced to particular genetic factors. Even though genes are important, they do not work independently of the environment. Research shows that genes are activated and suppressed by many environmental factors; furthermore, even the *effects* of genes inside the human body are influenced by numerous environmental factors.

Genes are neither autonomous nor the sole causes of important, real-life outcomes associated with our bodies and what they do. The influence of genes is regulated by chemicals that exist in cells as well as other chemicals, such as hormones, that come from other parts of the body. These chemicals and hormones are influenced, in turn, by a wide range of external environmental factors. For example, when a mother rat licks and grooms her infant, these actions initiate biochemical processes that activate genes regulating the physical growth of the infant rat. Therefore, geneticists have concluded that the operation and effects of genes cannot be separated from the environment that switches them on and off and influences their effects (Davids and Baker, 2007).

The point is this: genes do not exist and operate in environmental vacuums. This is true for genes related to diseases and genes related to jumping. Furthermore, we know that physical actions such as jumping, running and shooting a basketball all involve one or more clusters of multiple genes. To explain overall success in a sport such as basketball or football requires an investigation of 'at least 124 genes and thousands, perhaps millions, of combinations of those genes', and this would provide only part of an explanation (Farrey, 2005). The rest would involve research on why people choose to do certain sports, why they are motivated to practise and excel, how they are recognized and identified by coaches and sponsors, and how they are able to perform under particular conditions.

This means that discovering jumping genes would be exciting, but it would *not* explain why one person jumps higher than another, *nor* would it explain why people from one population jump, on average, higher than people from other populations. Furthermore, no evidence shows that particular genes related to jumping or other complex sport performances vary systematically with skin colour or any socially constructed ideas about race and racial classifications.

Jumping is more than a physical activity

Jumping is much more than a mechanical, spring-like action initiated by a few leg muscles. It is a total body movement involving the neck, shoulders, arms, wrists, hands, torso, waist, hips, thighs, knees, calves, ankles, feet and toes. Jumping also involves a timed co-ordination of the upper and lower body, a particular type of flexibility, a 'kinaesthetic feel' and a total body rhythm. It is an act of grace as much as power, a rhythmic act as much as a sudden muscular burst, an individual expression as much as an exertion, and it is tied to a sense of the body in harmony with space as much as simply overcoming resistance through physical force.

Athletes in different sports jump in different ways. Gymnasts, volleyball players, figure skaters, skateboarders, mogul skiers, BMX bikers, basketball players, ski jumpers, high jumpers, long jumpers, triple jumpers and steeplechase runners all jump, but their techniques and styles vary greatly from sport to sport and person to person. The act of jumping among people whose skin colour and ethnic heritage have been given important social meanings is especially complex because race and ethnicity are types of performances in their own ways. In other words, performing race and ethnicity often involves physical expressions and body movements that are integrally related to the cultural–kinaesthetic histories of particular groups.

Noted scholar Gerald Early (1998) explains that playing sports is an *ethnic performance* because the relevance and meaning of bodily movements vary from one cultural context to another. For example, jumping is irrelevant to the performances of world leaders, CEOs of major corporations, sports team owners, coaches, doctors and university lecturers. The power, influence and resources that these people possess do not depend on their jumping abilities. The statement that 'White men can't jump' is not defined as a racial slur by most whites, because jumping deficiencies have not stopped them from dominating the seats of power in the UK. Outside of a few sports, jumping ability has nothing to do with success in everyday life or achieving positions of power and influence. White CEOs making millions of pounds a year do not care that someone says they cannot jump. As Public Enemy rapped in the 1998 film, *He Got Game*, 'White men in suits don't *have* to jump.' And, of course, as Jonathan Edwards proved when he broke the world record in the men's triple jump, white men *can* jump (see Fleming, 2001).

To study the physical aspects of jumping, sprinting and distance running is important because it helps us understand human biology more fully. But this research will not explain why people in some social and cultural populations jump well in certain sports and not others, or not at all. Such explanations must take into account the historical, cultural and social circumstances that make jumping and running important in some people's lives and why some people work so hard to develop their jumping and running abilities. There certainly are genes related to jumping, but it is wrong to assume that they operate independently of environmental factors, that they are connected with skin colour or that they correspond with the racial categories that people have constructed for social and political purposes (also see Carrington and McDonald, 2001; Fleming, 2001). Knowledge about genes is important, but it will never explain for us the complex physical and cultural performance of slam dunks orchestrated by the England Basketball 2007 players of the year, Alfredo Ott and Stephanie Gandy. Nor will it explain the amazing vertical leaps and hang time of the European, Brazilian, Chinese and Japanese volleyball players who have won so many international events. Nor will it tell us why whites have always won America's Cup yachting races (see Cartoon 9.1) *What do you think?*

Such complacent tolerance of racism creates a climate in which the Spanish coach Luis Aragones can casually dismiss the Arsenal and French striker Thierry Henry as 'a black shit'.

(Jason Cowley, journalist, 2004, p. 1)

This statement is laughable when made about whites. However, similar statements about blacks have been used by scientists as a basis for hundreds upon hundreds of studies over the last century. As a result, racial ideology has influenced the process of knowledge production as well as everyday explanations of social worlds and the actions of individuals

Cartoon 9.1 *'Of course, white folks are good at this. After 500 years of colonizing the world by sea, they've been bred to have exceptional sailing genes!'*

Racial ideology and a sense of athletic destiny among black British men

Does racial ideology influence how black Britons interpret their own physical abilities and potential as athletes? This is a controversial question. Statements by athletes and coaches combined with research suggest that many young blacks, especially men, grow up believing that the black body is special and superior when it comes to physical abilities in certain sports (Cashmore, 2007a; Harrison and Lawrence, 2004; Harrison et al., 2004; Lawrence, 2005; Liddle, 2003; Stone et al., 1997, 1999). This belief might inspire some young people to think that playing certain sports and playing them better than anyone else in the world is part of their biological and cultural destiny. This inspiration is intensified when young blacks feel that their occupational future might involve low-wage, dead-end jobs on the one hand, or riches and respect gained from goal-scoring records or Olympic sprint victories on the other. Even boxing might look better than a demeaning, minimum wage job! However, it should be noted that the largest ethnic minority groups in the UK, those of Asian descent, are not involved in these sports to the same extent. This is something that we discuss further in the section on 'Sport participation among Asian Britons' (p. 331).

Figure 9.1 outlines a hypothesized sociological explanation of the athletic achievements of black British male athletes. The top section of the figure shows that racial stereotypes about innate physical abilities among blacks have been a part of UK history. When this fact is combined with limited opportunities in mainstream occupations and access to opportunities to develop skills in certain sports, many young blacks are motivated to play those sports; indeed, over time, they come to believe that it is their destiny to play them better than anyone else, especially whites (see the middle section of Figure 9.1). If this sense of destiny is strong and pervasive enough, it could push blacks to accomplish great things and set records in certain sports (see the last section of Figure 9.1).

This sense of personal and cultural destiny could be a powerful force driving millions of black Britons to dedicate the very fabric of their being to achieving greatness in certain sports. Is this what has led to the notable achievements of black British men in football, athletics and boxing? Is this the reason why they have won medals in certain Olympic events for many years? Is this why black British women are following in their men's footsteps in certain sports? When social worlds are organized to foster a sense of destiny among particular people, *it should not be surprising when they achieve notable things in the pursuit of their perceived destiny.*

When these three social and cultural conditions are added together:

A long history of racial ideology that has emphasized
'black male physicality' and innate, race-based physical abilities among blacks

+

A long history of racial segregation and discrimination, which has limited
the opportunities for black men to achieve success and respect in society

+

The existence of widespread opportunities and encouragement
to develop physical skills and excel in a few sports

There are two intermediate consequences:

Many blacks, especially young men, come to believe
that it is their biological and cultural destiny to become great athletes

+

Young black men are motivated to use every opportunity
to develop the skills they need to fulfill their destiny as athletes

The resulting hypothesis is this:

The sense of biological and cultural destiny, combined with
motivation and opportunities to develop certain sport skills,
leads some black males, especially those with certain physical
characteristics, to be outstanding athletes in certain sports

The challenge of escaping racial ideology in sports

The most effective way to defuse racial ideology is to bring people from different ethnic backgrounds together under conditions that enable them to deal with one another as individuals and discover that ideologies obscure important aspects of people and the realities of their lives. However, this is difficult when teachers, coaches and employers maintain a belief in the myth of black natural physical talent and a lack of cerebral skills. Social scientist Ellis Cashmore (2005) illustrates this with an experience of receiving a telephone call from a black journalist writing for a prestigious broadsheet newspaper. The journalist asked why no one actually expressed what he believed to be an absolute truth: that black athletes have a 'natural edge'. The very fact that a talented black journalist believed this defective theory is testament to its power and the difficulties in escaping expectations based on racial ideology. When such myths maintain credibility in society, black people are regarded as unsuited to, or unwanted for, study, work and other activities that demand mental rather than physical skills.

Such persistent racism effectively closes down perceived choices for black youth when they are considering career choices, and may lead to them being academically marginalized. Many black youths will commit to sports as a viable career path because they know that sport, along with entertainment, has traditionally been an area where black people were able to achieve success, and they have many positive role models of black sports stars. Such commitment means that many do achieve some level of success, but elite sports status is, by definition, difficult to achieve and so the majority inevitably fail. In addition, it remains the case that, even within sports, relatively few black players progress into administrative, management or coaching positions (see Jones, 2002).

Racial ideology, therefore, has a uniquely powerful impact on life choices for black people in the UK. In addition, its consequences are frustrating for young black people who want to expand their social identities beyond sports, or who do not even play sports, but find it difficult to have these aspirations taken seriously because of the colour of their skin. More research is needed on this issue, but it seems that it is difficult for some people to escape the subtle racial ideology which supports widely accepted stereotypes about the potential and abilities of blacks and whites, especially when it comes to sports (Brown et al., 2003; Stone et al., 1997, 1999). We need to know more about the conditions under which this occurs and how it affects everyone involved.

As Ellis Cashmore has noted, the achievements of some black performers in sports is not necessarily a positive feature of British society because they mask the fact that far more fail than achieve a successful sporting career, and because too many blacks channel their energies into sports at the expense of developing other important skills. Of course, the same may be said of white male working-class youths, a point we discuss in Chapter 10. The point is not that blacks should avoid playing sports but that the uncritical acceptance of racial ideology distorts perceptions among blacks and whites in ways that perpetuate the racial status quo and undermine the possibility of creating a fair and just society.

Racial ideology and sports choices among whites

A few years ago, Jay invited five children to be on a youth sports panel in his sports in society course; all were white 10- to 12-year-olds who were heavily involved in sports. During the discussion, a 12-year-old boy known in his nearly all-white school for his sprinting and basketball skills was asked if he would play those sports in high school. Surprisingly, he said no. When asked to explain, he said, 'I won't have a chance because the black kids will beat me out.' He said this did not upset him because he would play football and run the 1500 metres in track and field athletics. He also said that he had never played sports with black peers in school, but he had watched television and seen blacks play basketball and win Olympic sprint medals. This had helped him to develop ideas about race, and his decisions about sports clearly took into account his whiteness and racial ideology as it applies to sport.

A similar application of racial ideology to understanding sports performance was made by cricketers in a British league. Several of the white players drew heavily upon stereotypes about race, physical abilities and the chance for success in their sport. This strongly influenced perceptions of difference between themselves and black and Asian players, as illustrated in the following three quotations:

> Mentally, English players handle pressure better, but they are not so naturally talented and are less physical.

> More flamboyancy with Asian or ethnic players than you get with the stodgy English performer.

> White English players have to rely more on technique and tactics because we are physically inferior to the West Indies.
>
> *(All cited in Long and Hylton, 2002, p. 94)*

These players' whiteness, a taken-for-granted characteristic in the rest of their lives, strongly influenced beliefs about their athletic abilities. It is possible that these kinds of beliefs may also be why the official times of white runners in certain sprints and long-distance road races have actually become slower since the 1950s and 1960s. Whites' genes have not changed, but their perceived choices and motivation appear to have changed as black athletes have become successful participants in these events (Bloom, 1998; George, 1994; Merron, 1999; Weir, 2000).

Research suggests that racial ideology and the stereotypes that it spawns influence sports participation choices and how people perform in sports (Harrison and Lawrence, 2004; Harrison et al., 1999; Stone et al., 1997, 1999), but this is a tricky issue to study. Racial ideology exerts subtle and indirect influence that often is difficult to detect. Therefore, researchers must use creative methods to examine how racial ideology affects people's lives and the organization of the social worlds in which choices are made.

Racial ideology, gender and social class

There are complex interconnections between racial and gender ideologies in the social world of sports. For example, research suggests that the implications of racial ideology for black men are different from those for black women (Bruening, 2005; Carrington, 2007b; Daniels, 2000; Majors, 1998; Winlock, 2000). This is true partly because the bodies of black men have historically been viewed and socially constructed differently from the bodies of black women.

Many white people in the UK have grown up fearing the power of black male bodies, feeling anxious about their sexual capacities, and being fascinated by their movements. Ironically, this aspect of racial ideology has created circumstances in which black male bodies have come to be valuable entertainment commodities, first in music and later on sports fields. Black female bodies, on the other hand, have been socially constructed in sexualized terms that have not made them valuable entertainment commodities in sports (Winlock, 2000).

Race and gender have influenced the lives of black British men in another way. Because they have systematically been denied opportunities enabling them to be successful breadwinners and providers for partners and families, some black British men have learned to construct complex racial and masculine identities in order to negotiate the challenges of white racism and be able to succeed in a racist society. For example, Naseem Hamed, the former world boxing heavyweight champion, carefully manipulated his arrogance, particularly through his posturing as 'Prince Naz', gaining fame and marketability. For other black men, rather than seeking acceptance by the white community, masculine and racial identities are deliberately constructed to resist racism. Findings from studies in the north of England of a boxing gym (Woodward, 2004) and a predominantly black cricket team (Carrington, 2007b) suggest that the competition between black and white men in these sporting contexts became both symbolic and very real contests of masculine and racial pride.

Educator Richard Majors suggests that some black men have developed a presentation of self that he describes as 'cool pose'. This presentation of self is organized around 'unique, expressive, and conspicuous styles of demeanour, speech, gesture, clothing, hairstyle, walk, stance, and handshake' (Majors, 1998, p. 17). It emerges out of the frustration, self-doubt, anger and marginalization in schools and the mainstream economy that has emasculated many black men. Cool pose is all about achieving a sense of significance and respect through *interpersonal* strategies when one is denied significance and success in jobs, politics and education. Cool pose is also about being tough, detached and in control. Cool pose says different things to different people. To the white man, it says, 'Although you may have tried to hurt me time and time again, I can take it (and if I am hurting or weak, I'll never let you know).' It also says, 'See me, touch me, hear me, but, white man, you can't copy me' (Majors, 1986, pp. 184–5). The cool pose of footballer Ian Wright and athlete Linford Christie is a style that has become popularized and imitated (see Polley, 1998). Cool pose also is an interpersonal strategy through which masculinity is portrayed by black boys and men who face status threats in everyday life. Research with British footballers suggests that one consequence of this is that many black players will also avoid speaking out against racism in order to avoid being seen as 'too sensitive' (see Andersson, 2007; Back et al., 2001; Garland and Rowe, 2001).

Black female athletes face some of the same challenges faced by black men. However, as Sheila Scraton identifies, black British women are largely invisible in the sport research literature, as most studies of 'race' focus on *male* experiences and most studies of gender focus on *white* women. The lack of such important research means that black female athletes remain marginalized. There is certainly a need for greater understanding of how being black, British and female has been socially constructed within patriarchal, post-colonial societies such as the UK (see Ismond, 2003; Mirza, 1997; Scraton, 2001). Such research might usefully focus on the following questions:

- How do social stereotypes influence the position of black women in British sports?
- What are the processes by which sports become racially gendered?

■ How do women position themselves in relation to these processes? (Adapted from Brah, 1994; Scraton, 2001.)

In a study of women's football, Scraton et al. (2005) demonstrate the dominance of white women in playing positions and white men in the decision-making positions in women's football clubs which, they argue, impacts on the experiences of black and Asian players. The Football Association has attempted to address this by introducing academies and football festivals targeting black and minority ethnic girls and women. The women in this study identify how their experiences of football were both gendered and racialized, and many had stories to tell of sexist and racist incidents which had constrained their involvement in the sport. For example, many of the players experienced multiple layers of discrimination by being female in a male-dominated game, and suffering racist chants such as 'nigga', receiving bananas as gifts (reflecting the racist view that black people are synonymous with monkeys), and being stereotyped as 'naturally fast' because of their skin colour and as a consequence being channelled into positions requiring speed. Scraton et al. (2005) argue that this results in gender, race and ethnicity being woven into the social identities and sporting experiences of these women.

As social conditions change, so do ideas and beliefs about race and the bodies of athletes. Successful British boxers today are just as likely to be white and Asian as black, while the dominance of white British middle-distance runners in international competition during the 1980s has been replaced in recent years by black African athletes. At the same time, Africans are widely recruited by previously all-white men's football clubs in the UK and elsewhere in Europe, and minority ethnic athletes are succeeding in the previously white-dominated golf and Formula One men's competitions.

Furthermore, studies of black and minority ethnic groups in the UK suggest that the over-representation of minority ethnic groups in lower social classes means that an appreciation of class is central to understanding the sports opportunities and choices of different groups (Fleming, 1995; McGuire et al., 2001). For example, in a study of black and Asian cricketers in Britain, Malcolm (1997) identified the 'stacking' of black players into low-status bowling positions, and Asian players into the higher-status position of batsman which, he argues, reflects specific class relations from British colonialism. While cricket was introduced into African and Caribbean colonies through slavery and a position of white power and privilege, the relationship with the Asian countries in the British Empire contained a more even power balance which, Malcolm argues, was reflected in the differential introduction of black and Asian cricketers to Britain. The classed nature of sports participation is an issue that we return to in Chapter 10.

To explain all these trends, we must understand social and cultural changes along with shifts in racial, ethnic, gender and political ideologies. Information on genes may not help much, if at all, when developing our theories.

It seems an iron law that the more expensive and exclusive the sport, the whiter are its participants and spectators.

(Martin Jacques, journalist, 2007, p. 55)

Sports Participation among Minority Ethnic Groups in the UK

Sports in the UK have long histories of racial and ethnic prejudice, constraint and exclusion (Carrington, 2007a; Holt and Mason, 2000; Polley, 1998). While Britain has a long history of multiculturalism largely stemming from its imperial role, many of the early ethnic groups (predominantly Irish and Jewish) were less visible than the later immigration of people with discernible physical differences – most particularly skin colour – which created new prejudices and social challenges. Britain has only had a numerically significant non-white population since the end of the Second World War, and this new ethnic diversity raised questions of national identity and what it meant to 'be British', and created 'issues of accommodation, assimilation, discrimination, and hostility' (Polley, 1998, p. 137). This was encapsulated in the title of Paul Gilroy's (1991) first book, *There Ain't No Black in the Union Jack*, which was a popular racist chant aimed at early black British players on national football teams.

Men and women in all ethnic minorities traditionally have been under-represented at all levels of competition and management in most competitive sports, from school teams and sports clubs through to the national teams. When members of minority groups played sports, they often played among themselves in games and events segregated by choice or by necessity (Carrington, 2007b; Holt and Mason, 2000; Tomlinson and Fleming, 1996). For example, the exclusion of young British Asian men from the nation's most popular sport, football, has caused many to form their own teams to protect themselves from individual and institutional racism in the game (Johal, 2001; McGuire et al., 2001). In recent years, new questions regarding ethnicity and national identity have been raised by the increased numbers of continental Europeans in the UK, and the changing relationships between the four home country nations.

Sports participation among black Britons

Data on sport participation in the UK is limited, in part because of the difficulties in defining ethnic groups. For example, a survey of sports participation by ethnic group in England found that a large minority of respondents did not identify with any of the ethnic categories on the survey (see Rowe and Champion, 2000). However, the survey did identify that people identifying as Black African and Black Other matched or exceeded national participation rates, with particularly high figures for males in these categories. In contrast, those identifying as Indian, Pakistani and Bangladeshi have participation rates below the national average, and women in these groups were least likely to be involved in sports.

The participation of black people in sport has also been concentrated in a limited range of activities, with black people under-represented in most sports at most levels of competition. This is often overlooked because people watch professional football, Olympic track and field, and boxing, and see black athletes. However, these sports make up only a very small proportion of overall sports participation in the UK. There is a similar pattern in other European countries with strong sporting traditions.

Many people forget that there is a virtual absence of black athletes – male or female – in archery, motor racing, badminton, bowls, canoeing/kayaking, cycling, diving, equestrian events, figure skating, golf, gymnastics, hockey, rowing, sailing, shooting, swimming, skiing, table tennis, tennis, volleyball, water polo, yachting, most field events in track and field, and the majority of alternative sport events. How many black medal winners have there been in the Winter Olympics? This raises the question: 'Why are there so few black athletes in sports?'

The exceptions to this pattern of exclusion stand out because they *are* exceptions. The under-representation of blacks in this list of sports is much greater than the under-representation of whites in sports such as basketball and football. Finding black rowers at a regatta is almost impossible, and even though nearly all the athletes, coaches and spectators are white, nobody refers to these races as white events. In a *white-centred* cultural setting where the lives of whites are the expected focus of attention, it is not even noticed that some sports are exclusively white. And in a *white-dominated* and *white-identified* setting where the characteristics of whites are used as the standards for judging qualifications, black athletes must play, drive, think and act like whites to be accepted as participants who are doing it the right way. But this is often the case for anyone breaking a long-standing barrier related to race, ethnicity or gender.

The alternative option taken by some black athletes has been to 'turn inward' and form black-only teams as a response to the racist backdrop to their sports experiences. For example, the all-black Accra Football Club was formed in Brixton in the 1990s to help young black men to prepare for the difficulties of living in a racist society (see Tomlinson and Fleming, 1996). Similarly, Carrington's research into the Caribbean Cricket Club in Leeds describes how this was formed as a black community space by West Indian war veterans who had settled in the city after the Second World War, and remained an arena for the expression of black identity relatively free from white racism (see Carrington, 2007b). In each of these cases, black women remained relatively marginalized.

Through British sports history, the participation of black females has been severely limited and has received little attention, apart from that given to occasional Olympic medal winners in track events. Black women suffer the consequences of gender and racial ideologies. Apart from a handful of studies, little is known about the unique experiences of black British female athletes, even those participating today (Scraton, 2001).

Overall, sports participation rates in middle- and upper-middle-income white communities in the UK are much higher than those in most predominantly black communities, especially those where resources are scarce. Racial ideology causes many people to overlook this fact. Many people see only the black male athletes who make high salaries in high-profile sports, and then assume that they have 'taken over' sports and that discrimination is gone. This exemplifies how dominant racial ideology influences what people see in their social worlds and what they define as problems.

Sports participation among Asian Britons

There were more than 2.3 million people with Asian backgrounds in the UK in the 2001 population census, the largest non-white ethnic group in the population. The global migration of labour has brought people from many Asian cultures to the UK and other nations around the world. In the UK, most British Asians live in cities where they have been attracted by job opportunities. However, the cultural heritage and the individual histories of British Asians are very diverse.

The differences between many of the Asian cultural groups in the UK are socially significant. However, most non-Asian Britons tend to erase these differences by referring generally to

'Asians', and the diversity is often ignored in media coverage and sometimes ignored in research. Many non-Asian Britons envision stereotypical habits and dress such as eating spicy foods, wearing loose-fitting full-length clothing, and also often adopt the racial ideology that Asians are less physically able than other ethnic groups, except in sports such as hockey, badminton and cricket. British Asians do not necessarily share similar lifestyles or cultures, and this is reflected in sports participation which is affected by a number of factors including religion, family relationships, social class and gender (see Burdsey, 2007; Fleming, 2001, 2007).

Although British Asians have made significant achievements in certain sports over the past century, it remains the case that those identifying as 'Asian' have the lowest participation rates in sport of any ethnic group in the UK (Sporting Equals, 2005). In addition, and perhaps relatedly, public recognition of British Asian athletes has often been limited to those few who have been standout athletes on the national cricket team and in the boxing ring. The recent success and popularity of a few Asian and British Asian athletes has raised important issues about ethnic dynamics in sports. The success of athletes like Amir Khan in boxing and Monty Panesar in cricket suggests that it is possible for athletes from a range of Asian backgrounds to develop a strong fan base in the UK.

Research is now needed to examine the impact of these players on ethnic relations in the sports grounds and communities where they live and play. In addition, the success of British Asian players, particularly in cricket, has become an important dimension of the contestation of national identities, with many players and supporters expressing a nationalistic pride not only for British sporting success but also for that of their country of descent (particularly in the cases of India and Pakistan). Since, in the case of cricket, this country would previously have been a colony of the British Empire, beating a British team on the cricket field enables cultural pride over the former 'masters' (see Malcolm, 1997; Werbner, 1996).

Although some transnational corporations have been hesitant to offer endorsement contracts to British Asian athletes, a growing number of companies now see some of these athletes as having global commercial appeal and value. For example, Amir Khan caught the attention of teenage fans and the media during the summer Olympic Games in Athens in 2004, where he won silver in the lightweight category at the age of 17. His popularity, anchored in his exciting performances, may also be tied to how he has seemingly forged a hybrid ethnic identity with which he is comfortable. This is attractive to many people who have done the same or face the challenge of doing so in the UK where living with a mixed-ethnic heritage, in Khan's case identifying with being both 'British' and 'Asian', is an increasingly common experience.

The participation of Asian-born athletes in elite sports has elicited prejudiced statements from some athletes. Professional golfer Jan Stevenson, a native of Australia, said in 2003 that Asian women golfers 'are killing our tour'. She explained that the Asian professionals did not promote women's golf because they lacked emotional expressiveness, refused to speak English, even when they could do so, and rarely spoke to fans and reporters (Adelson, 2003; Blauvelt, 2003). In 2008, professional women's golf raised, although eventually dropped, a requirement that players should be required to take an English language proficiency test to qualify for the tour. While sentiments such as these are rare, they point to the challenges faced when people from different cultural and ethnic backgrounds participate in sports that are organized around the cultural orientations and traditions of Europeans and North Americans. (See discussions of globalization in Chapter 13, p. 000.)

At this point, research is needed on how images of Asian and British Asian athletes are taken up and represented in the British media and in the minds of people around the country. Research is also needed on the dramatic rise in popularity of various martial arts in the UK. Karate, judo, tae kwon do and other sports with Asian origins have become especially popular among children. Has participation in these martial arts had an impact on children's knowledge and awareness of Asian cultures, on ethnic relations in schools and on the stereotypes used or challenged among children and others who participate in these sports? Or have these sport forms become so Anglicized that their Asian roots are lost or ignored by participants?

Research on British Asians shows the diversity of the traditions and norms that revolve around gender and sports participation for girls and women from various Asian cultures. Parents may feel that playing sports is contrary to their cultural traditions and prevents their daughters from doing household tasks such as caring for siblings, assisting with meal preparation and cleaning the house – none of which their brothers are expected to do. Furthermore, playing sports is a luxury in households where meeting expenses is a struggle and transportation to practices and games is unavailable or costly.

For some girls and women with Muslim beliefs, participation in sporting activities presents a specific set of challenges. A study of Muslim women in Norway demonstrates that for those women who identify in terms of their religion, physical activity was viewed positively because it is in line with Islam's stance on health. In contrast, for those women who regard their ethnicity as a source of identity, they had little interest in sports because they challenge the boundaries of femininity and cultural identity (Walseth, 2006). It also remains the case that the conditions in which sporting activities take place are crucial to their acceptability. In particular, more fundamentalist Muslims believe that men should not be allowed to look at women in public settings, and women must cover their bodies with robes and headscarves, even when they exercise. As a result, physical activities in many Muslim nations are sex segregated, but this tradition may be more difficult to maintain in some areas of British society, and this influences British Muslim women's opportunities to engage in sporting activities in a way which is consistent with their cultural and religious beliefs (see Kay, 2006; Wray, 2002). The connection between gender, sport and Islam is discussed further in the box 'Allah's will' (pp. 334–335).

Young Asians are more likely than their peers in past generations to see good athletes who look like them. Sometimes, there is media coverage of Asians such as Kiran Matharu in golf and Aman Dosanj in football, but these reports generally focus only on the rarity of British Asian sporting role models. Instead most of their inspiration comes from older sisters and neighbouring girls who play sports. Research on the experiences of British Asians is important because it helps us understand more fully the dynamics faced by young women caught up in the experience of immigration and making their way in a new society and culture. We know little about the experiences of these young women as they combine family life with school, sports and jobs.

The experiences and sports participation patterns of British Asians differ, depending on their immigration histories. Research must be sensitive to these differences and the ways that they influence sport participation patterns and experiences. Gender issues also are important to study across a range of sports (Wong, 1999). Applied research is needed to assist coaches with British Asian athletes.

reflect on SPORTS   *Allah's will: dilemmas for Islamic women in sports?*

Imagine winning an Olympic gold medal, receiving death threats from people in your country who brand you as an immoral and corrupt woman, and then being forced to live in exile. At the same time, imagine that you are a heroine to many young women, who see you as inspirational in their quest for equal rights and opportunities to play sports.

This was the situation faced by Hassiba Boulmerka, the gold medallist in the 1500 metres at the 1992 Olympic Games in Barcelona, Spain. As an Algerian Muslim woman, she believed that being an international athlete did not require her to abandon her faith or her commitment to Islam. But many of those who condemned Boulmerka said that although it is permissible for women to participate in sports, it was not permissible to do so in shorts or T-shirts, or while men are watching, or when men and women train together, or when facilities do not permit total privacy, or if you are married, unless your husband gives his permission (Beiruty, 2002).

To complicate matters, Boulmerka has also been rejected by some Islamic feminists, who see her as a woman co-opted and used by a sports system that is grounded in men's values and sponsored by powerful corporations that promote a soulless, worldwide consumer culture. To participate in such a system, they say, is to endorse global forces that are dangerously oppressive to all humankind.

Boulmerka supporters are primarily liberal feminists and others who want to revise the restrictive norms governing many Muslim women. They promote women's rights and the transformation of societies and communities in which women live without a voice, without public legitimacy and without power (Hargreaves, 2000). However, Boulmerka has also been embraced by those who do not know or understand Islam and reject Muslim ways of life because of their own ethnocentrism and religious beliefs.

This complicated, real-life scenario illustrates how religious beliefs often define expectations related to femininity and masculinity. These expectations then regulate bodies and, in the case of Muslim women, their bodies have become 'contested terrain'. They are at the centre of deep political, cultural and religious struggles about what is important, what is right and wrong, and how social life should be organized. These struggles have an impact on sports participation patterns in societies and between cultures, and are embodied and personified in women athletes. A few scholars in the sociology of sport have studied the influence of Islamic beliefs on the participation of Muslim women (Hargreaves, 2000; Nakamura, 2002; Pfister, 2001). On the one hand, these athletes are active subjects who assert new ideas about what it means to be a Muslim woman. On the other hand, they are passive objects that are the focus of debates about morality and social change in the world today.

The varied experiences of Muslim women in sport are illustrated by the fact that while Muslim nations in many parts of Central and Southeast Asia have no religious restrictions on girls and women playing sports, Islamic beliefs in other parts of the world legitimize patriarchal structures, and maintain definitions of male and female bodies that discourage girls and women from playing sports and restrict their everyday access to sport participation opportunities (Fatwa Bank, 2004; Good, 2002; Moore, 2004; Taheri, 2004). This is why national Olympic teams from some Muslim nations have few or no women athletes. For example, in 1992, 35 nations, half of them Muslim, sent no women to the Olympic Games in Barcelona. In 2004 only four Muslim nations had no women on their teams, but the total number of women from Muslim nations was the lowest since the 1960 Olympics (Taheri, 2004). The nations with the tightest restrictions include Iran, Afghanistan, Oman, Kuwait, Pakistan, Qatar, Saudi Arabia, the United Arab Emirates and Sudan. However, Iran regularly holds events exclusively for women, the latest being the Fourth Women Islamic Games in September 2005. But these games are not televised because the women are allowed to dress as they wish, and there is a fear that men may watch them. No men are allowed in or near the event, and armed women guards guarantee that men keep their distance.

The popularity of sports among men in Islamic countries is often tied to expressions of political and cultural nationalism rather than religious beliefs (Stokes, 1996). Similarly, when Muslims migrate from Islamic countries to the UK, or elsewhere in Europe or North America, they participate in sports, but their participation is tied more to learning about life and gaining acceptance in their new cultures than expressing Muslim beliefs through sports. Muslim girls and women in non-Islamic countries have very low sports participation rates (Nakamura, 2002; Verma and Darby, 1994), and Muslim organizations are unlikely to sponsor sports for their members. However, some people, including scholars in the sociology of sport, have organized programmes that enable Muslim women to train and play sports under conditions consistent with their modesty norms. So far, these programmes have been successful in attracting and providing participation opportunities for girls and young women (Weaver, 2005).

This leaves us with a series of currently unanswered questions. Is there social and cultural space in Islamic nations for Hassiba Boulmerka and others like her? Is it possible to merge Islamic beliefs with ideas about equal rights and sport participation among women? Can the Qur'ān (Koran) be interpreted in ways that give women the power to make choices in their lives? Can people live peacefully together as they interpret the Qur'ān in different ways?

Sociologist Jennifer Hargreaves (2000) explains that intervening in the struggles to answer these questions is a major challenge and must be undertaken with sensitivity and cultural awareness. Efforts to promote change from outside Islam are risky because they are easily linked with ethnocentric beliefs about the superiority of Western values and the need to reform cultural practices that seem strange. This means that intervention must occur through and with Muslim organizations that can make changes in their ways and on their terms. Hargreaves notes that these changes may not take the forms envisioned by Western observers, but if they free women from oppressive forms of social control, they will represent progress.

Many Muslims, including Muslim women, continue to disagree with each other about such changes. Therefore, struggles over issues of religion and gender will continue into the future. Understanding and coming to terms with 'Allah's will' is not easy and creates dilemmas for Islamic women athletes. *What do you think*?

Throughout my life, I've never worried about people's race, colour or religion. I just took people for who they are, my only concern is that they should respect each other when respect is deserved.

(Kelly Holmes, Olympic double gold medallist, 2006, p. 117)

Sports participation, ethnicity and national identity in the 'United' Kingdom

The UK is a complex, multi-layered society, consisting of the three nations of Great Britain (England, Scotland and Wales), together with Northern Ireland and islands such as the Isle of Man, Guernsey and Jersey. There are also dependent areas including a number of Caribbean islands, Gibraltar and the Falkland Islands. The UK is a member of the European Union, but remains outside the European Economic and Monetary Union (the euro).

Some sociologists have argued that the complexity of the UK is creating a crisis of national identity. This is partly because of the immigration of those from the former colonies of the

British Empire, as discussed in the previous sections, but also because of the so-called 'Celtic fringe' of Scotland, Wales and Ireland asserting their national identities, with some even calling for the dissolution of the 'United' Kingdom. An additional feature of the ethnic make-up of contemporary British society is the presence of continental Europeans, some of whom are ancestors of Romany communities and maintain travelling lifestyles, and some recent migrants who have arrived within the context of the complex relationship between the UK and the European Union (see Tuck, 2003b). Many of these developments, and the resultant challenges to national identity, are played out in sporting contexts.

For example, in some sporting competitions such as the Olympic Games, a combined team of Great Britain and Northern Ireland enters. In events such as the Commonwealth Games, each home nation (and the Isle of Man, Guernsey and Jersey) enter separate teams. In rugby union, there are separate home nation teams for most competitions, but there is a combined 'Ireland' team representing Northern Ireland and the Republic of Ireland, and quadrennially a combined British/Irish 'Lions' team competes, apparently unifying the home nations and an otherwise divided Ireland. Where there are separate home nations teams, this allows for the expression of a unique cultural and ethnic identity, with the playing of the 'home national anthems', different team strips, and fans often wearing clothing representing their home nation allegiance. In particular, sport is often used as a site for the expression of anti-English sentiments from the other home nations (Dimeo and Finn, 2001; Finn and Guilianotti, 1998). Success in specific sports enables the expression of a more local ethnocultural identity, such as golf in Scotland, and the historical importance of rugby in Wales. (See Chapter 13 for further discussion of the sports policies and priorities of the home countries.)

In sectarian Northern Ireland, the expression of national identity is particularly complex. Where sports are organized on an all-Ireland basis, different sports make different choices regarding the use of the Republican, Ulster and British flags and anthems. Sports such as football have separate national teams, but are equally popular among the Catholic and Protestant, Northern and Republican populations. In contrast, others sports are more divided along ethno-religious lines. For example, Protestants are more likely to play sports which have a British tradition, such as cricket and hockey. Meanwhile, Gaelic sports such as Gaelic football, hurling and camogie are played by the Catholic population and are seen as an expression of support for an Irish Republic. The historical structure and organization of Gaelic Games has deliberately excluded Protestant Unionists (see Chapter 3, p. 84). In this way, sports have facilitated the ethno-sectarian divisions in Northern Irish society and contributed to the maintenance of distinctive national identities (see Bairner, 2003; Cronin, 2002).

Such sectarianism has also crossed the sea into Scotland where large communities of Irish workers settled in the nineteenth century. In particular, the football club Glasgow Celtic is a traditionally Catholic club with strong Irish roots, while Glasgow Rangers maintains a connection to Protestantism. As a result, Celtic has been the focal point of anti-Irish racism largely deriving from Rangers supporters, to the extent that the club has even been blamed for introducing sectarianism into Scotland (see Dimeo and Finn, 2001). One significant feature of Gaelic ethnic groups, including those who have migrated, is that they are primarily white and so are not visible minorities, and as a result they are sometimes overlooked in discussions of racism.

Consideration of migrating communities must also take into account the extension of the European Union, which has led to increased immigration of people from continental and particularly Eastern European nations to the UK. This has had a significant impact on the multi-culturalism of the UK, even though most are also white and so are not visible minority ethnic groups. Currently, little is known about the sporting behaviour of these people. More research on the sports experiences of immigrants from the European Union is important because they constitute the fastest-growing ethnic populations in the UK. We also know little about Gypsies and Travellers, predominantly white 'mobile' communities whose ancestors would originally have arrived in the UK from Europe, or about the sporting activities which are popular in these groups, such as boxing, horse trotting and quoits. Nor, indeed, has any research been conducted into the sports behaviour and requirements of refugees and asylum seekers, who experience new forms of racism and sectarianism in British society (see Swinney and Horne, 2005). Each of these migrating groups affect, and are affected by, definitions of British national identity/ies. Physical educators, coaches and sports development officers would benefit from further research, as would people in sports management and commercial sports where there is an emphasis on attracting new customers and fans.

The Dynamics of Racial and Ethnic Relations in Sports

Racial and ethnic relations in most sports settings are better today than in the past, but many changes are needed before sports are a model of inclusion and fairness. The challenges faced today are different from those faced 20 years ago, and experience shows that when current challenges are met, a new social situation is created in which new challenges emerge. For example, once national borders are opened up to people from a variety of nations, they must learn to live, work and play with each other despite diverse experiences and cultural perspectives. Meeting this challenge requires a commitment to equal treatment, *plus* learning about the perspectives of others, understanding how they define and give meaning to the world around them, and then determining how to form and maintain relationships while respecting differences, making compromises and supporting one another in the pursuit of goals that may not always be shared. None of this is easy, and challenges are never met once and for all.

Many people think in fairy-tale terms when it comes to racial and ethnic relations: they believe that opening a door so that others may enter a social world is all that is needed to achieve racial and ethnic harmony. However, this is merely a first step in a never-ending process of nurturing relationships, producing an inclusive society and sharing power with others. Racial and ethnic diversity brings potential vitality and creativity to a team, organization or society, but this potential does not automatically become reality. It requires constant awareness, commitment and work to achieve and maintain it.

The following sections deal with three major challenges related to racial and ethnic relations in sports today: (1) eliminating racial and ethnic exclusion in sports participation, (2) dealing with and managing racial and ethnic diversity by creating an inclusive culture on sports teams and in sports organizations, and (3) integrating positions of power in sports organizations.

Eliminating racial and ethnic exclusion in sports

Why are some sports characterized by disproportionately high rates of participation by racial and ethnic minorities, whereas others have little or no racial or ethnic diversity? When

American sociologist Harry Edwards (1973) answered this question in the early 1970s, he said that certain sports had built-in characteristics that made them easier to desegregate. These remain timely and include the following.

- The people who control teams in commercial sports can maximize their profits when they employ the best players regardless of skin colour or ethnicity.
- Athletes' performances can be measured in concrete, objective terms that are not usually influenced by racial ideology.
- All players on a sports team benefit when a teammate performs well, regardless of the teammate's skin colour or ethnicity.
- When minority athletes excel on the playing field, they are not automatically promoted into leadership positions where they would have control over white players.
- Friendships and off-the-field social relationships between teammates are not required for team success.
- Ethnic minority athletes are controlled by coaches, managers, administrators and owners who are almost always white.

These six characteristics limit the threats that cause whites in non-sports situations and organizations to fear and resist racial and ethnic desegregation in non-sports situations and organizations. Therefore, when the people who controlled professional teams realized that they could benefit financially from recruiting ethnic minority players without giving up power and control, and without disrupting the existing structure and relationships in their sports, they began to do so.

Desegregation occurs more slowly in sports that lack the characteristics listed above. Golf, tennis, swimming and other sports played in private clubs where social interaction is personal and often involves male–female relationships have been slow to welcome racial and ethnic diversity. As social contacts become increasingly close, people are more likely to enforce various forms of exclusion. This is why informal practices of racial and ethnic exclusion still remain in many private sports clubs and why it remains difficult to name more than a few black women and men playing on the major professional golf and tennis tours. This is also part of the reason why Lewis Hamilton has already received so much publicity during his relatively short career. Motor-racing sports in the UK are composed almost exclusively of whites, and many of them want to show that there is no racism in the sports. However, even in 2008, Formula One and other motor-racing events have very few black participants.

The most significant forms of racial and ethnic exclusion in sports today occur at the community level where they are hidden behind the fees and other resources required for sports participation. People can claim to have open sports programmes when in reality their location, fees and the lack of accessible transportation preclude ethnically inclusive participation. Eliminating forms of exclusion related to socio-economic status that also overlap with race and ethnicity is one of the most difficult challenges of this century. This is one of the points made in 'Breaking barriers', opposite.

Diversity does not breed interaction.

(Tim Layden, journalist, Sports Illustrated, *2001)*

breaking BARRIERS
Point-of-entry barriers: *we are out there*

American swimmer Toni Davis was training for the 2004 Paralympics in Athens. She had heard about Martiza Correia, a new member of the Athens-bound US Olympic swimming team. Correia had broken US swimming records held by the highly touted Amy Van Dyken and Jenny Thompson in the 50- and 100-metre freestyle. When Davis looked online for information about the new record-setting swimmer, she discovered that Correia was an African-American like her. Davis was heartened and declared proudly, *'We are out there.'*

When Davis referred to 'we', she meant *black swimmers*. She knew that a black person on a swimming team caused many people to do a double take. She also knew that when people saw her – a black swimmer with only one arm – they often did a triple take.

Davis says that she gets more looks for having one arm than for being black, but she knows that race influences choices and opportunities in sports. 'I'm not afraid to speak out and get black swimmers more attention, more participation', she says, but 'I also want to get more notice for the Paralympics' because many people do not know it exists. 'What we need to do for minority kids', Davis explains, is to have low-cost programmes that enable them to be in the water, and receive the instruction they need to develop their abilities (Schaller, 2005).

Davis knows that sports participation always has a point of entry – a time and place at which a person is hooked up with an opportunity. In the case of people with a disability, the point of entry is often made available through rehabilitation, occupational therapy and medical care programmes, or through a local network of friends and family.

Taking advantage of an entry opportunity is never automatic. People from ethnic minority backgrounds are most likely to enter a programme when they see others who will understand them and with whom they can identify. If everyone in a programme, including administrators and coaches, is white, they will think twice before taking a first step towards participation. 'Fitting in' is always an issue when initiating or continuing participation.

Point-of-entry opportunities have complex dynamics related to race, ethnicity, healthcare, trusting medical providers, transportation, and the 'look and feel' of disability sport programmes. If ethnic inclusiveness is not apparent, black and minority ethnic people may back off to avoid being labelled as 'different'. Playing sports is fun, but it becomes tedious when people constantly do triple takes when they see you.

Eliminating point-of-entry barriers related to race and ethnicity is a major challenge in sports for people with disabilities. As in most sports organizations, there is a need to recruit coaches and administrators from under-represented ethnic minorities. Inclusiveness must be apparent so that prospective participants can see people who look like them. Additionally, there is a need to create new entry points that are part of the structure of everyday life in neighbourhoods and communities where ethnic minorities live and work. Churches, schools, hospitals, medical clinics and veterans' organizations are sites at which institutionalized entry points can be created. Once they exist, more people from ethnic minority backgrounds will join Toni Davis in declaring proudly, 'We are out there.'

Dealing with and managing racial and ethnic diversity in sports

As sports become more global, as teams recruit players worldwide and as global migration creates pressures to develop racially and ethnically sensitive policies related to all aspects of sports, there will be many new racial and ethnic challenges faced by players, coaches, team administrators and, even, spectators. It is naive to think that the racial and ethnic issues that exist around the world today have no impact on sports or that sports can effectively eliminate these issues once and for all time. A brief look at sports and racial issues in football in the UK illustrates this point.

History shows that, since Arthur Wharton and Andrew Watson became the first black footballers to play in England and Scotland respectively at the end of the nineteenth century, there were many new challenges faced by the football leagues, players throughout the leagues and spectators attending games. The number of black players in professional British football steadily increased following the period of significant immigration after the Second World War and, in particular, during the 1970s and 1980s when those born in Britain reached an age where they could play professionally.

Many of these early players had to endure unspeakable racism by opponents, spectators and racists in the general population. As the number of black players on teams increased, so did the level of racism among supporters. This was often enabled by far right-wing groups such as the National Front and the British National Party, who used football terraces to recruit and disseminate their views. When John Barnes became the first high-profile black player signed to Liverpool FC, the team was labelled 'Niggerpool' by local rival club Everton, a club whose fans also proudly chanted 'Everton are white' (a reference to the lack of black players on their own team). Many players experienced chants of animal noises, peanuts and bananas being thrown onto the pitch, booing and racial taunts (Back et al., 2001; Jones, 2002). Even the former England manager Ron Atkinson, who famously signed three black players to West Bromwich Albion in the 1970s and was popularly regarded as a champion of black players, had to resign from his job as a football commentator in 2004 when a post-match conversation was mistakenly recorded and broadcast, during which he stated of Marcel Desailly, a black French player on the Chelsea team: 'He's what is known in some schools as a f...... lazy thick nigger.'

Black players have often felt disadvantaged in team politics because all the coaches, managers, trainers and owners were white. The positions that blacks and whites played have traditionally fitted patterns tied to racial ideologies: blacks played peripheral wing positions, requiring speed and quick reactions, whereas whites played the positions believed to require intelligence and decision-making skills. These position placements, or 'stacking' patterns, prevented most blacks from playing the positions that led players to be identified as good candidates for coaching jobs after they retired (see Guilianotti, 1999; Maguire, 1991; Norris and Jones, 1998). The lack of black managers and coaches remains an issue in football today (see Back et al., 2001; Jones, 2002). There are also very few Asian players in the professional game, despite its popularity among the Asian community at the amateur and recreational level. An additional trend is the number of anti-Semitic incidents, primarily in London clubs where there are large Jewish communities, and which increased at Chelsea Football Club following the brief appointment of Avram Grant, an Israeli Jew, to manager in 2007.

This example of one professional sport illustrates that racial and ethnic issues are never settled permanently. Challenges met today create new challenges tomorrow. Football coaches now often have players from several national and cultural backgrounds, some teams have played an entirely non-British side and increasing numbers of coaches are also not British. These players and coaches sometimes hold negative racial and ethnic stereotypes at the same time as they have customs that other players and staff may define as strange. Translators are used on teams, cultural diversity training is needed, coaches must learn new ways to communicate effectively, and the marketing departments for teams must learn how to promote an ethnically diverse team to predominantly white fans. Ethnic and cultural issues enter into sponsorship considerations and the products sold at games. Cultural and ethnic awareness is now an important qualification for employees who handle team advertising and sponsorship deals.

This is not only the case at club level. National teams in the UK, and elsewhere in Western Europe, also increasingly face the challenge of coping with new racial and ethnic tensions created by high rates of migration from Africa and Eastern Europe. These challenges are related to matters of national identity, labour migration and citizenship status. Populist leaders in some nations do not want their national teams to include players whose ancestors may have come from another country, and some fans use players with African or South Asian backgrounds as scapegoats for social and economic problems in their lives. In turn, many of these players will not challenge any racism that they experience, in order to avoid being seen as a troublemaker or a black person with a 'chip on their shoulder', and so be accepted into clubs and the playing culture of some British sports (see King, 2004). For example, in cricket, few black players have challenged the common practice of 'sledging' – the term given to describe a range of tactics used to deliberately distract an opponent and undermine their game – even when this takes the form of overtly racist comments and behaviour (Carrington and McDonald, 2001).

Many people are aware of these issues although there have been few public discussions about them. Race is not something that people in the UK feel comfortable talking about in public settings, even though they do talk about it in private, often among friends from the same racial or ethnic background. Research shows that avoiding discussions of race and ethnicity is not due to personal prejudices or underlying racism as much as it is due to a civic etiquette that discourages public discussions of these issues (Eliasoph, 1999). This etiquette keeps racial and ethnic issues 'off the table' and prevents people from discussing them thoughtfully and publicly – even in many university lecture theatres. Initiatives in football such as the 'Kick Racism Out of Football' and 'Football Against Racism in Europe' (FARE) racial awareness campaigns, along with the selling of interlocking black and white wristbands with 'Stand Up Speak Out' stamped on them, have raised public consciousness of some of these issues. However, challenges related to managing racial and ethnic relations in sports are here to stay, although they will change over time.

Integrating positions of power in sports organizations

Despite progressive changes in many sports, positions of power and control are held primarily by white men. There are exceptions to this pattern, but they do not eliminate pervasive and persistent racial and ethnic inequalities related to power and control in sports. Data on who holds positions of power change every year, and it is difficult to obtain consistent information from sports teams and organizations.

The BME Sports Network East (2005) published a survey of research into the involvement of black and minority ethnic people in sports in this region of the UK. The findings suggest that almost all physical education teachers, leisure centre managers and local authority sports officials are white. Similarly, very few black and minority ethnic people are involved in the organization and governance of sport through national governing bodies at national and county level.

The Football Association is probably the most advanced in reviewing its inclusion of black and minority ethnic members across all levels of involvement. In men's football, the year 1993 saw the launch of the 'Kick it Out' campaign, the first black captain of England in Paul Ince, and the first black managers of league clubs. However, the recruitment procedures adopted in football generally appear to effectively close senior administrative positions to those outside the club, including members of minority ethnic communities (Bradbury, 2001). For example, approximately one-third of clubs said that they used existing personal contacts to recruit senior administrative staff, which effectively discriminates against applicants from minority ethnic backgrounds and also against women, ensuring the ongoing dominance of white males in senior posts. A survey of black and minority ethnic players by the Professional Footballers' Association found that one-third felt that the lack of black coaches in the game was due to institutional racism (PFA, 2003). It is, therefore, not surprising that there was no black English manager in the Premiership/Premier League until Paul Ince's brief appointment to Blackburn Rovers in 2008, no black members of the ruling council of the Football Association and very few black referees.

Similarly, research into women's sport conducted by the Women's Sport Foundation (2007c) found that only 5 per cent of female coaches surveyed were from black and minority ethnic groups. Encouragingly, however, the current coach of the England women's football team, Hope Powell, is black.

 There is no place for racism in football or modern society.

(Richard Caborn, former Sports Minister, 2004)

Prospects for change

People do not give up racial and ethnic beliefs easily, especially when they come in the form of well-established ideologies rooted deeply in their cultures. Those who benefit from dominant racial ideology often resist changes in the relationships and social structures that reproduce it. This is why certain racial and ethnic inequities have remained a part of sports.

Sports may bring people together, but they do not automatically lead them to adopt tolerant attitudes or change long-standing mechanisms of social exclusion. For example, white team owners and managers in the UK worked with black athletes for many years before they ever hired black coaches or administrators. It often requires social and legal pressures to force people in power positions to act more affirmatively in their recruitment practices. In the meantime, blacks and other ethnic minorities remain under-represented in coaching and administration.

Although there is resistance to certain types of changes in sports, many sports organizations are more progressive than other organizations when it comes to many aspects of racial and ethnic relations. However, good things do not happen automatically or as often as many think; nor do changes in people's attitudes automatically translate into changes in the overall organization of sports. Challenging the negative beliefs and attitudes of individuals is one thing; changing the relationships and social structures that have been built on those beliefs and attitudes is another. Both changes are needed, but neither occurs automatically just because sports bring people together in the same changing rooms and stadiums.

Racial and ethnic relations will improve in sports only when those who have power work to bring people together in ways that confront and challenge racial and ethnic issues. This means that changes must be initiated and supported by whites as well as members of ethnic minorities, or else they will fail (Oglesby and Schrader, 2000). It has never been easy for people to deal with racial and ethnic issues, but if it can be done in sports, it would attract public attention and possibly inspire changes in other spheres of life.

Change also requires a new vocabulary to deal with racial and ethnic diversity in social life and promote inclusive practices and policies. A vocabulary organized around the belief that skin colour or ethnicity signifies a unique biological essence only perpetuates racial and ethnic discrimination. In connection with sports, there is a need for research to go beyond documenting racial and ethnic performance differences and explain how social and cultural factors, including racial ideologies, create and perpetuate differences. Simply documenting differences without explaining them too often reproduces the very racial ideologies that have caused hatred, turmoil and confusion in much of the world for nearly 300 years. This is why many scholars in the sociology of sport now ask research questions about the meanings that people give to physical and cultural characteristics, and how those meanings influence actions, relationships and social organization.

The racial and ethnic diversity and equality policies of recent years have produced some changes, but promoting positive changes in intergroup relations today requires owners, managers and coaches to create more inclusive cultures and power structures in sports organizations. This means that equality policies and practices should go beyond athletes and referees, to include everyone from team owners to the people in middle management, coaching, marketing and public information. There also needs to be consistency across different regions and sports to clearly reinforce the messages.

For example, in 2002 the Scottish Executive launched the 'One Scotland – Many Cultures' campaign against racism, in no small part to encourage foreign workers to move to Scotland, and to address the racism and sectarianism experienced by refugees, asylum seekers and migrants from the European Union. Specific policies for sport include the Social Inclusion Partnerships (SIP) and 'Sport 21', which is the sportscotland social inclusion agenda. However, the success of these policies has been limited by a need for more 'joined-up thinking'. First, approaches to racial equality are not consistent across local authorities; second, limited research has been carried out to discover the needs of black and minority ethnic populations; and, third, many regions adopt a 'no problem here' approach because of the small number of black and minority ethnic people in some areas of Scotland (see Dimeo and Finn, 2001; Swinney and Horne, 2005).

Even people who are sensitive to diversity issues require opportunities to learn new things about the perspectives of those whose experiences and cultures are different from our own. This means that for policies and training sessions to be effective, they should be organized, in part, around the perspectives of racial and ethnic minorities. An attempt to expose people to the views of another ethnic group has been attempted in Northern Ireland, where the Sports Council launched the 'Sport Without Prejudice' campaign in 1998 to address sectarianism within sport, and Youth Sport Omagh which developed a sports complex to be used by young people from both sides of the community (Northern Ireland Assembly, 2001). These kinds of strategies are essential if positive changes are to occur. When making things better means doing them to fit the interests of those currently in power, real change is unlikely.

Summary: Are Race, Ethnicity and National Identity Important in Sports?

Racial, ethnic and national identity issues exist in sports, just as they exist in most other spheres of social life. As people watch, play and talk about sports, they often take into account ideas about skin colour and ethnicity. The meanings given to skin colour and ethnic background influence access to sports participation and the decisions that people make about sports in their lives. *Race* refers to a category of people identified through a classification system based on meanings given to physical traits among humans; *ethnicity* refers to collections of people identified in terms of their shared cultural heritage. Racial and ethnic *minorities* are populations that have endured systematic forms of discrimination in a society, and whose presence creates challenges to traditional notions of *national identity*.

The idea of race has a complex history, and it serves as the foundation for racial ideology, which people use to identify and make sense of 'racial' characteristics and differences. Racial ideology, like other social constructions, changes over time as ideas and relationships change. However, over the past century in the UK, dominant racial ideology has supported the notion that there are important biological and cognitive differences between people classified as 'black' as opposed to 'white,' and that these differences explain the success of blacks in certain sports and sports positions.

Racial ideology influences the ways that many people connect skin colour with athletic performance. At the same time, it influences sports participation decisions, achievement patterns in sports and explanations of sports performances.

Sports participation patterns among black and Asian Britons, and among the different home countries and migrating continental Europeans, each have unique histories. Combinations of historical, cultural and social factors have influenced those histories. However, sports participation in ethnic minority populations usually occurs under terms set by the dominant ethnic population in a community or society. Minority populations are seldom able to use sports to challenge the power and privilege of the dominant group, or the dominant view of national identity, even though particular individuals may experience great personal success in sports.

The fact that some sports have histories of racially and ethnically mixed participation does not mean that problems have been eliminated. Harmonious racial and ethnic relations never occur automatically, and ethnic harmony is never established once and for all. As current problems are solved, new relationships and new challenges are created. This means that racial and ethnic issues require regular attention if challenges are to be anticipated accurately and dealt with successfully. Success also depends on whether members of the dominant ethnic

The Irish Football Association began in 2000 to use football as a site for eradicating the Protestant versus Catholic sectarianism that has led to decades of violence and terrorism in Northern Ireland. Aaron Hughes, captain of Northern Ireland's National Football Team, and his teammates work with young people to promote equality and diversity. The team motto is 'Sectarianism and racism in Northern Ireland Football is not welcome and will not be tolerated' (*Source*: Mike Collins, Irish Football Association, Northern Ireland)

population see value in racial and ethnic diversity, and commit themselves to dealing with diversity issues alongside those who have different ethnic backgrounds.

Sports continue to be sites for racial and ethnic problems, which are often expressed through narrow definitions and displays of national identity. However, it is important to acknowledge that, despite problems, sports can also be sites for challenging racial ideology and transforming ethnic relations. This happens only when people in sports plan strategies to encourage critical awareness of ethnic prejudices, racist ideas and forms of discrimination built into the cultures and structures of sports organizations. This awareness is required to increase ethnic inclusion in sports, deal with and manage ethnic diversity, and integrate ethnic minorities into the power structures of sports organizations. Without this awareness, ethnic relations often become volatile and lead to overt forms of hostility.

Website resources

Note: Websites often change. The following URLs were current when this book was printed. Please check our website (***www.mcgraw-hill.co.uk/textbooks/coakley***) for updates and additions.

www.mcgraw-hill.co.uk/textbooks/coakley Click on Chapter 9 for additional materials related to race, ethnicity and national identity.

www.britsoc.co.uk/equality/ The website of the British Sociological Association, which offers guidelines for appropriate language when discussing issues of 'race' and ethnicity.

www.equalityhumanrights.com This is the website for the Equality and Human Rights Commission, which was formed in 2007 from the merger of three previous commissions including the Commission for Racial Equality, Disability Rights and Equal Opportunities. It contains resources and advice for addressing discrimination and promoting equity, including in sport.

www.farenet.org/ Football Against Racism in Europe.

www.home.earthlink.net/~prometheus_6/RaceReadings.htm This site contains a series of short essays dealing with race; the essays are authored by people from many academic disciplines. They are very helpful for anyone wishing to understand race as a concept and as lived experience.

www.kickitout.org The website of the Let's Kick Racism Out of Football campaign.

www.le.ac.uk/fo/resources/factsheets/index.html A series of factsheets by the Sir Norman Chester Centre for Football Research at the University of Leicester, including several on black players and racism in football.

www.menter.org.uk/html/sports.html A regional network for black and minority ethnic groups, with links to information about sports projects and funding.

www.pbs.org/race/000_General/ 000_00-Home.htm The site for the three-part series, *Race – The Power of An Illusion*, first shown in 2004; the site contains information for students and instructors; each part of the series is summarized in links provided through this site. Also there are many resources links for those wishing to explore the topic of race in more detail.

www.sportengland.org/ethnic_survey.pdf The link to the national survey of sports participation rates by ethnic group in England.

www.sportingequals.org.uk Sporting Equals is a national initiative supported by Sport England which has a mission to eradicate racial inequalities in sport. Provides links to key policy and resource documents, and several factsheets.

www.sportscoachuk.org/About+Us/Policies/Racial+Equity+Policy.htm Information on sportscoach UK's race equity policy, workshops and research.

Chapter 10

Social class: do money and power matter in sports?

(*Source*: Elizabeth Pike)

 Participation rates have remained stubbornly static and inequities in participation between different social groups have continued largely unchanged over the last 30 years or so.

(*Nick Rowe, Head of Research, Sport England, 2004, p. 2*)

Learning Centre Resources

Visit *Sports in Society*'s Online Learning Centre (OLC) at **www.mcgraw-hill.co.uk/ textbooks/coakley** for additional information and study material for this chapter, including:

- Self-grading quizzes and essay questions
- Learning outcomes
- Related websites
- Additional readings

Chapter contents

Social class and class relations
Sports and economic inequality
Social class and sports participation patterns
Global inequalities and sports
Economic and career opportunities in sports
Sports participation and occupational careers among former athletes
Summary: do money and power matter in sports?

> The decline in PE curriculum time … will affect children from less well off backgrounds the most … who will be least likely to be able to take up the opportunities offered by extra-curricular and club sport.
>
> *(Sport England, 2001, p. 1)*

> [Sport] serves to reproduce social and economic distinctions and preserve the power and influence of those who control resources in society.
>
> *(Alan Tomlinson, sociologist, University of Brighton, 2007, p. 4695)*

People like to think that sports transcend issues of money, power and economic inequalities. They see sports as open to everyone, watch them on 'free' television, and define success on the playing field in terms of individual ability and hard work. However, all organized sports depend on material resources, and those resources must come from somewhere. Therefore, playing, watching and excelling in sports depend on resources supplied by individuals, families, governments or corporations.

More than ever before, it takes money to play sports and develop sport skills. Tickets are expensive and spectators often are divided by social class in the stadium: the wealthy and well connected sit in club seats and luxury suites, whereas fans who are less well-off sit in other sections, depending on their ability to pay for premium tickets or buy season tickets. Today it takes money to watch sports on television now that satellite and cable connections come with ever-increasing subscriber fees, and pay-per-view costs skyrocket. This means that sports and sports participation are closely connected with the distribution of economic resources in society.

Many people also believe that sports are a new path to economic success for people from all social classes. Rags-to-riches stories are common when people talk about athletes. However, these beliefs and stories distract attention from the ways in which sports reflect and perpetuate existing economic inequalities.

This chapter deals with matters of money and wealth, as well as larger sociological issues related to social class and socio-economic mobility. Our discussion focuses on the following questions:

- What is meant by *social class* and *class relations*?
- How do social class and class relations influence sports and sport participation?
- Are sports open and democratic in the provision of economic and career opportunities?
- Does playing sports contribute to occupational success and social mobility among former athletes?

Social Class and Class Relations

Understanding social class and the related concepts of social stratification, socio-economic status and life chances is important when studying social worlds. Economic resources are related to power in society, and economic inequalities influence many aspects of people's lives.

Social class refers to *categories of people who share a position in society based on a combination of their income (earnings), wealth (savings and possessions), education, occupation and social connections.* People in a particular social class also share similar **life chances**, that is, *similar odds for achieving economic success, status and power in society.* Social classes exist in all industrial societies because life chances are not equally distributed across all populations.

Social stratification refers to *structured forms of inequalities that are part of the organization of everyday social life.* In other words, in comparison with people from higher social classes, people from lower social classes have fewer opportunities to achieve economic success and power. Children born into wealthy, powerful and well-connected families are in better positions to become wealthy, powerful and well-connected adults than are children born into poor families that lack influence and social networks connecting them with educational and career opportunities.

Most of us are aware of economic inequalities in society. We see them all around us and on television in programmes like *Posh Swap* and *The Secret Millionaire* (in which people try to 'pass' in different social class settings). We know they exist and influence people's lives, but there are few public discussions about the influence that social class has on our views of ourselves and others, our social relationships and our everyday lives (Perrucci and Wysong, 2003). In other words, we do not discuss **class relations**, that is, the many *ways that social class is incorporated* *into* our *everyday lives.* We often hear about the importance of equal opportunities in society, but there are few discussions about the ways that people in upper socio-economic classes use their income, wealth, status and power to maintain their privileged positions in society and pass that privilege from one generation to the next. Instead, we hear 'rags-to-riches' stories about individuals who overcame a lower-class background to become wealthy and stories about 'millionaires next door' and chief executive officers (CEOs) who are 'regular guys' who happen to make £10 million a year. Ignored in the media and popular discourse are the oppressive effects of poverty and the limited opportunities available to those who lack economic resources, access to good education and well-placed social connections. Those stories are too depressing to put in the news, claim executives for the commercial media – people do not like to hear about them and they lower the audience ratings. However, social-class differences are real; they have real consequences for life chances, they affect nearly every facet of people's lives, and all this is clearly documented by valid and reliable data (Perrucci and Wysong, 2003; Sernau, 2005).

People in many post-industrial societies often shy away from critical discussions of social class and class relations because they are uneasy about acknowledging that equality and equality of opportunity is largely a myth in their society. This is especially true in regard to sports and sports participation – a sphere of life in which most people would like to believe that money and class-based privilege does not matter.

The discussion of social class and class relations in this chapter is grounded in critical theories. The focus is on economic inequality, the processes through which it is reproduced, how it benefits wealthy and powerful people, and how it affects sports and the lives of people associated with sports.

 We are already in a situation where we are expecting children to play games they cannot afford to watch.

(Harry Edwards, sociologist/social activist, 2000, p. 29)

Sports and Economic Inequality

Money and economic power exert significant influence on the goals, purpose and organization of sports in society (Bairner, 2007; Gruneau, 1999; Sugden and Tomlinson, 2000; Tomlinson, 2007). Many people believe that sports and sports participation are open to all people and that inequalities related to money, position and influence have no influence on the organized games we play and watch. However, formally organized sports could not be developed, scheduled or maintained without economic resources. Those who control money and economic power use them to organize and sponsor sports. As they do so, they give preference to sports forms that reflect and maintain their values and interests.

The wealthy aristocrats who developed the Olympic Movement and sponsored the modern Olympic Games even used their power to establish a definition of *amateur* that favoured athletes from wealthy backgrounds. This definition, which excluded athletes who used their sports skills to earn a living has been revised over the years so that participants can include those who are not independently wealthy. However, money and economic power now operate in different ways as elite-level training has become increasingly privatized and costly in many countries.

Additionally, powerful corporations use the Olympics to expand profits by linking their logos and products to particular athletes and global sports images that serve their interests.

Elite and powerful people have considerable influence over what 'counts as sport' and how sports are organized and played in mainstream social worlds. Even when grass-roots games and physical activities become formally organized as sports, they are not widely sponsored or promoted unless they can be used to reaffirm the interests and ideologies of sponsors with resources. The informal games played by people of all ages often depend on the availability of facilities, equipment and safe play spaces. These are more plentiful in the everyday lives of people from upper- and upper-middle-income families and neighbourhoods. Low-income families and neighbourhoods often lack the resources and well-maintained public spaces needed to initiate and sustain informal activities; they do not have large lawns at their homes, cul-de-sacs without traffic or well-maintained parks where they can play. This is why it is important that we understand the dynamics of class relations when we study sports and patterns of sports participation. The ways in which social divisions have been maintained in sports in the UK throughout history are summarized in Table 10.1.

The dynamics of class relations

To understand the dynamics of class relations is to think about the way that age relations operate in sports. For example, even though young people are capable of creating and playing games on their own, adults intervene and create organized schemes. These schemes emphasize the things that adults think are best for their children. As noted in Chapter 5, adults have the *resources* to develop, schedule and maintain organized youth schemes that reflect their ideas of what children should be doing and learning. Children often enjoy these adult-controlled sports, but their participation occurs in a context that is determined by adults and organized to legitimize and reproduce adult control over the lives of children.

Age relations are especially apparent in youth sports when participants do not meet adult expectations or when they violate the rules developed by adults. The adults use their power to define deviance, identify when it occurs, and demand that children comply with rules and expectations. Overall, the adults use their superior resources to convince young people that 'the adults' way' is 'the right way' to play sports. When young people comply with adults' rules and meet the adults' expectations, they are rewarded and told that they have 'character'. This is why many adults are fond of elite coaches who are autocratic and controlling. These coaches reaffirm the beliefs that it is normal and necessary for adults to control young people and that young people must learn to accept that control. In this way, sports reproduce a hierarchical form of age relations with adult power and privilege defined as normal and necessary aspects of social worlds.

Class relations work in similar ways. People with resources sponsor sports that support their ideas about 'good character', individual responsibility, competition, achievement and proper social organization. In fact, whenever people obtain power in a social world they define 'character' in a way that promotes their interests. For example, if wealthy and powerful people play sports in exclusive clubs, it is important that everyone believes that this is the way that society and sports should be organized and that wealthy and powerful people deserve their privilege to play sports as they do. Similarly, they sponsor sports that can be presented in ways

Table 10.1 **Sports development by social status**

Era	High social status	Social division maintained by	Low social status
Thirteenth century to eighteenth century	Master, lord, landowner, aristocrat, gentry	Royal proclamation, civil law, by-laws, game laws, commercial pressure	Man, peasant, tenant, servant, employee
Early nineteenth century	Gentleman Leisure used as badge of social superiority Pure amateur (no money)	Taking over and gentrifying sport, including working men in subservient positions	Working men Leisure used as a rest from work Quasi-amateur (money in prizes and expenses)
Mid-nineteenth century	New gentlemen in public schools and suburban recreation	Withdrawal into recreation and away from 'open' competition	Pseudo-professional (broken-time payments)
Late nineteenth century	Establishment of gentlemanly amateur governing bodies Clubs for gentlemen amateurs only	Redefining 'amateur' and enforcing exclusion through 'blackballing' and high cost	Establishment of alternative governing bodies and clubs for tradesmen, amateurs (prizes only) and professionals (wages)
Twentieth century (up to Second World War)	Upper/middle class	Social divisions remain but governing bodies encouraged co-operation due to international competition	Working class
Twentieth century (post-Second World War)	Socio-economic groups A, B and C	The Sports Council (1965) imposes a 'sport for all' policy	Socio-economic groups D and E
Early twenty-first century	NS-SEC[1] categories I, II and IIIN	Sports Equity Index and Active People Survey monitor social exclusion and provide basis of new policies	NS-SEC[1] categories IIM, IV and V

Note:

[1] NS-SEC is the National Statistics Socio-Economic Classification system introduced in 2000 to replace the old classifications of Social Class (based on occupation) and Socio-Economic Group (based on social and economic status) (for an explanation of the categories, see www.statistics.gov.uk).

Source: adapted from Wigglesworth, 2007, p. 93

that reaffirm the existing class structure in society and the ideology that supports it. This is partly why popular spectator sports worldwide today emphasize the neo-liberal values of competition and individualism, and reward highly specialized skills, the use of technology and dominance over opponents. When these values and cultural practices are widely accepted, average people are more likely to believe that the status and privilege of the wealthy and powerful are legitimate and deserved. Sports that emphasize partnership, sharing, open participation, nurturance and mutual support are seldom sponsored because sponsors do not want to promote values that reaffirm equality and horizontal forms of social organization in society.

Class ideology in the UK

Sociologists define **class ideology** as a *web of ideas and beliefs that people use to understand economic inequalities, identify their class position and evaluate the impact of economic inequalities on the organization of social worlds*. Dominant class ideology in the UK has long been organized around a social hierarchy, grounded in a legacy of birthright and land ownership, and manifested in sports arenas through amateur codes. More recently, this has combined with an ideal that the UK is becoming a meritocracy.

The **amateur/professional** dichotomy in sports was used historically as a means of social class distinction. Its definition has been complex and varied between different sports. For example, in rowing the notion of an amateur was to exclude those who rowed for a living from competition with gentlemen who rowed only for sport. Other sports variously defined as

Since 2003 the annual Homeless World Cup has been held in different cities where national teams comprising homeless people, mostly men, compete during a three-day tournament. This event was initiated by two editors of newspapers that serve homeless people. Their readers sometimes played informal soccer games, so they recruited sponsors and have organized the event each year. In 2007, teams from 48 countries were funded to play in Copenhagen, Denmark. In addition to being a sport event, the tournament is a site for sustaining political strategies advocating the rights of homeless people worldwide (*Source*: Jay Coakley)

professional anyone who worked for a wage from the 'gentleman amateur', in order to segregate the social classes and dignify upper-class athletes. The 'great schism' between the two codes of rugby – league and union – was largely based in a north/south, professional/amateur divide, and the ethos of the two sports traditionally reflected class differences. This is discussed in more detail in Chapters 3 and 11.

A **meritocracy** *is a form of social organization in which rewards and positions of leadership and power go to people who deserve them due to their abilities and qualifications.* Believing that the UK is a meritocracy legitimizes the economic inequalities that are inevitably created in a capitalist economy. It helps people explain and justify economic inequalities, and it supports the assumption that success is rightfully earned and failure is caused by poor choices and a lack of ambition.

Sustaining widespread beliefs that the UK is a meritocracy requires that people also believe that individual ability, qualifications and character are objectively proven through competitive success, that humans are naturally competitive and that competition is the only fair way to allocate rewards in a society. This is why people with money and power like to use sports as a metaphor for life – it identifies winners like them as deserving individuals who have outperformed others in a natural process of individual competition and achievement that has taken them to the top of the class structure. Additionally, it promotes the belief that the economy, like sports, is organized so that only the best, brightest and hardest workers make it to the top, and that those at the top deserve what they receive.

Figure 10.1 shows that class ideology in the UK today increasingly consists of a web of ideas and beliefs grounded in the legacy of the amateur/professional dichotomy and the emerging belief that the UK is a meritocracy. It explains inequality as a result of people receiving what they deserve and that success is achieved only when people develop abilities and work hard. As a consequence, it justifies inequality as a natural result of competition in a society where merit counts.

One of the outcomes of such an ideology is that competitive success comes to be linked with moral worth. People assume that 'you get what you deserve, and you deserve what you get'. This belief, of course, works to the advantage of people with wealth, because it implies that they deserve what they have and that inequality is a natural outcome of competitive processes. A related belief is that as long as competition is free and unregulated as in 'free-market' terms, only the best will succeed and only the lazy and unqualified will fail.

Promoting this ideology is difficult when it conflicts with the real experiences of many who work hard and have not achieved success or have failed due to factors beyond their control. Therefore, people in the upper classes are most likely to retain their position and status if they can create widespread agreement that competition is a 'natural' and fair way to allocate rewards and that the winners in competitive processes deserve the rewards they receive – even when they are excessive. This, of course, is how sports come to be connected with class relations in society. Sports offer 'proof' that inequalities are based on merit, that competition identifies winners, and that losers should work harder or change themselves if they want to be winners, or simply get up and try again. Most important, sports provide a metaphor for society that portrays social class as a characteristic of individuals rather than an economic structure that is linked with cultural beliefs and practices.

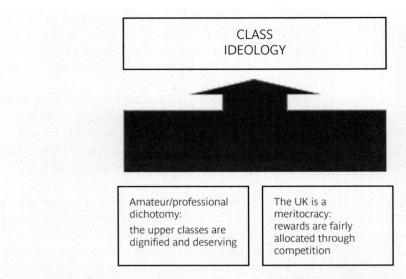

Figure 10.1 **Major beliefs that inform and support class ideology in the United Kingdom**

Alan Tomlinson, a British sociologist who has studied power and social class for decades, has noted that sport, as it is sponsored and played today, 'ultimately serves to reproduce social and economic distinctions and preserve the power and influence of those who control resources in society'. As a result, he says, sports today 'cannot be fully understood unless this key influence and core dynamic is fully recognized' (2007, p. 4695).

The reality of most British sports practices is that they are probably far from meritocratic and are designed to maintain social distinctions rather than reward those with sporting ability. Those in elite groups continue to be able to control resources, maintain power over the organization of sports, and ensure that some sporting spaces are inaccessible to others. This is illustrated in the case of private golf clubs in Scotland, whose membership is often protected by the privileged members of committees in order to ensure that the clubs and courses maintain their social exclusivity (see Jarvie, 2006; Jarvie and Burnett, 2000; Maguire et al., 2002). This is discussed further in the next section.

Class relations and who has power in sports

Sport decisions are made at many levels, from sport in the community schemes to the International Olympic Committee. Although scholars who study sports in society identify those who exercise power in various settings, they usually do not develop lists that rank powerful people in sports. But such lists do exist. For example, the *Sporting News*, a national weekly newspaper in the USA, publishes an annual list of 'the most powerful people in sports'.

The list includes four 'emperors', so identified because they have vast power over sports around the world. All these emperors are white men, demonstrating that gender and racial ideology also influence who has power in sports – when it comes to power in sports, it is a white man's world. We can understand more about the dynamics of power in sports by taking

The belief that wealth and power are achieved through competitive success infers that being wealthy and powerful is proof of one's abilities, qualifications and overall moral worth. Exclusive sports clubs reaffirm this belief and the class privilege enjoyed by powerful and wealthy people – and they are sites for establishing useful relationships in addition to being opulent places to play sports (*Source*: Jay Coakley)

a closer look at one of the four white men identified as 'emperors' by the *Sporting News*: Rupert Murdoch.

Rupert Murdoch is chairman of DirecTV, and chairman and CEO of News Corporation. As a major owner of these companies, he is the most powerful media person in the world. His ownership includes BSkyB and SkySports in the UK, companies that arguably transformed the spectator sports market (discussed further in Chapter 12). In addition, Murdoch owns US companies Fox Network, DirecTV (the largest US satellite television provider), Fox News Channel, Fox Sports Net, Fox Soccer Channel, Fox Sports en Español, Fox Sports en Latinoamérica, and cable, broadcast, Internet and satellite systems and channels (such as the National Geographic Channel) across Asia, Europe, Latin America and Australia. Murdoch's companies decide what football games will be seen by billions of people in more than 160 nations. News Corporation also owns hundreds of major newspapers, and controls sports teams and leagues around the world, including the *Sun* and *The Times* and the rights to transmit Premier League Football in the UK. Murdoch's decisions influence the sports that become popular and the sports that do not receive media coverage and come to be defined as 'second class'. His companies make things happen and prevent things from happening in sports. On any given day, Murdoch can deliver a message or programming to over 70 per cent of the world's population. No other person on Earth can make such a claim.

Murdoch, and others like him who control economic resources around the world, make decisions that influence the visibility of sports, the ways in which they are organized, and the images and meanings associated with them. Although these decisions do not ignore the interests of common folk around the world, their main purpose is to establish and expand the power and profitability of the organizations represented by the decision makers. Therefore, sports tend to revolve around the meanings and orientations valued by those with economic resources and power while providing enjoyable and entertaining experiences to people like us.

Even the National Lottery ('Lotto') in the UK, which ostensibly funds 'good causes', appears in reality to have contributed to social class divisions. For example, while the lottery draws predominantly working-class support in terms of ticket sales, the prize money is disproportionately biased towards upper- and middle-class sporting tastes (see Jarvie, 2006). And, of course, the Lotto is itself managed by a large private corporation, Camelot. The National Lottery 'Dream Ticket', along with a local council tax, is also making a significant contribution to the costs of hosting the London 2012 Summer Olympic Games. While the public substantially subsidize major sporting events in this way, the benefits are mostly felt by those already with wealth and power. As journalist Andrew Jennings (1996a, p. 293) has suggested: 'the IOC will take its profits, the sponsors and television network will make theirs and the local taxpayers will foot the bill'.

This is why some critical theorists have described sports as cultural vehicles for developing 'ideological outposts' in the minds of people around the world: when large and transnational corporations become the primary providers of popular pleasure and entertainment, they can use the very things that give people joy and excitement to deliver messages about what should be important in people's lives. This is a clear manifestation of class relations and the process of hegemony at work.

 There is good reason for believing that sport and social class have been mutually reinforcing categories in British society for a long time.

(Grant Jarvie, sociologist, 2006, p. 305)

Social Class and Sports Participation Patterns

In all capitalist societies, social class and class relations influence who plays, who watches, who consumes information about sports, and what information about sports is available in the mainstream media. Patterns of sports participation, whether they include playing, watching or consuming media coverage of sports, are closely associated with money, power and privilege. At a basic level, organized sports are a luxury item in the economies of many nations, and they are most prevalent in wealthy nations where people have discretionary money and time.

Active sports participation, attendance at events and consuming media sports are positively correlated with a person's income, education and occupational status (Booth and Loy, 1999; Donnelly and Harvey, 2007; Scheerder et al., 2002; Wilson, 2002). For example, Olympic athletes and officials have generally come from more privileged groups in society (Collins and Buller, 2003; Kidd, 1995), and an analysis of British medallists at the 2000 Sydney Olympic Games estimated that 80 per cent of these athletes had attended private school (*Guardian*, 21 August 2004, p. 4).

Even the health and fitness movement, often described as a grass-roots phenomenon in the UK, involves mostly people who have higher-than-average incomes, education and qualifications, and work in professional or managerial occupations. For the most part, people in lower-income jobs do not run, bicycle or swim as often as their high-income counterparts. Nor do they play as many organized sports during their lunch hour, after work, at weekends or during holidays. This pattern holds true throughout the life course, for younger and older people, men and women, racial and minority ethnic populations, and disabled people: social class is related strongly to participation among all categories of people (see Table 10.2).

Over time, economic inequality in society leads to the formation of class-based lifestyles that involve particular forms of sports (Bourdieu, 1986a, 1986b; Dukes and Coakley, 2002; Laberge and Sankoff, 1988). For the most part, sports participation in various lifestyles reflects patterns of sponsorship and access to participation opportunities. For example, the lifestyles of wealthy people routinely include golf, tennis, swimming, sailing and other sports that are self-funded and played at exclusive clubs and resorts. These sports often involve the use of expensive facilities, equipment and/or clothing, and generally require that people have jobs and/or lives in which they have the control, freedom and time needed to participate; some people also combine sports participation with their jobs, such as going to the club, gym, match (executive box) and tournament with business associates. They even use the company credit card to pay for these things, and the company then deducts a portion of the expenses so it pays less income tax, thereby decreasing tax receipts that could be used to fund sport programmes for people who do not own golf, tennis or elite health club memberships.

The lifestyles of middle-income and working-class people, on the other hand, tend to include sports that by tradition are free and open to the public, or available through state schools. When these sports involve the use of expensive equipment or clothing, participation occurs in connection with various forms of financial sacrifice. For instance, buying a mountain bike often means working overtime for six months and not taking a holiday this year.

Some sports are stratified within themselves. For example, horse-racing generally sees upper-class owners, middle-class trainers and working-class followers gambling in the bookmakers, while greyhound racing has also attracted predominantly working-class supporters across the UK, to the benefit of the middle-class owners of the stadiums. These are two examples of sports with strong links with gambling cultures, which offer the dream of a windfall and better life, and so often appeal more to working-class followers.

There are some regional variations in sports participation patterns in the UK. For example, in Scotland sports participation rates are generally considered to be higher than in the other home countries. This is largely due to high numbers of people of all socio-economic groups involved in walking as a leisure-time activity, an activity which 'counts' in the sports participation statistics. However, there remain social class differentials, with sports such as curling, skiing and cricket popular among the Scottish higher classes, and ice skating, ice hockey and angling popular among the lower classes (sportscotland, 2001).

Throughout all the home countries, the lifestyles of low-income people and those living in poverty seldom involve regular forms of sports participation. Life chances clearly vary by social class, and when people spend much of their time and energy coping with the challenges of everyday life, they have few resources left to develop lifestyles that revolve around sports participation. Spending money to play or watch sports is a luxury that many people cannot afford. At

Table 10.2 **British physical activity levels by social class**

Physical activity	Socio-economic classification									
	Higher managerial	Higher professional	Lower managerial/ professional	Intermediate	Small employers	Lower supervisory	Semi-routine	Routine	Unemployed	Total
	Percentage participating in the four weeks before interview									
At least one (excl. walking)	59	59	51	43	43	38	31	30	26	43
At least one activity	75	75	68	58	57	54	46	44	38	58

Source: Office for National Statistics, 2004a

the same time, those who are successful in the economy like sports because they reaffirm a class ideology that works to their advantage. This is partly why they are willing to spend thousands of pounds each year to buy club memberships, season tickets and executive boxes in sport stadiums, or have their companies buy them.

Home-making, child-rearing and earning a living: class and gender relations in women's lives

The impact of social class on everyday lives often varies by age, gender, race and ethnicity, and geographic location (see also Chapters 8 and 9). For example, married women with children are less likely than their male counterparts to have the time and resources needed to play sports (Raisborough, 2006; Thompson, 1999a, 1999b). When they join a netball team that schedules training early in the evening, they may wonder if it is OK with their families because they are the family chefs, chauffeurs and tutors. 'Time off for good behaviour' is not a principle that applies to married women with children.

On the other hand, married men with children are less likely to feel such constraints. When they play football or squash after work, their wives may delay family dinners or keep dinners warm until they arrive home. When they schedule a golf game on a Saturday morning, they expect that their wives will take care of the children and everything else around the house in their absence.

Women in middle- and lower-income families are most constrained by home-making and child-rearing responsibilities. Unable to pay for childcare, domestic help and sports participation fees, these women have few opportunities to play sports. They also lack time, transportation to and from sport facilities, access to gyms and playing fields in their neighbourhoods, and the sense of physical safety that enables them to feel secure enough to leave home and travel to places where they can play sports. When playing a sport requires multiple participants, the lack of resources among some women affects others, because it reduces their prospects for assembling the requisite number of players. This also is true for men, but women from middle- and lower-income families are more likely than their male counterparts to lack the network of relationships out of which sports interests and participation emerge and are supported.

Women from upper-income families, on the other hand, usually face few constraints on sports participation. They can afford childcare, domestic help, takeaway dinners and sports fees. They participate by themselves and with friends and family members. Their social networks include other women who also have resources to play sports. Women who grow up in these families play sports during their childhoods and attend schools with good sports curricular. They seldom experience the same constraints as their lower-income counterparts, even though their opportunities may not equal those of their upper-income male peers.

The sports participation of girls and young women also is limited when they are expected to shoulder responsibilities at home. For example, in low-income families and families in certain ethnic groups (see Chapter 9), teenage daughters often are expected to care for younger siblings after school until early evening when their parents return from work. This is particularly the case in single-parent families. Divorce rates in Britain are the highest in the European Union, and it is generally women who end up as the 'single parent' and shoulder the majority of domestic responsibilities. Single mothers are one of the social groups most vulnerable to

The sports played by young people from low-income households often occur in public areas such as this school playground. Young people from upper-income backgrounds usually have resources to purchase access to privately owned sport facilities and spaces. This results in different sport experiences and different sport participation patterns from one social class to another in society (*Source*: Tini Campbell)

poverty and this impacts on their physical activity levels and those of their children, especially their daughters (see Collins and Kay, 2003).

Boys and girls from higher-income families seldom have household responsibilities that force them to drop out of sports. Instead, their parents drive them to practices, lessons and games; make sure they have all the equipment they need; and then help them obtain cars so that they can drive themselves to training and matches.

The implications of social class dynamics become very serious when health and obesity issues are considered. Limited opportunities to exercise safely and play sports are among the factors contributing to a rapid rise in obesity, diabetes and heart disease, especially among girls and women from low-income households (Office for National Statistics, 2004b). The availability of facilities, safe spaces, transportation and sports activities all vary by social class, and girls and women in low-income households experience the effects of social class in different and more profound ways when it comes to involvement in physical activities and sports.

> My only brother was not required to help out around the house, but was encouraged to go out and play football with his friends.

(Dr Beatriz Vélez, 2003)

Being respected and becoming a man: class and gender relations in men's lives

Many boys and young men learn to use sports to establish a masculine identity, but the dynamics of this process vary by social class. For example, in a qualitative analysis of essays written about sports by 15- and 16-year-old French Canadian boys in the Montreal area, Suzanne Laberge and Mathieu Albert (1999) discovered that upper-class boys connected their sports participation with masculinity because playing sports, they said, taught them leadership skills, and being a leader was central to their definition of masculinity. Middle-class boys said that playing sports provided them with opportunities to be with peers and gain acceptance in male groups, which fitted their ideas of what they needed to do to establish identities as young men. According to working-class boys, playing sports enabled them to display toughness and develop the rugged personas that matched their ideas about manhood. In this sense, social class influences the ways that sports and sports experiences are integrated into young men's lives.

Social historians Holt and Mason (2000, p. 8) have noted similar trends in UK culture, suggesting that 'sport remained a defining element of male culture throughout the second half of the [twentieth] century'. Sports are favourite topics of conversation for men, since they provide for discussion of a shared passion without emotional intimacy, so enabling sociability consistent with heterosexual male norms. More recently, such males have been described as the 'New Lads' – a deliberate response to the politically correct and feminist aware 'New Man' – the New Lads displaying traditionally masculine working-class behaviours of heavy drinking, heterosexist and often homophobic discourse, frequently played out in the sporting arena and on the terraces. However, this is still a class-based experience, with working-class males remaining more committed to sports such as football and boxing, while upper- and middle-class males might be more absorbed in following rugby union and golf fixtures.

Social class factors may also create social conditions under which young men from lower-income backgrounds have more at stake when it comes to playing sports. In a study of former elite male athletes from low-income backgrounds in the USA, Messner (1992) found that many often saw sports participation as a way to obtain 'respect'. However, this was not as important among males from middle-class backgrounds. What he did not mention is that the development of sports skills often requires material resources that do not exist in low-income families. Therefore, unless equipment and training are provided in state school physical education classes, young men from low-income groups stand little chance of competing against upper-income peers, who can buy equipment and training if they want to develop skills – except in sports such as football and athletics that are still provided in many schools in lower-income areas.

In fact, young people from upper-income households often have so many opportunities that they seldom see sports as high-stakes career-related activities in their lives. For someone who has a car, nice clothes, money for university tuition and good career contacts for the future, playing sports can be fun, but it is not perceived as necessary for economic survival, gaining respect or establishing an identity (Messner, 1992). Therefore, young men from middle- and upper-income backgrounds often choose to disengage gradually from exclusive commitments to becoming professional athletes. When these young men move through adolescence and into adulthood, opportunities often take them in a variety of directions. For them, playing sports does not hold the same life significance as it does for their peers from working-class or low-income households. This is clearly illustrated in the next section.

Fighting to survive: class, gender and ethnic relations among boxers

Chris Dundee, a famous American boxing promoter, once said, 'Any man with a good trade isn't about to get himself knocked on his butt to make a dollar' (in Messner, 1992, p. 82). What he meant was that middle- and upper-class boys and men have no reason to play a sport that destroys their brain cells, that boxers always come from the lowest and most economically desperate income groups in society, and that boxing gyms are located in neighbourhoods where desperation is most intense and life piercing (Scambler, 2005; Sugden, 1996; Wacquant, 2004).

The dynamics of becoming and staying involved in boxing have been studied and described by British sociologist John Sugden (1996) and French sociologist Loïc Wacquant (1992, 1995a, 1995b, 2004). The findings of their research studies are summarized in Chapter 7. Sugden worked with boxers around the world, but his research included time spent in Belfast, Northern Ireland. Wacquant spent over three years training and hanging out at a boxing gym in a black ghetto area in Chicago in the USA, documenting the life experiences of 50 professional boxers.

Both of these studies demonstrate that the motivation to dedicate oneself to boxing can be explained only in terms of a combination of class, gender and, in some cases, race relations. Sugden (1996, p. 17) argues that the reason men choose to engage in such a violent activity is a consequence of the 'prevailing social and economic conditions'. In other words, for men who live in poor and harsh social circumstances, the boxing ring is not dramatically different from the rest of their lives. In addition, the possibility of financial reward and celebrity status is even more attractive for those with limited life opportunities. This helps us to understand why professional boxing has been dominated by working-class (and mostly black) men. Statements by the boxers themselves illustrate the influence of their life circumstances on their choice of sport:

> Right [in the area where I lived] it was definitely rough, it was dog-eat-dog. I had to be a mean dog … young guys wan'ed to take yer money and beat ya up an' you jus' had to fight or move out the neighbo'hood. I couldn't move, so I had to start fightin'.
>
> *(In Wacquant, 1992, p. 229)*

The alternative to boxing for many young men was often the violence of the streets. When Wacquant asked one boxer where he would be today if he had not started boxing, he answered with these words:

> If it wasn't for boxin', I don't know where I'd be … Prob'ly in prison or dead some-where, you never know. I grew up in a tough neighbo'hood, so it's good for me, at least, to think 'bout what I do before I do it. To keep me outa the street, you know. The gym is a good place for me to be every day. Because when you're in d'gym, you know where you are, you don' have to worry about getting into trouble or getting shot at.
>
> *(In Wacquant, 2004, p. 239)*

Similarly, one of the trainers interviewed by Sugden explained that:

> There's a lot of bad things go on in Belfast, in all areas, Catholic and Protestant. If the kids stay at the club, come training three or four times a week, they're not getting into trouble with the police, getting involved in mischief, or falling into the wrong hands.
>
> *(Sugden, 1996, p. 101)*

Wacquant explains that most boxers know they would not be boxing if they had been born in households where resources and other career opportunities existed. 'Don't nobody be out there fightin' with an MBA', observed a trainer-coach at the gym (in Wacquant, 1995a, p. 521). Wacquant notes that these men see boxing as a 'coerced affection, a captive love, one ultimately born of racial and class necessity' (1995a, p. 521). Many of the boxers realized that, despite their personal commitment to boxing, their sport involved exploitation. As one boxer noted, 'Fighters is whores and promoters is pimps, the way I sees it' (in Wacquant, 1995a, p. 520).

When Wacquant asked one boxer what he would change in his life, his answer represented the feelings of many men at the gym:

> I wish I was born taller, I wish I was born in a rich family, I … wish I was smart, an' I had the brains to go to school an' really become somebody real important. For me I mean I can't stand the sport, I hate the sport, [but] it's carved inside of me so I can't let it go.
>
> *(In Wacquant, 1995a, p. 521)*

The boxers were attached to their craft, but over 80 per cent did not want their children to be boxers. One said,

No, no fighter wants their son [to box], I mean ... *that's the reason why you fight, so he won't be able to fight* ... It's too hard, jus' too damn hard ... If he could *hit the books* an' study an' you know, with me havin' a little background in school an' stuff, I could help him. My parents, I never had nobody helpin' me.

(In Wacquant, 1995a, p. 523, original emphases)

There is little doubt that a survey of amateur and professional boxing is one of the quickest ways of discovering which groups are the poorest of the poor in the modern industrial world (Sugden, 1996, p. 187) (*Source:* McGraw-Hill)

These mixed feelings about boxing were pervasive; the men were simultaneously committed to and repulsed by their trade, and their participation was clearly connected with the dynamics of social class in their lives. We can understand the sports participation of men like those in the studies of Sugden and Wacquant only in terms of the social class contexts in which they lived their lives and how those contexts influenced their identities as working-class (and in many cases, black) men. Boxing and the gym provided them refuge from the violence, hopelessness and indignity of the poverty that framed their lives since birth.

Class relations in action: the decline of school sports and physical education

In Chapter 5, we noted that the quantity and quality of physical education in school curricular is often limited to less than the minimum two hours a week proposed by the government. This is not unique to the UK. A study by Hardman and Marshall (2000) reviewed the state of physical education in several countries around the world, and concluded that there is an overall decrease in the time, budget, resources, status and perceived value of physical education in school curricula. Such trends seem to particularly impact on children from low-income families, as indicated in the concern expressed by Sport England (2001c, p. 1) that 'the decline in PE curriculum time ... will affect children from less well off backgrounds the most ... who will be least likely to be able to take up the opportunities offered by extra-curricular and club sport'.

Outside of the school curriculum, young people's choices are also limited. Fear of 'stranger danger' means that children have decreased opportunities for unsupervised play. The myth that living in rural areas facilitates active play is also being challenged because of geographical isolation from other children, lack of facilities and fear over unsupervised use of open spaces (see Smith and Barker, 2001).

Young people from low-income families indicate that their opportunities to participate in sport are particularly limited by responsibilities which include housework, childcare for younger siblings and taking part-time jobs, all of which are essential to the economy of poorer households. Girls, in particular, are constrained by expectations to undertake domestic responsibilities. In addition, many suggest that the neighbourhoods in which they live do not provide anywhere safe to play, and more formal facilities cost too much (see Collins and Kay, 2003).

While school sport opportunities in middle- and upper-income areas also may be threatened by financial problems, parental interest and funding mean that more of these schools are likely to benefit from schemes which link children with sports clubs or youth groups enabling out-of-school sporting opportunities. In poorer areas, there is a need for more deliberate intervention by public or voluntary agencies, and these schemes have variable success. For example, the Nottinghamshire Sports Training Scheme (NSTS) was established to increase the number of young people participating in sports. However, an analysis of the scheme illustrated that children from well-off areas had a much higher chance of becoming NSTS participants than children from areas of social need. While this was a study of only one region, Nottinghamshire is fairly typical of many regions of the UK, and it was a well-organized scheme, suggesting that such social inequalities are structural (see Collins and Kay, 2003).

These apparently nationwide trends highlight the importance of social class. When it comes to sports participation, the socio-economic status of the family you are born into has never been more important – participation is a family affair and is driven by family resources. This often is the case for people with disabilities, as explained in 'Breaking barriers', opposite.

Class relations in action: the cost of attending sports events

It is still possible to attend some sports events for free. Many local club events in the UK remain affordable for many people. But tickets to most major professional events are beyond the means

Children in middle-class suburban areas often have safe streets on which they can play. The boys in this cul-de-sac have access to many portable basketball goals, and they often recruit friends to play full-court games in the street. Of course, they also skateboard, play football and may take skiing or surfing holidays with their families. Sports may be important in their lives, but they are not seen as a means of economic survival (*Source*: Jay Coakley)

breaking BARRIERS

Resource barriers: *I'm trying to make do*

We occasionally hear heartening stories about people using assistive devices made of Kevlar, carbon fibre and other high-tech materials. These materials are now used to make light and fast racing chairs, revolutionary running prostheses, and racing mono-skis that can be manoeuvred down steep slopes.

This technology is seductive for those who see it for the first time – so seductive that they focus on the device and overlook the person using it (Belson, 2002). However, as most athletes know, technologies are only as good as the people who use them. And most people with disabilities know that adaptive technologies for sports are prohibitively expensive.

American athlete, Diane Cabrera, discovered this when cancer took her leg in 2001. A new prosthesis enabled her to walk, but it cost US$11 000, and her medical insurance covered only US$4000 per year. She spread payments over two years and struggled to find US$2200 for additional payments related to diagnostics, fitting, tuning and maintaining the device. When she needed a new leg socket in 2005, because her original prosthesis no longer fitted correctly, she put it off due to cost. When asked about this, Diane said with resignation, 'I'm trying to make do right now.'

'Make do right now.' That's what many people do today when they need prostheses. Unless you are wealthy or have private healthcare that covers specialist prosthetic limbs, you quickly learn to 'make do'. This is because, while standard prostheses are available on the National Health Service, prosthetic limbs and adaptive devices for sports involve additional costs. Sport prosthetics require replacement every year or two, and other prosthetic limbs should be replaced every four to six years. Racing wheelchairs cost about £3000, and Kevlar wheels push the cost up even higher.

The cost of equipment is a real barrier to sports participation among many people with disabilities. Accentuating resource barriers in the UK are the following facts (see Collins and Kay, 2003; Thomas, 2002).

- The unemployment rate among people with disabilities is approximately double the rate among people without disabilities.
- Approximately 75 per cent of people with disabilities depend on welfare and are defined as 'poor'.
- People with disabilities often have additional living and care costs, and are less likely to have regular access to transportation.
- Community sports schemes are scarce, even if people have transportation to play sports regularly.

These are the realities of social class and disability in the UK. For young elite athletes, there are a few sponsorships available from companies that develop and manufacture prostheses and other adaptive technologies. This is one way for a select few to bypass resource barriers. But for others who do not have wealthy and connected advocates the barriers are formidable. Their goal is simply to 'Make do right now.'

of many people. The cost of attending these events has increased far beyond the rate of inflation over the past decade.

Table 10.3 shows that, between 1996 and 2006, the average ticket prices for tennis, football and rugby increased 371 per cent, 210 per cent and 200 per cent respectively. During the same time period, inflation was 14 per cent. Ticket prices increase as players' wages have escalated, and new stadiums and arenas are built to attract wealthier spectators. Team owners want to 'capture' the people who have money to spend. Therefore, these new facilities are shopping malls built around a playing surface. They house expensive luxury executive suites and sections of club seating, where upper-income spectators have special services available to them: private waiting service, complementary drinks, private toilet facilities, plasma screen televisions, wireless Internet access, private entrances with no queues or turnstiles, special parking areas, and other things that make going to a game no different than going to a private club.

As ticket prices increase and as spectators are increasingly segregated by their ability to pay, social class and class relations become more evident in the stands (see Chapter 11). Spectators may cheer at the same times and experience similar emotions, but this is the extent to which social-class differences are transcended at the events, and the reality of social class returns as soon as people leave the stadium. For example, when Roman Abramovich, the Russian billionaire owner of Chelsea Football Club, was photographed in 2007 watching a game in the stands among regular supporters, this did not change the fact that after the game he was driven in one of his expensive cars to one of his luxury mansions, while the spectators surrounding him returned to their far more modest lifestyles.

Efforts to lower ticket prices seldom work because people in executive boxes, club seats and other premium seats do not want to be identified with fans who cannot afford high-priced tickets and concessions. Expensive tickets are now status symbols for wealthy spectators. They *want* class distinctions to be preserved in connection with attending games, and they are willing to pay, for example, £50 000 per season for an executive box at a Premier League football club to conspicuously display their status and experience the game without mixing with average fans. Attendance and seating at many events, from the opening ceremonies at the Olympics to Ascot horse racing and the Henley Royal Regatta, also are tied to conspicuous displays of wealth, status and influence. As long as this is the case, efforts to make games affordable to everyone will fail, and this may have consequences if people try to challenge these trends, as discussed in 'Social class and spectator behaviour' (p. 372).

Table 10.3 **Escalating ticket prices versus inflation in the United Kingdom, 1996–2006**

Average ticket price increase (percentage)	
Tennis	371
Athletics	215
Football	210
Cricket	208
Rugby	200
Golf	195
Horse racing	142
Inflation rate, 1996–2006: 14 per cent	

Source: adapted from Wigglesworth, 2007, p. 142

'I thought they said "Sport brings everyone together" when they increased our council tax to build this place!'

Cartoon 10.1 **As they sit at the top of the stands and spot wealthy people in luxury executive boxes and hospitality suites, these fans discover that the dynamics of social class operate in ways that privilege some people more than others. To say that 'sports unite the social classes' is to ignore the dynamics that often separate people from different social class backgrounds**

Global Inequalities and Sports

When we discuss social class and sports, it is essential to think beyond our own society. Inequalities exist at all level of social organization – in families, groups, organizations, communities, societies and the world. Global inequalities related to per capita income, living standards and access to developmental resources cause many of the most serious problems that we face today. Research shows that the gap between the richest and poorest nations is growing wider. For example, people in the UK, *on average*, spend about £45 per day to live as they do (Office for National Statistics, 2005). In the 39 nations classified as 'less developed countries' (LDCs), people spend about 30 pence a day to live as they do. In terms of consumption, an average person in the UK spends about 150 times more than nearly half the individuals in the world spend per day.

Another way to look at social class in global terms is to determine how many of the 6.7 billion people (in mid-2008) live on less than US$1 or US$2 a day, an amount that international organizations agree is clearly below basic subsistence levels in any country, regardless of cost of living. In 2008, about 2.6 billion lived on less than US$2 per day, and 1 billion of them lived on less than US$1 a day (Gore, 2002, 2004; www.globalisationguide.org/03.html). As a point

reflect on SPORTS   *Social class and spectator behaviour: is social inequality expressed on the terraces?*

Different sports often attract participants and followers from different social classes. Violent sports such as boxing have traditionally appealed to those from the working classes, with supporters celebrating the hero who fights his way out of material deprivation. Similarly, pub-based social sports such as darts have also been strongly connected with the working classes. At times, marketing strategies appear to have been deliberately developed to exploit presumed working-class followings and lifestyles, as was the case when Tetley Bitter made the decision to sponsor rugby league, based on an apparent assumption that this was a working-class sport and that followers would consume this drink (see Polley, 1998).

In some cases, the sports terrace has also provided a space for contesting social class inequalities. For example, English cricket, a traditionally upper-class sport, now has a following of the 'Barmy Army', predominantly middle-class supporters who reflect a broader trend of 'New Laddism'. Their behaviour is consistent with that more usually associated with traditional masculine working-class supporters – loud chants, replica kit and other visible displays of team allegiance, and high levels of alcohol consumption. Interestingly, Tetley Bitter has more recently chosen to sponsor cricket, along with the more traditionally middle-class code of rugby union, as well as rugby league. The related commercialism and sports tourism of these 'new' followers of national cricket teams will be discussed in more detail in Chapter 11.

Cricket is not the only sport to witness such apparent social changes in the demography of its supporters. The exclusive arena of Wimbledon tennis has recently introduced the 'People's Sunday' midway through the tournament, which is an unofficial opportunity for a wider social spectrum of people to gain access to tickets, and witnesses spectators who are more vocal and visible in their support of players than the polite handclap of the traditional upper-middle-class spectators. In this way, these spectators have begun to claim traditional upper-class sports as their own.

Occasionally, the challenge to social inequalities is less carnivalesque and more violent than these examples of tennis and cricket. The game of football has traditionally been associated with the British working classes, both as players and spectators. A small but visible minority of spectators have engaged in violent behaviour which is now commonly termed 'football hooliganism'. While the causes of football hooliganism are complex and not fully agreed upon, most sociologists agree that social class dynamics are central to understanding some aspects of this phenomenon. Figurational sociologists such as Eric Dunning suggest that hooliganism should be understood as the expression of a working-class-based violent masculine style, akin to that discussed in the section of this chapter 'Fighting to survive' (p. 364). Some Marxist sociologists have argued that hooliganism is an explicit outcome of social class relations. In particular, that the so-called bourgeoisification of the game – all-seater stadiums, high-paid performers, increased ticket prices and increased numbers of middle-class supporters – met with resistance among the traditional working-class supporters who attempted to reclaim their sport through violent clashes (these theories are discussed in more detail in Chapter 7). *What do you think?*

of comparison, the *median* income in UK households was around £50 per day (approximately US$85) in 2005 (Office of National Statistics, 2005).

The meanings given to this global gap between the wealthy and poor differ depending on the ideologies that people use to guide their understanding of world affairs. But apart from ideological interpretations, it is clear that about 40 per cent of all people in the world have few resources to use on anything but basic survival. Those who are not sick or disabled may engage in physical play or games, but they do not have resources for organizing and playing sports as we know them. For these people, the sports played in the UK and other post-industrial nations are clearly out of reach. They cannot understand why David Beckham can make £27 million in 2006, an amount that is spent over an entire year by more than 100 000 poor people in their country. Neither would it be understood by people in other countries who make less than 50 pence an hour producing the balls, shoes and other equipment and clothing used by most British people who play sports, including professional athletes (Weiner, 2004). This inequality was the target of an international campaign in 2008, in particular the 'violation of worker's rights during the production of Olympic-related merchandise' for the Beijing Games (www.playfair.org).

However, when a dirt football pitch or basketball court exists in communities where people struggle to survive, it often attracts young people who may have seen televised football or basketball games. This has not escaped the attention of people who identify potential elite athletes for professional football and basketball teams in wealthy nations. According to an article in the American magazine, *Sports Illustrated* (Wahl, 2004), the scouts that visit these areas are 'on safari for 7-footers'. When they find a good prospect, they know that he has no agent to represent him and will sign a contract for a low sum of money in 'Western' terms, and be thankful to do so. Only a few of these prospects have made it to the top professional leagues, and many of those who do make it use much of their money to buy food and medical care for people in their home village. This is one of the ways that class relations operate on a global scale.

> Who has the motive to invest in the ... long lasting success of African football? African governments ... have more important things to worry about. When they have some spare cash, they are not usually thanked by their impoverished peoples for sinking it into fancy new stadiums.
>
> *(David Runciman, political scientist, Cambridge University, 2006)*

Economic and Career Opportunities in Sports

Do sports and sports organizations provide opportunities for upward social-class mobility in society? **Social mobility** is a term used by sociologists to refer to *changes in wealth, education and occupation over a person's lifetime or from one generation to the next in families.* Social mobility can occur in downward or upward directions. On a general level, career and mobility opportunities exist in sports and sports organizations. However, as we consider the impact of sports on mobility in the UK, it is useful to know the following things about sports-related opportunities.

- The number of career opportunities in sports is limited, and the playing careers of athletes are short term.
- Opportunities for women are growing but remain limited on and off the field.
- Opportunities for blacks and other ethnic minorities are growing but remain limited on and off the field.

These points are discussed in the following sections.

After hearing about the millions of pounds earned by footballers, many people in the UK forget that sports are a luxury item. At least half the people in the world do not have regular access to the time, resources, equipment, or spaces enabling them to play sports. These boys live in Kibera (Nairobi, Kenya), the largest slum in Africa by population. Here, you play only if you make a ball (*Source*: Kevin Young)

Career opportunities are limited

Young athletes often have visions of playing professional sports, and their parents may have similar visions. But the chances of turning these visions into realities are remote. The actual odds for a person to become a professional athlete are difficult to calculate, and many different methods have been used. For example, sometimes the odds may be calculated for athletes playing at a lower level in a particular sport, for athletes from particular racial or ethnic groups, or for any male or female in a particular age group of the total population in a society. The calculations may be based on the number of players in the top league in a sport, such as the English Premier League in football, or they may take into account that there are professional football leagues elsewhere in the UK and the world and minor professional leagues in England. The calculations may or may not take into account the number of football players that come from different countries. This is important because, on average, 17 members of each of the Premier League clubs grew up outside the UK.

All calculations must be qualified, but this does not change the fact that playing at the professional level in any sport is a long shot. To put this in perspective, if you saw similar odds for a horse at a racetrack, you would never bet on it unless you had money to burn – and, if you placed a bet with such bad odds, people would wonder about your sanity.

Additionally, professional sports opportunities are short term, averaging three to seven years in team sports and three to 12 years in individual sports. People do not always see this because the media focus on the best athletes in the most popular sports, and they have longer playing careers than others in their sports. In contrast, little coverage is given to those who play for one or two seasons before being dropped or forced to quit for other reasons, especially injuries. As a result, we hear about the long careers of popular footballers, but little about the numerous players whose contracts are not renewed. The reality is that the average age of players in the England football team is approximately 25 years old, and there are few players older than 35 in the Premier League. This means that, after playing careers end, there are about *30 additional years* in a person's work life. Unfortunately, many people, including athletes, coaches and parents, ignore this aspect of reality.

Opportunities for women are growing but remain limited

Career opportunities for female athletes are limited relative to opportunities for men. Tennis and golf provide opportunities for women, but the professional competitions for these sports draw athletes from around the world. For women in the UK, this means that the competition to make a living in these sports is great. There were more than 1100 players who competed in Women's Tennis Association (WTA) tournaments in 2008 but, of the 100 top-ranked players in February 2008, none was British (the highest was ranked at 123). Players ranked beyond the top 100 are unlikely to win sufficient prize money to cover their expenses for the year (www.wtatour.com/thewtatour/). In golf, the British Women's Open has been won by a British player only three times in the years from its inception in 1976, and very few women from the UK make enough prize money to cover their expenses as professional golfers.

There are expanding opportunities in professional track and field athletics, cycling, football and skiing, but the number of professional female athletes or leagues remains very low, and only a few women make large amounts of money. For example, Paula Radcliffe had to break the world marathon record in order to be offered £300000 to race in the London Marathon, whereas some Premier League football players will earn that amount every week – a comparison that says much about opportunities, gender and cultural values. Overall, the advice for women who aspire to make a living as professional athletes is have a backup plan and be ready to use it.

What about other careers in sports? There are jobs for women in coaching, training, officiating, sports medicine, sports information, public relations, marketing and administration. As noted in Chapter 8, most of the jobs in women's sports continue to be held by men, and women seldom are hired for jobs in men's sports, except in support positions. Women in most post-industrial nations have challenged the legacy of traditional gender ideology, and some progress has been made in various administrative positions in some sports organizations. However, a heavily gendered division of labour continues to exist in nearly all organizations (McKay, 1997, 1999). In traditional and developing nations, the record of progress is negligible, and very few women hold positions of power in any sports organizations (White and Henry, 2004; Women's Sports Foundation, 2007b, 2007c).

Opportunities for women in sports will continue to shift towards equity, but people continue to resist the ideological changes that would open the door to full equity. In the meantime, there will be gradual increases in the number of women coaches, sports broadcasters, sport therapists, administrators and referees. Changes will occur more rapidly in community-based recreation and fitness schemes where salaries are low, and in certain sport industries that target women as consumers and need women employees to increase their sales and profits. But the gender ideology used by influential decision makers *inside* many sports organizations will continue to privilege those perceived as tough, strong, competitive and aggressive, and men are more likely to be perceived in such terms.

Many women who work in sports organizations continue to face the burden of dealing with organizational cultures that are primarily based on the values and experiences of men. This contributes to low job satisfaction and high job turnover among women. Professional development programmes, workshops and coaching clinics have been developed since the late 1990s to assist women as they live in and try to change these cultures and make them more inclusive. However, full equity will not occur until more men in sports and sports organizations change their ideas about gender and its connection with sports and leadership (McKay, 1997).

Opportunities for ethnic minorities are growing but remain limited

The visibility of black athletes in certain spectator sports often has led to the conclusion that career opportunities for black Britons are abundant in UK sports. Anecdotal support for this conclusion comes from some successful black athletes who attribute their wealth and fame to sports. However, the extent to which job opportunities for blacks exist in sports has been greatly overstated. Very little publicity is given to the actual number and proportion of blacks who play sports for a living or make a living working in sports organizations. Also ignored is the fact that sports provide very few career opportunities for black women.

A review of professional spectator sports shows few blacks in any professional sports apart from boxing, football, and track and field athletics. Apart from football, some of the most lucrative sports for athletes remain almost exclusively white. Tennis, golf and motor racing are examples, where the high-profile figures of American athletes such as Serena and Venus Williams and Tiger Woods, together with Briton Lewis Hamilton, are the exception rather than the rule.

Despite the dismal odds of becoming a professional athlete, young blacks often aspire to reach that goal. Of course, this does not mean that they ignore other goals as they pursue their sport dreams, but it does suggest a need to emphasize that educational goals and career opportunities outside sports should not be ignored (Collins, 2004; Early, 1991; Edwards, 1993; Hoberman, 1997; McCallum, 2002; Platt, 2002; Sailes, 1998). With the sports images that come into the lives of young people every day, sports dreams can be very seductive, especially when other dreams are absent. Unfortunately, some young black Britons see so little hope and justice in the world around them that they focus on televised images of successful black athletes in the Premier League, the boxing ring and on the track. Those images are powerful because they are among the only positive images of black men that they see regularly in the media.

Furthermore, when it comes to employment off the field, opportunities are limited. For example, there had never been a black English manager of a Premier League football team until the appointment of Paul Ince at Blackburn Rovers in 2008, and only approximately 1 per cent of senior coaching staff in football teams are black. These trends are paralleled in many other sports (see Chapter 9). Research in sociology has shown that, when CEOs recruit candidates for top management positions, they often look for people who think as they do so that they can work closely and supportively (Cunningham and Sagas, 2005). This is why they often hire people they have known for many years, who have familiar and shared backgrounds, and are perceived as predictable and trustworthy. Therefore, if the CEO is a white male, he may question the job qualifications of candidates from racial or ethnic backgrounds different from his, backgrounds he may know little about. He may wonder if he could trust them to be supportive and fit in with others. If he has *any* doubts, conscious or unconscious, he will choose the candidate he believes is most like himself. These dynamics exist in sports and other organizations, and if they continue, minority men and all women will remain under-represented in power positions in sports.

As a result, the success of someone like Ian Wright is the exception rather than an indication of genuine opportunities for black Britons in sport. Wright's progress from a working-class and troubled youth to success as a football player and media celebrity should be understood in the context of the extensive racial abuse and class-related constraints he experienced throughout his career, and his construction of a media-friendly identity which conformed to dominant British values (see Carrington, 2001).

The dynamics of ethnic relations in every culture are unique (see Chapter 9). Making generalizations about ethnic relations and opportunities in sports is difficult. However, dominant sport forms in any culture tend to reproduce dominant cultural values and the social structures supported by those values. This means three things: (1) members of the dominant social class in a society may exclude or define as unqualified those who have characteristics and cultural backgrounds different from their own, (2) ethnic minorities often must adopt the values and orientations of people in the dominant social class if they want to be hired and promoted in sports organizations, and (3) the voices of ethnic minorities are seldom represented in the stories that people tell one another about themselves. In any case, blacks are likely to perceive that they have fewer career opportunities than their white counterparts, and they may have higher levels of job dissatisfaction (Cunningham and Sagas, 2005).

People in the UK with Asian backgrounds also are under-represented in many sports and sports organizations (Fleming, 2001, 2007). One reason for this is that many people still feel uncomfortable with ethnic diversity in situations in which they must trust co-workers. This is due to a lack of knowledge about people from various ethnic backgrounds and about the ways that ethnic diversity can make positive contributions to the operation and overall culture of an organization.

Sports Participation and Occupational Careers among Former Athletes

What happens in the occupational careers of former athletes? Are athletes' career patterns different from the patterns of others? Is sports participation a stepping-stone to future occupational success and upward social mobility? Does playing sports have economic pay-offs after active participation is over?

These are difficult questions to answer, and only a few studies have compared former athletes with others on issues related to social class and social mobility. Those studies suggest that young people who play sports experience no more or less occupational success than others from comparable social class and educational backgrounds. This does not mean that playing sports has never helped anyone in special ways; it means only that research does not indicate that former athletes have a systematic advantage over comparable peers in their future occupational careers.

Research on this topic becomes out of date when the meaning and cultural significance of sports participation change over time; such changes are likely to influence the links between playing sports and success in later careers. However, past research suggests that, *if* playing sports is connected with future career success, the reason may involve one or more of the following factors (see Coakley, 1983a, 1998, for references to 30 of these studies).

- Playing sports under certain circumstances (see the numbered list below) may teach young people *interpersonal skills*, which carry over and enable them to succeed in jobs requiring those skills.
- The people who hire employees may define former athletes as good job prospects and give them opportunities to develop and demonstrate work-related abilities, which then serve as the basis for career success.
- Former high-profile athletes may have reputations and references that help them obtain and succeed in certain jobs.
- Playing sports under certain circumstances (see the numbered list below) may enable athletes to develop social networks consisting of social relationships that help them obtain good jobs after retiring from sports.

After reviewing much of the research on this topic, our sense is that playing sports is positively related to future occupational success and upward mobility when it does the following:

1 increases opportunities to complete academic degrees, develop job-related skills and/or extend one's knowledge about the world outside of sports
2 increases support from significant others for *overall* growth and development, not just sports development
3 provides opportunities to develop social networks that are connected with career opportunities outside of sports and sports organizations
4 provides material resources and the guidance needed to successfully create and manage opportunities
5 expands experiences, identities and abilities unrelated to sports
6 minimizes risks of disabling injuries that restrict physical movement or require expensive and/or chronic medical treatment.

This list suggests that playing sports can either expand *or* constrict a person's overall development and future career possibilities (see Chapter 4). When expansion occurs, athletes develop abilities and both social and cultural capital that lead to career opportunities and success. When constriction occurs, abilities and social and cultural capital may be so limited that career opportunities are scarce and unsatisfying.

Highly paid athletes and career success after playing sports

Conclusions about sports participation, career success and social mobility must be qualified in light of the following recent changes related to elite and professional sports in the UK and other wealthy societies.

- ■ An increase in salaries that began in the mid-1970s has enabled athletes to save and invest money that can be used to create future career opportunities.

- ■ An increase in the media coverage and overall visibility of sports has created greater name recognition than past athletes enjoyed; therefore, athletes today can convert themselves into a 'brand' that may lead to career opportunities and success.

- ■ Athletes have become more aware that they must carefully manage their resources to maximize future opportunities.

Of course, many professional athletes have short careers or play at levels at which they do not make much money. When they retire, they face the same career challenges faced by their age peers, and they experience patterns of success and failure similar to patterns among comparable peers who did not play sports. This means that playing sports neither insures nor boosts one's chances of career success, but it does not mean that playing sports was a waste of time.

In Chapter 4 it was explained that retirement from sports is best described as a process rather than a single event, and most athletes do not retire from sports at a moment's notice – they disengage gradually and revise their priorities as they disengage. Although many athletes handle this process smoothly, develop other interests and move into relatively satisfying occupations, some encounter adjustment problems that interfere with occupational success and overall life satisfaction.

When American sociologist Mike Messner interviewed former elite athletes, he found that those who had been heavily involved in sports since childhood encountered serious adjustment problems as they tried to make the transition out of sports. A former player in the American football league (NFL) highlighted these problems with the following explanation:

> [When you retire] you find yourself scrambled. You don't know which way to go. Your light ... has been turned out ... Of course you miss the financial deal, but you miss the camaraderie of the other ballplayers. You miss that – to be an elite, to be one of a kind ... The game itself ... the beating and all that ... you don't really miss. You miss the camaraderie of the fellas. There's an empty feeling ... The one thing that has been the major part of your life is gone ... You don't know how people are going to react to you ... You wonder and question.
>
> *(In Messner, 1992, pp. 120–1)*

The two challenges that face many retiring athletes are (1) reaffirm or reconstruct identities in terms of activities, abilities and relationships that are not directly related to sports participation, and (2) nurture or renegotiate relationships with family and friends so that new identities can be established and reaffirmed. Messner's study also indicated that young men from low-income families were more likely to have problems when retiring from sports because they had fewer material resources to use in the transition process and they were more likely to have identities deeply rooted in sports. The men from middle-class backgrounds, on the other hand, had greater material resources and support that enabled them to take advantage of opportunities and social connections; and they were less likely to have identities exclusively rooted in sports.

Studies also show that adjustment problems are most likely when injuries force an athlete to retire without notice (Coakley, 1983b; Lavallee et al, 2000; Swain, 1999; Weisman, 2004). Injuries link retirement with larger issues of health and self-esteem, and propel a person into life-changing transitions before they are expected. When this occurs, athletes often need career-related assistance.

When athletes encounter problems transitioning out of sports into careers and other activities, support should be and occasionally is provided by the sports organizations that benefited from their labour (Dacyshyn, 1999). Some sports organizations in the USA, including universities and national governing bodies, are beginning to do this through career transition programmes that involve workshops focusing on career self-assessments, life skills training, career planning, CV writing, job search strategies, interviewing skills, career placement contacts and psychological counselling. Retiring athletes often find it helpful to receive guidance in identifying the skills they learned in sports and how those skills can be transferred to subsequent careers, and this is a feature that needs to be developed in the UK.

Cartoon 10.2 **Only a few former athletes can cash in on their athletic reputations. The rest must seek opportunities and work just like the rest of us. Those opportunities vary, depending on qualifications, experience, contacts and connections, and a bit of luck**

Summary: Do Money and Power Matter in Sports?

Social class and class relations are integrally involved in sports. Organized sports depend on resources, and those who provide them do so in ways that support their interests by establishing economic arrangements that work to their advantage. This is why dominant sports forms in the UK and other nations with market economies promote an ideology based on the belief that 'you always get what you deserve, and you always deserve what you get (meritocracy)'.

This ideology drives a combination of individual achievement and consumption, along with corporate expansion, in society. Using it leads to favourable conclusions about the character and qualifications of those who are wealthy and powerful, but it disadvantages the poor and powerless. Furthermore, it leads to the conclusion that economic inequality, even when it is extreme and oppressive, is natural and beneficial in society as a whole.

Class relations also are tied to patterns of sports team ownership, event sponsorship and media coverage of sports. Sports events are one of the vehicles these people can use to transfer public money into their own hands. At the same time, economic and political elites, including powerful transnational corporations, are perceived as those who sponsor the teams, events and media coverage that bring people pleasure and excitement. Although fans do not always give sports the meaning that sponsors would like them to, fans seldom subject sports to critical analysis, and usually do not see them as perpetuating a class ideology that justifies inequality and serves as a basis for public policies that foster it.

Sports participation patterns worldwide are connected with social class and the distribution of material resources. Organized sports are a luxury that people in many regions of the world cannot afford. Even in wealthy societies, sports participation is most common among those in the middle and upper classes, and class-based lifestyles often go hand-in-hand with staging and participating in certain sports.

Sports participation patterns also are connected with the intersection of class, gender, and race and ethnicity in people's lives. This is seen in the case of girls and women who have low participation rates when resources are scarce, and among lower-income men who see sports as a means of obtaining respect when they are living on the social and economic margins of society. Boxing provides an example of a sport in which class, gender, race and ethnicity intersect in a powerful combination. As a result, the boxing gym often becomes a safe space that offers temporary refuge for minority men who live in poor neighbourhoods where poverty, community conflict and despair spawn desperate acts of violence among their peers.

Patterns of watching sports also are connected with social class and class relations. This is demonstrated by the increased segregation of fans in stadiums and arenas. Executive boxes, club seating and patterns of season-ticket allocations separate people by a combination of wealth and power so that social class often is reaffirmed when people attend sport events.

Opportunities for careers that hold the hope of upward social mobility exist for some people in sports. For athletes, these opportunities often are scarce and short-lived, and they reflect patterns of class, gender and ethnic relations in society. These patterns take various forms with regard to careers in sports organizations. Although opportunities in some of these jobs have become increasingly open over the past decade, white men still hold most of the power positions in sports organizations. This will change only when the organizational cultures of sports teams become more inclusive and provide new ways for women and ethnic minorities to participate fully in shaping the policies and norms used to determine qualifications in sports, and to organize social relations at the workplace.

Research generally indicates that people who use sports participation to expand their social and cultural capital often have an advantage when seeking occupational careers away from sports. However, when sports participation constricts social and cultural capital, it is likely to have a negative effect on later career success. The relevance of this pattern varies by sport and is affected by the resources that athletes can accumulate during their playing careers.

Ending athletic careers may create stress and personal challenges, but most people move through the retirement process without experiencing *excessive* trauma or difficulty. Problems are most likely when identities and relationships have been built exclusively in connection with sports. Then professional help may be needed to successfully transition into satisfying careers and relationships in which mutual support encourages growth and the development of new identities. Otherwise, it is possible to become stuck in the 'glory days' of being an athlete instead of facing the challenges presented in life after sports.

In conclusion, sports are clearly tied to patterns of class, class relations and social inequality in society. Money and economic power do matter, and they matter in ways that often reproduce existing patterns of social class and life chances.

Website resources

Note: Websites often change. The following URLs were current when this book was printed. Please check our website (***www.mcgraw-hill.co.uk/textbooks/coakley***) for updates and additions.

www.imdb.com/title/tt0286499/ and ***www.imdb.com/title/tt0082158/*** These sites give information on the films *Bend it Like Beckham* and *Chariots of Fire*, both British-based films which provide a personalized look at social class, gender, ethnicity and national identity issues in the lives of young sports people.

www.playfair.org Report and recommendations on wages and working conditions in the global sportswear industry, with specific attention to the production of merchandise for Beijing 2008.

www.sportdevelopment.org.uk/dupsocialcontext.pdf The site of 'Driving up Participation', examining key trends in sports participation in the UK.

www.sportingnews.com/features/powerful The *Sporting News*, a US weekly, presents annual lists of the 100 most powerful people in sports; the lists are intended to be international, but they focus primarily on power in sports from a US perspective, and they are only one picture of power in the world of sports.

www.sportengland.org/sports_equity_index_regular.pdf The link to the sport England 'Sports Equity Index' with information on levels of sports participation among different social groups.

www.sportengland.org/index/get_resources/research/segmentation_main_page/segments_and_priority_groups.htm This link outlines Sport England's priority groups (including identified social classes) and how they are incorporated into strategies to raise participation in sport.

www.sportengland.org/resources/pdfs/publicat%5FEng%5FJune03.pdf Economists provide a report entitled 'The value of the sports economy in England: a study on behalf of Sport England'; it provides an example of how researchers study the economic impact of sport in an entire nation.

www.scotland.gov.uk/Topics/Statistics/Browse/Tourism-Culture-Sports/TrendSportParticipation The findings of a survey of participation rates in sport in Scotland.

11

Sports and the economy: what are the characteristics of commercial sports?

(*Source*: **Elizabeth Pike**)

Chapter contents

Emergence and growth of commercial sports
Commercialization and changes in sports
Owners, sponsors and promoters in commercial sports
Legal status and incomes of athletes in commercial sports
Summary: what are the characteristics of commercial sports?

Learning Centre Resources

Visit *Sports in Society*'s Online Learning Centre (OLC) at **www.mcgraw-hill.co.uk/ textbooks/coakley** for additional information and study material for this chapter, including:

- Self-grading quizzes and essay questions
- Learning outcomes
- Related websites
- Additional readings

> Take away sponsorship and commercialism from sport today, and what is left? A large sophisticated engine developed over 100 years – with no fuel.
>
> *(Dick Pound, member of the International Olympic Committee, 2004, p. 25)*

> The new post of commercial director is critical to our ability to deliver this company's key strategic aim of converting more fans to consumers and leveraging the club's brand through our global commercial activities.
> *(David Gill, Chief Executive of Manchester United Football Club, in Treanor, 2003)*

> Sporting events establish a strong bond between team members from across the organisation, encouraging colleagues to share information, which can produce useful business leads. Business relationships can often be cemented whilst talking sport, playing sport, or attending a sporting event. Recruitment and HR consultancy thrive on relationships, so it is vital for us to build that trust and friendship with clients in social situations. Sport is a perfect vehicle for that.
> *(Rob Chandler, Head of Human Resources, Hudson Recruitment Consultancy, in SIRC, 2006, p. 47)*

Sports have been used as a form of public entertainment throughout history. However, sports have never been so thoroughly commercialized as they are today. Never before have economic factors so totally dominated decisions about sports, and never before have economic organizations and corporate interests had so much power and control over the meaning, purpose and organization of sports.

The economic stakes for athletes and sponsors have never been higher than they are today. The bottom line has replaced the goal line. As a board member of Sport England notes:

> The sporting pound is very important to the economic health of the nation. More people are using their wages to go and watch matches, buy sports clothing or splash out on the latest sports equipment. More importantly, new jobs are being created and sports clubs are benefiting from increase[s] in subscriptions.
>
> *(In Brady, 2008)*

Sports today are evaluated in terms of gate receipts, merchandise sales, licensing fees, media rights contracts and website hits. Games and events are evaluated in terms of media criteria such as market share, ratings points and the cost of commercial time. Athletes are evaluated in terms of their entertainment value as well as their physical skills. Stadiums, teams and events are increasingly named after corporations and are associated with corporate logos instead of people and places that have historical meaning.

Corporate interests now more pervasively influence team colours, uniform designs, event schedules, media coverage and the comments of announcers during games and matches. Media companies sponsor and plan events, and they own a growing number of sports teams. Many sports are corporate enterprises, tied to marketing concerns and processes of global capitalist expansion. The mergers of major corporate conglomerates that began in the 1990s and now continue into the twenty-first century have connected sports teams and events with media and entertainment companies. The names of transnational corporations are now synonymous with the athletes, events and sports that bring pleasure to the lives of millions of people.

Because economic factors are so important in sports, this chapter focuses on the following questions:

- Under what conditions do commercial sports emerge and prosper in a society?
- What changes occur in the meaning, purpose and organization of sports when they become commercial activities?
- Who owns, sponsors and promotes sports, and what are their interests?
- What is the legal and financial status of athletes in commercial sports?

Emergence and Growth of Commercial Sports

In order to discuss the relationship between commercial sports and the economy, it is important to define what is meant by these terms. In this chapter, the **economy** refers to *the production and distribution of wealth in a society*, and the general acceptance that there is never enough money to satisfy the desire of all citizens. **Commercialization** refers to *financial transactions and the exploitation of goods for profit*, to underpin the economy. Commercial sports therefore are those organized and played to make money as entertainment events. They depend on a combination of gate receipts, sponsorships and the sale of media broadcasting rights, and other revenue streams associated with sport images and personalities. Therefore, commercial sports grow and prosper best under five social and economic conditions.

First, they are most prevalent in market economies where material rewards are highly valued by athletes, team owners, event sponsors and spectators.

Second, commercial sports usually exist in societies that have large, densely populated cities because they require high concentrations of potential spectators. Although some forms of commercial sports can be maintained in rural, agricultural societies, their revenues would not support full-time professional athletes or sport promoters.

Third, commercial sports are a luxury, and they prosper only when the standard of living is high enough that people have time and resources they can use to play and watch events that have no tangible products required for survival. Transportation and communications technologies must exist for sponsors to make money. Therefore, commercial sports are common in wealthy, urban and industrial or post-industrial societies; they seldom exist in labour-intensive, poor societies where people must use all their resources to survive.

Fourth, commercial sports require *large amounts of capital* (money or credit) to build and maintain stadiums and arenas in which events can be played and watched. Capital can be accumulated in the public or private sector, but in either case, the willingness to invest in sports depends on anticipated pay-offs in the form of publicity, profits or power. *Private* investment in sports occurs when investors expect financial profits; *public* investment occurs when political leaders believe that commercial sports serve their interests, the interests of 'the public' or a combination of both (see Chapter 13).

Fifth, commercial sports are most likely to flourish in cultures where lifestyles involve high rates of consumption and emphasize material status symbols. This enables everything associated with sports to be marketed and sold: athletes (including their names, autographs and images), merchandise, team names and logos. When people express their identities through clothing, other possessions, and their associations with status symbols and celebrities, they will spend money on sports that have meaning in their social world. The success of commercial sports depends on selling symbols and emotional experiences to audiences, and then selling audiences to sponsors and the media (Burstyn, 1999; Horne, 2006; Jackson and Andrews, 2005).

Sports are played in all cultures, but professional sports seldom exist in labour-intensive, poor nations around the world. The Afghan horsemen here are playing buzkashi, a popular sport in their country, but Afghanistan lacks the general conditions needed to sustain buzkashi as a professional sport with paid athletes and paying fans (*Source*: Efren Lukatsky, AP/Wide World Photos)

Class relations and commercial sports

Which sports become commercialized in a society? As noted in Chapter 10, priority is usually given to the sports that are watched or played by people who control economic resources in society. For example, golf is a major commercial sport in the UK, even though it does not lend itself to commercial presentation. It is inconvenient to stage a golf event for a live audience or to televise it. Camera placement and media commentary are difficult to arrange, and live spectators see only a small portion of the action. Golf does not involve vigorous action or head-to-head competition, except in rare cases of match play. Usually, if you do not play golf, you have little or no reason to watch it.

But golfers include relatively wealthy and powerful people who are important to sponsors and advertisers because they make consumption decisions for themselves, their families, their businesses and thousands of employees who work under their supervision. They buy luxury cars and other high-end products for themselves; more important to advertisers, however, is that they buy thousands of company cars and computers for employees, and make investment decisions related to pensions and company capital.

Golfers as a group have economic clout that goes far beyond their personal and family lives. This makes golf an attractive sport for corporations that have images and products that appeal to consumers with money and influence. This is why major golf events such as the Ryder Cup and Professional Golfers' Association (PGA) tours are sponsored by companies which sell expensive jewellery and cars. This also is why major television networks cover golf tournaments: they can sell commercial time at a high rate per minute because those watching golf have money to spend – their money *and* the money of the companies, large and small, that they control.

Market economies always privilege the interests of those who have the power and resources to influence which sports will be given cultural significance in a society. A sport will not come to be known as a 'national pastime' or become associated with ideal personal character, community spirit, civic unity and political loyalty unless it is favoured by people with resources. For example, hunting in the name of 'sport' has been a controversial activity for many years in the UK. Despite this, Scotland has seen a spread of sporting estates (private hunting reserves), largely due to their support by land-owning and social elites. Sporting estates constitute approximately half of privately owned land in Scotland, and the proprietors stock their reserves with game for exclusive hunting. The estates have also become commodified and commercialized with, for example, the invention of estate tartans and tweeds to mimic the indigenous culture of the Highlands and Islands of Scotland. While such estates contribute to the local economy, they do so in a way which enables members of the upper classes to maintain large expanses of land exclusively for their own recreation, and in the face of broader social debates regarding the morality of 'blood sports' (see Wightman et al., 2002).

Furthermore, unless people with power and resources want to play, sponsor or watch a sport, it will not be commercialized on a large scale, nor will it be selected for promotion or media coverage. For example, while football has a long tradition of popular working-class support, the large-scale commodification of the game is relatively recent in the history of the sport. The so-called 'gentrification' of football, including the development of all-seater stadia, executive boxes, extensive merchandising, together with the highly paid 'celebrity' players, have been witnessed on a large scale only since the 1990s. Similar trends have been witnessed in other sports. For example, while the professionalization of rugby union in the 1990s appeared to offer the opportunity for working-class men to play full-time with a salary, in reality the professional game has become a commercial enterprise with expensive tickets and merchandise supporting its continued status as a middle-class sport. These trends celebrate and privilege the values and experiences of the people, usually men, who control and benefit from corporate wealth and power in the UK. Take the England cricket team supporters' 'Barmy Army', which presents itself as a socially inclusive group. It has been carefully developed by some entrepreneurial men who copyrighted the name 'England's Barmy Army' along with a logo, and who then developed their own brand of merchandise. In addition, the Barmy Army have enabled the expansion of sports tourism for supporters who travel to international matches, which means that in reality this is a socially exclusive group which continues to privilege middle-class (and predominantly white male) supporters (see Parry and Malcolm, 2004; Polley, 1998).

These sorts of trends help us to understand why men will pay thousands of pounds to buy expensive season tickets to games, why male executives use corporation money to buy expensive blocks of 'company tickets' to football games, and why corporation presidents write £100 000 cheques to pay for executive boxes and club seats for themselves, friends and clients. Sports are entertaining for them but, more importantly, they reproduce an ideology that fosters their interests.

Women who want to be a part of the power structure often find that they must learn to 'talk sports'. If female executives do not go to corporate sports events, take clients with them and know the language of the sport, they risk being excluded from the 'masculinity loop' that constitutes the core of corporate culture and communication. When they go to work every Monday, they know that being able to talk about the weekend's sporting fixtures keeps them in touch with many of the men around them.

The creation of spectator interest in sports

What leads people to become sports spectators? Why do they look to sports for entertainment? These questions have multiple answers, and many sociologists have conducted studies on the experience of consuming sport as a spectator or 'fan' (see Horne, 2006, for a summary of research into fans and sports consumption). However, spectator interest is related to four factors in modern and post-industrial societies: a general quest for excitement, a cultural emphasis on material success, early life experiences in sports and easy access to sports through the media.

The quest for excitement

When social life becomes highly controlled and organized, everyday routines often cause people to feel emotionally constrained. This fosters a search for activities that offer tension-excitement and emotional arousal. According to sociologists Eric Dunning and Norbert Elias, historical evidence suggests that this occurs in modern societies. Sports, they contend, provide activities in which rules and norms can be shaped to foster emotional arousal and exciting actions, thereby eliminating boredom without disrupting social order in society (Dunning, 1999; Elias and Dunning, 1986).

Sports generally are characterized by a tension between order and disruption. To manage this tension, norms and rules in sports must be loose enough to break boredom, but not so loose that they permit violence or other forms of destructive deviance. When norms and rules are too controlling, sports are boring and people lose interest; when they are too loose, sports become sites for reckless and dangerous actions that jeopardize health and social order. The challenge is to find and maintain a balance. This explanation of spectator interest raises the question, why do so many people give priority to sports over other activities in their quest for excitement? Critical theorists suggest that answers can be found by looking at the connection between ideology and cultural practices. This leads us to consider other factors.

Success ideology and spectator interest

Many people watch games or follow them in the media, but spectator involvement is highest among those who believe in a meritocratic ideal: the idea that success is always based on skills and hard work, and skills and hard work always lead to success. This belief supports a widely held class ideology in societies with capitalist economies (see Chapter 10). Those who hold it often use sports as a model for how the social world should operate. When sports promote the idea that success is achieved only through hard work and skill, their ideology is reaffirmed and they become more secure in their beliefs. This is why sport media commentators emphasize that athletes and teams succeed when they work hard and have talent. This also is why corporations use the bodies of elite athletes to represent their public relations and marketing images; the finely tuned bodies of athletes are concrete examples of skill, power and success as well as the use of science and technology (Hoberman, 1994). When high-profile athletes can deliver this message for corporations, lucrative endorsements come their way.

Youth sports schemes and spectator interest

Spectator interest often is created and nurtured during childhood sports participation. When organized youth sports schemes emphasize skills, competition and success, participants are likely to grow up wanting to watch elite athletes. For young people who continue to play sports, watching elite athletes provides them with models for playing and improving skills. For those who discontinue participation, watching elite athletes provides continuous connections with the images and experiences of success that they learned when they played sports in their youth. In 2008, the British government launched 'International Inspiration', a £9 million Olympic legacy plan to encourage young people in five developing nations to become involved in sport. It will be interesting to see whether this plan influences spectating as well as participation, and the impact this might have on the growth of commercial sports in these nations.

Media coverage and spectator interest

The media promote the commercialization of sports by publicizing and covering events in ways that sustain spectator interest among many people. Television increases spectator access to events and athletes worldwide, and it provides a unique 're-presentation' of sports. Camera coverage enables viewers to focus on the action and view replays in slow motion as they listen to the 'insider' comments of announcers – all of which further immerses spectators into vicarious and potentially exciting sport experiences.

On-air commentators serve the media audience as fellow spectators who embellish the action and heighten identification with athletes. Commentators provide inside stories, analyse strategies, describe athletes as personalities and present the event in ways that magnify its importance.

Television recruits new spectators by providing a means of learning the rules and strategies of a sport without purchasing tickets. Furthermore, newcomers to a sport can do their learning at home with family and friends. Overall, television provides a painless way to become a spectator, and it increases the number of people who will buy tickets, regularly watch televised games, pay for cable and satellite sports programming, and even become pay-per-view customers in the future.

Commercial sports and the economy of the UK

The large numbers of spectators who consume commercial sports in various ways has increased the economic significance of these sports within developed nations. This is seen most clearly in the USA which dominates the global sports economy, but the UK, together with Germany and Japan, share the domination of retail sales for sports goods. For example, while the USA has 42 per cent of the global market in sports clothing and shoes, the European nations of the UK, France, Germany, Italy and Spain have 35 per cent of these sales. These sales are worth approximately US$3 billion to the UK each year (see Horne, 2006; Ohl and Tribou, 2004).

It is difficult to know the precise economic significance of sport in the UK. Coalter (2007) suggests that there are four dimensions to the relationship between sport and the economy: (1) economic profits from income and expenditure on sports, (2) the economic benefits of having an active and healthy population, (3) hosting mega sports events, and (4) urban regeneration and the building of sport stadia.

There are many surveys which provide some information on how much money is spent on sports in the UK, taking into account admissions, subscriptions, equipment and gambling, but these are only estimated figures. For example, the UK government's official survey of expenditure estimates that the average household expenditure on sports is £5 per week, which equates to a total weekly expenditure of approximately £121 million in the UK (Office for National Statistics, 2006). Membership of private health clubs alone has enabled companies such as Cannons and David Lloyd to achieve a turnover in the region of £2 billion per year (Jeffries, 2004). In addition, sports contribute to the economy by providing employment in various forms which accounts for approximately 400 000 jobs or 2 per cent of all employment in England alone, and provides households in England with nearly £6 billion (or 1 per cent) of disposable income (Cambridge Econometrics, 2003).

Of course, there is also a significant economic investment in many sports from initial government and lottery funding. A survey of the economic investment and return from mega sports events found that for every pound invested in an event, there was an average return of £3.20. This money comes from spectators purchasing food, drink and merchandise, and mostly benefits the local economy (see UK Sport, 2006). Many people will travel to a region to watch a sports event, and will spend money on accommodation, meals in restaurants and other entertainment. Sport tourism is now big business.

Many companies who do not have anything to do with sports directly, also see a value in encouraging their employees to be participants and spectators of sports. A study published in 2006 suggested that sports have a positive effect on the workplace, and some companies sponsor individuals and teams to engage in sports, and even allow staff time off during major sports events to watch matches, believing that this will boost morale and productivity. For example, Kirsty Leyland, the Head of Colleague Policy for the supermarket ASDA, says:

In recognition of the immense impact the World Cup will have on ASDA, we've introduced a special 'World Cup Leave' policy ... We're ensuring our staff are motivated and productive during the World Cup by allowing them to choose the times they work. In this way, we simultaneously ensure all our customers still receive the excellent service they've come to expect. We expect the World Cup to have an impact on our sales, but it's a key part of our strategy to ensure that we also boost staff morale and harness the nation's excitement to sustain and even increase our productivity.

(SIRC, 2006, p. 46)

Economic factors and the globalization of commercial sports

In addition to the impact on the national economy, commercial sports are now global in scope. Globalization has occurred because (1) those who control, sponsor and promote sports seek new ways to expand markets and maximize profits, and (2) transnational corporations use sports as vehicles for introducing their products and services around the world. This makes sports a form of global cultural trade that is exported and imported in a manner similar to other products.

Sports organizations look for global markets

Commercial sports organizations are businesses, and their goal is to expand their operations into as many markets as possible. For example, profits for the rugby football union premiership and the county cricket league could expand significantly if the leagues were able to sell broadcasting rights to television companies worldwide, and licensed merchandise (hats, shirts, jackets, and the like) to people in countries outside the UK. This already occurs to some extent, but the continued commercial success of major sports organizations requires that they create spectators worldwide. Success also depends on using the media to export a combination of game knowledge and athlete identification. In this way, sports organizations become exporters of culture as well as products to be consumed. The complex export–import processes that occur in connection with sports are now topics studied by scholars in the sociology of sport (see Chapter 13).

The Fédération Internationale de Football Association (FIFA) has a long history of global expansion (Sugden and Tomlinson, 1998, 1999). Football teams such as Manchester United and Chelsea have clearly used strategies to expand their global marketing reach. Chelsea was bought by the Russian billionaire Roman Abramovich for approximately £140 million in 2003, and he has since invested several more millions into the club, which has won several titles since his takeover. When Malcolm Glazer, a US billionaire, paid US$1.47 billion to purchase 75 per cent of Manchester United in 2005, he anticipated additional global expansion of the 'Man U' brand. He had bought an American gridiron football team, the Tampa Bay Buccaneers, for US$192 million in 1995 and saw the team value skyrocket to US$779 million in 2004, so he knew that capitalist expansion could pay returns. Manchester United now has dedicated websites for China, Japan and Korea, as does Chelsea, which also has dedicated Russian and American sites. These websites are produced in the national languages to ensure the teams succeed as a global brand. They have been so successful that they are valued at US$500 million more than any North American sport team franchise (as of 2005). There are now several Premier League teams owned by overseas investors seeking to benefit from the global success of this brand. Controversially, in 2008 the Premier League's chief executive, Richard Scudamore, announced a proposal for some Premier League matches to be played outside Europe to spread the global appeal of the league, with the inevitable financial benefits.

While British teams have expanded their commercial operations overseas, sports from other countries have had success in the UK. For example, the spirit of global expansion has led teams from the North American football, basketball, ice hockey and baseball leagues to play games in England. Furthermore, powerful sports organizations like the International Olympic Committee, have turned themselves and their sports into a global brand. The IOC gradually has incorporated national Olympic committees from more than 200 nations, and has turned the Olympic Games into the most successful and financially lucrative media sports events in history. This has had serious implications for the Paralympic Games, as explained in 'Breaking barriers' on pages 394–395.

> We very much want to build a brand, particularly in Asia, but also in North America and South America, as well as Europe.

(Tom Hicks, owner of Liverpool Football Club, 2007)

Corporations use sports as vehicles for global expansion

Because certain sports capture the attention, emotions and allegiance of so many people worldwide, corporations have been eager to sponsor them. Corporations need symbols of success, excellence and productivity that they can use to create 'marketing hooks' for their

In 2007, the New York Giants and the Miami Dolphins NFL teams played a game at Wembley Stadium in London. Statues of the players were situated around the city, such as this one at Victoria Train Station, to promote the game and attract spectators (*Source*: Elizabeth Pike)

breaking Barriers

Brand barriers: *there was nothing we could do*

When is a flag not a flag? Dr Jens Bromann discovered in 1983 that this is not a trick question. As a representative of disabled athletes, he attended a meeting called by Juan Antonio Samaranch, the president of the International Olympic Committee (IOC). Samaranch told Bromann and others from disability sports organizations that they could no longer use Olympic images at the Paralympics or the trials leading up to them. Samaranch explained that, among other things, the Olympic flag and the five interlocking rings were symbols that now represented a global brand with its own commercial interests and goals. The flag, therefore, was not so much a flag as it was a licensed logo, and it could be used only by those who paid for the right to do so. As Bromann left the meeting, he told reporters that the Olympics was now an exclusive commercial brand, and 'there was nothing we could do' to maintain the interests of the Paralympics (Jennings, 1996a).

Upset, but not wanting to cut ties with the IOC, Bromann and his peers in disability sports turned their attention to the Paralympic Games that would follow the 1984 Los Angeles Olympics. But neither the Los Angeles Olympic Organizing Committee nor the United States Olympic Committee (USOC) would support them and their event. So they left Los Angeles and split their events between New York and Stoke Mandeville, England. They also formed the International Coordinating Committee of World Organizations for the Disabled (ICC) and made it the governing body for the Paralympic Games.

As president of the new ICC, Bromann focused on organizing the 1988 Paralympic Games in Seoul, Korea. With support from Korean Olympic officials, the games were a huge success, bringing together over 3000 athletes from 61 nations. At the opening ceremonies, Bromann, who had once competed in sports for blind athletes, received from the Korean organizers a flag that they had designed specifically for the Korean Paralympic Games. It was white and had five *tae geuks*, or traditional Korean line symbols, that resembled teardrops in the same positions and colours as the five interlocking rings on the Olympic flag. This was meant to show that the Paralympics were related to the Olympic movement and that Paralympians train and compete as Olympians do (Sheil, 2000).

The ICC reorganized in 1989 and after the 1992 Paralympic Games in Barcelona, Spain, it became the International Paralympic Committee (IPC). In the meantime, it continued to use the *tae geuks* flag as its symbol, but this infuriated the IOC. The flag, claimed IOC officials, was too similar to their brand

(A)   (B)   (C)

These are the flags that have been used by the Paralympics. Because of brand confusion that might discourage sponsors, the IOC demanded that the five-teardrop flag (A) be changed. The three-teardrop flag (B) was used between 1994 and 2004, and the new Spirit in Motion flag (C) was used at the Beijing Paralympic Games in 2008 (*Source*: Flag images courtesy of the International Paralympic Committee)

logo. In 1991 the IOC told the ICC to change its flag or face sanctions. This prompted investigative journalist Andrew Jennings to ask sarcastically, 'Sanctions against the disabled? What would they do? Shoot some guide dogs? Smash up a few wheelchairs?' (1996a, p. 228). But the ICC knew the sanctions meant there would be no more funding from the IOC – an action that would destroy many disability sports.

To appease the IOC, a new symbol with three *tae geuks* was officially launched at the 1994 IPC World Championships. The *tae geuks* again appeared as teardrops, but officials explained that they now represented the Paralympic motto: 'Mind, Body, and Spirit'. This flag was used for the 2004 Paralympic Games in Athens. But in 2003, after years of failed attempts to gain full IOC recognition and support, the IPC separated from the IOC and adopted a new symbol and flag to represent the unique purpose and identity of the Paralympic Games. It consisted of three elements in red, blue and green – the colours most often used in national flags. The elements are known as *Agitos* (a Latin word meaning, I move), and they appear to be in motion around a central point, representing a dynamic, global 'Spirit in Motion' – the new motto of the Paralympics. This new representation emphasizes that the IPC goal is to sponsor sports that bring together athletes from all regions of the globe. The Spirit in Motion flag flew at the 2008 Paralympics in Beijing, and there was nothing the IOC could do to prevent it.

Today, the IPC uses a commercial model of sports as a survival strategy. Its flag is now a licensed logo – like the IOC flag. But this change raises the question of who will benefit from and be hurt by the commercialization of elite disability sports. Athletes who can attract spectators and sponsors will certainly benefit, but will this inspire sports participation among others or will it turn them into spectators? Will people be inclined to donate money to elite athletes, leaving everyone else to say, 'There's nothing we could do'? Hopefully, this is not where commercialization will lead.

products and services, and public goodwill for their policies and practices. For example, David Beckham's image has been attached to Police sunglasses and Pepsi, among other products, and many people associate the Olympics with Coca-Cola. For many athletes, the crowning Olympic achievement is to have their image associated with a product or brand. Status among many children depends on wearing expensive shoes and clothing with official logos and other sports images on them.

Scholars and sports writers have identified US basketball player Michael Jordan as a key figure in the process of corporations' using sports to boost bottom lines (Andrews, 2001; Andrews and Jackson, 2001). People around the world still associate Michael Jordan with the 'Air Jordan' trademark copyrighted by Nike. It is argued that Jordan:

> commercialised his sport and himself, turning both into brands for an emerging legion of sports marketers ... In his own way, Jordan ... spread an ideology. It was that sports are not just games but tools for advertisers. It was that basketball isn't a playground thing, but a corporate thing.
>
> *(In Weiner, 1999, p. 77)*

Companies whose profits depend on the sales of alcohol, fast food, soft drinks and sweets are especially eager to have their products associated with the healthy image of athletes and sports (Dewhirst and Sparks, 2003). This enables them to counter negative publicity related to the nutritional value of their products. They want people to think that 'if the sports we love are brought to us by beer, cigarettes, sugar-based soft drinks, beef burgers, deep-fried foods and chocolate bars, these things must have some redeeming qualities'.

We now live in an era of transnational corporations (TNCs). About half the world's 100 largest economies (in terms of annual revenues) are corporations; the other half are nation states (Anderson and Cavanagh, 2000). The majority of the most powerful corporations are based in the USA. For example, General Motors, Chevron-Texaco, Wal-Mart, Exxon Mobile, Mitsubishi, Mitsui and Ford Motor Company each has more economic resources and power than over 60 per cent of all nations. The 200 largest corporations in the world control over one-third of the economic activity around the globe. The executives in these corporations make decisions that influence the economies of entire nations and even regions of the world. They affect who has jobs, the kinds of work people do, their salaries, working conditions, the products that they can buy, where they can buy them and what they cost.

When these corporations enter the world of sports, they negotiate deals that promote their interests and increase their power. Their power over the last few decades has grown largely unchecked. Free-trade agreements now enable many companies to move capital at will and operate largely outside the laws of any single nation. As corporations and the multibillionaires who own or control them do business around the world, they need to create global images of themselves as both citizens and leaders. Sports serve as a site through which they can do this.

Corporate branding is pervasive in sports today. Corporations that sell fast food, sweets and alcohol are especially eager to sponsor sports because they want their products associated with activities defined as healthy and wholesome. The beer company, Heineken, is clearly visible as the main sponsor of a rugby union competition at Twickenham Stadium (*Source*: Elizabeth Pike)

This is partly why corporations pay millions of pounds every year to sponsor sports, and why they spend significantly more sponsoring sports than other cultural events. In the UK, it is estimated that sports sponsorship is worth approximately £500 million (see Horne, 2006). Globally, companies like General Motors and Coca-Cola each spent nearly US$2 billion to sponsor Olympic sports between 1998 and 2008. Like other transnational corporations, they want to promote the belief that enjoyment and pleasure in people's everyday lives depend on corporations and their products. Their goal is to use this belief as the foundation for ideological outposts in the minds of people around the world (see Chapter 4). Corporate executives realize that they can use such outposts to defuse opposition to corporate policies and deliver ideological messages about what is and should be happening in the world. This is a useful strategy for global corporations that want to defuse resistance to products that may not be compatible with local attitudes and cultural practices. For example, when Coca-Cola and Kentucky Fried Chicken face anti-American attitudes in Islamic Pakistan, they can associate their products with international sports rather than US culture and foreign policy.

When a Coca-Cola executive gave a presentation to IOC officials before the 1996 Olympic Games in Atlanta, he assumed that, after nearly 80 years of sponsoring the Olympics, the officials owed loyalty to Coke. So he told the officials the following:

> Just as sponsors have the responsibility to preserve the integrity of the sport, enhance its image, help grow its prestige and its attendance, so too, do you [in sports] have responsibility and accountability to the sponsor.
>
> *(In Reid, 1996, p. 4BB)*

The IOC officials knew that drinking cola did not meet the nutritional needs of elite athletes or the health goals of the Olympic movement, but they did not resist the soft-drink executive's message. Coca-Cola had worked for eight decades to colonize their minds and establish the outposts through which this message was transmitted. More recently, the Olympic Games in Beijing were awash with Coca-Cola imagery as outposts were being established in the heads of 1.3 billion potential consumers of soft drinks.

Outposts in action: branding sports

When ranchers want to show ownership of animals, they burn logos into the animals' hides. The brand is their mark of ownership. Corporations have done the same things with sports.

The naming of stadiums and arenas after sponsors is a relatively recent practice in the UK compared to the USA where there are at least 175 major stadiums and arenas which have sold naming rights to corporate sponsors for deals worth up to US$10 million per year. The first football stadium in the UK to be named after its sponsor was Scarborough, whose ground became the McCains Stadium, after the frozen chip company, in 1988. However, the club went out of business in 2007 after accruing debts of approximately £2.5 million. Current (2008) football stadia include the Emirates (Arsenal), JJB (Wigan), Liberty (Swansea), Reebok (Bolton Wanderers) and Walkers (Leicester). Deals vary, but the Emirates agreement with Arsenal football club is one of the most lucrative, and is estimated to be worth £90 million for the 15-year duration from 2006 to 2021. The deals include signage in and around the venue, the use of executive boxes and club seats, and promotional rights for events.

Omega, the Swiss watch manufacturer, has paid for the rights to be the 'official timekeeper' of the Olympic Games, and is able to associate the company with the Olympic movement and use the Olympic rings in its advertising, as seen in this photograph taken at Hong Kong airport the day before the Beijing 2008 Olympic Games commenced (*Source*: Elizabeth Pike)

The branding of sports also exists inside stadiums, where nearly every available surface is sold to corporate sponsors. At the Wimbledon Lawn Tennis Championships, Robinsons is the 'official soft drink' while Nescafé is the 'official coffee', Lanson is the 'official champagne' and Häagen-Dazs the 'official ice cream'. The balls are supplied by Slazenger, Polo Ralph Lauren is the outfitter for all the officials, Rolex is the official timekeeper, Philips is the official supplier of all televisions, Hertz is the official car to get players to the championship and G4S is the official security services provider to take care of players on arrival. The names of these sponsors appear throughout the grounds, and surfaces without corporate messages are now defined as wasted space, even in publicly owned facilities.

As corporations brand public spaces, community identities often come to be linked with brands, thereby converting the physical embodiments of local traditions and histories into highly visible signs that promote consumption and identify corporations as the source of pleasure and excitement. In the process, the public good is replaced by the corporate good, even in spaces owned by citizen-taxpayers.

Sports events also are branded, and so people now compete in and watch the Barclays Premier League, the Flora London Marathon, the LV (Liverpool Victoria financial services) County Cricket Championship, the RBS (Royal Bank of Scotland) Rugby Union Six Nations Championship, and the Volvo Ocean Race, among many others. In 2005, the sportswear company adidas-Salomon paid US$351 million to secure the rights to all FIFA events until 2012. Formula One motor racing has always been heavily branded. Racing cars are billboards with surface spaces which are purchased by companies, who will pay anything from US$16 million to US$60 million to advertise their products on television in front of billions of viewers. Bernie Ecclestone, who is largely credited with the commercialization of Formula One, is now a multibillionaire, appearing 24th in the list produced by *The Times* in 2008 of the richest people in the UK. The athletes in all these sports are also thoroughly branded, wearing corporate logos on their shirts, shoes, headwear and equipment.

Corporations brand teams worldwide in football, cycling, rugby and many other sports. Because British football was televised for many years by the BBC, which is a public service television station that has no commercials, corporations put their logos on the players themselves and all around the pitches (playing fields) so that spectators would see them constantly. This tradition continues. For example, in 2006, AIG (American International Group) paid the highest recorded shirt sponsorship deal of £56.5 million to have its name on the kit of Manchester United players for four years. Manchester United, with over 50 million fans worldwide, also has sponsorship deals with Nike (US$450 million for 13 years, 2002–15), Budweiser and Audi. Similarly, seven-time Tour de France winner Lance Armstrong and his cycling teammates rode for the Discovery Channel. Professional baseball teams in Japan are named after corporations, not cities. Players and even referees in most sports wear the corporate logos of sponsors on their uniforms.

'This is Pepsi McDonald at Spielberg Jurassic Park, where the Microsoft Raiders will battle the Tesco Titans. Team captains, Nike Jones and Budweiser Williams, prepare for the Lloyds TSB Coin Toss, right after this message from our sponsor, EDF Energy – giving you power on demand!'

Cartoon 11.1 Televised versions of commercial sports have become inseparable from the logos and products of corporate sponsors. It is not too far-fetched to imagine this scene in the near future

Corporate branders now give priority to sports that appeal to younger demographics. So the British Surfing Association is now sponsored by Calypso soft drinks, along with a range of clothing companies such as Animal, Billabong and Gul. Many companies will attach their name to specific skateboard and BMX parks and promotional events.

Sports agents today tell athletes that they can be brands in themselves and that their goal should be to merge with other commercial entities rather than simply endorse another company's products. Michael Jordan was the first to do this. He initially endorsed Nike products, but gradually became a brand in his own right. Today he has his own line of products in addition to 'Air Jordan'. David Beckham and his wife Victoria Beckham have both developed lines of children's clothing. However, this strategy is possible only for those athletes whose celebrity is so great that it can be converted into a brand name, like 'Brand Beckham' (see 'Reflect on sports', p. 401).

The most extensive sponsorship of sports occurs in the USA, not least in the National Football League (NFL). The culmination of the professional NFL season is the Super Bowl. This event is now too expensive for even a large corporation to brand on its own, and it is known as much for its advertisements as for the game itself. Corporate sponsors of the 2009 Super Bowl paid US$3 million or more for 30-second commercial spots during the telecast of the game – that is US$100 000 per second! This generated over US$160 million in revenues for NBC and General Electric, which owned the 2009 television rights. Corporate sponsors paid this amount because their advertisements received exposure beyond the game itself – in terms of previews,

This skate park has a number of local and national sponsors eager to have their name prominently displayed in an area popular with young people (*Source*: Elizabeth Pike)

summaries, highlights, evaluations and rankings in other media coverage – and they will be available for years on the Internet where people can see every advertisement starting with the 1969 Super Bowl. Anheuser-Busch (Budweiser) spent over US$25 million for commercial time during the 2009 game, not including the money spent to produce the commercials. Corporations have branded the Super Bowl to such an extent that it has been described as a programme where the commercials are the entertainment, and the entertainment is the commercials.

Future forms of corporate branding are difficult to predict because it is hard to say where people will draw the line and prevent corporations from colonizing their lives. Advertisements during television coverage are now inserted digitally on the field, court and other surfaces of arenas and stadiums so that viewers cannot escape them even when they record events and delete commercials. Corporations spend more of their advertising money today to purchase brand-placement rights, so their names, logos and products appear directly in the content of sports. This means that we will see more branding of playing fields/spaces, uniforms and athletes' bodies. For example, boxers have gone into the ring with henna tattoos of corporations on their backs. English football player Robbie Savage has an Armani logo tattooed on his arm. Snooker

Reflect on SPORTS 'Brand Beckham'

Smart (2003, p. 77) argues that branding is not simply the selling of a product, it also 'promotes a way of living, a way of doing something, a way of being'. In UK sports, this is perhaps illustrated most clearly in the case of David Beckham. Beckham's lifestyle, from his clothing, hairstyles, pop star wife and playing for a top-flight Premiership football team before moving to continental Europe and then the USA, has enabled him to become 'a vision of the good life to which others aspire' (Cashmore, 2002, p. 6). In the early days of Beckham's success, he was able to associate his name with the global brand of Manchester United, one of the world's best-known football teams (see Andrews, 2004; Horne, 2006). It was not long before 'Brand Beckham' became a global brand in its own right. By 2003, just before Beckham left Manchester United to move to Real Madrid, he was endorsing products including adidas clothing (£3 million per annum), Marks & Spencer (£3 million per annum), Pepsi drinks (£2 million per annum), Police sunglasses (£1 million per annum) and Vodafone (£1 million per annum). In the same year he made a trip to Japan with his wife, and 'Brand Beckham' secured endorsements of a range of products including Meiji chocolate, which was reportedly worth £10 million, making him the highest-paid foreign sporting celebrity (see O'Connor, 2004; Smart, 2005). Advertisements draw on his sporting stature and family values, and the corporations in turn have seen significant sales increases following his endorsement (Cashmore, 2002). The football teams that employ Beckham also see substantial profits. For example, estimates from Beckham's time playing at Real Madrid suggest that sales of the number 23 shirt that he wore enabled the club to recoup his £25 million transfer fee within one year. When Phil Anschutz, the owner of Los Angeles Galaxy, paid US$27.5 million for Beckham in 2007, he was not paying for Beckham's abilities as a footballer, but for the potential increase in earnings that 'Brand Beckham' offered for his other businesses in property, hospitality, newspapers and entertainment.

Beckham is one part of a global celebrity industry. Some would argue that this is for the benefit of the corporations whose products he endorses, and the teams he plays for, which make large sums of money from the sale of his merchandise. Others have suggested that associating with global celebrities offers people a sense of meaning and feeling of empowerment in the uncertain and risky worlds in which many of us now live. *What do you think?*

The goal of branding is to establish outposts in people's heads by connecting pleasure and excitement with corporations and their products. Corporations sponsor sports because many people are emotionally tied to athletes and teams. This man's emotional connection with Manchester United is inscribed permanently on his body. Vodafone, the club's primary corporate sponsor at the time this photograph was taken, uses such connections to their advantage. (*Source*: Luca Bruno, AP/Wide World Photos)

player Jimmy White changed his name by deed poll to James Brown to secure sponsorship from a sauce manufacturer during the Masters tournament in 2005 (see Horne, 2006). Action sports legend Shaun Palmer, arguably the best athlete in the world, has Cadillac tattoos because he likes old Cadillacs. However, what would happen if Cadillac used a photograph of his body in one of their ads? Who owns Shaun Palmer's body and the images on its surface? Does he, the artist who created the tattoos, or Cadillac which owns copyrights on Cadillac images? There have already been lawsuits filed in cases like this, and we will see more in the future.

The limits of corporate branding

Can corporations go too far in their branding of sports? Olympic officials, dedicated to health and fitness, did not turn down $65 million from McDonald's in a deal naming it the Official Restaurant of the 2004 and 2006 Olympics in Athens, Greece and Torino (Turin), Italy. However, people did object when the journalists from American television network CBS wore Nike logos on their jackets as they covered the 1998 Winter Olympics in Nagano, Japan. And, in 2007, the British government introduced new legislation prohibiting the sale of replica sports shirts to children if they carry the logo of an alcoholic drink. But despite a few cases of resistance, sports generally are for sale, and corporations are willing buyers when deals boost their power and profits and promote consumption as a lifestyle.

One interesting development in the sponsorship of British sport was the significance of banning cigarette advertising on television in 1965. The almost immediate response of tobacco companies was to increasingly sponsor sports events and so have their product names highly visible without breaching legislation. In particular, several Formula One teams were sponsored by tobacco companies, they raced under the colours of the company and displayed the corporate name on the cars. This loophole was effectively closed in 2002 with the introduction of the Tobacco Advertising and Promotion Act. Many felt that there was an incongruence between the healthy image of sports and the sponsorship by tobacco companies, with the known health-damaging properties of their products, and that this particular form of corporate branding should be banned. However 'global events' such as Formula One and world snooker were given longer to arrange new sponsorship deals because the sports had become so dependent on the money from the tobacco companies. Notably the Ferrari team still races in the red and white colours of Marlboro, with the company name displayed when racing in territories where tobacco sponsorship is still permitted.

Corporate executives realize that sports produce enjoyable and emotional identifications with athletes, teams, events and places. Therefore, they think it makes economic sense to brand sports so that people will recognize corporate names and products, and associate them with the things that provide excitement and pleasure in their lives (Pennington, 2004). In less than a generation, sports have been so thoroughly branded that many people, especially those under 30 years old, see this situation as 'normal' – as the way it is and should be. Does this mean that corporations have established ideological outposts in people's heads to the point that they accept corporate power as inevitable and even desirable? If so, corporate hegemony is deeply entrenched, even if a few people say it is unwise to turn sports over to entities accountable only to market forces. If so, commercial sports are sites where people with political and financial resources can package their values and ideas and present them in a form that most people see as a taken-for-granted part of life.

Commercialization and Changes in Sports

What happens to sports when they shift from being activities organized for players to being activities organized for paying spectators and sponsors? Do they change, and, if so, in what ways?

When a sport is converted into commercial entertainment, its success depends on spectator appeal. Although spectators have many reasons for watching sports, their interest usually is tied to a combination of four factors:

1 attachment to those involved ('Do I know or like players and/or teams?')

2 the uncertainty of an event's outcome ('Will it be a close contest?')

4 the risk or financial rewards associated with participating in an event ('How much money, ego or personal well-being is at stake in the contest?')

4 the anticipated display of excellence, heroics or dramatic expression by the athletes ('Are the players and/or teams skilled and entertaining?') .

When spectators say they saw 'a good game', they usually are talking about one in which (1) they were attached personally or emotionally to people involved, (2) the outcome was in doubt until the last minutes or seconds, (3) the stakes were so high that players were totally committed to and engrossed in the action, or (4) there were skilled and dramatic performances. Events containing all four of these factors are remembered and discussed for many years.

Because attachment, uncertainty, high stakes and performance attract spectators, successful commercial sports are organized to maximize the probability that all four factors will exist in an event. To understand how this affects sports, we consider the impact of commercialization on the following three aspects of sports:

1 the internal structure and goals of sports
2 the orientations of athletes, coaches and sponsors
3 the people and organizations that control sports.

Internal structure and goals of sports

Commercialization influences the internal structure and goals of newly developed sports, but it has less influence on long-established sports. Among new sports developed explicitly for commercial purposes, it is clear that rules are designed to promote on-the-field action that will be defined as entertaining by a targeted audience.

Entertainment is not the only issue that influences the internal structure and goals of new sports, but it is the *primary* issue. This is apparent in the case of the X Games where the rules are designed to maximize 'big air', dangerous and spectacular moves, and the technical aspects of equipment, often manufactured by event sponsors. The drinks company Red Bull has been particularly keen to associate itself with a variety of newly developed entertainment sports, and the company sponsors everything from the more traditional sport of Formula One to newer sports such as snowboarding, surfing, cliff diving and the Flugtag aerobatic competition. The company's trademark phrase is 'it gives you wings' while the company motto states 'break through the extreme, express the potential'. It is clear that Red Bull, along with many other sponsors, is most interested in promoting sports as entertainment, and a research study of consumers' perceptions of sports sponsors found that most spectators associated Red Bull with words such as 'exciting' and 'trendy' (IDG, 2007).

The rules in established sports also undergo changes to make the action more exciting and understandable for spectators, but the changes seldom alter the basic internal organization and goals of the sports. Changes in all commercialized spectator sports usually do one or more of six things: (1) speed up the action, (2) increase scoring, (3) balance competition, (4) maximize drama, (5) heighten attachment to players and teams, and (6) provide strategic breaks in the form of 'commercial time-outs'. A review of rule changes in many sports shows the importance of these factors. For example, the points available for a rugby try were increased to encourage players to run the ball rather than kick for goal. Football rules were changed to prevent matches in major competitions from ending in ties, with the introduction of the 'golden goal' and 'silver goal' in extra time, and penalty shootouts. Tennis scoring was changed to meet the time requirements of television schedules. In cricket, the English Cricket Board introduced the Twenty20 game in 2003, which limits the number of overs to 20 per side, making the game a spectator-friendly length of approximately three hours. In national football tournaments such as the FA Cup, the Premier League teams do not enter the competition until the later rounds to establish interest in the teams from the lower leagues who might be successful in some 'giant killing'.

In addition, some new competitions have been created in order to attract more spectators. In international athletics, the International Association of Athletics Federations (IAAF) introduced the Golden League series of grand prix meetings in 1998 to ensure the best competitors competed against each other in regular meets. And, in 2008, the newly formed Indian Premier League (IPL) for Twenty20 cricket offered lucrative fees for players (including some British cricketers) which were enabled by broadcasters and sponsors signing deals with the league for a 10-year period. The IPL was viewed as potentially undermining the English Premier League (EPL) which paid significantly lower wages and so was likely to lose many top-flight players attracted by the large pay packets on offer in India. The IPL proposed a partnership with the EPL, allowing players to compete in India in the spring and England in the summer in newly created Twenty20 Super Leagues, played at times to suit live and television spectators. Both the Golden League and the Twenty20 Premier Leagues were supported by multimillion-pound television and sponsorship deals, but they have not yet replaced other competitions or changed the fundamental rules or scoring of the sports.

Although these changes are grounded in commercialization, they have not altered the internal structure and goals of long-established sports: teams remain the same size with similar positions, and outscoring opponents remains the primary goal. Some of these changes also reflect the concerns of athletes, who have more fun when there is more action, more scoring and a closer contest. In addition, some of the changes are to protect the health and well-being of athletes, such as the 'blood replacement' in rugby which was introduced to ensure that injured athletes get treatment without compromising the team, and to avoid participants being exposed to the blood of another player.

Because sports are social constructions, they change in connection with shifts in social conditions and power relations in the society as a whole. This means that people have and always will establish rules for sports. And those people are always influenced by social and cultural conditions at the time that they make or revise rules. However, commercial issues are carefully considered today when changes are suggested, discussed and made.

Another change that has come with commercialization is that many events today are organized intentionally as *total entertainment experiences*. There is loud music, attractive and rapidly changing video displays, cheerleaders and mascots who plan entertaining performances, light displays, and announcers who heighten drama with excited verbal descriptions of the action. This entertainment package represents a change, but it affects the context surrounding a game or match rather than the structure and goals of the sport itself.

Orientations of athletes, coaches and sponsors

Commercialized sports exist in a 'promotional culture' created to sell athletic performances to audiences and to sell audiences to sponsors. These sports are promoted through marketing hype based on stories, myths and images created around players, teams and even stadiums or arenas. Athletes become entertainers and the orientations of nearly everyone in sports shift towards an emphasis on heroic actions and away from aesthetic actions.

The shift towards heroic orientations is necessary to attract a mass audience to buy tickets or watch televised events. Entertaining a *mass* audience is difficult because it contains many people who lack technical knowledge about the complex physical skills and strategies involved in a sport. Without technical knowledge, hype and drama become primary sources of entertainment for the audience. Hype and drama are easily understood, and spectators are entertained when athletes take risks and face clear physical danger. Spectators are impressed by the dramatic expressions of athletes, and they are awed by athletes dedicated to the game and to victory, regardless of personal cost. They are more impressed by athletes who collapse as they surpass physical limits than by athletes who know their limits so well that they can play for years without going beyond them. Spectators without technical knowledge about a sport enjoy watching athletes project exciting or controversial personas, and they often rate performances in terms of a player's style as much as his or her technical proficiency.

When spectators lack technical knowledge about football, for example, they are entertained more by a striker's corner-post dance after a goal than by the midfielder's pass that enabled the striker to score. Those who know little about the technical aspects of ice skating are entertained more by triple and quadruple jumps than routines carefully choreographed and practised until they are smooth and flawless. Without dangerous jumps, naive spectators become bored because they are not aware of subtle differences in the skills of skaters. Those who lack technical knowledge about rugby are more likely to talk about a single try than the well co-ordinated defence that enabled the team to win a game. Players know this and realize that their tries will be shown on news replays, regardless of who plays a technically good game. Thus, try-mania rules, and fans are disappointed when they see a 'kicking game' rather than a 'running game'; they want to see the heroic more than the aesthetic aspects of sports.

Figure 11.1 illustrates that when a sport depends on entertaining mass audiences, the athletes, coaches and team administrators often revise their ideas about what is important in athletic performances. The danger of movement becomes important in addition to the beauty of movement; style and dramatic expression become important in addition to fundamental skills; pushing beyond personal limits becomes important in addition to exploring limits; and commitment to victory for the team and sponsor becomes important in addition to commitment to participation. When sports become commercialized, most people associated with them develop heroic orientations in addition to aesthetic orientations; they even describe games and matches as 'showtime'. This does not mean that aesthetic orientations cease to be important or that people are no longer impressed by beauty and skills in sports, but it does mean that heroic orientations enter the mix of what constitutes a good sports performance. Heroic actions are what attract a mass audience.

Many athletes realize the dangers associated with heroic orientations, and some even try to limit the emphasis on heroic actions in their sports. For example, some figure skaters want restrictions on the number of triple jumps required in skating programmes. They worry that the quest for commercial success is putting their bodies on the line. Other skaters, however, adopt heroic orientations to please audiences, and conform to shifts in the orientations of judges, coaches and other skaters (Mihoces, 2005). Thus, it is not surprising that figure skaters train to hit a long succession of triple jumps and hope to perform occasional quad jumps without breaking bones or destroying the continuity of their skating programmes. Aesthetic orientations still exist, but heroic orientations are becoming more central in defining the 'quality' of figure skaters. One additional outcome of the heroic orientation of supporters is that they are then interested to see whether performers will be successful in their heroic actions, and many are willing to gamble money on the outcome of this. This is discussed in the box 'Sports and the gambling economy' (p. 408).

> I have obligations to my sponsors and, if I don't achieve certain things, I lose my sponsors.

(Jason Gardener, British track and field athlete, 2004, p. 45)

The people and organizations that control sports

Commercialization changes the location of control in and over sports. When sports depend on the revenues they generate, the control centre in sports organizations shifts away from the athletes and towards those who have the resources to produce and promote sports. Athletes in heavily commercialized sports generally lose effective control over the conditions of their own sport participation. These conditions are controlled by a combination of general managers, team owners, corporate sponsors, agents, advertisers, media personnel, marketing and publicity staff, professional management staff, accountants and agents.

The organizations that control commercial sports are designed to co-ordinate these people so that profits are maximized. This means that decision making in commercial sports promotes economic interests and deals with athletes as commodities to be managed. The power to affect these decisions is grounded in resources that may not even be connected with sports. Therefore, athletes in many commercial sports find themselves cut out of decision-making processes, even when the decisions affect their health and the rewards they receive for playing.

As decision making in sports organizations moves further away from athletes, there is a need for athletes and their supporters to develop strategies to represent their interests, financial

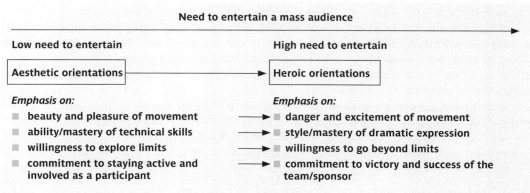

Note: The orientations associated with many commercial spectator sports today have shifted from the aesthetic to the heroic. Many people in a mass audience do not have enough technical knowledge about a sport to be entertained by aesthetic action; instead, they seek and focus on heroic action. Therefore, athletes and others associated with the game emphasize heroic orientations in their performances. 'Heroic' as it is used in this chapter and figure refers to 'villains' and others who emphasize dramatic expression in their sport performances.

Figure 11.1 **Shifting orientations: what happens when there is a need to entertain a mass audience.**

reflect on SPORTS   *Sports and the gambling economy* • • • • • • • • • •

The development of commercialized sport has also led to the expansion of a parallel industry of sports gambling. People who gamble on sports may be driven by pure economics and a belief that they can predict the outcome of an event and so win money, or by the drama and entertainment of the spectacle with their attachment to a team or individual heightened by having money resting on the outcome. In either case, sports gambling reflects the broader relationship between commercialization and the economy of sports. Gambling on the outcome of sporting events is not a new phenomenon (see Cashmore, 2007b). In the seventeenth century, people would bet on the outcome of duels between soldiers returning from the English Civil War. Gambling on other forms of face-to-face combat such as pugilism and boxing has always been commonplace. In the nineteenth century, betting on blood sports became popular. Although dogfighting, cockfighting, bear-baiting and other animal sports are now illegal, betting on animal sports such as horse and greyhound racing remains popular. One of the main developments in sports gambling was the introduction of 'the football pools' in the 1930s, where people would select a specified number of drawn games, and their betting forms could be collected from their homes. This remained popular until the introduction of the National Lottery (more recently rebranded as 'Lotto') in the 1990s.

The Lotto is a tremendously popular form of gambling and promotes itself as underpinning good causes. However, it is often described as a regressive tax, since it is played mostly by those on low wages but benefits the wealthy. One additional concern with the Lotto is that those who play have no mechanism to force discussions with politicians for how profits are spent (unlike more formal taxation); including, for example, the decision to use Lotto funding to contribute to the £9 billion price tag of the London Olympic Games in 2012, and the subsequent reduction of funding to the tune of nearly £100 million to non-Olympic sports ventures and £112 million to the arts.

The appeal of these convenient types of gambling has provided a large audience for the increasing number of Internet gambling sites, and in 2000 the first duty-free Internet football betting website was launched, enabling customers to gamble on football leagues online from anywhere in the world. It is estimated that gambling in the UK is worth in excess of £20 billion, while the online gambling and gaming industry may be worth as much as US$11 billion (see Beech and Chadwick, 2004; Robinson, 2008). In 2007, a government survey of family expenditure in the UK estimated that approximately £3.60 per week, or one-third of the money spent on sport-related activities, is actually on gambling (Office for National Statistics, 2008)!

Sports gambling has many positive benefits, including increased spectating from those who seek to make money from sport. However, there are also serious concerns about betting on sports. Gambling has led to accusations of match-fixing and other forms of cheating, as well as 'underground' sports competitions specifically focused on gambling (in particular animal sports and illegal fighting – see Chapter 6). Also, for some people, the thrill of gambling is so great that compulsive gambling is now a recognized addiction, akin to that of alcohol or drugs, and there have been many high-profile cases of athletes such as Michael Owen and Wayne Rooney who are known gamblers. Some argue that the negative consequences of gambling outweigh the pleasure and economic gains that benefit the few. *What do you think?*

and otherwise. In Spain, professional football teams are connected with a club structure which incorporates public ownership, and fans have organized lobbying groups to express their interests. A relatively recent development in the UK is the online membership system for Ebbsfleet United Football Club. Individuals can pay for membership of the club, and this entitles them to joint ownership of the team. Members are able to vote on key business decisions and have access to financial information. As the club's website states: 'Own the club, pick the team and be part of the first website community takeover in the world' (www.myfootballclub. co.uk). Moves such as this reflect some people's concerns with the commercialization of sports, and an attempt to resist the dominant commercial model in which corporations set the terms and conditions of playing sports at the highest levels of competition. While commercialization may not change the structure and goals inside the activities and games, it dramatically changes the cultural and organizational contexts in which they are played.

Owners, Sponsors and Promoters in Commercial Sports

Commercial sports are organized in different ways from one society to the next, but in all cases, owners, sponsors and promoters significantly influence the conditions under which professional athletes perform. In this section, we focus on the overall control structure that exists in most visible professional sports in the UK.

Professional sports in the UK

Professional sports in the UK have the characteristics of a mixed economy (see Horne et al., 1999). In principle, sports are controlled by their governing bodies, although this is subject to meeting commercial and other demands. In reality, some sports clubs are publicly owned while others are owned by private businesses. In some cases, there is a combination of the two, where a club might be owned by shareholders, while the venue in which the events are played may be owned by a private corporation, and they may have special arrangements with sponsors and media companies. Where the athletes themselves fit into this system is also complicated. Athletes may be owned by the clubs (for the duration of their contract), by managers or operate as free agents. The complexity of the system of sports ownership is illustrated in Table 11.1.

Owners include large corporations, partnerships and wealthy individuals whose assets range from hundreds of millions to billions of pounds. Owners can make good to excellent returns on their investments, and support from media companies and corporate sponsors almost guarantees financial success at this level of ownership. There have been many entrepreneurs who, therefore, see professional sports as a wise financial investment. This is not only about the income from ticket sales and merchandise, but also the potential from the acquisition of shares, and property development surrounding the most successful clubs. In men's football, the financial investment of entrepreneurs has contributed to the dominance in recent years of 'The Big Four': Arsenal, Chelsea, Liverpool and Manchester United. Each of these clubs has non-UK citizens who own significant shares and have a place on the board of directors.

Similarly the large corporations that sponsor particular events, from major golf and tennis tournaments to Formula One and European athletics races, know the costs and benefits that are involved. Their association with top events not only provides them advertising platforms but also connects them with clearly identified categories of consumer (see Cartoon 11.2). Television companies also will sponsor events so that they can control their own programming, as in the case of Premier League football.

Table 11.1 **Ownership structures**

Type of ownership	Explanation	Sporting example
Consolidation	The acquisition of several elements or subunits of a market sector	Frank Warren, boxing promoter and owner of Frank Warren Sports Network, which has the television rights to fights involving his boxers
Vertical integration	Ownership of a range of facilities, or having power at several levels of the business	Rupert Murdoch's ownership of BSkyB and various sports television networks, several newspapers and sports teams
Horizontal integration	Ownership of several facilities, giving power at one level across a range of clubs, teams, etc.	The ownership by United Racecourses of Epsom, Sandown Park and Kempton Park
Diversification	The development of business interests by expanding into new areas	Roman Abramovich, Russian oil billionaire who purchased Chelsea Football Club in 2003

Source: adapted from Horne et al., 1999, p. 273

'Winning at sports is easy when you own them and can prevent others from playing.'

Cartoon 11.2 **The growth and profitability of commercial sports around the world have little to do with athletes. Owners, sponsors and media executives control sports today, and they make money when governments allow them to operate as cartels and keep competitors out of the game**

Sport sponsorships enable companies that sell tobacco, alcohol and foods with questionable nutritional value to link their products and logos to popular activities. Because people associate sports with healthy and strong bodies instead of cancer, heart disease, diabetes, obesity, tooth decay and other forms of poor health related to their products, these companies are eager to be sponsors. It increases their legitimacy in society and defuses resistance to corporate policies, practices and products.

Investments in sports and sport events are motivated by many factors. In some cases, investors are sports fans with money looking to satisfy lifelong fantasies, build their egos or socialize with celebrity athletes. Owning or sponsoring sports gains them more enjoyment and prestige than other business ventures, often making them instant celebrities in their cities. Those who invest in sports seldom are so carried away with fun and fantasy that they forget business or capitalist expansion. They do not enjoy losing money or sharing power. They may look at their athletes as heroes, but they want to control them and maximize investment returns. They may not agree with fellow owners and sponsors on all issues, but they do agree on the need to protect their investments and maximise profits. This was illustrated clearly at Chelsea football club where the owner, Russian billionaire Roman Abramovich, was famously accused of repeatedly intervening in the decisions of his former manager, Jose Morinho, including which players to purchase and field. While Abramovich was often witnessed passionately supporting his team, his main interests were clearly also about maximizing the return on his financial investment.

Professional sports leagues in the UK have always tended to be 'open', meaning that the teams and players who are most successful during the designated season are likely to be promoted or sustain their position within a league, while the less able will be relegated. This contrasts with the system in the USA, where leagues are 'closed' and limited to a designated number of teams and franchises, and entry to the league is largely determined by access to funds. Of course, the reality in the UK is that those teams who have access to financial resources can afford better

Jose Morinho and Roman Abramovich share a joke (*Source*: Phil Cole/Getty Images)

players, facilities and support staff and so are more likely to be successful. And as these clubs become increasingly successful, so they also dominate the media coverage and the share of television revenues, which facilitates their further dominance and the generous salaries of the players and shareholders (this is discussed further in Chapter 12).

There have also been many financial disasters, where clubs have gone out of business, leaving many owners, sponsors and promoters in debt. For example, Leeds United football club was among the 'top flight' clubs, reaching the UEFA Champions League semi-final in 2001. The club's owners took out large loans in the anticipation of television and sponsorship revenues, but when Leeds failed to qualify for UEFA in the following season it was unable to pay off its debts. The club was forced to sell several key players, and eventually its training ground and stadium. Inevitably Leeds United was relegated from the Premiership, and by 2007 was in Coca-Cola League One (the third of the three leagues) with a deduction of 15 points for the financial maladministration, and its funding crisis still not fully resolved. Of course, this is only one example of those who have lost money in sports.

Professional sports venues

The belief that cities must have professional sports teams, big sports events and appropriate arenas and stadiums to be 'world class' has led to public support for sports organizations (Silk, 2004). This has been particularly significant in areas of the UK where the decline in the manufacturing industries led many cities to turn to sport to 're-image' the city to attract tourists and address economic decline. For example, Sheffield developed substantial facilities for the World Student Games in 1991, and Manchester hosted the Commonwealth Games in 2002. Disused industrial land has also been used to build sports stadiums, such as the Emirates Stadium, the home of Arsenal football club, and many of the facilities for the London 2012 Olympic Games, all under the guise of 'urban regeneration'. As noted in Chapter 10, 'stadium socialism' enables wealthy and powerful capitalists to use development facilities for personal gain. In contrast to the USA where most facilities are publicly owned, largely through local taxation, and rented to teams, in the UK sports teams and clubs are largely expected to provide their own facilities.

Owners justify the development of professional sports venues with five arguments (Lavoie, 2000).

1 A stadium and professional team creates jobs; those who hold the jobs spend money and pay taxes in the city.

2 Stadium construction infuses money into the local economy; this money is spent over and over again as it circulates, generating tax revenues in the process.

3 The team attracts businesses to the city and brings in visitors who spend money.

4 The team attracts regional and national media attention, which boosts tourism and contributes to economic development.

5 The team creates positive psychological and social benefits, boosting social unity, and feelings of pride and well-being in the local population.

These arguments often are supported by studies that are commissioned by those with a vested interest in the development of sports and facilities. However, *independent* studies do *not* always support them (see Coalter, 2007). Independent studies generally conclude the following.

■ Teams and stadiums create jobs, but apart from highly paid athletes and team executives, these jobs are low paying and seasonal. As a result the ushers, car park attendants and ticket agents do not make full-time living wages. Additionally, many athletes do not live in the city or spend their money there.

■ The companies that design and build stadiums are seldom local, and construction materials and workers on major projects often come from outside the region; they spend most of what they earn in other places.

■ Stadiums attract other businesses, but most are restaurant and entertainment franchises headquartered in other cities, even other countries. These franchised businesses often drive out locally owned businesses. Spectators come from out of town, but most live close enough to make day trips to games, so they do not spend much money outside the stadium and the immediate area.

■ Stadiums and teams generate public relations for the city, but this has mixed results for tourism because some people stay away from cities on game days. Most important, *regional* economic development often is limited by a new facility because fans who spend money at and around the stadium have fewer pounds to spend in their neighbourhoods. A stadium helps nearby businesses, but it often hurts outlying businesses (Hudson, 2001).

■ A professional sports team makes some people feel better and may enhance general perceptions of a city, but this is difficult to measure. Additionally, feelings often vary with the success of teams, and some people are unimpressed by the male-orientated heroics that are glorified in some men's sports.

The people who object to stadium development seldom have the resources to oppose the well-financed, professionally packaged proposals developed by experienced political advisers hired by team owners. The social activists who might lead the opposition already deal full-time with problems related to unemployment, underfunded schools, homelessness, poor health, drug use and the lack of needed social services in cities. They cannot take leave from these tasks to lobby against using public money to benefit billionaire team owners and millionaire celebrity athletes. And yet, building these new sport facilities will not cut poverty rates, improve schools or increase the availability of safe, low-cost housing for those who are often most affected by them. Often, they simply force poor people to move to another area of town while developers build on condemned properties that they buy for little money. For example, building the Cardiff Millennium Stadium involved the demolition of a low-cost public swimming pool, which was replaced by exclusive retail and food franchises. At the same time, sports writers publish stories about the great public service of athletes who visit classes in dilapidated schools in the city.

 I'm 100% for regeneration if it's for East Enders, but we have to make sure that it's not just another name for giving big business carte blanche to make a killing out of the Olympics.

(Long-term resident of East London, London East Research Unit, 2006, p. 14)

Sources of income for sports owners

The owners of top professional teams in the major men's sports make money from (1) gate receipts, (2) media revenues, (3) stadium revenue, (4) licensing fees and (5) merchandise sales. The amounts and proportions of each of these revenue sources vary from sport to sport.

Stadiums which have been built in recent years are based on the demands of owners who require venues that can generate new revenue streams. This is why new stadiums resemble a shopping mall built around a playing field. Sociologist George Ritzer (2005) describes them as 'cathedrals of consumption' designed so that consumption is seamlessly included in spectator experiences. These stadiums offer restaurants, bars, museums, tours and, even, the opportunity to pay for all this on a club credit card to further 'support the team'! Owners see this as important because it enables them to capture a greater share of the entertainment pound in a highly competitive urban market. The more a spectator 'supports their team', the more this contributes to the bank accounts of the multimillionaire owners and players. The Rugby Football Union (RFU) uses Twickenham stadium to raise money through ticket sales and corporate hospitality. People buying into the 'Twickenham Experience Ltd' get the best seats and a nice lunch. In return, the corporate industry provides the RFU with approximately £25 million, which accounts for a third of the RFU's total annual revenue (Wigglesworth, 2007).

One fairly recent extension of this is the expansion of the sports tourism industry. This is multifaceted, with some people choosing to take holidays to visit a specific sporting venue, or to incorporate watching a major sports competition. In addition, some sports clubs (both professional and amateur) will travel for training and competition purposes. And, of course, there are large numbers of sporting holidays particularly related to fishing, golfing, mountaineering,

Twickenham rugby ground offers a museum, retail store, and numerous food and drink outlets to encourage spectators to spend money beyond the cost of their ticket to watch the event (*Source*: Elizabeth Pike)

skiing and walking, which provide a multimillion-pound sport-related industry, especially in Scotland and Wales (see Gratton and Taylor, 2000). This was not lost on the organizers of the London 2012 Olympic Games, and in 2007 a document entitled *Winning: A Tourism Strategy for 2012 and Beyond* was produced by the Department for Culture, Media and Sport. This document opens by stating:

> Our aim is to improve the quality of life for all through cultural and sporting activities, support the pursuit of excellence, and champion the tourism, creative and leisure industries.
>
> *(Department for Culture, Media and Sport, 2007, p. 1)*

The strategy proposed by the government is to develop the sports tourism infrastructure of facilities, accommodation and transport, in order to attract more visitors and businesses through sport in a way which is environmentally sustainable. Of course, this is underpinned by the awareness of a £85 billion tourist economy which the UK 'must grasp with both hands' (DCMS, 2007, p. 2)!

Amateur sports in the UK

Amateur sports do not have owners, but they do have commercial sponsors and governing bodies that control events and athletes. Generally, the sponsors are corporations interested in using amateur sports for publicity and advertising purposes. The governing bodies of amateur sports operate on a non-profit basis although they use revenues from events to maintain their organizations and power over amateur sports.

Centralized sports authorities administer amateur sports in most countries. They work with the national governing bodies (NGBs) of individual sports, and together they control events, athletes and revenues. Furthermore, although the UK government has been less keen to subsidize professional sports teams to pay their players and attract revenue, they have been more involved in amateur sports. Sport England, Sport Northern Ireland, sportscotland and the Sports Council for Wales are examples of centralized authorities which have a 'quasi-autonomous' link with the government; they develop the policies that govern the various national sports organizations in the UK. This is explained further in Chapter 13. Local authorities have played a significant role in providing fields, swimming pools and indoor spaces for sporting activities, which may be used by clubs.

All amateur sports organizations share an interest in controlling two things: (1) the athletes in their sports, and (2) the money generated from grant applications, sponsorships and competitive events. A major source of income for amateur sports comes from the National Lottery. In 1999, the Sport England Lottery Fund was set up to develop both 'sport for all' and international sporting success through to 2009. In part this is a response to the relative decline in safe sporting spaces and the increasing numbers of commercialized sporting activities, not least in the form of private fitness gyms and health clubs, which are available only to those with sufficient funds to pay the subscriptions (see Smith Maguire, 2008). Approximately £200 million is available each year from the National Lottery, of which £150 million is invested in community projects, with the remainder given to the 'world class fund'. Community projects funded through the Lottery include school sports, sports for social inclusion and regeneration projects, and a range of health-related physical activity projects. These aim to increase opportunities for sporting physical activity among those who have limited access and funds to otherwise engage in such schemes. The world class programmes have contributed to the development of facilities such as the Millennium Stadium in Cardiff, Hampden Park in Glasgow and the facilities for the London 2012 Olympic Games (see Roberts, K., 2004). In principle, these facilities are also open to amateur sports clubs and performers at designated times.

Sponsorship patterns in amateur sports take many forms. The NGBs of amateur sports are increasingly dependent on corporate sponsorship money, to supplement Lottery and other sources of funding to pay for athlete training, operating expenses and competitive events. Corporate logos now appear on the clothing and equipment of amateur athletes. As this model of corporate sponsorship is increasingly used, the economics of sports becomes tied closely to the fortunes and fluctuations of market economies and large corporations. Corporations sponsor only sports that foster their interests, and economic conditions influence their ability and willingness to maintain sponsorships.

The voluntary sector

The UK has a long history of amateur sports, which were largely dependent on volunteers. We have identified in the previous section the increasing role of public funding and sponsorship in amateur sports, but the development of many sports is still dependent on unpaid volunteers working in non-profit organizations outside the government and commercial sectors. The voluntary sector is very diverse, incorporating some NGBs, organizations for specific groups (such as youth sports or sports for disabled athletes), regular sports clubs, and occasional sports events organized and run by volunteers. Research suggests that people engage in volunteer work in sports partly to serve a shared need and partly for economic reasons. In either case, volunteering may enable a sports activity to take place which might not otherwise happen, and this usually suits the needs of the volunteer personally or those of their children or partner. Sports which are most likely to have high numbers of volunteers are those in a formal club which manages its own facilities, such as bowls or cricket (see Nichols, 2001). Because volunteer work is diverse and unpaid, it is difficult to know the extent of volunteering in the UK, but it is estimated that there are nearly 6 million volunteers working in sports in England alone, contributing more than 1 billion hours in time each year, which is worth £14 billion to the sports industry (Sport England, 2003b). Volunteering is becoming increasingly encouraged and structured, and 2005 was designated the Year of the Volunteer in the UK.

Legal Status and Incomes of Athletes in Commercial Sports

When sports are commercialized, athletes are entertainers. Professional athletes are paid for their efforts, whereas amateur athletes receive rewards within limits set by the organizations that govern their lives. This raises two questions: (1) what is the legal status of the athlete-entertainers who work in 'amateur' sports, and (2) how are athlete-entertainers rewarded for their work? Many people do not think of athletes as workers, and they overlook owner–player relations in professional sports as a form of labour relations. This is because people associate sports with play in their lives, and they see sports as fun rather than work. However, when sports are organized to make money, players are workers, even though they may have fun on the job (Zimmer and Zimmer, 2001). This is not unique; many workers enjoy their jobs. But regardless of enjoyment, issues of legal status and fair rewards for work are important.

Professional athletes

Legal status: team sports

The legal status of participants in professional men's football has become a controversial issue in the UK in recent years. In 1961 the maximum wage was abolished, and this was followed in 1963 by the 'Eastham Case' which was a High Court ruling limiting the power of clubs to own players and restrict their trade. Perhaps the most significant case is the 'Bosman ruling' in the 1990s, which redefined the legal status of contracts, club ownership of players, the quota system and the ways that players transferred between clubs and across national borders. This also has implications for other sports.

The Bosman ruling was the outcome of a legal case brought by a Belgium football player, Jean-Marc Bosman, to the European Court of Justice (ECJ). Bosman had secured a transfer from his Belgian club to a French team in 1990, but the deal collapsed when his Belgian team failed to apply to the Belgian Football Association for the necessary clearance certificates to enable Bosman to move to France, and then suspended him without a salary in accordance with the rule of the Belgian Association. Bosman started proceedings in the domestic courts and his case was eventually heard in the ECJ. His case was interesting because it did not introduce any new legislation, it simply argued that the existing systems in professional football were incompatible with European law, specifically Article 48 of the EC Treaty which agrees freedom of movement of workers between member states. The Bosman ruling of 1995 confirmed that the quota system in football, which limited the number of 'foreign' players on a team, and the transfer system which required the payment of a fee for an out-of-contract player, did breach Article 48. Since the Bosman ruling, the governing bodies of all European sports have had to operate within this new legal environment which allows freedom of movement for those working within sports, including those working as athletes (for a detailed overview of the implications of the Bosman ruling, see Parrish and McArdle, 2004).

The Bosman case gave increased power to players and increased their ability to negotiate lucrative contracts. As a result, the system of transferring players between football clubs has become a significant economy in itself. As one football agent stated: 'The whole transfer system has become an incredibly complicated industry. Quite often you have a deal and several parties want to get involved. It's getting worse because the money is greater' (Rachel Anderson, in Roderick, 2006b, p. 125). In turn, this has created additional legal issues: the problems of 'illegal' tactics, and the role of sports agents.

The most common aspect of 'illegal' processes in transfers is that of 'tapping'. This is the system where a coach or manager will contact a player or their agent informally, in order to establish whether the player would consider transferring to their club. One of the most famous cases of 'tapping up' was when Chelsea football club was fined £300 000 in 2005 for illegally speaking with Ashley Cole and his agent without speaking with Arsenal football club, with whom he had a contract at the time. Cole did subsequently move to Chelsea.

Sports agents are playing an increasingly visible role in the negotiations of players' transfers and other aspects of their sporting and celebrity commercial ventures. Agents will often deal with managers in connection with legal and contractual issues on behalf of the player, represent the player in interviews with the media, and help with pensions and insurance, all in return for significant personal financial gain. It is, therefore, in the interests of the agent that the player earns a large salary, and encouraging players to regularly change clubs is one way of doing this. In the case of Ashley Cole, the chair of the Football Association's Premier League stated that he had been relatively lenient with Cole, believing that Cole had been manipulated by his agent to engage with the illegal 'tapping up' move. Agents also have a legal hold over players, as once a player has signed with an agent they cannot then sign with a different agent as this will be in breach of their contract (see Roderick, 2006b). While this is not new, it is an increasing aspect of commercial and global sports as athletes become commodities to be sold for the financial gain of themselves and those who work with them.

Legal status: individual sports

The legal status of professional athletes in individual sports varies greatly from sport to sport and even from one athlete to another. Although there are important differences among boxing, bowling, golf, tennis, motor racing, horse racing, track and field, skiing, cycling, and a number of recently professionalized alternative and action sports, a few generalizations are possible.

The legal status of athletes in individual sports largely depends on what athletes must do to train and qualify for competition in their sports. For example, few athletes can afford to pay for all the training needed to develop professional-level skills in a sport. Furthermore, they do not have the knowledge or connections to meet the formal requirements to become an official competitor in their sport, which may include having a recognized agent or manager (as in boxing), being formally accepted by other participants (as in most motor racing), obtaining membership in a professional organization (as in most bowling, golf and tennis tournaments) or gaining a special invitation through an official selection group (as in professional track and field meets).

Whenever athletes need sponsors to pay for their training or have others help them meet participation requirements, their legal status is shaped by the contracts they sign with sponsors, agents and the groups that regulate participation. This is why the legal status of athletes in individual sports varies so much.

Let us use boxing as an example. Because many boxers come from low-income backgrounds, they do not have the resources to develop high-level boxing skills or arrange official bouts with other boxers. Therefore, they need trainers, managers and sponsors. The support of these people always comes with conditions that are written in formal contracts or based on informal agreements. In either case, they require the boxers to forfeit control over much of their lives and a portion of the rewards they may earn in future bouts. This means that few boxers, even those who win large amounts of money, have much control over their careers. They are forced to trade control over their bodies and careers for the opportunity to continue boxing. This is an example of how class relations operate in sports: when people lack resources, they cannot negotiate the conditions under which their sports careers occur.

The legal status of athletes in individual sports usually is defined in the by-laws of professional organizations such as the Professional Golf Association (PGA), the Ladies' Professional Golf Association (LPGA), the Association of Tennis Professionals (ATP) and the Amateur Boxing Association (ABA). Because athletes control many of these organizations, their policies support athletes' rights and enable them to control some of the conditions under which they compete. Without these organizations, athletes in these sports would have few rights as workers.

Income: team sports

Despite the publicity given to the supercontracts of some athletes in the premier football leagues in Europe, and the major sports leagues in North America, salaries vary widely across the levels and divisions in professional team sports. The potential for salary earnings in team and individual sports is indicated in Table 11.2.

It is important to recognize that while it is clearly the case that a handful of players will earn significant sums of money from their sporting careers, most professional athletes earn relatively little. And even those who do make a lot of money will earn far more for their employers than for themselves. For example, Kimi Raikkonen, Fernando Alonso, Valentino Rossi and Lewis Hamilton appear on this list and, together with other Formula One racing drivers, they contributed to the multibillion fortunes of Bernie Ecclestone. While David Beckham was at Manchester United, his personal multimillion earnings also contributed to Manchester United's status as the richest sports team in the world, and to the far greater personal wealth of Martin Edwards, the former chair of the club. It is also worthy of note that the highest-paid competitors are mostly from the USA, and all are men. The highest-earning female competitor is Maria Sharipova, the Russian tennis player, who ranks at number 34 with earnings of US$21.8 million. Additionally, these are seasonal jobs with few benefits. Clearly commercialization is not as good for most athletes as it is for the special few (see Cartoon 11.3).

The dramatic increase in salary at the top level of professional sports since 1980 is due to two factors: (1) changes in the legal status and rights of players, which have led to free agency and the use of a salary arbitration process, and (2) increased revenues flowing to some leagues and owners. Salaries in each major men's team sport since 1970 show that increases in salary levels correspond closely with court decisions and agreements over working conditions that changed the legal status of competitors and gave them bargaining power in contract negotiations with team owners and managers. The development of the European Union (EU) is one important aspect of this. Unions and legal cases have worked for some competitors, as they have for many workers in other industries.

Income: individual sports

As with team sports, publicity is given to the highest-paid athletes in individual sports. However, not all players in these sports make enough money from tournament winnings to support themselves comfortably. Many golfers, tennis players, track and field athletes, motor and motorcycle racers, figure skaters and others must carefully manage their money so that they do not spend more than they win as they travel from event to event. When tournament winnings are listed in the newspaper, nothing is said about the expenses for air fares, hotels, food and transportation, or about other expenses for coaches, agents, managers and various support people. The top money winners do not worry about these expenses, but most athletes in individual sports are not big money winners.

Typical of many individual sports, the disparity between the top money winners and others has increased considerably on the men's and women's golf and tennis tours. In 2007 Tiger

Table 11.2 **Best-paid competitors**

Name	Sport	Nation	Salary (US$ million)
1. Tiger Woods	Golf	USA	128.0
2. Phil Mickelson	Golf	USA	62.4
3. David Beckham	Football	UK	48.2
4. Kimi Raikkonen	Motor racing	Finland	46.0
5. LeBron James	Basketball	USA	40.5
6. Floyd Mayweather	Boxing	USA	40.2
7. Ronaldinho	Football	Brazil	37.5
8. Lionel Messi	Football	Argentina	35.8
9. Kobe Bryant	Basketball	USA	35.5
10. Roger Federer	Tennis	Switzerland	35.1
=11. Fernando Alonso	Motor racing	Spain	35.0
=11. Shaquille O'Neal	Basketball	USA	35.0
=11. Alex Rodriguez	Baseball	USA	35.0
14. Valentino Rossi	Motor racing	Italy	34.0
15. Yao Ming	Basketball	China	31.8
16. Kevin Garnett	Basketball	USA	31.0
17. Peyton Manning	American football	USA	30.5
18. Cristiano Ronaldo	Football	Portugal	30.3
19. Derek Jeter	Basketball	USA	30.0
20. Ichiro Suzuki	Baseball	Japan	27.6
21. Lewis Hamilton	Motor racing	UK	27.6
22. Dale Earnhardt	Motor racing	USA	27.2
23. Allen Iverson	Basketball	USA	27.1
24. Thierry Henry	Football	France	26.1
25. Kevin Durant	Basketball	USA	26.0

Note: these figures include salaries winnings, bonuses, endorsements and appearances.

Source: Freedman, 2008

SIDELINES

©1982 M.T.F.-T.W.S.-Lakewood, CO

'I make £10 million a year, and I don't feel guilty!'

Cartoon 11.3 Most athletes generate revenues that match their salaries or prize money. Like other entertainers, a few of them have benefited from national and international media exposure. Sports events are now marketed in connection with the celebrity status and lifestyles of high-profile athlete-entertainers

Woods made US$10.6 million in prize money and US$87 million in endorsements. Golfer Lorena Ochoa, who won eight tournaments in 2007, made about US$14.5 in prize money and endorsements, about 15 per cent of Woods' annual earnings. Maria Sharapova, the highest-paid woman athlete in 2007, won US$1.7 million but had endorsements of about US$20 million. But these are unique cases. Many people are surprised to learn that the top 15 to 20 players on the Women's Tennis Association (WTA) Tour make as much prize money as the other 1800 registered WTA players during the tour year.

The vast majority of men and women playing professional tennis, golf and other individual sports do not make enough money to pay their competition expenses each year, although some have sponsors who pay for training and travel expenses. Some athletes with sponsors may be under contract to share their winnings with them. The sponsors/investors cover expenses during the lean years but then take a percentage of prize money when the athletes win matches or tournaments. This often occurs with boxers, most of whom never make enough money to live comfortably. Additionally, boxers have no unions, pensions or health insurance. Journalist Jack Newfield notes that for every big-name boxer who becomes rich 'there are 1000 you never hear of who end up with slurred speech, failing memory and an empty bank account' (2001, p. 14).

Sponsorship agreements cause problems for professional athletes in many individual sports. Being contractually tied, for example, to an equipment manufacturer or another sponsor often puts athletes in a state of dependency. They may not have the freedom to choose when or how often they will compete, and sponsors may require them to attend social functions, at which they talk with fan-consumers, sign autographs and promote products. For example, when Kim Clijsters (Belgium), the world's number two-ranked tennis player, discovered that she would not be allowed to wear her sponsor's logo'd clothing during the 2004 Olympics, she withdrew from the Games.

Overall, a few athletes in individual sports make good money, whereas most others struggle to cover expenses. Only when sports events are broadcast on television can athletes expect to compete for major prize money and earn large incomes, unless they are amateurs.

Amateur athletes in commercial sports

The status of amateur athletes in commercial sports often is confusing and contradictory. Understanding their situation requires knowledge of their legal status and the restrictions they face when it comes to income related to their sports.

Legal status of amateur athletes

The primary goal of amateur athletes is simple: to train and compete. However, achieving this goal has not always been easy because amateur athletes have little control over the conditions of their sports participation. Instead, control rests in the hands of amateur sports organizations, each setting rules that specify the conditions under which training and competition may occur. Although many rules ensure fairness in competition, others simply protect the power and interests of governing organizations and their leaders.

The majority of sports clubs in the UK continue to be organized on an amateur, and often volunteer, basis and so there have been recent attempts to support and protect the clubs and their athletes. Since 2002, sports clubs can apply to be designated 'Community Amateur Sports Clubs', which provides them with some of the financial benefits of charitable status including tax relief. Such clubs are required to have a constitution, insurance, written records and meet other legal requirements (including child protection).

While this has helped many clubs, athletes themselves still have a relative lack of power or rights. For example, while amateur athletes in Olympic sports have made some strides to gain control over their training and competition, the centres of power move further and further away from athletes as the sports become more commercialized. Athletes are now included on advisory boards for NGBs, but NGBs take a back seat to sponsors and media in the case of commercial events. The paradox for athletes is that, as they gain more resources to train and compete, the control of their training and competition moves further away from them. The exceptions are those athletes with national visibility and the individual power to negotiate support that meets their interests.

Income of amateur athletes

Amateur athletes in commercial sports face another paradox: they generate money through their performances, but they cannot directly benefit financially from participating in sports. Although elite international athletes may receive stipends for living expenses while they train, many amateur athletes receive no compensation, even when they create revenues. This is not new, but there are times now when amateurs compete in multimillion-pound events such as the Olympics, and receive relatively little revenue in comparison to their professional counterparts, irrespective of level of performance and achievement. The unfairness of this situation for certain athletes promotes under-the-table forms of compensation.

International rules now permit athletes to be paid living expenses. However, they cannot make money beyond approved cost-of-living stipends and travel expenses related to training and competition. Therefore, if a 16-year-old Olympic figure skater participates in a professional skating competition, her amateur status may be revoked, even if she accepted no money. This would make her ineligible for future Olympic competitions. This makes it difficult for many athletes from lower-income backgrounds to maintain amateur status and continue doing the sports they love (Sokolove, 2004c).

Questions about the fairness of this situation have been raised by an increasing number of athletes. Canadian economist Mark Lavoie (2000) has noted that there may be a time 'when the so-called amateur athletes will threaten to go on strike in order to get their share of the huge revenues generated by worldwide mega-events such as the Olympic Games' (p. 167).

Summary: What are the Characteristics of Commercial Sports?

Commercial sports are visible parts of many contemporary societies. They grow and prosper best in urban, industrial societies with relatively efficient transportation and communications systems, a standard of living that allows people the time and money to play and watch sports, and a culture that emphasizes consumption and material status symbols. Spectator interest in commercial sports is based on a combination of a quest for excitement, ideologies emphasizing success, the existence of youth sports programmes, and media coverage that introduces people to the rules of sports and the athletes who play them.

The recent worldwide growth of commercial sports has been fuelled by sports organizations seeking global markets and corporations using sports as vehicles for global capitalist expansion. This growth will continue as long as it serves the interests of transnational corporations. As it does, sports, sports facilities, sports events and athletes are branded with corporate logos and ideological messages promoting consumption and dependence on corporations for excitement and pleasure.

Commercialization leads to changes in the internal structure and goals of certain sports, the orientations of people involved in sports, and the people and organizations that control sports. Rules are changed to make events more fan-friendly. People in sports, especially athletes, emphasize heroic orientations over aesthetic orientations and use style and dramatic expression to impress mass audiences. Overall, commercial sports are packaged as total entertainment experiences for spectators, mostly for the benefit of spectators who know little about the games or events they are watching.

Commercial sports are unique businesses. At the minor league level, most of them do not generate substantial revenues for owners and sponsors. However, team owners, event sponsors and promoters at the top levels of professional sports are involved with commercial sports to make money while having fun and establishing good public images for themselves or their corporations and corporate products, policies and practices.

Commercialization makes athletes entertainers. Because athletes generate revenues through their performances, issues related to players' rights and receiving revenues generated by their performances have become very important. As rights and revenues have increased, so have players' incomes. Media coverage has been key in this process.

Most athletes in professional sports do not make vast sums of money. Players outside the top men's sports and golf and tennis for women have incomes that are surprisingly low. Income among amateur athletes is limited by the rules of governing bodies in particular sports. In other amateur sports, athletes may receive direct cash payments for performances and endorsements, and some receive support from the organizations to which they belong, but relatively few make large amounts of money.

The structure and dynamics of commercial sports vary from nation to nation. Commercial sports in most of the world have not generated the massive revenues associated with a few high-profile, heavily televised sports in Western Europe, North America, Australia, and parts of Latin America and eastern Asia. Profits for owners and promoters around the world depend on supportive relationships with the media, large corporations and governments. These relationships have shaped the character of all commercial sports, professional and amateur.

The commercial model of sports is not the only model that might provide athletes and spectators with enjoyable and satisfying experiences. However, because most people are unaware of alternative models, they continue to express a desire for what they get, even though people with commercial and corporate interests largely determine it (Sewart, 1987). Therefore, changes will occur only when spectators and people in sports develop visions for what sports could and should look like if they were not shaped by economic factors.

Website resources

Note: Websites often change. The following URLs were current when this book was printed. Please check our website (***www.mcgraw-hill.co.uk/textbooks/coakley***) for updates and additions.

See the OLC, ***www.mcgraw-hill.co.uk/textbooks/coakley***, for an annotated list of readings related to this chapter.

www.mcgraw-hill.co.uk/textbooks/coakley Click on Chapter 11 for information on 'outposts in action' and financial data on escalating franchise fees and franchise values, discussions of top athletes' salaries and endorsements, and why ticket prices to top events are increasing so rapidly.

www.footballeconomy.com A website on the political economy of football, with statistics on clubs, their turnover, prize money, match attendance, television and broadcasting.

www.forbes.com/lists/ Go to link for sport lists to see the values of teams and players in global football, as well as several North American sports.

www.sirc.org/ This is the site of the Social Issues Research Centre based in Oxford. There are several downloadable publications, including one on sport and the workplace.

www.sportbusiness.com This site contains a variety of information on sports events, marketing and media, with information on specific sports, and across a range of countries.

www.sportengland.org/resources/pdfs/publicat%5FEng%5FJune03.pdf Economists provide a report entitled, 'Value of the sports economy in England: a study on behalf of Sport England'; it provides an example of how researchers study the economic impact of sport in an entire nation.

Chapter 12

Sports and the media: could they survive without each other?

(*Source*: Elizabeth Pike)

Chapter contents

Characteristics of the media
Sports and the media: a two-way relationship
Images and narratives in media sports
Audience experiences with media sports
The profession of sports journalism
Summary: could sports and the media survive without each other?

Learning Centre Resources

Visit *Sports in Society*'s Online Learning Centre (OLC) at **www.mcgraw-hill.co.uk/textbooks/coakley** for additional information and study material for this chapter, including:

- Self-grading quizzes and essay questions
- Learning outcomes
- Related websites
- Additional readings

Television sport is probably the most spectacular and regular vehicle for conveying and communicating both global and national culture.

(David Rowe, sociologist, 2004a, p. 88)

Of the millions [of pounds] that circulate in the media sport industry, only a small proportion is ever used to nurture grassroots sport ... [Elite] sport is now, more than ever, the playground of corporate capitalism.

(Gary Whannel, media scholar, 2002, p. 215)

The media is a creator of heroes, of role models, of the profile which enables sports-people and events to inspire young people, to influence their daily decisions, to spread the messages.

(Lord Sebastian Coe, 2006)

The media, including newspapers, magazines, books, films, radio, television, video games and the Internet, pervade culture. Although each of us incorporates media into our lives in different ways, the things we read, hear and see in the media are important parts of our experience. They frame and influence many of our thoughts, conversations, decisions and experiences.

We use media images and narratives as we evaluate ourselves, give meaning to other people and events, form ideas and envision the future. This does *not* mean that we are slaves to the media or passive dupes of those who control media content and the ways it is re-presented to us. The media do not tell us what to think, but they greatly influence *what we think about* and, therefore, what we talk about in our relationships. Our experiences and our social worlds are clearly informed by media content, and if the media did not exist, our lives would be different.

Sports and the media are interconnected parts of our lives. Sports provide valuable media content, and many sports depend on the media for publicity and revenues. In light of these interconnections, five questions are considered in this chapter:

1   What are the characteristics of the media?
2   How are sports and the media interconnected?
3   What images and messages are emphasized in the media coverage of sports in the UK?
4   Do the media influence sports-related choices and actions?
5   What are the characteristics of sports journalism?

Characteristics of the Media

Revolutionary changes are occurring in the media. Personal computers, the Internet and wireless technology have propelled us into a transition from an era of sponsored and programmed media for mass consumption to an era of multifaceted, on-demand, interactive and personalized media content and experiences. The pace and implications of this transition are significant, and college students are among those whose experiences are on the cutting edge of this media revolution. Although it is important to discuss new trends and explain what may occur in the future, our discussions should be based on a general understanding of the traditional media and their connections with sports.

Media research in the past often distinguished between print and electronic media. **Print media** included *newspapers, magazines, fanzines, books, catalogues, event programmes* and, even, *trading cards* – words and images on paper. **Electronic media** included *radio, television and film*. But video games, the Internet, mobile phones and online publications have nearly eliminated the dividing line between these media forms. Today, media provide *information, interpretation, entertainment* and *opportunities for interactivity*. On some occasions they provide all these features simultaneously. When media content is provided for commercial purposes, entertainment is emphasized more than information, interpretation or opportunities for interactivity. In the process, media consumers become commodities sold to advertisers with the goal of promoting lifestyles based on consumption.

The media also put us in touch with information, experiences, people, images and ideas outside the realm of our everyday, real-time lives. But media content is edited and 're-presented' to us by others – producers, editors, programme directors, programmers, camera operators, writers, journalists, commentators, sponsors, bloggers and website providers. These people provide information, interpretation, entertainment and, even, opportunities for interactivity to achieve one or more of five goals: (1) making profits, (2) shaping values, (3) providing a public service, (4) building their own reputations, and (5) expressing themselves in technical, artistic or personal ways.

In nations where most media are privately owned, the dominant goals are to make profits and to distribute content that promotes the ideas and beliefs of people in positions of power and influence. These are not the only goals, but they are the most influential. Media expert Michael Real explains that there has been no greater force in the construction of media sport reality than 'commercial television and its institutionalised value system [emphasizing] profit making, sponsorship, expanded markets, commodification, and competition' (1998, p. 17). As the Internet and wireless technology extend content and access, media sport reality is being constructed in diverse ways. This can be a contentious process as corporations and powerful individuals attempt to control online access and content. The resulting struggle is a crucial feature of contemporary social worlds.

In nations where media are controlled primarily by the state, the primary goals are to provide a public service and promote identification with the state and its officials (Lund, 2007). However, state control of the media has steadily declined as television companies and newspapers have become privatized and deregulated, and as more individuals obtain online access to information, interpretation, entertainment and opportunities for interactivity.

Power relations in society also influence the priority given to the five goals that drive media content. Those who make decisions about content act as filters as they select and create the images and messages that they present in the media. In the filtering and presentation process, these people usually emphasize images and narratives consistent with ideologies that support their interests in addition to attracting large audiences. As deregulation and private ownership have increased, the media have become hyper-commercialized, and media content has focused more on consumption, individualism, competition and class inequality as natural and necessary in society. Seldom included in the content of commercial media is an emphasis on civic values, anti-commercial activities and political action (McChesney, 1999; Walker, 2005). In fact, when groups with anti-commercial messages want to buy commercial time on television, media corporations and networks have refused to sell it to them (Lasn, 2000).

There are exceptions to this pattern, but when people use the media to challenge dominant ideologies, they can expect some form of backlash. This discourages counter-hegemonic programming and leads people to censor media content in ways that defer to the interests of those with power. Even when there is legal protection for freedom of speech, as in the UK, those who work in the media often think carefully before presenting images and messages that challenge the interests of those who have power and influence in society, especially when those people own the media or sponsor programmes for commercial purposes.

This does not mean that those who control the media ignore what consumers think and 'force' media audiences to read, hear and see things unrelated to their interests. But it does mean that, apart from content that individuals create online, average people influence the media only through programme ratings. Therefore, the public receives edited information, interpretation, entertainment and interactive experiences that are constructed to boost profits and maintain a business and political climate in which commercial media can thrive. In the process, people who control media are concerned with what attracts readers, listeners and viewers within the legal limits set by government agencies and the preference parameters of individuals and corporations that buy advertising time. As they make programming decisions, they see audiences as collections of consumers that can be sold to advertisers (see Cartoon 12.1).

 Sport and the media must surely be the most potent combination of forces amongst the key factors in the globalization game. They have a unique synergy.

(Robert Davies, chief executive, International Business Leaders Forum, 2002b)

In the case of sports, those who control media not only decide which sports and events to cover but also the kinds of images and commentary that are presented in the coverage (Andrews and Jackson, 2001; Arsenault and Castells, 2008; Bernstein and Blain, 2003; Brookes, 2002; Martzke and Cherner, 2004; Rowe, 2004a, 2004b; Whannel, 2002). When they do this, they play an important role in constructing the overall frameworks that people in media audiences use to define and incorporate sports in their lives.

Most people do not think critically about media content. For example, when we watch sports on television, we do not often notice that the images and messages we see and hear have been carefully presented to heighten the dramatic content of the event and emphasize dominant ideologies in British society. The pre-game analysis, the camera coverage, the camera angles, the close-ups, the slow-motion shots, the attention given to particular athletes, the announcers' play-by-play descriptions, the colour commentary, the quotes from athletes, and the post-game summary and analysis are all presented to entertain media audiences and keep sponsors happy.

Television commentaries (narratives) and images in the UK, for example, highlight action, competition, aggression, hard work, individual heroism and achievement, playing despite pain, teamwork and competitive outcomes. Television coverage has become so seamless in its representations of sports that we often define televised games as 'real' games, more real even than the games seen in person at the stadium. Magazine editor Kerry Temple explains:

> It's not just games you're watching. It's soap operas, complete with story lines and plots and plot twists. And good guys and villains, heroes and underdogs. And all this gets scripted into cliffhanger morality plays … And you get all caught up in this until you begin to believe it really matters.
>
> *(1992, p. 29)*

'Quick! Bring the camera – this crash will boost our ratings!'
Cartoon 12.1 Media representations of sports are carefully selected and edited. Commentary and images highlight dramatic action, even when it is a minor part of an event. Some media people are quite effective in seeking out pain and tragedy because it attracts viewers.

Temple's point is more relevant today than it was in 1992. The focus on profits has increased soap-opera storytelling as a means of developing and maintaining audience interest in commercial media sports coverage. Sports programming is now 'a never-ending series of episodes – the results of one game create implications for the next one (or next week's) to be broadcast' (Wittebols, 2004, p. 4). Sports rivalries are hyped and used to serialize stories through and across seasons; conflict and chaos are highlighted with a predictable cast of 'good guys', 'bad guys' and 'redemption' or 'comeback' stories; and the storylines are designed to reproduce ideologies favoured by upper-middle-class media consumers – the consumers that corporate sponsors want to reach with their advertisements.

Even though the media coverage of sports is carefully edited and represented in total enter-tainment packages, most of us believe that, when we see a sports event on television, we are seeing it 'the way it is'. We do not usually think that what we see, hear and read is a series of narratives and images selected for particular reasons and grounded in the social worlds and interests of those producing the event, controlling the images and delivering the commentary (Crawford, 2004; McCullagh, 2002). Television coverage provides only one of many possible sets of images and narratives related to a sports event, and there are many images and messages that audiences do not receive (Knoppers and Elling, 2004). For example, if we went to an event in person, we would see something quite different from the images that are selected and repre-sented on television, and we would develop our own descriptions and interpretations, which would be very different from those carefully presented by media commentators.

This point was clearly illustrated in the coverage of the 1996 Olympics in Atlanta by the US television company NBC, which was then sold on to British and other national networks. NBC strategically created entertaining drama by representing what media analysts have described as 'plausible reality' in its broadcasts. To do this, it deliberately withheld information so that it could frame events in its terms, even though it knew those terms were contrary to what was real for the athletes and others involved. It gave priority to entertainment over news and factual information. Former Olympic swimmer Diana Nyad, who was in Atlanta for the event, observed, 'Compared to the TV audience, the people in Atlanta have seen a completely different Olympics' (Nyad, 1996). She also noted that television and other media coverage revolves around a focus on gold medals, which distorts the actual experiences and priorities of athletes and spectators alike.

New York Times writer Robert Lipsyte (1996a, 1996b) describes televised sports as 'sportainment' – the equivalent of a television movie that purports to be based on a true story but actually provides fictionalized history. In other words, television constructs sports and viewer experiences. But the process occurs so smoothly that most television viewers believe they experience sports in a 'true and natural' form. This, of course, is the goal of the directors, editors and on-camera announcers who select images and narratives, frame them with the stories they wish to tell and make sure they do not alienate sponsors in the process.

To illustrate this point, think about this question: what if all prime-time television programmes were sponsored by environmental groups, women's organizations and trades unions? Would programme content be different from the way it is now? Would the political biases built into the images and commentary be the same as they are now? It is unlikely that they would be the same, and we would be quick to identify all the ways that the interests and political agendas of the environmen-talists, feminists or trades unionists influenced images, narratives and overall programme content.

Now think about this: capitalist corporations sponsor nearly 100 per cent of all sports programming in the media, and their goals are to create consumers loyal to capitalism and generate profits for corporations and their shareholders. As media consumers realize the implications of this approach, they often turn to the Internet and seek content provided by bloggers and independent journalists. Of course, online content is presented for many reasons, and those who want to use it as an alternative to the content in commercial media must critically assess its validity and reliability. For those who remain 'tuned in' to the commercial media, their experiences as spectators are heavily influenced – that is, 'mediated' – by the decisions of those who control the media.

The X Games were created by ESPN, which is shown in the UK via Sky. ESPN is owned by ABC. ABC is owned by the Walt Disney Company. The power behind the X Games makes it difficult for the athletes to maintain the culture of their sports on their terms (*Source*: Becky Beal)

> Journalists are like stockbrokers. We thrive on movement in our individual markets. What you don't want is a plateau in people's fortunes. So you do have this crazy situation where someone is a hero one minute and is a zero the next minute. The Dutch call it the tall poppy syndrome, when the poppy grows high enough they chop its head off.
>
> *(Henry Winter, journalist, in* Sports Dirty Secret, *video, 2007)*

New media and sports

New media, including the Internet, extend and radically change media representations of sports because they provide virtual access to potentially unlimited and individually created and selected information, interpretation and entertainment. Additionally, the interactivity of being online is like having open voice, video and text connections with everyone in the world who is also online.

In the case of sports, online access can provide active involvement with sports content. We can interact with fellow fans in chat rooms, ask questions of players and coaches, identify scores and statistics, and play online games that either simulate sports or are associated with real-time sports events around the world. We can even create media content to match our interests and the interests of others worldwide. This gives us control in ways that radically alter media experiences and mediated realities (Crawford, 2004; Halverson and Halverson, 2008).

Although people often access online sports content to complement content they consume in traditional media, many now use new media to replace traditional content. This shift in consumption patterns concerns people in media companies that broadcast live sports worldwide, because their revenues in the past have depended on controlling this content and maintaining large audiences to sell to advertisers. At the same time, sports organizations such as the English Premier Football League are becoming more active in managing media representations of their sports so they can directly control information, analysis and entertainment to promote themselves on their terms.

As we are witnessing today, content in the new media often blurs the lines between entertainment, journalism and marketing so that it invariably promotes lifestyles of consumption (Halverson and Halverson, 2008; Maguire et al., 2008a, 2008b; Scherer, 2007; Scherer and Jackson, 2008). This was illustrated in 2008 when NBCOlympics, which bought the rights to the Beijing Olympics, provided over 1.2 billion online pages and over 72 million video streams giving online access to 2200 hours of live events and all 3600 hours of video (and much commentary) taken during the Games (Stetler, 2008).

At the same time that corporations try to maximize control over online representations of sports, YouTube and other sites provide people with video cameras opportunities to upload their own representations of alternative and action sports. For over three decades, young people in alternative sports have found ways to photograph, film and distribute images of their activities. In the past, photos and video-cassette recorder (VCR) tapes were mailed and passed person-to-person, but distribution today occurs online with images accessible worldwide. Although these images represent what may be described as 'performance sports', they are central to the media experiences of many young people who find highly structured, overtly competitive sports such as football or rugby to be constraining and uncreative.

In some cases, young people use new media to represent sports involving transgressive actions such as skating in empty car parks at night or doing **parkour** (and 'free-running'), *an activity in which young men and a few young women use their bodies to move rapidly and efficiently through existing landscapes*, especially in urban areas where walls, buildings and other obstacles normally impede movement (www.urbanfreeflow.com; www.parkour.org.uk). Research on the new media representations of these activities is sorely needed.

The major sociological question related to the Internet and new media generally is this: will they democratize social life by enabling people to freely share information and ideas, or will they become tools controlled by corporations to expand their capital, increase consumption, reproduce ideologies that drive market economies and maintain the illusion that we need them to provide pleasure and excitement in our lives? Sociologist Brian Wilson suggests that open and accessible avenues of online communication create 'an immense revolutionary potential in sport-related contexts, and [also] for sociologists (of sport) interested in contributing to activist projects' (Wilson, 2007, p. 457) – and this is the last thing that commercial providers want.

New media account for the dramatic growth of online 'fantasy leagues'. Although the first fantasy sport league, invented in 1979 by a baseball fan, did not require online access, most fantasy sports today are played online. If we use football as an example, playing fantasy football makes every participant a 'team owner' who selects real players for positions on their fantasy teams. The weekly performance statistics of the players on an owner's team are converted into points so that each fantasy team owner competes against other team owners. Usually, all participants pay fees to one of many online services that compile players' statistics, compute scores and keep track of team records.

An estimated 15 to 18 million people play fantasy sports. Players are mostly college-educated white men (93 per cent) between 25 and 50 years old with higher than average incomes. Collectively, they spend over £4 billion annually to obtain data about players and compete in organized fantasy leagues. Individually, each owner devotes many hours to watching sports and managing his team, a portion of which occurs at work (Ballard, 2004; Petrecca, 2005; Wendel, 2004).

Fantasy sports alter sport consumption patterns (Levy, 2005; Wendel, 2004). Real games often matter little to fantasy players who focus on the performance statistics of their players who play on many different teams in real-life games. Although they often subscribe to expensive cable and satellite television 'sports packages' that enable them to watch their players, they are not too concerned about the outcomes of those games. While they watch, they also check out other players and take note of injuries because during the season they can cut, trade and acquire new players on their fantasy team.

Fantasy sports also reposition fans relative to players (Davis and Duncan, 2004; Halverson and Halverson, 2008; Kusz, 2001; Zirin, 2008). They provide the white men who play them with a sense of power and control over players unlike them, and at the same time connect them with others who share their interests and backgrounds (Bell, 2008; Levy, 2005).

Overall, issues related to access will cause the Internet to be contested terrain well into the future as people struggle over the rights of users to share information and ideas (Totilo, 2008). Sports leagues and teams will use the Internet more widely in the future, but they will charge fees for access to events for which they have also sold media rights to television and radio. Furthermore, sponsors of television and radio broadcasts will oppose Internet coverage that interferes with selling products and services to their sports audiences.

As media technology becomes more accessible, new forms of Internet-based sports coverage will emerge. For example, grandparents in distant locations will be able to watch their grandchild play a school netball game simply by logging on to the school website. The filming, commentary and production of the game might be done for credit by students on a media course. This could lead to creative, non-commercial or non-profit forms of sports media coverage. How this will change the reality of mediated sports and our experience of them remains to be seen.

The future is difficult to predict. Will people choose 500-channel, high-definition digital television over the medium of the Internet? Will InternetTV replace television as we know it today? Will the economics of technology and the 'digital divide' between technology haves and have-nots segregate spectators even further by social class? Will the culture of the Internet favour some people over others, or will it enable all spectators to create realities that fit their interests and preferences?

Answers to these questions depend on the social, political and economic forces shaping the future of the Internet. Economic forces guarantee that the first people to enjoy new spectator experiences and realities will be those who can buy the hardware, software and bandwidth to move around the Internet at will. Social class will influence Internet access to spectator experiences because broadband providers overlook lower-income neighbourhoods where profits are scarce. But progressive public policies could mandate the provision of access in these neighbourhoods or provide wireless access as a public service, thereby blurring class differences in future access to the Internet. This latter possibility, however, depends on the public good being given priority over the corporate good when it comes to online access. All of us will participate in the creation of the future, either actively or passively, as we make our choices and influence political decisions and regulations.

 Know the media. Change the media. Be the media.

(Adbusters, 2004)

Video games and virtual sports

Sports also come into our lives through video games and virtual experiences. Sport video games are popular in wealthy nations, and some people have even participated in virtual sports of various types although most virtual sports are experimental and not available for general participation.

The images in digital games have become increasingly lifelike, and those who play them have uniquely active spectator experiences, even when they occur in solitude. Social science research has focused mostly on violence and gender issues, and there is little information about the actual experiences of people who play video games modelled after 'real' sports.

Video games that simulate sports have become so realistic that some athletes even use them to train. The games offer high-definition graphics, intense interactivity, control of the action, and opportunities to create, train and be your own player competing with and against representations of 'real' players.

Organized, online video sports tournaments now attract thousands of players worldwide, many of whom identify themselves as cyberathletes and participate in gaming tournaments (Snider, 2007). They train regularly, have fans and agents, and if they are high-profile players, endorse products related to the games. Between 1997 and 2008 the Cyberathlete Professional

League sponsored about 50 major international tournaments and awarded over £6 million in prizes to competitors. Events in Major League Gaming have attracted audiences of hundreds of thousands, and participants have come from many parts of the world (Caplan and Coates, 2007).

It is clear that sports video games provide different experiences from consuming televised sports or playing sports. For example, golf fans can match their video golf skills with the physical skills of professional golfers by going online and golfing on the same course as Tiger Woods or other high-profile players whose shots have been represented and archived through digitized images. This is a new media experience, and research has not been done to show how people integrate such experiences into their lives.

Those who play video sports are usually regular consumers of standard sports media events. Their interest and enjoyment of the video games is tied to their knowledge about a sport, sports teams and athletes. However, the experience of digital gaming is changing as more people play one another on the Internet in organized tournaments while others watch.

Interactive video games will be continuously modified to attract new consumers. Older fans will match football stars of the past with those of today (Schiesel, 2007), others will have opportunities to manage their favourite teams in virtual games (Schiesel, 2006), controlling David Beckham's body and managing the LA Galaxy football team as 'he' plays for them in the USA. We do not know if interactive sport video games will eventually replace or simply extend other forms of sports media consumption (Crawford, 2004). This and related issues are discussed in the box 'Win at any cost', opposite.

Game players have choices, but those choices are not unlimited, nor are they ideologically neutral. The experiences of video game players are influenced by the ethos that underlies the programmed images and actions in the games. The games clearly highlight corporate brands, affirm traditional masculinity and support other values associated with most major media sports today (Baerg, 2007; Scherer, 2007). It is important that we increase our understanding of how people integrate video game experiences into their lives.

Studies of virtual sports have not been done in the sociology of sport. But as the technology for creating virtual reality evolves, people will become immersed in physical activities in new ways. Although we do not know exactly what this means, it is possible that many people in the future will prefer virtual sports to what we define as sports today. Instead of going to a gym or fitness centre, people may go to virtual sports complexes where they can put on lightweight headsets that provide visual spaces enabling them to physically engage in sport challenges that transcend time and space.

This futuristic arcade will allow cyclists in the year 2050 to race with Lance Armstrong's granddaughter as they pedal and sweat their way along the virtual roads of the Tour de France on bikes and in environments where they experience feelings of speed, wind and rain in their faces, and the excitement of developing and carrying out strategies with virtual teammates in the Tour de France. Other sports will merge virtual and real spaces in other ways, changing the meaning of reality when it comes to sports (Marriott, 2004). The Wii gaming console and Wii Fit represent a minor step in that direction and provide a basic introduction to new forms of gaming. But future virtual sport possibilities will replace Wii in rapid succession and provide experiences going far beyond responding to video images.

In the meantime, it is important to understand the relationship between sports and the media in the early twenty-first century and to know how each has influenced the other.

reflect on SPORTS   *'Win at any cost': video games as simulated sports*

When developers create video games, they consult top athletes so that game situations and players' movements are lifelike simulations. Most top players co-operate with game developers because they want their moves and actions accurately portrayed in the video game. Even unique mannerisms related to their dramatic on-field personas are filmed so that they can be included in the action just as they are in 'real' commercialized sports. However, a major issue for game developers is obtaining the rights to use the names and images of athletes and sport leagues in their games.

Some professional team coaches worry that video games are so popular among their players that they are distractions from real games. On the other hand, Formula One, and other motor-racing video games are so realistic that some racing drivers use the games to prepare for the split-second responses required during actual races. Game designers want to create for players the audio, visual and emotional experiences matching those of the athletes.

The financial stakes associated with creating realistic and entertaining games are significant. This constantly pushes designers to refine graphics, action and game possibilities. It also leads them to talk with potential sponsors about product placements and advertisements built into the storylines and actions in the games. As more young people play these games and watch fewer television broadcasts, corporations see video games as tools for developing outposts in the heads of game players and fostering their commitment to a lifestyle based on consumption (Richtel, 2005). Product placement in games is now a major advertising venue and a valuable source of revenue for game designers.

Meanwhile, a growing number of children are being introduced to sports through video games. They learn rules and game strategies as they play. They see the moves involved in a sport as they manipulate images in the games, and their initial emotional experiences in certain sports are felt in front of computer monitors or televisions rather than on playing fields. For those of us in the sociology of sport, this raises important research questions: after playing video sports for two years, will 6-year-olds be willing to listen to whistle-blowing coaches when they are accustomed to being in complete control of players, game strategies and game conditions? Will children bring new forms of game knowledge to the situations in which they play informal and formally organized games? How will that knowledge influence the games they play? Will some children simply stay home in front of their monitors and televisions as they control their own games without having to accommodate the wishes of teammates or obey the commands of coaches? Will they know that, when they do this, they are taking for granted the ideologies of the people who developed the games they play? To whom are game developers accountable other than market forces?

Adult game players outnumber children who play, and the majority of players are males between the ages of 12 and 30. Many male college students are regular game players to the point that their status on campus sometimes reflects prowess in video game sports. Playing these games also provides regular social occasions similar to those provided by 'real' sport events.

As high-speed Internet connections become more widespread, cybersports will become more popular. Technology now enables players to compete with opponents around the world and even form teams with players who have never met one another in person. Spectators can watch games online and even listen to the voices of the players as they compete. If bookies developed betting odds and took bets on video sport game outcomes, it would not be surprising.

At this point, studies of simulated sports and video games are rare. We know little about the experiences of players, the social settings created around the games, and what players learn about themselves and others during their experiences. Future research is likely to be inspired by many questions such as the following: will playing video games influence how people play real-time sports? Will the norms in real-time sports be influenced by players' experiences in simulated sports? Will children be introduced to sports through video games rather than informal games? If so, will video game experiences influence what they will expect in real-time games? Will game designers and manufacturers eventually have more power than the big media companies today? *What do you think?*

Sports and the Media: a Two-way Relationship

The media and commercialization are closely related topics in the sociology of sport. The media intensify and extend the process and consequences of commercialization. For this reason, much attention has been given to the interdependence between the media and commercialized forms of sports. Each of these spheres of life has influenced the other, and each depends on the other for part of its popularity and commercial success.

Sports depend on the media

People played sports long before the media covered sports events. When sports exist just for the participants, there is no urgent need to advertise games, report the action, publish results and interpret what happened. The players already know these things, and they are the only ones who matter. It is only when sports become forms of commercial entertainment that they depend on the media to re-present them. Take, for example, snooker, which is the second highest rating sport in UK television (to football) in terms of total number of hours of coverage. Snooker's breakthrough came with colour television, which made it attractive to viewers. Snooker is easy to televise, requiring few cameras or media personnel, and so can fill hours of television time cheaply. Following the arrival of colour television in most people's living rooms from the 1970s onwards, the prize fund for the World Championships rose from a few thousand pounds to more than a million pounds over the next three decades. Elite snooker players are now dependent on television coverage to maintain their substantial prize funds and millionaire lifestyles.

Commercial sports are unique in that they require the media to provide a combination of coverage and news. For example, when a stage play is over, it is over – except for a review after opening night and the conversations of those who attended the play. When a sports event is over, many people wish to know about and discuss statistics; important set pieces, records and standings; the overall performances of the players and teams; upcoming games or matches; the importance of the outcome in terms of the season as a whole and the post-season and the next season, and so on. The media provide this knowledge and facilitate these discussions, which in turn generate interest that can be converted into revenues from the sale of tickets, executive boxes, club seats, concessions, parking, team logo merchandise and licensing rights. After games or matches are played, the scores become news, and interpretations of the action become entertainment for fans, regardless of whether they saw an event or not. This is the case worldwide – for bullfights in Spain, ice hockey games in Canada, cricket matches in Australia, South Africa and the Caribbean, and sumo wrestling in Japan.

Sports promoters and team owners know the value of media coverage, and they provide free access to reporters, commentators and photographers. For example, the Beijing Organizing

Committee credentialed 4500 written press journalists and 1100 photographers for the 2008 Olympic Games. Credentialed media personnel often are given comfortable seats in press boxes, access to the playing field and changing rooms, and summaries of statistics and player information. In return, promoters and owners expect, and usually receive, supportive media coverage.

Although commercial spectator sports depend on the media, some have a special dependence on television because television companies pay fees for the rights to broadcast games and other events. Table 12.1 and Figure 12.1 indicate that rights fees provide sports with predictable, significant and increasing sources of income. Once 'rights contracts' are signed, revenues are guaranteed regardless of bad weather, injuries to key players and the other factors that interfere with ticket sales and on-site revenue streams. Without television contracts, spectator sports seldom generate profits.

Television revenues also have greater growth potential than revenues from gate receipts. The number of seats in a stadium limits ticket sales, and ticket costs are limited by demand. But television audiences can include literally billions of viewers now that satellite technology transmits signals to most locations worldwide. For example, it is estimated that 3.7 billion people in 220 countries watched television coverage of the 2004 Olympic Games in Athens. The audience was attracted by more than 4000 hours of coverage supplied by 180 broadcasting organizations that paid about US$1.5 billion in rights fees to the International Olympic Committee (IOC). These organizations covered 300 events with over 12000 personnel, 1000 cameras, 450 videotape machines and nearly 60 trailers of equipment.

The goal of the IOC and other sports mega events is to turn the entire world into an audience that can be sold to sponsors. The size of the potential television audience and the deregulation of the television industry are the reasons that television rights fees have increased at phenomenal rates since the early 1970s. For example, the US rights fees paid to televise the 1984 Olympic Games in Los Angeles amounted to US$287 million – 10 times *more* than were paid to televise

Table 12.1 **Escalating annual media rights fees for major commercial sports**

Sport	Broadcast rights	Cost*
Rugby union	Sky TV	US$323 million (2006 – 10)
IPL	Sony and World Sport Group (shown on Setanta in UK)	US$1 billion (2008 – 18)
Premier League football	BSkyB Setanta	£1314 million £392 million 2007 – 10 (worth approximately £28 million per club per year)
Formula One	BBC	Approximately £40 million per year 2009 – 13

Note:

*These amounts are not inflation adjusted. Data come from multiple sources. Amounts change whenever new contracts are negotiated.

the 1976 Olympic Games in Montreal, and nearly seven times *less* than the US$1.9 billion that has been paid to televise the 2012 Olympic Games in London; and London will also receive at least US$700 million from other media companies worldwide.

This growth in television rights fees makes commercial sports more profitable for promoters and team owners, and increases the attractiveness of sports as sites for national and global advertising. Increased attention allows professional athletes to demand higher salaries and turns some of them into national and international celebrities, who then use their celebrity status to endorse products sold around the world. For example, the global celebrity and endorsement value of David Beckham is primarily due to the invention of satellite television.

As the quality of video streaming improves and sports events are widely available on the Internet, there will be interesting changes in how and with whom media rights are negotiated. The global reach of the web creates new possibilities for large corporations wanting to 'teach the world' to consume. However, it also creates challenges because new corporations will compete with traditional media companies for the video rights to sports. This is why NBC developed NBCOlympics.com in 2008, a portal enabling consumers to view events in the 2008 Olympic Games in Beijing, along with on-demand replays and highlights. Coverage was available on mobile devices and cable video on demand (VOD) packages, and other features were available for consumers interested in athlete profiles and gaming experiences. This is also why Rupert Murdoch and his global News Corporation is buying websites that attract people worldwide; he wants to combine the immediacy and interactivity of the web with the traditional allure of television, and he will use sports programming to attract InternetTV subscribers (Hansell, 2005). As this approach is used more frequently, traditional television coverage may become obsolete.

Have commercial sports sold out to the media?

Most commercial sports depend on television for revenues and publicity. In many cases, more than 50 per cent of revenue comes from the media. The English Cricket Board claims to be the sport most dependent on the media, stating that 80 per cent of its total revenue is from broadcasting rights. However, television money comes with strings attached.

Accommodating the interests of commercial television has required many changes in the ways that sports are organized, scheduled and re-presented. Some of these changes include the following.

- The schedules and starting times for many sport events have been altered to fit television's programming needs.
- The timings of certain sports have been shortened to keep television viewers tuned to events, either through shorter half-time periods or, in the case of cricket, creating new formats of one-day or limited-over games.
- Prearranged schedules of time-outs have been added to games and matches to make time for as many commercials as possible.
- Teams, leagues and tournaments have been formed or realigned to take advantage of regional media markets and build national and international fan support for sports, leagues and teams. One example of this is the India Premier League for Twenty20 cricket which was formed in 2008, and subsequently led to the creation of a Twenty20 Champions League starting in 2009 including England, Australia and South Africa.

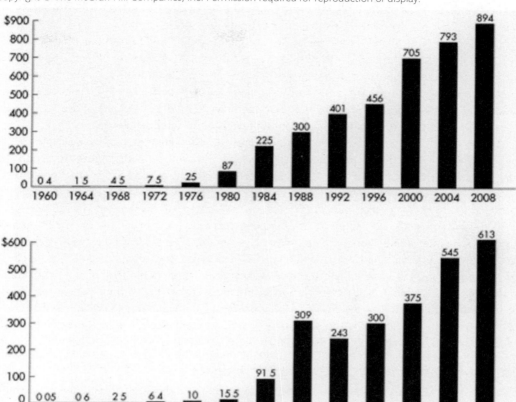

Figure 12.1 **Escalating media rights fees paid by US media companies to televise the Summer (top) and Winter (bottom) Olympics (in millions of US dollars).**
Note:

The local organizing committee for the Olympic Games also receives rights fees from other television companies around the world. Europe, Japan and continental Asia are paying increasingly higher fees. For example, in 1984 ABC paid US$225 million and other media companies worldwide paid an additional US$62 million to the Los Angeles Olympic Organizing Committee; in 2010 NBC will pay US$820m in for Vancover and in 2012 NBC will pay a total of US$1.2 billion in television rights fees and other media companies worldwide will pay about $700 million to the London Organizing Committee of the Olympic Games (LOCOG).

In other cases, the lure of television money has encouraged changes that eventually would have occurred in the course of commercializing sports. For example, various sports have extended their seasons by adding games and play-offs for relegation and promotion between leagues. But these changes probably would have occurred without the influence of television money. Commercial sports would have added games and extended seasons simply to increase gate receipts and venue revenues, but television money increased the stakes associated with these changes and hurried them along. The same is true for the additions of sudden-death extra-time periods in some sports, the tie-breaker scoring method in tennis, the addition of medal play and powerplay in golf, the bowl-off in Twenty20 cricket, and the penalties after extra time in

Approximately 100 000 people watched this game on screens placed in open areas near the Eiffel Tower in Paris, while the French national rugby team played a few miles away in the Stade de France. This is a new spectator phenomenon, which is likely to be regulated by leagues and media corporations in the future to gain financial benefit (*Source*: Jay Coakley)

football. These changes are grounded in general commercial interests, but television expands and intensifies the financial stakes associated with producing more marketable entertainment for all spectators and a more attractive commercial package for sponsors and advertisers.

Most changes associated with television coverage have been made willingly by sports organizations. The trade-offs usually are attractive for both players and sponsors. In fact, many sports and athletes not currently receiving coverage gladly would make changes if they could gain the attention and/or money associated with television contracts. Are there limits to what they would change for television coverage? Yes, but limits are always negotiated around the issue of sharing control over the conditions of sports participation. For example, surfers have turned down television contracts because they would not allow television companies to dictate the conditions under which they would compete. The companies did not care if waves were too dangerous because they wanted to stay on schedule and provide live coverage. But surfers up until now have decided that selling control over their sports participation and being forced to risk their lives in competitions was not worth television coverage.

Have the media corrupted sports?

Some people complain that dependence on the media, especially television, corrupts the true nature of sports. However, these people fail to take into account two factors.

1 *Sports are not shaped primarily by the media in general or by television in particular.* The idea that television by itself has somehow transformed the essential nature of sports does not hold up under careful examination. Sports are social constructions, and commercial sports are created over time through interactions among and between athletes, facility directors, sports team owners, event promoters, media representatives, sponsors, advertisers, agents and spectators – all of whom have diverse interests. The dynamics of these interactions are grounded in power relations and shaped by the resources held by different people at different times. It is unrealistic to think that those who control the media determine sports to fit their interests alone, but it is equally unrealistic to ignore their power.

2 *The media, including television, do not operate in a political and economic vacuum.* People who control the media are influenced by the social, political and economic contexts in which they do business. Government agencies, policies and laws regulate the media in most countries. Although government regulations have been loosened or lifted in recent years, the media must negotiate contracts with teams and leagues under certain legal constraints. For example, in the UK, sports events are categorized by the government into Group A and Group B (see Table 12.2). Those events in Group A must be free to air, and available to at least 95 per cent of the population of the UK in accordance with the Television Broadcasting Regulations (2000). Those in Group B may be sold to pay-television companies, but they must still offer highlights to free-to-air television. Economic factors also constrain the media by setting limits on the values of sponsorships and advertising time, and by shaping the climate in which pay-per-view sports and cable and satellite subscriptions might be profitable. Finally, the media are constrained by social factors, which influence people's decisions to consume sports through the media.

Connections between the media and commercial sports are grounded in complex sets of social, economic and political relationships, which change over time and vary from culture to culture.

Table 12.2 **Categories of sports events**

Group A (available only to free-to-air television companies)	Group B (available to pay television, but highlights must be offered to free-to-air companies)
The Olympic Games	Cricket test matches played in England
The FIFA World Cup Finals tournament	Non-finals play in the Wimbledon tournament
The FA Cup Final	All other matches in the Rugby World Cup Finals tournament
The Scottish FA Cup Final	Six Nations Rugby tournament matches involving home countries
The Grand National	The Commonwealth Games
The Derby	The World Athletics championship
The Wimbledon Tennis Finals	The Cricket World Cup – the final, semi-finals and matches involving home nations' teams
The European Football Championship Finals tournament	The Ryder Cup
The Rugby League Challenge Cup Final	The Open Golf championship
The Rugby World Cup Final	

These relationships influence the media's impact on sports. In other words, the conclusion that the media corrupt sports is based on an incomplete understanding of how the social world works and how sports are connected with social relations in society.

With that said, it is also important to remember that nearly all of the most powerful people in sports around the world are CEOs or owners of major, global corporations. Nearly all of them are white men from English-speaking nations, and each wants to offer programming that people around the globe will watch and that corporations will sponsor. The sports selected for national and global coverage depend on the media for their commercial success, and the salaries and endorsement income of top athletes also depend on media coverage (Delaney and Eckstein, 2008; Jeanrenaud and Kesenne, 2006; Nicholson, 2007; Raney and Bryant, 2006; Trumpbour, 2007). However, there are two sides to this process.

The media enable some athletes to become global celebrities and benefit from windfall income related to their popularity. They know that their celebrity depends on using and maintaining close connections with the media. Danielle Brown, a Paralympic archery gold medallist in Beijing 2008, is seen here talking to the media, but she may not have the same opportunities for celebrity status because of her disability (*Source*: Katherine Bond)

> Rare is the postmodern sporting hero or icon that interrogates or rebels against 'his' hyper-commodification, let alone renounces the rewards and celebrity that ensue.
>
> *(Graham Scambler, sociologist, 2005, p. 175)*

The media depend on sports

Most media do not depend on sports coverage. This is especially true for magazines, books, radio, films and the Internet, although it is less true for newspapers and television. The Internet does not depend on sports, but certain online services make money when sports fans use the Internet to get up-to-the-minute scores, obtain insider information about particular events, place bets with offshore bookies, access coverage of events, and enter exclusive online discussions about athletes, teams and events.

Neither book publishing nor the film industry depends on sports. Until recently, there were very few successful books or films about sports. The urgency and uncertainty that are so compelling in live sports are difficult to capture in these media. However, since the late 1980s, both publishers and film studios have produced projects with tragic, inspiring or outrageous stories about sports figures.

Many radio stations give coverage to sports only in their news segments, although local football, cricket and select other events often are broadcast live on local radio stations. However, there are some dedicated sports radio stations, such as talkSPORT and Radio Five Live, that mostly attract listeners from a demographic that is attractive to certain advertisers – that is, young men with higher than average incomes. Most magazines devote little or no attention to sports coverage, although the number of general- and special-interest sport magazines and 'fanzines' in the UK and other countries is significant. A visit to a local newsagents shows that magazines are devoted to information about football, cycling, skiing, motor racing and dozens of other sports.

The media most dependent on sports for commercial success are newspapers and television.

Newspapers

Newspapers at the beginning of the twentieth century had a sports page, which consisted of a few notices about upcoming activities, a short story or two about races or club matches, and possibly some scores of local games. Today, there are daily and weekly newspapers devoted exclusively to sports, and nearly all daily newspapers have sport sections often making up about 25 per cent of their news content.

Major British newspapers give more daily coverage to sports than any other single topic of interest, including business or politics. The sports section is the most widely read section of the paper. It attracts advertisers who want to reach young to middle-aged males with advertisements for car supplies, airline tickets for business travellers, alcoholic beverages, power tools, building supplies, sporting goods, hair-growth products, Viagra, testosterone and hormone therapies. Additionally, there are advertisements for bars or clubs providing naked or near-naked female models and dancers, all-night massage parlours, and organizations offering gambling advice and opportunities (see a sample of, mainly tabloid, newspapers to confirm this). Advertisements for all these products and services are unique to the (men's) sports section, and they generate considerable revenues for most newspapers.

It is difficult to predict the future of newspapers' dependence on sports. As the Internet becomes a primary source of information about sports nationally and worldwide, newspapers may focus mostly on local sports, including school, university and other youth sports.

Television

Some television companies also have developed a dependence on sports for programming content and advertising revenues. For example, sports events are a major part of the programming schedules of the major terrestrial stations in the UK and many cable and satellite-based stations.

Sports account for a growing proportion of income made on the sales of commercial time by television companies. Many cable and satellite companies have used sports programmes to attract subscribers from particular segments of the viewing public and then sell the audiences to advertisers for a nice profit. For example, in 2005 the US-based company ESPN had multiple networks showing over 5100 hours of live sports and 2300 live or taped sports events. These were watched by about 95 million people each week in 192 countries, and these people received sports information and event broadcasts in 12 languages.

Media corporations also use sports programmes to attract commercial sponsors that might take their advertising money elsewhere if television stations did not cover certain sports. For example, games in major men's team sports are ideal for promoting the sales of beer, cars and car insurance, computers, credit cards, male hair and shaving products, and air travel. The people in the advertising departments of major corporations realize that sports attract male viewers. They also realize that most business travellers are men and that many men make family decisions on the purchases of beer, cars, computers and insurance. Finally, advertisers also may be interested in associating their product or service with the culturally positive image of sports. This is especially important for products such as beer and fast foods, which are frequent targets of health advocates, among others.

Golf and tennis are special cases for television programming. These sports attract few viewers, and the ratings are exceptionally low, with the notable exception of the Wimbledon championships which attracts broader viewing figures for the two-week duration of the tournament. However, the audience for these sports is attractive to certain advertisers. It is made up of people from the highest income groups, including many professionals and business executives. This is why television coverage of golf and tennis is sponsored by companies selling luxury cars and high-priced sports cars, business and personal computers, and trips to exclusive vacation areas. This is also why some networks continue to carry these programmes despite predominantly low ratings. Advertisers are willing to pay high fees to reach high-income consumers and corporate executives who make decisions to buy thousands of 'company cars' and computers. With such valued viewers, these programmes do not need high ratings to stay on the air.

In the mid-1990s, television executives 'discovered' women viewers and women's sports. Data indicate that women have made up more than half the viewing audiences for both Winter and Summer Olympic Games since 1988. This led the American television network NBC, which has bought the rights to most recent Olympic Games, to hype women's sports, appeal to female viewers during subsequent telecasts of the games and emphasize gender equity in scripted studio commentary, although on-site coverage of events has always favoured men (Eastman and Billings, 1999).

Other women's sports also attract television coverage although the coverage they receive pales in comparison with coverage of men's sports. Women's events do not receive more coverage partly because female viewers of women's games have not been identified as a target demographic by advertisers. Furthermore, men make up over half the viewing audience for most women's sports, and they watch men's sports, so sponsors have already bought access to them when they advertise during men's events.

Over the past two decades, television companies have paid rapidly increasing amounts of money for the rights to televise certain sports. This was shown in the data in Table 12.1 and Figure 12.1. The contracts for these rights are negotiated every few years. In the case of the major men's spectator sports, contracts involve hundreds of millions of pounds for the Olympics, the football and rugby World Cups, and the Premier League. Even though there are cases when television companies lose money on sports, profits are generally good. Furthermore, regular sports programming is a platform to promote other programmes and boost ratings during the rest of the week; and it enhances the image and legitimacy of television among people who watch little other than sports.

As choices for sports television viewing have increased, audiences have fragmented and ratings for many sports have declined, even as the total number of people watching television sports has remained relatively steady. This means that rights fees for the very large events will remain high, but fees for other events, including 'special interest' events (such as bowls, swimming championships and international skiing races) will be limited. When interest in special events is especially strong among particular viewers, pay-per-view (PPV) sports programming pushes rights fees to high levels, as in the case of championship boxing bouts. Pay-per-view can generate massive revenues, but events must be chosen selectively because most people are not willing to pay upfront for a single event on television. In the meantime, pay television has become part of people's lives in the form of subscription fees for cable and satellite connections and special sports channels and packages.

Finally, sports programming has been used as a centrepiece for the global expansion of emerging sports networks. For example, in 1994, Rupert Murdoch, owner of the Fox Television Network, successfully used the coverage of sports as part of a global expansion strategy. He has been successful, and his News Corp conglomerate is the most powerful media organization in the world (see Chapter 10, p. 357). Other corporations have used their ownership of sports rights and programming as a key component of their mergers and acquisitions in the entertainment, news, sports, television and Internet industries. This influences the sports programmes that we see and do not see, what we hear and do not hear in commentary, the sites that we visit on the Internet, and the corporate messages presented in connection with athletes, teams, events and sports places. More important, it has implications for the viability of democracy around the world because democracy depends on the free flow of information from diverse sources. When only a few corporations control the media, the flow of ideas follows the channels constructed by corporate executives.

Sports and the media: a relationship fuelled by economics and ideology

Commercial spectator sports depend heavily on the media, although non-commercial sports continue to exist and often thrive without media coverage. Similarly, some media companies that publish daily newspapers in the UK and produce television programmes depend on sports to generate circulation and viewer ratings.

When large corporations control the media, the interdependence of sports and the media revolves around revenue streams and profits. Sports generate identifiable audiences that can be sold to capitalists seeking consumers for products and services. In turn, the media generate revenues for sports organizations and create sports-related images, which can be sold in connection with everything from coffee mugs and credit cards to shoes and footballs.

Since the 1970s, global economic factors have intensified the interdependence between commercial sports and the media. Major transnational corporations have needed vehicles to develop global name recognition, cultural legitimacy and product familiarity. They also want to promote ideologies that support a way of life based on consumption, competition and individual achievement. Media sports offer global corporations a means of meeting these needs: certain sports events attract worldwide attention; satellite technology takes television signals around the world; sports images are associated with recognizable symbols and pleasurable experiences by billions of people; sports and athletes usually can be presented in politically safe ways by linking them with local identities and then using them to market products, values and lifestyles related to local cultures or popular forms of global culture. Therefore, powerful transnational corporations now spend billions of pounds annually to sponsor the media coverage of sports, especially on television (it will be the Internet in the future). This in turn gives global media companies significant power over sports worldwide (see Cartoon 12.2).

An important source of corporate sponsorship money for sports comes from the alcohol and fast-food industries. For them, the sports media are key vehicles for presenting and promoting their products in connection with activities defined as healthy by most people around the world. This enables them to present positive corporate and brand images, which they hope will counteract negative images about their products. We find these images most frequently in print media and stadium signage. They regularly appear in the prime advertising space of sports magazines and on the surfaces of stadiums and other facilities that host car, dog and horse races.

Finally, many male executives of large media corporations are dedicated sports fans, and they like to be associated with sports as sponsors. Masculine culture is deeply embedded in most of the corporations that they control, and they use their sponsorship money to receive VIP (very important person) treatment at sports events. Furthermore, they use sports events to entertain clients, fellow executives and friends, and pay all the bills with company credit cards. This combination of masculine ideology and government-supported tax deductions for sports entertainment in the UK is a key factor in the media dependence on sports.

The long-time marriage of sports and the media is clearly held together and strengthened by vast amounts of money from corporations whose executives use sports as tools for promoting profits and ideologies consistent with their personal and corporate interests. Ideology is a key factor in the sports–media marriage. This is not a marriage based solely

Cartoon 12.2 **A few powerful global media companies control most of the media representations of sports worldwide. This has serious implications for what sports we see or do not see, especially in developing nations. Some people wonder what this will mean in the long run, whereas others do not give it much thought as they watch what the media re-present**

on money, but the goal of the sports–media partnership is to create a global family of eager consumers.

Images and Narratives in Media Sports

To say that sports are 'mediated' is to say that they consist of selected images and narratives. Much research in the sociology of sport has deconstructed these images and narratives and analysed the ideas or themes on which they are based. The scholars who have done these studies assume that media sports are symbolic constructions, much like Hollywood action films, television soap operas and Disney cartoons (Andrews and Jackson, 2001; Crawford, 2004; McCullagh, 2002; Rowe, 2004a, 2004b; Wenner, 1998; Whannel, 2002).

To say that television coverage of a football game is a symbolic construction means that it presents the ideas that certain people have about football, values, social life and the characteristics of the viewing audience. Although each of us interprets media images and narratives in different ways, many people use mediated sports as reference points as they form, revise and extend their ideas about sports, social life and social relations.

Because media sports are part of everyday experience in today's societies, it is important to consider the following:

- the media construction of sports
- the ideological themes underlying media coverage
- the influence of media coverage on those who consume it.

The media construction of sports?

When media are privately owned and organized to make financial profits, sports are selected for coverage on the basis of their entertainment value and revenue-generating potential. Media images and narratives are presented to provide as much of the event as possible and fit the perceived interests of the audience and sponsors. Sports that are difficult to cover profitably usually are ignored by the media or covered only with selected highlights, emphasizing spectacular and heroic injuries or achievements.

Sports magazines and the sports sections of newspapers provide scores, statistics, accounts of big plays and individual heroics, and behind-the-scenes stories; they use photographs to depict action. Television coverage focuses on the ball (or puck and so on) and individual athletes, especially those who are currently winning the game, match, meet or race. Television announcers provide narratives designed to entertain a mass audience. The major differences between print and broadcast media are summarized in Table 12.3.

Sports media generally present images and narratives that hype sports by exaggerating the spectacular, inventing and focusing on rivalries, and manufacturing reasons that events are important. Furthermore, they strive to create and maintain the celebrity status of athletes and teams. Cultural studies scholar Garry Crawford explains the strategy used in this process:

> The mass media construction of celebrity often lacks depth of character, as figures are frequently painted in one-dimensional terms ... Much of the language used to describe sport stars ... draws on the narrative of melodrama. Heroes rise and fall, villains are defeated, and women play out their roles as supporting cast members to men's central dramatic roles.
>
> *(2004, p. 133)*

Narratives even redeem villains who demonstrate that they can be heroic warriors, with commentators often describing them as 'loyal blue-collar players', 'willing to take figurative bullets for their teammates' and 'always being there when the chips are down', even if they sometimes have been nasty and broken rules in the past.

The major media also emphasize elite sports competition (Crawford, 2004; Horne and Manzenreiter 2006; Lowes, 1999). For example, British newspapers and television networks increased their coverage of professional sports through the twentieth century and decreased coverage of amateur sports. This shift was accompanied by a growing emphasis on the importance of winning and heroic actions, and the desire to attract corporate sponsors and a mass audience. It is important to understand this process and the ways that particular images and narratives in media coverage inform popular ideas about sports and about social relations and social life in general. This topic is discussed below and in the 'Breaking barriers' box on page 452.

Ideological themes in media images and narratives?

Sports are complex and are represented in the media through images and narratives that are selected from a vast array of possibilities (Knoppers and Elling, 2004). The traditional media resemble windows through which we view what others choose to put in our range of sight and hear what others choose to say. Therefore, the only way to avoid being duped is to become a

Table 12.3 **Differences between newspaper/magazine and radio/television coverage of sports**

Newspaper/magazine coverage	Radio/television coverage
Emphasizes information and interpretation	Emphasizes entertainment
Offers previews and summaries of events	Offers play-by-play images and narratives
Provides written representation of events	Provides real-time representations of events
Success depends on credibility	Success depends on hype and visual action
Highlights facts and dominant ideology	Highlights heroic plays and dominant ideology
Most likely to provide criticism of sports and sports personalities	Most likely to provide support for sports and sports personalities

Source: based on material in Koppett, 1994

critical media consumer or work with others to create grass-roots media representations of sports.

To become a critical media consumer involves learning to identify the ideologies that guide others as they construct media representations for us. In the case of sports, the most central ideologies that influence what we see and hear are those related to success, gender, race, ethnicity and nationality.

People in the media often treat the Paralympics as a special-interest story rather than a sports story. This is not an effective way to break down stereotypes, and it does not give the athletes the credit they deserve for their training and achievements (*Source*: David Biene; photograph courtesy of Ossur)

breaking BARRIERS

Image and narrative barriers: *from a special interest story to a sports story*

Athletes with a disability receive little or no media coverage. While there is some limited television and newspaper coverage of the Paralympics, this event occurs only once every four years. World Championships and other major events receive no mainstream-media coverage.

Most people who make decisions about media coverage assume that covering disability sports is a poor commercial risk. Additionally, most media people have never played or even seen disability sports, so they lack the words and experiences that would enable them to provide coverage that might build a media audience.

Research shows that when disability sports have been covered in mainstream media, athletes often are portrayed as 'courageous victims' or as 'heroic supercrips' who engage in inspiring athletic performances – it is always 'inspiring'. When sociologist Ian Brittain (2004) analysed this coverage he found that media images and narratives usually fell into one of the following categories.

Patronizing: 'Aren't they marvellous!'
Curiosity: 'Do you think she can really do that?'
Tragedy: 'On that fateful day, his life was changed for ever.'
Inspiration: 'She's a true hero and a model for all of us.'
Mystification: 'I can't believe he just did that!'
Pity: 'Give her a hand for trying so hard.'
Surprise: 'Stay tuned to see physical feats you've never imagined!'

Images and narratives organized around these themes construct disability in terms of a medical model – focused on personal impairments that must be overcome. This treatment ignores *why* particular social meanings are given to disabilities and *how* they shape the lives of many people with specific impairments (Brittain, 2004; Smith and Thomas, 2005). Consequently, media coverage often perpetuates the belief that disabilities are abnormalities and that people with disabilities have one-dimensional identities based on abnormalities.

Despite these misguided media representations, most athletes with a disability would accept distorted coverage rather than have no coverage at all. Like other athletes, they want to be acknowledged for their physical competence, but they also hope that by becoming visible in the media, they can challenge traditional stereotypes and make people aware of the need to maximize access and inclusion in all spheres of society.

Developing a media audience, says Jil Gravink, begins at the local, recreational level. Gravink is the founder and director of Northeast Passage, an American organization that develops community-based schemes to increase the relevance of disability sports among people with disabilities and among the general population. The schemes provide opportunities for people with a disability and able-bodied people to interact, play sports and identify one another in terms of multiple characteristics and abilities.

Gravink explains that only when average people with disabilities play sports and become fully integrated into the community can disability sports 'move from a special interest story to a sport story' (in Joukowsky and Rothstein, 2002a, p. 98). Then poster people and 'supercrips' will be exposed for the myths they are.

Success as a theme in media representations of sports

Media coverage of sports in the UK emphasizes success through competition, hard work, assertiveness, domination over others, adherence to rules, obedience to authority, and 'big plays' such as hitting a six, scoring a try and single-handed goals. The idea that success can be based on empathy, support for others, sharing resources, autonomy, intrinsic satisfaction, personal growth, compromise, incremental changes or the achievement of equality is seldom included in media representations of sports, even though they are there.

Journalists and commentators in the UK focus on competitive rivalries between teams and individuals, together with sudden-death play-offs, dominating others, and the 'big plays' or big hits. References to learning, enjoyment and competing with others are rare, even when players see their participation in these terms, and many do. Thus, the media do not 'tell it like it is' as much as they tell it like people interested in productivity in the form of competitive success want to see and hear it. This ideological bias does not mean that most people do not enjoy media sports. Enjoyment is central and it drives media sports consumption. However, there are many ways to enjoy sports, and the media highlight the ways that fit popular and corporate interests simultaneously. Discovering other ways to enjoy sports is left to individuals and groups, who are curious enough to seek alternatives to commercialized media sports.

Gender themes in media representations of sports

Masculinity rules in media sports (Kian et al., 2008). Men's sports receive about 95 per cent of the coverage in all the media, and both images and narratives tend to reproduce traditional ideas and beliefs about gender (Duncan and Messner, 1998, 2000, 2005; Women's Sports Foundation, 2007a). Men's football dominates television and newspaper coverage of sports. Coverage of women's sports is not a priority in the media, except for the Olympics, major tennis, and track and field meetings. Sports magazines have been notoriously slow to cover female athletes and women's sports although they frequently have images of women as sex objects in advertisements for alcohol, men's toiletries and other products (Bishop, 2003). This pattern of under-representation of women's sports in the media exists around the world (see Urquhart and Crossman, 1999).

Progress has occurred in some cases, but it is uneven and does not represent a pattern of consistent growth. For example, in television and radio there are regular appearances from female sports reporters, and the BBC estimates that approximately one-quarter of staff in its sports department are female. The increased number of sports channels offers opportunities for women's sports to be showcased, and the women's rugby and football World Cups have been televised, although to nowhere near the extent of coverage given to the men's events. In 2006, there was also a landmark deal between England netball and Sky Sports to show weekly coverage of the Netball Superleague (see Women's Sports Foundation, 2007a).

However, it remains the case that everyday coverage of women's sports continues to make up only about 5 per cent of total sports coverage across all media. The women's sports covered regularly are tennis, netball, and track and field athletics. These are traditionally seen as sports emphasizing grace, balance, co-ordination and aesthetics, all of which are attributes consistent with traditional images of femininity. This pattern is not as clear as it has been in the past, but it remains. For example, when Maria Sharapova won the Wimbledon Championship in 2004, she received extensive coverage. A commentator introduced one segment of a sports show by saying, 'She's young, she's talented, and very beautiful, but can [she] stay focused tonight'; another sports news 'teaser' before a commercial said, 'They slapped her on a billboard that read "the closer you get, the hotter it gets"' (in Duncan and Messner, 2005, p. 15). Despite some male announcers being unable to describe Sharapova as they describe Roger Federer or other physically attractive male athletes, most television coverage of women's sports now takes female athletes and their events more seriously than it did in the 1980s. Sports talk shows still make women the butt of jokes, but this is accepted only among men who have trouble accepting women as athletes and like to pretend that they are still in the changing room having adolescent male fantasies about 'girls'.

Olympic and Commonwealth Games media coverage in the UK tends to highlight stereo-typically feminine sports such as track and field, gymnastics and swimming. Some scholars have noted that other sports receive attention when linked to nationalism (Andrews, 1998; Wensing and Bruce, 2003), which in the UK means that medal hopefuls in sports such as rowing and cycling in the Summer Games, and skeleton and curling in the Winter Games have received some coverage. Individual sports continue to be given priority over team sports in the coverage, and the coverage of women's Olympic sports continues to reinforce gender stereotypes. For example, the media coverage of the women's team who won the gold medal in 2002 in curling made repeated references to performing housework tasks: a reference to the role of the 'sweeper' in curling.

The men's sports most often covered in the media emphasize physical strength, speed, size, and the use of physical force and intimidation to dominate opponents – all qualities consistent with traditional images of masculinity. For example, football is by far the most popular televised men's sport in the UK, and television coverage emphasizes traditional notions of masculinity.

Coverage of women's sports often contains commentaries that highlight the personal charac-teristics of the athletes, such as their attractiveness, their spouses and children, their domestic interests and skills, and their vulnerabilities and weaknesses (Eastman and Billings, 1999; Weiler and Higgs, 1999). For example, when Shelley Rudman won the silver medal in the skeleton event in the 2006 Olympics, her male partner – who competed in the same event but did not win a medal – featured in most of the stories about her success, under headlines including 'Our Tea Tray Romance', or 'And All Because the Lady Loves Tea Tray' (*Mail on Sunday*, 19 February 2006). This not only served to prioritize Rudman's personal life over her athletic triumph, but also trivialized her sport in its reference to the skeleton as a 'tea tray'. In this example, as elsewhere, journalists covering women's sports refer to female athletes by their first names and as 'girls' or 'ladies', although this pattern is changing as researchers have called attention to its sexist implications.

Commentators for men's sports seldom refer to male athletes by their first names, and almost never call them 'boys' or 'gentlemen'. It is assumed that playing sports turns boys into men, and it is hoped that playing sports does not keep women from being ladies. Similarly, references to physical strength have been much more common in commentaries about male athletes, although women clearly demonstrate strength and power, even in sports such as golf, tennis, and track and field events. A recent exception to this has been the coverage given to Venus and Serena Williams. After white media personnel were able to look beyond the beads in their hair and the fact that they did not present themselves as if they were raised in country club settings, they began to refer to their strength, power and speed.

Coverage of sports by the media reproduces traditional gender ideology in the culture
(*Source*: **Alamy**)

Men's sport events often are promoted or described as if they had special historical importance, whereas women's sports events usually are promoted in a less dramatic manner. Men's
events usually are unmarked by references to gender and represented as the events, whereas
women's events almost always are referred to as women's events. For instance, there has always
been 'The World Cup' and 'The Women's World Cup' in football and rugby coverage. This terminology reflects the low priority given to women's sports in all media.

Erasing homosexuality

Homosexuality is ignored in nearly all media coverage, whereas heterosexuality is regularly
acknowledged directly and indirectly among men and women in sports. Heterosexual female
athletes are constantly shown with husbands, children, fiancés, boyfriends and dates; for heterosexual men their heterosexuality is so widely taken for granted that it is mentioned only in
passing. Gay athletes are not erased as much as they are assumed not to exist (Anderson, 2005;
LeBlanc and Jackson, 2007). Lesbian images, however, are carefully erased from coverage, even
though the partners of players and coaches are known and visible to many spectators (Collins,
2004). Lesbian relationships are ignored for fear of offending media audiences.

Lesbian athletes in golf, tennis, and track and field are never profiled in ways that
acknowledge partners or certain aspects of their lifestyles – those parts of their personal stories
are not told. In media-constructed sports reality, lesbians and gay men in sports generally are
invisible unless they publicly come 'out' as gay. Even then, they are marginalized in coverage.
As media studies scholar Pam Creedon notes, 'Homosexuality doesn't sell' (1998, p. 96).
Meanwhile, heterosexual athletes and their partners are discussed and pictured in everything

from the sports magazines to the television coverage of post-game victory celebrations, and nobody accuses these heterosexual athletes of pushing their values and agendas on others. Living in a heterosexual-dominated culture is especially difficult for female coaches and players who would like to acknowledge the support that they have received from long-time partners. Their partners, instead of sharing the moment in public like heterosexual spouses often do, sit in the stands or at home wondering if their very existence could jeopardize their partners' careers. Completely unknown are the men who discreetly watch their male partners win World Cups and league titles.

Media organizations are gendered

Traditional gender patterns in media coverage have been slow to change partly because sports media organizations worldwide have cultures and structures that are deeply gendered. They have been organized and scheduled around men's sports, just like the work routines and assignments of sport reporters. Therefore, the coverage of women's events often requires changes in institutionalized patterns of sports media work. Furthermore, the vast majority of sports media personnel are men, and the highest-status assignments in sports media are those that deal with men's sports.

Even female reporters and commentators know that their upward mobility in the sports media industry demands that they cover men's events in much the same ways that men cover them. If they insist on covering only women's events or if they are assigned only to women's events, they will not advance up the corporate ladder in media organizations (Coventry, 2004). Advancement also may be limited if they insist on covering men's sports in new ways that do not reaffirm the 'correctness' of the coverage patterns and styles developed by men. Although women in the print media regularly cover men's sports, there remain relatively few women who do regular commentary for men's sports in the electronic media.

When it comes to issues of masculinity, most sports coverage uses images and narratives that reproduce dominant ideas about manhood. The television broadcasts of most male team sports are presented as soap operas for men. The vocabularies and storylines construct a symbolic male community that draws meaning from the culture of men's spectator sports and allows men to apply those meanings to themselves in ways that women spectators cannot, even if they are dedicated fans.

The sports coverage most often consumed by boys depicts aggression and violence as normal and exciting, portrays athletes who play in pain as heroes, uses military metaphors and terminology, and highlights conflict between individuals and teams. Women are seldom seen except when portrayed as sex objects, spectators, and supportive mothers and spouses on the sidelines. The role of the supporting female has received so much coverage that the term 'WAGs' (wives and girlfriends) has entered general vernacular.

Overall, gender ideology informs media representations of sports. This is highlighted in the box 'Meet the press' (opposite). However, it is important to note that few of us accept media representations at face value. We make sense of representations in our own terms although we are heavily influenced by the cultures in which we have been socialized. When we have special knowledge or personal connections with a sport or the athletes involved, we often give our own meanings to media representations, even if we are not critical in our assessments of them (Bruce, 2007; van Sterkenburg and Knoppers, 2004).

In 2001, just before the start of the Women's British Open squash tournament, a media frenzy broke out surrounding the appearance of one of the players in a black thong and bra which she claimed was less restrictive than other underwear and would help improve her performance. The player in question, Vicky Botwright, was ranked eighteenth in the world at the time, and her behaviour was publicly condemned by the chief executive of WISPA (the Women's International Squash Players Association). In fact, the whole event was a publicity stunt organized by WISPA to try to encourage press interest for a sport in which British women were successful but unable to secure sponsorship. While Botwright's image appeared in several newspapers under the headline of 'Lancashire Hot Bot', she subsequently lost her place on her local team, suffered negative publicity and, despite moving up in the world rankings, neither she nor the sport sustained any long-term media interest.

Botwright is not the only athlete to have posed naked or semi-naked as a way of raising funding and sponsorship for her sport. Denise Lewis, Olympic gold medallist in the Sydney heptathlon, was pressured by her sponsors to pose topless for a magazine save from being body-painted with the Union Flag.

Like Botwright and Lewis, many young female athletes face a dilemma when people in the media insist on sexualizing them. They must decide if they should just play sports and hope they will be rewarded as athletes, or if they should also present their bodies in sexualized terms to attract attention, sponsors and media support. For example, the British badminton player Gail Emms and heptathlete Kelly Sotherton have both repeatedly had to resist pressure from their sponsors to wear more revealing clothing in competitions and so have decided against allowing their bodies to be sexualized, but believe they probably lose out on media coverage and sponsorship as a result. They are also critical of their peers who have their hair and make-up attended to before they compete. While this raises concerns about the methods that some female athletes must go to in order to raise the profile of their sport and to secure funding to support it, other female athletes either conform to or exploit expectations based on traditional ideas and beliefs about what women should be. As a result, there remain athletes like Sharapova who clearly benefit from conforming to gender stereotypes and the subsequent media coverage and sponsorship deals.

Many people find it difficult to analyse these issues. What are the guidelines and limits for media representations of athletes' bodies? More to the point, who should determine those guidelines and limits, and what can be done to increase the chances that those determinations will be based on critically informed choices? Gail Emms refuses to wear sexy clothing, at least in front of a camera under conditions that she had not chosen. But, if other athletes choose to be represented as sexy in the media, should they be targets of criticism and defined as sex objects instead of athletes?

These questions are best answered if we consider issues of power and ideology. If female athletes had the power to control how they are represented in the media and they critically understood the importance of media images in our culture, it would be much easier for them to meet the press. But that leaves the toughest question unanswered: how do women gain that power in sports and society? *What do you think?*

Race and ethnicity themes in media representations of sports

Just as gender ideology influences media coverage, so does racial and ethnic ideology and the stereotypes associated with it (Bruce, 2004, 2007; Curry et al., 2002; Davis and Harris, 1998;

Kian et al., 2008; van Sterkenburg and Knoppers, 2004). For example, in 1935, Grantland Rice, often identified by white American journalists as the best sports writer of the early twentieth century in the USA, described black heavyweight boxing champion Joe Louis as the 'brown cobra' and wrote that Louis brought into the boxing ring 'the speed of the jungle, the instinctive speed of the wild' (in Mead, 1985, p. 91). Louis was described very differently in the black American press, but millions of whites read Rice's words and accepted them without question.

Ideology and stereotypes changed during the second half of the twentieth century, and white announcers commonly described black athletes as having natural abilities, good instincts, unique physical attributes and tendencies to be undisciplined players; references to 'jungle' and 'the wild' were replaced with 'ghetto'. Meanwhile, Asian athletes have been described as methodical, mechanical, machine-like, mysterious, industrious, self-disciplined and intelligent. Their achievements are often attributed to cognitive rather than physical abilities, and stereotypes about height and other physiological characteristics are sometimes used to explain success or failure in sports. In contrast, there is a tendency to describe Latin American athletes as flamboyant, exotic, emotional, passionate, moody and hot blooded (Blain et al., 1993). When it comes to white athletes, they are often described as hard working, intelligent, highly disciplined and driven by character rather than instincts (Davis and Harris, 1998).

Research in the 1970s and 1980s discredited the assumed factual basis of racial and ethnic stereotypes at the same time that media studies identified the ways that ideology influenced sports stories and commentaries, particularly in reference to black athletes. This made journalists and commentators increasingly aware of the need to avoid words, phrases and inferences based on stereotypical ideas and beliefs (Sabo et al., 1996). People in the print media chose their words more carefully, and broadcasters doing live commentary on talk radio and during games became sensitive to the racial implications of what they said. But making these changes was difficult for media people who accepted dominant racial ideology and never viewed it critically or from the perspectives of black or Asian populations. Therefore, some made mistakes and a few were fired for them. An extreme example of this was in 2004 when Ron Atkinson was fired as a television football commentator and journalist for describing the Chelsea captain Marcel Desailly as a '-----lazy, thick nigger', not realizing that he was still broadcasting live (see chapter 9).

Avoiding stereotypes and covering racial and ethnic relations in an informed way are two different things. Sports coverage today pretends that race and ethnicity do not exist; it is assumed that everyone in sports faces the same challenges and odds for success. But in actuality, race and ethnicity influence experiences and perspectives to such an extent that people cannot talk about them without discovering real, meaningful and socially important racial and ethnic differences in what they think and feel. Ignoring this story about real differences allows whites in the media and media audiences to be comfortably colour-blind, and deny the legacy and continuing relevance of skin colour and cultural heritage in British society and in sports. At the same time, blacks and British Asians are reminded that acceptance in the dominant culture requires them to 'be like whites' in how they think, talk and act. They understand that to be embraced by the media and white fans they should smile in accommodating ways on camera and during interviews, just like Ian Wright and Kelly Holmes have done so effectively for many years (see Carrington, 2001; Davis and Harris, 1998). But they also admire athletes who express their racial or ethnic identities and 'do not forget where they came from'. This creates tension for ethnic minority athletes, and unique social dynamics in sports where players are racially and ethnically mixed. This is a newsworthy story, but it would make many people, especially white sports fans, uncomfortable, and it would be difficult for most journalists to tell. But as long as it remains untold, white privilege in sports will persist without being recognized, and anyone who does talk about it will be accused of 'playing the race card'.

Pretending to be colour-blind in a culture where a skin-colour-based racial ideology has existed for the past three centuries is a sure way to guarantee that white privilege is seamlessly incorporated into the media coverage of sports. It allows the sports media to avoid asking why so many sports at the professional level are exclusively white. Ethnic studies scholars refer to this new insistence that we should ignore skin colour as racism that is based on completely denying the existence of the history and relevance of skin colour and ethnicity in societies where they influence everything from the distribution of income and wealth to where and how people live (Bonilla-Silva, 2001, 2003; Brown et al., 2005; Doane and Bonilla-Silva, 2003). Colour-blind coverage in sports misses a significant dimension of sport reality and reproduces the racial and ethnic status quo. But it allows people to use sports as forms of social escapism, as whitewashed worlds devoid of the complex, messy issues that characterize real everyday life. In this way, the sports media do not 'tell it like it is' as much as they tell it like many people want to hear it.

Making changes

The most effective way to reduce subtle forms of racial and ethnic bias in the media is to hire ethnic minority reporters, editors, photographers, writers, producers, directors, camerapersons, commentators and statisticians (Rowe, 2004a, 2004b). Lip-service is paid to this goal, and progress has been made in certain media, but members of racial and ethnic minorities are clearly under-represented in most sports newsrooms, press boxes, broadcast booths and media executive offices. This is unfortunate because ethnic diversity among people who represent sports through the media would enrich stories and provide multiple perspectives for understanding sports and the people who play and coach them. When ethnic diversity has existed, it has resulted in more accurate and insightful coverage (Thomas, 1996).

Many editors and producers are fond of saying that skin colour is irrelevant to the quality of journalists, and most people agree with them. But if there are fewer than a handful of black reporters covering the Premier League, which has a large number of black players, the definition of quality becomes an issue. Are experiences that enable a reporter to understand the backgrounds, orientations and actions of players included in the definition of quality? Is it important for a player to feel that a reporter understands who he is and how he views the world when he is interviewed? Is it important for the media to provide coverage from different vantage points, angles and perspectives? If so, reporters and broadcasters defined as qualified should bring diverse ethnic perspectives to sports coverage.

In addition to critically examining the definition of quality used to hire people in sports media, current reporters and broadcasters must do their racial and ethnic homework if they wish to keep their jobs. This involves learning what it means to work in a white-dominated/identified/centred organization and cover sports organized around the values and experiences of white men. It involves learning to view the world through the eyes of the people whom you write and talk about. For whites, this means learning as much as possible about the history and heritage of everyone from athletes to owners, and even reading classic books written by ethnic minority authors and recent research on race and ethnicity. Neither skin colour nor gender precludes knowledge about sports or the people involved in them, but knowledge is based on a combination of experience and the richness of the perspectives one has to make sense of the ethnically and racially diverse social worlds that are covered by the media.

National identity themes in media representations of sports

Although some sports reporters and broadcasters around the world are careful to avoid using national stereotypes in their representations of athletes and teams, evidence suggests that subtle stereotypes regularly influence sports coverage (Mayeda, 1999; McCarthy et al., 2003; Sabo and Jensen, 1998; Sabo et al., 1996; van Sterkenburg and Knoppers, 2004). Images and narratives clearly emphasize nationalism and national unity grounded in traditional British loyalty and patriotism. This has become particularly significant in periods when the sense of 'Britishness' is under threat: for example, by increasing devolution of the so-called 'Celtic fringe' from the UK, globalization and specifically Americanization processes, and the gradual integration into the European Union (see Bloyce, 2005; Tuck, 2003b). In fact, the sports that were 'invented' in the UK – football, cricket and rugby – are the most widely televised sports in the country. Other sports are covered, but if they do not match traditional ideas about what it means to be British, they do not receive priority coverage.

When British teams and athletes are competing against teams and athletes from other countries, events are usually framed in an us-versus-them format. This is particularly evident when British teams are playing their traditional 'enemies' of Germany and Argentina, with whom they have a history of military conflict (see Maguire, 2005; Maguire et al., 1999). When British teams or athletes win, reporters and broadcasters declare proudly, 'We won.' Of course, this is complicated when the home nations compete against each other, rather than as one unified British or UK team (see Chapter 13).

Other ideological themes in media sports

Research using critical theories has identified other ideological themes around which images and narratives in media sports have been constructed. In addition to the themes that we have already discussed (success, gender, race and ethnicity, and nationalism), others include, individualism, teamwork, aggression and consumption (Andrews and Jackson, 2001; Kinkema and Harris, 1998; Real, 1998; Rowe et al., 1998).

These themes should not surprise anyone who has consumed media sports in the UK. Media images and narratives emphasize individual efforts to achieve competitive victories, even in the coverage of team sports. Matches are promoted with announcements such as 'It is Rooney against Gerrard in the all-Red final.' This emphasizes the idea that individuals must take responsibility for what happens in their lives and that team failures can be traced to the failures and flaws of one or more individuals.

Images and narratives in sports coverage also stress teamwork, which usually means following a game plan developed by a coach/leader, being loyal to the team and being willing to make sacrifices for the good of the team (Kinkema and Harris, 1998). Media coverage clearly identifies coaches as the organizers and controllers of teams. Commentators praise athletes as 'team players' when they follow the game plan; similarly, they praise coaches for their ability to fit players into team roles that lead to victories. This ideological approach to teamwork matches the ideology underlying most business organizations: teamwork means loyalty to the organization and productivity under the direction of a leader-coach.

The importance of mental and physical aggression is another ideological theme around which images and narratives are constructed in media sports. Rough, aggressive play is assumed to be a sign of commitment and skill, and aggressive players are praised as 'warriors' (Messner et al., 1999). The vocabulary stresses 'bone-crushing tackles' and 'hard hits' in rugby and football. These actions are represented as necessary parts of the game and as skills needed by players if they are to play the game well.

When the games are reported in highlights and news programmes, they are full of violent images: the teams as 'troops at battle', 'annihilating the opposition', engaging in 'shootouts' and on and on. The scores sound like the results of military operations during a war. In fact, much of the language used in the media to represent sports in the UK is taken from the realm of violence, the military and warfare, particularly when British teams are playing against another nation's team (see Maguire, 2005; Tuck, 2003b; Cartoon 12.3). Aggression is celebrated, whereas kindness and sensitivity are seen as weakness. This is even extended to supporters, particularly in the media coverage of football-related spectator disorder, where the media appear to amplify so-called 'football hooliganism' since it makes a good story (see Poulton, 2005, 2006).

Finally, the emphasis on consumption is clear in the media coverage of sports: a significant proportion of televised sports on the commercial channels consists of commercial time, advertisements fill newspapers and magazines, and Internet sites use multiple strategies to present

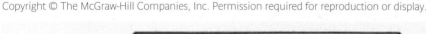

'Yes, I KNOW you watch Spooks and the Bill, but this rugby game contains real violence, so off to your room now!'

Cartoon 12.3 **This father distinguishes between fictional and real-life violence on television. If video games are rated for violent content, why is the same not done for sport events in which the violence is real and has real consequences for players and their families?**

advertisements mixed with scores, commentary and links. The audiences for media sports are encouraged to express their connections to teams and athletes by purchasing thousands of branded objects, particularly team shirts displaying the logo of the sponsor.

Media impact on sports-related behaviours

We know that media images and narratives influence people, but we do not know much about who is influenced or in what ways people are influenced. Media coverage is part of our experience, and experiences influence who we are and what we think, feel and do. However, in this section, we focus only on the connections between consuming sports media and either playing sports or attending events.

Active participation in sports

Do the media cause people to be more active sports participants or turn them into couch potatoes? This is an important issue, given the high rates of obesity, diabetes and heart disease in the UK. More people watch sports on television than ever before, and the rates of obesity and diabetes are the highest in British history. This is not to say that watching sports on television causes obesity and the health problems associated with it, but it suggests issues that should be studied.

When children watch sports on television, some copy what they see if they have or can make opportunities to do so. Children are great imitators, with active imaginations, so when they see and identify with athletes, they may create informal activities or seek to join youth sports programmes to pursue television-inspired dreams. Participation grounded in these dreams does not last long, especially after children discover that it takes years of tedious, repetitive and boring practice to compete successfully and make those glorious trips to the victory podium. However, other motives may develop in the process and inspire healthy sports participation patterns. But we do not know how many children decide to avoid or quit sports because they cannot meet performance expectations formed as they watch highly skilled athletes in the media.

Many adults who watch sports on television do not play anything that they watch, whereas others are active participants in one or more sports (Wenner and Gantz, 1998). Interestingly, there is little research on this issue. Therefore, the safest conclusion at this point is that consuming sports through the media is connected with each outcome in different situations and with different people.

Attendance at sports events

Match attendance is related to many factors, and its relationship to the media is complex. On the one hand, some professional sports have been able to limit live television coverage of matches based on the belief that television coverage hurts attendance and ticket sales. In support of this belief, many people say that they would rather watch certain sport events on television than attend them in person. On the other hand, the media publicize sports, promote interest, and provide the information that people need to identify with athletes and teams and become potential ticket buyers for events (Wann et al., 2001; Weiss, 1996; Zhang et al., 1998).

The most logical conclusion is that people who watch more games on television also attend more games in person (Zhang and Smith, 1997). However, this conclusion has two qualifications. First, as ticket prices increase and the number of elite, 'live' games increases across various sports, people may limit attendance when there is the option of watching a lower-league match or an alternative sport on television. Second, because the media focus attention on elite sports, such as professional football, they may undermine attendance at less elite events such as local club and school games. Thus, the media may be positively related to attendance at the top levels of competition but negatively related to attendance at lower levels of competition (Zhang et al., 1997). Research is needed to explore this issue in more depth.

Audience Experiences with Media Sports

Media sports provide topics of conversation, sources of identity and heroes (Melnick and Jackson, 2002), feelings of success when favourite teams win, opportunities to express emotions, occasions for getting together with others and a focus for those who are passing time alone (Wenner and Gantz, 1998). We actually know very little about the audiences for media sports (Ang, 1991) but we do know that adults integrate media sports into their lives in a variety of ways (Obel, 2001; Wenner and Gantz, 1998). Although studies have identified some adults, more men than women, who focus considerable attention on watching sports, overall patterns indicate that watching television sports is a major activity for a relatively limited segment of the overall population in the UK. Furthermore, those studies do not tell us much about the ways that people include the consumption of media sports in their lives (Crawford, 2004; Wann et al., 2001).

Research summarized by Wenner and Gantz (1998) shows that men and women who live together often watch televised sports together and that this usually is a positive activity in their relationships. In other words, 'football widows' are not as common as many people believe. Men watch sports more than women do and are more likely to be committed fans. However, when women are highly committed fans, they watch and respond to sports on television in ways that are similar to patterns among men. Research suggests that being a fan is more important than gender or any other factor when it comes to people's viewing experiences. Some couples experience conflicts related to viewing sports, but most couples resolve them successfully. Partners usually learn to accommodate each other's viewing habits over time, and when differences are associated with problems, it usually is in relationships that have other problems unrelated to their patterns of watching sports on television.

Future studies will tell us more about the ways that media sports experiences are integrated into people's lives and when media sports become important sites at which social relationships occur. The use of the Internet and video games should be included in these studies.

The Profession of Sports Journalism

Some people trivialize sports journalism by saying that it provides 'entertaining material about people and events that don't really matter too much' (Koppett, 1994). However, sports do matter – not because they produce a tangible product or make essential contributions to our survival, but because they represent ideas about how the world works and what is important in life. Therefore, sports journalists do things that matter when it comes to ideology and public consciousness.

Sports journalists on the job: relationships with athletes

As televised sports have increased, sports writers have had to create stories that go beyond the action and scores in sports. This leads them to seek information about the personal lives of the athletes, and this in turn has influenced relationships between journalists and athletes. For example, athletes today realize that they cannot trust writers to hold information in confidence, even if it was disclosed in the privacy of the changing room. Furthermore, the stakes associated with 'bad press' are so great for athletes and teams that everyone in sports organizations is on their guard when talking with journalists. Clinton Doaks, a long-time sports writer in the USA explains that 'today's sports world is so driven by public relations that there are very few stories to report. Every player, coach, and team is so image conscious … that they all offer the same homogenous quotes week in and week out, game after game' (Doaks, 2004).

As journalists seek stories that athletes do not want to tell, it creates tensions in their relationships with athletes. Tension is also caused by differences in the salaries and personal backgrounds of players and sports writers. For example, wealthy black football players without a university degree have little in common with white, middle-class, university-educated writers. As a result, writers feel less compelled to protect or empathize with athletes in their stories, and athletes feel that they must be wary of the motives of journalists.

Team owners and managers are so conscious of tensions between athletes and media personnel that they now provide players with training on how to handle interviews without saying things that sound bad or can be misinterpreted. However, tensions sometimes reach a point that players threaten people from the media, and sports writers, in particular, quit their jobs to find less stressful occupations.

Tensions also call attention to ethical issues in sports journalism. Responsible journalists, including writers and announcers, are now sensitive to the fact that they should not jeopardize people's reputations simply for the sake of entertainment. This does not mean that they avoid criticism that might hurt someone, but they are less likely to hurt someone unintentionally or without good reason. Unfortunately, journalists constantly face grey areas in which ethical guidelines are not clear, and the need to present attractive stories often encourages them to push ethical limits.

Sports writers and sports commentators: a comparison

Different media have slightly different goals and strategies. The print media focus on entertaining people with information and in-depth analysis – and, in the case of tabloid newspapers, with personal interest stories – whereas radio and television entertain people with images and commentary, which create on-the-spot urgency. The implications of these differences are summarized in Table 12.4.

Although differences between sports writers and commentators are often difficult to identify, the print media usually hire writers who can tell reliable and thorough stories, whereas broadcast companies hire commentators who can excite and entertain an audience with rapid commentary (see Cartoon 12.4). This is why newspaper and magazine writers (especially the latter) usually do more thorough investigative reporting, whereas commentators talk with a sense of urgency to entertain viewing or listening audiences. However, some writers go beyond information and analysis and write strictly to entertain, particularly in the case of tabloid

Table 12.4 **Sports writers and sports commentators: a comparison of roles**

Role characteristics	Sports writers*	Sports commentators†
Job security	High	Low
Salary	Low	High
Popularity/public recognition	Low	High
Freedom of expression in job	Moderately restricted	Heavily restricted
Purpose of role	Entertain and provide information	Entertain and 'sell' sport events
Role expectations	Be trustworthy investigators	Be knowledgeable entertainers
Management expectations	Do not offend advertisers	Do not offend sponsors
Opportunities to do investigative reporting	Occasionally	Rarely
On-the-job contacts	Copy desk editors and sub-editors	Broadcast executives, team management, sponsors/advertisers
Relationships with players	Often tense and antagonistic	Often friendly and supportive
Attachment with public	Based on style and writing skills	Based on credibility and personality

Notes:

*The primary focus here is on newspaper reporters. Magazine writers have similar jobs, but they are different in that they often cover issues and topics in greater depth.

†The primary focus here is on television commentators. Radio commentators have similar jobs, but they are different in that they must focus more on description in their commentary and less on interpretation.

Source: adapted from Koppett (1994)

newspapers, and some television and radio personalities work on investigative stories in which information and analysis are as important as entertainment.

The efforts of television companies to provide a combination of play-by-play commentary and entertainment lead them to hire popular retired athletes and coaches to be commentators. Media companies cover sports as 'infotainment' rather than news, and those who commentate on matches must be entertainers. But they must be credible entertainers who can provide insider interpretations and stories. This is why commentators may be former athletes and coaches who fans perceive to be credible. However, all radio and television commentators are expected to self-censor their commentary so that they stay within limits set by teams and television companies. Consequently, commentators seldom stray from a fairly standard entertainment approach, and they provide no critical comments about sports as social phenomena as we watch them on television. For people who consume sports primarily through the popular media, critical discussions of sports, such as the ones in this book, may create defensiveness or discomfort.

'This may be my first time reporting on the news, but I know how to report on violence, drug abuse and corruption – I used to cover the sports for BSkyB.'

Cartoon 12.4 The media coverage of sports news is much like other news in that it contains representations of violence and drama. Such representations are not accurate indicators of what generally happens in sports or our communities

SUMMARY: Could Sports and the Media Survive without Each Other?

To understand social life today, we must give serious attention to the media and media experiences. This is why we study the relationship between sports and the media.

Media sports, like other parts of culture, are social constructions. They are created, organized and controlled by human beings whose ideas are grounded in their social worlds, experiences and ideologies. The media do not reflect reality as much as they provide re-presentations of selected versions of reality. Power relations in society influence these representations. Therefore, the images and narratives that comprise the media often reaffirm dominant ideologies and promote the interests of those who benefit most from them. The possible exception to this is the Internet, a medium that offers revolutionary potential for people to create their own media content.

Video games and virtual sports are important components of the new media. At this time, they complement existing media, but they will gradually provide sports-related experiences that are unique and unrelated to other media. As technology makes possible the exploration of virtual realities and participation in physical challenges with virtual teammates and opponents, sports will occur more frequently in virtual worlds (Leonard, 2006; Lomax, 2006; McDaniel and Sullivan, 1998).

Sports and the media have grown to depend on each other as both have become more important parts of cultures in many societies. They could survive without each other, but they would be different from what they are now. Commercial sports have grown and prospered because of media coverage and the rights fees paid to sports organizations by media companies. Without the publicity and money provided by the media, commercial sports would be local business operations with much less scope than they have today, and less emphasis would be given to elite forms of competitive sports. Without exposure to sports through the media, people would probably give lower priority to organized power and performance sports in their everyday lives, and they might give higher priority to pleasure and participation sports.

The media also could survive without sports. But they, too, especially newspapers and television, would be different if they did not have sports to make their programming attractive to young male audiences and the sponsors who wish to buy access to them. Without sports, newspaper circulation would decrease, and television programming on weekends and holidays would be different and less profitable for television companies.

The symbiotic relationship between sports and the media suggests that we will continue to see many commercialized sports covered by the media and the major media presenting regular coverage of sports. However, history also shows that this relationship has developed within a larger cultural context, one in which priority is given to commercial profits and the creation of mega media events. Furthermore, the relationship between sports and the media has been created in connection with the ever-changing interactions among athletes, agents, coaches, administrators, sports team owners, sponsors, advertisers, media representatives and a diverse collection of spectators. The power dynamics in these interactions have an important impact on the sports–media relationship.

Sports covered by the electronic media are represented to audiences with dramatic, exciting and stylized images and narratives designed to be entertaining for audiences and attractive to sponsors. The influence of these media sports in our lives depends on how we integrate them into our relationships and routines. Direct experiences with sports influence how we interpret and use what we read, listen to and view in the media. If we have little direct experience with and in sports, the media play a more central role in creating our sports realities and influencing how those realities are integrated into the rest of our lives.

Research suggests that dominant ideologies related to success, gender, race and ethnicity, nationalism, individualism, teamwork, violence and consumption are perpetuated through the images and narratives represented in the media coverage of sports in the UK. These ideologies support the interests of corporate sponsors, males and white people in the UK, and they are presented seamlessly in sports coverage so that the current distribution of power and privilege seems to be normal and natural. Future research will tell us more about how people use media content as they form ideas about sports, their social relationships and the social world.

Especially important in the future will be research on how people use the Internet and video games as sites for constructing their experiences in and with sports. Some 13-year-olds would much rather play sport video games than watch games on television. In the future, some of them will do both at the same time. And some 25-year-olds enjoy the sports-related interactive experiences that they have on the Internet more than the games themselves. Media sports and the experiences associated with them are changing rapidly, and it is important to study them in ways that promote critical media literacy rather than the uncritical celebration of media technology and culture (Kellner, 2003a, 2003b, 2004; Leonard, 2006; Scherer, 2007).

Website resources

Note: Websites often change. The following URLs were current when this book was printed. Please check our website (***www.mcgraw-hill.co.uk/textbooks/coakley***) for updates and additions.

See the OLC, ***www.mcgraw-hill.co.uk/textbooks/coakley***, for an annotated list of readings related to this chapter.

www.culture.gov.uk This is the website for the Department for Culture, Media and Sport, and provides links to each of the main groups in the department, the 2012 Olympic Games and creative industries.

http://iplt20.com The official website of the India Premier League, where viewers can register and watch matches online, and follow links to the websites of the league's sponsors.

www.i-uk.com/servlet/Front?pagename=OpenMarket/Xcelerate/ShowPage&c=Page&cid=1 006977151753 This site gives a brief description of the organization of sports in the UK. There are links to articles and factsheets on sport and the media.

www.mediauk.com/radio/317/bbc-five-live-sports-extra This site provides details of radio stations, shows and television stations that are involved in the sporting industry.

Chapter 13

Sports, politics and globalization: how do governments and global processes influence sports?

(*Source*: Elizabeth Pike)

Learning Centre Resources
Online

Visit *Sports in Society*'s Online Learning Centre (OLC) at **www.mcgraw-hill.co.uk/ textbooks/coakley** for additional information and study material for this chapter, including:

- Self-grading quizzes and essay questions
- Learning outcomes
- Related websites
- Additional readings

Chapter contents

The sports – government connection
Sports and global political processes
Politics in sports
Summary: how do governments and global processes influence sports?

> Sport is a powerful and often under-used tool that can help Government to achieve a number of ambitious goals.
>
> *(Tony Blair, former British Prime Minister, in DCMS Strategy Unit, 2002, p. 5)*

> Unquestionably sport can mobilize groups and publics. This is why it is a ready source of both profits and political kudos. Furthermore, the fact that sport can be used strategically to serve the system or vested interests via money and power implies the possibility of lifeworld resistance and change.
>
> *(Graham Scambler, sociologist, 2005 p. 181)*

> We have waged a lengthy and tireless battle to create a [revolutionary] sports culture … This is what has allowed our country to reach a place of honour in sports … recognized by the entire world.
>
> *(Fidel Castro, president of Cuba, 2001)*

Organized competitive sports have long been connected with politics, governments and global processes. **Politics** refers to the *processes and procedures of making decisions that affect collections of people, from small groups to societies and even multiple societies that are unified for certain purposes*, such as the European Union consisting of 27 nations with shared policies, and some of which share a common currency. In a sociological sense, politics involves processes through which power is gained and used in social life. Therefore, people in the sociology of sport study politics in families, communities, local and national sports organizations, societies and large non-government organizations (NGOs) such as the International Olympic Committee (IOC) or Fédération Internationale de Football Association (FIFA), the international governing body for football.

Governments are *formal organizations with the power to make and enforce rules in a particular territory or collection of people.* Because governments make decisions affecting people's lives, they are political organizations by definition. Governments operate on various levels from local towns to nation states, and they influence sports whether they occur in a local public park or privately owned stadiums that host international competitions. People in the sociology of sport often refer to '**the state**' because this concept *includes the formal institution of a national government plus those parts of civil society – such as education, family, media and churches – that teach values and ideologies that extend the influence and control of the political agencies that make and enforce laws and govern a society.*

Politics often involve the actions and interactions of governments but rule-making in sports today often transcends the boundaries of nation states and occurs in connection with global processes. For example, football became a global sport as British workers, students and teachers took the game to South America and British soldiers took it to Africa, Asia, the West Indies and other colonized areas of the nineteenth-century British Empire. Therefore, football was introduced to people around the world through the global processes of migration, capitalist expansion, trade links, British imperialism and colonization. These processes clearly involve politics. Governments usually are involved, but the processes often transcend particular governments as people, products, ideas, technologies and money move so rapidly across national borders that time and space become compressed.

This chapter focuses on the relationships between sports and politics. The goal is to explain the ways in which sports are connected with governments, the state and global political processes. Chapter content focuses on four major questions:

1 Why do governments often sponsor and control sports?
2 How are sports connected with global politics that involve nation states, transnational corporations and non-governmental organizations?
3 What is the role of the Olympic movement in global politics and processes?
4 What are the ways that political processes occur in sports and sports organizations?

As you read this chapter, remember that power and authority are the key concepts used when studying politics and political processes. **Power** refers to *an ability to influence people and achieve goals, even in the face of opposition from others* (Weber, 1968/1922). **Authority** is *a form of power that comes with a recognized and legitimate status or office in a government, an organization or an established set of relationships.* For example, a large corporation has power if it can influence how people think about and play sports and if it can use sports to achieve its goals. Sports organizations such as the IOC, FIFA, BUCS, and a local parks and recreation department have *authority* over the sports that they administer as long as people associated with those sports accept the organizations as legitimate sources of control. This example alerts us to the fact that, in this chapter, *politics* refers to the power to make decisions that affect sports and sports participation at all levels of involvement.

The Sports – Government Connection

When sports become popular community activities, government involvement often increases. Many sports require sponsorship, organization and facilities – all of which depend on resources that few individuals possess on their own. Sport facilities may be so expensive that regional and national governments are the only entities with the power and resources to build and maintain them. Therefore, government involvement in sports often is a necessity. Government involvement also occurs when there is a need for a third party to regulate and control sports and sports organizations in ways that promote the overall good of people in a community or society.

The nature and extent of government involvement in sports varies by society, but it generally serves one or more of the following purposes (adapted from Houlihan, 2000):

- safeguard the public order
- maintain health and fitness among citizens
- promote the prestige and power of a group, community or nation
- promote a sense of identity, belonging and unity among citizens
- reproduce values consistent with dominant ideology in a community or society
- increase support for political leaders and government
- promote economic development in a community or society
- serve as a foreign policy tool.

Safeguard the public order

Governments often make rules determining the legality of sports, where they may and may not be played, the safety equipment that must be used, who must have opportunities to play, and who can use public sports facilities at certain times. Ideally, these rules promote safety and reduce conflict between multiple users of particular spaces. For example, a government might ban bullfighting, bare-knuckle boxing or bungee jumping off public bridges. In the case of commercial sports, governments may regulate the rights and duties of team owners, sponsors, promoters and athletes. Local governments may regulate sports participation by requiring permits to use public facilities and playing fields. Likewise, local officials may close streets or parks to the general public so that sports events can be held under controlled and safe conditions. For example, marathons in London and New York City require the involvement of the government and government agencies such as the local police forces.

Governments may pass laws or establish policies that safeguard public order by protecting the participation rights of citizens. *Game Plan* and the *National Framework for Sport* in the UK are examples of government (re)distribution policies intended to promote social inclusion in and through sports.

Safeguarding public order also involves policing sport events. Local police or even military forces may be called on to control crowds and individuals who threaten the safety of others. During the Olympics, for example, the host city and nation provide thousands of military and law enforcement officials to safeguard public order. In the face of possible protests and terrorist actions, it is estimated that the Chinese government spent up to £13 billion to police and monitor the Beijing area in connection with the 2008 Olympic Games – more than the £3 billion spent by Athens, Greece to secure, the 2004 Olympic Games (Latimer, 2008; Waterford, 2004). The government also employed over 43 000 soldiers, 47 helicopters, 74 aeroplanes and 33 naval ships, 6000 security guards on 18 000 buses, 30 000 guards at bus stops and terminals, and tens of thousands of surveillance cameras in Beijing and other cities, as well as the personnel to monitor them.

Some governments attempt to safeguard public order by sponsoring sports events and programmes for at-risk youths. Sports, they believe, keep youths off the streets, thereby lowering crime rates, vandalism, loneliness and alienation. However, these programmes generally fail because they do not deal with the deprivation, racism, poverty, dislocation, unemployment, community disintegration and political powerlessness that often create 'at-risk youths' and social problems in communities and societies (Coakley, 2002; Coalter, 2007; Hartmann, 2001, 2003b). Finally, sports are used in military and police training so that the soldiers and police will be more effective protectors of public order (Mangan, 2003). Military academies in the UK and many nations traditionally sponsor sports for cadets, and the World Police and Fire Games are held every two years because people believe that sports participation keeps law enforcement officials and firefighters physically fit and prepared to safeguard public order.

Maintain health and fitness

Governments also become involved in sports to promote health and fitness among citizens. Nations like the UK, which have government-funded health insurance programmes, promote and sponsor certain sports to improve physical health in the general population and thereby reduce the cost to the National Health Services.

Similar motives underlie government sponsorship and organization of fitness and sports programmes in other nations. Many people believe that sports participation improves fitness, fitness improves health, and good health reduces medical costs. This belief persists in the face of the following factors (Waddington, 2000a, 2007).

- Many illnesses that increase healthcare costs are caused by environmental factors and living conditions that cannot be changed through sports or fitness programmes.
- Certain forms of sports participation do not produce physical fitness or identifiable health benefits.
- The win-at-all-cost orientation in certain competitive sports often contributes to injuries and increased healthcare costs (see Chapter 6).
- The demand for healthcare often increases when people train for competitions because they seek specialized medical care to treat and rehabilitate sport injuries.

These factors lead governments to be cautious and selective when they sponsor sports for health purposes. Most governments now emphasize non-competitive physical activities and exercise with clear aerobic benefits instead of competitive sports. The relationship between sports participation and overall health and fitness is a complex one. Although research clearly shows that physical exercise has health benefits, competitive sports involve more than mere exercise.

Local authorities often regulate the circumstances under which certain sports can occur. This skate park is an area of a city where skateboarding is permitted, but there are strict 'conditions of use' (*Source*: Elizabeth Pike)

Competitive sports can promote overall health when athletes value physical well-being over performance and competitive success. Playing sports is beneficial when it helps us understand our bodies and maintain physical well-being; it is not beneficial when it involves overtraining, the use of bodies as weapons and overconformity to the norms of the sport ethic (as explained in Chapter 6). This is why health professionals sometimes disagree when it comes to recommending government involvement in sports to promote health and fitness.

Promote the prestige and power of a group, community or nation

Government involvement in sports frequently is motivated by the desire to overcome political isolation and/or a quest for recognition and prestige (Allison, 2004; Bairner, 2005). This occurs on local, national and even global levels. For example, the 1996 Olympic Games were used by Atlanta to present itself as a world-class city symbolizing the 'new South', now open to all people regardless of race or national background. Sydney, host of the 2000 Summer Games, presented itself as a city with clean air in a country with a pleasant climate and vital business connections with emerging nations in Asia. Salt Lake City used the 2002 Winter Olympics to present itself as an economically progressive area and an attractive tourist destination. Athens used the 2004

Summer Games to show the world that Greece was part of the new Europe and that it was a nation that had more than monuments of a past era. When Germany hosted the men's Football World Cup for the second time in 2006, it was intended to be a showcase of the new reunited Germany. At the same time, this event was seen as an ideal opportunity to erase the powerful memory of two previous incidents related to sports events on German soil: the 1936 'Nazi' Olympics, and the terrorist attack on Israeli athletes during the 1972 Summer Olympic Games in Munich (Merkel, 2006). China, according to some estimates, spent over £30 billion to present itself during the 2008 Olympic Games in Beijing as a new world power and a dynamic nation that is ideal for business investments and tourism (Brownell, 2008; Price and Dayan, 2008).

This quest for identity, recognition and prestige also underlies government subsidies for national teams across a wide range of sports, usually those designated as Olympic sports. Government officials use international sports to establish their nation's legitimacy in the international sphere, and they often believe that winning medals enhances their image around

Quantifying and measuring the long-term social impact of sports is difficult. These supporters are demonstrating an allegiance to an Irish team at a rugby match against a French team which took place in England. Will their identities and sense of Ireland's place in the world be changed because of the success of their team? Sports provide immediate and temporary emotional experiences, but it takes careful planning to make those experiences the basis for real change in a city or nation (*Source*: Elizabeth Pike)

the world. This is why many governments provide cash rewards to their athletes who win medals. At the 2008 Olympic Games in Beijing, Greek athletes were promised US$300 000 for gold, US$200 000 for silver and about US$107 000 for bronze medals, plus civil service jobs and advertising contracts worth up to US$500 000. Russia paid US$50 000, US$30 000 and US$20 000 for medals, but medal winners also received bonuses amounting to about US$500 000. The US Olympic Committee paid US$25 000, US$15 000 and US$10 000 to gold, silver and bronze medal winners, although the largest financial rewards are given to gold medal winners by corporations seeking celebrity endorsements. In China the rewards for medals came from the national, provincial and city governments, and from a foundation that traditionally awards medal winners with US$80 000 and a kilo of gold. Many other nations had and continue to maintain similar reward systems for medal winners (Grohmann, 2008).

Attempts to gain recognition and prestige also underlie local government involvement in sports. Cities may fund sports clubs and teams and then use them to promote themselves as good places in which to live, work, locate a business or holiday. Many people feel that, if their city does not have one or more major professional sports teams, it cannot claim world-class status (Delaney and Eckstein, 2003; Silk, 2004; Silk and Andrews, 2008). However, when governments fund sports and sports facilities to boost the profile of a city or nation, they often become caught in a cycle where increased funding is regularly required to compete with other cities and nations doing the same thing with bigger budgets or newer facilities (Bourdieu, 1998; Hall, 2006). This continuously pushes up the funds and other resources that must be allocated to sports, and it decreases resources for schemes having more direct and concrete positive impact on citizens. Government officials often find that using this strategy to boost prestige for a city or nation is costly relative to the public benefits created, especially when most of the benefits go to a relatively small and predominantly wealthy segment of their constituency.

Promoting identity and unity

Groups, organizations, towns, cities and nations use sports to express collective sentiments about themselves (Allison, 2000, 2004; Bairner, 2001, 2005; Jutel, 2002; Maguire, 1999, 2005; Maguire et al., 1999; Poulton, 2004; Sam, 2003; Sato, 2005; Silk and Andrews, 2008). An athlete or team representing a larger collection of people has the potential to bring individuals together and to create emotional unity among them.

When a nation's football team plays in the World Cup, citizens share a sense of 'we-ness', regardless of their race, religion, language, education, occupation or income. This emotional sense of 'we-ness', or unity, is connected with their feelings of attachment to the nation's history and traditions, and even about its destiny in the world order. However, this emotional unity seldom lasts long, and it often serves the interests of people with power and influence because they use sports as occasions to highlight the images, traditions and memories around which national identities are expressed and then say that the status quo must be preserved lest we endanger the things that make us who 'we' are as a nation.

> Sport is an important tool for 'imagining' nationhood. It is a perfect forum for constructing identity.

(Annemarie Jutel, physical educator, 2002, p. 195)

When government involvement in sports is intended to promote identity and unity, it usually benefits some people more than others. For example, when men's sports are sponsored and women's sports are ignored, the sense of national identity and unity among men may be strong, but women may feel alienated (Adams, 2006). When sports involve participants from only one ethnic group or a particular social class, there are similar divisions in the 'imagined community' and 'invented traditions' constructed around sports.

National and local identity is political in that it can be constructed around many different ideas about who or what the city or nation is. Of course, these ideas can vary widely between particular categories of people. Furthermore, neither the identity nor the emotional unity created by sports changes the social, political and economic realities of life. When games end, people go their separate ways. Old social distinctions become relevant again, and the people who were disadvantaged prior to the game or tournament remain disadvantaged after it (Smith and Ingham, 2003). But this raises an interesting set of questions: do privileged people feel more justified in their privilege, and do people who are systematically disadvantaged in a city or nation feel less justified in making their disadvantage a political issue because everyone, even the rich and powerful, is part of the big 'we' that is reaffirmed at sport events? The identity and unity created by sports clearly feels good to many people, and it can inspire a sense of possibility and hope, but it may obscure the need for social transformations that would make social worlds more fair and just.

Local government involvement in sports is also motivated by concerns to promote and express particular forms of identity. Club football teams in Europe often receive support from local governments because the teams are major focal points for community attention and involvement. The teams reaffirm community identity among local citizens, and games often are social occasions at which people renew old acquaintances and maintain social networks. In this way, sports are *invented traditions* that people use to reaffirm social relationships.

The recent growth of global labour migration has intensified interest in the relationship between sports and national identity. As globalization has blurred national boundaries and made them less relevant for many people, government officials have used sports and national teams to rekindle the idea of nationhood at the same time that they have used sports and multinational teams to inspire identification with newly created political and economic entities (Houlihan, 1994; Maguire, 1999, 2005). For example, as European nations sponsor national sports to reinvigorate old feelings of national identity at a time when immigrant workers bring diverse identities to various nations, representatives of the 27-nation European Union use golf's Ryder Cup, pitting Team Europe against Team USA, to promote the formation of a European identity. Satellite and cable companies (Eurosport and Sky Sports) that serve most European nations have fostered both forms of identification with their sports programming, depending on which one will increase ratings.

These developments complicate national identity and make it more difficult to study and understand its connection with sports. Governments continue to use sports to promote identity and unity, but the long-term effectiveness of this strategy is difficult to assess. Many government officials *believe* that sports create more than temporary good feelings of national 'we-ness', but nearly all these officials are men, and the sports they support usually have long histories of privileging men. Multiple layers of politics are associated with sports.

Reproduce values consistent with dominant political ideology

Governments also become involved in sports to promote certain political values and ideas among their citizens. This is especially true when there is a need to maintain the idea that success is based on discipline, loyalty, determination and hard work, even in the face of hardship and bad times. Sports are useful platforms to promote these values and foster a particular ideology that contains taken for granted assumptions about the way social life is organized and how it does and should operate.

It is difficult to determine the extent to which people are influenced by sports that are presented in specific ideological terms, but we do know that in capitalist societies, such as the UK, sports provide people with a vocabulary and real-life examples that are consistent with dominant ideology. The images, narratives and the often repeated stories that accompany sports in market economies emphasize that competition is clearly the best and most natural way to achieve personal success and allocate rewards to people, whereas alternative approaches to success and allocating rewards – democratic socialism, socialism, communism and the like – are ineffective, unnatural and even immoral.

A classic example of a government's use of sport to promote its own political ideology occurred in Nazi Germany in 1936. Most countries hosting the Olympic Games use the occasion to present themselves favourably to their own citizens and the rest of the world. However, Adolf Hitler was especially interested in using the games to promote the Nazi ideology of 'Nordic supremacy' through the 'Berlin Games', which preceded the Second World War. The Nazi government devoted considerable resources to training German athletes, who won 89 medals in Berlin: over four times as many as any other country won during the Games. This is why the performance of Jesse Owens, an African-American, was so important to countries not aligned with Germany at that point in history. Owens's four gold medals and world records challenged Hitler's ideology of Nordic (white) supremacy, although it did not deter Nazi commitment to a destructive political and cultural ideology.

The Cold War era following the Second World War was also a time when nations, especially the USA, the former Soviet Union and East Germany, used the Olympics and other international sports competitions to make claims about the superiority of their political and economic ideologies. Today, such claims are less apt to be associated with international sports because the Cold War is over. Furthermore, some corporations are now more powerful than many nations, and use the Olympic Games and other major international events to make claims about the superiority of their products and services and the 'naturalness' of capitalist, free-market principles and lifestyles based on consumption.

Increase support for political leaders and government

Government authority rests ultimately in legitimacy. If people do not perceive political leaders and the government as legitimate, it is difficult to maintain social order. In the quest to maintain their legitimacy, political officials may use their connections with athletes, teams and particular sports to boost their acceptance in the minds of citizens. They assume, as Antonio Gramsci predicted they would, that if they support the sports that people value and enjoy, they can increase their legitimacy as leaders. This is why so many political leaders present themselves as friends of sport, even as faithful fans or active participants. They attend highly publicized sport events and associate themselves with high-profile athletes or teams that win major competitions. British prime ministers traditionally have associated themselves with successful athletes and teams, and have invited champions to Downing Street for photo opportunities.

Some male former athletes and coaches in the UK have used their celebrity status from sports to gain popular support for their political candidacy. For example, Lord Sebastian Coe, who led the bid for London to host the Olympic Games in 2012, is an ex-Olympic gold medallist and a former Conservative Member of Parliament. The former leader of the Liberal Democrat Party, Sir Menzies Campbell, is also an ex-athlete who captained the British team and held the national 100-metre record. These, and other former athletes and coaches, are able to use their status from sports and their sports personas to increase their legitimacy as 'tough', 'hard working' and 'loyal' candidates who are 'decisive under pressure' and 'dedicated to being winners'.

Promote economic development

Since the early 1980s, government involvement in sports often has occurred to facilitate a particular form of urban economic development (Delaney and Eckstein, 2003; Gold and Gold,

In 2008, the Olympic torch was taken to Downing Street as part of its world tour from Olympia to Beijing. Prime Minister Gordon Brown was photographed with Olympic and Paralympic athletes (*Source:* Peter Macdiarmid/Getty Images)

2007; Hall, 2006; Horne and Manzenreiter, 2006; Lenskyj, 2000, 2008; Schimmel, 2000, 2002, 2006; Silk and Andrews, 2008). National and city governments spend millions of pounds on their bids to host the Olympic Games, Commonwealth Games, World Cup tournaments, world or national championships, golf tournaments, and track and field meets. For example, the government of South Korea saw sports as a way to boost the image of the country overseas, and successfully bid to host the 1988 Summer Olympic Games in Seoul and co-host, with Japan, the 2002 men's Football World Cup. The social, cultural and political significance as well as the economic impact of these two mega events are well documented and have been widely investigated (e.g. Horne and Manzenreiter, 2002; Manzenreiter and Horne, 2004; Perryman 2002). The staging of these sport spectacles has also yielded direct and indirect, short- and long-term economic benefits, for example, through increased foreign investment and exports, and the creation of additional employment. The Football World Cup also contributed to an expansion of South Korea's tourist infrastructure, improved the image of Korean brands and products, and provided a showcase for the country's information technology products.

Although the experience of South Korea and some other nations indicates that it is possible for sports events to create economic development, the pattern is that events often provide only a temporary boost to the economy and too often leave local citizens with public debt and facilities that require annual subsidies to keep the doors open. Using sports for economic development is risky and controversial. Many cities have failed to meet any of the optimistic economic projections used to convince local voters and officials to dedicate public money for events, facilities and subsidies for sports team owners (Lenskyj, 2000, 2002; Schimmel, 2002). Recent evidence shows that the forms of economic development associated with sports often benefit relatively few people, usually those who are already wealthy and powerful (see Chapters 10 and 11).

For example, when Nagano, Japan, bid to host the 1998 Winter Olympics, Yoshiaki Tsutsumi, the richest man in the world at that time, heavily influenced the IOC selection committee. Tsutsumi owned many high-end ski areas, golf courses and resort hotels in the Nagano region of northern Japan, and would make hundreds of millions of pounds if the government would spend the equivalent of approximately £8 billion to build a new 120-mile bullet train line from Tokyo to Nagano. The story of how Tsutsumi influenced Japan's government and the IOC so that Nagano was named the Olympic host city and the train line was built is a long one, but the story ends with overuse threatening the natural environment of the Nagano region and Tsutsumi's wealth increased (Jennings, 1996a; Jennings and Sambrook, 2000). This is neither a new story nor an old one – similar things occurred in Utah, USA, in connection with the 2002 Winter Olympics (Jennings and Sambrook, 2000), and there is speculation about the activities surrounding the bid and developments for London 2012. Sports can be used for economic development, but the critical questions always are, who benefits and who pays?

Serve as a foreign policy tool

Political tensions and conflicts have long accompanied modern sports, whether in the form of communism and capitalism (Riordan and Arnaud, 1999), integration and separatism (Hargreaves, 2000; Sugden and Bairner, 1995) or nationalism and internationalism (Merkel, 2003). During the twentieth century, ideological tensions and conflicts overshadowed a large number of international events as several nations employed sports in their foreign policy and international relationships. Sports are attractive tools of foreign policy as they are cheap and low risk, but have a high profile due to the global media interest. Sports events not only provide a stage for political and ideological rivalries, tensions and conflicts, but can also facilitate co-operation. This was particularly clear during the Cold War era when communist countries used sports to promote relations with pro-communist countries and win support among developing countries. For example, while it is well documented that relations between the USA and the former Soviet Union were famously played out in the sporting arena, and particularly in the 'tit for tat' boycotts of the 1980 and 1984 Olympic Games, the Soviet Union also forged links with China and Cuba through sports, and Cuba in turn has developed relations with Namibia.

The ways in which sports may increase understanding, bridge profound differences, break down stereotypes and confine conflicts to the playing field rather than the battlefield is perhaps illustrated most powerfully in the First World War Christmas truce of 1914. Although it has often been dismissed as though it was merely a myth, there is now plenty of historical evidence that a truce between the opposing soldiers did take place, and that during this time the British and German soldiers played a football match (Brown and Seaton, 1994; Jürgs, 2003; Weintraub, 2002).

The end of the Cold War in the early 1990s did not lead to a general depoliticization of sports. However, there is growing evidence that sports are also able to play a new and more positive role in international relations, as reflected in the Wrestling Diplomacy between Iran and the USA (2002), the Cricket Diplomacy between Pakistan and India (2004) and the increased use of sports to keep the reunification theme in the public discourse in divided Korea (since 2000).

Critical issues and government involvement in sports

Government involvement in sports is justified because it serves the 'public good'. It would be ideal if governments promoted equally the interests of all citizens, but differences between individuals and groups make this impossible. Therefore, public investments in sports often benefit some people more than others. Those who benefit most are those capable of influencing policy makers. This does not mean that government policies reflect only the interests of wealthy and powerful people, but it does mean that policies are often contentious and create power struggles among various segments of the population in a city or society.

Government involvement in sports occurs in many ways, from funding local parks for recreation and sports participation to supporting elite athletes for national teams. When there are debates over policies and priorities, those who represent elite sports often are organized, generally have strong backing from other organized groups and can base their requests for support on visible accomplishments achieved in the name of the entire country, community or club. Those who represent masses of recreational and general-ability sports participants are less likely to be politically organized and supported by powerful organizations, and they are less able to give precise statements of their goals and the political significance of their programmes. This does not mean that government decision makers ignore mass participation, but it does mean that 'sport for all' usually has lower priority for funding and support (Green, 2004; Green and Houlihan, 2004; Sam, 2003).

Those who believe the myth that there is no connection between sports and government are most likely to be ignored when government involvement does occur. Those who realize that sports have political implications and that governments are not politically neutral arbitrators of differences are most likely to benefit when government involvement occurs. Sports are connected with power relations in society as a whole; therefore, sports and politics cannot be separated.

The governance of sports in the UK

Sports play a significant role in the history, culture, economy and politics of the UK (Craig and Beedie, 2008; Houlihan, 2008). The UK government has invested considerable resources into developing a wide range of policies for sports. However, many of these policies are politically contentious since they privilege some groups and individuals more than others. It is important to consider how and why the British government has developed particular policies at particular times, how they are communicated to the public and in turn how they are accommodated, negotiated and/or resisted. In this section we outline the key agencies involved in establishing policies for sports, recreation and physical activity in the UK.

The organization of sport in the UK comes under the broad umbrella of the government's *Department for Media, Culture and Sport (DCMS)* (see Figure 13.1). The DCMS claims to be: 'committed to providing access to sport and work to encourage the take-up of sport across communities and by children and young people in particular' (www.culture.gov.uk/about_us/ sport/). The main policy document for sport under the New Labour government is *Game Plan: A Strategy for Delivering Government's Sport and Physical Activity Objectives* (DCMS/Strategy Unit 2002), which has a focus on both social inclusion and elite sporting success. In 2007, the government requested that Sport England review the fitness for purpose of its systems, and in 2008 it produced the *Sport England Strategy 2008–2011* (Sport England, 2008b) to meet a government remit to produce a 'world leading community sport system' in time for the 2012 Olympic Games to be hosted in London. In addition to this broad agenda, the government has also committed to underwriting the costs of these Olympic Games. The production of the Games will not be the direct responsibility of the government, but will be through the London Organizing Committee for the Olympic Games (LOCOG), but this is still politically contentious since some groups will gain from the Olympics while others will lose out. In addition to these groups, the main provision of sports facilities is largely operated through local, rather than national, government policies and organization.

The main sports bodies in the UK are the sports quangos (quasi autonomous non-governmental organizations), which work in partnership with the government. *UK Sport* is responsible for managing and distributing public and lottery funds, with a stated mission to 'work in partnership with the home country sports councils and other agencies to lead sport in the UK to world-class success' (www.uksport.gov.uk). The regional sports councils for the home nations set priorities for the development of sport in their own country. These are: *Sport England, Sports Council for Northern Ireland, sportscotland* and *Sports Council for Wales.* Each of these has quite distinct national strategies. Sport England's main priority is the production of sporting excellence as it prepares for London 2012, and the nurturing of talent is largely the responsibility of the English Institute of Sport (EIS); sportscotland and the Sports Council for Wales have more of a focus on policies to encourage a physically active nation. The Sports Council for Northern Ireland has at its heart community integration, with sport taking a role in developing understanding and inclusivity in the years following 'The Troubles'. School sports are influenced by each of these bodies, and by the government Department for Children, Schools and Families.

There is also one powerful, independent body, the *Central Council of Physical Recreation (CCPR)*. This acts on behalf of national governing and other bodies for sport to lobby for the interests of sport and physical activity at all levels.

Each of these national bodies is also influenced by international agencies, such as the International Olympic Committee, the International Paralympic Committee, various international federations, and the relationship between sport and global politics and ideologies.

Sports and Global Political Processes

Most people have lofty expectations about the impact of sports on global relations. It has long been hoped that sports would serve diplomatic functions by contributing to cultural understanding and world peace. Unfortunately, the realities of sports have not matched the ideals. Nations and transnational corporations regularly use sports to promote ideologies favouring their special interests, and global political realities have changed so that now a few dozen corporations have assets and budgets surpassing those of most nations worldwide. Furthermore, sports themselves have become much more global, with teams recruiting athletes outside their national borders and sports equipment being manufactured in developing nations where labour is often exploited. Issues related to these global processes often are linked with politics, so it is useful to understand them when studying sports in society.

International sports: ideals versus realities

Achieving peace and friendship among nations was emphasized by Baron Pierre de Coubertin, the main instigator of the modern Olympic Games in 1896, although somewhat ironically de Coubertin was also seeking an efficient way of improving the physical fitness of French youths to prepare them for the next war against their main enemy, Germany. Through the twentieth century, many people have hoped that sports would do the following things:

- create open communication lines between people and leaders from different nations
- highlight shared interests among people from different cultures and nations
- demonstrate that friendly international relationships are possible
- foster cultural understanding and eliminate the use of national stereotypes
- create a model for cultural, economic and political relationships across national boundaries
- establish working relationships that develop leaders in emerging nations, and close the resource gap between wealthy nations and poorer nations.

During the past century, it has become clear that sports can be useful in the realm of **public diplomacy** because it creates *public expressions of togetherness in the form of cultural exchanges and general communication among officials from various nations*. However, sports have very little impact in the realm of **serious diplomacy**, which involves *discussions and decisions about political issues of vital national interest*. In other words, international sports provide political

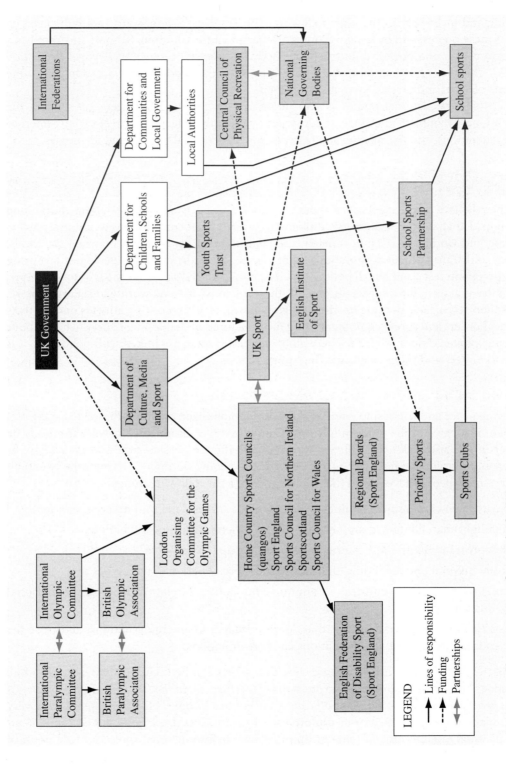

Figure 13.1 The governance of sports in the UK

leaders from different nations with opportunities to meet and talk, but sports do not influence their discussions or decisions. Sports bring together athletes, who may learn from and about one another, but athletes make no political decisions and their relationships with one another have no serious political significance. For example, sports have been used in Northern Ireland as both an expression of cultural identity and a way of developing cross-community under-standing in a sectarian society. While there are projects aimed at reducing the impact of sectarianism, sports are not seen as solutions to the political problems that Northern Ireland has faced throughout its history (see Bairner, 2004). Northern Ireland is certainly not unique as a divided country, or one in which sports have played a role in sectarianism. The British-based Football For Peace (F4P) project was developed with the aim of bringing together Jewish and Arab children living in Northern Israel in a sporting environment. The aims of the project include providing an opportunity for social contact across community boundaries. However, the project recognizes that this cannot impact on political relations between the different groups in Israel, and the project requests that political and ideological views are left outside the sporting arena (Sugden and Wallis, 2007; www.footballforpeace.org.uk).

Recent history shows that most nations use sports and sports events, especially the Olympic Games, to pursue self-interests rather than international understanding, friendship and peace. Nationalist themes going beyond respectful expressions of patriotism have been clearly evident at many events, and most nations have used sports events regularly to promote their own military, economic, political and cultural goals. This was particularly apparent during the Cold War era following the Second World War and extending into the early 1990s. During these years, the Olympics were extensions of 'superpower politics' between the USA and its allies and the former Soviet Union and its allies.

The connection between international sports and politics was so blatant in the early 1980s that Peter Ueberroth, president of the Los Angeles Olympic Organizing Committee, said that 'we now have to face the reality that the Olympics constitute not only an athletic event but a political event' (Ueberroth, 1983). Ueberroth was not being prophetic; he was simply summa-rizing his observations of events leading up to the 1984 Olympics in Los Angeles. He saw that nations were more interested in self-interest than global friendship and peace. The demon-stration of national superiority through sports was a major focus of world powers.

Wealthy and powerful nations are not the only ones to use international sports to promote political self-interest. Many nations lacking international political and economic power have used sports in a quest for international recognition and legitimacy. For them, the Olympics and other international sports have been stages for showing that their athletes and teams can stand up to and sometimes defeat athletes and teams from wealthy and powerful nations. For example, when the cricket teams from the West Indies or India play teams from England, the athletes and people from the West Indies and India see the matches as opportunities to show the world that they are now equals to the nation that once colonized their land and controlled their people. When their teams win, it is cause for political affirmation and great celebration.

National leaders know that hosting mega sports events such as the Olympics is a special opportunity to generate international recognition, display national power and resources to a global audience, and invite investments into their economies. This is why bid committees from prospective host cities and nations have regularly used gifts, bribes and financial incentives to encourage IOC members to vote for them in the bid selection process. Illegal and illicit

The Irish Football Association (IFA) uses football as a site for eradicating the Protestant-versus-Catholic sectarianism that has caused decades of violence and terrorism in Northern Ireland (*Source*: Michael Boyd, Irish Football Association, Northern Ireland)

strategies reached their peak during the bidding for the 2002 Winter Olympics when officials from Salt Lake City offered to IOC members and their families money, jobs, scholarships, lavish gifts, vacations and the sexual services of 'escorts' as they successfully secured the votes needed to host the games (Jennings, 1996a, 1996b; Jennings and Sambrook, 2000).

The political goals of the nations hosting major international events are especially clear when nations boycott the Olympics and other international sport events. For example, the 1980 Moscow Games were boycotted by the USA and 62 of its political allies to protest the Soviet Union's decision to send armed forces to Afghanistan in order to support the relatively weak Communist regime against the regional warlords and other Islamic rebels who were subverting Soviet control of the region. The boycotting nations supported the autonomy of Afghanistan and armed the rebels, and the boycott of the Olympic Games in Moscow was intended to show support for the rebels and demonstrate that these nations were clearly opposed to unilateral invasions. While the British team has never boycotted an Olympic Games, the Conservative government of the time under Margaret Thatcher's leadership did not support the attendance of the athletes who took part in 1980. The British team entered the opening ceremony and received their medals under the Olympic flag and anthem, instead of the Union flag and national anthem, to reflect their independent decision to attend the Games, and their objection to the Soviet invasion of Afghanistan. In retaliation, the Soviet Union and at least 14 of its allies boycotted the 1984 Olympic Games in Los Angeles to protest the commercialization of the games and avoid terrorist actions they expected from jingoistic Americans. Each of these Olympic Games was held despite the boycotts, and each host nation unashamedly displayed its power and resources to the world and touted the fact that they topped the medal count for the respective games. Neither the boycotts nor hosting the games had any major effects on American or Soviet political policies, although they did intensify Cold War feelings and fears.

Increased global media coverage has intensified and added new dimensions to the connection between sports and politics (Jackson and Haigh, 2008). For example, television companies have traditionally attracted viewers to their Olympic coverage by stressing political controversies along with national interests and symbols. These themes are now accompanied and sometimes obscured by images and narratives promoting capitalist expansion and the products and services of transnational corporations. These issues are discussed in the box 'Olympism and the Olympic Games' (p. 488).

Nation states, sports and ideological hegemony

Global politics often revolve around issues of ideological hegemony, that is, whose ideas and beliefs are most widely accepted worldwide and used to guide everything from world trade to who starts wars with whom. In this process, sports usually serve the interests of wealthy and powerful nations. For example, when nations with few resources want to participate in major international sports, they must look to wealthy nations for assistance in the form of coaching, equipment and training support. As this occurs, people in poorer nations often de-emphasize their traditional folk games and focus on the global sports developed around the values and experiences of nations powerful enough to export their games around the world and make them the centrepieces of international competitions. To the extent that this makes them dependent, sports become vehicles for economically powerful nations to extend their control over important forms of popular culture worldwide – and to claim that it is part of the 'foreign aid' that they give to assist poor people and struggling nations (Miller et al., 2001, 2003).

When people in traditional cultures want to preserve their native games, they resist the ideological influence associated with this form of 'cultural imperialism', but resistance is difficult when popular international sports have rules and customs grounded in the ideologies of powerful nations (Ben-Porat and Ben-Porat, 2004; Mills and Dimeo, 2003). For example, when a British sport such as football is introduced to another country, it comes with an emphasis on ideas about individual achievement, competition, winning, hierarchical authority structures, physical power and domination, the body and the use of technology to shape bodies into efficient machines. These ideas may not be completely accepted by those learning to play or watch football. Although it is difficult to believe nowadays, when football first arrived in Germany in the late nineteenth century as a by-product of British engineering, mining and textile know-how, this new sport was first met with indifference and later with open hostility. The reason was that the Germans had already established their own, very distinctive form of physical culture, *Turnen* (gymnastics), a vital part of their national identity, which they felt was threatened by this new team sport (Merkel, 2003). However, it is often the case that the introduction of new sports will eventually encourage orientations that privilege the values which are usually those of developed 'Western' nations such as the UK, and give low priority to the co-operative values more common in traditional cultures.

reflect on SPORTS *Olympism and the Olympic Games: are they special?*

According to the Olympic Charter, the Olympic Games are based on a special philosophy described in these words:

> Olympism is a philosophy of life, exalting and combining in a balanced whole the qualities of body, will and mind. Blending sport with culture and education, Olympism seeks to create a way of life based on the joy found in effort, the educational value of good example and respect for universal fundamental ethical principles.

The fundamental principles of the Olympic Charter are simple and straightforward. They emphasize that the Olympics should provide opportunities for people worldwide to learn about and connect with one another. This is important because our future and the future of the Earth itself depends on global co-operation.

The spirit of Olympism emphasizes learning to understand and appreciate human diversity and working to sustain healthy and safe lifestyles worldwide. If the Olympic Games inspire this spirit, they are indeed special. But nationalism and commercialism exert so much influence on today's Olympic Games that the goals of global understanding and health promotion receive only token attention (Carrington, 2004b; Lenskyj, 2008).

One of the factors undermining Olympism is the current method of selling media broadcasting rights for the Olympic Games (Andrews, 2007; Real, 1996). Television companies buy the rights to take the video images they want from the Olympics and combine them with their own narratives to attract audiences in their countries. So instead of bringing the world together around a single unifying experience, the coverage consists of many heavily nationalized and commercialized versions of the Olympic Games. Of course, media consumers give their own meanings to this coverage, but they all have the same images and narratives as starting points for making sense of and talking about the Olympics.

Media consumers who want to use the Olympics to visualize a global community constructed around cultural differences and mutual understanding can do so, but current television coverage provides little assistance in this quest. Most coverage highlights the association between human achievement, selected cultural values and corporate sponsors. In the process, many people come to believe that corporations really do make the Olympics possible. As they watch the events, a significant proportion of television time presents messages from those corporations, the companies that, in the words of the announcers, 'bring you the Olympics'.

People do not accept media images and narratives in literal terms, but corporate sponsors bet hundreds of millions of pounds every two years that connecting their logos with the Olympic rings discourages criticism of their products, encourages people to consume those products regularly, and fosters audience acceptance of consumption as a lifestyle.

The overt commercialism in the Olympics has led some people to question the meaning of the Olympics. As one multiple medal-winning Olympian says: 'The Olympics is not about sports any more.

It's about who can win the most money. It's like going to Disneyland' (in Reid, 1996, p. 4BB). A high-ranking Olympic official makes similar observations:

> I'm on the verge of joining those who think it's time for the Olympics, in their present context, to die. And they need to die for the same reason the ancient Olympic Games died – greed and corruption.
>
> *(In Reid, 1996, p. 4BB)*

In 1992, the USA sent a team of all-professional players to compete in the men's basketball in the Barcelona Olympics. The team became known as the 'Dream Team' and they easily won all of their games and the Olympic gold medal. Charles Barkley, who was an outspoken member of the 'Dream Team', noted in 1992 that the purpose of the games had little to do with Olympic ideals. He said,

> I know why we're here. We're here to spread basketball internationally and make more money for somebody … We're going to win the gold medal, but there won't be any life changing decisions made because of it … [P]oor people will still be poor and racism and sexism will still exist.
>
> *(In DuPree, 1992, p. 7E)*

Kevin Walmsley, director of the International Centre for Olympic Studies, supports these observations by saying that the Olympic Ideal 'is an empty vessel filled up by the ideas of the day' (in Price, 2004, p. 56).

These statements support the need to change the Olympic Games. The IOC issues regular press releases full of rhetoric about friendship and peace, but it has made no concerted effort to develop programmes and processes making it clear to athletes and spectators that the games are about cultural understanding and working together in socially responsible ways. Bruce Kidd, a former Olympian who is now a physical and health educator at the University of Toronto in Canada, has made this point. Kidd (1996a) argues that if the Olympic Games are to be special, they must be used to highlight global injustice and promote social responsibility worldwide.

Kidd suggests that athletes should be selected to participate in the Olympics on the basis of their actions as global citizens as well as their athletic accomplishments. There also should be a curriculum enabling athletes to learn about fellow competitors and their cultures. The games should involve formal, televised opportunities for intercultural exchanges, and athletes should be ready to discuss their ideas about world peace and social responsibility during media interviews. The IOC should sponsor projects enabling citizen-athletes to build on their Olympic experiences through service to others around the world. A proportion of windfall profits coming from rapidly escalating television rights fees could fund such projects, thereby giving IOC members opportunities to talk about real examples of social responsibility connected with the Olympics. The personal stories that television companies present during coverage of the games could then highlight the ways that athletes are socially responsible, rather than focusing on soap opera-like personal tragedies and triumphs. Television viewers may find such coverage more entertaining and hopeful than tabloid-like stories focusing on training and trauma.

Additionally, the IOC could control nationalism and commercialism more carefully as it organizes the games and sells broadcasting rights. There is no single best way to do this, but we offer the following suggestions for consideration.

1   *Eliminate national uniforms for athletes.* Let athletes choose from uniforms created by selected designers to express cultural themes from various regions of the world. This change would reduce nationalism, highlight creativity and cultural learning, and incorporate art into the Olympics – effects that the Ancient Greeks would endorse. The specially designed uniforms could be trademarked and sold by an 'Olympic Artists Foundation', with incoming revenue used to support artists in developing regions of the world and to empower the workers who make sport equipment and apparel for less than a living wage under oppressive conditions.

2   *Revise the opening ceremonies so that athletes enter the arena by event instead of by nation.* This would emphasize global unity rather than the nation states into which the athletes were born by chance. Artists from around the world would be commissioned to design flags for various sports. National flags would be displayed collectively in the middle of the field to emphasize difference amid unity.

3   *Eliminate national anthems and flags during the award ceremonies.* Present medals in the stadium at the end of each day of competition in such a way that awards' ceremonies emphasize athletes first as representatives of all humanity and second as representatives of their nations. Most people are nationalistic enough without encouragement during an event that is declared to highlight global unity, not the superiority of some nations over others.

4   *Promote a fair method of calculating medal counts.* National medal counts are contrary to the spirit and official principles of the Olympic movement. They foster chauvinism, present the achievements of athletes in divisive rather than unifying ways, and privilege large, wealthy nations with the resources to create excellence in sports. To defuse the meaning that people give to traditional medal counts, members of the Olympic Academy (scholars who study Olympism) should publish an 'official medal count' in which the size and/or wealth of nations is statistically controlled. Table 13.1 provides an example of how rankings would change if only national population size were controlled. Column A ranks nations in traditional terms – by the total number of medals won in all the Olympic Games from 1896 through 2004. But Column B ranks nations in terms of the medals won per capita (for every 10 million people, in this case). Therefore, if a nation with 10 million people has an athlete who wins one medal, it would have the same significance as a nation with 100 million people having athletes who win 10 medals.

Table 13.1 **Olympic medal count by total medals and medals per capita, 2007**

Total medals rank		Medals per 10 million people*	
Nation	**Medals**	**Nation**	**Medals**
1. USA	2309	1. Liechtenstein	2669
2. France	670	2. Norway	864
3. UK	**664**	3. Finland	839
4. Sweden	577	4. Sweden	641
5. Italy	568	5. Hungary	448
6. Germany	560	6. Switzerland	382

7. Hungary	449	7. Austria	303
8. Finland	438	8. Denmark	298
9. Norway	398	9. Bulgaria	269
10. Australia	354	10. St Kitts & Nevis	257
11. Canada	326	11. Estonia	217
12. Japan	296	12. Bahamas	199
13. Switzerland	286	13. New Zealand	185
14. Netherlands	282	14. Australia	176
15. Romania	266	15. Netherlands	172
16. Austria	248	16. Bermuda	153
17. Poland	247	17. Belgium	140
18. China	245	18. Jamaica	135
19. Russia	214	19. Cuba	120
20. Bulgaria	200	20. Romania	119
21. Korea, South	174	21. Greece	118
22. Denmark	162	22. France	111
23. Belgium	145	**23. UK**	**109**
24. Cuba	137	24. Luxembourg	106
25. Greece	126	25. Trinidad & Tobago	102

Note:

*In the per capita list, the United States ranks at number 31 (79 medals per 10 million people), behind Iceland (26), Canada (27), Italy (28), Virgin Islands (29) and Tonga (30). If per capita income was also taken into account, the list would shift and the USA would drop much lower than 31 (see www.symworld.com/medals/index.php?sort=totalnormal and www.billmitchell.org/sport/medal_tally_2008).

Source: adapted from four data sets provided by NationMaster: www.nationmaster.com/graph/spo_sum_oly_med_all_tim-summer-olympic-medals-all-time (retrieved 10 June 2008). The data cover all medals won from 1896 to 2004. This is problematic because many countries today did not exist prior to the end of the First World War and the Second World War when the victors split or combined existing nations to meet their interests and concerns.

5   *Eliminate or revise team sports.* Organizing team sports by nation encourages players and spectators to perceive games in we-versus-they terms. Therefore, eliminate all team sports or develop methods of choosing teams so that athletes from different countries play on the same teams and athletes from a particular nation play on different teams. Then 'dream teams' would emphasize

international unity rather than specific national and commercial interests. And athletes might make more friends worldwide and learn about other cultures.

6   *Add to each games 'demonstration sports' native to the cultural regions where the games are held.* The IOC should specify that all media companies purchasing broadcasting rights and receiving press credentials must devote 5 per cent of their coverage to these native games. Because the media influence the ways that people imagine, create and play sports around the world, this would provide expanded images of physical activities, and facilitate creative approaches to sport participation worldwide. At present, many Olympic sports are simply a legacy of former colonial powers that had the power to export their games around the world (Bale and Christensen, 2004).

7   *Use multiple sites for each Olympic Games.* The cost of hosting the summer Olympic Games was approximately £8 billion in Athens in 2004 and well over £20 billion for Beijing in 2008. The predicted costs of London 2012 trebled within the first year after being awarded the Games, and are likely to exceed £10 billion. Such costs privilege wealthy nations and prevent less wealthy nations from hosting the games and highlighting their cultures. If Olympic events were split into three successive 'event packages', it would be possible for some developing nations to host one of the event packages and enjoy the benefits of staging the events at the same time that media spectators would see a wider range of cultural settings as they viewed events over the 18 days of coverage. When one nation hosts the entire games, it is required to build massive, highly specialized facilities that may never be regularly used or filled to capacity in the future. This is economically and ecologically irresponsible and often leaves citizens in cities or smaller nations with a legacy of massive debts and underused facilities.

8   *Emphasize global responsibility in media coverage.* Television contracts should mandate an emphasis on global social responsibility. Athlete committees – working with committees from the Olympic Academy, which includes scholars committed to the spirit of Olympism – could include individuals, organizations and corporations that have engaged in noteworthy forms of social responsibility and assist media companies in producing coverage of these cases. Additionally, a mandated amount of media time should be dedicated to public service announcements from non-profit human rights groups that work with athletes and sports organizations to promote social justice and sustainable forms of development. This would guarantee that media consumers would have access to messages that are not created or censored by corporations and market forces.

9   *Integrate the Olympics and Paralympics.* Just as the Olympic Movement supports gender equality and opposes racial apartheid in sports, it should include people with disabilities in the Olympic Movement (Wolff, 2005). This could be done by having common opening and closing ceremonies, awarding the same Olympic medals to athletes in both events, and referring to both as 'Olympics'. This would send a powerful message to the world saying that the full inclusion of people with disabilities is an achievable goal in all spheres of life.

10 *Reinvigorate the Olympic Village.* Athletes traditionally all lived in a purpose-built Olympic Village during the Games, where they interacted with people from all over the world. Increasingly, athletes from wealthier nations are choosing to stay in exclusive hotels and only travel to the Olympic site for their competitions, limiting the opportunities to appreciate the lifestyles and values of people from different cultures.

People will say that these suggestions are idealistic or that the IOC, the global media and corporate sponsors constitute a power base that cannot be challenged successfully. However, the Olympic movement was founded on idealism and intended to inspire visions of what our world could and should be; additionally, it emphasizes that progress comes only through effort and participation. If the Olympic

Games of today are little more than global marketing opportunities for transnational corporations and a stage for global power displays by wealthy nations with medal-winning athletes, now is a good time to take action. A good starting point would be to replace 'Citius, Altius, Fortius' ('Faster, Higher, Stronger') with 'Excellence, Unity and Peace' as the new Olympic motto. *What do you think?*

Ideally, sports facilitate cultural exchanges through which people from different nations share information and develop mutual cultural understanding. But true 50–50 sharing and mutual understanding are rare when nations have unequal power and resources. Therefore, sports often become cultural exports from wealthy nations incorporated into the everyday lives of people in other nations. These imported sports may be rejected, but they are usually revised and reinterpreted to fit with local values and lifestyles (Ben-Porat and Ben-Porat, 2004; Denham, 2004; Maguire, 2005). However, even when revisions occur, people in traditional cultures become increasingly open to the possibility of importing and consuming additional goods, services and ideas from the wealthy nations (Jackson and Andrews, 2005). Unless political power and economic resources are developed in connection with this process, poorer

In 2008, the Olympic Torch relay was greeted by large numbers of protesters in several of the countries visited. When the relay reached London, people lined the streets to protest against China's records on human rights and, in particular, the presence of China in Tibet (*Source:* Elizabeth Pike)

nations become increasingly dependent on wealthy nations, and it becomes difficult not to adopt many of their values and ideologies. This is a complex process, involving many issues in addition to those related to sports.

New political realities in an era of transnational corporations

Global politics have changed dramatically since the 1970s. Massive corporations are now among the largest economies in the world today, and they share the global political stage with nation states. This change occurred as nation states embraced a policy of deregulation, lifted trade restrictions, lowered tariffs, and made it easier for capital, labour and goods to flow freely around the globe. Although nation states remain central in global relations, the differences between national and corporate interests and identities have nearly disappeared in connection with sports. This was implied by Phil Knight, CEO of US-based Nike, when he discussed a shift in his fan loyalties during the men's football World Cup:

> We see a natural evolution … dividing the world into their athletes and ours. And we glory ours. When the US played Brazil in the World Cup, I rooted for Brazil because it was a Nike team. America was Adidas.
>
> *(In Lipsyte, 1996a, p. 9)*

For Knight, teams and athletes now represent corporations as much or more than nations; and corporate logos have become more visible than national flags at international events. When Nike paid US$200 million to sponsor Brazil's national team (in 2003) and used its players to market Nike products worldwide, Knight was pushing consumption and brand loyalty over patriotism and public service as the most important global values. For him, sports were outposts in the heads of sport fans worldwide and could be used as receptors and transmitters for the messages coming from Nike and other corporate sponsors seeking further global capitalist expansion. Like executives from other transnational corporations (TNCs), he believes that sports contribute to the growth of global well-being when they are used to promote a lifestyle of consumption and the ideologies that support it.

Corporate sponsors now exert significant influence over sport events, at least to the point of directing sports images and narratives towards spectator-consumers rather than spectator-citizens. Sports that cannot be covered in this way – such as those that are not organized to attract spectators with high purchasing power, or those that do not emphasize competitive outcomes and setting performance/production records – are not sponsored. When spectators and potential media audiences are not valued consumers, and when sports do not represent an ideology of competition and success, corporations do not become sponsors and commercial media have no reason to cover them.

The global power of transnational corporations is neither unlimited nor uncontested. There are documented cases where local populations have used their own cultural perspectives to make sense of the images and narratives that come with global sports and global advertising, and give them meanings that fit with their lives (Foer, 2004; Maguire, 1999, 2005). However, those who use critical theory note that global media sports and the commercial messages that accompany them often cleverly fuse the global and the local through thoughtfully and carefully edited images that combine local traditions, sports action and consumer products in seamless and technically brilliant media representations (Andrews and Silk, 1999; Carrington and Sugden, 1999; Jackson and Andrews, 2005; Jackson and Hokowhitu, 2002; Jackson and Scherer, 2002; Miller et al., 2001, 2003; Silk, 1999; Tomlinson, 2005). These scholars argue that such fused images tend to 'detraditionalize' local cultures by representing local symbols and lifestyles in connection with consumer products.

The process of destabilizing local cultures and creating a culture of consumption is based on the corporate application of research findings in anthropology, sociology and psychology (Goodman, 2001; Klein, 2002) – and it occurs in a broader context than traditional cultures in developing regions of the world. For example, a company that produces shoes and apparel suited for physical activity may hire qualitative researchers to observe young people and identify new, popular activities that they have invented and incorporated into their lives. When an activity is identified, it is described in fine detail, and the 'homemade' apparel of participants is carefully studied. Then the company 'produces' a version of the shoes and apparel that represents the culture created around the activity, and gives 'samples' to the most popular participants and asks them to try them out. People from the company hope that after they have taken the creations of the young people and used them to produce consumer items, they can sell the items to the young people at a high price. Additionally, they patent, trademark and copyright the items so that what was originally created by the participants in the locally created activity is now owned and controlled by the company and used to make profits.

On a slightly less subversive level, Coca-Cola claims that it sponsors the Olympics because it wants the whole world 'to sing', to 'live Olympic', to experience 'unity on the Coke side of life', to be 'red around the world', to 'go red for China' or to be 'friends for ever', but when Coke executives envision 'one world one dream', they see 6.7 billion people drinking Coke after Coke for life. McDonald's uses a similar approach as the Official Restaurant of the Olympic Games from 1996 to 2012.

Corporations that sponsor global sports and use them as advertising platforms know that sooner or later the images and narratives associated with sources of pleasure and entertainment in people's lives will in some form enter the imaginations and conversations of those who see and hear them. Commercial images and messages do not dictate what people think, but they certainly influence what people think about, and in this way they become a part of the overall discourse that occurs in cultures around the globe.

This description of new global political realities does not mean that sports have fallen victim to a worldwide conspiracy hatched by transnational corporations. It means only that transnational corporations have joined nation states in the global political context in which sports are defined, organized, promoted, played, presented and given meaning around the world (Jackson and Scherer, 2002; Silk, 1999).

Other global political issues

As sports become increasingly commercialized and national boundaries become less relevant, more athletes become global migrant workers. As they increasingly go where they can develop their skills and earn rewards for them, the global migration of athletes has raised new political issues for sports. Similarly, as the demand for sports equipment and clothing has increased in wealthy nations, transnational corporations have opted to cut costs for those products by

Coca-Cola sponsored the Beijing Olympic Games, which had the motto 'One World One Dream', in the hope of ensuring that people like these at a booth in Guangzhou, China, will continue to drink Coca-Cola throughout their lives (*Source*: Elizabeth Pike)

manufacturing them in poor countries where wages are extremely low and workers plentiful. One result of these two developments is a clear split between the world's haves and have-nots when it comes to sports. Those born into privilege in wealthy nations manage and host sports and consume sports products, and those born into disadvantaged circumstances struggle to make a living on the field or in the factory. This gap between rich and poor is not new, but it reminds us that sports are integrally linked with global political processes in many ways.

Athletes as global migrant workers

Human history is full of examples of labour migration, both forced and voluntary. Industrial societies, in particular, have depended on mobile labour forces responsive to the needs of production. Now that economies are more global, the pervasiveness and diversity of labour migration patterns have increased. This is true in sports and many other occupational categories (Maguire, 2004, 2005; Maguire et al., 2002; Stead and Maguire, 2000).

Athletes frequently move from their home towns when they are recruited to play elite sports, and then they may move many times after that as they are traded from team to team or seek continuing opportunities to play their sports. This migration occurs from region to region within nations, as well as from nation to nation within and between continents (Bale and Maguire, 1994; Maguire, 2004; Maguire and Stead, 2005). Each of these moves raises issues related to (1) personal adjustments by migrating athletes, (2) the rights of athletes as workers, (3) the impact of talent migration on the nations from and to which athletes migrate, and (4) the impact of athlete migration on the identities of athletes and fans.

Some migration patterns are seasonal, involving temporary moves as athletes travel from one climate area to another to play their sports. Patterns may follow annual tour schedules as athletes travel from tournament to tournament around a region or the world, or they may involve long-term or permanent moves from one region or nation to another. For example, cricketers and snow-skiers may travel alternately to the northern and southern hemispheres to play or ski year-round.

The range of personal experiences among migrating athletes is great. They vary from major forms of culture shock and chronic loneliness to minor homesickness and lifestyle adjustments. Some athletes are exploited by teams or clubs, whereas others make great amounts of money and receive a hero's welcome when they return home in the off-season. Some encounter prejudice against foreigners or various forms of racial and ethnic bigotry, whereas others are socially accepted and make good friends. Some cling to their national identities and socialize with fellow athletes from their homelands, whereas others develop more global identities unrelated to one national or cultural background. In some cases, teams and clubs expect foreign athletes to adjust on their own, whereas others provide support for those who need to learn a new language or become familiar with new cultural settings (Klein, 1991; Maguire, 2004, 2005).

Athletic talent migration also has an impact on the nations involved. For example, football has the highest rate of talent migration of all sports, particularly within Europe. The impact of this migration on national talent pools, and the ability of local clubs and teams to maintain economically viable sports programmes is complex. Talent migration usually benefits the nation to which athletes move more than it benefits the nation from which athletes come, but this is not always the case. In the UK, and especially England, there are many who argue that the large number of non-British players in the elite leagues limits the opportunities for British players to develop and play at the highest level which, in turn, undermines the performance of the national teams. In contrast, players who migrate to the British leagues (and especially the Premier League) are exposed to the highest level of competition, which may benefit their national teams when they represent their country of origin in international tournaments.

The global migration of athletes also may influence how people think about and identify themselves in connection with nation states, but this topic has not been studied. Many people appreciate athletic talent regardless of the athlete's nationality (Cyphers, 2003), but they may also have special affection for athletes born and raised in their own nation. Does this make people more open-minded and knowledgeable about other cultures, or does it make them more defensive and ethnocentric? This question becomes important because many teams and leagues recruit players from a wide range of national and cultural backgrounds. For example, in the 2006–07 season more than half the starting line-ups and goal scorers in the Premier League were players from outside the UK.

Like other forms of labour migration, the global recruitment and migration of athletes blurs national borders. But, in sports, it also blurs the meaning of success in both national and international events (Bale and Maguire, 1994; Maguire, 2004; Maguire and Stead, 2005). These trends worry some people. This is why some leagues have quotas that limit the number of foreign-born or foreign-nationality players that teams may sign to contracts, and the FA is considering reintroducing a quota system to enable domestic talent to play high-level football. This is not unique to football or the UK. For example, in basketball in 1996 England lifted all quotas for both men's and women's professional basketball teams. However, in the same time period, Japan banned US female basketball players from its professional league, and professional leagues in Italy, Spain and France allowed their teams to have up to two foreign players.

As commercial sports organizations expand their franchise locations across national borders and recruit athletes worldwide, the global migration of athletes will continue to increase. Researchers in the sociology of sport have studied some of the implications of this migration, but much remains to be learned (Elliott and Maguire, 2008; Takahashi and Horne, 2006; Taylor, 2007).

Global politics and the production of sports equipment and apparel

Free-trade agreements allowing money and goods to flow back and forth across national borders without the constraints of taxes and tariffs have created a new global economic environment. This change makes it even more cost-effective for large corporations selling products to people in wealthy nations to locate production facilities in labour-intensive, poor nations. Workers in these nations are desperate for jobs and will work for low wages under conditions that would be considered oppressive by everyone who buys the products.

Through the first few years of this century, many athletic shoes costing well over £50 a pair in the UK were cut and sewn by Chinese, Indonesian and Thai workers, some of them children, making less than £1 per day (Sage, 1999). Children in Pakistan, India and Bangladesh, where working conditions and pay were reprehensible, stitched footballs. Outrage among people who became aware of these situations in the late 1990s led to widespread social activism, much of which was fuelled by Internet communication. After years of confronting and struggling with companies such as Nike, Reebok, adidas and others, human rights activists forced some of these corporations to enact anti-child labour policies and to allow their factories to be monitored so that working conditions meet minimal standards of acceptance. But child labour and sweatshop conditions continue to exist, and a wide range of sporting goods and apparel consumed in wealthy nations is made by people living below local poverty levels and working under conditions that make individual and family survival a daily challenge (Oxfam International, 2008; Play Fair, 2008; WRC, 2007).

Workers' rights continue to be a significant global issue. Research shows that it is possible to improve working conditions among people who produce sporting goods and other products if enough people in wealthy nations participate in actions that make corporations accountable and provide exploited workers the resources they need to demand higher wages and better working conditions. Sociologist of sport George Sage (1999) has documented the impact of the Nike Transnational Advocacy Network, an Internet-based form of political activism that mobilized people worldwide to force Nike to meet certain standards of social responsibility in the way they treated production workers. Sage's study is heartening because it shows that change is possible, even when dealing with multibillion-pound corporations and the autocratic governments of nations that allow corporations to exploit their people. The study also is provocative because it indicates that unless consumers in wealthy nations are socially concerned about how their products are made, there is little to stop transnational corporations that operate in an under-regulated global marketplace from pursuing profits in whatever ways they wish.

When activists such as the Maquila Solidarity Network, the Global March Against Child Labour and other social justice groups sparked global pressure to stop companies from using children to sew soccer balls in India and Pakistan, some sewing operations moved to Africa where people are desperate for jobs and not yet organized to demand fair wages. Instead of setting up factories, companies contract with individuals who work in their homes or small local facilities like this one outside Nairobi, Kenya (*Source*: Kevin Young)

Making sense of political realities

It is not easy to explain all the changes discussed in this chapter. Are sports simply a part of general globalization processes through which various forms of sport come together in many combinations? Are we witnessing the modernization of sports? Are sports being Americanized? Europeanized? Asianized?

Do global processes involve the diffusion of sports throughout the world, with people in some countries emulating the sports played in other countries, or do they involve the use of sports in connection with capitalist expansion and new forms of cultural imperialism? Are sports used to make poorer nations dependent on wealthier ones, or do they provide emerging nations with opportunities to establish cultural and economic independence? As globalization occurs, will traditional sports and folk games around the world be replaced by the competitive sports favoured by wealthy and powerful nations?

Finding answers to these questions requires research at local *and* global levels. Existing studies suggest that sports that are favoured by wealthy nations are not simply imposed on people worldwide. Even when people play sports that come from powerful nations, they give them meanings that are grounded in local cultures and the experiences of the people who play them. Global trends are important, but so are the local expressions of and responses to those trends (Bale and Christensen, 2004; Bale and Cronin, 2003; Ben-Porat and Ben Porat,

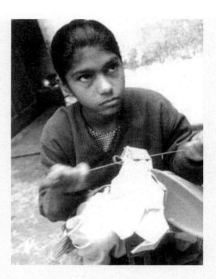

In the mid-1990s, many people became aware of the exploitive labour practices used to produce sports equipment and apparel. These photos, provided by the Global March Against Child Labour, show a 12-year-old girl in India sewing a football. The ball is stamped with the claim that it is made with 'Child Free Labour'. Sweatshop labour is still used to produce sport products consumed by people in wealthy nations, but global social activism has stopped some companies from using child labour (*Source*: Global March Against Child Labour)

2004; Denham, 2004; Donnelly, 1996a; Foer, 2004; Hastings et al., 2005; Maguire, 1999, 2004, 2005; Okubu, 2004). Power is a process, and it is always exercised through relationships and current forms of social organization. Therefore, research on sports worldwide must examine the processes through which powerful nations exert control over sports in other nations as well as the processes through which people worldwide integrate sports and sports experiences into their lives on their own terms.

Politics in Sports

The term *politics* usually is associated with formal government entities in the public sphere. However, politics include all processes of governing people and administering policies, at all levels of organization, public and private. Therefore, politics are an integral part of sports, and many local, national and international sports organizations are referred to as 'governing bodies'.

Most sports organizations provide and regulate sports participation opportunities, establish and enforce policies, control and standardize competitions and acknowledge the accomplishments of athletes. This sounds like a straightforward set of tasks, but they seldom are accomplished without opposition, debate and compromise. Members of sports organizations agree on many things, but conflicts often arise as decisions are made in connection with the following questions:

- What qualifies as a sport?
- What are the rules of a sport?
- Who makes and enforces the rules in sports?
- Who organizes and controls sports events?
- Where do sports events take place?
- Who is eligible to participate in a sport?
- How are rewards distributed to athletes and others associated with sports?

These questions are inherently political because the answers affect different people in different ways. Most people understand this, but they complain about politics in sports only when the answers are not the ones they want to hear. This becomes clear in the following sections.

What qualifies as a sport?

As noted in Chapter 1, there is no universal agreement on the definition of sports. What is considered a sport in a society or a particular event, such as the Olympics, is determined through political processes (Donnelly, 1996b). The criteria used to identify sports reflect the ideas and interests of some people more than others. In the Olympics, for example, a competitive activity or game for men must be played in at least 75 countries on four continents to be considered for inclusion in the Olympic Games; an activity or a game for women must be played in at least 40 countries on three continents. It also must have an officially designated international governing body, a requisite number of national governing bodies and a history of international championships before the IOC will consider recognizing it as an Olympic sport. However, IOC decisions about what qualifies as a sport can be changed, as seen in 2005 when baseball and softball were eliminated from the programme for the 2012 Olympics in London.

In these days of multibillion-pound media contracts, an activity or a game is more likely to be recognized as a sport if it is attractive to younger viewers, who will bring new advertisers and corporate sponsors to the Olympics and the television coverage of the Games. It also helps if women play the activity because more women than men watch the Olympics and the IOC knows it must highlight gender equity if it is to avoid negative publicity for the Olympics as a whole.

This method of determining what qualifies as a sport favours nations that historically have emphasized competitive games and had the resources to export their games around the world. Former colonial powers are especially favoured because they used their national games to introduce their cultural values and traditions to people in the regions that they colonized. Wealthy and powerful nations today not only have their national sports broadcast on satellite channels around the world but also have the resources to subsidize the development of these sports worldwide. Therefore, when the IOC uses its method of recognition, the sports from wealthy nations are at the top of the list. When these sports are recognized as official Olympic sports, the cultural values and traditions of wealthy and powerful nations are reaffirmed. In this way, the sports in wealthy and powerful nations become part of an emerging global culture that favours their interests. This also is why native games in traditional cultures are not a part of the Olympics. Games played only in limited regions of the world do not qualify for recognition as sports. Therefore, if people from nations with traditional cultures want to participate in the Olympics, they must learn to do sports as they are done in wealthy nations. If people in traditional cultures lack access to the equipment and facilities needed to train in their homelands, they must depend on support from people and organizations in wealthy nations to become athletes in recognized 'international' sports. In this way, sports enable people and organizations in wealthy nations to gain a cultural foothold in other nations and use it to promote changes that foster their interests.

This type of political process also occurs in other contexts. For example, for well over 100 years, the men who have controlled school physical education curricula have used a power and performance model to designate certain activities as appropriate school sports. They have organized these sports to emphasize competition and physical dominance, so they reaffirm male notions of character and excellence. This way of defining and organizing sports seldom has been questioned, but if power and performance sports attract fewer girls and women than boys and men, it may be time to ask critical questions about what qualifies as appropriate physical education for school children and why. Some educators are doing this, but changes are slow and localized. When we ask these questions, we need to be sensitive to the politics that have long worked to the advantage of men in sports. Trying to change taken-for-granted political realities always creates resistance among those who have benefited from them. Ironically, many men say that people who challenge traditional realities are slaves to 'political correctness'. What they mean, however, is that they do not want to change the insensitive and self-interested ways of doing things that allow them to ignore the needs of others.

The development of criteria underlying the meaning and organization of sports also occurs on a global scale. Sociologist Peter Donnelly (1996b) illustrates this in his analysis of how the ideologies of 'Olympism' and 'professionalism' have been combined to form a global sports monoculture, which he calls 'prolympism'. Prolympism is now the model for determining what qualifies and is funded as 'sports' in nations around the world. This occurs even in nations where prolympism is clearly inconsistent with traditional games. In this way, the politics of defining sports are both local and global in impact.

What are the rules of a sport?

Sports are social constructions because people create them as they interact with one another within the constraints of culture and society. The rules that govern sports also are social constructions created through political processes. Why should a basketball rim be 10 feet above the ground? Why should the top of a volleyball net be 88⅛ inches off the ground in international women's volleyball? Why can pole vaulters not use any type of pole they want? Why can tournament golfers not use any golf club or golf ball they want? Why is 6 centimetres the maximum height for the sides of bikini bottoms worn by women in beach volleyball when men wear long shorts? This list of questions could go on and on. The point is that the rules of sports can be based on many concerns, and this makes them political. Because sports have more rules than many human activities, they are especially political.

Who makes and enforces the rules in sports?

The rules of an 'official' sport are determined by a recognized governing body that makes decisions affecting the sport and its participants. The process of becoming recognized as the *sole* governing body of a sport clearly involves politics. Governing bodies have power, status and control over resources, so it is common for more than one organization to claim that it is the rightful rule-making body for a sport. The simultaneous existence of various governing bodies creates confusion for athletes and spectators. Professional boxing, for example, has at least four governing bodies (the WBO, the WBU, the WBF and the IBO), each with its own weight categories and championships and each claiming to be the official rule-making body for boxing. 'New' sports, such as skateboarding, snowboarding, in-line skating and BMX (biking), each have had at least two organizations vying to be official governing bodies. As organizations seek power over sports and the athletes who participate in them, they battle one another to recruit dues-paying members and sponsor competitive events, especially national and international championships. In the process, their policies confuse athletes and limit participation opportunities. When this occurs, people clearly see politics in sports.

When rules exist, there is a need for rule enforcement. This adds another political dimension to sports. Anyone who has ever refereed or officiated a game or match will tell you that rule violations are seldom clear-cut. Identifying violations is difficult, and few people see violations the same way. Rule violations occur on a regular basis in many sports, but the best referees learn when to call fouls or penalties in connection with these violations. In fact, referees and officials discuss when they should or should not call fouls during games and matches. They realize that it is a political challenge to make sports appear to be fair to athletes and spectators.

Enforcing off-the-field rules is also a political challenge. The process of investigating rule violations, determining innocence or guilt and punishing rule violators involves judgements based on ideas about fairness, moral principles, economic interests, personal reputations, organizational prestige or other factors. How these factors are considered and which ones prevail in the rule enforcement process are political matters.

Who organizes and controls sports events?

Representatives of official governing bodies often organize and control sports events. Standards emerge when the governing body is stable, but standards do not exist once and for all time. For example, even though governing bodies devise formal standards for judging performances in figure skating, diving and gymnastics, research shows that the votes of judges are influenced by political loyalties, personal connections, coercion and bribes (Jennings, 1996a; Jennings and Sambrook, 2000). This has been a serious issue in many Olympic Games, but it became widely publicized in 2002 when a judge for the figure skating pairs competition allegedly favoured a Russian couple over a Canadian couple. Her scores determined who received the gold and silver medals, respectively. After much debate, the International Skating Union (ISU) awarded the Canadian couple a gold medal without taking the gold medal away from the Russian couple. Then the ISU changed its rules to discourage unfair judging in the future, but the changes were widely criticized and were revised at least twice between 2003 and the following Winter Olympics in Turin in 2006.

When international politics influence judges, it is disheartening to athletes, but it should be no more disheartening than the knowledge that 'cuteness', 'hairstyles', 'body build' and 'eye colour' can also influence judges when it comes to female athletes in certain events. This is a form of cultural politics that forces some athletes to spend thousands of pounds on everything from braces to straighten their teeth to plastic surgery, if they wish to be successful. Politics come in many forms.

Now that sports are heavily commercialized, official governing bodies and a combination of corporate sponsors and media production people organize and control events. The location and timing of events, event schedules, the awarding of press credentials, and the choices of which television companies will broadcast the events and which corporate logos will be displayed are resolved through political processes. The participants in those processes and their interests change from one event to the next; this means that there is never an end to politics in sports.

Where do sports events take place?

Site selection decisions have become increasingly political recently because more 'places' now bid to host teams and events. The selection of Olympic sites has always been political, as clearly demonstrated by the site selection, vote-buying scandal involving the IOC and the Salt Lake Olympic Organizing Committee during the 1990s. As the stakes for hosting the Olympic Games have increased, bid committees have been willing to wine, dine, bribe and pressure IOC members, whose votes determine which city hosts a particular Games (Jennings, 1996a; Jennings and Sambrook, 2000; Simson and Jennings, 1992). The politics of site selection also operate in other ways. For example, when Atlanta was selected to host the 1996 Games instead of the city of Athens that had hosted the first modern Olympic Games exactly 100 years previously, it was clear to many people worldwide that the selection process was influenced by the television rights fees anticipated from NBC and the location of Coca-Cola's international headquarters in Atlanta. Coca-Cola had a 67-year history of paying hundreds of millions of US dollars to support the IOC and sponsor the Olympics, and IOC members felt indebted to the corporation. During the Games, the red-and-white Coke logo was so evident in Atlanta and Olympic venues that many observers described them as the 'Coca-Colympics'.

The selection of Beijing, China, for the 2008 Summer Olympic Games involved political considerations and complex political processes. China was desperate to host the games because it wanted to showcase its culture, solicit tourism and business investments, and claim political legitimacy as a global power. The members of the IOC selection committee were influenced by many considerations: China was home to nearly 20 per cent of the world's population, it had never hosted an Olympic Games, bringing Olympism to China would strengthen the Olympic movement, and the potential economic benefits of awarding the games to China were very high because corporate sponsors would see China as a prime site for capitalist expansion. NBC, the US network with the rights to televise the 2008 Games, saw China as an attractive site for marketing its coverage. NBC knew that by 2008 many people would be very interested in China because of its size, power, culture and economic growth potential. NBC also knew it could use that interest to boost ratings and sell high-priced advertising time to transnational corporations.

Site bids for other large international events may not cost as much as bids to host the Olympics, but they are just as political. In many parts of the world, these politics reflect environmental issues. For example, the use of open space or agricultural land for golf courses is being contested in Europe, Japan and, even, North America. As one researcher claims, 'golf has acquired the status of a four-letter word because of the havoc it has wrought across the globe' (www.twnside.org.sg/title2/ttcd/TA-06.doc). The Global Anti-Golf Movement (www.antigolf.org/) is fuelled by widespread objections to the use of chemical fertilizers and massive water resources to keep grass soft and green for golfers representing the economic elite in societies. It is a loosely organized collection of lobbying groups, often focused on environmental issues in densely populated regions of India and South-east Asia.

Ski resort expansion in Europe, North America and Japan also has been resisted for environmental reasons. The organizers of the 2000 Sydney Games faced severe criticism when they failed in important ways to live up to the environmental principles developed by the original bid committee (Lenskyj, 2000). Such examples highlight the fact that the politics of place in sports often involve local opposition to hosting events and building sports facilities.

Who is eligible to participate in a sport?

Who plays and who does not is a hotly contested issue in sports. As people in governing bodies make eligibility decisions, they use criteria such as gender, age, weight, height, ability (and disability), place of residence, citizenship, educational affiliation, social status, income or, even, race and ethnicity to determine participation eligibility. Such questions are increasingly common today as athletes have parents from different nations and a birthplace that differs from the nations where they live, train, attend school or get married (Layden, 2005; Wertheim, 2004). Although eligibility policies often are presented as if they were based on unchanging truths about human beings and sports, they are grounded in political agreements. This is true in local youth sports schemes and the Olympics.

People often debate the seeming arbitrariness of eligibility rules. Even in youth sports, there are frequent debates about the age and weight rules used to determine eligibility. These have increased as children of immigrants want to play youth sports and have none of the formal birth records that are routinely kept in the UK. As global mobility increases, there will be more questions about eligibility as it is related to citizenship, nationality and place of residence. Amateur sports have long been the scene for debates over the meaning of amateur and who qualifies as an amateur athlete. Athletes with disabilities regularly challenge rules prohibiting their participation in certain sports. Within events such as the Paralympics there are frequent debates about disability classifications and eligibility, and even what it means to be disabled (see Howe and Jones, 2006). This is discussed in 'Breaking barriers', opposite. Because these meanings are socially determined, they change over time and from place to place. This is another reason why politics will always be a part of sports.

How are rewards distributed to athletes and others?

The distribution of rewards is an issue at all levels of sports participation. Coaches, league administrators, sports writers, judges, team owners, arbitrators, tournament committees and parents decide who will receive special commendations, certificates of accomplishment, trophies, scholarships, contracts, pay increases and so on. 'Who gets what?' is a political question, and the answers are not always clear-cut. People discuss and sometimes argue about rewards. As the level of competition increases, so do the stakes associated with decisions. At the highest levels of competition, these decisions can involve massive amounts of money and status.

With the increased commercialization of sports, there are heated debates about the ways that revenues should be distributed among sports organizations, organization officials, owners and promoters, athletes and others connected with sports. As noted in Chapter 11, the political processes associated with the distribution of revenues in commercial sports are complex and never ending. These processes take various forms and come to different resolutions in different countries and sports.

Debates revolve around questions such as these: why should some professional sports team owners make more money than the best players on their teams? What percentage should agents receive when they negotiate player contracts? Why should a talented athlete who risks his health and endures pain and injury while generating millions of pounds for his team be ineligible for compensation when his club refuses to renew his contract, leaving him with few career prospects? Why should Olympic athletes not be paid for their participation when they collectively generate millions of pounds during the Games? Why should the IOC receive 33 per cent of the revenues from every Olympics, and why should the United States Olympic Committee (USOC) receive 12.8 per cent of the money paid by US television companies for the rights to broadcast the Olympics (about US$114 million in 2008) when the USA already has more athlete-training money than any other nation? Should athletes receive compensation when their images and uniform numbers are used in video games? These and hundreds of similar questions show that the 'politics of rewards' are an integral part of sports.

Sometimes rewards involve status or prestige rather than money, such as being selected to a hall of fame. Even youth league teams have 'politics of status' awards for 'the most improved player of the year', 'the most valuable player', 'the most dedicated player' and so on. When people agree on who should receive these awards, they forget that the selection process is political. It is only when they do not agree that they complain about politics in sports.

breaking BARRIERS

Political barriers: *I think ... this opens some doors for people*

When we talk about sports and people with a disability, we must talk politics. Consider the legal case of PGA golfer Casey Martin. In 1994 as a student at Stanford University, he was voted captain of the golf team and led it to the collegiate championship. Tiger Woods joined the team in 1995, and Martin was his roommate when Stanford played tournaments away from Palo Alto and its home course. Martin won the US Intercollegiate Golf Championship that year and led Stanford to the NCAA finals.

But all was not well with Martin. A congenital defect in his right leg prevented normal blood circulation, and was gradually eroding his bone and causing him increasingly severe and chronic pain. There were times when he could barely walk, so his coach convinced him to use a golf cart, which was permissible under the rules of the National Collegiate Athletic Association (NCAA) – the US equivalent of BUCS – given his medical condition.

After graduating, Martin played professional golf and by 1997 found that there were times when he could not walk and needed a motorized cart to complete 18 holes. But the PGA ruled that Martin had to walk or quit. Martin sued and won an injunction allowing him to use a cart. The PGA appealed and the case eventually went to the US Supreme Court. In a split decision, the court ruled in 2001 that under the Americans with Disability Act of 1990, Martin must be allowed to use a cart because it did not force the PGA to make an unreasonable accommodation in his case.

Martin spent over US$100 000 of his money to play politics with the PGA for four years. His pain and fatigue continued to increase and he played only nine tournaments between 2001 and late 2005. Today at 36 years old (in 2008), he is the men's golf coach at the University of Oregon. He knows that a leg amputation is needed, but he puts it off because, as he puts it, 'I'm attached to it' (Yocom, 2008).

In the meantime, Nike has established the Casey Martin Nike Award, which honours an individual with a disability who has taken a public stand and engaged in political battles to inspire or expand sports participation rights for people with disabilities. Nike's position is that, 'If you have a body, you are an athlete.'

The Casey Martin story is not unique. As we discussed in Chapter 6, the South African athlete Oscar Pistorius also had to 'get political' with the IOC to overturn a decision which had banned him from competing with 'able-bodied' athletes in the Olympic Games. People with disabilities have always fought political battles to avoid being invisible in the world of sport (DePauw, 1997). For example, in 2005 when London competed with Madrid, Moscow, New York and Paris to be chosen by the IOC to host the 2012 Olympics and Paralympics, Madrid was actually the only one of these bidding cities which mentioned the Paralympics in their overall plan. Invisibility was in plain sight, even in the bid of London, which won the right to host the Games.

After the Supreme Court decision in 2001, Casey Martin said, 'I'm thrilled ... I think in the future this opens some doors for people.' However, in the real world of sports where decisions are made about everything from eligibility and the rules of the game to where eligibility rules are frequently exclusive, people with disabilities know that if they do not play politics, they may not play at all.

Summary: How Do Governments and Global Processes Influence Sports?

Sports and politics are inseparable. Government involvement in sports is generally related to the need for sponsorship, organization and facilities. The fact that sports are important in people's

Politics are related to sports for people with disabilities in many ways. War, land mines and dangerous working conditions continue to be leading causes of disabilities worldwide. Elliot Mujaji of Zimbabwe lost his arm when he was electrocuted in an accident at work. He won gold medals in the 100-metre race in both Sydney and Athens (*Source*: David Biene; photograph courtesy of Ossur)

lives and can be sites for social conflict often leads to government involvement. The forms of involvement vary by society, but their purposes are generally to (1) safeguard the public order, (2) maintain health and fitness among citizens, (3) promote the prestige and power of a group, community or nation, (4) promote a sense of identity, belonging and unity among citizens, (5) reproduce values consistent with dominant ideology, (6) increase support for political leaders and government structures, (7) promote economic development, and (8) serve as a foreign policy tool.

The rules, policies and funding priorities set by government officials and agencies reflect political differences and struggles among groups within a society. This does not mean that the same people always benefit when government involvement occurs, but involvement seldom results in equal benefits for everyone. For example, when funds are dedicated to the development and training of elite athletes, fewer funds are available to support general participation schemes. Funding priorities could favour mass participation instead of elite sports, but the priorities themselves are subject to debate and negotiation. This political process is an inevitable part of organized sports.

History shows government intervention in sports usually favours groups with the greatest quantity of resources and the highest degree of organization, and with goals that support the ideological orientations of public officials. The groups least likely to be favoured are those that fail to understand the connection between sports and politics or lack resources to effectively influence political decisions. When people believe the myth that sports and politics are unrelated, they are unlikely to be pleased when officials develop policies and allocate funds.

The connection between sports and global political processes is complex. Ideally, sports bring nations together in contexts supportive of peace and friendship. Although this can and does occur, most nations use sports to satisfy their own interests. Displays of nationalism have been and continue to be common at international events. The Olympic Games are a good case in point. People who work with, promote or follow the Olympics often focus on national medal counts and use them to support their claims for national status.

If mega events such as the Olympics are indeed special events with positive potential, efforts should be made to maximize that potential. Limiting nationalism and commercialism, and emphasizing the interdependence of nations and people would be helpful and could be done by any number of strategies.

Powerful transnational corporations have joined nation states as major participants in global political processes. As a result, sports are used increasingly for economic gains as well as political purposes. Nationalism and the promotion of national interests remain part of global sports, but consumerism and the promotion of capitalist expansion have become more important since the early 1990s and the end of the Cold War. Within the context of global relations, athletes and teams now are associated with corporate logos as well as nation states. Global sports events have political and economic implications. They are sites for presenting numerous images and narratives associated with the interests of nation states *and* corporate sponsors. The dominant discourses associated with sports in the UK are clearly consistent with the interests of corporate sponsors, and they promote an ideology infused with the capitalist values of individualism, competition, achievement and consumption.

Global political processes also are associated with other aspects of sports such as the migration patterns of elite athletes and the production of sporting goods. Political issues are raised when athletes cross national borders to play their sports, and when transnational corporations produce sports equipment and clothing in labour-intensive, poor nations and then sell these products in wealthy nations.

These and other issues associated with global political processes are best understood when they are studied on both global and local levels. Data in these studies help determine when sports involve reciprocal cultural exchanges leading to mutual understanding among people and when they involve processes through which powerful nations and corporations exercise subtle influence over the social life and political events in less powerful nations.

Politics are also part of the very structure and organization of sports. Political processes exist because people in sports organizations must answer questions about what qualifies as a sport, the rules of a sport, procedures for enforcing rules, organization and control of sport events, locations of sport events, eligibility criteria for participants and distribution of rewards. These political issues are central to sports, and they illustrate why the organizations that make decisions about sports are often described as governing bodies. This is another example highlighting that sports are inseparable from politics and political processes.

Website resources

Note: Websites often change. The following URLs were current when this book was printed. Please check our website (***www.mcgraw-hill.co.uk/textbooks/coakley***) for updates and additions.

See the OLC, ***www.mcgraw-hill.co.uk/textbooks/coakley***, for an annotated list of readings related to this chapter.

www.mcgraw-hill.co.uk/textbooks/coakley Click on Chapter 13 for information on sports and international relations, gift giving and the Olympic scandal, and politics and the Paralympic movement.

http://europa.eu.int/comm/sport/index_en.html The site of Sport and European Union covers issues related to the development of sport through the European Union; information about programmes, government influence on sports, and the politics of co-ordinating national sport governing bodies with this international governing body.

www.footballforpeace.org.uk The website of the F4P project, organized in the UK for Arab and Jewish children in Northern Israel.

www.globalmarch.org/campaigns/worldcupcampaign/Index.php This is the site of the Global March Against Child Labour, an international movement based in India and focused on eliminating exploitive work that condemns millions of children to lives of servitude and suffering; this site takes you to its 2002 World Cup project.

www.iwg-gti.org The site of the International Working Group on Women and Sport; contains information on programmes, policy issues and problems faced by girls and women in nearly 100 countries; information reveals different patterns of government involvement as well as the cultural issues that influence programmes, policies and problems; key links to other international sport organizations.

www.london2012.com The website for the London 2012 Olympic Games, with details of the organization of the Games.

www.olympic.org The site of the International Olympic Committee; has links to National Olympic committees around the world and information about the IOC and its programmes.

http://olympicstudies.uab.es/eng/index.asp This is the site of the Olympic Studies Centre at the Universitat Autònoma de Barcelona; has many links to official information about the Olympics.

www.policyalternatives.ca/index.cfm?act=news&do=Article&call=163&pA=BB736455 Olympic costs and benefits: a cost–benefit analysis of the proposed Vancouver 2010 Winter Olympic and Paralympic Games, by Marvin Shaffer, Alan Greer and Celine Mauboules. Vancouver: Canadian Centre for Policy Alternatives, February 2003.

http://purl.access.gpo.gov/GPO/LPS28875 (PDF is at *http://purl.access.gpo.gov/GPO/LPB28876*) The Beijing Olympics and human rights: roundtable before the United States Congressional–Executive Commission on China, 107th Congress, second session, 18 November 2002.

www.sportdevelopment.org.uk/html/rg_policy.html Provides links to key policy documents for sport in the UK.

www.ucalgary.ca/library/ssportsite/ Scroll down to 'National Sport Structures and Organisations' and find links to nearly every established organization in the world, including National Olympic Committees and government sports organizations around the world.

www.uksport.gov.uk/ The website for UK Sport, the organization that works in partnership with the home country sports councils to work towards world-class sports performance. UK Sport distributes public funds, and is accountable to Parliament through the Department for Culture, Media and Sport.

www.un.org/Depts/dhl/resguide/r58.htm This site has links to two UN resolutions: 'Building a Peaceful and Better World Through Sport and the Olympic Ideal' (A/RES/58/6) and 'Sport as a Means to Promote Education, Health, Development and Peace' (A/RES/58/5); to find them, start at the bottom of the list and move up.

www.un.org/sport2005/ This URL changes yearly from, for example, 2005 to 2006; the site contains up-to-date news related to sports and issues of development around the world; there are links to the latest reports and projects; also a link to a Sport for Development and Peace report entitled, 'Sport as a tool for development and peace: towards achieving the United Nations Millennium Development Goals' (33 pages).

Sports in the future:
what can we create?

Chapter contents

Envisioning possibilities for the future
Current trends related to sports in society
Factors influencing trends today
Envisioning possibilities and creating futures
Summary: what can we create?

Online
Learning Centre Resources

Visit *Sports in Society*'s Online Learning Centre (OLC) at **www.mcgraw-hill.co.uk/ textbooks/coakley** for additional information and study material for this chapter, including:

- Self-grading quizzes and essay questions
- Learning outcomes
- Related websites
- Additional readings

> The primary goal of futurists is not to predict the future but to uncover images of possible, probable, and preferable futures that enable people to make informed decisions about their lives.
>
> *(Wendell Bell, futurist, 1997. p. 1)*

> Sport is the most dynamic activity in the world today, with the potential to contribute powerfully to a better world ... The power and influence of sport is only just being understood.
>
> *(Robert Davies, chief executive, International Business Leader Forum, 2002a)*

> Sport is not so much a power on its own, more a movement, which has a pivotal role to play in improving the values of the society we live in.
>
> *(Jacques Rogge, IOC president, 2003)*

Discussions of the future often involve exaggerations. Predicting dramatic changes is always more exciting than declaring that tomorrow will look much like today. Therefore, people often describe the future in science fiction terms revolving around extreme hopes or fears. This sparks our interest and sometimes leaves us temporarily awestruck, but such images of the future are rarely helpful.

For better or worse, the future seldom unfolds as rapidly or dramatically as some forecasters would have us believe. Instead, changes occur in combination with emerging social conditions and the efforts of people to create a future that fits their visions of what life should be like. Of course, some people have more power and resources to create the future than others, but they seldom want revolutionary changes because their privileged positions depend on stability and controlled change. This often impedes progressive changes in favour of increasing the efficiency and profitability of existing ways of life. In the case of capitalist societies, this involves fostering growth in the production and distribution of consumer goods.

Although power relations cannot be ignored, many aspects of sports are contested as people integrate them into their lives. Accordingly, the goal of this chapter is to respond to the following questions:

- What models of sports might we use to envision possibilities for the future?
- What current trends must be acknowledged as we consider the future of sports?
- What major factors underlie existing trends, and how will they influence the future of sports?
- How can we become effective agents in creating the future of sports?

Envisioning Possibilities for the Future

Sports are social constructions. This means that dominant sports at any particular place and time are consistent with the values, ideas, interests and experiences of those who have power in a group or society. However, dominant sports are not universally accepted in many social worlds. History shows that people often modify them or develop alternatives in the process of resisting or challenging them.

Dominant sports in most societies have been and continue to be grounded in the values and experiences of men who value military conquest, political control and economic expansion. As noted in previous chapters and explained in Chapter 4, these sports are based on a **power and performance model**. However, people may reject all or part of dominant sports forms as they seek experiences grounded in alternative values and experiences. Many of these people create sports organized around one or more elements of a **pleasure and participation model**.

These two models do not encompass all the possibilities for envisioning sports in the future. But they represent two popular conceptions of sports in contemporary societies, and they are practical starting points for envisioning and thinking about what we would like sports to be in the future.

Power and performance sports

Power and performance sports will continue to be highly visible and publicized sports forms in the near future. They are based on key aspects of dominant ideologies in many post-industrial societies as demonstrated by their emphasis on strength, power, speed, competition and competitive outcomes.

Although power and performance sports take many forms, they are all built upon the idea that excellence is proved through competitive success and achieved through dedication, hard work and a willingness to take risks. They stress setting records, pushing human limits, using the body as a machine and employing science and technology. According to many athletes in power and performance sports, the body is to be disciplined and monitored to meet the demands of sports. Sports are defined as battles in which the goal is to defeat opponents.

Power and performance sports are exclusive in that participants are selected for their physical skills and abilities to achieve competitive success. Those who lack these 'qualities' are dropped or relegated to lower-status programmes. Organizations and teams have hierarchical authority structures in which athletes are subordinate to coaches and coaches are subordinate

Club sports and intramurals may include elements from both power and performance sports and pleasure and participation sports. Ultimate frisbee is a good example of this (*Source*: **Bob Byrne, Ultimate Players Association**)

to owners and administrators. It is widely accepted that coaches can exceed standard normative limits when motivating and training athletes to outperform others. Athletes are expected to obey coaches and show that they are willing to make sacrifices in their quest for competitive success.

The sponsors of power and performance sports stress the value of winning; being endorsed by winning athletes and teams is important when selling products and promoting the sponsor's brand. Sponsors assume that their association with winning athletes and teams enhances their status and makes them special in the eyes of people they wish to impress and influence. As long as current sponsors desire this connection, power and performance sports will remain dominant for the foreseeable future in most societies.

Pleasure and participation sports

Although power and performance sports are highly visible, many people realize that there are other ways to organize and play sports that more closely match their values and interests. This realization has led to the creation of numerous sport forms organized around *pleasure and participation,* and emphasizing freedom, authenticity, self-expression, enjoyment, holistic health, support for others and respect for the environment. They focus on personal empowerment and the notion that the body is to be nurtured and enjoyed in a quest to experience challenges rather than trained and subordinated in a quest to achieve competitive success.

Pleasure and participation sports tend to be inclusive, and skill differences among participants often are accommodated by using 'handicaps' that allow everyone to experience exciting challenges associated with organized physical activities. Sports organizations and teams based on this model have democratic decision-making structures characterized by co-operation, power sharing, and give-and-take relationships between coaches and athletes. Humiliation, shame and derogation are inconsistent with the spirit underlying these sports.

Pleasure and participation sports are characteristically sponsored by public and non-profit organizations and by corporations seeking exposure to a defined collection of consumers. Additionally, some corporations may sponsor these sports as part of an overall emphasis on social responsibility and a commitment to health promotion, among other commendable goals.

Current Trends Related to Sports in Society

Becoming aware of current trends and the factors that influence them is the starting point for being effective agents in creating the futures we want to see. The complexity of social worlds complicates the identification of trends, so it is useful to think of the factors that support the growth of power and performance sports, on the one hand, and pleasure and participation sports, on the other. Making this distinction helps us clarify our goals and use social theories more effectively as we participate in the process of influencing the culture and organization of sports.

Factors supporting the growth of power and performance sports

There are strong vested interests in power and performance sports among those who have power and influence in wealthy post-industrial societies. For example, when the goal is to use strength, power and speed to outperform others, sports reaffirm gender differences and a form of gender ideology that privileges men. As long as men control corporate resources there will be an emphasis on sponsoring power and performance sports. Currently, this helps to explain why men's football, the classic embodiment of these sports, has become the most popular spectator sport in the UK and continues to attract millions of pounds in television rights fees and other revenues. Athletes in the Premier League and other power and performance sports are portrayed in the media as heroic figures, as warriors that embody a corporate emphasis on productivity, efficiency and dedication to performance in the face of all barriers. Spectators are encouraged to identify with these athletes and express their identification through the consumption of licensed merchandise and other products.

Because power and performance sports often involve pushing human and normative limits, they are relatively easy to market and sell when combined with storylines that resonate with the experience of consumers. This is why the media now emphasize the personal lives of athletes and their families. Dedicated, lifelong fans may be satisfied with coverage focused on games, scores and statistics, but new and less knowledgeable fans often are attracted to more dramatic and tabloid-style information about players' lives. For instance, David Beckham is one of the most widely recognized athletes in the world. The media attention to his captaincy of the England football team, and performances on the pitch for Manchester United, Real Madrid and

LA Galaxy, are matched by stories about his dress, hairstyles and personal life. In particular, newspaper and television reports focus on his marriage to a member of the Spice Girls, one of the world's most successful all-female pop music groups, and their three (in 2008) children. In 2004, Beckham's performance in the European men's football tournament, and specifically his failure to score crucial penalties, was linked in media reports to an alleged affair between Beckham and a former assistant. These stories maintain the interest of readers and viewers who do not know much about football, but who can still be attracted to reports of 'Brand Beckham'. Such coverage has become typical in nearly all other power and performances sports, and it serves to keep them popular.

Factors supporting the growth of pleasure and participation sports

Sports have always been social occasions in people's lives, and people incorporate into them the things that give them pleasure or reaffirm their values. Pleasure and participation sports today are popular to the extent that people define them as attractive alternatives to the more culturally dominant power and performance sports. Factors that motivate this search for alternatives today are (1) concerns about health and fitness, (2) participation preferences among older people, (3) values and experiences brought to sports by women, and (4) groups seeking alternatives to highly structured, competitive sports that constrain their experiences.

Concerns about health and fitness

As healthcare policies and programmes around the world emphasize prevention rather than expensive cures, people become more sensitive to health and fitness issues. This encourages people to more actively seek alternatives to power and performance sports and increase participation in pleasure and participation sports for which health benefits are much higher (Waddington, 2000b, 2007).

In the UK, new concerns about health, fitness and obesity are reviving interests in forms of physical education that focus on lifetime activities, non-competitive challenges, inclusive participation philosophies, respect and support for other participants, and responsible attitudes towards the environment – all of which are characteristics of pleasure and participation sports. If these concerns continue to grow, they will influence the sports preferences of people through the life course. If this happens, they will demand subsidized memberships of local leisure facilities rather than season tickets to Premier League games or expensive cable packages allowing them to sit on a sofa and watch hundreds of hours of sports each year.

If people realize that healthy exercise can be organized to create family fun and a sense of community, there will be powerful incentives for them to give priority to a wide array of pleasure and participation sports in their lives. But this depends on how people choose to create the future.

Participation preferences among older people

As the median age of the population in many societies increases, as people live longer and as older people represent an increasingly larger proportion of the world's population, there will be more interest in sports that do not involve intimidation, the use of physical force, the domination of opponents and the risk of serious injuries.

As people age, they are less likely to risk physical well-being to establish a reputation in sports. Older people are more likely to see sports as social activities and make them inclusive rather than exclusive. Older people also realize that they have but one body, and it can be enjoyed only if they cultivate it as though it were a garden rather than driving it as though it were a racing machine or a bulldozer.

People such as baby boomers in the UK, who grew up playing competitive sports, are not likely to completely abandon their interest in those sports as they age, but they will avoid participation in power and performance sports that have high injury rates. Most will play modified versions of competitive activities in which rules emphasize the pleasure of movement, connections between people and controlled challenges. Many older people also will engage in walking, swimming, strength training, yoga, tai chi and similar activities, which will be taken seriously but done in settings where the focus is on health, fitness and social connections rather than setting records, using the body to dominate opponents or bragging about who sweats the most during their Bikram yoga sessions.

Pleasure and participation sports will be sites where older people will challenge dominant ideas about ageing. Ageing has often been seen as a process that involves increasing dependency and incapacity, but the sports participation of older people supports the idea that ageing does not automatically mean becoming weak and incapacitated. 'Veterans' and 'masters' sport programmes will increase as people demand them. As a result, images of older people who are fit, healthy and accomplished athletes will become more visible and serve as models for others.

Values and experiences brought to sports by women

As women gain more power and resources in sports, many will reject the culture that often accompanies traditional power and performance sports. In the process, they will challenge the very gender ideology on which such sports are organized. A possible outcome of this will be new norms and structures that emphasize dimensions of pleasure and participation sports. For instance, when women play sports such as rugby, football and hockey, they often emphasize inclusiveness and support for teammates and opponents in explicit ways that are seldom present in men's versions of these sports. The 'in-your-face' power and performance orientation exhibited by some men is replaced by an orientation that is expressive of the joy and connections resulting from participation.

Women face difficulties when recruiting sponsors for sports that differ from men's power and performance sports. Without an emphasis on physical domination, women's sports are often seen as second-rate or not 'real' enough to attract the attention that sponsors seek. However, if women choose such sports in greater numbers, sponsors may respond if they see benefits for their bottom lines. If they do, pleasure and participation sports will receive increased support.

Groups seeking alternative sports

People who reject power and performance sports or certain dimensions of them also will contribute to the growth of sports organized more closely around the pleasure and participation model. There is evidence of this in the unique sport subcultures that have been developed around many alternative sports. Studies of skateboarders and snowboarders show that some young people resist attempts to turn their sports into commercialized, competitive forms (Beal,

1995; Honea, 2005). As illustrated in Cartoon 14.1, athletes in these sports can feel frustrated if they are pressured by sponsors to say things that do not represent their experiences.

People sometimes resist attempts to change the pleasure and participation emphasis in their activities. They do not want competition and the domination of opponents to replace the expression and support of fellow participants. For example, when a 12-year-old snowboarder was asked about adding his sport to the Olympics, he said, 'Don't kill the ride, dude. Let us be free.' Even at age 12, he knew that the ideology of power and performance would subvert desired elements of pleasure and participation in his sport. After snowboarding was added to the Olympics in 1996, Terje Haakonsen, reputedly the best boarder in the world, refused to compete in Nagano, Japan. He said, 'Snowboarding is about fresh tracks and carving powder and being yourself and not being judged by others; it's not about nationalism and politics and money' (in Perman, 1998, p. 61).

After skateboarding had been turned into a traditional competitive sport by the X Games, legendary skater Tony Hawk declared that 'it's about time the riders took the competitions into their own hands' because others were destroying many of the expressive and pleasurable elements of boarding (in Higgins, 2005). Hawk organized his Boom Boom HuckJam tour to preserve the spirit of action and lifestyle sports in a format that could generate revenues to support elite athletes as well as media coverage to grow the sports. Similarly, Terje Haakonsen and other snowboarders created 'Ticket To Ride' (www.ttrworldtour.com/) in 2002 – a series of rider-controlled events designed to preserve the ethos of their sports through 'a movement

'I love the X Games ... because they're all about ... freedom and individual expression.'
Cartoon 14.1 Some athletes in alternative sports are uneasy about what happens when their sports become commercialized and represented in terms that fit the interests of sponsors

connected to the core of snowboarding's identity [and an emphasis on a] sense of fun and friendship, the appreciation of nature, the travel and the unique experiences, the freedom and creativity'. The challenge for these sports today is to resist those who want to align with corporate sponsors and incorporate into their activities more power and performance elements that will attract mass audiences.

People with a physical or intellectual disability have developed alternative sports and adapted dominant sports to fit their interests and needs. Although some of these sports emphasize power and performance, others emphasize pleasure and participation. Concern and support for teammates and opponents, as well as inclusiveness related to physical abilities, characterize these latter sports.

When people with a disability participate with able-bodied people in sports organized around a power and performance model, it presents an opportunity for all athletes, regardless of age or ability, to deal with the reality that human relationships always involve accommodating difference and uniqueness. Dealing with this reality requires making a choice: maintain power and performance sports as they are and marginalize those with a disability or revise them with features from the pleasure and performance model to be inclusive. It is difficult to predict how people in different situations and at different points in their lives will handle this choice, but it is certain that their decisions will create at least part of sports' future.

Athletes with a disability will participate in sports in greater numbers. Creatively designed equipment will permit new forms of sports involvement for both the able-bodied and the disabled, as shown in this photo of trail riders (*Source:* Rob Schoenbaum)

The Gay Games, the World Outgames and the EuroGames provide additional examples of alternative sport forms emphasizing participation, support, inclusiveness and the enjoyment of physical movement. The seventh quadrennial Gay Games in Chicago and the First World Outgames in Montreal each drew over 10 000 athletes in 2006, and the EuroGames draws nearly 3000 athletes to its annual event. Participants include lesbians, gay men, bisexuals and transsexuals (LGBTs) in sports emphasizing inclusion and other aspects of the pleasure and participation model. Lesbians, gay men, bisexuals and transsexuals also organize sports at the community level to provide experiences free of the homophobia that can destroy enjoyment in other sports (Ravel and Rail, 2007).

The range of sports that incorporate elements of the pleasure and participation model will grow if more people realize that sports are social constructions that can be created to fit even temporary interests and passing situations. Although it often is a challenge to find corporate sponsors, forms of pleasure and participation sports usually survive because people are creative enough to find the resources to maintain them. Furthermore, corporate or media sponsors are needed only when a sport hires administrators, focuses on national and international tournaments, and requires equipment and travel expenses. When a sport is done simply for pleasure and participation, the primary resource needed is people wishing to play it. This resource has existed through human history.

Trends in sport spheres

Predicting the future is less important than knowing about current trends and using that knowledge to participate in creating the future. For instance, some people study trends so that they can more effectively plan strategies to create sports that are humane, accessible, inclusive and democratically organized. Others have different goals, but in any case, our knowledge of current trends in various sports spheres is useful. If the result is *multiple futures*, that is ideal.

Professional sports

Current trends in professional sports involve the following:

- profit-driven national and global expansion
- staging expensive total entertainment events
- building facilities designed as hospitality and leisure venues
- contentious negotiations between players and owners over working conditions.

Although people think they have little control over these trends, most professional sports exist in democratic societies where citizens have some influence on the use of public funds to build sports stadiums and arenas. They also elect political representatives who determine the legal environment in which businesses, including professional sports, operate. This means that people could organize and pressure local legislators to impose ceilings on prices to use facilities built with public money. Legislators could also mandate that a lottery be used to sell tickets to major events, as has been the case at the Wimbledon tennis championships in recent years, rather than letting corporations buy all the good seats and run up prices. If people learn to act as citizens before professional leagues and team owners convert them into consumers, they will create futures more in line with their interests and resources.

Youth sports

Current trends in organized youth sports involve the following:

- declining public programmes due to government cuts that create local budget crises
- increased privatization favouring people who can pay club and facility fees
- struggles over gender equity
- increasing elitism favouring skilled and highly specialized athletes
- fewer opportunities for children in low-income families and communities
- more children seeking alternatives to adult-controlled organized sports.

These trends mimic trends in society as a whole. As ideology emphasizes individualism and a form of 'family values' that calls for every family to provide for itself, those who have resources will use them to create playgrounds in their fenced gardens and to buy access to private programmes and facilities for their sports. They do not need public parks or publicly funded programmes and seldom vote to support them. As a result, public services, including sports and parks, are cut back or eliminated. The future of youth sports will involve escalating social-class divisions unless people decide they want something different. Debates about the meaning, purpose and organization of school sports often are also contentious, and this has impacted on the curriculum, delivery of school sports to male and female students, and relationships between schools, clubs and national governing bodies (NGBs) of sports. Decisions similar to this will determine many aspects of our collective futures, not just youth sports.

Sports for people with a disability

Current trends in sports for people with a disability involve the following:

- increasing numbers of people disabled by war, land mines, lack of medical care and poverty
- increasing numbers of people living longer, with age-related disabilities
- increasing recognition that people with a disability want to play sports and have a right to do so
- continuing use of sports participation as therapy
- more visible examples of sports for elite athletes with a disability
- new technologies that facilitate sport participation
- emerging ideas, vocabularies and orientations that support people with a disability and their participation in sports.

There is a growing popular awareness that disability is multifaceted and more common than previously recognized. As a result, emerging ideas, vocabularies and orientations are supportive of opportunities for people with a disability to play sports. The use of the medical model that encouraged people to seek technical or medical 'fixes' and 'cures' for disability is slowly giving way to a social model recognizing that impairments are a normal part of the human condition and that there is a need for changes that increase access to sports participation across all ability levels (Howe, 2008; Nixon, 2007). This change of thinking is leading more people to view ability

breaking BARRIERS

Vision barriers: *I have to believe*

When Ben Quilter was 7 years old, he took up judo in order to take part in the same sport as his brother. By the time he was 12 he was competing in national and regional competitions. Between the ages of 12 to 15, Ben's eyesight had deteriorated sufficiently that at the age of 16 he was categorized as a visually impaired competitor. The rules of judo are adapted for visually impaired participants so that they start bouts 'gripped up', and there are some changes to the judo ring. However, Ben explains that these changes are sufficiently minor for visually impaired and sighted athletes to train and compete with each other. In addition, the organization and funding of judo is similar for sighted and visually impaired participants. In 2008, Ben was selected for the Paralympic Team for the Beijing Games, and the team was announced at the same press launch as the judo team for the Olympic Games. As Ben says, in judo, 'Everything's the same, just train full time with the guys, I'm treated like everyone else really, you wouldn't even know that I had a visual problem.'

Ben's experience of judo is an example of how sports can be organized so that people with disabilities feel that they are treated on equal terms. The Disability Sports Events (DSE) was established in 1961 to enable competitions in a range of sports between people with any impairment at any age. In 2008, DSE hosted the twenty-fifth 'mini games' multi-sport event for children aged between 6 and 12 years old. The event includes a series of inclusive sports and games to try to encourage more young disabled people to become involved in sports. Able-bodied young people and volunteers are available

Ben Quilter represented Great Britain in the 2008 Paralympic Games in judo, achieving fourth place in his category. He is photographed here as a sports celebrity promoting sports for 'more people', regardless of ability or disability, as the UK prepares for the 2012 Olympic and Paralympic Games in London (*Source*: Elizabeth Pike)

to assist players if the need arises. One of the sports included is zonal tag rugby, which is an adapted form of the game of rugby to enable participants with different levels of (dis)ability to participate and compete in a safe and challenging sporting competition. However, the organization does not receive any government funding, and relies on fund-raising and sponsorship.

The kind of idealism seen in judo and the DSE events is heartening to those who know a disabled child who cannot play in some existing sports schemes because these are not appropriately adapted or inclusive. It is also heartening to the thousands of veterans returning from Iraq and Afghanistan with amputated limbs, sight and hearing impairments, and injuries that impair walking. Making sports accessible to them would seem to require little imagination, even among those who lack idealism. As veterans return to communities, universities, gyms, parks and workplaces, idealism is essential if barriers are to be broken.

Jayne Craike, who competes on the New Zealand Equestrian Federation national dressage circuit and represents her country in the Paralympics, encourages people to be idealistic as they envision and work to create the future. She says, '*I have to believe* that there is still more to come in a world that is continually changing, and that we can make a difference' (Joukowsky and Rothstein, 2002b, p. 55, emphasis added; see also, www.lupus.org.nz/PersonalExperiences.htm). Craike knows that sports are more than therapeutic tools for people with (dis)abilities. In cultures where sports participation is highly valued, they are normalizing activities; they enable people to establish important identities; and they are sites for meeting others and forcing everyone who watches to acknowledge that (dis)abilities are a normal part of the human condition. It may be idealistic to envision and work for universal accessibility, but who wants to settle for the alternative?

in terms of a continuum rather than simply reducing it to the two mutually exclusive categories of able-bodied and disabled. As more people think this way, many futures become possible, as illustrated in the 'Breaking barriers' box, above.

Spectators and spectator sports

Current trends related to spectators and spectator sports involve the following:

- continuing commitment to watching sports as a central leisure activity
- increasing use of the Internet and other technologies that provide spectator experiences
- defining spectators as consumers who are receptive to advertising messages.

Spectator sports are deeply embedded in many cultures. However, people can decide how much they will pay in terms of money, time and effort to be spectators; what meanings they will give to their experiences; and how they will integrate those experiences into their lives. They also can envision futures that deviate from those envisioned by corporate sponsors and media executives. For example, if people voted to bring free or low-cost wireless (Wi-Fi) Internet access to their communities, the future would involve incredibly diverse spectator experiences. But if people allow giant cable and telecommunications corporations to control the conditions of broadband access, their futures as spectators will be limited and expensive. Imagine futures in which broadband access is publicly provided like other essential services, such as roads and schools, and is available to people worldwide. This future is much more feasible than building roads worldwide, and as more people share this vision, spectator sports will change dramatically.

Factors Influencing Trends Today

When creating futures it is useful to know about factors that influence current trends. This enables us to anticipate possibilities, avoid resistance and make more informed decisions as we participate in social worlds.

Many factors influence trends in sports, but the discussion here is limited to five: technology, telecommunications and electronic media, a widespread commitment to organization and rationalization, a cultural emphasis on commercialism and consumption, and the demographic characteristics of communities and societies.

Technology

Technology is the *application of scientific or other organized knowledge to solve problems, expand experiences or alter the conditions of reality*. It is used to make sports safer, detect and treat injuries more effectively, assess physical limits and potential, expand the experiences available in sports, train bodies to perform more efficiently, provide athletes with more control of their bodies, increase the speeds at which bodies move, decrease the risks involved in sports, enhance the size and strength of bodies, alter bodies to match the demands of particular sports, identify rule infractions and enforce rules more accurately, measure and compare performances with precision, and improve the durability and functionality of equipment (Assael, 2007c; Atkinson, 2007; Dimeo, 2007; Pennington, 2007; Yessis, 2006).

The major issue related to technology is when and how to use and regulate it. The governing bodies of sports try to regulate the technologies used by coaches, officials, trainers and athletes, but the rapid expansion of new technologies makes this difficult. Assessing the full implications of particular technologies is not easy (Crouse, 2008; Magdalinski, 2008). Consistent and sensible decisions about them are made only when we know what we want sports to be in the future. Consider genetic-enhancement technologies. They can be used to improve human performance, heal injured bodies and correct certain physical impairments. If we want to create a future in which sports are organized around the power and performance model, the framework and criteria for assessing genetic enhancement would be different from the way they would be if we want sports organized around a pleasure and participation model. This is why it is important to have a clear sense of the place of sports in society and the purpose we want sports to serve in our lives and the world as a whole.

> The use of drugs, and, perhaps more startling, the engineering of genes to enhance performance, raises questions about the notion of what an athlete is.

(Richard Sandomir, journalist, 2002)

Telecommunications and electronic media

Television, computers, the Internet, mobile phones and other handheld devices are technologies with implications for sports. Television and the Internet, for instance, provide visual images and narratives that many people use to imagine future possibilities for sports; the same is true for video games. Some people even use electronic images to inform their choices about participation and formulate standards for assessing sports experiences. Therefore, media producers worldwide have considerable power to create the future. The events, athletes and stories represented in the media influence popular discourse about sports, and it is out of that discourse that people form their ideas about what sports could and should be in the future.

To understand this process, imagine that football was the only sport you ever saw on television. You would have a seriously limited sense of what sports are and what they could be. A version of this occurs as media companies select for coverage only those sports that generate profits on commercial television. As a result, those are the sports that dominate popular discourse and influence what we envision for the future. For example, when the media do not cover women's sports, people are less likely to talk about them, learn about the athletes and teams, and incorporate them into the experiences they use to envision the future.

If we realize this, we can seek images and narratives about sports that are not represented exclusively through commercial media. This expands our experience and enables us to think more creatively about the present and future. The more versions of sports we see and talk about, the more we can create futures to match our interests and circumstances.

Organization and rationalization

All sports contain the element of play. But sports today focus so much on purpose, planning and productivity that play has been pushed to the sidelines. 'Fun' in organized, purpose-driven sports is associated with achieving goals rather than emotional expression and joy. Process is now secondary to product, and the journey is secondary to the destination.

People in post-industrial societies live with the legacy of industrialization. They emphasize organization according to rational principles based, whenever possible, on systematic research.

The future of sports is difficult to predict. Will children prefer video games and virtual sports over the dominant sport forms of today? (*Source*: Elizabeth Pike)

Being organized and making plans to accomplish goals is so important that spontaneity, expression, creativity and joy – the elements of play – are given low priority or may even be considered frivolous by event planners, coaches and spectators. This is why legendary snowboarder Terje Haakonsen decided against participating in the Olympics, because he felt that it was a form of sport in which organization and rationalization had subverted play. His thoughts about this are summarized in his description of snowboarding:

> That was a fun time … I was always learning new tricks, figuring out ways to get better. When I'm having fun snowboarding, it's like meditation. I'm not thinking about anything but what I'm doing right now. No past, no future … [But today, too many] people get stuck and all they do the whole year is pipe, and that's too bad for them. They do the same routine over and over, get the moves down. It becomes like this really precise, synchronised movement, like they're little balle-rinas or something. It's no longer this spontaneous sport, like when you're a kid screwing around.
>
> *(In Greenfeld, 1999)*

Haakonsen felt that fun and effort merge together in sports when they are done on terms set by participants; this merger breaks down when sports are done for judges using criteria that ignore the subjective experience of participation.

When we are creating sports, these are important things to keep in mind because there is a tendency in post-industrial cultures to organize them so that they make sense for the purposes of rationally assessing skills and performances. Working to improve physical skills so we can expand possibilities for new experiences is one thing, but spending years perfecting a specialized skill to conform to someone else's idea of technical perfection is another. Once we 'feel' this distinction in our own sport participation, we become more creative when thinking about the future.

Commercialism and consumption

Many people today are so deeply embedded in commercial culture that they think of themselves as customers instead of citizens. This changes the basis for evaluating self, others and experi-ences. When commercial ideology pervades sports, play becomes secondary to play-offs and pay-offs; games, athletes and sports participation itself become commodities – things bought and sold for bottom-line purposes. Participation then revolves around the consumption of equipment, lessons, clothing, nutritional supplements, gym and club memberships and other material things. Status is based on where you do sports, the equipment that you use and the clothing that you wear – not the joy of playing.

Many people are turned off by this approach, but unless they have experienced alternatives, it may be difficult to envision sports devoid of commercialism and consumption. This is why it is important to have public spaces where people can play sports that do not require fees, permits or memberships (Bale and Vertinsky, 2004). Creativity thrives in such spaces. In this sense, public policies at all levels of government can create or subvert possibilities for non-commercial sports futures.

Trying to improve skills on your own terms is different from doing a routine over and over to meet someone else's idea of technical perfection. Once we 'feel' this distinction in our own sport participation, we become much more creative as we think of how to do sports and incorporate them into our lives (*Source*: McGraw-Hill)

Demographic characteristics of communities and societies

Sports are social constructions, and some of the richest sport environments are those in which people have diverse cultural backgrounds and sports experiences. Even when people play the same sport, strategies and styles often vary with their cultural backgrounds. For example, the English sport of rugby was adapted by people in the USA to fit their preferences; the result was American football, a game that is relatively unique in the world (Riesman and Denny, 1951). In 2008, the Indian Premier League for cricket was established, surrounded by an exuberant 'Bollywood'-style culture which underpinned the media coverage, the cheerleaders, the advertising and the style of play – markedly different to the traditional English colonial game which is played on village greens and stops for afternoon tea.

Although demographic diversity presents challenges, it also presents possibilities for creating new forms and versions of sports. As geographical mobility, labour migration and political turmoil push and pull together people from diverse backgrounds, there will be many opportunities to borrow and blend different sports, styles of play and game strategies. If people take advantage of those opportunities without systematically privileging games from one culture and marginalizing games from other cultures, it will be possible to envision and create sports that fit a wide range of interests and abilities.

At the same time that global blending occurs, there will be increased divisions between people from different social classes and certain racial and ethnic groups within societies where inequalities are great. As a result, people from certain ethnic minorities will play only a few sports, whereas those in the dominant population will have diverse opportunities to play sports and develop skills.

Envisioning Possibilities and Creating Futures

Robert Davies, chief executive of the International Business Leaders Forum, an organization dedicated to promoting global social responsibility, tells corporate leaders worldwide that the visibility and popularity of sports at the local and global levels provides opportunities to improve health, develop communities, boost education and literacy, and empower girls and women. He says that 'the power and influence of sport is only just being understood' by people concerned with social responsibility (Davies, 2002a). He also told an international assembly of journalists and media representatives that 'high profile global sporting events are seen as a frontier for raising issues of injustice and social responsibility' and that the media have a responsibility to explore that frontier (Davies, 2002b).

As Davies thinks about the future from the perspective of corporate social responsibility, he sees possibilities for changing sports and using them to facilitate changes beyond playing fields and changing rooms. Other perspectives alert us to even more possibilities. To assess them and work to convert selected possibilities into realities, there is a need to understand connections between sports and the rest of the world. This is why social theories are especially useful; they provide frameworks to identify and explain those connections. This, in turn, enables people to develop focused and consistent strategies for creating the future.

Using social theories to create futures

Each of the theories discussed in Chapter 2 provides a different perspective for understanding connections between sports and social worlds, identifying problems and selecting approaches to create sports in terms of their anticipated consequences in people's lives. The following sections provide only brief summaries of how those theories may be used for these purposes.

Functionalist theory

Functionalist theory continues to be used to envision sports in the future. For example, when Robert Davies talks to corporate leaders, he bases many of his ideas on a functionalist approach. This appeals to those leaders and to others with power and influence because such an approach takes the existing social system for granted and explains how sports help to preserve and improve that system. A functionalist approach to the future emphasizes that existing sport forms should be supported and maintained through the use of conservative and reformist strategies.

A **conservative strategy** is *based on the belief that sports reaffirm traditional values and established forms of social organization, and therefore should be strengthened and expanded rather than transformed.* The focus is on management issues designed to make sports and sports organizations more efficient while maintaining the culture and structure of sports as they are. Conservative strategies are very common in sports because few people view sports in critical terms and because the people who control sports and have the resources to influence them in the future are advocates of growth, not social and cultural transformation.

A **reformist strategy** is *based on a similar belief about the merits of sports, but it focuses on eliminating problems, promoting fairness, controlling cheating and drug use, urging athletes to be* *positive role models and making sports organizations more efficient.* In this way, more people will have access to sports participation and experience its benefits. In other words, eliminate problems but keep the culture and structure of sports as they are. For example, women, people with disabilities, and others who have lived on the margins of mainstream sports and wish to be included in existing structures, programmes and organizations frequently use reformist strategies. Reformers focus mostly on issues such as equality of opportunity and social justice.

The Women's Sport and Fitness Foundation (WSFF) in the UK is an example of an organization that often uses reformist strategies based on a functionalist approach. The WSFF lobbies for gender equity so that girls and women have equal opportunities to participate in sports, and it calls attention to the need for more women in decision-making positions in existing sports organizations. Because the WSFF is a charity which depends on members and some support from Sport England and its sponsors, it is very careful when it uses more radical strategies based on critical and feminist theories. It does not want to alienate the majority of their supporters who favour a functionalist approach and want sports to be maintained much the way they are today.

Conflict theory

Conflict theory is seldom used when British people think about sports and society. Although some intellectually orientated people today think that it is fashionable to discuss injustices related to race and gender, discussion of injustices related to social class and class relations can make them uncomfortable (hooks, 2000). Conflict theory, with its explicit focus on social class, challenges the very ideologies on which their class privilege rests and forces them to think about problems inherent in a capitalist economy that survives on profits made by paying workers as little as possible.

Conflict theory focuses attention on class relations in sports and the ways that sports are used to preserve and disguise basic social-class divisions in society. People using conflict theory to create sports adopt a particular form of **radical strategy** in *which the goal is to transform the economic organization of society so that class differences fade away.* This would make possible forms of sport in which there are no constraints on freedom, creativity and enjoyment. The profit motive would be gone, so there would be no reason to exploit or oppress people.

Nearly everyone who uses conflict theory in the UK understands that eliminating capitalism is unrealistic at this point in history. Therefore, they favour specific strategies through which citizens, athletes and spectators organize themselves and challenge those who have used wealth and economic power to shape sports in ways that maintain their privilege. Over the past half century, people using conflict theory have worked with like-minded reformers and people using other radical strategies to reduce racism, sexism, nationalism and militarism in sports.

Outside the UK, conflict theory remains popular among many people. In cultures where people are less devoted to consumption as a form of status expression, class-related and economic ideologies are more open and widely discussed. This makes them more sensitive to the social and political implications of extreme gaps between the very wealthy and powerful and everyone else. It also makes them less resistant to using conflict theory to envision possibilities that do not depend on commercialism and the use of large amounts of capital.

Critical theory

People who use critical theory are concerned with the processes through which culture is produced, reproduced and changed. Therefore, they focus their attention on issues related to ideologies, representation and power in society. They are especially interested in the ways that people use power to maintain cultural practices and social structures that represent their interests and the ways that people resist or oppose those practices and structures.

Critical theory helps people envision possibilities for sports that are free of exploitation and oppression; organized to be inclusive in connection with age, gender, race, ethnicity, religion and (dis)ability; and used to empower people to participate actively in the social worlds in which they live. Reformist and radical strategies are used because the goal is to transform sports so that a diverse range of participation opportunities is available to all people. For example, radical strategies are used to disrupt and transform the structure and dynamics of social relations related to gender, race, class, sexuality and (dis)ability so that previously marginalized or under-represented categories of people have equal opportunities to create and participate in sports that fit their interests and needs.

The radical strategies favoured by people using critical theory emphasize eliminating inequities, creating democratic forms of participation and making ideological and structural changes in sports and society as a whole. These strategies usually involve efforts to redistribute power and give voice to previously disenfranchised segments of the population in social worlds.

Motorized sports impact the environment and the experiences of hikers, cross-country skiers and other wilderness users. As more people incorporate technology into their sports and leisure, critical theories provide a useful basis for asking questions and doing research on these issues (*Source*: Jay Coakley)

People with power and wealth usually strongly oppose radical strategies because they are designed to transform the ideas, beliefs and forms of social organization on which their power and wealth depend. Privileged people dislike radicals because privilege depends on preserving the ideologies that legitimize elitist lifestyles and maintain the structures through which power is exercised over others. Their success in opposing radical strategies depends primarily on convincing most other people in society that the current, dominant ways of thinking and doing things are natural, normal and supportive of everyone's interests in society. This is a primary reason why radical strategies are seldom used in sports; they are very risky because those who use them become targets of those who have power and influence in society. Furthermore, most people who favour radical strategies dedicate all their attention and resources to issues of poverty, homelessness, universal healthcare, quality education for children, accessible public transportation, full employment and guaranteed minimum standards of living. However, a few radicals who are concerned with ideological issues have used sports as sites for the following purposes: challenging dominant definitions of masculinity and femininity, raising questions about the meaning of race, highlighting the difficulties of preserving democracy in the face of a growing gap between the haves and have-nots in society, destroying long-held stereotypes about (dis)abilities, and encouraging people to think critically about the anti-democratic features of the exclusive and hierarchical structures that characterize most organized sports today.

Critical feminist theory

People who use critical feminist theory are concerned with gender, gender relations and gender ideology. They see sports as sites where dominant forms of masculinity and femininity may be reproduced or transformed. Therefore, much of their attention is focused on struggles over gender equity and issues related to changing sports.

Critical feminist theory focuses on transforming sports and gender ideology so that women are not systematically disadvantaged. It helps people envision what sports could be if there were no sexism, misogyny, heterosexism or homophobia. People guided by critical feminist theory use reformist and radical strategies – reformist strategies to promote equity, and radical strategies to resist and transform the dominant gender ideology, which privileges men and gives high priority to all sports based on the values and experiences of men, especially those in positions of power. Both strategies are used to push the boundaries of gender and expand accepted ways of 'doing gender' in sports and everyday life.

The International Working Group on Women and Sport (IWG) is grounded primarily in critical feminist theory. Its members around the world use many strategies, including radical strategies aimed at changing ideologies and institutions that systematically exclude women from sports and disadvantage women when they do play sports. Strategies vary from nation to nation because the problems faced by women are different in various societies (Hargreaves, 2000). The IWG uses reformist strategies to increase opportunities for girls and women to play sports and to advance women into positions of power in society and in sports organizations. Radical strategies are used to transform the gender ideologies on which male privilege is based and female disadvantage is guaranteed in many cultures around the world.

Interactionist theory

When people use interactionist theory, they focus on social processes through which social worlds are created. They view those worlds, including the ones created around sports, through the eyes of the participants themselves. They assume that socialization occurs in and through sports experiences, that people give meaning to sports and sports participation as they interact with each other, and that people form identities as they integrate their experiences into their sense of who they are and how they are connected with the rest of the world.

Interactionists view the future in terms of the possibilities for social interaction associated with sports. They may use *conservative*, *reformist* or *radical* strategies to facilitate the creation of sports in which participants have representative control over the meaning, purpose and organization of the sports they play. For example, reformist or radical approaches have been used to create sports and sports organizations that are democratic and inclusive (Birrell, 2000; Donnelly and Coakley, 2003). As this has been done, ideas have often been borrowed from other theories, especially critical and critical feminist theories.

reflect on SPORTS   *Athletes as change agents: does it happen?*

Athletes are visible and popular. Some have the highest name and face recognition of any human beings in history. This puts them in good positions to be change agents in society – or does it?

The visibility and popularity of athletes depends heavily on media coverage and overall public image. Teams and corporations use athletes' images to promote events and products, but this does not mean that athletes can readily convert their celebrity status into power related to serious social, political or economic issues.

The 'context of sport celebrity' limits the extent to which athletes can be effective agents of change. If their words and actions do not match the interests of those who control their images, they risk losing the coverage and support that sustains their visibility and popularity. Team owners and corporate sponsors shy away from players who speak out on social issues; owners do not want to anger fans and corporations do not want to anger consumers.

When Tiger Woods was selected by *Time* magazine as one of 'the 25 most influential Americans' in 1997, he was widely condemned for saying that 'Golf has shied away from [racism] for too long, [and] I hope ... [to] change that' (*Time*, 1997). His influence, he discovered, was limited to selling clothes and golf balls, not changing golf clubs run by powerful white men. Since 1997, Woods has supported only conservative approaches to change, if he talks about change at all. It is not surprising that athletes use conservative strategies based on a functionalist approach when they become involved in their communities. They focus on reaffirming dominant societal values and strengthening the status quo by building playgrounds, visiting children in hospitals, promoting literacy and delivering anti-drug messages in schools. Even when retired athletes enter politics, they generally represent conservative political positions aligned with preserving the status quo. If athletes in the UK used reformist or radical strategies based on critical or feminist theories, the British media would discredit and marginalize them, and their careers would be in jeopardy.

In 2008, the British Olympic Association tried to go a stage further by drafting a contract which banned all competitors going to the Beijing Olympics from commenting on any politically sensitive issues in China. It was forced to withdraw this after a backlash from athletes. Richard Vaughan, a British badminton player who signed a petition condemning China's inadequate response to the crisis in Darfur, said:

> Trying to bully athletes into not saying things is not the right way. It's very tough to keep a polite silence about a conflict that continues to cost so many lives.

(In Syed, 2008)

The most effective way for athletes to be agents of change is to work in or through established groups and organizations. For example, Surfers Against Sewage (SAS) started as a small campaign to improve the quality of water around the British coastline. This has now developed into an organized group, supported by professional surfers including Gary Elkerton, Rob Machado and Taylor Knox, and some high-profile sponsors. Surfers Against Sewage has pressured politicians, the Environment Agency, the House of Lords and even the European Parliament. This campaign has been effective in making improvements to the environment for cleaner, safer water and the reduction of sewage, chemicals and marine litter in recreational areas. It has demonstrated that athletes can be agents of change when they are part of an established and respected group that has resources to achieve goals.

However, recent history shows that even suggesting the need for ideological or structural changes can create problems for athletes. When Cassius Clay (Muhammad Ali) spoke against racism during the 1960s and, as a Muslim, refused induction in the military during the Vietnam War, he was stripped of his boxing title and sentenced to five years in prison. When 400-metre champions Tommy Smith and

Tommy Smith and John Carlos used this gesture to protest against global poverty and racism in the USA during the 1968 Olympics. As soon as the anthem was over, they were expelled from the Olympic village, sent back to the USA in disgrace, and widely condemned and rejected for over two decades. Then, in 2005, they received honorary doctorates from San Jose State University in the USA where a 23-foot-high statue was being built to commemorate what people now define as their courageous actions on the podium over a generation ago (*Source*: AP/Wide World Photos)

John Carlos protested racism and global poverty on the victory podium during the 1968 Olympics in Mexico City, they encountered over 20 years of contempt and rejection in the USA. Is this why athletes today choose to act as corporate plants instead of agents of change? *What do you think*?

Vantage points for creating futures

Creating futures is a never-ending process. Being an active agent in this process is always challenging, regularly frustrating, and sometimes rewarding. For those interested in creating futures related to sports and social life, strategies can be initiated from four vantage points (Hall et al., 1991).

1 *Work within the system of sports.* You can become involved in sports and sports organizations and then use your position or power to influence and initiate changes. Having an 'insider' vantage point can be very effective; sometimes, you can even use it to promote changes in society as a whole. However, becoming an insider often involves adopting the existing values and culture of the organization where you work. This means that, even though you may favour certain reforms or transformations, your commitment to actively promoting change may decrease as you move up the organization into positions of power. Once you reach a position that enables you to make changes, you often develop an interest in keeping things as they are and using a conservative strategy to slowly make things bigger and more efficient. This is not inevitable, but it is customary. Although an insider vantage point can be a good place from which to create futures, it is important to be realistic about what insiders can do. This is highlighted when we consider athletes as change agents. This issue is discussed in the box 'Athletes as change agents', above.

2 *Join 'opposition' groups.* You can become a change agent by forming or joining political groups that challenge unjust or exploitive sport policies and put pressure on sports organizations that have such policies and programmes. For example, opposition groups would lobby for the building of a community sports centre in a low-income neighbourhood or lobby against using public funds to build a stadium that would serve primarily the interests of already privileged people in a community. Opposition groups would apply pressure so that there would be a mandate to build low-cost housing and dedicate funds to economic development in low-income neighbourhoods in connection with hosting a major sports event, such as the Olympics. The possibilities for opposition are many.

3 *Create alternative sports.* You can reject or ignore dominant power and performance sports, and the organizations that sponsor them, and develop new sports grounded in the values and experiences of a wide array of different groups of people. This is often difficult because resources are seldom available when you choose this vantage point for making change. However, working from this vantage point can be effective even when it does not lead to concrete institutionalized changes because it provides clear-cut examples of new ways to look at and play sports, as well as new ways to look at and interact with other people. These examples then may inspire others to envision how they can create alternative sports in their own lives and communities. Former Olympian and current health and physical educator Bruce Kidd reminds us, 'The effort to create alternatives to the commercial sport culture will continue to be an uphill fight. But such alternatives do exist. They have a long, rich, and proud history' (1997, p. 270).

4 *Focus on transforming culture and social relations.* You can ignore sports and work directly on producing changes in the ideologies and social structures that support and legitimize the current organization of sports in society. For example, the Child Protection in Sport Unit has been working to lower abusive practices in sports in the UK by bringing pressure on other sports organizations to support policies that increase awareness of the problem and encourage progressive changes in coach–athlete relations.

Regardless of one's vantage point, being an effective agent of change always requires the following qualities:

1 visions of what sports and social life *could* and *should* be like
2 willingness to work hard on the strategies needed to turn visions into realities
3 political abilities to rally the resources that make strategies effective.

Bringing these qualities together requires individual and collective efforts. But unless we make these efforts, the meaning, purpose and organization of sports will be created for us by others, and the future is unlikely to match our visions of what sports should be.

Summary: What Can We Create?

Sports are social constructions. This means that we play a role in making them what they are today and what they will be in the future. We can play this role actively by envisioning what we would like sports to be and then working to make them so, or we can play it passively by doing nothing and allowing others to create sports as they would like them to be.

This chapter emphasized that the meaning, purpose and organization of sports will become increasingly diverse in the future, and that power and performance sports will remain dominant because they continue to attract wealthy and powerful sponsors. Pleasure and participation sports will grow in connection with demographic trends and ideological changes, but they will not attract as much sponsorship as is enjoyed by sports organized around the power and performance model.

Sports at all levels of participation will be sites for struggles over who should play and how sports should be organized. Current trends suggest that pleasure and participation sports are supported by concerns about health and fitness, the participation preferences of older people whose influence will increase in the future, the values and experiences brought to sports by women, and groups seeking alternative sports.

In all sport spheres, trends are influenced by many factors, including technology, telecommunications and electronic media, values supportive of organization and rationalization, a cultural emphasis on commercialism and consumption, and the demographic characteristics of communities and societies.

Futures come to be as people envision possibilities for what sports could and should be. Social theories are important in this process because they explain the connections between sports and social worlds, identify problems and help in the selection of strategies to turn visions of the future into realities.

Most people, especially those who are advantaged by the status quo, do not want to change sports as much as they want to expand and make them more efficient. This conservative strategy fits with the assumptions and goals of functionalist theory. Reformist and radical strategies are more apt to be inspired by conflict theory and combinations of interactionist, critical and critical feminist theories.

The effectiveness of people who want to be agents of change requires a clear understanding of the vantage point they occupy in the relationship between sports and society. The four major vantage points are in (1) sport organizations, (2) opposition groups, (3) groups that create new and alternative sport forms, and (4) groups working to transform the larger society in ways that will change in sports.

Regardless of one's vantage point, effectively creating the future depends on having a clear vision of what sports could and should be in the future, a willingness to work hard to turn visions into realities, and the political abilities to initiate and maintain strategies that produce results. Unless we work to create the sports we want in the future, sports will represent the interests of those who want us to play on their terms and for their purposes.

This leaves us with an interesting choice: we can be consumers who accept sports as they are, or we can be citizens who actively engage in the process of making the world and sports humane and sustainable. The goal of this book is to provide a foundation for informed and active citizenship.

Website resources

Note: Websites often change. The following URLs were current when this book was printed. Please check our website (***www.mcgraw-hill.co.uk/textbooks/coakley***) for updates and additions.

See the OLC, ***www.mcgraw-hill.co.uk/textbooks/coakley***, for an annotated list of readings related to this chapter.

www.mcgraw-hill.co.uk/textbooks/coakley Click on Chapter 14 to read information on the impact of technology on sports and athletes.

www.AforBW.org The site of Athletes for a Better World, an organization that now focuses primarily on self-change and making sports more ethical rather than on changing communities; there are no specific statements about the types of 'difference' athletes can or should make, other than just making things better.

www.bmxweb.com/ This site contains links to hundreds of sites used by BMX bikers; illustrates that athletes in the future will be able to form networks with fellow athletes around the world.

www.educatingforjustice.org This site was originally the home of the Olympic Living Wage Project, part of an international effort to make athletes in the 2000 Olympic Games in Sydney aware of labour abuses related to the production of their equipment and uniforms; today it is a non-profit organization that presents justice-orientated programming and content for educational purposes and to raise awareness that sparks social change.

www.gaygames.com The site of the Federation of Gay Games; links to the history of the games, and what happened in Montreal at the 2006 Gay Games.

www.hotrails.com/ The key site for aggressive in-line skaters; provides a 'feel' for the sport, who participates and the norms underlying participation; note gender, racial/ethnic and social-class patterns among participants because they provide information about the social dynamics of certain alternative sports as they develop.

www.paralympic.org The official website of the International Paralympic Committee.

www.sas.org.uk This is the site of Surfers Against Sewage, a campaign to improve the quality of water around the UK coastline, offering educational resources, information on its campaign and successes, and details of its sponsors.

www.sportsphilanthropyproject.com/ This is the site of the Sports Philanthropy Project; provides services to professional sports teams to set up foundations in their communities to enhance social development and community programmes.

www.the-arctic-challenge.com/ The site for snowboarders who resist dominant sport forms; use the TTR link to see the pleasure and participation philosophy of this Norway-based group; the group works on environmental issues as well as organizing events that emphasize expression, spontaneity and creativity.

www.un.org/Depts/dhl/resguide/r58.htm This site has links to two UN Resolutions: 'Building a Peaceful and Better World Through Sport and the Olympic Ideal' (A/RES/58/6) and 'Sport as a Means to Promote Education, Health, Development and Peace' (A/RES/58/5).

www.un.org/sport2005/ The site of the UN International Year for Sport and Physical Education 2005; also a link to a Sport for Development and Peace report entitled, 'Sport as a tool for development and peace: towards achieving the United Nations Millennium Development Goals' (33 pages).

References

Adams, M. (2006) 'The game of whose lives? Gender, race and entitlement in Canada's "national" game', in *Artificial Ice: Hockey, Culture, and Commerce*, D. Whitson and R. Gruneau (eds), Broadview Press, Peterborough, Ontario.

Adbusters (2004) www.adbusters.org.

Adelson, E. (2003) 'Driven', *ESPN The Magazine*, 22 December, 70–71.

Adler, P. and P. Adler (1998) *Peer Power: Preadolescent Culture and Identity*, Rutgers University Press, New Brunswick, NJ.

Aldred, T. (2006) 'It's inequality, love', *Guardian*, 26 June.

Alexander, C. (1996) *The Art of Being Black: The Creation of Black British Youth Identity*, Clarendon, Oxford.

Allison, L. (2000) 'Sport and nationalism', in *Handbook of Sports Studies*, J. Coakley and E. Dunning (eds), Sage, London.

Allison, L. (2004) *The Global Politics of Sport: The Role of Global Institutions in Sport*, Routledge, London.

American Academy of Pediatrics (2000) 'Intensive training and sports specialization in young athletes', *Pediatrics*, 106, 154–157.

American Anthropological Association (AAA) (1998) 'Statement on "Race"', Washington, DC: American Anthropological Association, www.aaanet.org/stmts/racepp.htm.

Anderson, E. (2000) *Trailblazing: America's First Openly Gay Track Coach*, Alyson, Hollywood, CA.

Anderson, E. (2002) 'Gays in sport: contesting hegemonic masculinity in a homophobic environment', *Gender and Society*, 16 (6), 860–877.

Anderson, E. (2004) 'Exploitation of the scholarship athlete', unpublished manuscript.

Anderson, E. (2005) *In the Game: Gay Athletes and the Cult of Masculinity*, State University of New York Press, Albany, NY.

Anderson, J. (2005) 'Most dangerous game', www.eye.net/eye/issue/issue_04.21.05/film/murderball.html.

Anderson, K. (1999) 'Snowboarding: the construction of gender in an emerging sport', *Journal of Sport and Social Issues*, 23 (1), 55–79.

Anderson, S. and J. Cavanagh (2000) *The Top 200*, Institute for Policy Studies, Washington, DC.

Andersson, M. (2007) 'The relevance of the black Atlantic in contemporary sport: racial imaginaries in Norway'. *International Review for the Sociology of Sport*, 42 (1), 65–81.

Andrews, D. (1996a) 'The fact(s) of Michael Jordan's blackness: excavating a floating racial signifier', *Sociology of Sport Journal*, 13 (2), 125–158.

Andrews, D. (ed.) (1996b) 'Deconstructing Michael Jordan: reconstructing postindustrial America', *Sociology of Sport Journal*, 13 (3), special issue.

Andrews, D. (1998) 'Feminizing Olympic reality: preliminary dispatches from Baudrillard's Atlanta', *International Review for the Sociology of Sport*, 33 (1), 5–18.

Andrews, D. (ed.) (2001) *Michael Jordan, Inc.: Corporate Sport, Media Culture, and Late Modern America*, State University of New York Press, Albany, NY.

Andrews, D. (ed.) (2004), *Manchester United: A Thematic Study*, Routledge, London.

Andrews, D. (2007) 'Sport as spectacle', in *Encyclopedia of Sociology*, G. Ritzer (ed.), Blackwell, London.

Andrews, D. and S.J Jackson (2001) *Sport Stars: The Cultural Politics of Sporting Celebrity*, Routledge, London.

Ang, I. (1991) 'Stalking the wild viewer', *Continuum: The Australian Journal of Media and Culture*, 4, 19–25.

Anonymous (1999) 'Confessions of a cheater', *ESPN The Magazine*, 1 November, 80–82.

Armour, K. and R. Kirk (2008), 'Physical education and school sport', in *Sport and Society: A Student Introduction*, B. Houlihan (ed.), Sage, London.

Armstrong, G. (2006) 'Football hooliganism', in *Encyclopedia of Sociology*, G. Ritzer (ed.), Blackwell, London.

Armstrong, K. and N. Perry (2008a) 'Key UW linebacker played entire season after his bloody print was tied to shooting', *Seattle Times*, 30 January.

Armstrong, K. and N. Perry (2008b) 'To Huskies fans a tragic hero, to the courts a wanted felon', *Seattle Times*, 30 January.

Armstrong, K. and N. Perry (2008c) 'Convicted of assault and accused of rape, star player received raft of second chances', *Seattle Times*, 31 January.

Arsenault, A. and M. Castells (2008) 'Switching power: Rupert Murdoch and the global business of media politics – a sociological analysis', *International Sociology*, 23 (4), 488–513.

Assael, S. (2003) 'Cut and run', *ESPN The Magazine*, 7 July, 40–49.

Assael, S. (2005) 'Shape shifter', *ESPN The Magazine*, 9 May 9, 88–96.

Assael, S. (2007a) *Steroid Nation: Juiced Home Run Totals, Anti-aging Miracles, and a Hercules in Every High School: The Secret History of America's True Drug Addiction*, ESPN Books, New York.

Assael, S. (2007b) 'Made in China', *ESPN The Magazine*, 18 October, 90–95.

Assael, S. (2007c) 'Business as usual', *ESPN The Magazine*, 26 March, 99–100.

Atkinson, M. (2007) 'Playing with fire: masculinity, health, and sports supplements', *Sociology of Sport Journal*, 24 (3), 165–186.

Atkinson, M. and K. Young (2005) 'Reservoir dogs: greyhound racing, mimesis and sports-related violence', *International Review for the Sociology of Sport*, 40 (3), 335–356.

Back, L., T. Crabbe and J. Solomos (2001) *The Changing Face of Football: Racism, Identity and Multiculture in the English Game*, Berg, Oxford.

Baerg, A. (2007) 'Fight night round 2: mediating the body and digital boxing', *Sociology of Sport Journal*, 24 (3), 325–345.

Bairner, A. (2001) *Sport, Nationalism, and Globalization: European and North American Perspectives*, State University of New York Press, Albany, NY.

Bairner, A. (2003) 'Sport, nationality and postcolonialism in Ireland', in *Sport and Postcolonialism*, J. Bale and M. Cronin (eds), Berg, Oxford.

Bairner, A. (2004) 'Inclusive soccer – exclusive politics? Sports policy in Northern Ireland and the Good Friday Agreement', *Sociology of Sport Journal*, 21 (3), 270–286.

Bairner, A. (ed.) (2005) *Sport and the Irish: Histories, Identities, Issues*, UCD Press, Dublin.

Bairner, A. (2007) 'Back to basics: class, social theory, and sport', *Sociology of Sport Journal*, 24 (1), 20–36.

Baker, A. (2003) 'Laureus awards: angry Grey-Thompson misses trip', www.telegraph.co.uk, 20 May.

Baker, J. and J. Côté (2006) 'Shifting training requirements during athlete development: the relationship among deliberate practice, deliberate play and other sport involvement in the acquisition of sport expertise', in *Essential Processes for Attaining Peak Performance*, D. Hackfort and G. Tenenbaum (eds), Meyer and Meyer, Aachen.

Baker, W. (1988) *Sports in the Western World*, University of Illinois Press, Urbana, IL.

Bale, J. and M. Christensen (eds) (2004) *Post-Olympism: Questioning Sport in the Twenty-first Century*, Berg, Oxford.

Bale, J. and M. Cronin (eds) (2003) *Sport and Postcolonialism*, Berg, Oxford.

Bale, J. and J. Maguire (eds) (1994) *The Global Sports Arena: Athletic Talent Migration in an Interdependent World*, Frank Cass, London.

Bale, J. and P. Vertinsky (eds) (2004) *Sites of Sport: Space, Place and Experience*, Routledge, London.

Ballard, C. (2004) 'Fantasy world', *Sports Illustrated*, 21 June 21, 80–89.

Barnes, S. (2005) 'A memo to those running both rugby codes: if we want real war, we turn to the front of the paper, www.timesonline.co.uk, 18 November.

Barnes, S. (2006) 'Football destined to remain the last bastion of homophobia – that's the straight truth of it', www.timesonline.co.uk, 6 October.

BBC (2001) 'Aggression is all the rage', http://news.bbc.co.uk/sport1/hi/funnyoldgame/.

BBC Sport Academy (2005) 'What is wheelchair rugby', http://news.bbc.co.uk/sportacademy.

Beal, B. (1995) 'Disqualifying the official: an exploration of social resistance through the subculture of skateboarding', *Sociology of Sport Journal*, 12 (3), 252–267.

Beal, B. and L. Weidman (2003) 'Authenticity in the skateboarding world', in *To the Extreme: Alternative Sports, Inside and Out*, R. Rinehart and S. Sydnor (eds), State University of New York Press, Albany, NY.

Beal, C. (1994) *Boys and Girls: The Development of Gender Roles*, McGraw-Hill, New York.

Beals, K. (2000) 'Subclinical eating disorders in female athletes', *Journal of Physical Education, Recreation and Dance*, 71 (1), 3–29.

Beech, J. and Chadwick, S. (2004) *The Business of Sport Management*, Pearson Education, Harlow.

Beiruty, H. (2002), 'Muslim women in sport', *Nida'ul Islam Magazine*, www.islamzine.com/women/women-sports.html.

Bell, J. (2008) 'Making it to the major league of fantasy sports', *New York Times*, 5 April, online, www.nytimes.com/2008/04/05/technology/05interview-web.html.

Bell, W. (1997) 'The purpose of future studies', *The Futurist*, 1 November, 1–19.

Belson, M. (2002) 'Assistive technology and sports', in *Raising the Bar*, A. Joukowsky and L. Rothstein (eds), Umbrage Editions, New York.

Ben-Porat, G. and A. Ben-Porat (2004) '(Un)bounded soccer: globalization and localization of the game in Israel', *International Review for the Sociology of Sport*, 39 (4), 421–436.

Benedict, J. (1997) *Public Heroes, Private Felons: Athletes and Crimes against Women*, Northeastern University Press, Boston, MA.

Benedict, J. (1998) *Athletes and Acquaintance Rape*, Sage, London.

Benedict, J. (2004) *Out of Bounds: Inside the NBA's Culture of Rape, Violence, and Crime*, HarperCollins, New York.

Bernstein, A. and N. Blain (eds) (2003) *Sport, Media, Culture: Global and Local Dimensions*, Frank Cass, London.

Berra, L. (2005) 'This is how they roll', *ESPN The Magazine*, 5 December.

Bick, J. (2007) 'Looking for an edge? Private coaching, by the hour', *New York Times*, 25 February.

Bilger, B. (2004) 'The height gap', *New Yorker*, 5 April.

Birley, D. (1995) *Playing the Game: Sport and British Society, 1910–1945*, Manchester University Press, Manchester.

Birrell, S. (2000) 'Feminist theories for sport', in *Handbook of Sport and Society*, J. Coakley and E. Dunning (eds), Sage, London.

Bishop, R. (2003) 'Missing in action: feature coverage of women's sports in *Sports Illustrated*', *Journal of Sport and Social Issues*, 27 (2), 184–194.

Bjerklie, D. and A. Park (2004) 'How doctors help the dopers', *Time*, 16 August.

Blackshaw, T. and T. Crabbe (2004) *New Perspectives on Sport and 'Deviance': Consumption, Performativity and Social Control*, Routledge, London.

Blain, N., R. Boyle and H. O'Donnell (1993) *Sport and National Identity in the European Media*, Leicester University Press, Leicester.

Blake, A. (1996) *The Body Language: The Meaning of Modern Sport*, Lawrence and Wishart, London.

Blauvelt, H. (2003) 'Stephenson says Asian players hurt LPGA tour', *USA Today*, 10 October.

Block, M. (1995) 'Americans with Disability Act: its impact on youth sports', *Journal of Health, Physical Education, Recreation and Dance*, 66 (1), 28–32.

Bloom, B. (1985) *Developing Talent in Young People*, Ballantine Books, New York.

Bloom, M. (1998) 'Slower times at American high schools', *New York Times*, 29 January.

Bloyce, D. (2005) '"That's your way of playing rounders, isn't it"? The response of the English press to American baseball tours to England, 1874–1924', *Sporting Traditions*, 22 (1), 81–98.

Blumenthal, R. (2004) 'Texas tough, in lipstick, fishnet and skates', *New York Times*, 1 August.

BME Sports Network East (2005) *Increasing BME Participation in Sport and Physical Activity by Black and Minority Ethnic Communities*, Ploszajski Lynch Consulting Ltd, Bedford.

Bolin, A. (1998) 'Muscularity and femininity: women bodybuilders and women's bodies in culturo-historical context', in *Fitness as Cultural Phenomenon*, K. Volkwein (ed.), Waxmann, Munster.

Bolin, A. (2003) 'Beauty or the beast: the subversive soma', in *Athletic Intruders: Ethnographic Research on Women, Culture, and Exercise*, A. Bolin and J. Granskog (eds), State University of New York Press, Albany, NY.

Bonilla-Silva, E. (2001) *White Supremacy and Racism in the Post-Civil Rights Era*, Lynne Rienner, Boulder, CO.

Bonilla-Silva, E. (2003) *Racism without Racists: Color-blind Racism and the Persistence of Racial Inequality in the United States*, Rowman and Littlefield, Lanham, MD.

Booth, D. and J. Loy (1999) 'Sport, status and style', *Sport History Review*, 30 (1), 1–26.

Bourdieu, P. (1986a) 'The forms of capital', in *Handbook of Theory and Research for the Sociology of Education*, J.G. Richards (ed.), Greenwood Press, New York.

Bourdieu, P. (1986b) *Distinction: A Social Critique of the Judgment of Taste*, Routledge, London.

Bourdieu, P. (1998) 'The essence of neoliberalism', trans. J.J. Shapiro, *Le Monde diplomatique*, December.

Brackenridge, C. (2001) *Spoilsports: Understanding and Preventing Sexual Exploitation in Sport*, Routledge, London.

Brackenridge, C. (2004) 'Women and children first? Child abuse and child protection in sport', *Sport in Society*, 7 (3), 322–337.

Brackenridge, C. and K. Fasting (eds) (2003) *Sexual Harassment and Abuse in Sport: International Research and Policy Perspectives*, Whiting and Birch, London.

Brackenridge, C., A. Pitchford, K. Russell and G. Nutt (2007a) *Child Welfare in Football: An Exploration of Children's Welfare in the Modern Game*, Routledge, London.

Brackenridge, C., I. Rivers, B. Gough and K. Llewellyn (2007b) 'Driving down participation: homophobic bullying as a deterrent to doing sport', in *Sport and Gender Identities: Masculinities, Femininities and Sexualities*, C. Carmichael Aitchison (ed.), Routledge, London.

Bradbury, S. (2001) 'The new football communities', Sir Norman Chester Centre for Football Research, University of Leicester.

Brady, K. (2008) 'Sports worth over £15 billion a year to nation's economy', www.sportengland.org/news/press_releases/sport_worth_over_15_billion_a_year_to_nation_s_economy_.htm.

Brah, A. (1994) 'South Asian young Muslim women and the labour market', in *The Dynamics of 'Race' and Gender: Some Feminist Transformations*, H. Asfhar and M. Maynard (eds), Taylor and Francis, London.

Brailsford, D. (1991) *Sport, Time and Society: The British at Play*, Routledge and Kegan Paul, London.

Bredemeier, B., E. Carlton, L. Hills and C. Oglesby (1999) 'Changers and the changed: moral aspects of coming out in physical education', *Quest*, 51 (4), 418–431.

Bridges, L. (2003) 'Out of the gene pool and into the food chain', in *To the Extreme: Alternative Sports, Inside and Out*, R. Rinehart and S. Sydnor (eds), State University of New York Press, Albany, NY.

Bristow, E. (2004) *Observer Sports Monthly*, 18 January, 51.

Brittain, I. (2004) 'Perceptions of disability and their impact upon involvement in sport for people with disabilities at all levels', *Journal of Sport and Social Issues*, 28 (4), 429–452.

Brookes, R. (2002) *Representing Sport*, Oxford University Press, Oxford.

Brooks, J., C. Fuller, S. Kemp and D. Reddin (2005) 'Epidemiology of injuries in English professional rugby union: Part 1 match injuries', *British Journal of Sports Medicine*, 39, 757–766.

Brown, A. (ed.) (1998) *Fanatics! Power, Identity and Fandom in Football*, Routledge, London.

Brown, G. (2008) www.youthsportstrust/org.page/media-news-detail/nssw/index.html.

Brown, M. and Seaton, S. (1994) *The Christmas Truce: Western Front, December 1914*, Papermac Books, London.

Brown, M., M. Carney, E. Currie, T. Duster, D. Oppenheimer, M. Schultz and D. Wellman (2005) *Whitewashing Race: The Myth of a Color-blind Society*, University of California Press, Berkeley, CA.

Brown, T., J. Jackson, K. Brown, R. Sellers, S. Keiper and W. Manuel (2003) '"There's no race on the playing field": perceptions of racial discrimination among white and black athletes', *Journal of Sport and Social Issues*, 27 (2), 162–183.

Brownell, S. (1995) *Training the Body for China: Sports in the Moral Order of the People's Republic*, University of Chicago Press, Chicago, IL.

Brownell, S. (2008) *Beijing's Games: What the Olympics Mean to China*, Rowman and Littlefield, Lanham, MD.

Bruce, T. (2004) 'Marking the boundaries of the "normal" in televised sports: the play-by-play of race', *Media, Culture and Society*, 26, 861–879.

Bruce, T. (2007) 'Media and sport', in *The Blackwell Encyclopedia of Sociology*, G. Ritzer, (ed.), Blackwell, London.

Bruening, J. (2005) 'Gender and racial analysis in sport: are all the women white and all the blacks men?', *Quest*, 57, 330–349.

Bryshun, J. and K. Young (2007) 'Hazing as a form of sport and gender socialization', in *Sport and Gender in Canada*, K. Young and P. White (eds), Oxford University Press, Oxford.

Buffington, D. (2005) 'Contesting race on Sundays: making meaning out of the rise in the number of black quarterbacks', *Sociology of Sport Journal*, 22 (1), 19–37.

Bull, A. (2007) 'The historic present', *Observer Sports Monthly*, 4 February.

Bull, C. (2004) 'The healer', *ESPN The Magazine*, 16 February.

Burdsey, D. (2007) *British Asians and Football: Culture, Identity, Exclusion*, Routledge, London.

Burstyn, V. (1999) *The Rites of Men: Manhood, Politics, and the Culture of Sport*, University of Toronto Press, Toronto.

Butler, J. (2004) *Undoing Gender*, Routledge, London.

Cambridge Econometrics (2003) *The Value of the Sports Economy in England 2000*, Cambridge Econometrics, Cambridge.

Cannella, S. (2006) 'Scorecard', *Sports Illustrated*, 105, 4 September.

Caplan, J. and T. Coates (2007) 'Tiger. Jordan. Hawk. Wendel?', *Time*, February.

Carlston, D. (1986) 'An environmental explanation for race differences in basketball performance', in *Fractured Focus*, R. Lapchick (ed.), Lexington Books, Lexington, MA.

Carrington, B. (2001) 'Postmodern blackness and the celebrity sports star: Ian Wright, 'race' and English identity', in *Sport Stars: The Cultural Politics of Sporting Identity*, D. Andrews and S. Jackson (eds), Routledge, London.

Carrington, B. (2004a) 'Introduction: race/nation/sport', *Leisure Studies*, 23 (1), 1–3.

Carrington, B. (2004b) 'Cosmopolitan Olympism, humanism and the spectacle of race' in *Post-Olympism: Questioning Sport in the Twenty-first Century*, J. Bale and M. Christensen (eds), Berg, Oxford.

Carrington, B. (2007a) 'Race and sport', in *The Blackwell Encyclopedia of Sociology*, G. Ritzer (ed.), Blackwell, Oxford.

Carrington, B. (2007b) 'Sport, masculinity and black cultural resistance, in *The Sport Studies Reader*, A. Tomlinson (ed.), Routledge, London.

Carrington, B. and I. McDonald (2001) 'Introduction: "race", sport and British society', in *'Race', Sport and British Society*, B. Carrington and I. McDonald (eds), Routledge, London.

Carrington, B. and J. Sugden (1999) 'Trans-national capitalism and the incorporation of world football', paper presented at the annual conference of the North American Society for the Sociology of Sport, Cleveland, OH, November.

Cashmore, E. (2002) *Beckham*, Polity, Cambridge.

Cashmore, E. (2005) *Making Sense of Sports*, Routledge, London.

Cashmore, E. (2007a) 'Black sportsmen', in *The Sport Studies Reader*, A. Tomlinson (ed.), Routledge, London.

Cashmore, E. (2007b) 'Gambling and sports', in *The Blackwell Encyclopedia of Sociology,* G. Ritzer (ed.), Blackwell, Oxford.

Castro, F. (2001) Speech available at, www.cuba.cu/gobierno/discursos/2001.

Caudwell, J. (2003) 'Sporting gender: women's footballing bodies as sites/sights for the (re)articulation of sex, gender, and desire', *Sociology of Sport Journal*, 20 (4), 371–386.

Caudwell, J. (ed.) (2006) *Queer Theory and Sport: Challenges and Controversies*, Routledge, London.

Chafetz, J. and J. Kotarba (1999) 'Little League mothers and the reproduction of gender', in *Inside Sports*, J. Coakley and P. Donnelly (eds), Routledge, London.

Chalip, L. and B. Green (1998) 'Establishing and maintaining a modified youth sport program: lessons from hotelling's location game', *Sociology of Sport Journal*, 15 (4), 326–342.

Charlesworth, H. and K. Young (2004) 'Why English female university athletes play with pain: motivations and rationalisations', in *Sporting Bodies, Damaged Selves: Sociological Studies of Sports-Related Injury*, K. Young (ed.), Elsevier, Oxford.

Charlesworth, H. and K. Young (2006) 'Injured female athletes: experiential accounts from England and Canada', in *Pain and Injury in Sport: Social and Ethical Analysis*, S. Loland, B. Skirstad and I. Waddington (eds), Routledge, London.

Chastain, B. (2004) *It's Not About the Bra*, Harper Resource, New York.

Christenson, M. and P. Kelso (2004) 'Soccer chief's plan to boost women's game? Hotpants', *Guardian*, 16 January, www.guardian.co.uk.

Chudacoff, H. (2007) *Children at Play: An American History*, New York University Press, New York.

Clarke, G. (2002) 'Difference matters: sexuality and physical education', in *Gender and Physical Education: Contemporary Issues and Future Directions*, D. Penney (ed.), London, Routledge.

Clarke, G. (2004) 'Threatening space: (physical) education and homophobic bodywork', in *Body Knowledge and Control: Studies in the Sociology of Physical Education and Health*, J. Evans, B. Davies and J. Wright (eds), Routledge, London.

Clarke, J. and Critcher, C. (1985) *The Devil Makes Work: Leisure in Capitalist Britain*, Macmillan, Basingstoke.

Clayton, B. and B. Humberstone (2006) 'Men's talk: a (pro)feminist analysis of male university football players' discourse', *International Review for the Sociology of Sport*, 41 (3–4), 295–316.

Coakley, J. (1983a) 'Play, games and sports: developmental implications for young people', in *Play, Games and Sports in Cultural Contexts*, J.C. Harris and R.J. Park (eds), Human Kinetics, Leeds.

Coakley, J. (1983b) 'Leaving competitive sport: retirement or rebirth?', *Quest*, 35 (1), 1–11.

Coakley, J. (1988–89) 'Media coverage of sports and violent behavior: an elusive connection', *Current Psychology: Research and Reviews*, 7 (4), 322–330.

Coakley, J. (1990) *Sport in Society: Issues and Controversies*, Times Mirror/Mosby, St Louis, MO.

Coakley, J. (1992) 'Burnout among adolescent athletes: a personal failure or social problem?', *Sociology of Sport Journal*, 9 (3), 271–285.

Coakley, J. (1993) 'Sport and socialization', *Exercise and Sport Science Reviews*, 21, 169–200.

Coakley, J. (1994) 'Ethics in coaching: child development or child abuse?', *Coaching Volleyball*, December–January, 18–23.

Coakley, J. (1998) *Sport in Society: Issues and Controversies*, McGraw-Hill, New York.

Coakley, J. (2002) 'Using sports to control deviance and violence among youths: let's be critical and cautious', in *Paradoxes of Youth and Sport*, M. Gatz, M.A. Messner and S.J. Ball-Rokeach (eds), State University of New York Press, Albany. NY.

Coakley, J. (2006) 'The good father: parental expectations and youth sports', *Leisure Studies*, 25 (2), 153–164.

Coakley, J. (2007a) 'Socialization and sports', in *Encyclopedia of Sociology*, G. Ritzer (ed.), Blackwell, London.

Coakley, J. (2007b) *Sports in Society: Issues and Controversies*, McGraw-Hill, London.

Coakley, J. (2008) 'Studying intercollegiate sport: high stakes, low rewards', *Journal of Intercollegiate Sport*, 1 (1), 14–28.

Coakley, J. and P. Donnelly (eds) (1999) *Inside Sports*, Routledge, London.

Coakley, J. and P. Donnelly (2004) *Sports in Society: Issues and Controversies*, 1st Canadian edition, McGraw-Hill Ryerson, Toronto.

Coakley, J. and A. White (1999) 'Making decisions: how young people become involved and stay involved in sports', in *Inside Sports*, J. Coakley and P. Donnelly (eds), Routledge, London.

Coalter, F. (2007) *A Wider Social Role for Sport: Who's Keeping the Score?* Routledge, London.

Coe, S. (2006) *Making Sport Matter for the Next Generation*, www.slv.vic.gov.au/programs/ltf/lectures/kmo/2006/transcript.html.

Cohen, L. (2005) *Without Apology: Girls, Women, and the Desire to Fight*, Random House, New York.

Cohen, S. (1972) *Folk Devils and Moral Panics*, Mac Gibbon and Kee, London.

Cole, C. (2000a) 'Body studies in the sociology of sport', in *Handbook of Sport Studies,* J. Coakley and E. Dunning (eds), Sage, London.

Cole, C. (2000b) 'The year that girls ruled', *Journal of Sport and Social Issues*, 24 (1), 3–7.

Collins, M. and J. Buller (2003) 'Social exclusion from high-performance sport: are all talented young sports people being given an equal opportunity of reaching the Olympic podium?', *Journal of Sport and Social Issues*, 27 (4), 420–442.

Collins, M. and T. Kay (2003) *Sport and Social Exclusion*, Routledge, London.

Collins, P. (2004) *Black Sexual Politics: African Americans, Gender, and the New Racism*, Routledge, London.

Collins, T. (1996a) 'How muscular Christianity met its match', *Journal of Association of Sports Historians*, 2.

Collins, T. (1996b) 'Myth and reality in the 1895 rugby split', *The Sports Historian,* 16 May, 33–41.

Collins, T. and W. Vamplew (2002) *Mud, Sweat and Beers: A Cultural History of Sport and Alcohol*, Berg, Oxford.

Connell, R. (1995) *Masculinities*, University of California Press, Berkeley, CA.

Côté, J. and J. Fraser-Thomas (2007) 'Youth involvement in sport', in *Introduction to Sport Psychology: A Canadian Perspective*, P. Crocker (ed.), Pearson Prentice Hall, Toronto.

Couser, G. (2000) 'The empire of the "normal": a forum of disability and self-representation – introduction', *American Quarterly*, 52 (2), 305–310.

Coventry, B. (2004) 'On the sidelines: sex and racial segregation in television sports broadcasting', *Sociology of Sport Journal*, 21 (3), 322–341.

Cowley, J. (2004) 'Should we care if our athletes have been pumped full of nandrolone?', *New Statesman*, 26 January.

Cox, B. and S. Thompson (2000) 'Multiple bodies: sportswomen, soccer and sexuality', *International Review for the Sociology of Sport*, 35 (1), 5–20.

Craig, P. and P. Beedie (2008) *Sport Sociology*, Learning Matters, Exeter.

Crawford, G. (2004) *Consuming Sport: Fans, Sport, and Culture*, Routledge, London.

Creedon, P. (1998) 'Women, sport, and media institutions: issues in sports journalism and marketing', in *MediaSport*, L. Wenner (ed.), Routledge, London.

Critcher, C. (1979) 'Football since the war', in *Working Class Culture,* J. Clark (ed.), Hutchinson, London.

Cronin, M. (1999) *Sport and Nationalism in Ireland: Gaelic Games, Soccer and Irish Identity Since 1884*, Four Courts Press, Dublin.

Cronin, M. (2002) 'Catholics and sport in Northern Ireland: exclusiveness or inclusiveness', in *With God on Their Side: Sport in the Service of Religion*, T. Magdalinski and T. Chandler (eds), Routledge, London.

Crouse, K. (2008) 'Scrutiny of suit rises as world records fall', *New York Times*, 11 April.

Cunningham, G. and M. Sagas (2005) 'Access discrimination in intercollegiate athletics', *Journal of Sport and Social Issues*, 29 (2), 148–163.

Curry, T. (1991) 'Fraternal bonding in the locker room: a profeminist analysis of talk about competition and women', *Sociology of Sport Journal*, 8 (2), 119–135.

Curry, T. (1993) 'A little pain never hurt anyone: athletic career socialization and the normalization of sports injury', *Symbolic Interaction*, 16 (2), 273–290.

Curry, T. (1996) 'Beyond the locker room: sexual assault and the college athlete', Presidential Address, North American Society for the Sociology of Sport Conference, Birmingham, AL.

Curry, T. (1998) 'Beyond the locker room: campus bars and college athletes', *Sociology of Sport Journal*, 15 (2), 205–215.

Curry, T., P. Arriagada and B. Cornwell (2002) 'Images of sport in popular nonsport magazines: power and performance versus pleasure and participation', *Sociological Perspectives*, 45 (4), 397–413.

Cushion, C. and R. Jones (2006) 'Power, discourse and symbolic violence in professional youth soccer: the case of Albion football club', *Sociology of Sport Journal*, 23 (2), 142–161.

Cyphers, L. (2003) 'Next', *ESPN The Magazine*, 22 December.

Dacyshyn, A. (1999) 'When the balance is gone: the sport and retirement experiences of elite female gymnasts', in *Inside Sports*, J. Coakley and P. Donnelly (eds), Routledge, London.

Daniels, D. (2000) 'Gazing at the new black woman athlete', *ColorLines*, 3, 25–26.

Dater, A. (2005) 'Female boxer, 34, dies after Golden Gloves bout', *Denver Post*, 5 April.

David, P. (2005) *Human Rights in Youth Sport*, Routledge, London.

Davids, K. and J. Baker (2007) 'Genes, environment and sport performance: why the nature–nurture dualism is no longer relevant', *Sports Medicine*, 37 (11), 961–980.

Davies. R. (2002a) 'Sports, citizenship and development: challenges and opportunities for sport sponsors', presentation at the World Sports Forum, Lausanne.

Davies, R. (2002b) 'Media power and responsibility in sport and globalisation', presentation made to the Third International Conference for Media Professionals in a Globalised Sport World, Copenhagen.

Davis, L. and O. Harris (1998) 'Race and ethnicity in US sports media', in *Media Sport,* LA Wenner (ed.), Routledge, London.

Davis, N. and M. Carlisle Duncan (2006) 'Sports knowledge is power: reinforcing masculine privilege through fantasy sport league participation', *Journal of Sport and Social Issues*, 30 (3), 244–264.

Deem, R. (1986) *All Work and No Play? The Sociology of Women and Leisure*, Open University Press, Milton Keynes.

Deford, F. (1997) 'Seasons of discontent', *Newsweek*, 29 December, www.newsweek.com. id/97770?tid=relatedcl.

Delaney, K. and R. Eckstein (2003) 'The devil is in the details: neutralizing critical studies of publicly subsidized stadiums', *Critical Sociology*, 29 (2), 189–210.

Delaney, K. and R. Eckstein (2008) 'Local media coverage of sports stadium initiatives', *Journal of Sport and Social Issues*, 32 (1), 72–93.

Delves, A. (1981) 'Popular recreation and social conflict in Derby 1800–1850', in *Popular Culture and Class Conflict 1590–1914,* E. Yeo and S. Yeo (eds), Harvester Press, Brighton.

Denham, B. (2004) 'Hero or hypocrite? United States and international media portrayals of Carl Lewis amid revelations of a positive drug test', *International Review for the Sociology of Sport*, 39 (2), 167–185.

Denham, B. (2007) 'Government and the pursuit of rigorous drug testing in Major League Baseball: a study in political negotiation and reciprocity', *International Journal of Sport Management and Marketing*, 2, 379–395.

Department for Culture, Media and Sport (DCMS) (1999) *Specialist Sports Colleges*, Cabinet Office, London.

Department for Culture, Media and Sport (DCMS) (2005) *Stars Launch Official School Sport Awards*, Cabinet Office, London.

Department for Culture, Media and Sport (DCMS) (2007) *Winning: A Tourism Strategy for 2012 and Beyond*, DCMS, London.

Department for Culture, Media and Sport (DCMS)/Strategy Unit (2002) *Game Plan: A Strategy for Delivering Government's Sport and Physical Activity Objectives*, Cabinet Office, London.

DePauw, K. (1997) 'The (in)visibility of disability: cultural contexts and 'sporting bodies'', *Quest*, 49 (4), 416–430.

Dewhirst, T. and R. Sparks (2003) 'Intertextuality, tobacco sponsorship of sports, and adolescent male smoking culture: a selective review of tobacco industry documents', *Journal of Sport and Social Issues*, 27 (4), 372–398.

Dimeo, P. (2007) *A History of Drug Use in Sport, 1876–1976*, Routledge, London.

Dimeo, P. and G. Finn (2001) 'Racism, national identity and Scottish football', in *'Race', Sport and British Society*, B. Carrington and I. McDonald (eds), Routledge, London.

DiPasquale, M. (1992) 'Editorial: why athletes use drugs', *Drugs in Sports*, 1, 2–3.

Director (2008) 'A great day at the Oscar(s). The National Center on Physical Activity and Disability', *NCPAD NEWS*, 7 (6), June.

Doaks, C. (2004) 'We can handle the truth', *Mile High Sport Magazine*, 10 November.

Dodd, M. (2002) 'Tiger: membership up to Muirfield', *USA Today*, 17 July.

Domi, T. (1992) 'Tough tradition of hockey fights should be preserved', *USA Today*, 27 October.

Donnelly, P. (1993) 'Problems associated with youth involvement in high-performance sports', in *Intensive Participation in Children's Sports*, B.R. Cahill and A.J. Pearl (eds), Human Kinetics, Leeds.

Donnelly, P. (1996a) 'Prolympism: sport monoculture as crisis and opportunity', *Quest*, 48 (1), 25–42.

Donnelly, P. (1996b) 'The local and the global: globalization in the sociology of sport', *Journal of Sport and Social Issues*, 20 (3), 239–257.

Donnelly, P. (1997) 'Child labour, sport labour: applying child labor laws to sport', *International Review for the Sociology of Sport*, 32 (4), 389–406.

Donnelly, P. (1999) 'Who's fair game? Sport, sexual harassment, and abuse', in *Sport and Gender in Canada*, P. White and K. Young (eds), Oxford University Press, Oxford.

Donnelly, P. (2000) 'Interpretive approaches to the study of sports', in *Handbook of Sport and Society*, J. Coakley and E. Dunning (eds), Sage, London.

Donnelly, P. (2004) 'Sport and risk culture', in *Sporting Bodies, Damaged Selves: Sociological Studies of Sports-Related Injury*, K. Young (ed.), Elsevier, Oxford.

Donnelly, P. and J. Coakley (2003) 'The role of recreation in promoting social inclusion', monograph in the Working Paper Series on Social Inclusion published by the Laidlaw Foundation, Toronto, Ontario.

Donnelly, P. and J. Harvey (2007) 'Social class and gender: intersections in sport and physical activity', in *Sport and Gender in Canada*, K. Young and P. White (eds), Oxford University Press, Oxford.

Donnelly, P. and K. Young (1999) 'Rock climbers and rugby players: identity construction and confirmation', in *Inside Sports*, J. Coakley and P. Donnelly (eds), Routledge, London.

Donohoe, H. (2003) *Women's Sports Foundation response to the Health Select Committee Inquiry on Obesity*, Women's Sports Foundation, London.

Drahota, J. and D. Eitzen (1998) 'The role exit of professional athletes', *Sociology of Sport Journal*, 15 (3), 263–278.

Dukes, R. and J. Coakley (2002) 'Parental commitment to competitive swimming', *Free Inquiry in Creative Sociology*, 30 (2), 185–197.

Duncan, M. and Messner, M. (1998) 'The media image of sport and gender', in *MediaSport*, L. Wenner (ed.), Routledge, London.

Duncan, M. and M. Messner (2000) *Gender in Televised Sports: 1989, 1993, and 1999*, Amateur Athletic Foundation, Los Angeles, CA.

Duncan, M. and M. Messner (2005) *Gender in Televised Sports: News and Highlights Shows, 1989-2004*, Amateur Athletic Foundation, Los Angeles, CA.

Dunning, E. (1986) 'Social bonding and violence in sport', in *Quest for Excitement: Sport and Leisure in the Civilizing Process*, N. Elias and E. Dunning (eds), Blackwell, Oxford.

Dunning, E. (1993) 'Sport in the civilising process: aspects of the development of modern sport', in *The Sports Process: A Comparative and Developmental Approach*, E. Dunning, J. Maguire and R. Pearton (eds), Human Kinetics, Leeds.

Dunning, E. (1999) *Sport Matters: Sociological Studies of Sport, Violence and Civilization*, Routledge, London.

Dunning, E. (2007) 'Sport, gender and civilization', in *The Sport Studies Reader*, A. Tomlinson (ed.), Routledge, London.

Dunning, E. and K. Sheard (1979) *Barbarians, Gentlemen and Players: A Sociological Study of the Development of Rugby Football*, University Press, New York.

Dunning, E. and I. Waddington (2003) 'Sport as a drug and drugs in sport: some exploratory comments', *International Review for the Sociology of Sport*, 38 (4), 351–368.

Dunning, E., P. Murphy, I. Waddington and A. Astrinakis (eds) (2002) *Fighting Fans: Football Hooliganism as a World Phenomenon*, University College Dublin Press, Dublin.

Dunning, E., P. Murphy and J. Williams (1988) *The Roots of Football Hooliganism: An Historical and Sociological Study*, Routledge and Kegan Paul, London.

DuPree, D. (1992) 'Controversy wears down Dream Team', *USA Today*, 5 August.

Duquin, M. (2000) 'Sport and emotions', in *Handbook of Sports Studies*, J. Coakley and E. Dunning (eds), Sage, London.

Dworkin, S. (2001) '"Holding back": negotiating a glass ceiling on women's muscular strength', *Sociological Perspectives*, 44, 333–351.

Dworkin, S. (2003) 'A woman's place is in the … cardiovascular room? Gender relations, the body, and the gym', in *Athletic Intruders: Ethnographic Research on Women, Culture, and Exercise*, A. Bolin and J. Granskog (eds), State University of New York Press, Albany, NY.

Early, G. (1991) 'Delusions of grandeur: young blacks must be taught that sports are not the only avenue of opportunity', *Sports Illustrated*, 75 (8), 19 August, 78.

Early, G. (1998) 'Performance and reality: race, sports and the modern world', *The Nation*, 267, 11–20.

Eastman, S. and A. Billings (1999) 'Gender parity in the Olympics: hyping women athletes, favoring men athletes', *Journal of Sport and Social Issues*, 23 (2), 140–170.

Edwards, H. (1973) *Sociology of Sport*, Dorsey Press, Homewood, IL.

Edwards, H. (1993) 'Succeeding against the odds', *Black Issues in Higher Education*, 10 (20), 136.

Edwards, H. (2000) 'The decline of the black athlete', as interviewed by D. Leonard, *ColorLines*, 3, 29–34.

Eitle, T. and D. Eitle (2002) 'Just don't do it: high school sports participation and young female adult sexual behavior', *Sociology of Sport Journal*, 19 (4), 403–418.

Eitzen, D. (2003) *Fair and Foul: Beyond the Myths and Paradoxes of Sport*, Rowman and Littlefield, Lanham, MD.

Elias, N. (1978) *The Civilizing Process: The History of Manners*, vol. 1, Basil Blackwell, Oxford.

Elias, N. (1982) *The Civilizing Process: State Formation and Civilization*, vol. 2, Basil Blackwell, Oxford.

Elias, N. (1986) 'An essay on sport and violence', in *Quest for Excitement*, N. Elias and E. Dunning (eds), Basil Blackwell, Oxford.

Elias, N. and E. Dunning (1986) *Quest for Excitement: Sport and Leisure in the Civilizing Process*, Blackwell, Oxford.

Eliasoph, N. (1999) '"Everyday racism" in a culture of political avoidance: civil society, speech, and taboo', *Social Problems*, 46, 479–502.

Elkind, D. (2007) *The Hurried Child*, Da Capo Lifelong Books, New York.

Elkind, D. (2008) *The Power of Play: Learning What Comes Naturally*, Da Capo Lifelong Books, New York.

Elling, A., P. de Knop and A. Knoppers (2003) 'Gay/lesbian sport clubs and events: places of homo-social bonding and cultural resistance?', *International Review for the Sociology of Sport*, 38 (4), 441–456.

Elliott, R. and J. Maguire (2008) '"Getting caught in the net": examining the recruitment of Canadian players in British professional ice hockey', *Journal of Sport and Social Issues*, 32 (2), 158–176.

Emms, G. (2006) 'What's sex got to do with it', *Observer*, 3 September, 12.

Engh, F. (1999) *Why Johnny Hates Sports*, Avery, New York.

English Institute of Sport (2006) 'The voice of experience', www.eis2win.co.uk/pages/news_hilaryrose.

Eriksson, S. (2004) 'FIFA probes racist chants', www.bbc.co.uk/sport2/football/internationals.

Eskes. T., M. Carlisle Duncan and E. Miller (1998) 'The discourse of empowerment: Foucault, Marcuse, and women's fitness texts', *Journal of Sport and Social Issues*, 22 (3), 317–344.

ESPN (1999) 'High school athletes: do jocks rule the school?', in *Outside the Lines*, T. Farrey (ed.), www.espn.com/gen/features/jocks.

ESPN The Magazine (2005) 'Special report: turning a blind eye to steroids – the inside story of baseball's open secret', *ESPN The Magazine*, 21 November, 69–84.

Evans, J., B. Davies and J. Wright (eds) (2004) *Body Knowledge and Control: Studies in the Sociology of Physical Education and Health*, Routledge, London.

Ewald, K, and R. Jiobu (1985) 'Explaining positive deviance: Becker's model and the case of runners and bodybuilders', *Sociology of Sport Journal*, 2 (2), 144–156.

Farber, M. (2004) 'Code red', *Sports Illustrated*, 22 March, 56–60.

Farhood, S. (2000) 'Typical girls', *Boxing Monthly*, 12, 1.

Farrey, T. (2005) 'Baby you're the greatest: genetic testing for athletic traits', *ESPN The Magazine*, 14 February, 80–87.

Farrey, T. (2007) 'The case for HGH', *ESPN The Magazine*, 29 January, 48–52.

Farrey, T. (2008) *Game On: The All-American Race to Make Champions of our Children*, ESPN Books, New York.

Fasting, K. (1996) '40,000 female runners: the Grete Waitz Run – sport, culture, and counter-culture', paper presented at International Pre-Olympic Scientific Congress, Dallas, July.

Fasting, K. and G. Pfister (2000) 'Female and male coaches in the eyes of female elite soccer players', *European Physical Education Review*, 1 (1), 91–107.

Fasting, K., C. Brackenridge and J. Sundgot Borgen (2000) *Sexual Harassment In and Outside Sport*, Norwegian Olympic Committee, Oslo.

Fasting, K, C. Brackenridge and J. Sundgot-Borgen (2004) 'Prevalence of sexual harassment among Norwegian female elite athletes in relation to sport type', *International Review for the Sociology of Sport*, 39 (4), 373–386.

Fatwa Bank (2004) 'Islam's stance on women's practicing sport', www.islamonline.net/fatwa/english/FatwaDisplay.asp?hFatwaID=48375.

Fausto-Sterling, A. (2000) *Sexing the Body: Gender Politics and the Construction of Sexuality*, Basic Books, New York.

Fenstermaker, S. and C. West (eds) (2002) *Doing Gender, Doing Difference: Inequality, Power, and Institutional Change*, Routledge, London.

Ference, R. and K. Muth (2004) 'Helping middle school females form a sense of self through team sports and exercise', *Women in Sport and Physical Activity*, 13 (1), 28–35.

Finger, D. (2004) 'Before they were next', *ESPN The Magazine*, 7 June, 83–86.

Finn, P. and R. Guilianotti (1998) 'Scottish fans, not English hooligans! Scots, Scottishness and Scottish football', in *Fanatics! Power, Identity and Fandom in Football*, A. Brown (ed.), Routledge, London.

Fish, M. (1993) 'Steroids riskier than ever', *Atlanta Journal-Constitution*, 26 September.

Fleming, S. (1995) *'Home and Away': Sport and Social Asian Male Youth*, Avebury, Aldershot.

Fleming, S. (2001) 'Racial science and South Asian and black physicality', in *'Race', Sport and British Society*, B. Carrington and I. McDonald (eds), Routledge, London.

Fleming, S. (2007) 'Sport and South Asian youth: the perils of "false universalism" and stereotyping', in *The Sport Studies Reader*, A. Tomlinson (ed.), Routledge, London.

Fleming, S. and A. Tomlinson (2007) 'Racism and xenophobia in English football', in *The Sport Studies Reader*, A. Tomlinson (ed.), Routledge, London.

Foer, F. (2004) *How Soccer Explains the World: An Unlikely Theory of Globalization*, HarperCollins, New York.

Football Association (2004) 'Becoming a professional', www.thefa.com/grassrootsnew/player/postings/2004/03/becomingaprofessional.

Foucault, M. (1961/1967) *Madness and Civilization*, Tavistock, London.

Fredrickson, B. and K. Harrison (2005) 'Throwing like a girl: self-objectification predicts adolescent girls' motor performance', *Journal of Sport and Social Issues*, 29 (1), 79–101.

Fredrickson, G. (2003) *Racism: A Short History*, Princeton University Press, Princeton, NJ.

Freedman, J. (2008) 'Fortunate 50', *Sports Illustrated*, 6 March.

Friedman, V., L. Martin and R. Schoeni (2004) 'An overview of disability in America', *Population Bulletin*, 59, 3.

Frosdick, S. and Marsh, P. (2005) *Football Hooliganism*, Willan, Cullompton.

Gardener, J. (2004) In 'British athletics', *Observer Sports Monthly*, August, 45.

Garland, J. and M. Rowe (2001) *Racism and Anti-Racism in Football*, Palgrave, Basingstoke.

Garrett, R. (2004) 'Negotiating a physical identity: girls, bodies and physical education', *Sport, Education and Society*, 9 (2), 223–237.

George, J. (1994) 'The virtual disappearance of the white male sprinter in the United States: a speculative essay', *Sociology of Sport Journal*, 11 (1) 70–78.

Gilroy, P. (1991) *There Ain't No Black in the Union Jack: The Cultural Politics of Race and Nation*, University of Chicago Press, Chicago, IL.

Gilroy, P. (2001) 'Foreword', in *'Race', Sport and British Society*, B. Carrington and I. McDonald (eds), Routledge, London.

Ginsburg, K. (2007) 'The importance of play in promoting healthy child development and maintaining strong parent–child bonds', *Pediatrics*, 119, 1.

Giordana, R. and K. Graham (2004) 'An early leg up', *Philadelphia Inquirer*, 24 February.

Give Us Back Our Game (2008) www.giveusbackourgame.co.uk.

Glock, A. (2005) 'The look of love', *ESPN The Magazine*, 20 June, 66–74.

Goffman, E. (1963) *Stigma: Notes on the Management of Spoiled Identities*, Prentice-Hall, Englewood Cliffs, NJ.

Golby, J. and A. Purdue (1984) *Civilization of the Crowd*, Batsford, London.

Gold, J. and M. Gold (2007) *Olympic Cities: City Agendas, Planning, and the World's Games, 1896–2012*, Routledge, London.

Good, R. (2002) 'Women's share at Olympic competitions drops', www.womensenews.org/article.cfm/dyn/aid/824.

Goodman, B. (2001) 'The merchants of cool: a report on the creators and marketers of popular culture for teenagers', www.pbs.org/wgbh/pages/frontline/shows/cool/.

Gore, C. (2002) *The Least Developed Countries Report, 2002: Escaping the Poverty Trap*, United Nations Publications, New York.

Gore, C. (2004) *The Least Developed Countries Report, 2004: Linking International Trade with Poverty Reduction*, United Nations Publications, New York

Gore, S. (2006) *Observer Sports Monthly*, 22 February.

Gorman, C. (2005) 'Why more kids are getting hurt', *Time*, 6 June, 58.

Goudsblom, J. (1977) *Sociology in the Balance*, Blackwell, Oxford.

Gramsci, A. (1971) *Selections from the Prison Notebook*, International Publishers, New York.

Gramsci, A. (1988) 'Selected writings: 1918–1935', Shocken, New York.

Grant, A. (2002a) 'Body shop', *ESPN The Magazine*, 4 February, 50–54.

Grant, A. (2002b) 'A painful reality', http://espn.go.com/magazine/grant_20020130.html.

Gratton, C. and P. Taylor (2000) *Economics of Sport and Recreation*, E&F Spon, London.

Graves, J. (2002) *The Emperor's New Clothes: Biological Theories of Race at the Millennium*, Rutgers University Press, New Brunswick, NJ.

Graves, J. (2004) *The Race Myth: Why We Pretend Race Exists in America*, Penguin Books, New York.

Green, M. and B. Houlihan (2004) 'Advocacy coalitions and elite sport policy change in Canada and the United Kingdom', *International Review for the Sociology of Sport*, 39 (4), 387–403.

Green, M. (2004) 'Power, policy, and political priorities: elite sport development in Canada and the United Kingdom', *Sociology of Sport Journal*, 21 (4), 376–396.

Greenfeld, K. (1999) 'Adjustment in mid-flight', *Outside*, February, www.outside.away.com.

Griffin, P. (1998) *Strong Women, Deep Closets: Lesbians and Homophobia in Sport*, Human Kinetics, Leeds.

Grohmann, K. (2008) 'Teams put a price on Beijing Games medals', *International Herald Tribune*, 5 March.

Grossfeld, S. (2005) 'New spin on rugby: quadriplegic athletes take sport to the extreme with wheelchair version', *Boston Globe*, 31 May.

Gruneau, R. (1988) 'Modernization or hegemony: two views of sports and social development', in *Not Just a Game*, J. Harvey and H. Cantelon (eds), University of Ottawa Press, Ottawa.

Gruneau, R. (1999) *Class, Sports, and Social Development*, Human Kinetics, Leeds.

Guilbert, S. (2004) 'Sport and violence: a typographical analysis', *International Review for the Sociology of Sport*, 39 (1) 45–55.

Guilianotti, R. (1999) *Football: A Sociology of the Global Game*, Polity, Cambridge.

Giulianotti, R. and G. Armstrong (2002) 'Avenues of contestation: football hooligans, running and ruling urban spaces', *Social Anthropology*, 10 (2), 211–238.

Gulick, L. (1906) 'Athletics do not test womanliness', *American Physical Education Review*, 11 (3), 158–159.

Guttmann, A. (1978) *From Ritual to Record: The Nature of Modern Sports*, Columbia University Press, New York.

Guttmann, A. (1986) *Sport Spectators*, Columbia University Press, New York.

Guttmann, A. (1988) *A Whole New Ball Game: An Interpretation of American Sports*, University of North Carolina Press, Chapel Hill, NC.

Guttmann, A. (1998) 'The appeal of violent sports', in *Why We Watch: The Attractions of Violent Entertainment*, J. Goldstein (ed.), Oxford University Press, Oxford.

Guttmann, A. (2004) *Sports: The First Five Millennia*, University of Massachusetts Press, Amherst, MA.

Hall, C. (2006) 'Urban entrepreneurship, corporate interests and sports mega-events: the thin policies of competitiveness within the hard outcomes of neoliberalism', *The Sociological Review*, 54, supplement 2, 59–70.

Hall, M. (2002) *The Girl and the Game: A History of Women's Sport in Canada*, Broadview Press, Peterborough, Ontario.

Hall, M., T. Slack, G. Smith and D. Whitson (1991) *Sport in Canadian Society*, McClelland and Stewart, Toronto.

Halverson, E.R. and R. Halverson (2008) 'Fantasy baseball: the case for competitive fandom', *Games and Culture*, 3 (3–4), 286–308.

Hansell, S. (2005) 'More people turn to the web to watch TV', *New York Times*, 1 August.

Hardman, K. and J. Marshall (2000) *A Worldwide Survey of the State and Status of School PE*, Manchester University Press, Manchester.

Hargreaves, J. (1986) *Sport, Power and Culture*, Polity Press, Cambridge.

Hargreaves, J. (1994) *Sporting Females: Critical Issues in the History and Sociology of Women's Sport*, Routledge, London.

Hargreaves, J. (2000) *Heroines of Sport: The Politics of Difference and Identity*, Routledge, London.

Hargreaves, J. (2007) 'Men and women and the gay games', in *The Sport Studies Reader*, A. Tomlinson (ed.), Routledge, London.

Hargreaves, J. and P. Vertinsky (eds) (2006) *Physical Culture, Power and the Body*, Routledge, London.

Harris, J. (2005) 'The image problem in women's football', *Journal of Sport and Social Issues*, 29 (2), 184–197.

Harris, J. and Clayton, B. (2002) 'Femininity, masculinity, physicality and the English tabloid press: the case of Anna Kournikova', *International Review for the Sociology of Sport*, 37 (4), 397–413.

Harrison, C. and Lawrence, S. (2004) 'College students' perceptions, myths, and stereotypes about African American athletes: a qualitative investigation', *Sport, Education and Society* 9 (1), 33–52.

Harrison, L., L. Azzarito and J. Burden (2004) 'Perceptions of athletic superiority: a view from the other side', *Race Ethnicity and Education*, 7 (2), 149–166.

Harrison, L., A. Lee and D. Belcher (1999) 'Race and gender differences in sport participation as a function of self-schema', *Journal of Sport and Social Issues*, 23 (3), 287–307.

Hart, M. (1981) 'On being female in sport', in *Sport in the Socio-cultural Process*, M. Hart and S. Birrell (eds), Brown, Dubuque, IA.

Hartmann, D. (2001) 'Notes on midnight basketball and the cultural politics of recreation, race, and at-risk urban youth', *Journal of Sport and Social Issues*, 25 (4), 339–371.

Hartmann, D. (2003a) 'The sanctity of Sunday afternoon football: why men love sports', *Contexts*, 2 (4), 13–21.

Hartmann, D. (2003b) 'Theorizing sport as social intervention: a view from the grassroots', *Quest*, 55 (2), 118–140.

Hasbrook, C. (1999) 'Young children's social constructions of physicality and gender', in *Inside Sports*, J. Coakley and P. Donnelly (eds), Routledge, London.

Hasbrook, C. and O. Harris (1999) 'Wrestling with gender: physicality and masculinity(ies) among inner-city first and second graders, *Men and Masculinities*, 1 (3), 302–318.

Hassan, D. (2003) 'Rugby Union, Irish nationalism and national identity in Northern Ireland', *Football Studies*, 6, 5–18.

Hastings, D., S. Cable and S. Zahran (2005) 'The globalization of a minor sport: the diffusion and COM modification of masters swimming', *Sociological Spectrum*, 25 (2) 133–154.

Hawes, K. (2001) 'Mirror, mirror', *NCAA News*, special report, 24 September.

Hayes, S. and G. Stidder (eds) (2003) *Equity and Inclusion in Physical Education: Contemporary Issues for Teachers, Trainees and Practitioners*, Routledge, London.

Henderson, J. (2004) 'Cycling's other race', *Denver Post*, 4 July.

Henricks, T. (2006) *Play Reconsidered: Sociological Perspectives on Human Expression*, University of Illinois Press, Urbana, IL.

Heywood, L. (1998) *Bodymakers: A Cultural Anatomy of Women's Bodybuilding*, Rutgers University Press, New Brunswick, NJ.

Heywood, L. and S. Dworkin (2003) *Built to Win: The Female Athlete as Cultural Icon*, University of Minnesota Press, Minneapolis. MN.

Hicks, T. (2007) In 'English tradition meets American ownership', R. Mahoney, *USA Today*, www.usatoday.com/sports/soccer/2007-05-16-soccer-cover_N.htm.

Higgins, M. (2005) 'A sport so popular, they added a second boom', *New York Times*, 25 July.

Higgins, P. (1992) *Making Disability: Exploring the Transformation of Human Variation*, Thomas, Springfield, IL.

Hnida, K. (2006) *Still Kicking: My Journey as the First Woman to Play Division I College Football*, Scribner, New York.

Hoberman, J. (1992) *Mortal Engines: The Science of Performance and the Dehumanization of Sport*, Free Press, New York.

Hoberman, J. (1994) 'The sportive-dynamic body as a symbol of productivity', in *Heterotopia: Postmodern Utopia and the Body Politic*, T. Siebers (ed.), University of Michigan Press, Ann Arbor, MI.

Hoberman, J. (1997) *Darwin's Athletes: How Sport Has Damaged Black America and Preserved the Myth of Race*, Houghton Mifflin, Boston, MA.

Hoberman, J. (2004) *Testosterone Dreams: Rejuvenation, Aphrodisia, Doping*, University of California Press, Berkeley, CA.

Holmes, K. (2006) *Black, White and Gold*, Virgin Books, London.

Holt, R. (1989) *Sport and the British: A Modern History*, Oxford University Press, Oxford.

Holt, R. and T. Mason (2000) *Sport in Britain: 1945–2000*, Blackwell, Oxford.

Honeyball, L. (2006) 'The impossible dreamer', *Observer Sports Monthly*, April.

Honea, J. (2005) 'Youth cultures and consumerism: sport subcultures and possibilities for resistance', Unpublished PhD dissertation, Colorado State University, Ft Collins.

Honea, J. (2007) 'Alternative sports', in *Encyclopedia of Sociology*, G. Ritzer (ed.), Blackwell, London.

hooks, b. (1992) 'Theory as liberating practice', *Yale Journal of Law and Feminism*, 4 (1), 1–12.

hooks, b. (2000) *Where We Stand: Class Matters*, Routledge, London.

Horne, J. (2006) *Sport in Consumer Culture*, Palgrave Macmillan, Basingstoke.

Horne, J. and W. Manzenreiter (2002) 'The world cup and television football', in *Japan, Korea and the 2002 World Cup*, J. Horne and W. Manzenreiter (eds), Routledge, London.

Horne, J. and W. Manzenreiter (2006) 'An introduction to the sociology of sports mega-events', in *Sports Mega-events: Social Scientific Analyses of a Global Phenomenon*, J. Horne and W. Manzenreiter (eds), Blackwell, Oxford.

Horne, J., A. Tomlinson and G. Whannel (1999) *Understanding Sport: An Introduction to the Sociological and Cultural Analysis of Sport*, Spon, London.

Houlihan, B. (1994) *Sport and International Politics*, Harvester Wheatsheaf, Hemel Hempstead.

Houlihan, B. (2000) 'Politics and sport', in *Handbook of Sports Studies*, J. Coakley and E. Dunning (eds), Sage, London.

Houlihan, B. (2004) 'Civil rights, doping control and the World Anti-Doping Code', *Sport in Society*, 7, 420–437.

Houlihan, B. (2008) *Sport and Society*, Sage, London.

Hovden, J. (2000) 'Gender and leadership selection processes in Norwegian sporting organizations', *International Review for the Sociology of Sport*, 35 (1), 75–82.

Howe, D. (2008) *The Cultural Politics of the Paralympic Movement*, Routledge, London.

Howe, P. (2003) 'Kicking stereotypes into touch: an ethnographic account of women's rugby', in *Athletic Intruders: Ethnographic Research on Women, Culture, and Exercise*, A. Bolin and J. Granskog (eds), State University of New York Press, Albany. NY.

Howe, P.D. (2004a) *Sport, Professionalism and Pain: Ethnographies of Injury and Risk*, Routledge, London.

Howe, P.D. (2004b) 'Welsh rugby union: pain, injury and medical treatment in a professional era', in *Sporting Bodies, Damaged Selves: Sociological Studies of Sports-Related Injury*, K. Young (ed.), Elsevier, Oxford.

Howe, P.D. (2006) 'The role of injury in the organization of Paralympic sport', in *Pain and Injury in Sport: Social and Ethical Analysis*, S. Loland, B. Skirstad and I. Waddington (eds), Routledge, London.

Howe, P.D. and C. Jones, (2006) 'Classification of disabled athletes: (dis)empowering the Paralympic practice community', *Sociology of Sport Journal*, 23 (1), 29–46.

Huang, C.-H. and I. Brittain (2006) 'Negotiating identities through disability sport', *Sociology of Sport Journal*, 23 (4), 352–375.

Hudson, I. (2001) 'The use and misuse of economic impact analysis: the case of professional sports', *Journal of Sport and Social Issues*, 25 (1), 20–39.

Hughes, R. and J. Coakley (1991) 'Positive deviance among athletes: the implications of overconformity to the sport ethic', *Sociology of Sport Journal*, 8 (4), 307–325.

Hughson, J. (2000) 'The boys are back in town: soccer support and the social reproduction of masculinity', *Journal of Sport and Social Issues*, 24 (1), 8–23.

Hui, S. (2004) 'Transsexual Olympiads', www.alternet.org/rights/19525/.

Hutchinson, J. (1975) 'Some aspects of football crowds before 1914', unpublished University of Sussex Conference Report, cited in Social Issues Research Centre, *Football in Europe*, SIRC, Oxford, p. 22.

IDG (2007) 'Sponsorship gives Red Bull wings', www.idg.com.

Ingham, A. and A. Dewar (1999) 'Through the eyes of youth: "deep play" in peewee ice hockey', in *Inside Sports*, J. Coakley and P. Donnelly (eds), Routledge, London.

Ingham, A., B. Blissmer and K. Davidson (1999) 'The expendable prolympic self: going beyond the boundaries of the sociology and psychology of sport', *Sociology of Sport Journal*, 16 (3), 236–268.

International Paralympic Committee (IPC) (2008) 'IPC position statement on IAAF's commissioned research on Oscar Pistorius', International Paralympic Committee, www.paralympic.org/release/Main_Sections_Menu/News/Press_Releases/2008_01_14_a.html.

Ismond, P. (2003) *Black and Asian Athletes in British Sport and Society: A Sporting Chance?* Palgrave, London.

Jackson, S.J. and D. Andrews (eds) (2005) *Sport, Culture and Advertising: Identities, Commodities and the Politics of Representation*, Routledge, London.

Jackson, S.A. and M. Csikszentmihalyi (1999) *Flow in Sports*, Human Kinetics, Leeds.

Jackson, S.J. and S. Haigh (eds) (2008) *Sport and Foreign Policy in a Globalising World*, special issue of *Sport in Society*, Routledge, London.

Jackson, S.J. and B. Hokowhitu (2002) 'Sport, tribes, and technology: the New Zealand All Blacks Haka and the politics of identity', *Journal of Sport and Social Issues*, 26 (2), 125–139.

Jackson, S.J. and J. Scherer (2002) 'Screening the nation's past: adidas, advertising and corporate nationalism in New Zealand', paper presented at the annual meetings of the North American Society for the Sociology of Sport, Indianapolis, November.

Jacques, M. (2004) 'Football's new world order', *Observer Sports Monthly*, June, 55.

Jacques, M. (2007) 'It's the same as Tiger: nothing will change', *Observer Sports Monthly*, June, 25.

James, C. (1984) *Beyond a Boundary*, Pantheon Books, New York.

Jarvie, G. (1991) *Highland Games: The Making of the Myth*, Edinburgh University Press, Edinburgh.

Jarvie, G. (2006) *Sport, Culture and Society: An Introduction*, Routledge, London.

Jarvie, G. and J. Burnett, (2000) *Sport, Scotland and the Scots*, Tuckwell Press, Edinburgh.

Jarvis, N. (2006) 'Ten men out: gay sporting masculinities in softball', in *Sport, Sexualities and Queer Theory: Challenges and Controversies*, J. Caudwell (ed.), Routledge, London.

Jeanrenaud, C. and S. Kesenne (eds.) (2006) *The Economics of Sport and the Media*, Edward Elgar, Northampton, MA.

Jeffries, S. (2004) 'The tyranny of the gym', *Guardian*, 5 January.

Jennings, A. (1996a) *The New Lords of the Rings*, Pocket Press, London.

Jennings, A. (1996b) 'Power, corruption, and lies', *Esquire*, May, 99–104.

Jennings, A. and C. Sambrook (2000) *The Great Olympic Swindle: When the World Wanted its Games Back*, Simon and Schuster, New York.

Johal, S. (2001) 'Playing their own game: a South Asian football experience', in *'Race', Sport and British Society*, B. Carrington and I. McDonald (eds), Routledge, London.

Johns, D. (1997) 'Fasting and feasting: paradoxes in the sport ethic', *Sociology of Sport Journal*, 15 (1), 41–63.

Jones, K. (2001) 'A key moral issue: should boxing be banned?', *Culture, Sport and Society*, 4 (1), 63–72.

Jones, R. (2002) 'The black experience within English semiprofessional soccer', *Journal of Sport and Social Issues*, 26 (1), 47–65.

Joukowsky, A. and L. Rothstein (eds) (2002a) *Raising the Bar*, Umbrage Editions, New York.

Joukowsky, A. and L. Rothstein (2002b) 'New horizons in disability sport', in *Raising the Bar*, A. Joukowsky and L. Rothstein (eds), Umbrage Editions, New York.

Jürgs, M. (2003) *Der kleine Frieden im Grossen Krieg. Westfront 1914: Als Deutsche, Franzosen und Briten gemeinsam Weihnachten feierten*, Bertelsmann, München.

Jutel, A. (2002) 'Olympic road cycling and national identity: where is Germany?', *Journal of Sport and Social Issues*, 26 (2), 195–208.

Kamila, G. (2000) 'The black edge: are athletes of African descent genetically superior?', *Salon*, 218, http://dir.salon.com/books/feature/2000/01/28/taboo/index.html.

Katz, J. (2003) 'When you're asked about the Kobe Bryant case', www.jacksonkatz.com/bryant.html.

Kay, J. and S. Laberge (2003) 'Oh say can you ski?', in *To the Extreme: Alternative Sports, Inside and Out*, R. Rinehart and S. Sydnor (eds), State University of New York Press, Albany, NY.

Kay, T. (2000) 'Sporting excellence: a family affair?', *European Physical Education Review*, 6 (2), 151–170.

Kay, T. (2003) 'Sport and gender', in *Sport and Society: A Student Introduction*, B. Houlihan (ed.), Sage, London.

Kay, T. (2006) 'Daughters of Islam: family influences on Muslim young women's participation in sport', *International Review for the Sociology of Sport*, 41 (4), 357–373.

Keating, P. (2004) 'Insurance run', *ESPN The Magazine*, 5 July, 70–73.

Keating, P. (2005) 'Baseball has solved its steroid problem – at least that's what they want you to believe', *ESPN The Magazine*, 5 December, 16.

Kellner, D. (2003a) 'Toward a critical theory of education', *Democracy and Nature*, 9 (1), 51–64.

Kellner, D. (2003b) *Media Spectacle*, Routledge, London.

Kellner, D. (2004) 'The sports spectacle, Michael Jordan, and Nike', in *Sport and the Color Line*, P. Miller and D. Wiggins (eds), Routledge, London.

Kelly, S. and I. Waddington (2006) 'Abuse, intimidation and violence as aspects of managerial control in professional soccer in Britain and Ireland', *International Review for the Sociology of Sport*, 41 (2), 147–164.

Kensler, T. (2005) 'Wie playing PGA Tour event seems out of bounds to some', *Denver Post*, 3 July.

Kian, E., J. Vincent and M. Mondello (2008) 'Masculine hegemonic hoops: an analysis of media coverage of March madness', *Sociology of Sport Journal*, 25 (2), 223–242.

Kidd, B. (1984) 'The myth of the ancient games', in *Five-ring Circus*, A. Tomlinson and G. Whannel (eds), Pluto Press, London.

Kidd, B. (1987) 'Sports and masculinity', in *Beyond Patriarchy: Essays by Men on Pleasure, Power, and Change*, M. Kaufman (ed.), Oxford University Press, Oxford.

Kidd, B. (1995) 'Inequality in sport, the corporation, and the state: an agenda for social scientists', *Journal of Sport and Social Issues*, 19 (3), 232–248.

Kidd, B. (1996a) 'Worker sport in the New World: the Canadian story', in *The Story of Worker Sport*, A. Kruger and J. Riordan (eds), Human Kinetics, Leeds.

Kidd, B. (1996b) 'Taking the rhetoric seriously: proposals for Olympic education', *Quest*, 48 (1), 82–92.

Kidd, B. (1997) *The Struggle for Canadian Sport*, University of Toronto Press, Toronto.

Kilvert, G. (2002) 'Missing the X chromosome', *Sports Illustrated Women*, 4, 21–22.

King, C. (2000) 'Trial by fire: a study of initiation rituals in English sport', unpublished MSc Sports Science thesis, Department of Physical Education, Sports Science and Recreation Management, Loughborough University.

King, C. (2004) 'Race and cultural identity: playing the race game inside football', *Leisure Studies*, 23 (1), 19–30.

King, K. (2002) 'The ultimate jock school', *Sports Illustrated*, 25 November, 48–54.

Kinkema, K. and J. Harris (1998) 'MediaSport studies: key research and emerging issues', in *MediaSport*, L.A. Wenner (ed.), Routledge, London.

Kirk, D. (2003) 'Sport, physical education and schools', in *Sport and Society: A Student Introduction*, B. Houlihan (ed.), Sage, London.

Kirk, D. (2004) 'Sport and early learning experiences', *Driving up Participation: The Challenge for Sport*, Sport England, London.

Kix, P. (2007) 'Muscling up', *ESPN The Magazine*, 21 May, 44.

Klein, A. (1991) *Sugarball: The American Game, the Dominican Dream*, Yale University Press, New Haven, CT.

Klein, A. (2008) 'Progressive ethnocentrism: ideology and understanding in Dominican baseball', *Journal of Sport and Social Issues*, 32 (2), 121–138.

Klein, N. (2002) *No Logo*, Picador, New York.

Knoppers, A. and A. Elling (2004) '"We do not engage in promotional journalism": discursive strategies used by sport journalists to describe the selection process', *International Review for the Sociology of Sport*, 39 (1), 57–73.

Koppett, L. (1994) *Sports Illusion, Sports Reality*, University of Illinois Press, Urbana, IL.

Koukouris, K. (1994) 'Constructed case studies: athletes' perspectives of disengaging from organized competitive sport', *Sociology of Sport Journal*, 11 (2), 114–139.

Krane, V. (1996) 'Lesbians in sport: toward acknowledgement, understanding, and theory', *Journal of Sport and Exercise Psychology*, 18 (3), 237–246.

Krane, V., P. Choi, S. Baird, C. Aimar and K. Kauer (2004) 'Living the paradox: female athletes negotiate femininity and muscularity', *Sex Roles*, 50 (5/6), 315–329.

Krane, V., J. Waldron, J. Michalenok and J. Stiles-Shipley (2001) 'Body image concerns in female exercisers and athletes: a feminist cultural studies perspective', *Women in Sport and Physical Activity Journal*, 10 (1), 17–54.

Kreager, D. (2007) 'Unnecessary roughness? School sports, peer networks, and male adolescent violence', *American Sociological Review*, 72 (5), 705–724.

Kusz, K. (2001) '"I want to be the minority." The politics of youthful white masculinities in sport and popular culture in 1990s America', *Journal of Sport and Social Issues*, 25 (4), 390–416.

Laberge, S. and M. Albert (1999) 'Conceptions of masculinity and of gender transgressions in sport among adolescent boys: hegemony, contestation, and social class dynamic', *Men and Masculinities*, 1 (3), 243–267.

Laberge, S. and D. Sankoff (1988) 'Physical activities, body *habitus*, and lifestyles', in *Not Just a Game*, J. Harvey and H. Cantelon (eds), University of Ottawa Press, Ottawa.

Lafferty, Y. and J. McKay (2004) '"Suffragettes in satin shorts"? Gender and competitive boxing', *Qualitative Sociology*, 27 (3), 249–276.

Lamb, L. (2000) 'Can women save sports? An interview with Mary Jo Kane', *Utne Reader*, 97, 56–57.

Lance, L. (2005) 'Violence in sport: a theoretical note', *Sociological Spectrum*, 25 (2), 213–214.

Laqueur, T. (1990) *Making sex*, Harvard University Press, Cambridge, MA.

Lasn, K. (2000) *Culture Jam*, Quill, New York.

Latimer, C. (2008) '"Before, I ran from danger and death. Now, I run for sport"', *Rocky Mountain News*, 8 August.

Laurendeau, J. (2004) 'The "crack choir" and the "cock chorus": the intersection of gender and sexuality in skydiving texts', *Sociology of Sport Journal*, 21 (4), 397–417.

Lavallee, D., P. Wylleman and D. Sinclair (2000) 'Career transitions in sport: an annotated bibliography', in *Career Transitions in Sport: International Perspectives*, D. Lavallee and P. Wylleman (eds), Fitness Information Technology, Morgantown, WV.

Lavoie, M. (2000) 'Economics and sport', in *Handbook of Sports Studies*, J. Coakley and E. Dunning (eds), London: Sage.

Lawler, J. (2002) *Punch: Why Women Participate in Violent Sports*, Wish, Terre Haute, IN.

Lawrence, S. (2005) 'African American athletes' experiences of race in sport', *International Review for the Sociology of Sport*, 40 (1), 99–110.

Layden, T. (2001) 'Does anyone remember the Titans?', *Sports Illustrated*, 15 October, 72–83.

Layden, T. (2005) '"I am an American"', *Sports Illustrated*, 103 (17), 60–69.

Leahy, M. (2008) 'The pain game', *Washington Post*, 3 February.

LeBlanc, R. and S.J. Jackson (2007) 'Sexuality as cultural diversity in sport organisations', *Special Issue of the International Journal of Sport Management and Marketing*, 2 (2), 119–133.

Lefkowitz, B. (1997) *Our Guys: The Glen Ridge Rape and the Secret Life of the Perfect Suburb*, University of California Press, Berkeley, CA.

Lehrman, S. (1997) 'Forget men are from Mars, women are from Venus', *Stanford Today Online*, www.stanford.edu/dept/news/stanfordtoday/ed/9705/9705fea401.shtml.

Lemos, G. (2002) 'David Beckham: s/he-ro', www.footballculture.net/players/profile_beckham.html.

Lenskyj, H. (1986) *Out of Bounds: Women, Sport and Sexuality*, Women's Press, Toronto.

Lenskyj, H. (1999) 'Women, sport, and sexualities: breaking the silences', in *Sport and Gender in Canada*, P. White and K. Young (eds), Oxford University Press, Oxford.

Lenskyj, H. (2000) *Inside the Olympics Industry: Power, Politics, and Activism*, State University of New York Press, Albany, NY.

Lenskyj, H. (2002) *The Best Olympics Ever? Social Impacts of Sydney 2000*, State University of New York Press, Berkeley, CA.

Lenskyj, H. (2003) *Out in the Field: Gender, Sport and Sexualities*, Women's Press, Toronto.

Lenskyj, H. (2008) *Olympic Industry Resistance: Challenging Olympic Power and Propaganda*, State University of New York Press, Albany, NY.

Leonard, D. (2006) 'An untapped field: exploring the world of virtual sports gaming', in *Handbook of Sports and Media*, A. Raney and J. Bryant (eds), Lawrence Erlbaum Associates, Mahwah, NJ.

Leonard, J. (2004) *Full Time: The Autobiography of a Rugby Legend*, CollinsWillow, London.

Levy, D. (2005) 'Fantasy sports and fanship habitus: understanding the process of sport consumption', paper presented at the annual conference of the American Sociological Society, Philadelphia, August.

Lewis, J. (2007) *Sports Fan Violence in North America*, Rowman and Littlefield, New York.

Lewis, N. (2004) 'Sustainable adventure: embodied experiences and ecological practices within British climbing', in *Understanding Lifestyle Sports: Consumption, Identity and Difference*, B. Wheaton (ed.), Routledge, London.

Liddle, E. (2003) 'Black is best', www.spectator.co.uk.

Ligutom-Kimura, D. (1995) 'The invisible women', *Journal of Physical Education, Recreation and Dance*, 66 (7), 34–41.

Lines, G. (2001) 'Villains, fools or heroes? Sports stars as role models for young people', *Leisure Studies*, 20 (4), 285–303.

Lipsyte, R. (1996a) 'One fell swoosh: can a logo conquer all?', *New York Times*, 7 February, 9.

Lipsyte, R. (1996b) 'Little girls in a staged spectacle for big bucks? That's sportainment!', *New York Times*, 4 August, 28.

Lipsyte, R. (2005) 'He's outraged at the steroid outrage', www.sociologycultureblog.blogspot.com.

Liston, K. (2006) 'Women's soccer in the Republic of Ireland: some preliminary sociological comments', *Soccer and Society*, 7 (2–3), 364–384.

Liston, K. (2007) 'Revisiting the feminist-figurational sociology exchange', *Sport in Society*, 10 (4), 623–645.

Liston, K., D. Reacher, A. Smith and I. Waddington (2006) 'Managing pain and injury in non-elite rugby union and rugby league: a case study of players at a British university', *Sport in Society*, 9, 388–402.

Lomax, R. (2006) 'Fantasy sports: history, game types and research, in *Handbook of Sports and Media*, A. Raney and J. Bryant (eds), Lawrence Erlbaum Associates, Mahwah, NJ.

London East Research Institute (2006) *Carrying the Torch*, London East Research Institute, London.

Long, J. and K. Hylton (2002) 'Shades of white: an examination of whiteness in sport', *Leisure Studies*, 21, 87–103.

Longman, J. (1996) 'Slow down, speed up', *New York Times*, 1 May, B11.

Longman, J. (2001) 'Getting the athletic edge may mean altering genes', *New York Times*, 11 May, www.nytimes.com/2001/05/11/sports/11GENE.html.

Longman, J. (2007) An amputee sprinter: is he disabled or too-abled? *New York Times*, 15 May, www.nytimes.com/2007/05/15/sports/othersports/15runner.html.

Lopiano, D. (1991) Presentation at the Coaching America's Coaches Conference, United States Olympic Training Center, Colorado Springs, CO.

Lowe, M.R. (1998) *Women of Steel: Female Bodybuilders and the Struggle for Self-definition*, New York University Press., New York.

Lowes, M.D. (1999) *Inside the Sports Pages: Work Routines, Professional Ideologies, and the Manufacture of Sport News*, University of Toronto Press, Toronto.

Lund, A.B. (2007) 'The political economy of mass mediated sports', keynote address at the ISHPES and ISSA Joint World Congress, Copenhagen, 3 August.

Lupton, D. (2000) 'The social construction of medicine and the body', in G. Albrecht, R. Fitzpatrick and S. Scrimshaw (eds), *The Handbook of Social Studies in Health and Medicine*, Sage, London.

MacArthur, L. (2008) 'The drive to strive: exploring the experiences of elite-level adolescent artistic performers', PhD dissertation, Department of Curriculum, Teaching, and Learning, Ontario Institute for Studies in Education of the University of Toronto.

MacNeill, M. (1999) 'Social marketing, gender, and the science of fitness: a case-study of ParticiPACTION campaigns', in P. White and K. Young (eds), *Sport and Gender in Canada*, Oxford University Press, Don Mills, ON.

MacPhail, A., T. Gorely, and D. Kirk (2003) 'Young people's socialisation into sport: a case study of an athletics club', *Sport, Education and Society*, 8, 251–267.

Madison, J.K. and Sarita, L.R. (2003) 'Exercise and athletic involvement as moderators of severity in adolescents with eating disorders', *Journal of Applied Sport Psychology*, 15 (3), 213–222.

Magdalinski, T. (2008) *Sport, Technology and the Body: The Nature of Performance*, Routledge, London and New York.

Maguire, J. (1988) 'Race and position assignment in English soccer: a preliminary analysis of ethnicity and sport in Britain', *Sociology of Sport Journal*, 5 (3), 257–269.

Maguire, J. (1991) 'Sport, racism and British society: a sociological study of England's elite male Afro-Caribbean soccer and rugby union players', in *Sport, Racism and Ethnicity*, G. Jarvie (ed.), Falmer, London.

Maguire, J. (1999) *Global Sport: Identities, Societies, Civilizations*, Polity Press, Cambridge.

Maguire, J. (2004) 'Sport labor migration research revisited', *Journal of Sport and Social Issues*, 28 (4), 477–482.

Maguire, J. (2005) *Power and Global Sport: Zones of Prestige, Emulation and Resistance*, Routledge, London.

Maguire, J., E. Poulton and C. Possamai (1999) 'Weltkrieg III? Media coverage of England versus Germany in Euro 96', *Journal of Sport and Social Issues*, 23, 439–454.

Maguire, J., G. Jarvie, L. Mansfield and J. Bradley (2002) *Sport Worlds: A Sociological Perspective*, Human Kinetics, Leeds.

Maguire, J. and D. Stead (2005) '"Cricketers of the Empire": cash crops, mercenaries and symbols of sporting emancipation?', in J. Maguire (ed.) *Power and Global Sport: Zones of Prestige, Emulation and Resistance*, Routledge, London/New York.

Maguire, J.A., S. Barnard, K. Butler and P. Golding (2008b) 'Celebrate humanity or consumers? Building markets, constructing brands and glocalising identities', *Social Identities*, 14(1) 63–77.

Maguire, J.A., K. Butler, S. Barnard and P. Golding (2008a) 'Olympism and consumption: an analysis of advertising in the British media coverage of the 2004 Athens Olympic Games', *Sociology of Sport Journal*, 25 (2), 167–186.

Mahany, B. (1999) 'Parents drive free time from lives of kids', *Chicago Tribune*, 27 May.

Mahiri, J. (1998) *Shooting for Excellence: African American Youth Culture in New Century Schools*, Teachers College Press, New York and London.

Majors, R. (1986) 'Cool pose: the proud signature of black survival', *Changing Men: Issues in Gender, Sex and Politics*, 17, Winter, 184–185.

Majors, R. (1998) 'Cool pose: black masculinity and sports', in G. Sailes (ed.), *African Americans in Sport*, Transaction, New Brunswick, NJ.

Malcolm, D. (1997) 'Stacking in cricket: a figurational sociological reappraisal of centrality', *Sociology of Sport Journal*, 14(3), 263–282.

Malcolm, D. (1999) 'Cricket spectator disorder: myths and historical evidence', *Sports Historian*, 19, 16–37.

Malcolm, D. (2002) 'Cricket and civilising processes: a response to Stovkis', *International Review for the Sociology of Sport*, 37, 37–57.

Malcolm, D. (2006) 'Sports medicine: a very peculiar practice? Doctors and physiotherapists in elite English rugby union', in *Pain and Injury in Sport: Social and Ethical Analysis*, S. Loland, B. Skirstad and I. Waddington (eds), Routledge, London.

Malcolm, D. and K. Sheard (2002) '"Pain in the assets": the effects of commercialization and professionalization on the management of injury in English rugby union', *Sociology of Sport Journal*, 19(2), 149–169.

Malcolmson, R.W. (1984) 'Sports in society: a historical perspective', *British Journal of Sport History*, 1 (1) 60–72.

Malloy, D.C. and D.H. Zakus (2002) 'Ethics of drug testing in sport – an invasion of privacy justified?', *Sport, Education and Society*, 2, 203–218.

Mangan, J.A. (ed.) (2003) *Militarism, Sport, Europe: War without Weapons*, Routledge, London and New York.

Manzenreiter, W. and Horne, J. (eds) (2004) *Football Goes East – Business, Culture and the People's Game in China, Japan and South Korea*, Routledge, London.

Maradona, D. (2006) *Observer Sports Monthly*, 24 April.

Markula, P. (1995) 'Firm but shapely, fit but sexy, strong but thin: the postmodern aerobicizing female bodies', *Sociology of Sport Journal*, 12 (4), 424–453.

Marriott, M. (2005) 'Cyberbodies: robo-legs', *New York Times*, 20 June 20, F1.

Marriott, M. (2004) 'Your shot, he said, distantly', *New York Times*, 26 August, 1.

Marsh, P. (1982) 'Social order on the British soccer terraces', *International Social Science Journal*, 34, 247–256.

Marsh, P. and A. Campbell (eds) (1982) *Aggression and Violence*, Basil Blackwell, Oxford.

Martzke, R. and R. Cherner (2004) 'Channeling how to view sports', *USA Today*, 17 August, 1C–2C.

Mayeda, D.T. (1999) 'From model minority to economic threat: media portrayals of major league baseball pitchers Hideo Nomo and Hideki Irabu', *Journal of Sport and Social Issues*, 23 (2), 203–217.

McCallum, J. (2002) 'Citizen Barkley', *Sports Illustrated*, 11 March, 38.

McCarthy, D., R.L. Jones and P. Potrac (2003) 'Constructing images and interpreting realities: the case of the black soccer on television', *International Review for the Sociology of Sport*, 38 (2), 217–238.

McChesney, R.W. (1999) 'The new global media: it's a small world of big conglomerates', *The Nation*, 269 (18), 11–15.

McClung, L.R. and E.M. Blinde (1998) 'Negotiation of the gendered ideology of sport: experiences of women intercollegiate athletes', paper presented at the annual conference of the North American Society for the Sociology of Sport, Las Vegas, November.

McCormack, J.B. and L. Chalip (1988) 'Sport as socialization: a critique of methodological premises', *Social Science Journal*, 25 (1), 83–92.

McCullagh, C. (2002) *Media Power*, Palgrave, New York.

McDaniel, S. and C. Sullivan (1998) 'Extending the sporting experience: mediations in cyberspace', in *Mediasport*, L. Wenner (ed.), Routledge, London.

McDonald, I. (2002) 'Critical sociology research and political intervention: moralistic versus radical approaches', in *Power Games: A Critical Sociology of Sport*, J. Sugden and A. Tomlinson (eds) Routledge, London.

McGarry, K. (2005) 'Mass media and gender identity in high performance Canadian figure skating', *The Sport Journal*, 8 (1), www.thesportjournal.org.

McGuire, B., K. Monks and R. Halsall (2001) 'Young Asian males: social exclusion and social injustice in British professional football', *Culture, Sport and Society*, 4, 65–80.

McHugh, J. (2007) 'Blade runner', *Wired*, March, www.wired.com/wired/archive/15.03/blade.html.

McKay, J. (1997) *Managing Gender: Affirmative Action and Organizational Power in Australian, Canadian, and New Zealand Sport*, State University of New York Press, NY.

McKay, J. (1999) 'Gender and organizational power in Canadian sport', in P. White and K. Young (eds), *Sport and Gender in Canada*, Oxford University Press, Don Mills, ON.

Mead, C. (1985) *Champion Joe Louis: Black Hero in White America*, Scribner, New York.

Melnick, M. and S.J. Jackson (2002) 'Globalization American-style and reference idol selection: the importance of athlete celebrity others among New Zealand youth', *International Review for the Sociology of Sport*, 37(4), 429–448.

Mendelsohn, D. (2004) 'What Olympic ideal?', *New York Times Magazine*, 8 August, www.nytimes.com/2004/08/08/magazine/WLN130551.html.

Mennesson, C. and J.-P. Clement (2003) 'Homosociability and homosexuality: the case of soccer played by women', *International Review for the Sociology of Sport*, 38(4), 311–330.

Merkel, U. (2003) 'The politics of physical culture and German nationalism: *Turnen* versus English sports and French Olympism', in *German Politics and Society*, 21 (2), 69–96.

Merkel, U. (2006) 'The 1974 and 2006 Soccer World Cups in Germany – commonalities, continuities and changes', in *Soccer and Society*, 1 (2), 14–28.

Merron, J. (1999) 'Running on empty', *SportsJones*, 3, June, www.sportsjones.com/running.htm.

Messner, M.A. (1992) *Power at Play*, Beacon Press, Boston, MA.

Messner, M.A. (2002) *Taking the Field: Women, Men, and Sports*, University of Minnesota Press, Minneapolis, MN.

Messner, M.A. (2007) *Out of Play: Critical Essay on Gender and Sport*, State University of New York Press, Albany, NY.

Messner, M.A. and M.A. Stevens (2002) 'Scoring without consent: confronting male athletes' violence against women', in M. Gatz, M.A. Messner and S.J. Ball-Rokeach (eds), *Paradoxes of Youth and Sport*, State University of New York Press, Albany, NY.

Messner, M.A., D. Hunt and M. Dunbar (1999) *Boys to Men: Sports Media Messages about Masculinity*, Children Now, Oakland, CA.

Meyer, J. (2002) 'Ward's fire within', *Denver Post*, 14 July, 1C, 12C.

Midol, N. and G. Broyer (1995) 'Toward an anthropological analysis of new sport cultures: the case of whiz sports in France', *Sociology of Sport Journal*, 12(2), 204–212.

Mihoces, G. (2005) 'Injured skaters struggle in world championships', *USA Today*, 15 March, www.usatoday.com/sports/olympics/winter/2005-03-14-skating-worlds_x.htm.

Miller, P.S. and G. Kerr (2003) 'The role experimentation of intercollegiate student athletes', *The Sport Psychologist*, 17 (2), 196–219.

Miller, T., G. Lawrence, J. McKay and D. Rowe (2001) *Globalization and Sport: Playing the World*, Sage, London.

Miller, T., D. Rowe, J. McKay and G. Lawrence (2003) 'The over-production of US sports and the new international division of cultural labor', *International Review for the Sociology of Sport*, 38 (4), 427–440.

Mills, J. and P. Dimeo (2003) '"When gold is fired it shines": sport, the imagination and the body in colonial and postcolonial India', in J. Bale and M. Cronin (eds), *Sport and Postcolonialism*, Berg, Oxford and New York.

Mirza, H. (1997) *Black British Feminism: A Reader*, Routledge, London.

Moore, D.L. (2002) 'Parents pay dearly to coach kids for stardom', *USA Today*, 26 July, 1A–2A, www.usatoday.com/educate/college/firstyear/casestudies/20040106-coaching.pdf.

Moore, K. (2004) 'Olympics 2004: Muslim women athletes move ahead, but don't leave faith behind', www.payvand.com/news/04/aug/1056.html (retrieved 5 July 2005).

Morris, G.S.D. and J. Stiehl (1989) *Changing Kids' Games*, Human Kinetics, Champaign, IL.

Morris, J. (1996) 'Introduction', in J. Morris (ed.), *Encounters with Strangers: Feminism and Disability*, Women's Free Press, London.

Munday, G. (2003) 'A semiotic analysis of the media portrayals of injured players in the 2002 World Cup', unpublished BA dissertation, University College Chichester.

Murphy, G.M., A.J. Petipas and B.W. Brewer (1996) 'Identity foreclosure, athletic identity, and career maturity in intercollegiate athletics', *Sport Psychologist*, 10 (3), 239–246.

Murphy, P. and I. Waddington (2007) 'Are elite athletes exploited?', *Sport in Society*, 10, 239–255.

Murphy, P., K. Sheard and I. Waddington (2000) 'Figurational/process sociology', in J. Coakley and E. Dunning (eds), *Handbook of Sports Studies*, Sage, London.

Murphy, P., J. Williams and E. Dunning (1990) *Football on Trial: Spectator Violence and Development in the World of Football*, Routledge, London.

Murphy, S. (1999) *The Cheers and the Tears: A Healthy Alternative to the Dark Side of Youth Sports Today*, Jossey-Bass, San Francisco, CA.

Nack, W. and L. Munson (1995) 'Sports' dirty secret', *Sports Illustrated*, 83 (5), 31 July, 62–75.

Nack, W. and L. Munson (2000) 'Out of control', *Sports Illustrated*, 93 (4), 24 July, 86–95.

Nack, W. and D. Yaeger (1999) 'Every parent's nightmare', *Sports Illustrated*, 91 (10), 13 September, 40–53.

Nakamura, Y. (2002) 'Beyond the hijab: female Muslims and physical activity', *Women's Sport and Physical Activity Journal*, 11 (2), 21–48.

National Statistics (2001) *Census*, Crown Copyright.

Nelson, M.B. (1994) *The Stronger Women Get, the More Men Love Football: Sexism and the American Culture of Sports*, Harcourt Brace, New York.

Nelson, M.B. (1998) *Embracing Victory: Life Lessons in Competition and Compassion*, Morrow, New York.

Newbery, L. (2004) 'Hegemonic gender identity and outward bound: resistance and re-inscription?', *Women in Sport and Physical Activity Journal*, 13 (1), 36–49.

Newfield, J. (2001) 'The shame of boxing', *The Nation*, 273, 13–22.

Newsweek (2004) 'Perspectives: entertainment', *Newsweek*, 29 December–5 January, 122.

Nichol, J.P., P. Coleman and B.T. Williams (1993) *Injuries in Sport and Exercise: Main Report*, Sports Council, London.

Nichols, G. (2001) 'The UK voluntary sector', in *Understanding the Leisure and Sport Industry*, C. Wolsey and J. Abrams (eds), Longman, Harlow.

Nichols, G. (2003) 'Crime reduction and sports programmes', *Recreation*, January/February, 20–23.

Nichols, G. (2007) *Sport and Crime Reduction: The Role of Sports in Tackling Youth Crime*, Routledge, London.

Nicholson, M. (2007) *Sport and the Media: Managing the Nexus*, Elsevier, London.

Nixon, H. (1993b) 'Accepting the risk of pain and injury in sport: mediated cultural influences on playing hurt', *Sociology of Sport Journal*, 10(2), 183–196.

Nixon, H.L. II (1993a) 'A social network analysis of influences on athletes to play with pain and injuries', *Journal of Sport and Social Issues*, 16 (2), 127–135.

Nixon, H.L. II (1996a) 'The relationship of friendship networks, sports experiences, and gender to expressed pain thresholds', *Sociology of Sport Journal*, 13 (1), 78–86.

Nixon, H.L. II (1996b) 'Explaining pain and injury attitudes and experiences in sport in terms of gender, race, and sports status factors', *Journal of Sport and Social Issues*, 20 (1), 33–44.

Nixon, H.L. II (2000) 'Sport and disability', in J. Coakley and E. Dunning (eds), *Handbook of Sport Studies*, Sage, London.

Nixon, H.L. II (2007) 'Constructing diverse sports opportunities for people with disabilities', *Journal of Sport and Social Issues*, 31 (4), 417–433.

Norris, J. and R. Jones (1998) 'Towards a clearer definition and application of the centrality hypothesis in English professional association football', *Journal of Sport Behaviour*, 21, 181–195.

Northern Ireland Assembly (2001) *Sectarianism and Sport in Northern Ireland*, Northern Ireland Assembly, Belfast.

Nyad, D. (1996) www.npr.org/templates/story/story.php?storyId=1030733.

Nylund, D. (2003) 'Taking a slice at sexism: the controversy over the exclusionary membership practices of the Augusta National Golf Club', *Journal of Sport and Social Issues*, 27(2), 195–202.

O'Connor, A. (2004) 'Is Beckham a pawn in the game?', *The Times*, 4 March.

O'Neill, M. (2004) 'Policing football in Scotland: the forgotten team', *International Review for the Sociology of Sport*, 39(1), 95–104.

Obel, C. (2001) 'From embankments to corporate boxes: watching sports', in *Sociology of Sport in Everyday Life in New Zealand*, C. Bell (ed.), Dunmore, Palmerston North.

Office for National Statistics (2004a) *Living in Britain: Results from 2002 General Household Survey*, TSO, London.

Office for National Statistics (2004b) *Obesity among Adults: By Sex and NS-SeC, 2001: Social Trends 34*, TSO, London.

Office for National Statistics (2005) *A Summary of Focus on Social Inequalities*, TSO, London.

Office for National Statistics (2006) *Family Spending: A Report on the 2004–5 Expenditure and Food Survey*, Palgrave Macmillan, Basingstoke.

Office for National Statistics (2008) *Family Spending 2007*, Palgrave Macmillan, Basingstoke.

Oglesby, C. and D. Schrader (2000) 'Where is the white in the Rainbow Coalition?', in *Racism in College Athletics: The African-American Athlete's Experience*, D. Brooks and R. Althouse (eds), Fitness Information Technology, Morgantown, WV.

Ohl, F. and G. Tribou (2004) *Les Marches du Sport: Consammateurs et Distributeurs*, Armand Colin, Paris.

Okubu, H. (2004) *Local Identity and Sport: Historical Study of Integration and Differentiation*, Academica Verlag, Sankt Augustin, Germany.

Oliver, M. (1996) *Understanding Disability: From Theory to Practice*, St Martin's Press, New York.

Olney, B. (2006) 'Why pitchers use', *ESPN The Magazine*, 3 July, 46–47.

Omi, M. and H. Winant (1994) *Racial Formation in the United States*, Routledge, New York and London.

Opdyke, J. (2007) 'Love & money: when a kid's game becomes your life', *Wall Street Journal Online*, 6 May, http://online.wsj.com/article/SB117840716307293503.html.

Ossur (2008) 'Oscar Pistorius – special feature', www.ossur.com/?PageID=6738.

Owen, G. (2006) 'Catching crabs: bodies, emotions and gay identities in mainstream competitive rowing', in *Sport, Sexualities and Queer/Theory*, J. Caudwell (ed.), Routledge, London.

Oxfam International (2008) *Offside! Labour Rights and Sportswear Production in Asia*. Oxfam International, Melbourne, www.oxfam.org/en/policy/briefingnotes/offside_labor_report.

Palmer, C. (2004) 'Death, danger and the selling of risk in adventure sports', in *Understanding Lifestyle Sports: Consumption, Identity and Difference*, B. Wheaton (ed.), Routledge, London.

Pappas, N., P. McKenry and B. Catlett (2004) 'Athlete aggression on the rink and off the ice', *Men and Masculinities*, 6, 291–312.

Parrish, P. (2002) 'The height of gaining an edge', *Rocky Mountain News*, 21 September, 1B, 12B–13B.

Parrish, R. and McArdle, D. (2004) 'Beyond Bosman: the European Union's. influence upon professional athletes' freedom of movement', *Sport in Society*, 7, 403–419.

Parry, J. (2006) 'The intentional infliction of pain in sport: ethical perspectives', in *Pain and Injury in Sport: Social and Ethical Analysis*, S. Loland, B. Skirstad and I. Waddington (eds), Routledge, London.

Parry, M. and D. Malcolm (2004) 'England's Barmy Army: commercialization, masculinity and nationalism', *International Review for the Sociology of Sport*, 39(1), 75–94.

Pastore, D., S. Inglis and K. Danylchuk (1996) 'Retention factors in coaching and athletic management: differences by gender, position, and geographic location', *Journal of Sport & Social Issues*, 20(2), 427–441.

Patrick, D. (2005) 'USOC lobbies for anti-doping agency funds', *USA Today*, 25 May, 7C.

PE and Sport Strategy for Young People (2008) Crown Copyright.

Pearson, G. (2000) 'Legislating for the football hooligan', in *Sport and the Law*, S. Greenfield (ed.), Frank Cass, London.

Pelak, C.F. (2002) 'Women's collective identity formation in sports: a case study from women's ice hockey', *Gender and Society*, 16 (1), 93–114.

Pelak, C.F. (2005) 'Athletes as agents of change: an examination of shifting race relations within women's netball in post-apartheid South Africa', *Sociology of Sport Journal*, 22 (1), 59–77.

Pennington, B. (2004) 'Reading, writing and corporate sponsorships', *New York Times*, 18 October, p. 1.

Pennington, B. (2005) 'Doctors see a big rise in injuries for young athletes', *New York Times*, section A, 22 February, 1.

Pennington, B. (2007) 'For athletes, the next fountain of youth?', *New York Times*, 29 March, www.nytimes.com/2007/03/29/sports/29stem.html.

Perman, S. (1998) 'The master blasts the board', *Time*, 19 January, 61.

Perrottet, T. (2004) *The Naked Olympics: The True Story of the Ancient Games*, Random House, New York.

Perrucci, R. and E. Wysong (2003) *The New Class Society*, Rowman and Littlefield, Lanham, MD.

Perryman, M. (ed.) (2001) *Hooligan Wars*, Mainstream, Edinburgh.

Perryman, M. (ed.) (2002) *Going Oriental – Football after World Cup 2002*, Mainstream, Edinburgh.

Petersen, A. (2007) *The Body in Question: A Socio-cultural Approach*, Routledge, London and New York.

Petrecca, L. (2005) 'Marketers tackle participants in fantasy football', *USA Today*, 25 August, 3B.

Pfister, G. (2001) 'Doing sport in a headscarf? German sport and Turkish females', *Journal of Sport History*, 27, 401–428.

Pike, E. (2004) 'Risk, pain and injury: "a natural thing in rowing"?', in *Sporting Bodies, Damaged Selves: Sociological Studies of Sports-related Injury*, K. Young (ed.), Elsevier, Oxford.

Pike, E. (2005a) '"Doctors just say 'rest and take Ibuprofen'": a critical examination of the role of non-orthodox health care in women's sport', *International Review for the Sociology of Sport*, 40(2), 201–219.

Pike, E. (2005b) 'Injury risk in women's sport', *Encyclopedia of World Sport*, Berkshire Publishing Group, Great Barrington.

Pike, E. (2007) 'Revisiting the "physical activity, sexual health, teenage identity construction" nexus'. *International Review for the Sociology of Sport*, 42 (3), 309–319.

Pike, E. and S. Beames (2007) 'A critical interactionist analysis of "youth development" expeditions', *Leisure Studies*, 26(2), 147–159.

Pike, E. and J. Maguire (2003) 'Injury in women's sport: classifying key elements of a "risk encounter"', *Sociology of Sport Journal*, 20(3), 232–251.

Pilz, G.A. (1996) 'Social factors influencing sport and violence: on the "problem" of football hooliganism in Germany', *International Review for Sociology of Sport*, 31 (1), 49–68.

Platt, L. (2002) *New Jack Jocks: Rebels, Race, and the American Athlete*, Temple University Press, Philadelphia.

Play Fair (2008) 'Clearing the hurdles: steps to improving wages and working conditions in the global sportswear industry', written by the Maquila Solidarity Network on behalf of the Play Fair 2008 Campaign, www.playfair2008.org/docs/Clearing_the_Hurdles.pdf.

Polley, M. (1998) *Moving the Goalposts: A History of Sport and Society Since 1945*, Routledge, London.

Poppen, J. (2004) 'Pro performance', *Rocky Mountain News*, 31 March, 6B.

Porterfield, K. (1999) 'Late to the line: starting sport competition as an adult', in J. Coakley and P. Donnelly (eds), *Inside Sports*, Routledge, London.

Portes, A. (1998) 'Social capital: its origins and applications in modern sociology.' *Annual Review of Sociology*, 24, 1–24.

Poulton, E. (2004) 'Mediated patriot games: the construction and representation of national identities in the British television production of Euro '96', *International Review for the Sociology of Sport*, 39 (4), 437–455.

Poulton, E. (2005) 'English media representation of football-related disorder: "Brutal, short-hand and simplifying"', *Sport in Society*, 8, 27–47.

Poulton, E. (2006) '"Lights, camera, aggro!": readings of "celluloid hooliganism"', *Sport in Society*, 9, 403–426.

Pound, D. (2004) *Observer Sports Monthly*, August, 25.

Preves, S.E. (2005) *Intersex and Identity: The Contested Self*, Rutgers University Press, New Brunswick, NJ.

Price, M. and A. Parker (2003) 'Sport, sexuality, and the gender order: amateur rugby union, gay men, and social exclusion', *Sociology of Sport Journal*, 2(1), 108–126.

Price, M.E. and D. Dayan (eds) (2008) *Owning the Olympics: Narratives of the New China*. University of Michigan Press, Ann Arbor, MI.

Price, S.L. (1997) 'What ever happened to the white athlete?', *Sports Illustrated*, 8 December, 31–55.

Price, S.L. (2004) 'Flag jumper', *Sports Illustrated*, 30 August, 54–56.

Probert, A., S. Leberman and F. Palmer (2007) 'New Zealand bodybuilder identities: beyond homogeneity', *International Review for the Sociology of Sport*, 42(1), 5–26.

Professional Football Association (PFA) (2003) 'Player survey', PFA.

Pronger, B. (1999) 'Fear and trembling: homophobia in men's sport', in P. White and K. Young (eds), *Sport and Gender in Canada*, Oxford University Press, Don Mills, ON.

Pronger, B. (2002) *Body Fascism: Salvation in the Technology of Physical Fitness*, University of Toronto Press, Toronto, Buffalo and New York.

Radcliffe, P. (2005) *My Story So Far*, Pocket Books, London.

Rail, G. (1998) *Sport and Postmodern Times*. State University of New York Press, Albany, NY.

Raisborough, J. (2006) 'Getting onboard: women, access and serious leisure', *The Sociological Review*, 54 (2), 242–262.

Ramella, M. (2004) *Positive Futures Impact Report: Engaging With Young People*, Home Office, London.

Raney, A. and J. Bryant (eds) (2006) *Handbook of Sports and Media*, L. Erlbaum Associates, Mahwah, NJ.

Ravel, B. and G. Rail (2007) 'On the limits of "gaie" spaces: discursive constructions of women's sport in Quebec', *Sociology of Sport Journal*, 24 (4), 402–420.

Real, M. (1996) 'The postmodern Olympics: technology and the commodification of the Olympic movement', *Quest*, 48 (1), 9–24.

Real, M. (1998) 'MediaSport: technology and the commodification of postmodern sport', in *MediaSport*, L.A. Wenner (ed.), Routledge, London.

Reid, E. (1997) 'My body, my weapon, my shame', *Gentlemen's Quarterly*, September, 361–367.

Reid, S. (1996) 'The selling of the Games', *Denver Post*, 21 July.

Reynolds, G. (2007) 'Give us this day our daily supplements', *New York Times Play Magazine*, 4 March.

Rice, R. (2005) 'Moment of impact', *ESPN The Magazine*, 6 June, 82–83.

Rich, E., R. Holroyd and J. Evans (2004) '"Hungry to be noticed": young women, anorexia and schooling', in *Body Knowledge and Control: Studies in the Sociology of Physical Education and Health*, J. Evans, B. Davies and J. Wright (eds), Routledge, London.

Richtel, M. (2005) 'A new reality in video games: advertisements', *New York Times*, 11 April.

Riesman, D. and R. Denny (1951) 'Football in America: a study of cultural diffusion', *American Quarterly*, Winter, 302–325.

Rigauer, B. (2000) 'Marxist theories', in *Handbook of Sports Studies*, J. Coakley and E. Dunning (eds), Sage, London.

Rinehart, R. (2000) 'Arriving sport: alternatives to formal sports', in *Handbook of Sports Studies*, J. Coakley and E. Dunning (eds), Sage, London.

Rinehart, R. and C. Grenfell (1999) 'Icy relations: parental involvement in youth figure skating', paper presented at the annual conference of the North American Society for the Sociology of Sport, Cleveland, November.

Rinehart, R. and C. Grenfell (2002) 'BMX spaces: children's grass roots' courses and corporate-sponsored tracks', *Sociology of Sport Journal*, 19(3), 302–314.

Rinehart, R. and S. Syndor (eds) (2003) *To the Extreme: Alternative Sports Inside and Out*, State University of New York Press, Albany, NY.

Riordan, J. (1996) 'Introduction', *The Story of Worker Sport*, in A. Krüger and J. Riordan (eds), Human Kinetics, Leeds.

Riordan, J. and P. Arnaud (1999) *Sport and International Politics: The Impact of Fascism and Communism on Sport*, Spon, London.

Ritzer, G. (2005) *Enchanting a Disenchanted World: Revolutionizing the Means of Consumption*, Pine Forge Press, Thousand Oaks, CA.

Rivers, I. (2004) 'Recollections of bullying at school and their long-term implications for lesbians, gay men and bisexuals', *Crisis*, 25, 169–175.

Roberts, K. (2004) *The Leisure Industries*, Palgrave Macmillan, Basingstoke.

Roberts, S. (2004) 'Augusta can't shield corporate executives from Burk', *New York Times*, 8 April.

Robinson, L. (1998) *Crossing the Line: Violence and Sexual Assault in Canada's National Sport*, McClelland and Stewart, Toronto.

Robinson, L. (2008) 'The business of sport', in *Sport and Society: A Student Introduction*, B. Houlihan (ed.), Sage, London.

Robinson, V. (2004) 'Taking risks: identity, masculinities and rock climbing', in *Understanding Lifestyle Sports: Consumption, Identity and Difference*, B. Wheaton (ed.), Routledge, London.

Roche, K. (1999) 'Neighborhood characteristics and social capital: influences on the association between parenting and fighting and delinquency among adolescent males', unpublished PhD dissertation, Department of Sociology, Johns Hopkins University, Baltimore, MD.

Roderick, M. (2004) 'English professional soccer players and the uncertainties of injury', in *Sporting Bodies, Damaged Selves: Sociological Studies of Sports-related Injury*, K. Young (ed.), Elsevier, Oxford.

Roderick, M. (2006a) 'The sociology of pain and injury in sport: main perspectives and problems', in *Pain and Injury in Sport: Social and Ethical Analysis*, S. Loland, B. Skirstad and I. Waddington (eds), Routledge, London.

Roderick, M. (2006b) *The Work of Professional Football: A Labour of Love*, Routledge, London.

Roderick, M., Waddington, I. and Parker, G. (2000) 'Playing hurt: managing injuries in English professional football', *International Review for the Sociology of Sport*, 35, 165–180.

Rogge, J. (2003) 'Foreword', *Olympic Review*, www.olympic.org.

Rose, D. (2004) 'Don't call me handicapped', http://news.bbc.co.uk, 4 October.

Rosenfeld, A. and N. Wise (2001) *The Over-scheduled Child*, St Martin's Griffin Edition, New York.

Roth, A. and S. Basow (2004) 'Femininity, sports, and feminism: developing a theory of physical liberation', *Journal of Sport and Social Issues*, 28 (3), 245–265.

Roversi, A. (1994) 'The birth of the "ultras": the rise of football hooliganism in Italy', in *Game without Frontiers: Football, Identity and Modernity*, R. Giulianotti and J. Williams (eds), Ashgate, Aldershot.

Rowe, D. (2004a) *Sport, Culture and the Media: The Unruly Trinity*, Open University Press, Maidenhead.

Rowe, D. (ed.) (2004b) *Sport, Culture and the Media: Critical Readings*, Open University Press, Maidenhead.

Rowe, D., J. McKay and T. Miller (1998) 'Come together: sport, nationalism, and the media image', in *MediaSport*, L.A. Wenner (ed.), Routledge, London.

Rowe, N. and R. Champion (2000) *Sports Participation and Ethnicity in England. National Survey 1999/2000 Headline Findings*, Sport England, London.

Runciman, D. (2006) 'They can play, but they can never win', *New Statesman*, 29 May, www.newstatesman.com.

Ryan, J. (1995) *Little Girls in Pretty Boxes: The Making and Breaking of Elite Gymnasts and Figure Skaters*, Doubleday, New York.

Sabo, D. (2004) 'The politics of sports injury: hierarchy, power, and the pain principle', in *Sporting Bodies, Damaged Selves: Sociological Studies of Sports-related Injuries*, K. Young (ed.), Elsevier, Oxford.

Sabo, D. and S. Jensen (1998) 'Prometheus unbound: constructions of masculinity in sports media', in *MediaSport*, L. Wenner (ed.), Routledge, London.

Sabo, D., S. Jansen, D. Tate, M. Carlisle Duncan and S. Leggett (1996) 'Televising international sport: race, ethnicity, and nationalistic bias', *Journal of Sport and Social Issues*, 20 (1), 7–21.

Sabo, D., K. Miller, M. Melnick and L. Heywood (2004) *Her Life Depends on It: Sport, Physical Activity, and the Health and Well-being of American Girls*, Women's Sport Foundation, New York.

Safai, P. (2003) 'Healing the body in the "culture of risk": examining the negotiation of treatment between sport medicine clinicians and injured athletes in Canadian intercollegiate sport', *Sociology of Sport Journal*, 20 (2), 127–146.

Sage, G. (1999) 'Justice do it! The Nike transnational advocacy network: organization, collective actions, and outcomes', *Sociology of Sport Journal*, 16 (3), 206–235.

Sage, G. (2000) 'Political economy and sport', in *Handbook of Sports Studies*, J. Coakley and E. Dunning (eds), Sage, London.

Sailes, G. (1998) 'The African American athlete: social myths and stereotypes', in *African Americans in Sport*, G. Sailes (ed.), Transaction, New Brunswick, NJ.

Sam, M. (2003) 'What's the big idea? Reading the rhetoric of a national sport policy process', *Sociology of Sport Journal*, 20 (3), 189–213.

Sandomir, R. (2002) 'Olympics: athletes may next seek genetic enhancement', *New York Times*, 13 November, www.nytimes.com.

Sapolsky, R. (2000) 'It's not all in the genes', *Newsweek*, 10 April, 68.

Saporito, B. (2004) 'Why fans and players are playing so rough', *Time*, 164, 30–34.

Sato, D. (2005) 'Sport and identity in Tunisia', *International Journal of Sport and Health Science*, 3, 27–34.

Scambler, G. (2005) *Sport and Society: History, Power and Culture*, Open University Press, Maidenhead.

Schaller, B. (2005) 'Toni Davis', www.blackathletesportsnetwork.net/artman/publish/article_0510. shtml.

Scheerder, J., B. Vanreusel, M. Taks and R. Renson (2002) 'Social sports stratification in Flanders, 1969–1999: intergenerational reproduction of social inequalities?', *International Review for the Sociology of Sport*, 37 (2), 219–246.

Scheinin, R. (1994) *Field of Screams: The Dark Underside of America's National Pastime*, Norton, New York.

Scherer, J. (2007) 'Globalization, promotional culture and the production/consumption of on-line games: engaging adidas's Beat Rugby campaign', *New Media and Society*, 9, 125–146.

Scherer, J. and S.J. Jackson (2008) 'Producing Allblacks.com: cultural intermediaries and the policing of electronic spaces of sporting consumption', *Sociology of Sport Journal*, 25 (2), 187–205.

Schiesel, S. (2006) 'Making virtual football more like the real thing', *New York Times*, 6 July.

Schiesel, S. (2007) 'With famed players, game takes on Madden's turf', *New York Times*, 17 September.

Schilling, M. (1997) 'Socialization, retirement, and sports', http://edweb6.educ.msu.edu/kin866/resschilling1.htm.

Schimmel, K. (2000) 'Take me out to the ball game: the transformation of production–consumption relations in professional team sport', in *Cultural Production and Consumption: Readings in Popular Culture*, C. Harrington and D. Bielby (eds), Blackwell, Oxford.

Schimmel, K. (2002) 'The political economy of place: urban and sport studies perspectives', in *Theory, Sport and Society*, J. Maguire and K. Young (eds), Elsevier Science, Oxford.

Schimmel, K. (2006) 'Deep play: sports mega-events and urban social conditions in the USA', *The Sociological Review*, 54 (2), 160–174.

Schultz, B. (1999) 'The disappearance of child-directed activities', *Journal of Physical Education, Recreation and Dance*, 70 (5), 9–10.

Schultz, J. (2004) 'Discipline and push-up: female bodies, femininity, and sexuality in popular representations of sports bras', *Sociology of Sport Journal*, 21 (2), 185–205.

Scraton, S. (1999) '"Boys muscle in where angels fear to tread" – girls' subcultures and physical activities', in *Understanding Sport: An Introduction to the Sociological and Cultural Analysis of Sport*, J. Horne, A. Tomlinson and G. Whannel (eds), Taylor and Francis, London.

Scraton, S. (2001) 'Reconceptualizing race, gender and sport: the contribution of black feminism', in *'Race', Sport and British Society*, B. Carrington and I. McDonald (eds), Routledge, London.

Scraton, S. and Flintoff, A. (2002) 'Sport feminism: the contribution of feminist thought to our understanding of gender and sport', in *Gender and Sport: A Reader*, S. Scraton and A. Flintoff (eds), Routledge, London.

Scraton, S., J. Caudwell and S. Holland (2005) '"Bend it like Patel": Centring "race", ethnicity and gender in feminist analysis of women's football in England', *International Review for the Sociology of Sport*, 40 (1), 71–88.

Scruton, R. (2004) 'In for a hound', *Observer Sports Monthly*, December.

Seal, R. (2005) 'Growing pains', *Observer*, 4 December.

Seeley, M. and G. Rail (2004) 'Youth with disabilities: rethinking discourses of the "healthy" body', paper presented at the annual meeting of the North American Society for the Sociology of Sport, Tucson, Arizona, November.

Selman, R. (1971) 'Taking another's perspective: role-taking development in early childhood, *Child Development*, 42, 1721–1734.

Sernau, S. (2005) *Worlds Apart: Social Inequalities in a Global Economy*, Pine Forge Press, Thousand Oaks, CA.

Sewart, J. (1987) 'The commodification of sport', *International Review for the Sociology of Sport*, 22 (3), 171–192.

Shakib, S. (2003) 'Female basketball participation: negotiating the conflation of peer status and gender status from childhood through puberty', *American Behavioral Scientist*, 46 (10), 1404–1422.

Shapin, S. (2005) 'Cleanup hitters: the steroid wars and the nature of what's natural', *New Yorker*, 18 April, 191–194.

Sharp, R. (2006) 'Football manager demands ban on women referees', *Observer*, 12 November, 2.

Shaw, S. (2007) 'Touching the intangible? An analysis of "The Equality Standard: A framework for sport"', *Equal Opportunities International*, 26 (5), 420–434.

Sheard, K. (2006a) 'Boxing in the Western civilizing process', in *Sport Histories: Figurational Studies of the Development of Modern Sports*, E. Dunning, D. Malcolm and I. Waddington (eds), Routledge, London.

Sheard, K. (2006b) 'Pain and injury in boxing: the medical profession divided', in *Pain and Injury in Sport: Social and Ethical Analysis*, S. Loland, B. Skirtad and I. Waddington (eds), Routledge, London.

Shaw, M. (2002) 'Board with sports', unpublished paper, University of Colorado, Colorado Springs.

Sheil, P. (2000) 'Shed a tear or two ... or else!', www.abc.net.au/paralympics/features/s201108.htm.

Shields, D. and B. Bredemeier (1995) *Character Development and Physical Activity*, Human Kinetics, Leeds.

Shields, D., B. Bredemeier, D. Gardner and A. Bostrom (1995) 'Leadership, cohesion, and team norms regarding cheating and aggression', *Sociology of Sport Journal*, 12 (3), 324–336.

Shilling, C. (1993) *The Body and Social Theory*, Sage, London.

Shilling, C. (2005a) *The Body in Culture, Technology and Society*, Sage, London.

Shilling, C. (2005b) 'The rise of the body and the development of sociology', *Sociology*, 39 (4), 761–768.

Shogan, D. and M. Ford (2000) 'A new sport ethics', *International Review for the Sociology of Sport*, 35 (1), 49–58.

Silk, M. (1999) 'Local/global flows and altered production practices', *International Review for the Sociology of Sport*, 34 (2), 113–123.

Silk, M. (2004) 'A tale of two cities: the social production of sterile sporting space', *Journal of Sport and Social Issues*, 28 (4), 349–378.

Silk, M. and D. Andrews (2008) 'Managing Memphis: governance and regulation in sterile spaces of play', *Social Identities: Journal for the Study of Race, Nation and Culture*, 14 (3), 395–414.

Simson, V. and A. Jennings (1992) *The Lords of the Rings: Power, Money and Drugs in the Modern Olympics*, Simon and Schuster, London.

Smart, B. (2003) *Economy, Culture and Society*, Open University Press, London.

Smart, B. (2005) *The Sport Star: Modern Sport and the Cultural Economy of Sporting Celebrity*, Sage, London.

Smedley, A. (1997) 'Origin of the idea of race', *Anthropology Newsletter*, November, www.pbs.org/race/000_About/002_04-background-02-09.htm.

Smedley, A. (1999) 'Review of Theodore Allen, the invention of the white race, vol. 2', *Journal of World History*, 10 (1), 234–237.

Smedley, A. (2003) PBS interview for the series, *Race – the Power of an Illusion*, www.pbs.org/race/000_About/002_04-background-02-06.htm.

Smith, A. and N. Thomas (2005) 'The inclusion of elite athletes with disabilities in the 2002 Manchester Commonwealth Games: an exploratory analysis of British newspaper coverage', *Sports, Education and Society*, 10 (1), 49–67.

Smith, A. and I. Waddington (2004) 'Using "sport in the community schemes" to tackle crime and drug use among young people: some policy issues and problems', *European Physical Education Review*, 10 (3), 279–298.

Smith, B. and A. Sparkes (2002) 'Men, sport spinal cord injury and the construction of coherence: narrative practice in action', *Qualitative Research*, 2 (2), 143–171.

Smith, F. and J. Barker (2001) 'Commodifying the countryside: the impact of out-of-school care on rural landscapes of children's play', *Area*, 33 (2), 169–176.

Smith, G. (2005) 'The shadow boxer', *Sports Illustrated*, 18 April, 58–68.

Smith, J. and A. Ingham (2003) 'On the waterfront: retrospectives on the relationship between sport and communities', *Sociology of Sport Journal*, 20 (3), 252–274.

Smith, M. (1983) *Violence and Sport*, Butterworths, Toronto.

Smith Maguire, J. (2008) *Fit for Consumption*, Routledge, London.

Snider, M. (2007) 'Gamers who mean business', *USA Today*, 14 August.

Social Issues Research Centre (SIRC) (2006) *The Impact of Sport on the Workplace*, Social Issues Research Centre, Oxford.

Sokolove, M. (2004a) 'In pursuit of doped excellence', *New York Times Magazine*, 18 January, 28–33.

Sokolove, M. (2004b) 'Built to swim', *New York Times Magazine*, 8 August, 20–25.

Sokolove, M. (2004c) 'The thoroughly designed American childhood: constructing a teen phenom', *New York Times*, 28 November, 80.

Solomon, A. (2000) 'Our bodies, ourselves: the mainstream embraces the athlete Amazon', *The Village Voice*, 19–26 April.

Sparkes, A. and B. Smith (2002) 'Sport, spinal cord injury, embodied masculinities, and the dilemmas of narrative identity', *Men and Masculinities*, 4 (3), 258–285.

Sparkes, A., J. Batey and D. Brown (2005) 'The muscled self and its aftermath: a life history of an elite, black, male bodybuilder', *Áuto/Biography*, 13 (2), 131–160.

Spitzer, G. (2006) 'Sport and the systematic infliction of pain: a case study of state-sponsored mandatory doping in East Germany', in *Pain and Injury in Sport: Social and Ethical Analysis*, S. Loland, B. Skirtad and I. Waddington (eds), Routledge, London.

Sport England (2000) *Positive Futures*, Sport England, London.

Sport England (2001a) *Disabled Young People's Participation in Sport*, Sport England, London.

Sport England (2001b) *Sport Equity Index*, Sport England, London.

Sport England (2001c) *Young People and Sport in England, 1999*, Sport England, London.

Sport England (2003a) *National Survey of Young People and Sport*, Sport England, London.

Sport England (2003b) *Sports Volunteering in England 2002*, Sport England, London.

Sport England (2004) *The Framework for Sport in England: Making England an Active and Successful Sporting Nation*, Sport England, London.

Sport England (2006) *Active People Survey*, Sport England, London.

Sport England (2008a) *School Sport: Schools Competition Development, Bulletin 2*, Sport England, London.

Sport England (2008b) *Sport England Strategy 2008–2011*, Sport England, London.

Sporting Equals (2005) *Increasing Participation in Sport and Physical Activity by Black and Minority Ethnic Communities*, Sporting Equals, Birmingham.

sportscotland (2001) 'Sports participation in Scotland 2000', *Research Digest*, 84. sportscotland, Edinburgh.

sportscotland (2005) *Continuous Sports Participation Survey*, sportscotland, Edinburgh.

Starr, M. and A. Samuels (2000) 'A season of shame', *Newsweek*, 29 May, 56–60.

Stead, D. and J. Maguire, (2000) '"Rite de passage" or passage to riches?', *Journal of Sport and Social Issues*, 24 (1), 36–40.

Sternheimer, K. (2006) *Kids These Days: Facts and Fictions about Today's Youth*, Rowman and Littlefield, Lanham, MD.

Stetler, B. (2008) 'Web audience for games soars for NBC and Yahoo', *New York Times*, 25 August.

Stevenson, C. (1999) 'Becoming an elite international athlete: making decisions about identity', in *Inside Sports*, J. Coakley and P. Donnelly (eds), Routledge, London.

Stevenson, C. (2002) 'Seeking identities: towards an understanding of the athletic careers of masters swimmers', *International Review for the Sociology of Sport*, 37 (2), 131–146.

St Louis, B. (2003) 'Sport, genetics and the "natural athlete": the resurgence of racial science', *Body and Society*, 9 (2), 75–95.

St Louis, C. (2007) 'Train like a pro, even if you're 12', *New York Times*, 19 July.

Stoelting, S. (2004) 'She's in control, she's free, she's an athlete: a qualitative analysis of sport empowerment and the lives of female athletes', paper presented at the annual conference of the American Sociological Society, San Francisco, August.

Stokes, M. (1996) '"Strong as a Turk": Power, performance and representation in Turkish wrestling', in *Sport, Identity and Ethnicity*, J. MacClancy (ed.), Berg, Oxford.

Stoll, S. and J. Beller (1998) 'Can character be measured?', *Journal of Physical Education, Recreation, and Dance*, 69 (1), 18–24.

Stoll, S. and J. Beller (2000) 'Do sports build character?', in *Sports in School: The Future of an Institution*, J. Gerdy (ed.), Teachers College Press, New York.

Stone, J., C. Lynch, M. Sjomeling and J. Darley (1999) 'Stereotype threat effects on black and white athletic performance', *Journal of Personality and Social Psychology*, 77 (6), 1213–227.

Stone, J., Z. Perry and J. Darley (1997) '"White men can't jump": evidence for the perceptual confirmation of racial stereotypes following a basketball game', *Basic and Applied Social Psychology*, 19 (3), 291–306.

Sugden, J. (1996) *Boxing and Society: An International Analysis*, Manchester University Press, Manchester.

Sugden, J. and Bairner, A. (1995) *Sport, Sectarianism and Society in Divided Ireland*, Leicester University Press, Leicester.

Sugden, J. and A. Tomlinson (1998) *FIFA and the Contest for World Football: Who Rules the People's Game?* Polity Press, Cambridge.

Sugden, J. and A. Tomlinson (1999) *Great Balls of Fire: How Big Money is Highjacking World Football*, Mainstream, Edinburgh.

Sugden, J. and A. Tomlinson (2000) 'Theorizing sport, social class and status', in *Handbook of Sport Studies*, J. Coakley and E. Dunning (eds), Sage, London.

Sugden, J. and J. Wallis (eds) (2007) *Football For Peace? The Challenges of Using Sport for Co-existence in Israel*, Meyer and Meyer Sport (UK) Ltd, Oxford.

Swain, D. (1999) 'Moving on: leaving pro sports', in *Inside Sports*, J. Coakley and P. Donnelly (eds), Routledge, London.

Sweeney, H. (2004) 'Gene doping', *Scientific American*, 291 (1), 69.

Swift, E. and D. Yaeger (2001) 'Unnatural selection', *Sports Illustrated*, 14 May, 87–93.

Swinney, A. and J. Horne (2005) 'Race equality and leisure policy discourses in Scottish local authorities', *Leisure Studies*, 24 (3), 271–289.

Swoopes, S. (2005) 'Outside the arc (as told to L.Z. Granderson)', *ESPN The Magazine*, 7 November, 120–125.

Syed, M. (2008) 'Memo to Tiger and the BOA: sport and politics do mix, so speak up', *The Times*, 14 February.

Taheri, A. (2004) 'Muslim women play only an incidental part in the Olympics', www.benadorassociates.com/article/6651.

Takahashi, Y. and J. Horne (2006) 'Moving with the bat and the ball: preliminary reflections on the migration of Japanese baseball labour', *International Review for the Sociology of Sport*, 41 (1), 79–88.

Talbot, M. (1986) 'Gender and physical education', *British Journal of Physical Education*, 17, 120–122.

Taub, D. and K. Greer (2000) 'Physical activity as a normalizing experience for school-age children with physical disabilities: implications for legitimating of social identity and enhancement of social ties', *Journal of Sport and Social Issues*, 24 (4), 395–414.

Taylor, I. (1982a) 'On the sports violence question: soccer hooliganism revisited', in *Sport, Culture and Ideology*, J. Hargreaves (ed.), Routledge and Kegan Paul, London.

Taylor, I. (1982b) 'Class, violence and sport: the case of soccer hooliganism in Britain', in *Sport, Culture and the Modern State*, H. Cantelon and R. Gruneau (eds), University of Toronto Press, Toronto.

Taylor, I. (1987) 'Putting the boot into a working-class sport: British soccer after Bradford and Brussels', *Sociology of Sport Journal*, 4 (2), 171–191.

Taylor, M. (2007) 'Football, migration and globalization: the perspective of history', *Idrottsforum*, http://idrottsforum.org/articles/taylor/taylor070314.html.

Temple, K. (1992) 'Brought to you by ...', *Notre Dame Magazine*, 21 (2), 29.

The Economist (2004) 'Real Money, David Beckham', *The Economist*, 13 March, www.economist.com.

Theberge, N. (1999) 'Being physical: sources of pleasure and satisfaction in women's ice hockey', in *Inside Sports*, J. Coakley and P. Donnelly (eds), Routledge, London.

Theberge, N. (2000) 'Gender and sport', in *Handbook of Sport Studies*, J. Coakley and E. Dunnings (eds), Sage, London.

Thing, L. (2001) 'The female warrior: meanings of play-aggressive emotions in sport', *International Review for the Sociology of Sport*, 36 (3), 275–288.

Thomas, C. (1999) 'Narrative identity and the disabled self', in *Disability Discourse*, M. Corker and S. French (eds), Open University Press, Milton Keynes.

Thomas, N. (2002) 'Disability sport policy area. Ill-defined and vulnerable?', *Inclusive Sport*, Spring, 36–37.

Thomas, R. (1996) 'Black faces still rare in the press box, in *Sport in Society: Equal Opportunity or Business as Usual?* R. Lapchick (ed.), Sage, London.

Thompson, S. (1999a.) *Mother's Taxi: Sport and Women's Labor*, State University of New York Press, Albany, NY.

Thompson, S. (1999b) 'The game begins at home: women's labor in the service of sport', in *Inside Sports*, J. Coakley and P. Donnelly (eds), Routledge, London.

Thomsen, S., D. Bower and M. Barnes (2004) 'Photographic images in women's health, fitness, and sports magazines and the physical self-concept of a group of adolescent female volleyball players', *Journal of Sport and Social Issues*, 28 (3), 266–283.

Thomson, R. (2000) 'Staring back: self-representations of disabled performance artists', *American Quarterly*, 52 (2), 334–338.

Thomson, R. (2002) 'Integrating disability, transforming feminist theory', *National Women's Studies Association Journal*, 14 (3), 1–32.

Thornton, A. (2004) '"Anyone can play this game": ultimate frisbee, identity and difference', in *Understanding Lifestyle Sports: Consumption, Identity and Difference*, B. Wheaton (ed.), Routledge, London.

Tibballs, S. (2007) 'Raising the game: the future of women's sport', www.wsff.org.uk.

Time (1997) 'Time's 25 most influential Americans', *Time*, 21 April, www.time.com.

Tinmouth, M. (2004) 'Initiation ceremonies in university sport in the UK', unpublished report, University of Southampton.

Todd, T. (1987) 'Anabolic steroids: the gremlins of sport', *Journal of Sport History*, 14 (1), 87–107.

Tomlinson, A. (2005) 'The commercialization of the Olympics: cities, corporations, and the Olympic commodity', in *Global Olympics: Historical and Sociological Studies of the Modern Games*, K. Young and K. Walmsley (eds), Elsevier, Oxford.

Tomlinson, A. (2007) 'Sport and social class', in *Encyclopedia of Sociology*, G. Ritzer (ed.), Blackwell, London.

Tomlinson, A. and S. Fleming (1996) 'Football, xenophobia and racism(s) – Europe and the old England', in *Racism and Xenophobia in European Football*, U. Merkel and W. Tokarski (eds), Meyer and Meyer, Aachen.

Torbert, M. (2004) 'A games model for facilitating a constructivist approach', in *The Child's Right to Play: A Global Approach*, R. Clements and L. Fiorentino (eds), Praeger, London.

Torbert, M. (2005) *Follow Me: A Handbook of Movement Activities for Children*, PLAY, Eagan, MN.

Totilo, S. (2008), 'Playing games', *The Nation*, 286 (21), 2 June, 25–30.

Tranter, N. (1998) *Sport, Economy and Society in Britain, 1750–1914*, Cambridge University Press, Cambridge.

Treanor, G. (2003) 'Manchester United hires former Disney executive', www.guardian.co.uk, 23 December.

Trujillo, N. (1995) 'Machines, missiles and men: images of the male body on ABC's Monday Night Football', *Sociology of Sport Journal*, 12 (4), 403–423.

Trulson, M. (1986) 'Martial arts training: a novel "cure" for juvenile delinquency', *Human Relations*, 39 (12), 1131–1140.

Trumpbour, R. (2007) *The New Cathedrals: Politics and Media in the History of Stadium Construction*, Syracuse University Press, Syracuse, NY.

Tuaolo, E. (2002) 'Free and clear', *ESPN The Magazine*, 11 November, 72–77.

Tuck, J. (2003a) 'Making sense of emerald commotion: rugby union, national identity and Ireland', *Identities: Global Studies in Culture and Power*, 10 (4), 495–515.

Tuck, J. (2003b) 'The men in white: reflections on rugby union, the media and Englishness, *International Review for the Sociology of Sport*, 38 (2), 177–199.

Tucker, R. and J. Dugus (2007a) 'Oscar Pistorius reaction: challenge the ban', *The Science of Sport*, 14 January, http://scienceofsport.blogspot.com/2008/01/oscar-pistorius-reaction-challenge-ban.html.

Tucker, R. and J. Dugus (2007b) 'Oscar Pistorius banned – IAAF result', *The Science of Sport*, 19 December, http://scienceofsport.blogspot.com/2007/12/oscar-pistorius-banned-iaaf-result.html.

Tucker, R. and J. Dugus (2007c) 'Oscar Pistorius – Science and engineering vs training. An evaluation of ALL the evidence', *The Science of Sport*, 11 July, http://scienceofsport.blogspot.com/2007/07/oscar-pistorius-science-and-engineering.html.

Tucker, R. and J. Dugus (2007d) 'Oscar Pistorius debut: the scientific facts and implications', *The Science of Sport*, 17 July, http://scienceofsport.blogspot.com/2007/07/oscar-pistorius-debut-scientific-facts_17.html.

Tucker, R. and J. Dugus (2008) 'Oscar Pistorius: a case where the science does not matter', *The Science of Sport*, 21 February, http://scienceofsport.blogspot.com/2008/02/oscar-pistorius-case-where-science-does.html.

Tucker, L. and J. Parks (2001) 'Effects of gender and sport type on intercollegiate athletes' perceptions of the legitimacy of aggressive behaviors in sport', *Sociology of Sport Journal*, 18 (4), 403–413.

Turner, B. (1997) *The Body and Society*, Sage, London.

Turner, R. (2006) 'We have to stop violent young players joining the professional game by weeding them out when they display violence', *Western Mail*, 6 October.

Ueberroth, P. (1983) 'US News & World Report', www.usnews.com.

UK Sport (2005) *UK National Anti-Doping Policy*, UK Sport, London.

UK Sport (2006) *Measuring Success 3: The Economic Impact of Major Sports Events*, UK Sport, London.

UK Sport (2007) *World Class Pathway*, UK Sport, London.

Urquhart, J. and J. Crossman (1999) 'The *Globe and Mail* coverage of the Winter Olympic Games: a cold place for women athletes', *Journal of Sport & Social Issues*, 23 (2), 193–202.

USOC (1992) *USOC Drug Education and Doping Control Program: Guide to Banned Medications*, USOC, Colorado Springs, CO.

Vamplew, W. (1988) *Pay Up and Play the Game: Professional Sport in Britain, 1875–1914*, Cambridge University Press, Cambridge.

Van Sterkenburg, J. and A. Knoppers (2004) 'Dominant discourses about race/ethnicity and gender in sport practice and performance', *International Review for the Sociology of Sport*, 39 (3), 301–321.

Veblen, T. (1899) *The Theory of the Leisure Class*, Macmillan, New York.

Vélez, B. (2003) 'Gender equity in Colombia', www.theglobalgame.com/velez.htm.

Verducci, T. (2002) 'Totally juiced', *Sports Illustrated*, 3 June, 34–48.

Veri, M. (1999) 'Homophobic discourse surrounding the female athlete', *Quest*, 51 (4), 355–368.

Verma, G. and D. Darby (1994) *Winners and Losers: Ethnic Minorities in Sport and Recreation*, Falmer Press, London.

Vertinsky, P. (1987) 'Exercise, physical capability, and the eternally wounded woman in late nineteenth century North America', *Journal of Sport History*, 14 (1), 7–27.

Vertinsky, P. (1994) 'Women, sport, and exercise in the 19th century', in *Women and Sport: Interdisciplinary Perspectives*, D. Costa and S. Guthrie (eds), Human Kinetics, Leeds.

Vincent, J. (2004) 'Game, sex and match: the construction of gender in British newspaper coverage of the 2000 Wimbledon championship', *Sociology of Sport Journal*, 21 (4), 435–456.

Vine, L. and R. Aust (2006) *Taking Part: The National Survey of Culture, Leisure and Sport*, Department for Culture, Media and Sport, London.

Viner, K. (2005) 'A year of killing', *Guardian*, 10 December 2005.

Wacquant, L. (1992) 'The social logic of boxing in black Chicago: toward a sociology of pugilism', *Sociology of Sport Journal*, 9 (3), 221–254.

Wacquant, L. (1995a) 'The pugilistic point of view: how boxers think and feel about their trade', *Theory and Society*, 24, 489–535.

Wacquant, L. (1995b) 'Why men desire muscles', *Body and Society*, 1 (1), 163–179.

Wacquant, L. (2004) *Body and Soul: Notebooks of an Apprentice Boxer*, Oxford University Press, Oxford.

Waddington, I. (2000a) 'Sport and health: a sociological perspective', in *Handbook of Sports Studies* J. Coakley and E. Dunning (eds), Sage, London.

Waddington, I. (2000b) *Sport, Health and Drugs: A Critical Sociological Perspective*, Routledge, London.

Waddington, I. (2006) 'Ethical problems in the medical management of sports injuries: a case study of English professional football', in *Pain and Injury in Sport: Social and Ethical Analysis*, S. Loland, B. Skirtad and I. Waddington (eds), Routledge, London.

Waddington, I. (2007) 'Health and sport', in *Encyclopedia of sociology*, G. Ritzer (ed.), Blackwell, London.

Wahidin, A and J. Powell (2003) 'Re-configuring old bodies: from the bio-medical model to a critical epistemology', *Journal of Social Sciences and Humanities*, 26 (2), 10–22.

Wahl, G. (2003) 'Inside soccer', www.sportsillustrated.cnn.com, 18 June.

Wahl, G. (2004) 'On safari for 7-footers', *Sports Illustrated*, 28 June, 68–78.

Walker, R. (2005) 'Extreme makeover: home edition – entertainment poverty', *New York Times*, 4 December.

Walseth, K. (2006) 'Young Muslim women and sport: the impact of identity work', *Leisure Studies*, 25 (1), 75–94.

Walseth, K. and K. Fasting (2003) 'Islam's view on physical activity and sport: Egyptian women interpreting Islam', *International Review for the Sociology of Sport*, 38 (1), 45–60.

Wann, D., G. Haynes, B. McLean and P. Pullen (2003) 'Sport team identification and willingness to consider anonymous acts of hostile aggression', *Aggressive Behavior*, 29, 406–413.

Wann, D., J. Hunter, J. Ryan and L. Wright (2001a) 'The relationship between team identification and willingness of sport fans to consider illegally assisting their team', *Social Behavior & Personality: An International Journal*, 29 (6), 531–537.

Wann, D., M. Melnick, G. Russell and D. Pease (2001b) *Sport Fans: The Psychology and Social Impact of Spectators*, Routledge, London.

Wann, D., R. Peterson, C. Cothran and M. Dykes (1999) 'Sport fan aggression and anonymity: the importance of team identification', *Social Behavior & Personality: An International Journal*, 27 (6), 597–602.

Wann, D., J. Royalty and A. Rochelle (2002) 'Using motivation and team identification to predict sport fans' emotional responses to team performance', *Journal of Sport Behavior*, 25 (2), 207–216.

Wann, D., P. Waddill and M. Dunham (2004) 'Using sex and gender role orientation to predict level of sport fandom', *Journal of Sport Behavior*, 27 (4), 367–377.

Waterford, R. (2004) 'Athens suffers old stereotypes', *USA Today*, 5 August.

Wearden, S. and P. Creedon (2002) '"We got next": images of women in television commercials during the inaugural WNBA season', *Sport in Society*, 5 (3), 189–210.

Weaver, P. (2005) 'Alma mater of Coe and Radcliffe brings sport to Muslim women', www.buzzle.com/editorials/2-23-2005-66148.asp.

Webb, E., C. Ashton, P. Kelly and F. Kamali (1996) *Alcohol and Drug Use in UK University Students*, University of Newcastle Upon Tyne. Newcastle Upon Tyne.

Weber, M. (1968/1922) *Economy and Society: An Outline of Interpretive Sociology*, trans. G. Roth and G. Wittich, Bedminster Press, New York.

Wedgewood, N. (2004) 'Kicking like a boy: schoolgirl Australian rules football and bi-gendered female embodiment', *Sociology of Sport Journal*, 21 (2), 140–162.

Weed, M. (2001) 'Ing-ger-land at Euro 2000: how "handbags at 20 paces" was portrayed as a full-scale riot', *International Review for the Sociology of Sport*, 36 (4), 407–424.

Weiler, K. and C. Higgs (1999) 'Television coverage of professional golf: a focus on gender', *Women in Sport and Physical Activity Journal*, 8 (1), 83–100.

Weiner, J. (1999) 'What do we want from our sports heroes?', *BusinessWeek*, 5 February, 77.

Weiner, T. (2004) 'Low-wage Costa Ricans make baseballs for millionaires', *New York Times*, 25 January, 3.

Weinstein, M., M. Smith and D. Wiesenthal (1995) 'Masculinity and hockey violence', *Sex Roles*, 33 (11/12), 831–847.

Weir, T. (2000) 'Americans fall farther behind', *USA Today*, 3 May.

Weise, E. (2003) 'Seniors seek vitality in growth hormone', *USA Today*, 4 November.

Weisman, L. (2004) 'Propelled to think past NFL', *USA Today*, 16 June.

Weiss, O. (1996) 'Media sports as a social substitution pseudosocial relations with sports figures', *International Review for the Sociology of Sport*, 31 (1), 109–118.

Wellard, I. (2006) 'Exploring the limits of queer and sport: gay men playing tennis', in *Sport, Sexualities and Queer/Theory*, J. Caudwell (ed.), Routledge, London.

Wellard, I. (ed.) (2007) *Rethinking Gender and Youth Sport*, Routledge, London.

Wendel, T. (2004) 'How fantasy games have changed fans', *USA Today*, 20 September.

Wenner, L. (1998) *MediaSport*, Routledge, London.

Wenner, L. and W. Gantz (1998) 'Watching sports on television: audience experience, gender, fanship, and marriage', in *MediaSport*, L. Wenner (ed.), Routledge, London.

Wensing, E. and T. Bruce (2003) 'Bending the rules: media representations of gender during an international sporting event', *International Review for the Sociology of Sport*, 38 (4), 387–396.

Weintraub, S. (2002) *Silent Night: The Remarkable Christmas Truce of 1914*, Pocket Books, New York.

Werbner, P. (1996) '"Our blood is green": cricket, identity, and social empowerment among British Pakistanis', in *Sport, Identity, and Ethnicity*, J. MacClancy (ed.), Berg, Oxford.

Wertheim, J. (2004) 'Globalization in sports: the whole world is watching (Part 1 of 4)', *Sports Illustrated*, 100 (24), 14 June, 72–86.

Wertheim, J. (2005) 'Gays in sports: a poll', *Sports Illustrated*, 18 April, 64–65.

Whannel, G. (2002) *Media Sport Stars: Masculinities and Moralities*, Routledge, London.

Whannel, G. (2007) 'Mediating masculinities: the production of media representations in sport', in *Sport and Gender Identities*, C. Carmichael Aitchison (ed.), Routledge, London.

Wheaton, B. (2004a) 'Introduction: mapping the lifestyle sport-scape', in *Understanding Lifestyle Sports: Consumption, Identity and Difference*, B. Wheaton (ed.), Routledge, London.

Wheaton, B. (2004b) '"New Lads"? Competing masculinities in the windsurfing culture', in *Understanding Lifestyle Sports: Consumption, Identity and Difference*, B. Wheaton (ed.), Routledge, London.

Wheaton, B. and B. Beal (2003) '"Keeping it real": subcultural media and the discourses of authenticity in alternative sport', *International Review for the Sociology of Sport*, 38 (2), 155–176.

Wheeler, G. (1996) 'Retirement from disability sport: a pilot study', *Adapted Physical Activity Quarterly*, 13 (4), 382–399.

Wheeler, G. (1999) 'Personal investment in disability sport careers: an international study', *Adapted Physical Activity Quarterly*, 16 (3), 219–237.

White, A. (2003) 'Women and sport in the UK', in *Sport and Women: Social Issues in International Perspective*, I. Hartmann-Tews and G. Pfister (eds), Routledge, London.

White, A. and C. Brackenridge (1985) 'Who rules sport? Gender divisions in the power structure of British sport from 1960', *International Review for the Sociology of Sport*, 20 (1), 95–107.

White, A. and I. Henry (2004) *Women, Leadership and the Olympic Movement*, Institute of Sport and Policy Research, Loughborough University.

White, M. and J. Kay (2006) 'Who rules sport now? White and Brackenridge revisited', *International Review for the Sociology of Sport*, 41 (4), 465–473.

White, P. (2004) 'The cost of injury from sport, exercise and physical activity: a review of the evidence', in *Sporting Bodies, Damaged Selves: Sociological Studies of Sports-related Injury*, K. Young (ed.), Elsevier, Oxford.

White, P. and K. Young (1997) 'Masculinity, sport, and the injury process: a review of Canadian and international evidence', *Avante*, 3 (2), 1–30.

Wiggins, B. (2004) *Observer Sports Monthly*, 45 January.

Wigglesworth, N. (2007) *The Story of Sport in England*, Routledge, London.

Wightman, A., P. Higgins, G. Jarvie and R. Nichol (2002) 'The cultural politics of hunting: sporting estates and recreational land use in the Highlands and Islands of Scotland', *Culture, Sport and Society*, 5 (1), 53–70.

Wightwick, A. (2008) 'Athletes frustrated over juggling sport and study', *Western Mail*, 14 February.

Williams, J. (2003) *The Liverpool Way*, Mainstream, London.

Williams, P. (2005) 'Genetically speaking', *The Nation*, 280 (24), 10.

Wilmore, J. (1996) 'Eating disorders in the young athlete', in *The Child and Adolescent Athlete*, O. bar-Or (ed.), Blackwell Science, London.

Wilson, B. (2007) 'New media, social movements, and global sport studies: a revolutionary moment and the sociology of sport', *Sociology of Sport Journal*, 24 (4), 457–477.

Wilson, D. (2008) 'Friendlier tone, but plenty of tough talk', *New York Times*, 16 January.

Wilson, T. (2002) 'The paradox of social class and sports involvement: the roles of cultural and economic capital', *International Review for the Sociology of Sport*, 37 (1), 5–16.

Winant, H. (2001) *The World is a Ghetto: Race and Democracy since World War II*, Basic Books, New York.

Winant, H. (2004) *The New Politics of Race: Globalism Difference Justice*, University of Minnesota Press, Minneapolis, MN.

Winant, H. (2006) 'Race and racism: towards a global future', *Ethnic and Racial Studies*, 29 (5), 986–1003.

Winlock, C. (2000) 'Running the invisible race', *ColorLines*, 3 (1), 27.

Wittebols, J. (2004) *The Soap Opera Paradigm: Television Programming and Corporate Priorities*, Rowman and Littlefield, Lanham.

Wolfe, T. (1979) *The Right Stuff*, Farrar, Strauss, Giroux, New York.

Wolff, A. (2003) 'The American athlete: age 10', *Sports Illustrated*, 6 October, 59–67.

Wolff, E. (2005) 'The 2004 Athens Games and Olympians with disabilities: triumphs, challenges, and future opportunities', presentation at the 45th International Session for Young Participants International Olympic Academy, Athens.

Wollaston, S. (2005) 'It's given me my life again', *Guardian*, 5 September.

Women's Sports Foundation (2007a) *WSF Factsheet: Women, Sport and the Media*, Women's Sport Foundation, London.

Women's Sports Foundation (2007b) *WSF Factsheet: Women into Sports Leadership*, Women's Sport Foundation, London.

Women's Sports Foundation (2007c) *WSF Factsheet: The Issues Surrounding Women and Coaching*, Women's Sports Foundation, London.

Wong, J. (1999) 'Asian women in sport', *Journal of Physical Education, Recreation and Dance*, 70 (4), 42–43.

Woodward. J. (2004) 'Professional football scouts: an investigation of racial stacking', *Sociology of Sport Journal*, 21 (4), 356–375.

Worker Rights Consortium (WRC) (2007) 'WRC factory investigation: Jerzees Choloma and Jerzees de Honduras', *Worker Rights Consortium*, www.workersrights.org/freports/JerzeesCholoma.asp.

Wray, S. (2002) 'Connecting ethnicity, gender and physicality: Muslim Pakistani women, physical activity and health', in *Gender and Sport: A Reader*, S. Scraton and A. Flintoff (eds), Routledge, London.

Wright, D. and K. Fitzpatrick (2006) 'Social capital and adolescent violent behavior correlates of fighting and weapon use among secondary school students', *Social Forces*, 4, 1435–1453.

Yessis, M. (2006) *Build a Better Athlete: What's Wrong with American Sports and How to Fix It*, Equilibrium Books, Terre Haute, IN.

Yocom, G. (2008) 'My shot: Casey Martin', *Golf Digest*, March.

Yorganci, I. (1993) 'Preliminary findings from a survey of gender relationships and sexual harassment in sport, in *Body Matters: Leisure Images and Lifestyles*, C. Brackenridge (ed.), Leisure Studies Association, Brighton.

Young, I. (1990) *Throwing Like a Girl and Other Essays in Philosophy and Social Theory*, Indiana University Press, Indianapolis, IN.

Young, I. (1998) 'Situated bodies: throwing like a girl', in *Body and Flesh: A Philosophical Reader*, D. Welton (ed.), Blackwell, London.

Young, K. (1993) 'Violence, risk, and liability in male sports culture', *Sociology of Sport Journal*, 10 (4), 373–396.

Young, K. (2000) 'Sport and violence', in *Handbook of Sport Studies*, J. Coakley and E. Dunning (eds), Sage, London.

Young, K. (2002) 'From "sports violence" to "sports crime": aspects of violence, law, and gender in the sports process', in *Paradoxes of Youth and Sport*, M. Gatz, M.A. Messner and S.J. Ball-Rokeach (eds), State University of New York Press, Albany, NY.

Young, K. (ed.) (2004a) *Sporting Bodies, Damaged Selves: Sociological Studies of Sports-related Injury*, Elsevier, Oxford.

Young, K. (2004b) 'Sports-related pain and injury: sociological notes', in *Sporting Bodies, Damaged Selves: Sociological Studies of Sports-related Injuries*, K. Young (ed.), Elsevier, Oxford.

Young, K. (2007a) 'Violence among athletes', in *Encyclopedia of Sociology*, G. Ritzer (ed.), Blackwell, London.

Young, K. (2007b) 'Violence among fans', in *Encyclopedia of Sociology*, G. Ritzer (ed.), Blackwell, London.

Young, K. and P. White (1995) 'Sport, physical danger, and injury: the experiences of elite women athletes', *Journal of Sport and Social Issues*, 19 (1), 45–61.

Zhang, J. and D. Smith (1997) 'Impact of broadcasting on the attendance of professional basketball games', *Sport Marketing Quarterly*, 6 (1), 23–29.

Zhang, J., D. Pease and E. Jambor (1997) 'Negative influence of market competitors on the attendance of professional sport games: the case of a minor league hockey team', *Sport Marketing Quarterly*, 6 (3), 31, 34–40.

Zhang, J., D. Pease and D. Smith (1998) 'Relationship between broadcasting media and minor league hockey game attendance', *Sport Management Quarterly*, 12 (2), 103–122.

Zimmer, M. and M. Zimmer. (2001) 'Athletes as entertainers', *Journal of Sport and Social Issues*, 25 (2), 202–215.

Zirin, D. (2008) 'The Super Bowl: who stole the soul?', *The Edge of Sports*, 1 February.

Zorpette, G. (2000) 'The chemical games', *Scientific American*, 11 (3), 16–23.

Index

AAA (American Anthropological Association) 317
about this book 2–3
    social life, sport and 3
Abramovich, Roman 94, 370, 392, 410–11
abstracts *see* summarizations
acceptance barriers 181–3
Accra Football Club, Brixton 331
action in games, increase in 164–5
Adams, M. 477
Adbusters 435
Adelson, E. 332
Adidas 26
Adler, P. and Adler, P. 153, 156
adult controlled sports for youth 151–2
    formal structure in 152
age
    older people, participation preferences among 517–18
    in organized sport 85
agents of socialization 101
aggression
    fan aggression, precipitation of 258
    themes in media representations of 461
    and violence in sports 227
Albert, Mathieu 363
alcohol consumption 200–201
Aldred, T. 276
Alexander, C. 313
Ali, Laila 233
Allison, L. 474, 476
Almada, Anthony 211
Alonso, Fernando 419, 420
alternative sports
    and action sports, increased interest in 148
    creation of 535
    groups seeking 518–19
    participation opportunities in 281–3
amateur athletes in commercial sports 422–3
    amateur sports in UK 415–16
    income of 422–3
    legal status of 422
    professional/amateur dichotomy 354–5
    see also athletes
American Academy of Pediatrics 154
anarchy 185

ancient sports *see* historical perspectives
Anderson, Eric 122, 291, 302–3, 304, 305, 455
Anderson, J. 236
Anderson, K. 282
Anderson, Rachel 417
Anderson, S. and Cavanagh, J. 396
Andersson, M. 328
Andrews, D. 128, 395, 401, 454, 488
Andrews, D. and Jackson, S.J. 128, 395, 429, 449, 460
Andrews, D. and Silk, M. 495
animal sports, violence as strategy in 240–41
Anschutz, Phil 401
antisocial deviance 190
Aragones, Luis 323
Armour, K. and Kirk, R. 160
Armstrong, G. 256
Armstrong, K. and Perry, N. 248
Armstrong, Lance 399, 436
Arnold, Thomas 80
Arsenault, A. and Castells, M. 429
Assael, S. 211, 215, 217, 525
Association for the Study of Sport and the European Union 29
athletes
    acceptance process for 105–6
    assaults by 248–50
    as change agents 533–5
    commercialization and orientations of 405–7
    focus on deviant behaviour among 202
    global migration of 495–8
    journalists' relationships with 464
    research on deviance among 197–205
    rewards of sports, distribution to 506
    student athletes 162–3
    support on gender issues for 283–4
Atkinson, M. 525
Atkinson, M. and Young, K. 240, 241
Atkinson, Ron 340, 458
attendance at events, media impacts on 462–3
audience experiences 463
authority, power and 471

Back, L. et al. 328, 340
Baerg, A. 436

Bairner, Alan 35, 85, 127, 336, 351, 474, 476, 485
Baker, A. 16, 67, 68, 73
Baker, J. and Coté, J. 149
Baker, W. 67, 68, 73
Bale, J. and Christensen, M. 7, 492, 499
Bale, J. and Cronin, M. 499
Bale, J. and Maguire, J. 496–7
Bale, J. and Vertinsky, P. 527
Ballard, C. 434
Bannister, Sir Roger 92
Barkley, Charles 489
Barnes, John 340
Barnes, Simon 225, 305
barriers to participation *see* breaking barriers
Basilio, Enrigueta 93
Batey, Joanne 123
BBC (British Broadcasting Corporation) 26, 238
    Sport Academy 236
    'Sports Personality of the Year' 10
Beal, B. and Weidman, L. 282
Beal, Becky 157, 432, 518
Beals, K. 274
Beckham, David 26, 187, 306, 321, 373, 395, 400, 401,
        419–20, 440, 516
    as brand 401
Beckham, Victoria 400
Beech, J. and Chadwick, S. 408
Beiruty, H. 334
Bell, Wendell 434, 513
Belson, M. 369
Ben-Porat, G. and Ben-Porat, A. 487, 493, 499
Benedict, J. 248
Benn, Nigel 242
Bernstein, A. and Blain, N. 429
Berra, L. 235
Best, George 244, 248
Bick, J. 140, 145
Biene, David 17, 70, 451, 508
Bilger, B. 318
biology
    biological notions of race 314, 317
    biological variation in humans 291–3
    of gender difference 299
Birley, D. 80
Birrell, S. 49, 288, 533
Bishop, R. 453
Bjerklie, D. and Park, A. 211
black people
    black-only teams 331
    British men, racial ideology and sense of athletic
        destiny for 324–5
    footballers, problems for 340

inferiority of, belief in 315
    swimmers 339
Blackshaw, T. and Crabbe, T. 200
Blain, N. et al 458
Blair, Tony 470
Blake, A. 21
Blankers-Koen, Fanny 92
Blauvelt, H. 332
Block, M. 158
Bloom, Benjamin 155
Bloom, M. 328
Bloyce, D. 460
Blumenthal, R. 235
BMC (bicycle motocross) 64–5, 116, 141, 148, 323,
        400, 503
BME Sport Network East 342
body
    bodybuilding 22
    contact between bodies, brutality in 229
    rationalization of 213
    shame in 275–6
    social construction of 22
    sports and meanings given to 21–3
Bolin, A. 299
Bolton Wanderers 26
Bond, Katherine 444
Bonilla-Silva, E. 459
Booth, D. and Loy, J. 358
borderline violence 229
Botwright, Vicky 457
Boulmerka, Hassiba 334, 335
Bourdieu, Pierre 359, 476
Bowyer, Lee 230
boxing
    class, gender and ethnic relations in 364–7
    control of violence 246
    violence within rules 244
Brackenridge, C. and Fasting, K. 250
Brackenridge, C. et al. 146, 229, 255, 258, 269, 302–3
Brackenridge, Celia 146, 186, 249, 250
Bradbury, S. 342
Brady, K. 385
Brah, A. 329
Brailsford, D. 77
breaking barriers
    acceptance barriers 181–3
    black swimmers 339
    body shame 275–6
    brands as barriers 394–5
    cultural barriers 16–18
    ideological barriers, wheelchair rugby and 236–8
    image barriers 452

impairment 59
  language barriers ('don't call me handicapped') 59
  mainstreaming barriers 158–9
  narrative barriers 452
  point-of-entry barriers 339
  political barriers 507
  resource barriers 369
  socialization barriers 131–3
  symbols as barriers 394–5
  vision barriers 523–4
  wheelchair rugby 236–8
Bredemeier, B. et al. 277
Brennan, Trevor 257–8
Bridges, L. 282
'Brighton Declaration' on gender equity 269–70
Bristow, Eric 201
British Sociological Association 319
Brittain, Ian 59, 86, 124–5, 452
Bromann, Dr. Jens 394
Brookes, R. 429
Brooking, Trevor 136
Brooks, J. et al. 51
Brown, A. 256
Brown, David 123
Brown, Gordon 162, 479
Brown, James 402
Brown, M. and Seaton, S. 481
Brown, M. et al. 320, 326, 459
Brownell, S. 21, 475
Bruce, T. 456, 457
Bruening, J. 327
Bruno, Luca 402
Bryant, Kobe 420
Bryshun, J. and Young, K. 193, 196
BSA (British Sociological Association) 29
BUCS (British Universities and Colleges Sport) 6
budget cuts, effect on participation 272
Buffington, D. 320
Bull, A. 78
Bull, C. 304
Bunker, David 155
Burdsey, D. 332
burnout among young athletes 109–10
Burstyn, Varda 15, 49, 82, 83, 125, 247, 290, 296, 307, 387
business relationships 385
  corporate interests in sports 386
  global expansion, business use of sports for 393–7
  transnational corporations, political realities in era of 494–5
Butler, J. 21, 293
Byrne, Bob 515

Caborn, Richard 342
Cabrera, Diane 369
Calzaghe, Joe 247
Cambridge Econometrics 391
Campbell, Sir Menzies 27, 479
Campbell, Tini 362
Cannella, S. 215
Cannon Company 391
Cantona, Eric 257
Caplan, J. and Coates, T. 436
careers in sport
  administrative jobs for women 284–7
  coaching jobs for women 284–7
  occupational careers among former athletes 378–80
  opportunities for 373–7
    ethnic minorities 376–7
    limitations on 374–5
    women's chances 375–6
  personal investment in 110–12
  success for highly-paid athletes in retirement 379–80
Carlos, John 93, 534
Carlston, D. 151
Carrington, B. and McDonald, I. 314, 315, 323, 341
Carrington, B. and Sugden, J. 495
Carrington, Bill 128, 311, 314, 315, 319, 320, 327, 328, 330, 331, 377, 458, 488
Cashmore, Ellis 32, 214, 215, 241, 321, 324, 326, 401, 408
Castro, Fidel 470
Catlin, Don 215
Caudwell, J. 51, 274, 293, 294, 297, 303, 304
Cawley (Goolagong), Evonne 93
CBS News 240
celebratory violence 254–5
Chafetz, J. and Kotarba, J. 156
Chalip, L. and Green, B. 167
Chambers, Dwain 211, 215
Chandler, Rob 385
change
  athletes as change agents 533–5
  career change as personal investment 110–12
  commercialization and changes in sports 403–9
  culture and ideology, strategies for changes in 305–8
  doing sports, change in ways of 307–8
  dominant gender ideology, resentment at change as threat to 272–3
  ethnicity themes in media representations, making changes 459–60
  football hooliganism, historical change and 256
  in gender relations 213

change – *continued*
  interests, values and opportunities, change in later years 79–80
  men and boys as agents of 289–91
  race, ethnicity and national identity issues, prospects for change in 342–4
  race themes in media representations, making changes 459–60
  social change in young people, sports as influence in 139–40
  sports as sites for 301–3
  sports organization, change in support of gender equity 307
  system of sports, changes from within 535
  television coverage and organizational changes to accommodate 440–42
  violence, cultural change and control of 232–3
  women and girls as agents of 288–9
changing room stories 120–21
Chapman, Katie 297
Charles I 74
Charlesworth, H. and Young, K. 118, 186, 214
Chastain, Brandi 274, 289
cheating 198–200
Chester Report (1966) 253
child-rearing 361–3
Christenson, M. and Kelso, P. 276–7
Christie, Linford 180, 328
Chudacoff, H. 138, 143
Clarke, Gill 127–8, 277, 302, 303
Clarke, J. and Critcher, C. 78, 83, 90
class ideology in UK 354–6
class relations
  in action 367–8, 368–71
  definition of 41, 350–51
  dynamics of 352–4
  power in sport and 357–8
  and social class 350–51
  young people and sports 41
Clay, Cassius (Mohammad Ali) 534
Clayton, B. and Humberstone, B. 201, 249
Clijsters, Kim 422
Coakley, J. and Donnelly, P. 53, 146
Coakley, J. and White, A. 107
Coakley, Jay 100, 107, 108, 109, 116, 139, 146, 154, 156, 163, 164, 170, 202, 252, 278, 284, 296, 326–7, 354, 357, 368, 378, 380, 442, 473, 531
Coalter, F. 391, 412, 473
Coca-Cola 26
Coe, Sebastian, Lord 24, 27, 119, 427, 479

Cohen, Leah 301
Cohen, S. 89
Cole, Ashley 417–18
Cole, C. 21, 289
Collins, M. and Buller, J. 358
Collins, M. and Kay, T. 204, 363, 367, 369
Collins, Mike 345, 486
Collins, P. 376, 455
Collins, T. 80, 81
Collins, T. and Vamplew, W. 200
Colorado Springs Gazette 8
commentators and writers, comparison of 464–5
commercial sports
  amateur athletes in 422–3
  class relations and 388–9
  emergence and growth of 386–403
  excitement, quest for 389–91
  income of athletes in 416–23
  legal status of athletes in 416–23
  media sellout by? 440–42
  owners, sponsors and promoters in 409–16
  UK economy and 391–2
commercialism
  economy and sports 385
  Olympianism and 489–92
  trends in 527
commercialization
  coaches and, orientations of 405–7
  definition of 386
  and violence in sports 232–5
community and cultural process
  politics as 126–7
  research as 127–8
  trends in 528–9
Condon, Paul Leslie, Lord 203
conflict theory
  approach to deviance in sports through 178–9
  future for sports 530
  weaknesses of 43–4
  young people and sports 41–4
Connell, R. 247
consumption
  themes in media representations 461–2
  trends in 527
contests and games
  in ancient Greece 66–8
  in ancient Rome 68–9
control
  and carry-over in off-field violence 245–7
  of media 429–30

of on-field violence 242–4
and organization of sports events 504
of sports, commercialization and 407–9
corporate branding in sport 398–402
limits of 402–3
Correia, Martiza 339
'cosmetic fitness' 273–5
cost of attending sports events 368–71
Coté, J. and Fraser-Thomas, J. 154, 155
Cotterill, James 230
Coubertin, Baron Pierre de 483
Couser, G. 131
Coventry, B. 456
Cowley, Jason 173, 176, 323
Cox, B. and Thompson, S. 297
Craig, P. and Beedie, P. 160, 482
Craike, Jayne 524
Crawford, Garry 252, 431, 433, 436, 449, 450, 463
Creedon, Pam 455
criminal activities 200
criminal violence 230
Critcher, C. 256
critical feminist theory 532
weaknesses of 51
critical theory
approach to deviance through 180–81
crowd violence and 256
freedom from exploitation or oppression 531
future for sports 531–2
radical strategies in 531–2
weaknesses of 48–9
young people and sports 44–9
Croker, Ted 266
Cronin, M. 84, 336
Crouse, K. 525
crowd dynamics 259–60, 261
crowd violence
control of 261–2
research and theories about 255–7
culture
cultural ideologies, definition of 46
definition of 4
diversity training, need for 340–41
and dominant racial ideology 321
exchange of cultures, sports and 493–4
and ideology, strategies for changes in 305–8
of risk 188
traditional cultures and native games 487–8
violence, cultural change and control of 232–3
working for transformation in 536
Cunningham, G. and Sagas, M. 377

Curry, T. 192, 249
Curry, T. et al 457
Cushion, C. and Jones, R. 122, 235
Cushion, Christopher 122
Cyphers, L. 497

Dacyshyn, A. 111, 380
Daily Mirror 187, 191
Daily Telegraph 196
Daley, Tom 5, 147
Daniels, D. 327
Dater, A. 242
David, P. 145, 146, 147, 167
Davids, K. and Baker, J. 322
Davies, Jonathan 189
Davies, Paul 236
Davies, Robert 429, 513, 529
Davis, L. and Carlisle Duncan, M. 434
Davis, L. and Harris, O. 457, 458
Davis, Toni 339
DCMS (Department for Culture, Media and Sports) 1, 99, 146, 415, 482
Strategy Unit 109, 117, 204, 470
de Lunden, Leon 206
Deem, R. 90
definitions
class relations 41, 350–51
commercialization 386
cultural ideologies 46
culture 4
deviance 184–5
disability 59
doping 209–10
economy 386
ethnicity 312
femininity, alternative definitions of 306
genocide 319
governments 471
handicap 59–60
hegemony 127
hybrid sports 163
impairment 59
masculinity, alternative definitions of 305–6, 308
national identity 313
performance-enhancing substances 209–10
politics 470–71, 501
power 471
race 312
racism 319
social class 350
social worlds 122

definitions – *continued*
   socialization 100–101
   society 4
   sports 4–11
      alternative approach to definition of 7–11
      traditional definition of 5–6
   theorization 34
   violence 226–7
Deford, Frank 45
Delaney, K. and Eckstein, R. 444, 476, 479
Delves, A. 78
demographics, trends in 528–9
Denham, B. 176, 493, 501
Dennelly, Peter 105, 106
DePauw, K. 60, 507
Desailly, Marcel 340, 458
deviance in sports 172–223
   acceptance barriers 181–3
   alcohol consumption in excess 200–201
   anarchy 185
   antisocial deviance 190
   athletes
      focus on deviant behaviour among 202
      research on deviance among 197–205
   body, rationalization of 213
   certification as 'well' in fight against substance
      abuse 219
   cheating 198–200
   codes of ethics, establishment of 219
   competition for distinction 187
   conflict theory, approach through 178–9
   constructionist approach to 184–97
   criminal activities 200
   critical theory, approach through 180–81
   culture of risk 188
   dedication above all to 'game' 186–7
   defining and studying, approaches to 176–81
   deviance, definition of 184–5
   deviant behaviour
      context and reflection on 201–2
      sports as cure for 204–5
   deviant overconformity 185–6, 190–92, 192–4,
      194–6, 196–7, 206–20
      control of 196–7
      deviant underconformity and 194–6
      encouragement of 214
      group dynamics and 192–4
      media constructs of 191
      reasons for 190–92
   deviant underconformity 185
      deviant overconformity and 194–6
   distinction, competition for 187

doping, definition of 209–10
drug testing
   arguments against 215–18
   as deterrent 214–18
   promotion of sports and 217–18
drug use education 219–20
ethic of sport, deviance and 186–90
   connection between 189–90
fascism 185
field sports and hunting 206–8
functionalist theory, approach through 176–8
gambling 198–200
'game' dedication above all to 186–7
gender relations, changes in 213
'harm reduction' approach 219
health and injury education programmes 219
herbs and natural substances 210
hubris 193
hunting and field sports 206–8
hypocrisy in sports 218–19
initiation ceremonies in sports teams 195–6
interactionist theory, approach through 180–81
media attention 174, 190, 200
norms, deviance and 184–5
nutritional supplements 210
obstacles, determination to overcome 188–9
off-the-field deviance, indulgence in 200–202, 206
on-the-field deviance, indulgence in 198–200
online Learning Centre resources 173
overconformity 185–6, 190–92, 192–4, 194–6,
   196–7, 206–20
   control of 196–7
   encouragement of 214
   group dynamics and 192–4
   media constructs of 191
   reasons for 190–92
   underconformity and 194–6
pain, playing through 188
painkillers 210
performance-enhancing substances 205–20
   availability of 212
   banning of 210–12
   definition of 209–10
power, organization of 213–14
research on deviance among athletes 197–205
risk, acceptance of 188
rule avoidance 198–200
rules against substance abuse, establishment of 219
self-medication 213
sports ethic and deviance 186–90
   connection between 189–90
sports-related deviance, examples of 202–3

studies of, problems for 174–6
substance control, challenge of 212–14, 218–20
substance use education 219–20
summarization 220–22
throwing of games 198–200
underage alcohol consumption 200–201
underconformity 185
  overconformity and 194–6
unfair conduct, indulgence in 198–200
WADA (World Anti-Doping Agency) 94, 211,
  215, 217–18
website resources 222–3
Dewhirst, T. and Sparks, R. 395
Di Pasquale, M. 218
digital games 435–6
Dimeo, P. 205, 525
Dimeo, P. and Finn, G. 336, 343
disability
  and alternative sports participation 520
  definition of 59
  disability sports, trends in 522–4
  in organized sport, historical view 85
  socialization and 131–3
disordered eating 119–20
distinction, competition for 187
Doaks, Clinton 464
Doane, A.M. and Bonilla-Silva, E. 459
Docherty, Drew 242
dog racing 240–41
domestic violence 251–2
Domi, Tie 248
dominant gender ideology
  resentment at change as threat to 272–3
  unfairness in 278–9
dominant political ideology 478
dominant racial ideology 320–21
Donnelley, P. and Young, K. 105
Donnelly, P. and Coakley, J. 533
Donnelly, P. and Harvey, J. 358
Donnelly, Peter 13, 15, 130, 145, 166, 501–2
Donohoe, H. 118
doping, definition of 209–10
Dosanj, Aman 333
Drahota, J. and Eitzen, D. 111
Drew, Mike 250
drug testing
  arguments against 215–18
  as deterrent 214–18
  promotion of sports and 217–18
Duff, Hillary 273–4
Dukes, R. and Coakley, J. 139, 145, 359
Duncan, M. and Messner, M. 453

Dundee, Chris 364
Dunn, Katherine 240
Dunning, E. and Sheard, K. 70
Dunning, E. and Waddington, I. 193, 201, 204
Dunning, E. et al. 256
Dunning, Eric 35, 54, 55, 55n3, 70, 80, 117, 198, 206,
  227, 228, 253, 256, 389
DuPree, D. 489
Duquin, M. 50, 307
Durrant, Kevin 420
Dworkin, S. 274, 277
Dyer, Kieron 230

Early, Gerald 323, 376
Earnhardt, Dale 420
EASS (European Association for the Sociology of
  Sport) 29
Eastman, S. and Billings, A. 447, 454
eating disorders 274
Ecclestone, Bernie 399, 419
The Economist 26
economy and sports 384–425
  amateur athletes in commercial sports 422–3
    income of 422–3
    legal status of 422
  amateur sports in UK 415–16
  Beckham as brand 401
  bottom lines, sports as boosts for 393–7
  brands as barriers 394–5
  business relationships 385
  coaches, commercialization and orientations of
    405–7
  commercial sports
    amateur athletes in 422–3
    class relations and 388–9
    emergence and growth of 386–403
    excitement and, quest for 389–91
    income of athletes in 416–23
    legal status of athletes in 416–23
    owners, sponsors and promoters in 409–16
    UK economy and 391–2
  commercialism 385
  commercialization
    and changes in sports 403–9
    definition of 386
    orientations of athletes and 405–7
  control of sports, commercialization and 407–9
  corporate branding in sport 398–402
    limits of 402–3
  corporate interests 386
  corporate use of sports for global expansion 393–7
  definition of 'economy' 386

economy and sports – *continued*
   economic conditions for commercialization 386–7
   economic factors and globalization of commercial
      sports 392–403
   economic inequalities and social class 351–8, 359
   economic opportunities in sports 373–7
   economic stakes for athletes and sponsors 385–6
   entertainment
      sports as 385
      as total experience 404–5
   funding, struggles over 90–91
   gambling economy 408
   global expansion, corporate use of sports for
      393–7
   global markets, sports organizations look for
      392–3
   globalization of commercial sports, economic
      factors and 392–403
   goals and internal structures of sports,
      commercialization and 404–5
   golf, commercialization of 388
   income
      of amateur athletes in commercial sports 422–3
      of athletes in commercial sports 416–23
      from individual sports 419–22
      sources for sports owners 413–15
      from team sports 419
   individual sports
      income from 419–22
      legal status of 418–19
   internal structures of sports, commercialization
      and 404–5
   investment in UK sports 411
   legal status of athletes in commercial sports
      416–23
   market economies, power and 388
   media and sports, economics and relationship
      between 448–9
   online Learning Centre resources 385
   organizations and people that control sports,
      commercialization and 407–9
   owners, sponsors and promoters in commercial
      sports 409–16
   ownership structures of UK sports 409–10
   participants in sports, commercialization and
      orientations of 405–7
   people and organizations that control sports,
      commercialization and 407–9
   power, resources and commercialization 388–9
   professional leagues in UK 411–12
   professional sports in UK 409–15
   'promotional culture' in sports 405–7
   rules and internal structures of sports,
      commercialization and 404–5
   social conditions for commercialization 386–7
   spectator interest
      creation of 389–91
      excitement and, quest for 389–91
      media coverage and 390–91
      success ideology and 390
      youth schemes and 390
   sponsorship 385
      commercialization and orientations of sponsors
       405–7
      in UK sports 411, 416
   sports and economic resources 349–50
   sports events, branding of 398–9
   sports organizations look for global markets 392–3
   sports personalities, branding of 400–402
   sports tourism 414–15
   stadiums for professional sports in UK 412–13
   summarization 423–4
   symbols as barriers 394–5
   team sports
      income from 419
      legal status of 417–18
   teams, branding of 399
   transnational corporations and sports 393–7
   venues for professional sports in UK 412–13
   voluntary sector 416
   website resources 424–5
Edwards, Harry 311, 319, 338, 351, 376
Edwards, Jonathan 323
Edwards, Martin 419
Eitle, T. and Eitle, D. 288
Eitzen, D. 80
electronic media
   in sports 428
   trends in 525–6
Elias, N. and Dunning, E. 206
Elias, Norbert 53–4, 55n3, 66, 389
Eliasoph, N. 341
elite athletes
   career success after retirement 379–80
   process of becoming 103–5
elite sports training schemes 145–6
Elkerton, Gary 534
Elkind, D. 143, 155
Elkington, John 2
Elling, A. et al. 303
Elliott, R. and Maguire, J. 498
Elliss, William Webb 4
Emms, Gail 271, 457
Engh, F. 147

English Institute of Sport 113
entertainment
    sports as 385
    as total experience in sports 404–5
    and violence in sports 233–4
equity
    'Brighton Declaration' on gender equity 269–70
    fairness and equity issues in gender 267, 278–87
    fundamentalist religion, equity and 280
    gender equity and women's football 269
    in gender issues, strategies for achievement of
        287–91
    participation and equity issues 267–91
    political challenges in gender equity 307
    sports organization, change in support of gender
        equity 307
Eriksson, Sven Goran 314
Eskes, T. et al. 289
ESPN The Magazine 212, 219, 246
ethics
    codes of, establishment of 219
    deviance and ethic of sport 186–90
        connection between 189–90
    performance ethic 142–3
    violence as deviant overconformity to norms of
        ethic of sport 230–32
ethnicity
    definition of 312
    diversity in sports 340–41
    ethnic relations, dynamics of 377
    exclusion in sports on ethnic or racial grounds,
        elimination of 337–8
    'mixed-race' people, erasure of 318–19
    and race, interchangeable use of terms 313
    racial and ethnic relations in sports, dynamics of
        337–44
    themes in media representations 457–60
        making changes 459–60
    see also race, ethnicity and national identity
Eubank, Chris 242
Euripides 63
EuroGames 521
Evans, J. et al. 21
Evans, John 119–20
everyday life
    conflict theory in 42–3
    critical feminist theory in 51
    critical theory in 48–9
    figurational theory in 56–7
    functionalist theory in 39–41
    interactionist theory in 53
Ewald, K. and Jiobu, R. 185

Ewald, Keith 185
examples of social worlds
    heroisim, learning to be a hero 122–3
    image is not everything 123
    man's world, living in shadow of 123–4
    media, portrayal of sports world in 124–5
    suviving in a ghetto 124

families
    family relationships, dynamics of 156
    parents, increased involvement and concerns
        among 146–7
    sports and family life 24, 25
fan aggression, precipitation of 258
fantasy sports 434
Farber, M. 242
Farrey, T. 147, 154, 155, 218, 322
fascism 185
Fashanu, Justin 305
Fasting, K. 268
Fasting, K. and Pfister, G. 284
Fasting, K. et al. 186, 250
Fatwa Bank 334
Fausto-Sterling, Anna 21, 291–2
Faviau, Christophe 213–14
Federer, Roger 420, 454
femininity
    alternative definitions of 306
    normative boundaries of 301
    in organized sport 82–3
feminist theory 49–51
Fenstermaker, S. and West, C. 293, 295
Ferdinand, Rio 214
Ference, R. and Muth, K. 289
Ferguson, Duncan 230
Ferguson, Sir Alex 203
field sports and hunting 206–8
FIFA World Cup™ 5, 26, 443
figurational theory 53–7
    weaknesses of 57
Finn, P. and Guilianotti, R. 336
Fish, M. 218
Fleming, S. and Tomlinson, A. 311
Fleming, Scott 128, 320, 323, 329, 332, 377
Flex 176
Flintoff, Ann 35
Foer, F. 494, 501
Football Association 136, 145, 146, 253, 258, 269,
    329, 342, 418
football hooliganism 256
Footwork Productions Ltd 26
Foucault, Michel 86

Frazier-Lyde, Jacqui 232
Fredrickson, B. and Harrison, K. 289, 306
Fredrickson, G. 314, 315, 319
Freedman, J. 420
Freud, Sigmund 44n1
Friedman, V. et al. 59
friendship influence 166
Frisk, Anders 258
Frosdick, S. and Marsh, P. 253
functionalist theory 529–30
    approach to deviance in sports through 176–8
    conservative strategy in 529
    reformist strategy in 529–30
    weaknesses of 41
    young people and sports 35–41
fundamentalist religion 280
Fung Ying Ki 18
future for sports 512–38
    alternative sports
        creation of 535
        groups seeking 518–19
    athletes as change agents 533–5
    change agents, athletes as 533–5
    commercialism, trends in 527
    communities, trends in 528–9
    conflict theory 530
    consumption, trends in 527
    creation of futures, visions of possibilities and
        529–36
    critical feminist theory 532
    critical theory 531–2
        freedom from exploitation or oppression 531
        radical strategies 531–2
    culture, working for transformation in 536
    demographics, trends in 528–9
    disability and alternative sports participation 520
    disability sports, trends in 522–4
    electronic media, trends in 525–6
    EuroGames 521
    exaggeration on 513
    factors influencing trends today 525–9
    forecasting 513–14
    functionalist theory 529–30
        conservative strategy 529
        reformist strategy 529–30
    future thoughts, using history 91–4
    Gay Games 521
    health and fitness, concerns about 517
    interactionist theory 533
    older people, participation preferences among
        517–18
    online Learning Centre resources 513

    online sports 435
    opposition, possibilities for 535
    organization, trends in 526–7
    participation preferences among older people
        517–18
    pleasure and participation sports 514, 515–16
        factors in growth of 517–21
    possibilities, visions of 514–16
    power and performance sports 514–15
        factors in growth of 516–17
    professional, trends in 521
    rationalization, trends in 526–7
    skateboarding for pleasure 518–19
    snowboarding for pleasure 519–20
    social relations, working for transformation in 536
    social theories in creation of future trends 529–33
    societies, trends in 528–9
    spectators and spectator sports, trends in 524
    sport spheres, trends in 521–4
    sports in society, current trends related to 516–24
    summarization 536–7
    system of sports, changes from within 535
    technology, trends in 525
    telecommunications, trends in 525–6
    values and experiences of women in sports 518
    vantage points for creating futures 535–6
    vision barriers, trends towards reduction in 522–4
    website resources 537–8
    women's values and experiences in sports 518
    World Outgames 521
    youth sports, trends in 522

Galen 118
gambling 198–200
    economy of 408
    throwing of games 198–200
games
    in ancient Greece 66–8
    in ancient Rome 68–9
    deviance and dedication above all to the 'game'
        186–7
    Gay Games 521
Gandy, Stephanie 323
Gardener, Jason 407
Garland, J. and Rowe, M. 328
Garnett, Kevin 420
Garrett, R. 274
Gascoigne, Paul 244, 248
gays
    and lesbians, 'out of bounds' 293
    male athletes, stories of 121–2
    men in sports 304–5

gender and sports 265–309
  administrative jobs for women 284–7
  alternative sports, participation opportunities in
      281–3
  appearance, cultural messages in promotion of 274
  athletes, support for 283–4
  biological variation 291–3
  body shame 275–6
  'Brighton Declaration' on gender equity 269–70
  budget cuts, effect on participation 272
  coaching jobs for women 284–7
  'cosmetic fitness,' emphasis on 273–5
  culture and ideology, strategies for changes in
      305–8
  doing sports, change in ways of 307–8
  dominant gender ideology
    resentment at change as threat to 272–3
    unfairness in 278–9
  eating disorders 274
  empowerment of women and girls 288–9
  equal rights, government legislation on 268
  equity, strategies for achievement of 287–91
  fairness and equity issues 267, 278–87
  female bodybuilders 298–300
  femininity
    alternative definitions of 306
    normative boundaries of 301
  'forever ladies' 297–8
  fundamentalist religion, equity and 280
  gender and gender relations, central topics 266–7
  gender boundaries, female challenges to 296–7
  gender classification 301
  gender equity and women's football 269
  gender identification 291–3
  gender ideology, blurring old boundaries 294
  gender relations, changes in 213
  gender themes in media representations 453–5
  gender trends in coaching and administration
      284–5
  global women and sports movement 268–70
  government legislation on equal rights 268
  health and fitness movement 270
  homophobia 277
  ideology and culture, strategies for changes in
      305–8
  ideology and power issues 267, 291–308
  informal sports, participation opportunities in
      281–3
  job satisfaction of women in sports 286–7
  lesbianism
    charges of 297–8
    fear of accusations of 277
  gays and lesbians, 'out of bounds' 293
  lesbians in sports 303–4
  mainstream sports, participation opportunities in
      279–81
  masculinity
    alternative definitions of 305–6, 308
    celebration of 295–6
  media coverage of women in sports 270–71
  men and boys as agents of change 289–91
  oestrogen 292–3
  online Learning Centre resources 266
  opportunities for participation 267–8
  organized sports, participation opportunities in
      279–81
  participation
    and equity issues 267–91
    increases, caution on future for 271–8
  physical variation 291–3
  political challenges in gender equity 307
  power in society, gender ideology in action 293–4
  professional sports, participation opportunities
      in 280
  racial ideology and gender 327–9
  sex categories 291–3
  sexual harassment 286–7
  sexy and feminine bodies, cultural messages about
      274
  society, gender ideology in 291–4
  sports, gender ideology in 294–308
  sports as sites for change 301–3
  sports organization, change in support of gender
      equity 307
  sports participation among girls and women
      267–91
  summarization 308–9
  support for athletes 283–4
  testosterone 292–3
  tomboys and lesbians 297–8
  trivialization of women's sports 276–7
  violence on the field and gender ideas 247–8
  website resources 309
  women and girls as agents of change 288–9
  women and girls as invaders in men's cultural
      centres 296–7
  women in decision-making positions, under-
      representation of 273
  women's football 269
  'women's sports,' non-threatening nature of 297
General Electric 26
genetic explanations for achievement 322–3
genocide, definition of 319
George, J. 328

Geraghty, Graham 239
Gerrard, Steven 460
Gibson, Althea 92
Gill, David 385
Gillette 26
Gilroy, Paul 312, 330
Ginsburg, K. 154
Giordana, R. and Graham, K. 140
Giulianotti, R. and Armstrong, G. 256
'Give Us Back Our Game!' campaign (2008) 166
gladiators in ancient Rome 68–9
Glazer, Malcolm 392
global expansion, corporate use of sports for 393–7
global inequalities, sports and 371–3
global markets, sports organizations and 392–3
global migration of athletes 495–8
global politics
    process of 483–501
    and production of sports equipment 498–9
global women and sports movement 268–70
globalization
    of commercial sports, economic factors and
        392–403
    see also politics and sports globalization
Glock, A. 274
Goffman, Erving 86
Golby, J. and Purdue, A. 79
Gold, J. and Gold, M. 479
golf, commercialization of 388
Good, R. 334
Goodman, B. 495
Gore, C. 371–2
Gorman, C. 140, 146
Goudsblom, J. 54
governance
    critical issues and government involvement 481–2
    economic development, responsibility for
        promotion of 479–80
    equal rights legislation 268
    foreign policy, sport as tool of 480–81
    government-sports connection 472–83
    governments, organisation of 471
    national prestige, responsibility for promotion of
        474–5
    public order safeguards, responsibility for 472–3
    recognition and prestige, responsibility for
        promotion of 474–5
    safeguarding public order, responsibility for 472–3
    of sports in UK 482–3
    support for sports 478–9
    unity, government responsibility for promotion
        of 476–7

Graf, Steffi 94
Gramsci, Antonio 44n1, 81, 126–7, 478
Grant, Avram 213, 340
Gratton, C. and Taylor, P. 415
Graves, J. 316
Gravink, Jil 452
Greek contests and games 66–8
Green, M. 481
Green, M. and Houlihan, B. 481
Greenfeld, K. 527
Grey-Thompson, Dame Tanni 16–18
greyhound racing 240–41
Griffin, Pat 277, 298, 303
Grohmann, K. 476
Grossfeld, S. 238
Gruneau, R. 64, 351
The Guardian 358
Guilbert, S. 238
Guilianotti, R. 340
Gulick, Luther 83
Guttmann, Allen 65, 69, 70, 71, 72, 78, 198, 227, 253
Guttmann, Ludwig 132

Haakonsen, Terje 27, 519
Hall, C. 476, 480
Hall, M. 277
Hall, M. et al. 535
Halverson, E.R. and Halverson, R. 433–4
Hamed, Naseem 328
Hamilton, Lewis 145, 147, 318, 321, 338, 376, 419,
    420
handicap, definition of 59–60
Hansell, S. 440
Hardman, K. and Marshall, J. 367
Hargreaves, J. and Vertinsky, P. 21
Hargreaves, Jennifer 35, 51, 59, 80, 83, 157, 266, 274,
    275, 307, 334, 335, 480, 532
Hargreaves, John 35
Harrington Report (1968) 253
Harris, J. 297
Harris, J. and Clayton, B. 271
Harrison, C. and Lawrence, S. 324, 327
Harrison, L. et al. 324, 327
Hart, M. 83
Hartmann, Doug 295–6, 473
Hasbrook, C. 157
Hasbrook, C. and Harris, O. 157
Hassan, D. 85
Hastings, D. et al 501
Hawes, K. 274
Hawk, Tom 519
Hawk, Tony 148

Hayes, S. and Stidder, G. 157
He Got Game (Spike Lee film) 323
health
    and fitness
        concerns about 517
        government responsibility for maintenance of
            473–4
        movement for 270, 359
    improvement through sport 117
    and injury education programmes 219
    physical well-being, improvement through sport
        117
    sport-health connection 117–8
heavy contact sports 232
hegemony 127
Henderson, J. 214
Henricks, T. 154
Henry, Thierry 154–5, 323, 420
Henry V (Shakespeare) 230–31
Henry VIII 115
herbs and natural substances 210
Heywood, L. and Dworkin, S. 270, 274
Heywood, Leslie 298–9
Hicks, Tom 393
Hickson, Paul 167, 250
Higgins, M. 519
Higgins, P. 59
high-performance sport schemes 166–7
Hill, Damon 173
historical perspectives 62–97
    age and disability in organized sport 85
    'character development' in sports participation
        81–2
    contests and games
        in ancient Greece 66–8
        in ancient Rome 68–9
    contests and games in ancient Greece 66–8
    contests and games in ancient Rome 68–9
    femininity in organized sport 82–3
    funding, struggles over 90–91
    future thoughts, using history 91–4
    games in ancient Greece 66–8
    games in ancient Rome 68–9
    gladiators in ancient Rome 68–9
    Greek contests and games 66–8
    history, thoughts about future 91–4
    Industrial Revolution 77–86
    interests, values and opportunities, change in later
        years 79–80
    lessons learned from history 75–6
    masculinity in organized sport 82–3
    meaning, social divisions and struggles over 87–8

medieval Europe
    masters and masses divide 71–3
    tournaments and games 71–3
medieval Europe, masters and masses divide 71–3
medieval Europe, tournaments and games 71–3
myths and sports in ancient Greece 66–8
nationality in organized sport 83–5
online Learning Centre resources 63
organised sport in UK, growth of 80–1
organization, struggles over 88–9
participation, struggles over 89–90
purpose, struggles over 88
race, impact on history of 317
Reformation 74–5
Renaissance 73–4
Roman contests and games 68–9
spectacles in ancient Rome 68–9
sport
    in early years, time and space for 77–9
    in later years, changing interests, values and
        opportunities 79–80
    participation in, 'character development' and
        81–2
    in society, understanding history of 64–5
sport in early years, time and space for 77–9
sport in later years, changing interests, values and
    opportunities 79–80
sport participation and 'character development'
    81–2
sports in society, understanding history 64–5
struggles continue, post 1920 87–91
summarization 94–6
time and space for sport in early years 77–9
tournaments and games in medieval Europe 71–3
UK sport, organised growth of 80–1
variety in sports by time and place 65–6
viewing sport, new way 80
violence in sports 227–8
website resources 96–7
Hnida, K. 248
Hoberman, J. 21, 205, 315, 377, 390
Holmes, Dame Kelly 318–19, 335, 458
Holroyd, Rachel 119–20
Holt, R. 77
Holt, R. and Mason, T. 315, 330, 363
home-making 361–3
Homeless World Cup 355
homophobia 277
homosexuality
    erasure in media representations 455–6
    see also gays; lesbianism
Honea, J. 282, 519

Honeyball, L. 187
hooks, bel 34, 530
hooliganism
    football hooliganism, historical change and 256
    and semi-organized confrontations 256–7
Horne, J. 274, 387, 389, 391, 397, 401–2
Horne, J. and Manzenreiter, W. 450, 480
Horne, J. et al 409–10
Houlihan, B. 211, 216, 472, 477, 482
Hovden, J. 286
Howe, P. David 117, 118, 120–21, 185, 186, 192, 219,
        277, 522
Howe, P.D. and Jones, C. 506
Huang, C.-H. and Brittain, I. 132
hubris 193
Hudson, I. 413
Hughes, R. and Coakley, J. 186
Hughson, J. 260
Hui, S. 301
hunting and field sports 206–8
Hurst, Geoff 93
Hutchinson, J. 253
hybrid sports 163
hypocrisy in sports 218–19

ICC (International Cricket Conference) 5
identity
    and control of violence in sports 247
    government responsibility for promotion of 476–7
    social theories 52
ideology
    and culture, strategies for changes in 305–8
    media images and narratives, ideological themes
        in 450–62
    nation states and ideological hegemony 487–94
    power and gender issues 267, 291–308
    and relationship between media and sports 448–9
    socialization and sport 125–8
    wheelchair rugby and ideological barriers 236–8
IDG 404
Ince, Paul 342, 377
income from sports see economy and sports
Industrial Revolution 77–86
informal sports
    alternative, informal and action sports,
        improvement of 163
    participation opportunities in 281–3
Ingham, A. 477
Ingham, A. and Dewar, A. 235
Ingham, A. et al. 107
initiation ceremonies in sports teams 195–6
injustice, crowd violence and perceptions of 261

institutionalization of violence in sports 238–41
interactionist theory
    approach to deviance in sports through 180–81
    crowd violence 256
    future for sports 533
    social theories 51–2
    weaknesses of 53
interconnections between media and sports 427–8
international sports, ideals and realities in 483–7
Internet 433–5, 440
intimidation 227
IOC (International Olympic Committee) 5, 6, 210,
        270, 285, 298, 358, 393, 489, 492, 501–2
IRB (International Rugby Board) 5
Irish Football Association 345
Islamic women in sports, dilemmas for 334–5
Ismond, P. 328
ISSA (International Sociology of Sport Association)
        29
ITV 26
Iverson, Allen 420

Jackson, Colin 297
Jackson, S.A. and Csikszentmihalyi, M. 130
Jackson, S.J. and Andrews, D. 387, 493, 495
Jackson, S.J. and Haigh, S. 487
Jackson, S.J. and Hokowhitu, B. 495
Jackson, S.J. and Scherer, J. 495
Jacques, Martin 310, 329
James, C.L.R. 46, 63
James I 74
Jarvie, G. and Burnett, J. 356
Jarvie, Grant 55, 88, 107, 111, 274, 356, 358
Jarvis, N. 122
Jeanrenaud, C. and Kesenne, S. 444
Jeffries, S. 391
Jennings, A. and Sambrook, C. 202, 212, 480, 486,
        504
Jennings, Andrew 5, 202, 358, 394, 480, 486, 504
Jeter, Derek 420
Jiobu, Robert 185
Johal, S. 330
John, Elton 276
Johns, D. 274
Johnson, Ben 180, 218
Jones, K. 244
Jones, Marion 297
Jones, Robyn 122, 313, 320, 321, 326, 340
Jones, Vinnie 232, 233
Jordan, Michael 395, 400
Joukowsky, A. and Rothstein, L. 18, 86, 452, 524
Jowell, Tessa 1

'jumping genes' 322–3
Jürgs, M. 481
Jutel, Annemarie 476

Kamtya, Gary 313
Kane, Mary Jo 284
Kaplan, Jason E. 237
Katz, J. 250
Kay, J. and Laberge, S. 282
Kay, T. 90, 157, 333
Keating, P. 212, 214
Kellner, D. 467
Kelly, Ruth 99
Kelly, S. and Waddington, I. 235
Kensler, T. 294
Khan, Amir 332
Kian, E. et al 453, 458
Kidd, Bruce 66, 82, 290–91, 296, 358, 489, 535
Kilvert, G. 283
King, Billie Jean 276
King, K. 140, 144, 145, 193, 196, 341
The King's Book of Sports (James I) 74
Kinkema, K. and Harris, J. 460
Kirk, D. 107, 157
Kix, P. 220
Klein, A. 319, 495, 497
Knight, Phil 494
Knoppers, A. and Elling, A. 431, 450
Knox, Taylor 534
Kohn, Alfie 7
Koppett, L. 451, 463, 465
Kornikova, Anna 274
Koukouris, Konstantinos 110
Krane, V. 298
Krane, V. et al. 275, 297
Kreager, Derek 246
Kusz, K. 434

LA Galaxy 321, 436, 517
Laberge, S. and Albert, M. 294, 363
Laberge, S. and Sankoff, D. 359
Laberge, Suzanne 363
Lafferty, Y. and McKay, J. 271
Lamb, L. 284
Lance, L. 235
Lang Report (1969) 253
language barriers ('don't call me handicapped') 59
Laqueur, T. 21
Lasn, K. 429
Latimer, C. 473
Laurendeau, J. 276
Lavallee, D. et al. 380

Lavoie, Mark 412, 423
Lawler, J. 239
Lawrence, S. 324
Layden, Tim 339, 505
Leahy, M. 242
LeBlanc, R. and Jackson, S.J. 455
LeBron, James 420
Lefkowitz, B. 248, 249
Lehrman, S. 298, 301
Leicester City 26, 253
Lemos, G. 306
Lenskyj, H. 48, 83, 277, 480, 505
Leonard, D. 466, 467
Leonard, Jason 188
lesbianism
    charges of 297–8
    fear of accusations of 277
    lesbians and gays, ‚out of bounds‘ 293
    lesbians in sports 303–4
    tomboys and lesbians 297–8
Levy, D. 434
Lewis, Denise 271, 457
Lewis, J. 253, 254
Lewis, N. 12
Leyland, Kirsty 391
Liddle, E. 324
life *see* everyday life
Ligutom-Kimura, D. 273
Lines, Gill 191
Lipsyte, Robert 205, 431, 494
Lister, Hilary 60
Liston, K. 193
Liston, K. et al. 188, 192
Liston, Katie 123–4, 273
LLoyd, David 391
LOCOG 441, 482
Lomax, R. 466
London Olympic Games (2012) 24, 26, 119, 408
Long, J. and Hylton, K. 327
Longman, J. 182, 190, 217
Lopiano, Donna 287–8
Lord of the Flies (Golding, W.) 139–40
Louis, Joe 458
Lowe, M.R. 289, 298, 299
Lowes, M.D. 450
Lukatsky, Efren 387
Lund, A.B. 429
Lupton, D. 21

MacArthur, L. 140, 143–4
McCallum, J. 377
McCarthy, D. et al. 460

McChesney, R.W. 429
McClellan, Gerald 242
McClung, L.R. and Blinde, E.M. 289
McCormack, J.B. and Chalip, L. 112
McCoy, Tony 186–7
McCullagh, C. 431, 449
McDaniel, S. and Sullivan, C.
McDonald, Ian 33, 35
McDonald's 26, 126, 143, 314, 315, 399, 402, 495
McElhone Report (1976) 253
McGarry, K. 296
McGuire, B. et al. 329, 330
Machado, Rob 534
McHugh, J. 182
McKay, J. 286, 376
MacNeill, M. 289
MacPhail, A. et al. 104, 105
Madison, J.K. and Sarita Ruma, L. 274
Magdalinski, T. 525
Maguire, J. and Stead, D. 496–7
Maguire, J. et al. 111, 297, 356, 433, 460, 496
Maguire, Joseph 35, 55, 64, 198, 340, 460, 461, 476,
        477, 493, 494, 496–7, 501
Mahany, B. 145
Mahiri, J. 59
Mail on Sunday 454
Majors, Richard 327, 328
Malcolm, D. 117, 219, 253, 329, 332
Malcolm, D. and Sheard, K. 186, 192
Malcolmson, R.W. 74
Malloy, D.C. and Zakus, D.H. 216
Manchester United 26, 94, 200, 257, 385, 392, 399,
        401, 402, 409, 419, 516
Mangan, J.A. 473
Manning, Peyton 420
Manzenreiter, W. and Horne, J. 480
Maradona, Diego 198
Markula, P. 273
Marriott, M. 275, 436
Marsh, P. 255
Marsh, P. and Campbell, A. 255
Martin, Casey 507
Martzke, R. and Cherner, R. 429–30
Marx, Karl 41, 44n1
masculinity
    alternative definitions of 305–6, 308
    celebration of 295–6
    masculine identity, establishment of 363–4
    in organized sport 82–3
    and violence in sports 235–8
Matharu, Kiran 333
Mayeda, D.T. 460

Mayweather, Floyd 420
Mead, C. 320, 458
media and sports 426–68
    active participation, media impacts on 462
    aggression, themes in media representations of
        461
    athletes, journalists' relationships with 464
    attendance at events, media impacts on 462–3
    audience experiences 463
    characteristics of media 428–37
    commentators and writers, comparison of 464–5
    commercial sports, media sellout by? 440–42
    consumption themes in media representations
        461–2
    control of media 429–30
    deviant overconformity, media constructs of 191
    digital games 435–6
    economics and relationship between 448–9
    electronic media 428
    ethnicity themes in media representations 457–60
        making changes 459–60
    fantasy sports 434
    female athletes and press coverage 457
    future for online sports 435
    gender themes in media representations 453–5
    homosexuality, erasure in media representations
        455–6
    ideological themes in media images and narratives
        450–62
    ideology and relationship between 448–9
    image and narrative barriers 452
    images in media sports 449–63
    interactive video games 436
    interactivity 428
    interconnections 427–8
    Internet and sport 433–5, 440
    media and corruption of true nature of sports
        442–5
    media attention and deviance in sports 174, 190,
        200
    media construction of sports? 450
    media content 428, 431
    media dependence on sports 445–7
    media images
        evaluative aspects of 427
        and narratives, ideological themes in 450–62
    media organizations, gendered nature of 456
    media rights fees 439–40, 441
    media sellout by commercial sports? 440–42
    narratives in media sports 449–63
    national identity themes in media representations
        460

new media and sport 433–5
newspapers, dependence of sports 445–6
online access to sport 433–5
online Learning Centre resources 427
participation, media impacts on 462
power relations in society and 429, 430–32
print media 428
profitability 428–9, 431
race themes in media representations 457–60
    making changes 459–60
relationship, two-way, between 438–49
simulated sports, video games as 437–8
social life, democtarization through online
        participation 434
social relationships and 442–5
'sportainment,' TV sports as 432
sports corruption, media and 442–5
sports dependence on media 438–45
sports journalism, profession of 463–5
sports-related behaviours, media impacts on 462–3
state control of media 429
stereotypes in media representations 458
success as theme in media representations 453
summarization 466–7
teamwork themes in media representations
        460–61
television
    commentaries on 430–31
    coverage by, and organizational changes to
        accommodate 440–42
    dependence of sports 446–7
    revenues from 439
video sports tournaments 435–6
violent images in media representations 461
virtual sports and video games 435–6
website resources 468
women in sports, media coverage of 270–71
writers and commentators, comparison of 464–5
medieval Europe
    masters and masses divide 71–3
    tournaments and games 71–3
Meier, Urs 258
Melnick, M. and Jackson, S.J. 463
men
    all-male sports, social dynamics in 249–50
    and boys as agents of change 289–91
    contact sports, violence as strategy in 238–9
    lives of, class and gender relations in 363–4
Mendelsohn, D. 66, 67
Mendes, Pedro 229
Mennesson, C. and Clement, J.-P. 301
Men's Fitness 176

Mérelle, André 154
meritocracy 355
Merkel, U. 475, 480, 487
Merron, J. 328
Messi, Lionel 420
Messner, M.A. and Stevens, M.A. 249
Messner, M.A. et al 461
Messner, Mike 117, 235, 247, 294, 295, 364, 379–80
Meyer, J. 214
Mickelson, Phil 420
Midol, N. and Broyer, G. 139
migration
    citizenship and national identity 341
    immigration into UK 315
    migrating communities, EU and 336–7
Millar, David 188
Miller, P.S. and Kerr, G. 123
Miller, T. et al 487, 495
Mills , J. and Dimeo, P. 487
Ming, Yao 420
minority groups 312–13
Mirza, H. 328
Modahl, Diane 215
Moggi, Luciano 202
Monie, John 186
Moore, Brian 188
Moore, D.L. 140
Moore, K. 334
Morinho, Jose 411
Morris, G.S.D. and Stiehl, J. 167
Morris, K. 59
Munday, G. 191
Munich Olympics, terrorism at 263–4
Murderball (Rubin-Shapiro documentary film) 236,
    238
Murdoch, Rupert 357–8, 410, 440, 447
Murphy, P. and Waddington, I. 186, 188, 190
Murphy, P. et al. 55, 112, 258
Murphy, Patrick 35
Murphy, S. 167
Murray, Andy 147
Murray, James 242
Murray, Jamie 147
Muscle and Fitness 176
Muslim women in sports, dilemmas for 334–5
myths and sports in ancient Greece 66–8

Nack, W. and Munson, L. 140, 147, 249
Nack, W. and Yaeger, D. 140
Nakamura, Y. 334, 335
NASSS (North American Society for the Sociology of
        Sport) 29

National Council for School Sport 6
national identity
   definition of 313
   nationality in organized sport 83–5
   themes in media representations 460
   see also race, ethnicity and national identity
nationalism, Olympianism and 489–92
native games and traditional cultures 487–8
Navratilova, Martina 303
NBC (National Broadcasting Company) 26, 271, 400,
     431, 433, 440, 441, 446, 504, 505
Nelson, M.B. 240, 277, 288
New York Times 431
Newbery, L. 7
Newell, Mike 272–3
Newfield, Jack 421
newspapers, dependence of sports 445–6
Newsweek 294
NFL (National Football League) 7, 379, 393, 400
Nichol, J.P. et al. 118
Nichols, Geoff 202, 204, 205, 416
Nicholson, M. 444
Nike 26, 191, 395, 399, 400, 402, 494, 498
Nixon, H.L. 117, 191, 240, 242, 522
Noah, Yannick 317
non-contact sports, violence as strategy in 238
Norris, J. and Jones, R. 340
Northern Ireland Assembly 344
NS-SEC (National Statistics Socio-Economic
     Classification) 353
nutritional supplements 210
Nyad, Diana 431
Nylund, D. 273

Obree, Graham 178
The Observer 189, 234
obstacles to participation *see* breaking barriers
Ochoa, Lorena 421
O'Connor, A. 401
oestrogen 292–3
off-field deviance 200–202, 206
off-field violence 244–50
O'Gara, Ronan 4
Oglesby, C. and Schrader, D. 342
Ohl, F. and Tribou, G. 391
Okuba, H. 501
Oliver, M. 59
Olney, B. 218
Olympianism 488–93
   commercialism and 489–92
Omi, M. and Winant, H. 314, 316
on-field deviance 198–200

on-field violence 228–44
'One Scotland - Many Cultures' campaign 343
O'Neal, Shaquille 420
O'Neill, M. 253
online access to sport 433–5
online Learning Centre resources
   deviance in sports 173
   economy and sports 385
   future for sports 513
   gender and sports 266
   historical perspectives 63
   media and sports 427
   politics and sports globalization 470
   race, ethnicity and national identity 311
   social class 349
   social theories 33
   socialization and sport 99
   sociology of sport 1
   violence in sports 225
   young people and sports 137
ONS (Office for National Statistics) 101, 360, 363,
     371, 372, 408
Opdyke, J. 140
opposition, future possibilities for 535
organized sports
   growth in UK of 80–1
   improvement of 163–4
   organization and control of sports events 504
   participation opportunities in 279–81
   people and organizations that control sports,
     commercialization and 407–9
   privatization of organized schemes 141–2
   trends in future for sports 526–7
   youth sports, origin and development of
     138–40
Ossur 17, 70, 133, 181–2, 451, 508
Ott, Alfredo 323
outlines *see* summarizations
overconformity 185–6, 190–92, 192–4, 194–6, 196–7,
     206–20
   control of 196–7
   encouragement of 214
   group dynamics and 192–4
   media constructs of 191
   reasons for 190–92
   underconformity and 194–6
Owen, G. 304
Owens, Jesse 92
ownership
   sponsors, owners and promoters in commercial
     sports 409–16
   structures in UK sports 409–10

pain
  playing through 188
  as price of violence in sports 241–2
painkillers 210
Palmer, C. 12
Palmer, Shaun 402
Panesar, Monty 332
Pappas, N. et al. 244
Paralympic Games 16–17, 109, 124, 146, 181, 200,
    279, 393, 394–5
Parrish, P. 217
Parrish, R. and McArdle, D. 417
Parry, J. 242
Parry, M. and Malcolm, D. 389
participation in sports
  active participation, media impacts on 462
  belief in 112–14
  budget cuts, effect on 272
  changing or ending 108–9
  decision for/against 107–8
  eligibility for 505–6
  equity issues and 267–91
  historical struggles over 89–90
  media impacts on 462
  opportunities for 267–8, 501
    in alternative sports 281–3
  participants in sports, commercialization and
      orientations of 405–7
  preferences among older people 517–18
  in sports, income and correlation between 358
  symbols as barriers to 394–5
  see also sports participation
past in sports see historical perspectives
Pastore, D. et al. 286
Patrick, D. 215, 217
PE and Sport Strategy for Young People (2008) 146
Pearson, G. 253
Pearson, Josie 236
Pelak, C.F. 289
Pennington, B. 140, 146, 403, 525
Pepsi 26, 48, 395, 399, 401
performance-enhancing drugs 205–20
  availability of 212
  banning of 210–12
  certification as 'well' in fight against substance
      abuse 219
  definition of 209–10
  substance control, challenge of 212–14, 218–20
  substance use education 219–20
performance ethic 142–3
Perman, S. 519
Perrottet, T. 67

Perrucci, R. and Wysong, E. 350, 351
Perryman, M. 253, 480
Petersen, A. 21
Petrecca, L. 434
PFA (Professional Footballers Association) 342
Pfister, G. 334
Phelps, Michael 183
Phillips, Bill 211
physical education 159–62
  decline in 367–8
Pike, E. and Beames, S. 113
Pike, E. and Maguire, J. 118
Pike, Elizabeth 43, 104, 111, 118, 129, 143, 162, 186,
    192, 204, 207, 213, 384, 393, 396, 398, 400,
    414, 426, 474–5, 493, 496, 523
Pike, Valerie 526
Pilz, G.A. 200, 239
Pipe, Andrew 301
Pistorius, Oscar 181–3, 507
Platt, L. 377
pleasure and participation sports
  factors in growth of 517–21
  future for sports 514, 515–16
Police 26, 395, 401
politics and sports globalization 469–511
  athletes
    global migration of 495–8
    rewards of sports, distribution to 506
  authority, power and 471
  commercialism, Olympianism and 489–92
  control and organization of sports events 504
  critical issues and government involvement
      481–2
  cultural exchange, sports and 493–4
  dominant political ideology, reproduction of
      values consistent with 478
  economic development, government responsibility
      for promotion of 479–80
  foreign policy, sport as tool of 480–81
  gender equity, political challenges in 307
  global migration of athletes 495–8
  global political process 483–501
  global politics and production of sports equipment
      498–9
  governance of sports in UK 482–3
  government and support for sports 478–9
  government-sports connection 472–83
  governments 471
  health and fitness, government responsibility for
      maintenance of 473–4
  identity, government responsibility for promotion
      of 476–7

politics and sports globalization – *continued*
international sports, ideals and realities in 483–7
location of sports events 504–5
nation states and ideological hegemony 487–94
national prestige, government responsibility for
promotion of 474–5
nationalism, Olympianism and 489–92
native games and traditional cultures 487–8
Olympianism 488–93
online Learning centre resources 470
organization and control of sports events 504
participation in sports
eligibility for 505–6
opportunities for 501
political barriers 507
political ideology, reproduction of values
consistent with 478
political leaders, sports and support for 478–9
political realities, making sense of 499–501
politics
actions and interactions of 471
definition of 470–71, 501
in era of transnational corporations 494–5
in sports 501–6
politics as community and cultural process 126–7
power, definition of 471
power and prestige, government responsibility for
promotion of 474–5
public order safeguards, government responsibility
for 472–3
qualification as a sport 501–3
recognition and prestige, government
responsibility for promotion of 474–5
rewards of sports, distribution of 506
rules of sports 503
making and enforcement of 503
safeguarding public order, government
responsibility for 472–3
sport as foreign policy tool 480–81
sports bodies in UK 482–3
sports equipment, global politics and production
of 498–9
sports events, organization and control of 504
state, concept of 471
summarization 507–10
traditional cultures and native games 487–8
transnational corporations, political realities in era
of 494–5
unity, government responsibility for promotion
of 476–7
website resources 510–11
Polley, Martin 75, 80, 328, 330, 372, 389

Ponsonby, Reverend Maurice 80
Poppen, J. 140
Popplewell Report (1985) 253
Porterfield, K. 107
Portes, A. 246
post-structuralism 44n1, 125n1, 128
Poulton, E. 232, 461, 476
Pound Dick 385
power
commercialization and power resources 388–9
definition of 471
organization of 213–14
and prestige, government responsibility for
promotion of 474–5
relations in society and media 429, 430–32
in society, gender ideology in action 293–4
in sports organizations, integration of 341–2
power and performance sports 514–15
factors in growth of 516–17
Preves, S.E. 21
Price, M. and Parker, A. 121, 304
Price, M.E. and Dayan, D. 475
Price, S.L. 321
print media 428
Probert, A. et al. 300
Probyn, Jeff 188
professional sport
amateur/professional dichotomy 354–5
participation opportunities in 280
professional leagues in UK 411–12
trends in 521
in United Kingdom 409–15
Pronger, B. 22, 291, 304
psychology of sport 12–14

qualification as a sport 501–3
quasi-criminal violence 229
Quilter, Ben 523

race, ethnicity and national identity 310–47
absence of black athletes in sports 330–31
Accra Football Club, Brixton 331
biological notions of race 317
black British men, racial ideology ans sense of
athletic destiny for 324–5
black footballers, problems of 340
black-only teams 331
black swimmers 339
change, prospects for 342–4
complex nature of issues of 311–12
cultural diversity training, need for 340–41
culture and dominant racial ideology 321

dominant racial ideology 320–21
dynamics of racial and ethnic relations in sports
    337–44
ethnic and racial diversity in sports 340–41
ethnic and racial exclusion in sports, elimination
    of 337–8
ethnic and racial relations in sports, dynamics of
    337–44
ethnicity
    definition of 312
    and race, interchangable use of terms 313
gender and racial ideology 327–9
genetic explanations for achievements of black
    athletes 322–3
genocide, definition of 319
history, impact of race on 317
ideas about genes, errors in 322–3
ideas and beliefs about 311, 314
immigration into UK 315
inferiority of black people, belief in 315
Irish Football Association 345
Islamic women in sports, dilemmas for 334–5
'jumping genes' 322–3
migrating communities, European Union (EU)
    and 336–7
migration, citizenship and national identity 341
minority groups 312–13
'mixed-race' people, erasure of 318–19
multi-layered society of UK 335–7
Muslim women in sports, dilemmas for 334–5
national identity, definition of 313
'One Scotland - Many Cultures' campaign 343
online Learning Centre resources 311
point-of-entry barriers 339
power in sports organizations, integration of
    341–2
race, definition of 312
race and ethnicity, interchangeable use of terms
    313
race and racial ideologies
    creation of 314–29
    problem with 316–19
race themes in media representations 457–60
    making changes 459–60
racial and ethnic diversity in sports 340–41
racial and ethnic exclusion in sports, elimination
    of 337–8
racial and ethnic relations in sports, dynamics of
    337–44
racial boundaries 315–16
racial classification models 317–18
racial ideology 314

in sports, challenge of escape from 326
    in United Kingdom 314–16
racial meanings, creation and use of 320
racial stereotypes 319
racism, definition of 319
racist language 320
sectarianism 336
self, 'cool pose' and presentation of 328
social class and racial ideology 327–9
social conditions, ideas and beliefs about race and
    329
social construction of race 318–19
social meanings and experiences 312
society, impact of race on 317, 319
sporting competitions, combined teams in 336
sports and 320–29
sports participation
    among Asian britons 331–3
    among black Britons 330–31
    among minority ethnic groups in UK 330–37
    in United Kingdom, race and 335–7
summarization of 344–5
traditional ideas about race 320
visible minorities 313
vocabulary of diversity, need for 343–4
website resources 346–7
whites, racial ideology and sports choices for
    326–7
women athletes and challenge of racial ideology
    328–9
Radcliffe, Paula 98, 375
rags-to-riches stories 350
Raikkonen, Kimi 419–20
Rail, G. 7
Raisborough, J. 361
Ramella, M. 204
Raney, A. and Bryant, J. 444
Ravel, B. and Rail, G. 521
Ravizza, Ken 137
Real, Michael 428, 460, 488
Real Madrid 26, 401, 516
Reasbeck, Nicola 230
Redgrave, Steven 94
Redknapp, Harry 229
reflections
    athletes as change agents 533–5
    Beckham as brand 401
    body, sports and meanings given to 21–3
    change agents, athletes as 533–5
    commercialism, Olympianism and 489–92
    consequences of sport 114–7
    contested activities, sports as 9–10

reflections – *continued*
    deviant overconformity, media constructs of 191
    dominant sport forms 69, 70
    experiences from sport 114–7
    female athletes and press coverage 457
    female bodybuilders 298–300
    field sports and hunting 206–8
    gambling economy 408
    gender equity and women's football 269
    gender ideas and violence on the field 247–8
    gender ideology 21–3
    genetic explanations for achievements of black
        athletes 322–3
    history, lessons learned from 75–6
    hunting and field sports 206–8
    ideas about genes, errors in 322–3
    Islamic women in sports, dilemmas for 334–5
    'jumping genes' 322–3
    lessons from history 75–6
    media constructs of deviant overconformity 191
    Munich Olympics, terrorism at 263–4
    Muslim women in sports, dilemmas for 334–5
    nationalism, Olympianism and 489–92
    Olympianism 488–93
    press coverage of female athletes 457
    reflections of society, sports and 47–8
    simulated sports, video games as 437–8
    social inequalities, spectator behaviour and 372
    society, sports and reflections of 47–8
    spectator behaviour and social class 372
    sponsorship matters 144
    sport forms, dominant 69, 70
    sport forms, unique 69, 70
    sport history, lessons learned from 75–6
    sports as contested activities 9–10
    terrorism and sports events 263–4
    video games as simulated sports 437–8
    violence on the field 247–8
    women's football 269
Reformation 74–5
Reid, E. 249
Reid, S. 397, 489
Renaissance 73–4
resource barriers 369
reviews *see* summarizations
rewards of sports, distribution of 506
Reynolds, G. 215
Rice, Grantland 458
Rice, R. 242
Rich, E., Holroyd, R. and Evans, J. 119–20
Rich, Emma 119–20
Richardson, James 198

Richtel, M. 437
Riesman, D. and Denny, R. 528
Rigauer, B. 81
Rinehart, R. 12, 139
Rinehart, R. and Grenfell, C. 139, 145, 148
Rinehart, R. and Syndor, S. 7, 12, 139, 282
Riordan, J. and Arnaud, P. 480
Riordan, James 69
risk, acceptance of 188
The Rites of Men (Burstyn, V.) 15
Ritzer, George 414
Rivers, I. 302
Roberts, K. 416
Roberts, S. 273
Robinson, L. 248, 408
Robinson, V. 189
Roche, K. 246
Rocky Mountain News 149
Roderick, M. 14, 186, 190, 235, 304, 417–8
Roderick, M. et al. 188, 189, 219
Rodriguez, Alex 420
Rogge, Jacques 513
Roman contests and games 68–9
Ronaldinho 420
Ronaldo, Cristiano 420
Rooney, Wayne 460
Rose, Damon 59–60
Rose, Hilary 113
Rosenfeld, A. and Wise, N. 144
Rossi, Valentino 419, 420
Roth, A. and Basow, S. 289
Roversi, A. 260
Rowe, D. et al 460
Rowe, David 427, 430, 449, 459
Rowe, N. and Champion, R. 330
Rowe, Nick 348
Rudman, Shelley 454
Rugby School 4
rules
    avoidance of 198–200
    and internal structures of sports,
        commercialization and 404–5
    of sports, making and enforcement of 503
    against substance abuse, establishment of 219
Runciman, David 373
Rusedski, Greg 140, 215
Russell, Kate 269
Ryan, Joan 146, 296–7

Sabo, D. 14
Sabo, D. and Jensen, S. 460
Sabo, D. et al 458

Safai, P. 219
Sage, George 81, 498
Sailes, G. 377
St Louis, C. 145, 321
Sam, M. 476, 481
Samaranch, Juan Antonio 394
Sandomir, R. 525
Santana, Wally 54
Sapolsky, Robert 322
Saporito, B. 254
Sato, D. 476
Savage, Robbie 401
Scambler, Graham 80, 254, 364, 445, 470
Schaller, B. 339
Scheerder, J. et al. 358
Scheinin, R. 198
Scherer, J. 6, 433, 467
Scherer, J. and Jackson, S.J. 433
Schiesel, S. 436
Schilling, M. 132
Schimmel, K. 480
Schoenbaum, Rob 520
school sports 159–62
    decline in 367–8
Schultz, B. 153, 274
Scraton, S. and Flintoff, A. 90
Scraton, S. et al. 329
Scraton, Sheila 15, 35, 328–9, 331
Scruton, Roger 207
Scudamore, Richard 393
Seal, Rebecca 187, 192
sectarianism 336
Seeley, M. and Rail, G. 131
Seles, Monica 94, 252, 297
self, ‚cool pose‘ and presentation of 328
self-medication 213
Selman, R. 154
Sernau, S. 351
Sewart, J. 424
sex categories 291–3
sexual assaults by athletes 248–50
sexual harassment in sports 286–7
Shakib, S. 274
Shapin, S. 210
Sharapova, Maria 273–4, 421, 453–4, 457
Sharp, R. 272–3
Shaw, Mark 148, 285
Sheard, K. 117, 244
Sheil, P. 394
Shields, D. and Bredemeier, B. 199, 239, 240
Shields, D. et al. 200, 240
Shilling, C. 21

Shogan, D. and Ford, M. 218
Silk, M. 412, 476, 495
Silk, M. and Andrews, D. 476, 480
Simson, V. and Jennings, A. 504
simulated sports, video games as 437–8
Six Nations Rugby 4
skateboarding for pleasure 518–19
Slaney, Mary Decker 190
Smart, B. 128, 401
Smedley, Audrey 315, 317, 319
Smith, A. and Thomas, N. 452
Smith, A. and Waddington, I. 204
Smith, Brett 276
Smith, F. and Barker, J. 367
Smith, G. 242, 301
Smith, J. and Ingham, A. 477
Smith, M. 257
Smith, Mike 229
Smith, Tommy 93, 534
Smith Maguire, J. 415
Snider, M. 435
snowboarding for pleasure 519–20
social class 348–83
    amateur/professional dichotomy 354–5
    boxing, class, gender and ethnic relations within
        364–7
    career opportunities in sports 373–7
        ethnic minorities 376–7
        limitations on 374–5
        women’s chances 375–6
    career success for highly-paid athletes after playing
        379–80
    child-rearing 361–3
    class ideology in UK 354–6
    class relations 350–51
        in action 367–8, 368–71
        definition of 350–51
        dynamics of 352–4
        power in sport and 357–8
    cost of attending sports events 368–71
    dynamics of, implications of 363
    economic inequalities 351–8, 359
    economic opportunities in sports 373–7
    economic resources, sports and 349–50
    elite athletes, career success after retirement
        379–80
    ethnic relations, dynamics of 377
    former athletes, sports participation and
        occupational careers among 378–80
    global inequalities, sports and 371–3
    health and fitness movement 359
    home-making 361–3

social class – *continued*
   Homeless World Cup 355
   masculine identity, establishment of 363–4
   men's lives, class and gender relations in 363–4
   meritocracy 355
   occupational careers among former athletes
      378–80
   online Lerning Centre resources 349
   participation in sports, income and correlation
      between 358
   physical education, decline in 367–8
   professional/amateur dichotomy 354–5
   racial ideology and 327–9
   rags-to-riches stories 350
   resource barriers 369
   school sports, decline in 367–8
   social class, definition of 350
   social stratification 350
   spectator behaviour and 372
   sport as defining element in male culture 363–4
   sports development by social status 353
   sports participation
      of former athletes 378–80
      patterns and 358–70
   status and violence off-field 245
   stratification of sports within themselves 359
   summarization 381–2
   ticket prices for sports events 369–71
   website resources 382–3
   women's lives, class and gender relations in 361–3
social conditions
   for commercialization of sports 386–7
   ideas and beliefs about race and 329
social construction of race 318–19
social inequalities, spectator behaviour and 372
social meanings and experiences 312
social psychological theories, crowd violence and
      255–6
social relationships
   media, sports and 442–5
   working for transformation in 536
social stratification 350
social theories 32–61
   British leadership in 35
   class relations, definition of 41
   in creation of future trends 529–33
   critical sociology of sport 33
   cultural ideologies, definition of 46
   disability, definition of 59
   everyday life
      critical feminist theory in 51
      critical theory in 48–9

      figurational theory in 56–7
      interactionist theory in 53
   feminist theory 49–51
   figurational theory 53–7
   handicap, definition of 59–60
   identity 52
   impairment, definition of 59
   interactionist theory 51–2
   language barriers ('don't call me handicapped') 59
   sport research
      critical feminist theory 49–50
      figurational theory 55–6
      interactionist theory 52
   summarization 36–8, 60–1
   theories, choice of 57–60
   theorization, definition of 34
   theory,choice of 57–60
   weaknesses of
      critical feminist theory 51
      critical theory 48–9
      figurational theory 57
      interactionist theory 53
   website resources 61
social worlds, examples of
   heroism, learning to be a hero 122–3
   image is not everything 123
   man's world, living in shadow of 123–4
   media, portrayal of sports world in 124–5
   surviving in a ghetto 124
socialization and sport 98–135
   agents of socialization 101
   athlete, process of acceptance 105–6
   barriers to socialization 131–3
   burnout among young athletes 109–10
   career, change in personal investment 110–12
   changing room stories 120–21
   community and cultural process
      politics as 126–7
      research as 127–8
   community and cultural process, politics as 126–7
   community and cultural process, research as 127–8
   disability and socialization 131–3
   disordered eating, stories of 119–20
   elite athlete, process of becoming 103–5
   emotional dimensions of socialization 130
   gay male athletes, stories of 121–2
   health, improvement from sport 117
   hegemony 127
      definition of 127
   ideology 125–8
   impact of sport 119
   interactionist model, definition of 102

involvement in sport 103
    attitude towards 112–14
involvement in sport, attitude towards 112–14
online Learning centre resources 99
participation
    belief in 112–14
    changing or ending 108–9
    decision for/against 107–8
physical well-being, improvement from sport 117
politics as community and cultural process 126–7
real-life experiences, stories of 119
research as community and cultural process 127–8
social change, influence on young people and
        sports 139–40
social worlds 122–5
    definition of 122
    examples of
    heroism, learning to be a hero 122–3
        image is not everything 123
        man's world, living in shadow of 123–4
        media, portrayal of sports world in 124–5
        surviving in a ghetto 124
socialization
    barriers to 131–3
    conflict theory approach 101–2
    definition of 100–101
    new approaches to 102–3
    research on 129–31
sport, getting out of 110
sport-health connection 117–8
sport-obesity connection 118–9
summarization 133–4
vocabulary of sports 130–31
website resources 134–5
society
    definition of 4
    gender ideology in 291–4
    impact of race on 317, 319
    multi-layered society of UK 335–7
    sports and reflections of 47–8
    sports in society, current trends related to 516–24
    top-down view of 44
    trends in 528–9
sociology of sport 11–18, 30
    amateurism 23
    approaches in 18
    barriers, breaking down of 16–18
    beliefs in cultures, sports and 19–24
    class ideology 23
    controversies created by 15–18
    cultural barriers, athletes and 16–18
    current status of 27–30

different approaches in 18
economy and sports 26
education and sports 24–6
family and sports 24, 25
gender ideology 20–21
health and sports 24–6
ideas in cultures, sports and 19–24
ideologies, importance of 19
images of sports 18–19
injury in sport, social reality and 14
insights developed through research in 14–15
media and sports 26
meritocracy 23
online Learning Centre resources 1
politics and sports 27
professionalism 23
psychology of sport and, differences between 12–14
publication sources for research 28–9
racial ideology 23
religion and sports 27
social life, sports connections to 24–7
special meaning of sports 18–19
sports and ideologies, complex connections 23–4
sports sciences 18
sports sociologists 18
stories of sports 18–19
summarization 30
talk about sports 19
uses of 14–15
website resources 30–31
youth sports, sociological questions on 153–6
Sokolove, Michael 140, 144, 145, 146, 173, 211, 215,
        217, 423
Solomon, A. 274
Sorenstam, Annika 294
Southerton, Kelly 457
Sparkes, A. and Smith, B. 275–6
Sparkes, A., Batey, J. and Brown, D. 123
Sparkes, Andrew 123, 276
spectacle
    in ancient Rome 68–9
    and violence in sports 233–4
spectator behaviour
    social class and 372
    spectator violence 250–62
spectator interest
    creation of 389–91
    excitement and, quest for 389–91
    media coverage and 390–91
    spectators and spectator sports, trends in 524
    success ideology and 390
    youth schemes and 390

Spitzer, G. 112
sponsorship 385
    commercialization and orientations of sponsors
        405–7
    importance of 144
    in UK sports 411, 416
Sport England 101, 110–11, 114, 117, 136, 204, 274,
    349, 367
sport research
    conflict theory 42
    critical feminist theory 49–50
    critical theory 46
    figurational theory 55–6
    functionalist theory 39
    interactionist theory 52
Sporting Equals 332
Sporting News 356, 357
sports
    alternative approach to definition of 7–11
    bodies in UK 482–3
    'character development' in sports participation
        81–2
    competitive activities 5
    consequences of 114–7
    constructionist approach to deviance in 184–97
    contested activities 9–10
    corruption of, media and 442–5
    as defining element in male culture 363–4
    definition of 4–11
    dependence on media 438–45
    development by social status 353
    dominant sport forms 69, 70
    drama of 6
    early years of, time and space for 77–9
    education and 159–63
    equipment for, global politics and production of
        498–9
    ethic of 186–90, 230–32
    experiences from sport 114–7
    experiences of young people in sport 148–53
    external rewards 6
    as foreign policy tool 480–81
    gender ideology in 294–308
    getting out of 110
    global markets, corporate interest in 392–3
    goals and internal structures, commercialization
        and 404–5
    history of, lessons learned from 75–6
    informal sports, participation opportunities in
        281–3
    institutionalized activities 5–6
    internal rewards 6

journalism, profession of 463–5
later years of, changing interests, values and
    opportunities 79–80
marginalization by 6–7
meaning of 9, 10–11
obesity-sport connection 118–9
organization of 5–6, 9, 10–11
    change in support of gender equity 307
participation 9
    among Asian Britons 331–3
    'character development' and 81–2
performance in 6
physical activities 5
play and 6
player- controlled sports 150–1
point-of-entry barriers 339
purpose of 9, 10–11
qualification as a sport 501–3
race, ethnicity and national identity and 320–29
sites for change 301–3
as social constructions 12, 13, 23–4
in society
    historical perspective on 64–5
    study of 18–27
specialized training schemes for young people
    145–6
sponsorship of 10, 26
sport-health connection 117–8
sport spheres, trends in 521–4
'sportainment,' TV sports as 432
system of, changes for future from within 535
traditional definition of 5–6
uniqueness of forms of 69, 70
variety in sports by time and place 65–6
venues for professional sports in UK 412–13
sports events
    branding of 398–9
    context of violence at 260
    historical background to violence at 253–4
    organization and control of 504
    situational factors and violence at 259–60
    violence and action in the event 257–8
    violence at 252–5, 255–7, 257–60
Sports Illustrated 321, 339, 373
sports participation
    among black Britons 330–31
    among girls and women 267–91
    among minority ethnic groups in UK 330–37
    of former athletes 378–80
    social class and patterns of 358–70
    see also participation in sports
sports personalities, branding of 400–402

sports-related behaviours, media impacts on 462–3
sports-related deviance, examples of 202–3
sports research
    as community and cultural process 127–8
    crowd violence, research and theories about 255–7
    on deviance among athletes 197–205
sports tourism 414–15
sportscotland 274, 359
stadiums for professional sports in UK 412–13
Starr, M. and Samuels, A. 200
state
    concept of 471
    control of media 429
    nation states and ideological hegemony 487–94
Stead, D. and Maguire, J. 496
Stead, Peter 239
stereotypes in media representations 458
Stetler, B. 433
Stevens Inquiry (2007) 203
Stevenson, Chris 103–4, 105, 107
Stevenson, Jan 332
Stewart, Jackie 145
Stoelting, S. 288
Stokes, M. 335
Stoll, S. and Beller, J. 112, 200
Stone, J. et al. 324, 326, 327
Strong Women, Deep Closets (Griffin, P.) 303
Sugden, J. and Bairner, A. 480
Sugden, J. and Tomlinson, A. 351, 392
Sugden, J. and Wallis, J. 485
Sugden, John 35, 124, 245–6, 364, 365, 367
summarizations
    deviance in sports 220–22
    economy and sports 423–4
    future for sports 536–7
    gender and sports 308–9
    historical perspectives 94–6
    media and sports 466–7
    politics and sports globalization 507–10
    race, ethnicity and national identity 344–5
    social class 381–2
    social theories 36–8, 60–1
    socialization and sport 133–4
    sociology of sport 30
    violence in sports 262–3
    young people and sports 168–70
The Sun 191, 357
Sunday Mirror 191
SustainAbility 2
Suzuki, Ichiro 420
Swain, D. 111, 380
Sweeney, H. 217

Swift, E. and Yaeger, D. 215, 217
Swinney, A. and Horne, J. 337, 343
Swoopes, S. 277, 303
Syed, M. 534
symbols as barriers to participation 394–5

Taheri, A. 334
Takahashi, Y. and Horne, J. 498
Talbot, M. 90
Taub, D. and Greer, K. 159
Taylor, G. 255–6
Taylor, Graham 230
Taylor, M.. 498
Taylor, Phil 10
Taylor Report (1989) 94, 253–4
team sports
    branding of teams 399
    communities and teams, connections between 261–2
    income from 419
    legal status of 417–18
teamwork themes in media representations 460–61
technology, future trends in 525
telecommunications, future trends in 525–6
television
    commentaries on 430–31
    coverage and organizational changes to accommodate 440–42
    dependence of sports 446–7
    revenues from 439
    viewers of, violence among 250–52
Temple, Kerry 430–1
terrorism and sports events 263–4
testosterone 292–3
Thatcher, Ben 229
Thatcher, Margaret (and Thatcherite policies) 256
Theberge, N. 240, 288, 289, 301
theories
    choice of social theories 57–60
    and young people in sports 33
    see also conflict theory; critical theory; critical feminist theory; figurational theory; functionalist theory; interactionist theory
There Ain't No Black in the Union Jack (Gilroy, P.) 330
Thing, Lone Friis 231–2
Thomas, C. 276
Thomas, N. 369
Thomas, R. 459
Thompson, Jenny 339
Thompson, S. 156, 361
Thomson, R. 132

Thornton, A. 7
Thorpe, Rod 155
Tibballs, Sue 266
ticket prices for sports events 369–71
Time magazine 533
The Times 230, 357, 399
Tinmouth, M. 193, 196, 201
Todd, T. 205
Tomlinson, A. and Fleming, S. 330, 331
Tomlinson, Alan 35, 349, 351, 356, 495
Torbert, M. 167
Total Sport 271
Totilo, S. 434
transnational corporations
    political realities in era of 494–5
    sports and commercialisation 393–7
Tranter, N. 77, 80
Treanor, G. 385
Trujillo, N. 191
Trulson, Michael 204–5, 246
Trumpbour, R. 444
Tuaolo, E. 304
Tuck, J. 85, 336, 460, 461
Tucker, L. and Parks, J. 240
Tucker, R. and Dugus, J. 182
Turner, B. 21
Turner, R.. 239
Tyson, Mike 234, 244

Ueberroth, P. 485
UK National Anti-Doping Policy (UK Sport) 217–18
UK Sport 109, 120, 217–18, 223, 273, 284, 330, 391,
    482, 511
underage alcohol consumption 200–201
underconformity 185
    overconformity and 194–6
unfair conduct, indulgence in 198–200
United Kingdom (UK)
    amateur sports in 415–16
    class ideology in 354–6
    commercial sports and UK economy 391–2
    governance of sports in 482–3
    immigration into 315
    investment in UK sports 411
    multi-layered society of 335–7
    organised sport in, growth of 80–1
    organized sports, growth in UK of 80–1
    ownership structures in UK sports 409–10
    professional leagues in 411–12
    professional sport in 409–15
    racial ideology in 314–16
    sponsorship in UK sports 411, 416

sport in, organised growth of 80–1
sports bodies in 482–3
sports participation
    of minority ethnic groups 330–37
    race and 335–7
stadiums for professional sports in 412–13
UK Athletics 16, 94, 180
Urquhart, J. and Crossman, J. 453
USOC (US Olympic Committee) 209

Vamplew, W. 82
Van Dyken, Amy 339
Van Sterkenburg, J. and Knoppers, A. 60, 456, 458
Vaughan, Richard *533*
Veblen, Thorstein 78, 80
Vélez, Dr Beatriz 363
Verducci, T. 214
Veri, M. 277
Verma, G. and Darby, D. 335
Vertinsky, P. 83
video games, simulated sports 437–8
video sports tournaments 435–6
Vincent, J. 271, 276
Vine, L. and Aust, R. 101
Viner, K. 244
violence in sports 224–64
    aggression 227
    all-male sports, social dynamics in 249–50
    animal sports, violence as strategy in 240–41
    assaults by athletes 248–50
    body contact, brutality in 229
    borderline violence 229
    boxing
        and control 246
        and violence within rules 244
    celebratory violence 254–5
    commercialization and 232–5
    control of on-field violence 242–4
    control vs carry-over, off-field violence 245–7
    criminal violence 230
    critical theories, crowd violence and 256
    crowd dynamics 259–60, 261
    crowd violence
        control of 261–2
        research and theories about 255–7
    cultural change and control of 232–3
    deviant overconformity, violence as 230–32
    dog racing 240–41
    domestic violence and watching sports 251–2
    entertainment and 233–4
    ethic of sport, violence as deviant overconformity
        to norms of 230–32

fan aggression, precipitation of 258
football hooliganism, historical change and 256
gender ideas and violence on the field 247–8
greyhound racing 240–41
group dynamics and control 247
heavy contact sports 232
historical perspective 227–8
hooliganism and semi-organized confrontations
    256–7
identity and control 247
ideological barriers, wheelchair rugby and 236–8
injury as price of 241–2
injustice, crown violence and perceptions of 261
institutionalization of 238–41
interactionist theories, crowd violence and 256
intimidation 227
masculinity and 235–8
men's contact sports, violence as strategy in 238–9
non-contact sports, violence as strategy in 238
off-field violence 244–50
on-field violence 228–44, 247–8
online Learning Centre resources 225
pain as price of 241–2
quasi-criminal violence 229
roots of playing-field violence 242–3
sexual assaults by athletes 248–50
social psychological theories, crowd violence and
    255–6
spectacle and 233–4
spectator violence 250–62
sports ethic, violence as deviant overconformity to
    norms of 230–32
sports events
    context of violence at 260
    historical background to violence at 253–4
    situational factors and violence at 259–60
    violence and action in the event 257–8
    violence at 252–5, 255–7, 257–60
statements about, contradictory nature of 226
status and violence off-field 245
summarization 262–3
teams and communities, connections between
    261–2
television viewers, violence among 250–52
terrorism and sports events 263–4
types of violence 229–30
violence, definition of 226–7
violence against women, social problem of 249–50
violent images in media representations 461
website resources 264
women's contact sports, violence as strategy in
    239–40

virtual sports and video games 435–6
visible minorities 313
vision barriers, trends towards reduction in 522–4
vocabulary of diversity, need for 343–4
voluntary sector in sports 416

Wacquant, Loïc 364, 365–6, 367
WADA (World Anti-Doping Agency) 94, 211, 215,
    217–18
Waddington, Ivan 35, 117, 186, 188, 192, 219, 242,
    473, 517
Wahidin, A. and Powell, J. 21
Wahl, G. 373
Walker, R. 429
Walkers Crisps 26
Walseth, K. 333
Walseth, K. and Fasting, K. 51
Wann, D. et al. 257, 462, 463
Warren, Frank 410
Waterford, R. 473
Watson, Andrew 340
Watson, Michael 242
Wearden, S. and Creedon, P. 270
Weaver, P. 335
Webb, E. et al. 201
Weber, Max 471
website resources
    deviance in sports 222–3
    economy and sports 424–5
    future for sports 537–8
    gender and sports 309
    historical perspectives 96–7
    media and sports 468
    politics and sports globalization 510–11
    race, ethnicity and national identity 346–7
    social class 382–3
    social theories 61
    socialization and sport 134–5
    sociology of sport 30–31
    violence in sports 264
    young people and sports 170–1
Wedgewood, N. 274, 289
Weed, M. 232
Weiler, K. and Higgs, C. 454
Weiner, T. 373, 395
Weinstein, M. et al. 239
Weintraub, S. 481
Weir, T. 328
Weise, E. 212
Weisman, L. 380
Weiss, O. 462
Wellard, I. 157, 304

Wendel, T. 434
Wenner, L. 449
Wenner, L. and Gantz, W. 462–3
Wennerstrom, Steve 300
Werbner, P. 332
Wertheim, J. 301, 505
Wesing, E. and Bruce, T. 454
Whannel, Garry 296, 427, 430, 449
Wharton, Arthur 340
Wheaton, B. 7, 105–6, 111, 282, 291
Wheaton, B. and Beal, B. 282
Wheeler, Garry 110
White, A. and Brackenridge, C. 285
White, A. and Henry, I. 376
White, Anita 107, 285
White, M. and Kay, J. 284, 285
White, P. 117, 242
White, P. and Young, K. 235, 239, 242, 290
Wie, Michelle 294
Wiggins, Bradely 188
Wigglesworth, N. 142, 353, 370, 414
Wightman, A. et al. 208, 388
Wightwick, A. 163
Wilkinson, Jonny 189
Williams, J. 269
Williams, P.. 317
Williams, Serena and Venus 376, 454
Wilmore, J. 274
Wilson, Brian 434
Wilson, D. 215
Wilson, T.. 358
Winant, H. 314, 315, 319
Winlock, C. 327–8
Winning: A Tourism Strategy for 2012 and Beyond
    (DCMS) 415
Winter, Henry 433
Wittebols, J. 431
Wolfe, Tom 191, 193
Wolfendon Report (1960) 89, 93
Wolff, A. 140, 144, 145
Wolff, E. 492
Wollaston, S. 60
women
    administrative jobs for women 284–7
    as agents of change 288–9
    challenge of racial ideology for women athletes
        328–9
    contact sports, violence as strategy in 239–40
    in decision-making positions, under-
        representation of 273
    empowerment of women and girls 288–9
    female bodybuilders 298–300

'forever ladies' 297–8
    as invaders in men's cultural centres 296–7
    job satisfaction of women in sports 286–7
    lives of, class and gender relations in 361–3
    media coverage of women in sports 270–71
    press coverage female athletes and 457
    sexy and feminine bodies, cultural messages about
        274
    trivialization of women's sports 276–7
    values of, experiences in sports and 518
    violence against, social problem of 249–50
    women's football 269
    'women's sports,' non-threatening nature of 297
Women's Physique World Magazine 300
Women's Sports Foundation 270, 273, 284, 285, 342,
    376
Wong, J. 333
Woods, Tiger 279, 318, 376, 419–20, 421, 533
Woodward, J. 320, 328
World Athletics Championships 16
World Outgames 521
World Police and Fire Games 473
Wray, S. 333
Wright, D. and Fitzpatrick, K. 246
Wright, Ian 128, 328, 377, 458
writers and commentators, comparison of 464–5

Yesalis, Chuck 217
Yessis, M. 525
Yocom, G. 507
Yorganci, I. 186
Young, I. 274, 289, 306
Young, K. and White, P. 240, 289
Young, Kevin 14, 105, 106, 117, 160, 229, 230, 231,
    239, 240, 242, 253, 256, 374, 499
young people and sports 136–71
    action increase 164–5
    adult controlled sports, formal 151–2
    alternative and action sports, increased interest in
        148
    barriers, mainstreaming 158–9
    burnout among young athletes 109–10
    class relations 41
    close scores, creation of 165
    conflict theory 41–4
        weaknesses of 43–4
    critical theory 44–9
    differences, analysis of 153
    elite sports training schemes 145–6
    everyday life
        conflict theory in 42–3
        functionalist theory in 39–41

experiences in sport 148–53
family relationships, dynamics of 156
friendship influence 166
functionalist theory 35–41
  weaknesses of 41
high-performance sport schemes, improvement
  of 166–7
hybrid sports, definition of 163
improvement of youth sports, prospects for 167–8
influence of social change 139–40
informal, alternative and action sports,
  improvement of 163
online Learning Centre resources 137
organized schemes, privatization of 141–2
organized sports, improvement of 163–4
organized youth sports, origin and development
  138–40
parents, increased involvement and concerns
  among 146–7
performance ethic 142–3
personal involvement increase 165
physical education 159–62
player-controlled sports, informal 150–1
post-war baby boom, growth in sport 138–9
readiness for competitive sports 153–6

recommendations for improving youth sports
  163–7
school sports 159–62
society, beyond needs of 44
sociological questions on youth sports 153–6
specialized sports training schemes 145–6
sponsorship matters 144
sport research
  conflict theory 42
  critical theory 46
  functionalist theory 39
sports and education 159–63
student athletes 162–3
summarization 168–70
theories 33
website resources 170–1
youth sports today, major trends 140–7, 522

Zerientes, Becky 240
Zhang, J. and Smith, D. 462
Zhang, J. et al. 463
Zidane, Zinadine 154–5
Zimmer, M. and Zimmer, M. 417
Zirin, D. 434
Zorpette, G. 214, 215, 217